050211
THE HENLEY COLLEGE LIBRARY

Hands On Java

A Self-Study Introduction to Java Programming

Alistair Stewart

Digital Skills
Milton
Barr
Girvan
Ayrshire
KA26 9TY

www.digital-skills.co.uk

Printed September 2001
Updated June 2001
Reprinted September 2003
Reprinted August 2004

Title : Hands On Java

ISBN : 1-874107-06-8

Other Titles Available

Hands On C++
Hands On XHTML
Hands On Pascal

Table of Contents

Introduction

Chapter 1 Background

Chapter 2 Starting Java

Chapter 3 Control Structures

Chapter 4 Functions

Chapter 5 Arrays

Chapter 6 Classes and Objects

Chapter 7 Class Relationships

Chapter 8 Basic Java Classes

Chapter 9 Advanced Features

Chapter 10 Handling Errors

Chapter 11 Streams

Chapter 12 Threads

Chapter 13 GUI Applications Using AWT

Chapter 14 The AWT Family Tree

Chapter 15 Layout Managers

Chapter 16 Listeners and Event Handlers

Chapter 17 Applets

Chapter 18 Swing

Introduction

Learn by Doing

The only way to become a programming expert is to practice. No one ever learned any skill by simply reading. Hence, this is not a text book where you can sit back in a passive way slowly reading through each chapter; rather it is designed as a teaching package in which you will do most of the work. The tasks embedded in the text are included to test your understanding of what has gone before and as a method of discovering for yourself some of the subtler aspects and techniques of the language. It is therefore important that you tackle each task since they are designed to test your knowledge and develop your skill. In addition, many of the short programs developed in the early chapters of the book are used to construct a final project in the last section of the text.

Who this Publication is For

This book is designed for the following groups:

- People new to programming who want to develop a high degree of skill in Java.
- People wanting to move on from other languages to Java.
- Students learning programming techniques using Java.
- Anyone requiring a practical introduction to object-oriented design and programming.

No previous knowledge of computers or programming is required, since what follows assumes you are new to these topics.

This text is designed for independent self-study by students in the first year of a degree or HNC/D Computing course, professional programmers who wish to develop skills in the most popular object-oriented language, as well as any individual curious to discover the fascinating world of Java.

The Contents

Chapter 1 covers some background material including number systems and a simple program definition language.

Chapters 2 to 5 cover the conventional aspects of Java.

Chapters 6 and 7 cover the basic concepts behind Object-Oriented programming.

Chapter 8 describes some of the basic classes supplied with the Java package.

Chapter 9 covers some of the more complex features of Object-Oriented programming in Java.

Chapter 10 covers error handling.

Chapter 11 covers file handling.

Chapter 12 is an introduction to the parallel processing features available using threads.

Chapters 13 to 16 cover the visual components available in the AWT package, layout managers and event handlers.

Chapter 17 shows how to create applets for a web page.

Chapter 18 takes a brief look at the Swing package.

Other topics mentioned within the text are: program testing, UML class diagrams, design documentation.

How To Get the Most out of this Package

Experience has shown that students derive most benefit from this material by approaching its study in an organised way. The following strategy for study is highly recommended:

1. Read a chapter or section through without taking notes or worrying too much about topics that are not immediately clear to you. This will give you an overview of the purpose of that chapter/section.

2. Re-read the chapter. This time take things slowly; make notes and summaries of the material you are reading (even if you understand the material, making notes helps to retain the facts in your long-term memory); re-read any parts you are unclear about.

3. Embedded in the material are a series of tasks. Do each task as you reach it (on the second reading). These are designed to test your knowledge and understanding of what has gone before. Do not be tempted to skip over them, promise to come back to them later, or to make only a half-hearted attempt at tackling them before looking up the answer (there are solutions at the end of each chapter). Once you have attempted a task, look at the solution given. Often there will be important points emphasised in the solution which will aid your understanding.

4. As you progress through the book go back and re-read earlier chapters since you will often get something new from them as your knowledge increases.

Language Syntax Diagrams

The text contains many syntax diagrams which give a visual representation of the format of various statements allowed in Java. These diagrams make no attempt to be complete but merely act as a guide to the format most likely to be used. The accompanying text and example should highlight the more complex options available.

Below is a typical diagram:

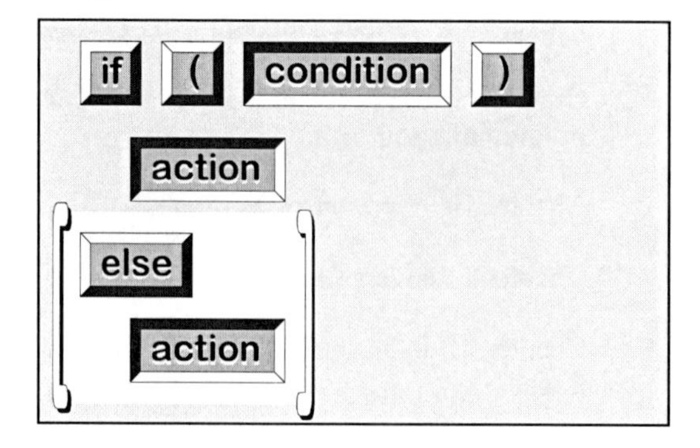

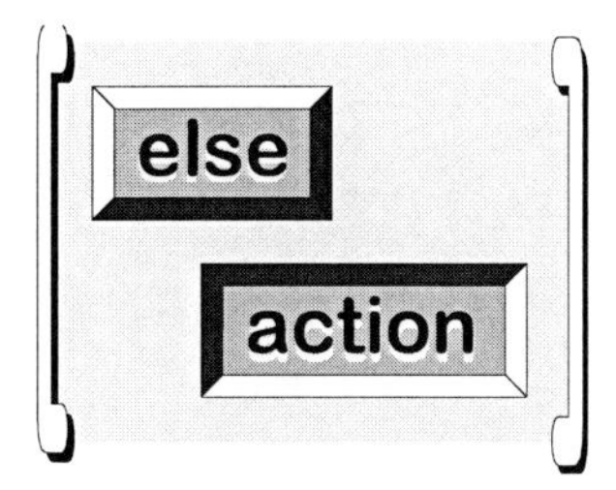

Each tile in the diagram holds a **token** of the statement. Raised tiles represent fixed terms in the statement which must be entered exactly as shown.

Sunken tiles represent tokens whose exact value is decided by you, the programmer, but again these values must conform to some stated rule.

Items enclosed in brackets may be omitted if not required.

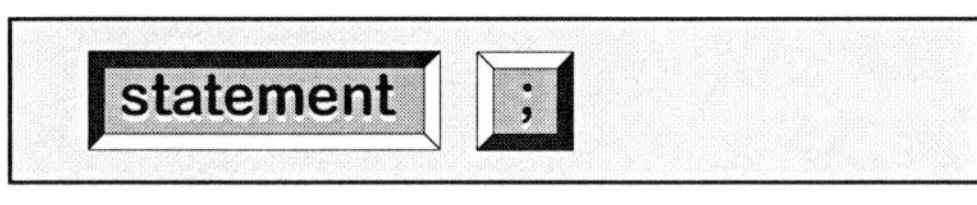

OR

Some tiles will be given a diagram of their own in order to explain their meaning in more detail. For example, the token, **action**, given above is defined in more detail by the diagram shown on the left.

This shows that **action** has two possible interpretations: either a single statement, or a series of statements enclosed in braces.

Where one or more tokens in a diagram may be repeated indefinitely, this is shown using the curved, arrowed line.

Java makes use of three types of brackets: ( ), { }, and [ ]. Rather than use this informal term, the correct names for each is used throughout this text. The correct terms are:

()	parentheses
{}	braces
[]	brackets

Occasionally a single line of code will have to be printed over two or more lines because of paper width restrictions; these lines are signified by a ↳ symbol. Enter these lines without a break when testing any of the programs in which they are used.

For example, the code

```
public class Act18_14 extends JFrame
  ↳implements ItemListener
```

should be entered as a single line.

CHAPTER 1

Background

This chapter covers the following topics:

Binary Numbers

Boolean Expressions

Boolean Operations on Binary Values

Character Codes

Control Structures

Converting between Number Bases

Designing Algorithms

Floating Point Numbers

Hexadecimal Numbers

Octal Numbers

Shift Operations

Stepwise Refinement

Designing Algorithms

Following Instructions

We're all used to following instructions: anything from fire evacuation procedures to how to assemble a flat-pack kitchen unit. Such a sequence of instructions is designed to allow us to perform some specific task. Sometimes the instructions we are carrying out are so familiar to us that we are not even aware of them. For example, driving a car requires us to perform various actions such as changing gear, pressing the brake or accelerator pedals, or turning the wheel. Other tasks, which are new to us, require a more deliberate adherence to the instructions given. For example, when we prepare a pre-packed meal from the freezer we are supplied with instructions such as:

```
Remove meal from carton
Remove lid
Preheat oven to 200°C
Place on baking tray in top half of oven
Leave for 35 minutes
```

A sequence of instructions designed to perform some specific task is known as an **algorithm**.

Every computer operates by following instructions. Such a set of instructions is known as a **computer program**.

The American spelling of program is used to differentiate a computer program from other types such as a TV programme.

Just as we may perform a great diversity of tasks by following a different set of instructions, so the computer can be made to carry out any task for which a program exists.

Computer programs are normally copied (or **loaded**) from a magnetic disk into the computer's memory and then executed (or **run**). Execution of a program involves the computer performing each instruction one after the other. This it does at impressively high rates, possibly exceeding 200 million instructions per second (200mips).

Depending on the program being run, the computer may act as a word processor, a database, a spreadsheet, a game, a musical instrument or one of many other possibilities.

Of course, as a programmer, you are required to design and write computer programs rather than use them.

Computer programs are written in a very formal style using a limited number of commands known to the computer. Like us, computers use many different languages; in this publication we use a relatively new programming language called **Java**.

Program Structures

Although programming is certainly complicated, there are only a few basic concepts and statements which you need to master before you are ready to start producing software. Luckily, the concepts are already familiar to you in everyday situations; all that is needed is to formalise their use to better suit a programming environment.

Sequence

The set of instructions from the frozen meal was given as:

```
Remove meal from carton
Remove lid
Preheat oven to 200°C
Place on baking tray in top half of oven
Leave for 35 minutes
```

This is an example of a **sequence** of instructions. In other words, instructions which are to be carried out one after another, beginning at the first and continuing, without omitting any, until the final instruction is completed.

> **Activity 1.1**
>
> Write down the set of instructions required to wash clothes in an automatic washing machine.

Binary Selection

Often a group of instructions in an algorithm should only be carried out when certain circumstances arise. For example, if we were producing a set of instructions to record a television programme onto video tape we might write:

```
Put a new tape in the machine if there isn't enough space on the
current tape.
```

Such a statement contains two components:

a condition : *there isn't enough space on the current tape*

and

an instruction : *put a new tape in the machine*

A condition is sometimes referred to as a **Boolean expression**

The instruction is only to be carried out if the condition is *true* and hence this is sometimes known as a **conditional instruction**. Although we could rewrite the above instruction in many different ways, when we produce a set of commands in a formal manner, as we are required to do here, then the following format is always used:

```
IF condition THEN
    conditional instructions (executed when condition is true)
ENDIF
```

Using this layout, the instruction to insert a new video tape would be written as:

```
IF there isn't enough space on the current tape THEN
    Put a new tape in the machine
ENDIF
```

Sometimes, there will be several instructions to be carried out when the condition specified is met. For example:

```
IF light bulb is not working THEN
    Switch off power
    Remove old bulb
    Insert new bulb
    Switch on
ENDIF
```

Of course, the conditional statement will almost certainly appear in a longer sequence of instructions. For example, the instructions for sitting an exam may be given as:

```
Write your name and class on the front sheet
When told to do so, turn over and read the exam paper
IF you have any questions THEN
    Raise your hand
    When the invigilator approaches you, ask any questions
ENDIF
Answer all questions in Section A of the paper
Answer only three questions from Section B of the paper
When you have finished, give your answer paper to the invigilator
Leave the room quietly
```

This longer sequence of instructions highlights the usefulness of the term **ENDIF** in separating the final conditional instruction, `When the invigilator approaches you, ask any questions`, from subsequent unconditional instructions.

Activity 1.2

Write a sequence of instructions to make a cup of tea. Start with the instruction `Fill kettle`, end with `Drink tea` and allow for options to add milk and sugar.

The **IF** structure is also used in an extended form to offer a choice between two alternative actions. For example, our earlier cooking instructions could give alternatives for using a conventional cooker or a microwave:

```
IF using a microwave THEN
    Place meal in microwave
    Set to HIGH
    Leave for 12 minutes
ELSE
    Preheat oven to 200°C
    Place on baking tray in top half of oven
    Leave for 35 minutes
ENDIF
```

If the condition is *true* then the statements following the term **THEN** are executed otherwise those following **ELSE** are carried out. The general form of this extended IF statement is:

```
IF condition THEN
    statements to be carried out when condition is true
ELSE
    statements to be carried out when condition is false
ENDIF
```

Activity 1.3

Write a set of instructions to write and post a letter. Start with `Write letter`, end with `Place letter in Post Box` and allow for the choice of sending by first or second class post.

Choosing between two alternative actions is called **binary selection**.

Multi-way Selection

Sometimes choosing from two alternatives is not enough. If our frozen food example gave separate instructions for gas and electric cookers as well as microwaves, we could use two **IF** statements to describe this:

```
IF using a microwave THEN
    Place meal in microwave
    Set to HIGH
    Leave for 12 minutes
ELSE
    IF using an electric oven THEN
        Preheat oven to 200°C
        Place on baking tray in top half of oven
        Leave for 35 minutes
    ELSE
        Preheat oven at gas mark 7
        Place on baking tray in bottom half of oven
        Leave for 40 minutes
    ENDIF
ENDIF
```

Where one IF statement occurs inside another IF statement this is termed **nested IFs.**

Although this is quite acceptable, it is rather difficult to follow. A better method would be to have labelled alternatives:

```
IF
    using microwave:
        Place meal in microwave
        Set to HIGH
        Leave for 12 minutes
    using an electric oven:
        Preheat oven to 200°C
        Place on baking tray in top half of oven
        Leave for 35 minutes
    using a gas oven:
        Preheat oven at gas mark 7
        Place on baking tray in bottom half of oven
        Leave for 40 minutes
ENDIF
```

Each option is explicitly named and only the one which is **true** will be carried out, the others will be ignored. Of course, we are not limited to merely three options; there can be as many as the situation requires.

Activity 1.4

Write a set of instructions to pay for items bought in a large store in which you have an account. Allow options to pay by cash, credit card, cheque or through your account. Start with *Find out total cost*, end with *Take purchases*. You should include statements such as *Hand over credit card, Sign authorisation slip*, *Give account number*, *Take change*, and *Show cheque card.*

When producing a program for a computer, all possibilities have to be taken into account. If we apply that approach to our instructions for cooking the meal, we have to allow for any other possible methods of preparing the meal. Since we cannot know exactly what other methods might be used (possibly portable gas stove, grilling etc.) we need an option which groups all the other possibilities together and supplies a set of instructions to deal with them.

```
IF
    using microwave:
        Place meal in microwave
        Set to HIGH
        Cook for 12 minutes
    using an electric oven:
        Preheat oven to 200°C
        Place on baking tray in top half of oven
        Cook for 35 minutes
    using a gas oven:
        Preheat oven at gas mark 7
        Place on baking tray in bottom half of oven
        Cook for 40 minutes
    ELSE:
        Heat meal until edible
ENDIF
```

The additional **ELSE:** option will be chosen only if none of the other options are applicable. This gives us the final form of:

```
IF
    condition 1 :
        statements to be carried out when condition 1 is met
    condition 2 :
        statements to be carried out when condition 2 is met
         .
         .
    condition x:
        statements to be carried out when condition x is met
    ELSE :
        statements to be carried out when none of the previous
        conditions are met
ENDIF
```

Choosing between several alternatives is known as **multi-way selection.**

Complex Conditions

Often the condition given in an **IF** statement may be a complex one. For example, if a college only admits a student to a course when he has the academic qualifications and good references, then this can be described in our more formal style as:

```
IF student has sufficient qualifications AND has good references
THEN
    Admit student to course
ELSE
    Reject student
ENDIF
```

Note the use of the word **AND** in the above example. **AND** (called a **Boolean operator**) is one of the terms used to link simple conditions in order to produce a more complex one. The conditions on either side of the **AND** are called the **operands**. Both operands must be **true** for the overall condition to be **true**. We can generalise this to describe the **AND** operator as being used in the form:

```
condition 1   AND   condition 2
```

The result of the **AND** operator is determined using the following rules:

1. Determine the truth of condition 1
2. Determine the truth of condition 2
3. IF both conditions are **true** THEN
       the result is **true**
   ELSE
       the result is **false**
   ENDIF

The results of the **AND** operator are summarised in TABLE-1.1.

TABLE-1.1

The AND Operator

condition 1	condition 2	condition 1 AND condition 2
FALSE	FALSE	FALSE
FALSE	TRUE	FALSE
TRUE	FALSE	FALSE
TRUE	TRUE	TRUE

Simple conditions may also be linked by the Boolean operator **OR** as in the instruction:

```
IF it's raining OR it's cold THEN
    Put on coat
ENDIF
```

Like **AND**, the **OR** operator works on two operands:

```
condition 1   OR   condition 2
```

When **OR** is used, only one of the conditions involved needs to be **true** for the overall result to be **true**. Hence the results are determined by the following rules:

1. Determine the truth of condition 1
2. Determine the truth of condition 2
3. IF any of the conditions are **true** THEN
        the result is **true**
    ELSE
        the result is **false**
    ENDIF

The results of the **OR** operator are summarised in TABLE-1.2.

TABLE-1.2

The OR Operator

condition 1	condition 2	condition 1 OR condition 2
FALSE	FALSE	FALSE
FALSE	TRUE	TRUE
TRUE	FALSE	TRUE
TRUE	TRUE	TRUE

The final Boolean operator which can be used as part of a condition is **NOT**. This operator is used to negate the meaning of a condition. Hence ***NOT*** *over 21* has the opposite meaning from *over 21*; that is to say that if *over 21* is **true** then ***NOT*** *over 21* is **false**. Unlike **AND** and **OR**, **NOT** is used with a single operand:

```
NOT condition
```

The results of the **NOT** operator are summarised in TABLE-1.3.

TABLE-1.3 The NOT Operator

condition	NOT condition
FALSE	TRUE
TRUE	FALSE

Complex conditions are not limited to a single occurrence of a Boolean operator, hence it is valid to have the statement:

```
IF it's raining OR it's cold OR it's windy THEN
    Put on coat
ENDIF
```

In this situation, the final result is produced by first determining the truthfulness of each simple condition. If we assume it's a dry, warm but windy day then the original expression can be reduced to:

it's raining **it's windy**

false OR false OR true

it's cold

Next, the result from each Boolean operation is substituted. The left-most operator is dealt with first giving:

it's raining **it's raining OR it's cold**

false OR false = **false**

it's cold

and replacing this result in the original expression gives:

it's raining OR it's cold

false OR true

it's windy

which has a result of:

true

it's raining OR it's cold OR it's windy

And, since the overall result is **true,** *Put on coat* is performed.

Finally, **AND**, **OR** and **NOT** operators may be used in any combination. For example, we might define people due to retire to be those which met the condition:

```
IF you are male AND aged over 65 OR
    you are female AND aged over 60
THEN
    You may retire
ENDIF
```

When various operators are used, **NOT** operations are performed first, followed by **AND** and finally **OR** operations. Where there is more than one identical operator these are calculated from left to right. In the above example, for a 53 year old female we get:

false AND false OR true AND false

Since there are no **NOT** operations, the **AND**s are determined first. Being more than one such operator, the left-most is handled first giving:

false OR true AND false

The second **AND** results in:

false OR false

which gives as a final result

false

Boolean operator priority is summarised in TABLE-1.4.

TABLE-1.4

Boolean Operator Priority

Operator	Priority
NOT	Highest
AND	
OR	Lowest

Sometimes the priority of operators works against what we are trying to express. For example, if an insurance company wants to add an excess to the premium of people under 25 living in Glasgow, Manchester or London, then we might be tempted to write:

```
IF living in Glasgow OR living in Manchester OR
    living in London AND under 25
THEN
    Add excess to premium
ENDIF
```

We would not expect a 26 year old living in Glasgow to pay the excess. But, if we look at the calculation for such a case, we get:

true OR false OR false AND false

the **AND** is calculated to give:

true OR false OR false

Next the left-most **OR** is reduced to give:

true OR false

Which finally reduces to **true**.

To achieve the correct results, we need the **OR** operations to be performed first and this can be done by giving the **OR** operators a higher priority than the **AND**.

Luckily, operator priority can be modified by the use of parentheses. Items in parentheses are always performed first. Rewriting the condition as:

```
IF (living in Glasgow OR living in Manchester OR
    living in London) AND under 25
THEN
    Add excess to premium
ENDIF
```

We now evaluate this as:

	(true	**OR**	**false**	**OR**	**false)**	**AND**	**false**
=	**(true**			**OR**	**false)**	**AND**	**false**
=	**true**					**AND**	**false**
=	**false**						

> **Activity 1.5**
>
> Write the expression for the conditions required in order for a laser printer to produce output. It will be necessary for the printer to be on-line and the toner should not be empty. There must also be paper in the main tray or in the auxiliary tray.

Iteration

There are certain circumstances in which it is necessary to perform the same sequence of instructions several times. For example, if a student sits three tests (each having a possible score of 100) and is given a pass only if his average mark for the tests is 50% or above, then we might describe the logic required in making such a decision as:

```
Set the total to zero
Read mark from test paper
Add mark to total
Read mark from test paper
Add mark to total
Read mark from test paper
Add mark to total
Calculate average as total divided by 3
IF average is not less than 50% THEN
    Student has passed
ELSE
    Student has failed
ENDIF
```

You can see from the above that two instructions,

```
Read mark from test paper
Add mark to total
```

are carried out three times; once for each test taken by the student. Not only does it seem rather time-consuming to have to write the same pair of instructions three times, but it would be worse if the student had sat 10 tests!

What is required is a structure which allows us to specify that a section of the instructions are to be repeated a fixed number of times. This is done using the **FOR..ENDFOR** structure:

FOR .. ENDFOR

Now the above can be rewritten as:

```
Set the total to zero
FOR 3 times DO
    Read mark from test paper
    Add mark to total
ENDFOR
Calculate average as total divided by 3
IF average is not less than 50% THEN
    Student has passed
ELSE
    Student has failed
ENDIF
```

The instructions between the terms **FOR** and **ENDFOR** are now carried out three times. Should the students have to sit 10 tests then all we need to do is rewrite the **FOR** statement as:

```
FOR 10 times DO
    Read mark from test paper
    Add mark to total
ENDFOR
```

The general form of this statement is:

```
FOR number of times required DO
    instructions to be repeated
ENDFOR
```

This structure is often referred to as a **loop structure** and the instructions to be repeated are known as the **loop body**.

Activity 1.6

Write a set of instructions to list the names of those students who achieve a score of less than 50% in an exam. There are exactly 20 students in the class. Your solution should contain the statements

```
Read mark and name
Add name to list of fails
IF mark is less than 50% THEN
```

REPEAT .. UNTIL

There are other circumstances in which, although we want to repeat instructions, the number of times we wish to do this cannot be specified. For example, if we were describing the action of playing a simple slot machine we might write:

```
Put coin in machine
Pull handle
IF you win THEN
    Collect winnings
ENDIF
Repeat the previous statements above until you want to stop
```

Although this describes exactly what is required, the final statement is too clumsy and informal. The instructions can be rewritten as:

```
REPEAT
    Put coin in machine
    Pull handle
    IF you win THEN
        Collect winnings
    ENDIF
UNTIL you want to stop
```

This is a better format since the start and end of the loop body are identified using the terms **REPEAT** and **UNTIL** respectively. The **UNTIL** statement also specifies the condition under which iteration is to stop; this is known as the **terminating condition**.

The general form of this structure is:

```
REPEAT
    loop body
UNTIL terminating condition
```

The terminating condition may use the Boolean operators **AND**, **OR** and **NOT** as well as parentheses, where necessary.

Activity 1.7

Write instructions to look through the articles in a magazine until one written by *Liz Herron* is found. Your solution should contain the instructions

```
Find start of article
Read the author's name
```

WHILE .. ENDWHILE

A final method of iteration, differing only subtly from the **REPEAT.. UNTIL** loop, is the **WHILE .. ENDWHILE** structure which has an **entry condition** at the start of the loop.

For example, when weighing out a half kilogram of individual wrapped sweets, most shopkeepers will empty out roughly the correct amount on to the scales and then add or remove individual sweets until the weight is correct. Using the WHILE structure to describe this action we get:

```
Empty approximately the correct weight of sweets onto the scales
WHILE the weight is incorrect DO
    IF the weight is over THEN
        Remove one sweet from scales
    ELSE
        Add one sweet to scales
    ENDIF
ENDWHILE
Place sweets in paper bag
```

The instruction between the **WHILE** and **ENDWHILE** will be carried out as long as the weight is incorrect. Once the weight is correct (that is, when the condition *weight is incorrect* is **false**) looping terminates and the statement following **ENDWHILE** is performed (*Place sweets in paper bag*).

The general form of this statement is:

```
WHILE continuation condition DO
    loop body
ENDWHILE
```

In what way does this differ from the **REPEAT** statement? There are two differences:

1. The condition is given at the beginning of the loop.
2. Looping stops when the condition is **false**.

The main consequence of this is that it is possible to bypass the loop body of a **WHILE** structure entirely without ever carrying out any of the instructions it contains. If the shopkeeper gets lucky and empties the correct amount onto the scales at the beginning then the condition, *the weight is incorrect*, will be **false** and hence control jumps directly to *Place sweets in paper bag*. In contrast, since the condition is at the end of the loop, the loop body of a **REPEAT** structure must be carried out at least once.

If we try to replace the **WHILE** loop directly with a **REPEAT** loop we get:

```
Empty approximately the correct weight of sweets onto the scale
REPEAT
    IF the weight is over THEN
        Remove one sweet from scales
    ELSE
        Add one sweet to scales
    ENDIF
UNTIL the weight is correct
Place sweets in paper bag
```

Note that the condition has been reversed from that in the original description.

But this doesn't work properly since, if the correct amount is placed on the scales at the beginning, we nevertheless go inside the **REPEAT** loop, find *the weight is over* to be **false** (since the weight is correct), jump to **ELSE** and *Add one sweet to the scales;* but now the condition, *the weight is correct*, in the **UNTIL** statement is no longer **true** and hence we go back round the loop structure to the **IF** statement where the condition, *the weight is over*, is now **true** and hence we remove a sweet. At this point, by first adding then removing a sweet, we have returned to the correct weight so that the condition in the **UNTIL** statement (*the weight is correct*) is at last **true** and the loop is exited and the sweets placed in the bag.

Although the **REPEAT** loop has produced the correct result in the end, it generated some unnecessary actions.

Activity 1.8

A game involves throwing two dice. If the two values thrown are not the same, then the die showing the lower value must be rolled again. This process is continued until both dice show the same value. Write a set of instructions to perform this game. Your solution should contain the statements

`Roll both dice`

and `Choose die with lower value`

Infinite Loops

A potential problem with REPEAT and WHILE loops is, since they do not specify exactly how many times the loop body is to be executed, it is possible to set up a loop structure which will never terminate. For example, we might attempt to describe the logic of weighing sweets as:

```
Empty approximately the correct weight of sweets onto the scale
WHILE the weight is incorrect DO
    Remove one sweet from scales
ENDWHILE
Place sweets in paper bag
```

The above logic is fine - as long as we don't put too few sweets on the scale at the beginning! Should that happen, removing a sweet will only take us further from the goal of getting the correct weight of sweets. With no chance of the condition, *the weight is incorrect,* being **false**, iteration will continue forever (although it won't be possible to keep removing sweets). This is known as an **infinite loop** and should be avoided. You can guard against such loops by mentally checking that some activity within the loop body will eventually result in the loop being exited.

Data

Imagine we need to write down instructions for a trainee insurance salesman who sells car insurance policies by phone. The caller will supply details of the car, his age and the city in which he lives. The salesman will calculate the premium due, adding any excess where necessary and tell the caller the cost. If the caller accepts the offer, the salesman will take additional personal details from the caller and fill out an application form which he then places in a *New Policies* tray on his desk. Our formal description of the operation might be:

```
Get details of car model, engine size, caller's age and city
Calculate premium as half the engine size in cc
IF (city is Glasgow OR Manchester OR London) AND
    age is under 25
THEN
    Calculate excess due as £50 for each year under 25
    Add excess to premium
ENDIF
Tell caller the amount of the premium
Ask if he wishes to accept the policy
IF policy accepted THEN
    Get caller's name, street, post code, phone number and car
    registration number
    Transfer details to policy form
    Get policy number from the top right hand of policy form
    Tell the policy number to caller
    Place form in New Policies tray
ENDIF
```

This example and the previous "test marks" example introduce the need to process facts and figures (known as **data**). In a computing environment most algorithms involve the processing of data. An item of data has two basic characteristics :

a name
and a value.

The name of a data item is a description of the type of information it represents. Hence *caller's name*, *caller's age* and *car registration number* are names of data items; *"Fred Bloggs"*, *27*, and *"M1 CKY"* are examples of the actual values which might be given to these data items.

Note that textual values are enclosed in double quotes while numeric values are not.

In programming, a data item is often referred to as a **variable**. This term arises from the fact that, although the name assigned to a data item cannot change, its value may vary.

Activity 1.9

List the names of five other data items in the insurance example above and give a possible value for each.

There are four basic operations which can be performed on data:

Input

The first involves obtaining a value for a data item. For example, the insurance salesman's instructions include *Get car model*. *Car model* is the name of a data item and the command requires the salesman to obtain a value which he may associate with that name from the caller. In a computer environment, the request to get a value for a data item requires the user of the computer to enter a value at the keyboard. We describe this as a value being **input** to a data item.

Calculation

The second operation involves calculating the value of a data item. For example, *Calculate premium as half the engine size in cc* produces a value for the data item *premium* by calculation. This calculation involves the value of another data item (*engine size*). If *engine size* had been given as 2000cc then *premium* would be £1000.00. Notice also that it is possible to modify the value of a data item; for instance, later in the algorithm we have the instruction *Add excess to premium*, which, for a 21 year-old living in London would result in an excess of £200.00 being added to *premium*; changing the value of that data item from £1000.00 to £1200.00. This is referred to as a **calculation operation**.

Comparison

The value of a data item may be compared against some other value. The insurance example compares the value given to *city* to see if it is equal to "Glasgow", "Manchester" or "London".

Output

The final operation is to disclose the value currently held in a data item. For example, the instruction, *Tell caller the amount of the premium*, is a request to state the value associated with the data item, *premium*. In a computer environment, the equivalent operation would normally involve displaying information on a screen or printing it on paper. This is called **output** of data.

Activity 1.10

Identify other input, calculation and output statements in the insurance premium example above.

When describing a calculation, it is common to use arithmetic operator symbols rather than English. Hence, instead of writing the word *subtract* we use the minus sign (-). A summary of the operators available are given in TABLE-1.5.

TABLE-1.5

Mathematical Operators

English	Symbol
Multiply	*
Divide	/
Add	+
Subtract	-

Like Boolean operators, mathematical operators are dealt with on a priority basis. Multiply and divide have the higher (and equal) priority; add and subtract, the lower.

As well as replacing the arithmetic operator words with symbols, the term `calculate`, is often replaced by the shorter but more cryptic symbol, :=

Using this abbreviated form, the instruction:

```
Calculate premium as half the engine size in cc
```

becomes

```
premium := engine size in cc / 2
```

Read the symbol := as "is assigned the value".

Levels of Detail

Although we might write the instructions for setting a video to record a program as:

```
Put new tape in video
Set timer details
```

this lacks enough detail for anyone unfamiliar with the operation of the machine. We could replace the first statement with:

```
Press the eject button
IF there is a tape in the machine THEN
    Remove it
ENDIF
Place the new tape in the machine
```

and the second statement could be substituted by:

```
Switch to timer mode
Enter start time
Enter finish time
Select channel
```

This approach of starting with a less detailed sequence of instructions and then, where necessary, replacing each of these with more detailed instructions can be used to good effect when tackling long and complex problems. By using this technique, we are defining the original problem as an equivalent sequence of simpler tasks before going on to create a set of instructions for each of these simpler problems. This divide-and-conquer strategy is known as **stepwise refinement**.

The following is a fully worked example of this technique:

Problem:
Produce a wage slip for an hourly paid worker. The worker gets paid £5.60 per hour when working between 0900 and 1700 Monday to Friday. If he works on Saturdays or after 1700 during the working week, he is paid £8.40 per hour. Sunday working pays a rate of £11.20 per hour. He has to pay 9% of his gross wage to superannuation, 10% of the gross wage to National Insurance. Of the remainder, the first £80.00 is tax free and the remainder is taxed at 25%.

Outline Solution

```
1.  Get details of hours worked
2.  Calculate gross wage
3.  Calculate deductions
4.  Calculate net wage
5.  Write details onto wage slip
```

This is termed a **LEVEL 1 solution**.

As a guideline we should aim for a LEVEL 1 solution with at most 20 statements - preferably significantly less.

Notice that each instruction has been numbered. This is merely to help with identification during the stepwise refinement process.

Before going any further, we must assure ourselves that this is a correct and full (though not detailed) description of all the steps required to tackle the original problem. If we are not happy with the solution, then changes must be made before we go any further.

Next, we examine each statement in turn and determine if it should be described in more detail. Where this is necessary, rewrite the statement to be dealt with, and below it, give the more detailed version. For example, *Get details of hours worked* would be expanded thus:

```
1.  Get details of hours worked
    1.1 Get hours at basic rate
    1.2 Get hours at time-and-a-half
    1.3 Get hours at double time
```

The numbering of the new statement reflects that they are the detailed instructions pertaining to statement 1. Also note that the number system is not decimal fraction so if there were to be many more statements they would be numbered 1.4, 1.5, 1.6, 1.7, 1.8, 1.9, 1.10, 1.11, etc.

It is important that these sets of more detailed instructions describe how to perform only the original task being examined - they must achieve no more and no less. Sometimes the detailed instructions will contain control structures such as IFs, WHILEs or FORs. Where this is the case, the whole structure must be included in the detailed instructions. That is to say, it is not possible to have, say, a FOR statement to start in the breakdown of statement 1 and the corresponding ENDFOR statement to appear in the breakdown of statement 2.

Having satisfied ourselves that the breakdown is correct, we proceed to the next statement from the original solution.

```
2.  Calculate gross wage
    2.1 Calculate gross wage as hours at basic rate * £5.60 +
        hours at time-and-a-half * £8.40 +
        hours at double time * £11.20
```

This time we haven't expanded into more statements but simply added detail to the original instruction.

The other statements expand as follows:

```
3.  Calculate deductions
    3.1 Calculate superannuation as 9% of gross wage
    3.2 Calculate national insurance as 10% of gross wage
    3.3 Calculate taxable pay as gross wage -
        (superannuation + national insurance + £80.00)
    3.4 IF taxable pay is greater than zero THEN
    3.5     Calculate tax due as 25% of taxable pay
    3.6 ELSE
    3.7     Set tax due to zero
    3.8 ENDIF
```

The **IF** statement allows for the possibility that the gross wage is not sufficient to incur tax.

Note that we have introduced a new data item, *taxable pay*, which although useful in arriving at *net wage* is not itself one of the data items required by the system. Such data items are called **temporary** or **local variables**.

```
4.  Calculate net wage
    4.1 Calculate net wage as gross wage -
        (superannuation + national insurance + tax due)
```

```
5.  Write details onto wage slip
    5.1 Write gross wage on payslip
    5.2 Write superannuation on wage slip
    5.3 Write national insurance on wage slip
    5.4 Write tax due on wage slip
    5.5 Write net wage on wage slip
```

Finally, we can describe the solution to the original problem in terms of the more detailed sequence of instructions:

```
1.1 Get hours at basic rate
1.2 Get hours at time-and-a-half
1.3 Get hours at double time
2.1 Calculate gross wage as hours at basic rate * £5.60
    + hours at time-and-a-half * £8.40
    + hours at double time * £11.20
3.1 Calculate superannuation as 9% of gross wage
3.2 Calculate national insurance as 10% of gross wage
3.3 Calculate taxable pay as gross wage -
    (superannuation + national insurance + £80.00)
3.4 IF taxable pay is greater than zero THEN
3.5     Calculate tax due as 25% of taxable pay
3.6 ELSE
3.7     Set tax due to zero
3.8 ENDIF
4.1 Calculate net wage as gross wage -
    (superannuation + national insurance + tax due)
5.1 Write gross wage on payslip
5.2 Write superannuation on wage slip
5.3 Write national insurance on wage slip
5.4 Write tax due on wage slip
5.5 Write net wage on wage slip
```

This is a LEVEL 2 solution. Note that a level 2 solution is produced by bringing together, in the correct order, the individual solutions of the LEVEL 1 instructions.

A Few Points to Note about Stepwise Refinement

For some more complex problems it may be necessary to repeat this process to more levels before sufficient detail is achieved. That is, statements in LEVEL 2 may need to be given more detail in a LEVEL 3 breakdown.

Not all statements need to be broken down to a lower level. For example, a LEVEL 1 solution might contain the statement `FOR 10 times DO` which may be left unaltered in a LEVEL 2 solution.

Activity 1.11

An orders clerk for a mail order company takes orders over the telephone. Customers begin by stating the number of different items they wish to purchase. For each item the clerk requests the catalogue number which, if given incorrectly, will require to be restated (it is possible that an invalid number will be given several times before the customer finally gives a recognised value). The clerk also asks the quantity required before checking if the item is in stock. If the item is out of stock or there is insufficient quantity, the clerk will offer an alternative if one is available. The clerk adds available items to an order list. Once the call is complete, the order list is sent to the dispatches department.

Continued on next page

Activity 1.11 (continued)

A possible LEVEL 1 solution to this task is:

```
1.  Get number of items
2.  FOR each item DO
3.      Get order details
4.      Process item
5.  ENDFOR
6.  Send order to dispatches department
```

Write a LEVEL 2 solution which should include statements such as:

IF item in stock AND sufficient quantity THEN
WHILE catalogue number is invalid DO
Check for alternative
IF alternative acceptable THEN

Summary

- Computers can perform many tasks by executing different programs.
- An **algorithm** is a sequence of instructions which solves a specific problem.
- A **program** is a sequence of computer instructions which usually manipulates data and produces results.
- **Three control structures** are used in programs :
  - Sequence
  - Selection
  - Iteration
- A **sequence** is a list of instructions which are performed one after the other.
- **Selection** is performed using the IF statement.
- **There are three forms of IF statement:**

```
IF condition THEN
    instructions
ENDIF
```

```
IF condition THEN
    instructions
ELSE
    instructions
ENDIF
```

```
IF
    condition 1:
        instructions
    condition 2:
        instructions
        .
        .
    condition x :
        instructions
    ELSE:
        instructions
ENDIF
```

- **Iteration** is performed using one of three instructions:

```
FOR number of iterations required DO
    instructions
ENDFOR

REPEAT
    instructions
UNTIL condition

WHILE condition DO
    instructions
ENDWHILE
```

- **An infinite loop** may result from an incorrectly formed iteration.
- A **condition** is an expression which is either **true** or **false**.
- **Simple conditions can be linked** using **AND** or **OR** to produce a complex condition.
- **The meaning of a condition can be reversed** by adding the word **NOT**.
- **Data items** (or variables) hold the information used by the algorithm.
- **Data item values** may be:

  Input
  Calculated
  Compared
  or Output

- **Calculations** can be performed using the operators:

Multiplication	*
Division	/
Addition	+
Subtraction	-

- **The symbol :=** is used to assign a value to a data item. Read this symbol as *is assigned the value.*
- In programming, a data item is referred to as a **variable**.
- The divide-and-conquer strategy of **stepwise refinement** can be used when creating an algorithm.
- **LEVEL 1 solution gives an overview** of the sub-tasks involved in carrying out the required operation.
- **LEVEL 2 gives a more detailed solution** by taking each sub-task from LEVEL 1 and, where necessary, giving a more detailed list of instructions required to perform that sub-task.
- **Further levels of detail** may be necessary when using stepwise refinement for complex problems.
- **Further refinement may not be required** for every statement.

- The order of priority of operators are:

Operator	Meaning	Priority
*	Multiply	1
/	Divide	1
+	Add	2
-	Subtract	2
NOT		3
AND		4
OR		5
:=	Is assigned the value	6

Items of equal priority are evaluated from left to right.

- The order of priority may be overridden using parentheses.

Number Systems

Introduction

The counting system we use today is the decimal or, more correctly, the **denary** system. It uses ten different symbols (0,1,2,3,4,5,6,7,8,9) to represent any value. The number of digits used in a number system is known as the **base** or **radix** of the system. Hence denary is a base 10 system.

In our number system, the position of a digit affects the value. Hence, 19 and 91, although containing the same digits, represent two different values.

In primary school we are often taught the theory of numbers by the use of column headings:

Thousands *Hundreds* *Tens* *Units*

To represent a value, we merely write the required numeric symbol in each of the appropriate columns. For example, to write down the number seven hundred and thirteen we place a 7 in the Hundreds column, a 1 in the Tens column and a 3 in the Units column:

Hundreds	*Tens*	*Units*
7	1	3

A more mathematical heading for these columns would be

10^2 is simply short-hand for 10*10.

The result of raising any number to the power zero is 1.

10^2	10^1	10^0
7	1	3

Note that the column value is based on the number radix being used. Hence, for any number system (say, to the base R) the value of the columns can be written as

$$\ldots \quad R^4 \quad R^3 \quad R^2 \quad R^1 \quad R^0$$

The Binary System

A modern computer stores all the information it holds, be it instructions, numbers or text, as a sequence of number codes. But the number system used by a computer has a base of two rather than ten. This is the **binary system** where every value is represented by only two digits: 0 and 1. Columns in this system have the values:

$$\ldots \quad 2^7 \quad 2^6 \quad 2^5 \quad 2^4 \quad 2^3 \quad 2^2 \quad 2^1 \quad 2^0$$

which replacing the powers of two headings, gives the column values:

128 64 32 16 8 4 2 1

The binary digits, 0 and 1, are referred to as **bits** (short for **b**inary dig**its**). Values are most often stored in eight bit groups.

This collection of eight bits is called a **byte**.

Converting from Decimal to Binary

From this information we can begin to see how we might represent a decimal number, say 23, in binary. Since 23 can be constructed from the values 16 + 4 + 2 + 1, we simply need to place a 1 in each of those columns, filling all other columns with zeros. Using the standard eight bit grouping the decimal value 23 is represented as:

128	*64*	*32*	*16*	*8*	*4*	*2*	*1*
0	0	0	1	0	1	1	1

Generalising this approach, we can construct a simple algorithm to convert any decimal number to its binary equivalent:

An ***integer*** value has no fractional part (i.e. a whole number).

```
Get positive decimal number
REPEAT
    Divide by 2, writing down integer part of the answer
    and whole number remainder
UNTIL the answer is zero
Write down the remainders in a line, last one first, from left to
right
```

The operation is shown in FIG-1.1.

FIG-1.1

Converting Decimal to Binary

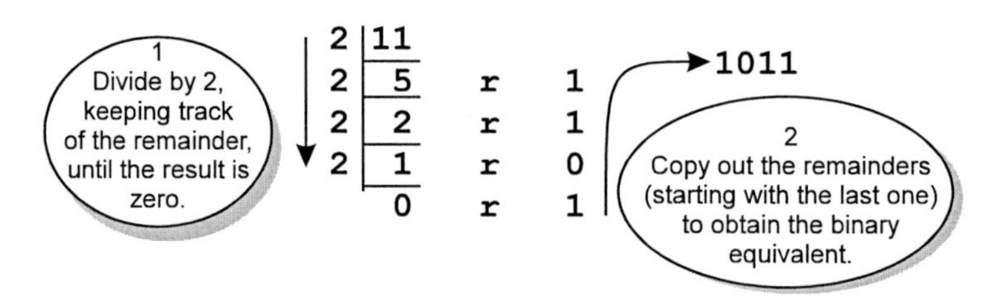

> **Activity 1.12**
>
> Convert the following numbers to 8-bit binary:
>
> 19
> 72
> 63

Binary to Decimal

To convert from binary to decimal, take the value of each column containing a one and add these values to arrive at the decimal equivalent. An example is shown in FIG-1.2.

FIG-1.2

Binary to Decimal Conversion

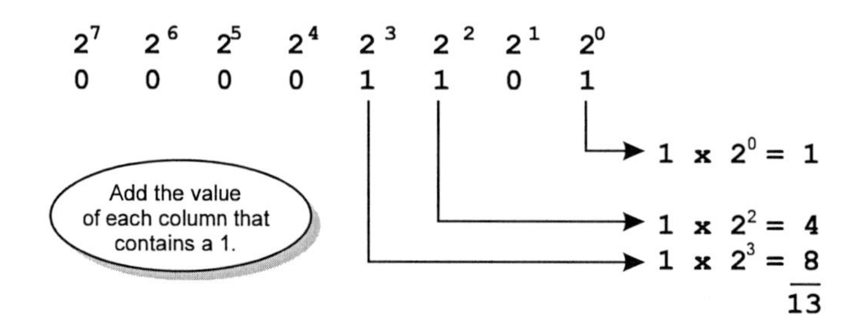

Activity 1.13

Convert the following binary values to decimal.

```
00101001
11111111
10101010
```

Converting Fractions

So far we have only looked at converting whole numbers (integers) but we also need to be able to represent decimal fractions in binary.

Decimal fractions have column values of

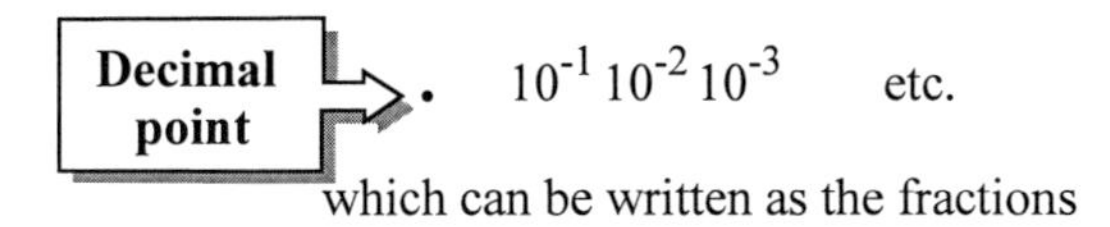

. $10^{-1}\ 10^{-2}\ 10^{-3}$ etc.

which can be written as the fractions

. $\frac{1}{10}\ \frac{1}{100}\ \frac{1}{1000}$

Binary fractions, on the other hand, have column values of

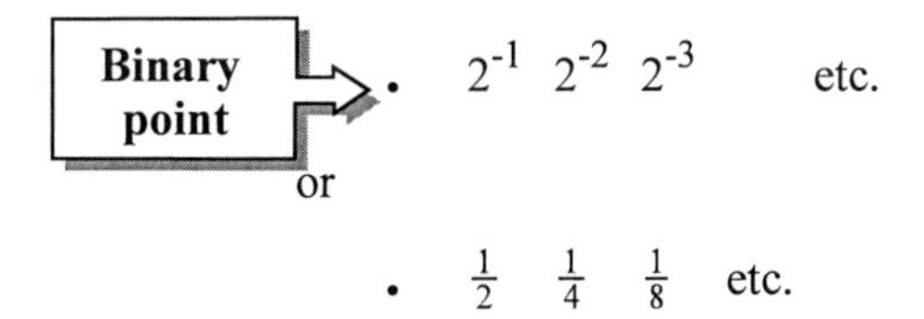

. $2^{-1}\ 2^{-2}\ 2^{-3}$ etc.

or

. $\frac{1}{2}\ \frac{1}{4}\ \frac{1}{8}$ etc.

To convert from a decimal fraction to the binary equivalent, the following algorithm can be employed:

```
Get decimal fraction
Copy decimal fraction to worked value
Write '0.'
REPEAT
    Multiply worked value by 2
    Write down integer part of the result
    Remove the integer part from the worked value
UNTIL worked value is zero OR required degree of accuracy obtained
```

The first iteration of this operation is shown in FIG-1.3.

FIG-1.3

Decimal Fraction to Binary

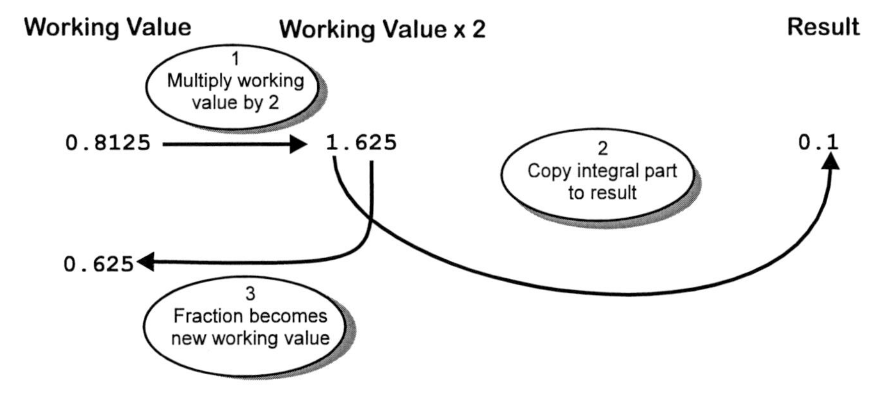

A full example of the conversion is shown below:

Value to be converted : 0.8125

Working value		*Working value x 2*	*Result*
			0.
0.8125	x 2	1.625	0.1
0.625	x 2	1.25	0.11
0.25	x 2	0.5	0.110
0.5	x 2	1.0	0.1101
0			

Activity 1.14

Convert the following decimal fractions to binary (stop after 6 binary places):

```
0.75
0.3125
0.38
```

Binary fractions to decimal present no problem since, like integers, it is simply a matter of adding the values of any column containing a 1.

To convert decimal numbers which contain a whole number and fraction part, such as 3.1415, simply split the number into its two parts, integer and fraction, and convert each separately.

Activity 1.15

1. Convert the binary value 0.01011 to decimal.

2. Convert the decimal value 12.625 to binary.

Hexadecimal

The **hexadecimal** system is another number system which is widely used in computing. It has a base of 16 which implies there are 16 different digits. However, since our own decimal system has only 10 digits, we are left with the problem of representing values between 10 and 15 (decimal) by a single digit. This is achieved by using the first 6 letters of the alphabet. Thus decimal 10 is represented by A, 11 by B and so on.

Column values in hexadecimal are

... 16^3 16^2 16^1 16^0

or

4096 256 16 1

Conversion from decimal to hexadecimal uses the same technique as that for binary, except this time we divide by 16 and any remainders greater than 9 are converted to the equivalent letter code. FIG-1.4 shows an example of decimal to hexadecimal conversion.

Hexadecimal to decimal uses the same method as with binary to decimal; only the column values are different (see FIG-1.5).

FIG-1.4

Decimal to Hexadecimal Conversion

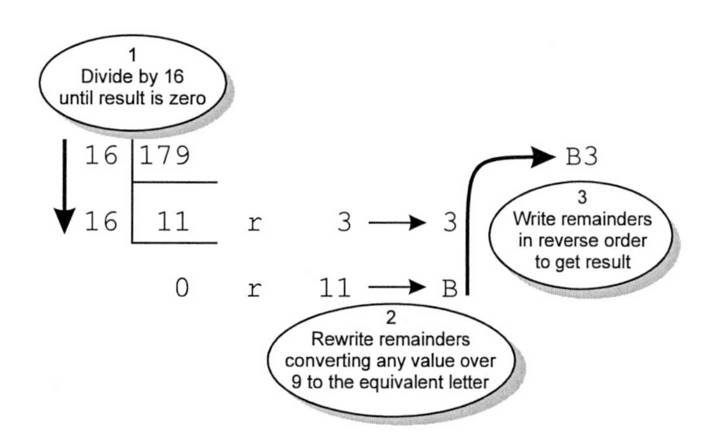

FIG-1.5

Hexadecimal to Decimal Conversion

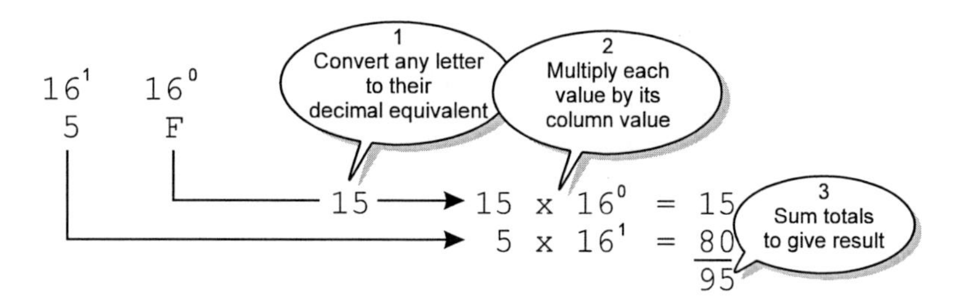

The most likely conversions when using hexadecimal are to and from binary. Four binary digits can range between 0000 and 1111 in value. Since this represents the values 0 to 15 we can use a single hexadecimal digit, 0 to F, to represent these four bits. Thus the contents of a single byte can be shown as two hexadecimal digits. The conversion technique is shown in FIG-1.6.

FIG-1.6

Binary to Hexadecimal Conversion

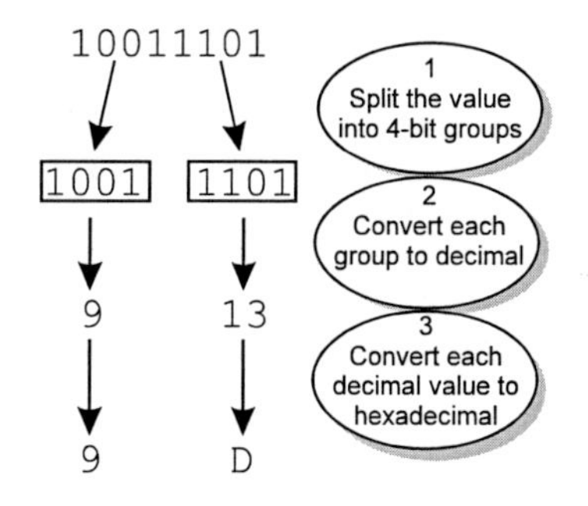

Conversion from hexadecimal to binary simply involves reversing this process as shown in FIG-1.7.

FIG-1.7

Hexadecimal to Binary Conversion

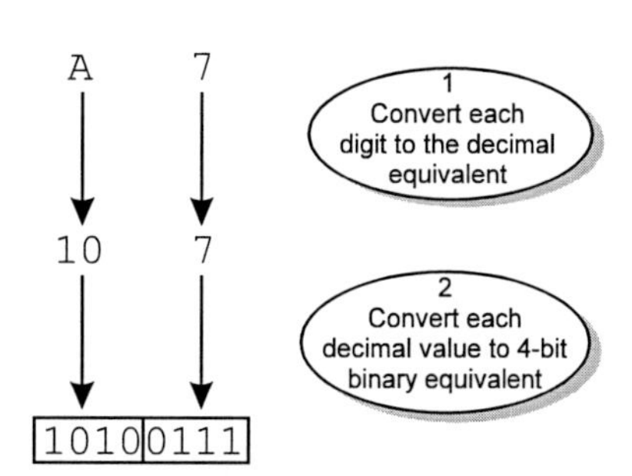

Activity 1.16

1. Convert the following binary values to hexadecimal:

```
01000111
11111111
11001011
```

2. Convert the following hexadecimal values to binary:

```
73
A2
FE
```

Octal

A final number system, which is useful in machines that use a 6 bit configuration rather than the more widespread 8 bit organisation, is **octal**. Octal is a base 8 numbering system using the digits 0 to 7.

Column values are

... 8^2 8^1 8^0

that is

... 64 8 1

Decimal to octal is achieved by continually dividing by 8 until a result of zero is arrived at and then copying out the remainders (last one being the most significant).

Octal to decimal is performed by multiplying each digit in the octal value by its column value and summing these values.

Binary to octal requires the binary value to be split into groupings of three bits. Grouping starts from the right-hand side; where the number of bits is not exactly divisible by three, the left-most group may have only one or two bits. Each group is converted to its decimal equivalent; these digits give the final result.

Octal to binary requires each octal digit to be converted to exactly three binary digits.

It will not be necessary to convert octal to or from hexadecimal.

Activity 1.17

1. Convert the following binary values to octal:

```
  101001
10011100
11111111
```

2. Convert the following octal values to decimal:

```
 75
121
333
```

Identify a Number's Base

Where a piece of text may refer to several number systems it is usual to include a subscript giving the number base being represented. Hence the decimal value 77 would be written as

77_{10}

while the hexadecimal value 57 would be shown as

57_{16}

Negative Numbers

In an 8 bit byte we can store any binary value between 00000000 and 11111111 which, in decimal, is 0 to 255. But how are negative numbers, such as -17, stored?

Imagine we are sitting in a car whose current journey odometer is set to 0000. If we drive forward one mile then we will have a reading of 0001. If, on the other hand, we were to drive in reverse for one mile the reading would be 9999. Now, if we consider moving forward in the car as equivalent to moving up through the positive numbers, while reversing is a movement through the negative range (as illustrated in FIG-1.8), then we can think of the reading on the odometer as representations of both positive and negative numbers (e.g. 0001 = +1; 9999 = -1). Some of the values are shown in TABLE-1.6.

FIG-1.8

Representing Positive and Negative Values on the Odometer

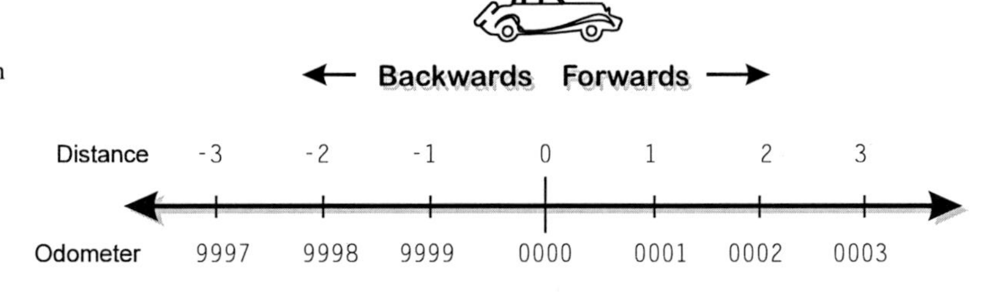

TABLE-1.6

Representation of Positive and Negative Values

Integer value	Reading
-3	9997
-2	9998
-1	9999
0	0000
1	0001
2	0002
3	0003

Of course, using this approach has a cost since the range of positive numbers we can represent has now been reduced. Readings such as 9996 no longer represent the value +9996 but rather -4. And what of the reading 5001? Does it represent the value +5001 or -4999? At some point on our readings we have to decide on a split between those which represent positive values and those which are negative. If we make the split half way (giving 5000 positive values - if zero is included; and 5000 negative values) we get the reading split as shown in TABLE-1.7.

TABLE-1.7

Negative and Positive Ranges

Reading	Integer value
0000	0
4999	4999
5000	-5000
9999	-1

This representation of negative values works rather well when performing arithmetic operations. For example, the subtraction:

47 -12

which can be rewritten as:

47 + (-12)

This is represented in our new system as:

0047 + (9988)

which, when added, gives:

0035

Remember, the odometer only has 4 digits, so the fifth digit (1) of the above addition is not stored in the result.

2's Complement

This same approach is used in binary where this method of representation is known as **2's complement**. With an 8 bit storage unit, values between -128 and +127 can be stored (as shown in TABLE-1.8)

TABLE-1.8

Negative and Positive Ranges

Byte	Integer value
00000000	0
01111111	127
10000000	-128
11111111	-1

Decimal to 2's Complement

We already have a technique for converting a positive whole number to its binary equivalent and this can be extended to find the 2's complement value for negative numbers. The algorithm required is:

```
Get negative value
Ignoring the sign, convert to binary using all bits
Starting at right hand digit
REPEAT
    Copy current digit into result
    Move to the next digit to the left
UNTIL digit copied is a 1
FOR each remaining digit DO
    Copy the opposite digit into the result
ENDFOR
```

Opposite digit means 1's are changed to zeros and vice versa.

For example, to find the 2's complement form of the value -68, we first find the binary representation of +68:

```
01000100
```

This example assumes the value is being stored in a single byte (8 bits).

Next copy every digit (from the right) unchanged up to and including the first 1:

```
     100
```

Finally, copy the remaining digits but changing 1's to 0's and vice versa:

```
10111100
```

Where a number is stored over 16 bits (2 bytes) this allows a larger range of values: -32,768 to 32,767 to be held, but the same 2's complement strategy is employed Hence, the value -68 would be stored in 16 bits as

```
11111111 10111100
```

> **Activity 1.18**
>
> Convert the following values to 2's complement form in both 8 and 16 bit format:
>
> ```
>   -3
>  -42
> -127
> ```

2's Complement to Decimal

Before converting a 2's complement value to decimal we must first decide if we are dealing with a negative value or a positive one. Looking back at TABLE-1.8 we can see that the left-most digit of all negative values is a 1 while it is 0 for positive values. Hence, where the left-most digit is a zero, conversion is achieved by following the same technique as that described earlier for positive binary values: add the values of each column containing a 1.

This means that, for negative values, we first convert the value to the equivalent positive value. Therefore, faced with the value

```
11001110
```

we begin by copying all the digits from the right up to and including the first 1

```
      10
```

and then changing each of the remaining digits

```
00110010
```

This results in the positive form of the original number which can then be converted in the usual way. Obviously, a minus sign must be placed in front of the result:

```
        128 64  32  16   8   4   2   1
         0   0   1   1   0   0   1   0

=   -(32 + 16 + 2)

=   -50
```

To summarise, whole numbers are stored in a computer's memory as a binary pattern. The representation used may not allow for negative numbers (the storage format is said to be **unsigned** or **absolute**). Alternatively, by using 2's complement (or **signed** format), both positive and negative values may be stored. If a value is stored in a single byte, using unsigned format ,any value between 0 and 255 can be represented, while 2's complement will allow values in the range -128 to +127.

When presented with a binary value it is necessary to know which of the above storage formats is being used before converting the value to decimal. For example, 11111111 represents the value 255 in unsigned format and -1 in 2's complement form.

Floating Point Values

Real numbers (those with fractional parts) are stored in a different format. The format used within the computer is similar to that employed when writing numbers in scientific notation. Numbers such as 12.8 are said to be written in **fixed point format** but the same number can also be written as 1.28E1. This is **scientific** or **floating point** notation. Although it may look somewhat unfriendly, if you're unfamiliar with this form, it is simply a formula for the original number. Hence,

$$\begin{aligned} & 1.28 \times 10^1 \\ = \ & 1.28 \times 10 \\ = \ & 12.8 \end{aligned}$$

The value 365.249 would be written as 3.65249E2 which is:

$$\begin{aligned} & 3.65249 \times 10^2 \\ = \ & 3.65249 \times 100 \\ = \ & 365.249 \end{aligned}$$

The first part of the floating point number (e.g. 3.65249) is termed the **mantissa**; the second part following the letter E is the **exponent**. The exponent represents the power of ten by which the mantissa must be multiplied to give the value being represented. The mantissa is always shown as a value greater than or equal to 1 and less than10. This is called the **normalised mantissa**.

For small numbers, such as 0.00013 the exponent will be negative:

$$\begin{aligned} & 0.00013 \\ = \ & 1.3E\text{-}4 \end{aligned}$$

For negative values, the mantissa is negative:

$$\begin{aligned} & -6712.8 \\ = \ & -6.7128E3 \end{aligned}$$

Again, conversion from fixed to floating point notation can be explained using a simple algorithm:

```
Get the fixed point value
The mantissa is the original number with the decimal point
moved between the first and second non-zero digit
Add an 'E'
IF the original value was less than 1 THEN
    Place a minus sign in front of the exponent
ENDIF
The exponent is the number of places the decimal point
had to be moved to change the original number into the
normalised mantissa
```

Activity 1.19

Convert the following values to floating point notation:

```
123.98
  6.9
 -0.00000001
```

When using floating point notation within the computer, the following approach is employed:

```
Get decimal value
Convert it to binary
Create the mantissa by moving binary point to left of the most
 significant 1
The exponent is the number of places the point was moved
 (written in binary)
IF the binary point was moved to the right THEN
    The exponent is negative
ENDIF
```

For example:

```
46.375
```

converts to

```
101110.011
```

giving a mantissa of

```
.101110011
```

and an exponent of

```
110
```

This format is changed slightly in most software to optimise the storage requirements and the efficiency of the algorithms used for manipulating floating point values.

There are two main changes. When storing real numbers in binary form, the exponent is usually held as a positive value. This is achieved by adding some value to the correct exponent, which may well be negative. For example, if the exponent occupies 8 bits of the space allocated to a real value, this allows for a range of values from -128 to 127 when 2's complement form is being used. However, if we add 128 to the exponent once it has been calculated and hold the value in unsigned format, a range of 0 to 255 can be accommodated. This is called a **biased exponent**. The mantissa is also modified slightly by omitting the most significant digit when it is stored. Since the first digit of the mantissa must be a 1, there is little point in actually storing it. This frees up one more bit to hold the remaining digits of the mantissa which results in slightly increased accuracy.

The storage format used is shown in FIG-1.9. The number of bits allocated to each component will depend on the implementation.

FIG-1.9

Floating Point Storage

Biased Exponent	Mantissa

Activity 1.20

Assuming floating point numbers are stored in 24 bits, the mantissa occupying 16 bits and the exponent 8 bits, show how the value 0.09375 would be stored. Assume an exponent with a bias value of 128.

Character Coding

As well as numbers, computers need to store characters. Since everything in the machine is stored in binary, this means that we need some coding system to represent these characters. This is much the same approach as employed in morse code where dots and dashes are used to represent letters.

ASCII stands for American Standard Code for Information Interchange

Although several coding methods are employed, originally the most universal one was the **ASCII** coding system. This uses a single byte (of which only seven bits are used) to store a letter in upper or lower case, or a punctuation character. This allows 128 different characters. For example the code for 'A' is

```
01000001
```

This is also the binary equivalent of the decimal value 65 and in order to correctly interpret a binary pattern stored in the machine, the computer needs to be aware of the type of value the pattern represents (a number or a character).

The IBM extended character set is an extension of the ASCII coding which makes use of the eighth bit to allow an extra 128 characters. Some of these codes are used for special European characters, others allow for simple graphics characters.

A new coding system using 16 bits is currently being finalised. This allocates codes to the characters of many other languages used throughout the world. The new coding system is referred to as **Unicode**. The first 128 characters in Unicode match exactly those of the still widely used ASCII coding system.

The full ASCII character set is shown in APPENDIX A.

Summary

- Computers store all data in **binary**.
- **Binary is a base 2 number system.**
- **Binary uses the digits 0 and 1.**
- **A binary digit** is often referred to as a **bit**.
- **Bits are most often organised into 8 bits**. A group of 8 bits is known as a **byte**.
- **Decimal to binary** conversion of integer values is achieved by continually dividing by 2 until a result of zero is achieved. The remainders (last one being the most-significant digit) form the result.
- **Decimal to binary** conversion of fractions is achieved by continually multiplying the remaining fraction by 2 until a result of zero or the required accuracy is achieved. The integral part of each result forms the binary value.

- **Real decimal values greater than 1** are changed to binary by converting the integer and fractional parts separately.
- Before converting from binary to decimal it is necessary to know which format is being used: **unsigned** or **2's complement** format.
- **For positive values,** binary to decimal conversion is achieved by summing the value of each column containing a one.
- **For negative values,** binary to decimal conversion is achieved by first converting to the positive equivalent.
- **Hexadecimal is a base 16 number system** using the digits 0 to 9, A to F.
- **A single byte can be represented by** two hexadecimal digits.
- **Decimal to hexadecimal** conversion is achieved by continually dividing by 16 until a result of zero is achieved. Any remainder over 9 is converted to the equivalent hexadecimal letter (10 = A, 11 = B etc.). The remainders (last one being the most-significant digit) represent the result.
- **Hexadecimal to decimal** conversion is achieved by summing the value of each column containing a non-zero digit.
- **Binary to hexadecimal** conversion is achieved by grouping the binary value into 4 bit groups; converting each group to the decimal equivalent; converting each decimal value to the hexadecimal equivalent.
- **Hexadecimal to binary** conversion is achieved by converting each hexadecimal digit to the decimal equivalent; converting each decimal value to the equivalent 4 bit binary value.
- **Octal is a base 8 number system** using the digits 0 to 7.
- **Decimal to octal** conversion is achieved by continually dividing by eight until a result of zero is achieved. The remainders (last one being the most-significant digit) represent the result.
- **Octal to decimal** conversion is achieved by summing the value of each column containing a non-zero digit.
- **Binary to octal** conversion is achieved by grouping the binary value into 3 bit groups; converting each group to the decimal equivalent.
- **Octal to binary** conversion is achieved by converting each octal digit to the equivalent 3 bit binary value.
- **The base of a value** can be shown as a subscript following the number.
- **Signed binary values** are held in 2's complement form.
- **Floating point values** are constructed from a mantissa and exponent.
- **Normalising a decimal mantissa** involves moving the decimal point until its value is not less than 1 and less than 10.
- **Normalising a binary mantissa** involves moving the binary point until the most significant 1 is to its immediate right.

- **The exponent represents** the number of places the mantissa's point must be moved to restore the original number. The exponent is negative if the point needs to be moved to the left.
- In the computer, **floating point values are often held with a biased exponent and the first 1 missing from the mantissa.**
- **The Unicode character set** is used by Java to allow the character sets of many writing systems to be represented.
- **Unicode characters** occupy 2 bytes each.
- **The earlier ASCII code** used a single byte to hold characters.
- **The first 128 characters in Unicode** match the ASCII character set.

Operations on Bits

As well as being able to perform arithmetic calculations using bits, it is also possible to perform logic operations such as AND and OR.

AND

As we saw earlier, when two Boolean expressions are ANDed together we get the result *true*, only where the original expressions were both *true*.

If we think of 0 (zero) as equivalent to *false* and 1 as equivalent to *true* then we can see that

```
1 AND 1 = 1
```

while

```
0 AND 1 = 0
```

The various combinations for the AND are summarised in TABLE-1.9

TABLE-1.9

The AND Operator

Bit 1	Bit 2	Bit 1 AND Bit 2
0	0	0
0	1	0
1	0	0
1	1	1

Rather than ANDing single bits, a more likely occurrence is that two integer values will be ANDed. A result is obtained by ANDing the bits in each column separately. An example is shown in FIG-1.10.

FIG-1.10

Using the AND Operator

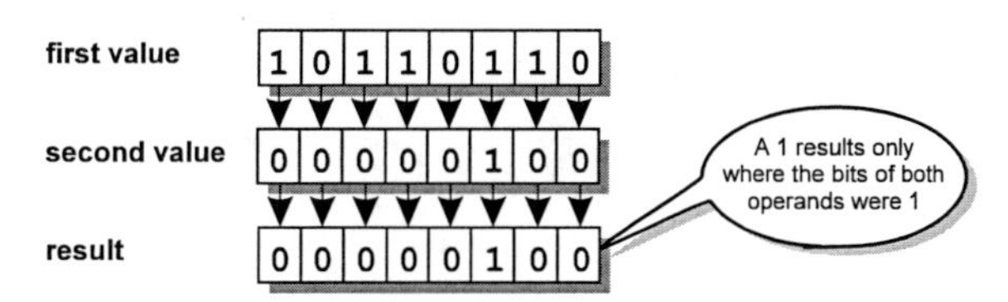

Activity 1.21

Write down the results of ANDing the following values:

a) `10101010 AND 01010101`
b) `10111101 AND 01001111`
c) `00100111 AND 11110011`

ANDing values can be of practical use when coding algorithms. For example, if we want to read in a number and then display the word "Odd" if the value entered is not even, then we might write

```
Read a number
IF number is odd THEN
    Display "Odd"
ENDIF
```

Assumes result is 8 bits.

But how would we determine if the number was odd? Well, every odd number, when held in binary must end with a 1 (the right-hand column is the only one with an odd value). So we could determine if a value is odd by writing

Actually, there is no need for the leading zeros and so we could write

number AND 1

```
Read a number
Calculate result as number AND 00000001
IF result is not zero THEN
    Display "Odd"
ENDIF
```

OR

OR returns a *true* result when any of the original Boolean expressions are *true*. Using binary, this means that a 1 is obtained if any of the values being ORed are 1.

Possible results when ORing two bits are shown in TABLE-1.10.

TABLE-1.10

The OR Operator

Bit 1	Bit 2	Bit 1 OR Bit 2
0	0	0
0	1	1
1	0	1
1	1	1

A typical ORing of two bytes is shown in FIG-1.11.

FIG-1.11

Using the OR Operator

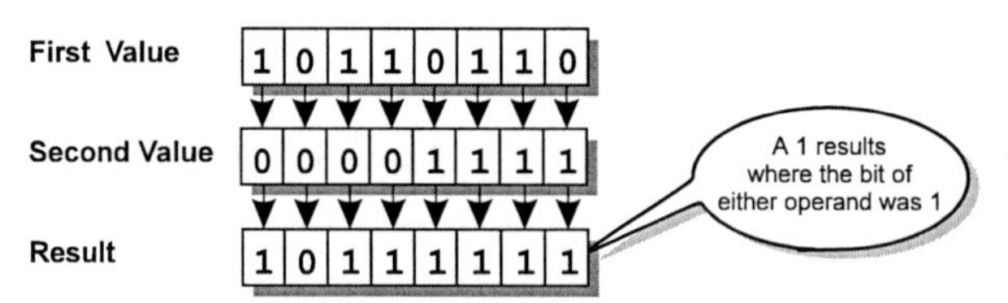

Activity 1.22

Write down the results of ORing the following values

a) 10101010 OR 01010101
b) 10111101 OR 01001111
c) 00100111 OR 11110011

NOT

NOTing a bit complements its value hence NOT 1 is 0 (zero) and NOT 0 is 1 (as shown in TABLE-1.11.

TABLE-1.11

The NOT Operator

Bit 1	NOT Bit 1
0	1
0	0

NOTing two bytes is shown in FIG-1.12.

FIG-1.12

Using the NOT Operator

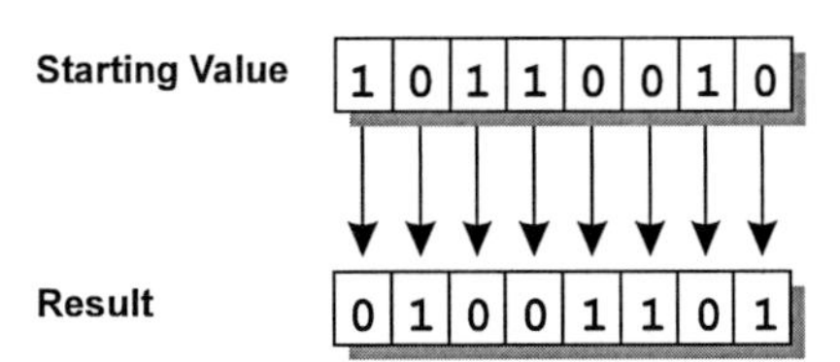

Activity 1.23

Write down the results of NOTing the following values:

a) 10101010
b) 11110000

Exclusive OR (XOR)

The exclusive OR operation, usually written as XOR, returns 1 when the two bits involved are different. Hence, 0 XOR 1 and 1 XOR 0 give the result 1; while two identical values give a zero: 0 XOR 0 = 0 and 1 XOR 1 = 0. This is summarised in TABLE-1.12.

TABLE-1.12

The XOR Operator

Bit 1	Bit 2	Bit 1 XOR Bit 2
0	0	0
0	1	1
1	0	1
1	1	0

XOR of two bytes is shown in FIG-1.13.

FIG-1.13

Using the XOR Operator

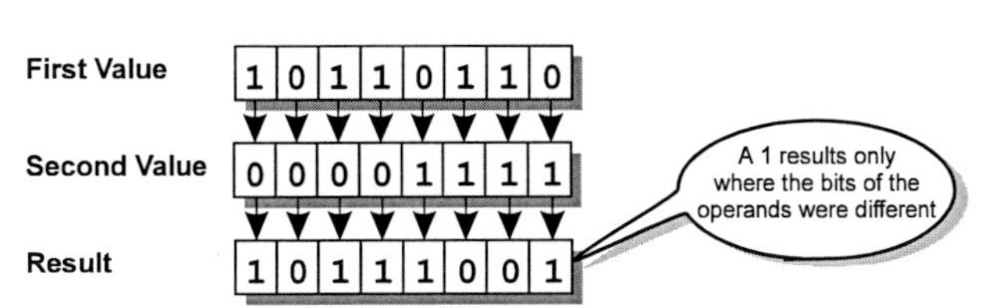

Activity 1.24

a) `10101010 XOR 01010101`
b) `10111101 XOR 01001111`
c) `00100111 XOR 11110011`

Take the result from b) and XOR it with 01001111

Left-Shift

The contents of one or more bytes can be left-shifted. The symbol used to achieve this varies between programming languages. In Java, two *less than* signs (<<) are used. This is known as the **left-shift** operator. Two values are required when using the left-shift operator: the value to be shifted and the number of places the bits are to be moved. An example is shown in FIG-1.14.

FIG-1.14

The Left-Shift Operator

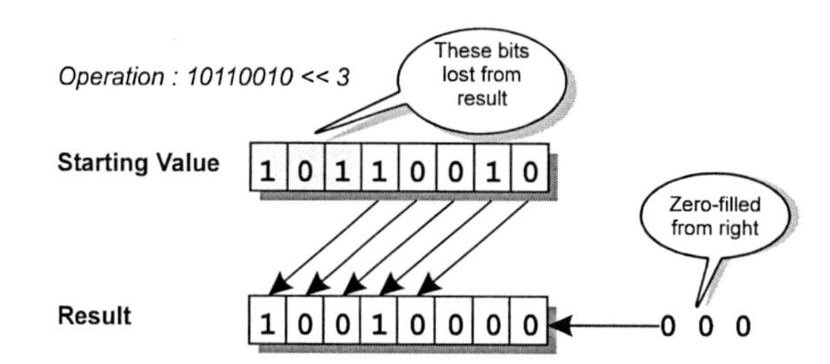

Notice that the left-hand bits of the original value are lost and that zeros are used to right fill the empty bits.

Where a small value is held (i.e. where the left-hand bits are zero, the left-shift operation allows a value to be multiplied quickly by a power of 2. For example, the value 3 in binary

```
11
```

when shifted left two places

```
1100
```

gives the value 12. That is, $3 * 2^2$.

Activity 1.25

Show the result of shifting value 00001101 three places to the left.

Write down the decimal equivalent of the original value and the result.

Right-Shift

A **right-shift** operation (using >>) moves a value a given number of places to the right. This is equivalent to integer division by some power of 2.

An example is shown in FIG-1.15.

FIG-1.15

The Right-Shift Operator

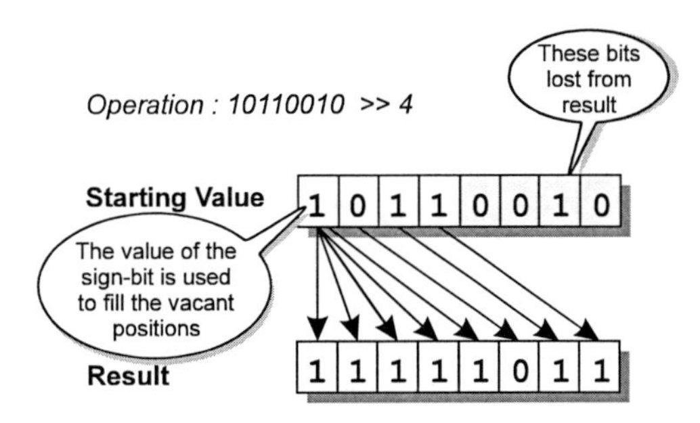

Notice from the example that the result is sign-filled from the left. That is, the sign-bit of the original value is used to fill the spaces left vacant by the move.

However, if the original value is an unsigned one, the shift operation will give an incorrect result.

To overcome this problem, a second, zero-fill, right-shift operator (>>>) is available in Java which always uses a zero when filling the vacant left-hand bits. An example is shown in FIG-1.16.

FIG-1.16

The Arithmetic Right-Shift Operator

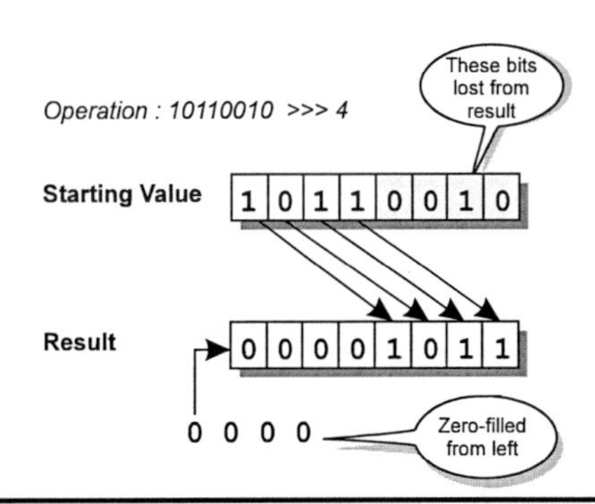

Summary

- **Logical operations** such as AND and OR can be performed on binary values.
- When performing these operations, **1 is equivalent of true** and **zero is equivalent to false.**
- **Each column in the result** is calculated independently.
- **The AND operator** gives a 1 result only when both other values are 1.
- **The OR operator** gives an 1 result when any of the other values is a 1.
- **The NOT operator** returns the complement of any value: 1s are changed to zeros; zeros to 1s.
- **The XOR operator** gives a 1 result when the other two values are different (i.e. 1 XOR 0 or 0 XOR 1).
- **A binary value can be shifted** left or right.
- **The left-shift operator** (<<) shifts value a given number of places to the left. Vacant positions are zero filled.

- **The arithmetic right-shift operator** (>>) shifts value a given number of places to the right. Vacant positions are filled with the sign-bit of the original value.
- **The right-shift operator** (>>>) shifts value a given number of places to the right. Vacant positions are zero filled.

SOLUTIONS

Activity 1.1

A possible solution is:

```
Open door of washing machine
Place clothes in washing machine
Put washing powder in powder tray
Close door
Choose required setting
When washing cycle complete, remove clothes from
machine
```

Of course, you will almost certainly have produced a solution which differs from the one above. But, as long as your logic is correct, (for example, it would be wrong to put the clothes in the machine before opening the door) then any solution is acceptable.
Remember to take a separate line for each instruction.

Activity 1.2

```
Fill kettle
Switch on kettle
Put tea in teapot
When water boils, pour into teapot
Wait for tea to infuse
Pour tea into cup
IF milk is required THEN
    Add milk
ENDIF
IF sugar is required THEN
    Add sugar
    Stir tea
ENDIF
Drink tea
```

Other solutions are possible but make sure the milk and sugar are dealt with by two separate IF statement, and that the ENDIF terms are included.

Activity 1.3

```
Write letter
Fold letter
Place letter in envelope
Seal envelope
Write address on envelope
IF sending first class THEN
    Stick first class stamp on envelope
ELSE
    Stick second class stamp on envelope
ENDIF
Take letter to post box
Post letter
```

Ensure you use an IF .. THEN .. ELSE structure when selecting the stamp.

Activity 1.4

```
Find out total cost
IF
    paying by cash:
        Give cashier sufficient money
        IF any change is due THEN
            Collect change
        ENDIF
    paying by cheque:
        Write out cheque
        Give cheque to cashier
        Show cheque card
    paying by credit card:
        Hand over credit card
        Sign authorisation slip
        Take back credit card
        Take credit transaction slip
    paying through account:
        Give account number
ENDIF
Take till receipt
Take purchases
```

Activity 1.5

```
printer on-line AND toner not empty AND
(paper in main tray OR paper in auxiliary
tray)
```

Activity 1.6

```
FOR 20 times DO
    Read mark and name
    IF mark is less than 50% THEN
        Add name to list of fails
    ENDIF
ENDFOR
```

Activity 1.7

```
REPEAT
    Find start of next article
    Read author's name
UNTIL author's name is "Liz Herron"
```

Activity 1.8

```
Roll both dice
WHILE both dice are not equal DO
    Choose die with lower value
    Throw die
ENDWHILE
```

Activity 1.9

Possible data items	Values
car model	Mini
engine size	1200cc
city	Glasgow
premium	299
street	14 High Street
post code	G2 8LD
phone number	0141-327-1199
policy number	9876541

Activity 1.10

Input statements:

```
Get caller's name, age, street, city, post
code, phone number, engine size, and car
registration number.

Get policy number from top right hand of
policy form
```

Calculation statements:

```
Calculate excess due as £50 for each year
under 25

Add excess to premium
```

Output statements:

```
Give the policy number to caller
```

Activity 1.11

Only two statements need to be expanded to give more detail:

```
3. Get order details
4. Process item
```

Possible expansions are:

```
3. Get order details
    3.1 Get catalogue number
    3.2 WHILE catalogue number is invalid DO
    3.3     Tell customer number is invalid
    3.4     Get catalogue number again
    3.5 ENDWHILE
    3.6 Get quantity required

4.  Process order
    4.1 IF item in stock AND sufficient quantity THEN
    4.2     Add details to order list
    4.3 ELSE
    4.4     Check for alternative
    4.5     IF there is an alternative THEN
    4.6     Tell customer details of
                alternative
    4.7         IF alternative acceptable THEN
    4.8             Add alternative's details
                    to order list
    4.9         ENDIF
    4.10    ELSE
    4.11        Tell customer item not available
    4.12    ENDIF
    4.13 ENDIF
```

This gives a final LEVEL 2 algorithm of:

```
1.      Get number of items
2.      FOR each item DO
3.1         Get catalogue number
3.2         WHILE catalogue number is invalid DO
3.3             Tell customer number is invalid
3.4             Get catalogue number again
3.5         ENDWHILE
3.6         Get quantity required
4.1         IF item in stock AND sufficient quantity
            THEN
4.2             Add details to order list
4.3         ELSE
4.4             Check for alternative
4.5             IF there is an alternative THEN
4.6                 Tell customer details of
                    alternative
4.7                 IF alternative acceptable THEN
4.8                     Add alternative's details
                        to order list
4.9                 ENDIF
4.10            ELSE
4.11                Tell customer item not available
4.12            ENDIF
4.13        ENDIF
5       ENDFOR
6.      Send order to dispatches department
```

Activity 1.12

```
00010011

01001000

00111111
```

Activity 1.13

```
41

255

170
```

Activity 1.14

```
0.11
0.0101
0.011000
```

Activity 1.15

1.
```
0.34375
```

2.
```
1100.101
```

Activity 1.16

1.
```
47
FF
CB
```

2.
```
01110011
10100010
11111110
```

Activity 1.17

1.
```
51
234
377
```

2.
```
61
81
219
```

Activity 1.18

8 bits	16 bits
11111101	1111111111111101
11010110	1111111111010110
10000001	1111111110000001

Activity 1.19

```
1.2398E2

6.9E0

-1.0E-8
```

Activity 1.20

```
01111101 1000000000000000
```

Remember the most-significant 1 in the mantissa is omitted.

Activity 1.21

a) 10101010 AND 01010101 = 00000000

b) 10111101 AND 01001111 = 00001101

c) 00100111 AND 11110011 = 00100011

Activity 1.22

a) 10101010 OR 01010101 = 11111111

b) 10111101 OR 01001111 = 11111111

c) 00100111 OR 11110011 = 11110111

Activity 1.23

a) NOT 10101010 = 01010101

b) NOT 11110000 = 00001111

Activity 1.24

a) 10101010 XOR 01010101 = 11111111

b) 10111101 XOR 01001111 = 11110010

c) 00100111 XOR 11110011 = 11010100

Result of b) is 11110010

11110010 XOR 01001111 = 10111101

(Note that this is the original value we started with in b).

In fact, the rule: XORing a value *x* with *y* (*x* XOR *y*) and XOR the result by *y* (*result* XOR *y*) will always produce the original value, *x*.

Activity 1.25

00001101 << 3 = 01101000

Original decimal value = 13

Shifted value = 104 (i.e. $13 * 2^3$)

Chapter 2
Starting Java

This chapter covers the following topics:

Arithmetic Operators

Assignment Operator

Basic Program Structure

Declaring Variables

Identifiers

Reading from the Keyboard

Outputting to the Screen

Java Reserved Words

Program Constants

Sample Programs

Variable Types

A Brief History Of Java

The immediate ancestor of Java is C++. These two languages share many features in common. In fact, Java has been referred to as *C++ with all the hard bits taken out.*

Java's story begins back in 1991 when a group of Sun engineers were asked to design a programming language which could be used to program a variety of hardware devices such as cable TV switchboxes. Because such devices tend to use a variety of processors, the language had to cope with the different architectures.

They returned to an idea which was used in the original Pascal implementation: a virtual machine. The idea of a virtual machine is to invent a whole machine code language for an abstract processor that doesn't actually exist and then create a piece of software that makes real processors act as if they were that abstract processor.

Unix is an operating system.

Because of their background in a Unix environment, the new language was based on C++. The language was to be called Oak, but a programming language of this name already existed, so the name was changed to Java.

Applets are small programs designed to be placed on a Web page.

In the end, Sun didn't persuade anyone producing intelligent machines to use their new language. However, around this time (1994) the Internet was taking off in a big way and Sun realised that Java could be used to create a browser and interpret ***applets*** downloaded onto any system. They created a browser called HotJava, but real success came when the market-leader in browsers, Netscape, released a Java enabled browser, Netscape Browser 2.0, in January 1996. All other major software manufacturers have since jumped on the bandwagon.

Java 1.02 was released in 1996, updates have followed: Java 1.1 in 1997 and Java 1.2 in 1998. As a major update, Java 1.2 was later renamed Java 2.

Sun later created version 1.3. To avoid confusion with what appears to be a backward step in version numbers, this release is referred to as Java 2 release 1.3.

Currently (2003), Java 2 version 1.4.1 is the latest release.

Java: Program Structure

An Overview

Every Java program is constructed from one or more classes. A class is a collection of data items and routines which operate on that data.

Before describing the basic elements of Java, we'll begin with a quick look at some code to give you the general structure of a simple Java application. The program in LISTING-2.1 displays the message *Hello world* on the screen. Most Java programs contain a mix of **keywords** (terms defined in the Java language); **identifiers** (terms defined by the programmer); **operators** (symbols used to perform calculations such as + - * /); **constants** (fixed values such as 7, "hello", -9.8) and **symbols** (special characters such as { ; .).

The program in LISTING-2.1 does not contain any operators.

LISTING-2.1

A Simple Java Program

```
public class First
{
   public static void main (String args[])
   {
      System.out.println("Hello world");
   }
}
```

An Explanation of the Code

Java keywords must be in lowercase.

`public class First`	Java programs are written as a set of one or more classes. The keyword `public` affects access to the class - we'll see more of this later. `class`, another keyword, marks the beginning of class definition. Next comes the identifier giving the name of the class - *First*. When we come to save the program the file name must be based on the class name and with the extension *.java*. Hence, this program will be saved as *First.java*. Java is a case-sensitive language, so remember to use a capital 'F' in *First*.
`{`	This symbol marks the start of the class declaration. In Java braces are used to mark the start and end of blocks of code.
`public static`	We'll ignore the meaning of these terms for the moment. They will be explained when we look at class definitions in more detail. At this point, all we need say is that these keywords must be included.
`void`	At this position in the statement the type of value returned by the function must be given. The term `void` is used when no value is returned by the function.
`main`	This is the name of the function. In a Java application, one class must contain a function called `main`. It is the

code within this function that is executed when a Java application is run.

`(String args[])`	This code specifies the parameters being passed to the function *main()*. Again, this is something we can ignore for the moment. However, it must always be given as the argument to *main*. Make sure you use a capital *S* in the word `String`.
`{`	Marks the beginning of a block of code. In this case the code for function *main*.
`System.out.println`	This term is used to produce screen output. Watch out for the capital *S* in `System` - you'll get an error if you use a lowercase *s*.
`( )`	The value(s) to be displayed must be enclosed in parentheses.
`"Hello world"`	Is the argument of the output statement and is the text string to be displayed. Note that strings are enclosed in double quotes.
`;`	The semi-colon ends a statement. Normally all statements in Java must end with the semi-colon.
`}`	Block terminator symbol. In this case, the end of the function *main*. **Note** that `}` is not followed by a semicolon.
`}`	The final brace marks the end of the declaration of the class *First*.

Activity 2.1

Create a new folder on your hard disk to contain your Java programs.
Name the folder using the format: ***Javayourname*** (e.g. ***JavaElizabeth***)
From DOS, make your Java directory the current directory with a command such as

```
CD C:\JavaElizabeth
```

In order to use Java on your machine the operating system will have to be able to find the Java Compiler (*javac.exe*). We'll do this by creating a batch file that adds that information to the *path* system variable.

Create a file called *jpath.bat* and enter the following line:

```
path = %path%;
```

Extend the line to include the full path to your Java compiler. For example, your completed line might be

```
path = %path%;C:\jbuilder4\java\bin
```

Save the file.
Now execute the file by typing

```
jpath
```

You are now ready to start creating Java programs.

NOTE: You will have to run *jpath.bat* every time you start a new java session.

If you're using your own machine, the *path* = line could be added to *autoexec.bat*. This would automatically set up the required path information every time you switched the machine on.

Activity 2.2

In this Activity we are going to run the program given in LISTING-2.1.

Open up a text editor (You must use a true text editor, not a word processor - in Windows you could use NotePad).

Type in the program in LISTING-2.1 exactly as shown (remember to use capital *F* and *S* at the appropriate points).

Save the program as *First.java*

Next we need to run the compiler to change our source code into bytecode.

If you're working in Windows, open a DOS window.

Move to the directory containing your program.

Type in ***javac First.java***

This calls up the java compiler (*javac*) and instructs it to compile *First.java.*

As a result the bytecode file *First.class* will be created. This has to be executed.

Load the Java Virtual Machine (JVM) by typing ***java First***

Your program should execute and the words *Hello world* appear on the screen.

For DOS users, you may get the error message *bad command or file name* when trying to compile your program. Assuming you've remembered to install the Java compiler, the most likely cause of this is that the path details are not set up to find the compiler.

The next program, (see LISTING-2.2) which sums two values, introduces program variables, comments, and calculations.

LISTING-2.2

Input, Variables and Assignment

```
public class Second
{
  public static void main (String args[])
  {
      /* A program to add two numbers */
      int no1, no2, ans;    //variables in main
      /* Assign values */
      no1 = 12;
      no2 = 5;
      ans = no1 + no2;
      /* Display results */
      System.out.println(no1+" + "+no2+" = "+ans);
  }
}
```

An Explanation of the Code

`int no1,no2,ans;` This defines the three variables, *no1*, *no2* and *ans* as integers.

`/*A program to add two numbers */`

This is a comment. Comments are enclosed between /* and */. Comments given in this format can span several lines of the program.

`//Variables in main`	An alternative to /* .. */ is to use two forward slashes (//) which makes the remainder of the current line a comment. The RETURN character marks the end of the comment.
`no1 = 12;` `no2 = 5;`	This assigns the values to the variables *no1* and *no2.*
`ans = no1 + no2;`	This assigns the sum of the contents of *no1* and *no2* to *ans*.
`(no1+" + "+no2+" = "+ans)`	Several values can be output in a single `println` statement. Use a plus sign to separate each value.

> **Activity 2.3**
>
> Type in and run this second program.

Summary

- **Java programs** are constructed from classes.
- **A class** is a structure containing data items and the routines which manipulate those data items.
- **A program can contain** several class definitions.
- **One class** must contain a function called *main.*
- **The function *main()*** will be executed when a Java application is run.
- **A Java application** must be saved to disk using the same name as the class containing *main()*.
- **A Java source file** must have the extension *.java.*
- **The compiler** (*javac*) converts the source code to bytecode.
- **The bytecode file** has the extension *.class*.
- **The Java Virtual Machine** (*java*) executes the .class file.

The Compilation Process

Since computers are only capable of recognising and executing commands given in their own native processor instruction set (known as **machine code**) and since computer programs are normally written in other languages, the computer is required to perform a translation process to convert the original program code (known as the **source code**) into the equivalent sequence of machine code instructions (the **object code**) which can then be executed by the computer.

This operation is known as **compilation** and is performed by a piece of software called a **compiler**.

The aim of Java is to create programs which can be executed on different operating systems using different computer hardware. So we can write a program in Java and then execute it from such diverse systems as Microsoft Windows, Unix or the Macintosh operating system.

So what's so special about that? Unlike Java, most compilers create a machine code program designed to be executed within a specific operating system. For example, Borland's C++ Builder creates programs which can only run under Microsoft Windows. Part of the reason for this restriction is that the object code produced by these compilers contains calls to specific operating system routines such as those necessary to display a drop-down menu or create a button.

Java programs make no such calls and hence remain independent of the operating system. It is said to be **platform-independent.**

To allow this independence, Java has its own set of classes to allow menus and buttons to be created. These classes are held in various files known as **packages.** To make use of a class, all that is required is that the appropriate package is included within the program.

To be platform-independent there's one other major problem: compilers generate object programs in the machine code of a specific processor. For example, a program compiled on a PC will produce instructions for an Intel Pentium while code compiled on a Macintosh will create Motorola 68000 machine code. If we want a program to be capable of running under any platform, the final machine code cannot be generated until we know the actual hardware being used at the time of execution.

Classes are held in packages in bytecode format.

Java tackles this problem by using a two stage translation process. Once a program has been written it is translated into something called **Java bytecode**. This is machine code for an abstract processor that doesn't actual exist.

This bytecode is then loaded into the machine on which the program is to be executed and there it is translated into the machine code of the actual processor involved. This is a relatively simple process since bytecode is similar in format to true machine code.

This translation is carried out by a piece of software known as the Java Virtual Machine (JVM). Usually, the translation is on a line by line basis as the program is being executed. Because translation occurs during execution, Java programs can sometimes be slow in operation. This is probably the greatest criticism levelled at the language.

Since the Java Virtual Machine must be translated from bytecode to actual machine code, it must be specific to that platform and hence separate JVM's must be written for each platform.

The compilation process is shown in FIG-2.1.

FIG-2.1

The Compilation Process

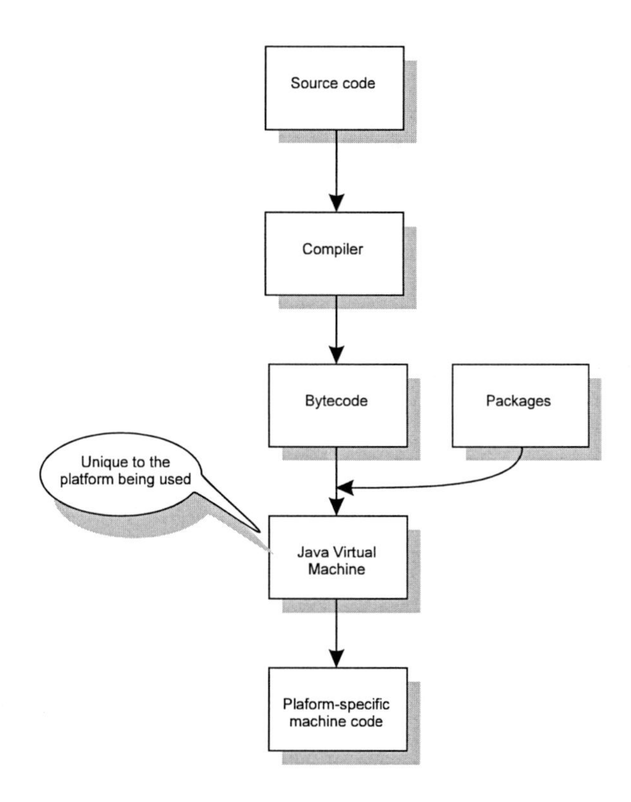

Java is capable of creating two types of programs : **applications** and **applets**.

An application is a full-blown program, capable of performing any task; an applet, on the other hand, is designed to be part of an Internet Web page. Applets are executed by a Web browser such as Internet Explorer or Netscape Navigator, both of which contain JVM software. Because this software is being downloaded and executed as soon as a web page is loaded, applets have some built-in security to stop them being used to tamper with your computer. For example, applets are not allowed to write to your disks.

Variables And Literals

Variables

What is a Variable?

Almost everyone has had to fill in a form similar to the one shown in FIG-2.2. Each

FIG-2.2

Part of a Typical Form

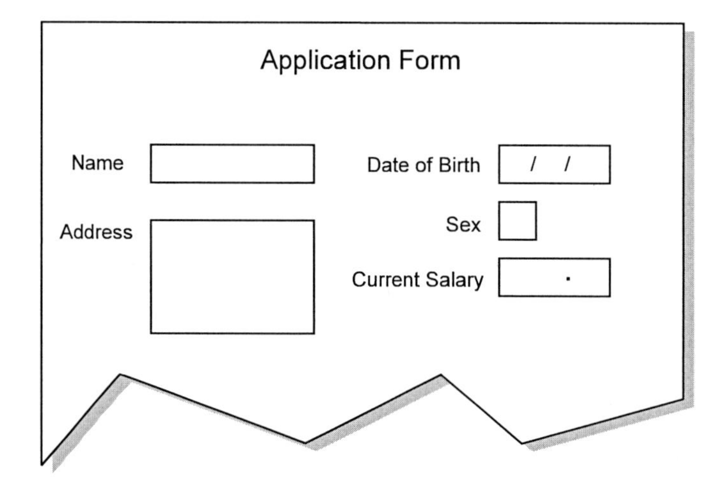

entry in the form has a boxed area in which we are required to enter information. Beside each box is a label (or name) giving us an indication of what information we are meant to place in that box. Each box differs in size and format depending on the type of information it is designed to hold. Hence the *address* box is long because it requires several lines of information whereas the *sex* box has sufficient space for only a single character ('M' or 'F') and the *date of birth* box contains two forward slash characters (/) to separate the day, month and year values.

If a computer program requires to store similar information, then it too needs areas in which to hold that information (more commonly called **data**). In a program, data is stored in variables and, like the boxes on the form, variables need to be given names. LISTING-2.2 (on page 48) defined three variables: *no1*, *no2* and *answer*.

Variable Types

Just as the boxes in the form are designed with the type of value they are going to hold in mind (such as a date, single character, amount of money etc.), so the type of value a program variable is to hold must also be specified.

Java recognises several types of values. Two value types are **integer** (whole numbers - positive or negative) and **real** (numbers containing fractional parts). The term `int` is used when defining integer variables; in LISTING-2.2 the three variables were defined as integers with the statement:

```
int no1, no2, ans;
```

Real values are defined using the term `float`. For example:

```
float angle, discount;
```

Naming Variables

The name given to a variable in a Java program must conform to the following rules:

- The first character must be a letter, underscore (_) or a dollar ($).
- Subsequent characters can be a letter, underscore, dollar or numeric.
- Capital and lower case **ARE** significant (*NO* and *no* are different).
- A variable name must **NOT** be a keyword.

A **keyword** is a word recognised by Java to have some specific meaning. A list of keywords is given in TABLE-2.1.

TABLE-2.1

Java Keywords

JAVA KEYWORDS				
abstract	double	import	private	throw
boolean	else	inner	protected	throws
break	extends	instanceof	public	transient
case	false	int	return	true
cast	final	interface	rest	try
catch	finally	long	short	var
char	float	native	static	void
class	for	new	super	volatile
const	future	null	switch	
continue	generic	operator	synchronized	
default	if	outer	this	

NOTE: All keywords in Java are in lowercase.

Activity 2.4

Indicate which of the following are invalid variable names:

```
no1
first_ans
3no
no_1
_result
try
final total
```

Memory Allocation

A byte consists of 8 bits.

Computer memory is often organised in bytes with each byte being allocated a unique identifying value known as the **memory address**.

Every variable defined in a program is allocated its own space in the computer's memory.

The amount of space allocated depends on the type of variable being defined. For example, a `float` requires more space than an `int`.

A single byte is not sufficient to store a reasonable range of numeric values and hence variables are normally allocated more than one byte.

Table 2.2 lists all the variable types available in Java, the number of bytes allocated to each type, and the range of values that each type can store.

TABLE-2.2

Java Variable Types

Variable type	Range of values	Number of bytes
Integer Types		
byte	-128 to 127	1
short	-32,768 to 32,767	2
int	-2,147,483,648 to 2,147,483,647	4
long	-9,223,372,036,854,775,808 to 9,223,372,036,854,775,807	8
Real Types		
float	$-3.4x10^{+38}$ to $3.4x10^{+38}$	4
double	$-1.7x10^{+308}$ to $1.7x10^{+308}$	8
Non-Numeric Types		
char	a single character	2
boolean	*false, true*	1

To summarise, every variable defined in a program has four characteristics associated with it:

- A name e.g. no1
- A type e.g. int
- A value e.g. -17
- An address in memory e.g. FFFF FFFD

Where the variable is allocated several bytes, the address associated with the variable is that of the first location allocated.

Literals

As well as variables, most programs make use of literals or constants; that is, fixed numeric or non-numeric values. For example, a program might use the value 3.1415 when calculating the area of a circle, or the message "Enter name" as a prompt for the user to key in a value. 3.1415 is a **numeric constant**; "*Enter name*" is a **string constant**.

Numeric Literals

There are two main classes of numeric literals: integer and real.

Integer Constants

An integer constant in Java is any non-negative whole number, hence 0, 7 and 124 are all examples of integer constants. Although integer values are, by default, assumed to be given in decimal (base 10), it is also possible to specify integer constants in hexadecimal (base 16) or octal (base 8). Hexadecimal values are preceded by 0x or 0X (zero X) (e.g. 0X8F). Octal values are simply preceded by 0 (zero) (e.g. 067).

Integer constants are held in `int` or `long` format depending on their value.

Constant values in the range 0 to 2,147,483,647 are stored in four bytes (i.e. in `int` format) while other values are held in `long` (8 bytes) format.

It is possible to force an integer constant to occupy a `long` format, irrespective of its value, by terminating it with the letter *L* (for `long`). Hence 213L will be stored in `long` rather than `int` format.

Real Constants

Real values may be given in fixed or floating point notation. For example, we may use 3.1415 or 0.31415E01 to represent the approximate value of π.

Irrespective of value, real constants default to `double` format storage. However, if the constant is terminated with the letter *F* (e.g. 3.1415F), then `float` format is employed. A lowercase *f* may also be used.

Negative Values

Where a negative value is required, for example, -12, most programming languages store this initially as a positive value (i.e. +12) and treat the minus sign as an arithmetic operator, changing the positive value which follows the operator to a negative one only when that line of code is executed. This operator is known as the **unary minus**.

Non-Numeric Literals

Non-numeric constants fall into two types: character and string.

Character Constants

A character constant is any single character and is normally shown enclosed in single quotes:

```
'a'
'*'
'9'
```

Character constants are stored in `char` format.

Some characters, such as **delete**, **newline** and **backspace** cannot be typed in directly. These characters are specified using a backspace character followed by a defining character. Collectively these are known as the **escape codes** . The full list of escape codes is shown in TABLE-2.3.

TABLE-2.3

Escape Codes

Escape Code	Meaning
\b	Backspace
\f	Form feed
\n	Newline
\r	Return
\t	Horizontal tab
\\	Backslash
\'	Single quote
\"	Double quote

The space, tab and newline characters are sometimes referred to as **whitespace** characters since all of them create gaps of some sort in any output produced.

Any character can be specified using the backslash character followed by the Unicode value of the required character given as a 4 digit hexadecimal. Hence the letter 'A' may be specified as \u0041 in hexadecimal.

You're probably best at this stage to stay within the first 127 characters of the ASCII code since other characters depend on the operating system's ability to display them.

String Constants

A string is a collection of zero or more characters enclosed in double quotes. For example,

```
"This is a string."
```

An empty string (i.e. a string with zero characters) is depicted as two adjacent double quote characters

```
""
```

A string may contain escape characters. The string, *"How are you?" he said*, would be written as

```
"\"How are you?\" he said"
```

Two or more string constants can be joined using the plus (+) symbol. For example,

`"The" + "ory"`	is equivalent to	`"Theory"`
`"to" + "get" + "her"`	is equivalent to	`"together"`

Strangely, Java will even create a string where one of the values beside the + operator is not itself a string. So,

`"Flat" + 23`	gives	`"Flat23"`
`12 + "a Baker Street"`	gives	`"12a Baker Street"`

However, this does not create a string if neither value is a string:

`2 + 7` performs a calculation and returns the integer value `9`

We'll have more to say about strings later.

Defining Variables

Every variable used in a Java program must be explicitly defined. A variable definition begins with the variable type followed by the variable name and ends with a semicolon. For example:

```
int    no;
float  square;
char   sex;
long   total;
```

As well as using meaningful names, it is advisable to add a comment explaining the purpose of a variable:

```
long   total; //*** Number of phone calls ***
```

Where several variables of the same type are required, they can be defined in a single statement using commas to separate each item.

```
int x1,y1,x2,y2;    //*** Co-ordinates of rectangle ***
```

This can be split over several lines to allow comments to be added to each variable:

```
int
    x1,     //*** x ordinate of top left corner ***
    y1,     //*** y ordinate of top left corner ***
    x2,     //*** x ordinate of bottom right corner ***
    y2;     //*** y ordinate of bottom right corner ***
```

Most commonly, in simple programs, definition will be done at the begin of the code:

```
public static void main(String args[])
{
    variables defined here
```

But, in fact, Java allows variables to be defined anywhere in a program. The only restriction being that a variable must be defined before it is referenced by another Java statement.

Initialising Variables

When a variable declared within a routine is allocated space in the computer's memory, the current content of that area of memory normally remains unchanged. This means that any binary pattern which happens to be contained in the memory allocated, is subsequently taken to be the starting value assigned to that variable. For example, if a program was to begin with the statements:

```
int num;
System.out.println(num);
```

then Java will display the compilation error message

```
Variable num may not have been initialized
```

Where no specific value has been assigned to a variable, it is said to be **uninitialised**. Although this is acceptable if the variable is subsequently given a value by an input or assignment statement, where the variable is needed as a count or total, then the variable will require to be initialised. Luckily, variables may be assigned a starting value in the definition statement. Hence, we could ensure a count begins at zero with the definition

```
int count = 0;
```

Any starting value can be assigned. Character constant values given to `char` variables must be enclosed in single quotes:

```
char code = 'A';
```

Where several variables of the same type have to be given the same value, each can be assigned separately as in:

```
int count = 0, total = 0, subtotal = 0;
```

It is also possible to initialise variables using a previously defined variable, or an expression:

```
int no1 = 7;
int no2 = no1;
int no3 = no2*3;
```

Octal or hexadecimal values can be assigned to a variable. For example:

```
int hexval = 0XA7;
int octval = 017;
```

The general format of a variable definition is shown in FIG-2.3.

FIG-2.3

Declaring Variables

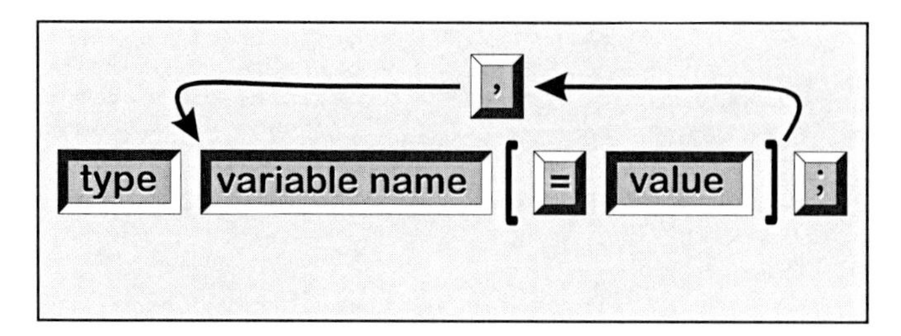

Activity 2.5

State which of the following definitions is invalid:

```
1. byte no = 12345;
2. char letter = "C";
3. float x = y = z = -6.812;
4.  int no = 13, no2 = 0, no3 = 6;
5. int x = 0XAE, int y = 015;
6. double m = 5.7312E02;
```

Summary

- **Variables are used to** hold values created or used in a program.
- **Variables have:** a name, a type and a value and are allocated an address in memory.
- **Variable names are constructed from** letters, numeric digits and the underscore character (_).

  They cannot begin with a numeric digit.

  They cannot be a Java keyword.
- **The following types are available:**

  ```
  byte
  short
  int
  long
  float
  double
  char
  boolean
  ```
- **The initial value held by a variable** is undefined.
- **Each variable is allocated an area of computer memory** where its value is stored. The size of this area depends on the variable's type.
- **Variables can be defined at almost any point** in a Java program.

- **Literals or constants** are fixed values.
- **Constants can be** integer, real, character, string or Boolean.
- **Integer constants can be specified in** decimal, hexadecimal or octal.
  Hexadecimal values begin with 0X (zero X) (e.g. `0X6F`).
  Octal values begin with 0 (zero) (e.g. `052`).
  Decimal values begin with any non-zero digit (e.g. `23`).
- **Integer constants are stored in** `int` or `long` format depending on the magnitude of the value.
- **The storage format can be forced** to `long` by the suffix L (e.g. `12L`).
- **Real constants are normally stored as** type `double`.
- **Real constants can be stored as** type `float` by adding the suffix F (e.g. `3.14F`).
- **Negative values** are stored as positive constants and changed to a negative value only when the line of code in which they are specified is executed.
- **A character constant** is a single character enclosed in single quotes (e.g. `'A'`).
- Certain characters, which cannot be entered directly from the keyboard have special methods of definition. These are called the **escape codes** (e.g. `'\n'` - the newline character).
- **A character can also be specified using \u** followed by the four-digit hexadecimal number identifying the Unicode character (e.g. `\u0041`).
- **String constants are enclosed in double quotes**. (e.g. `"This is a string")`.
- **Escape codes may be embedded in strings** (e.g. `"Line1\nLine2"`).
- **Strings can be joined** using the + operator (e.g. `"can" + "not"  = "cannot"`).
- Only one of the values needs to be a string when using the + operator (e.g. `"ext"+123 = "ext123"`   `12+"lbs" = "12lbs"`).
- **Spaces, tabs and newline characters** are collectively known as **whitespace** characters.
- **Variables may be initialised** (i.e. given a starting value) during definition (e.g. `int count = 0;`).

The Assignment Operators

The = Operator

Although variables may be assigned values when they are defined, it is also possible to modify the value of a variable later in the program using the basic assignment operator (=). For example, assuming a program contains the definition

```
int no1 = 0;        //*** Initial value of zero ***
```

then the statement

```
no1 = 5;        //*** New value is 5 ***
```

changes the contents of the variable *no1* from zero to 5.

The assignment statement takes the form defined in FIG-2.4.

FIG-2.4

The Assignment Operator (=)

Execution of an assignment statement results in *value* being copied to the memory allocated to *variable name*. Any previous value held by *variable name* is lost.

value must be one of the following:

a literal,
another variable
or an expression

Literal

Where value is a constant, that fixed value is assigned to the variable. For example:

```
int     no1,no2;
double  rno1, rno2;
char    letter;

no1     = 6;
no2     = -10;
rno1    = -4.891;
letter  = 'D';
```

Variable

Alternatively, the value held in one variable can be copied into another. The contents of the right-hand variable are unaffected. For example:

```
int     no1=12,no2;
float   rno1=13.008F,rno2;
char    letter1='G',letter2;

no2     = no1;
rno2    = rno1;
letter2 = letter1;
```

Expressions

An expression is usually, but not always, an arithmetic expression containing constants, variables and arithmetic operators. The arithmetic operators, with one exception, are those already described in Chapter 1.

They are listed below:

	Addition	+
	Subtraction	-
	Multiplication	*
	Division	/
and	Remainder	%

However, two operators are worth a further explanation:

Division

The effect of the division operator (/) in Java is not always identical to its arithmetic counterpart: when used on two integer values, the division operator supplies an integer result. Hence:

8/3 will give a result of 2

However, if any of the operands are real, the result is also real. For example,

8.0/3 will give a result of 2.67

Where one of the values involved is negative, the result is the smallest negative integer greater than the actual result. For instance:

-8/5 will give a result of -1

Attempting to divide by zero generates an error.

The Remainder Operator (%)

The remainder operator (%) is used to determine the integer remainder after division. For example:

9 % 5
= 4

since 5 divides into 9 once with a remainder of 4.

Where both values have the same sign the result has that sign. Hence:

-8%-5
= -3

Where the two values have different signs, the result has the same sign as the first value. For example:

-8 % 5	8 % -5
= -3	= 3

The remainder operator may only be used with integer type values.

The remainder operator can also be used to perform the modulus operation. Remainder and modulus give the same result when the signs of both values are equal. However, when dealing with values of differing signs as in:

-7 modulus 3

the mathematical operator gives a result of 2,

while in Java

-7 % 3

gives a result of -1.

We can ensure that the % operator is equivalent to modulus by using the following algorithm:

```
Calculate the remainder when value1 is divided by value2
Add value2 to the result
Calculate the remainder when the modified result is divided by
value2
```

This translates into Java as:

```
result         = value1 % value2;
modifiedresult = result + value2;
answer         = modifiedresult % value2;
```

and can be reduced to a single, though more cryptic, statement:

```
result = ((value1 % value2) + value2) % value2;
```

Using the remainder operator where the second operand is zero will result in an error.

Activity 2.6

Determine the values of the following expressions:

8 / 4	8 % 4
9 / 4	9 % 4
9 / 4.0	9 % 4.0
7 / 0	7 % 0
0 / 7	0 % 7
2 / 8	2 % 8
-11 / 3	-12 % 3
-15 / -6	-15 % -6
9 / -2	9 % -2

As with Structured English, an arithmetic expression can contain an unlimited number of operators in any order. Normal operator precedence applies with the remainder operator given the same priority as multiplication and division. Operator precedence is overridden by the use of parentheses - expressions in parentheses being evaluated first. For example, in the expression

```
(no1 + 6) / 10
```

the addition operation will be performed before that of division.

Where there is more than one set of parentheses in an expression, such as

```
(no1 + 6) / (no2 + 10)
```

then the contents of the left-most parentheses are evaluated first.

Where parentheses are nested, as in

```
((no1 + 6) * (12 - no3) + 1) / (no2 + 10)
```

the contents of the inner most parentheses are evaluated first. For the expression above, the terms are evaluated in the order:

1. `(no1 + 6)`
2. `(12 - no3)`
3. `((no1 + 6) * (12 - no3) + 1)`
4. `(no2 + 10)`
5. `((no1 + 6) * (12 - no3) + 1) / (no2 + 10)`

The arithmetic operators and their precedences are given in TABLE-2.4.

TABLE-2.4

Arithmetic Operators

Operator	Description	Priority
( )	parentheses	3
*	multiplication	2
/	division	2
%	remainder	2
+	addition	1
-	subtraction	1

Several examples of expressions used with the assignment operator are given below:

```
int     no1 = 4, no2 = 5, no3, ans;
float   rno1 = 1.56, rno2 = 7.8, rno3, result;

no3    =  no1 + no2;
rno3   =  rno1 - rno2;
no1    =  23 * no2;
rno2   =  rno3 / 12;
result =  (rno1 + rno2) / rno3;
ans    =  ((no1 + 2) * 3 - 1) / (no3 - 2);
```

Automatic Numeric Type Conversion

So far, all the assignment examples have transferred values of the same type as the receiving variable. Java will also allow assignment between differing numeric types, so long as that conversion is from a weaker type to a stronger type. The classification is shown in FIG-2.5 below.

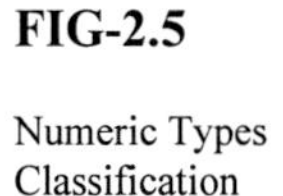

FIG-2.5

Numeric Types Classification

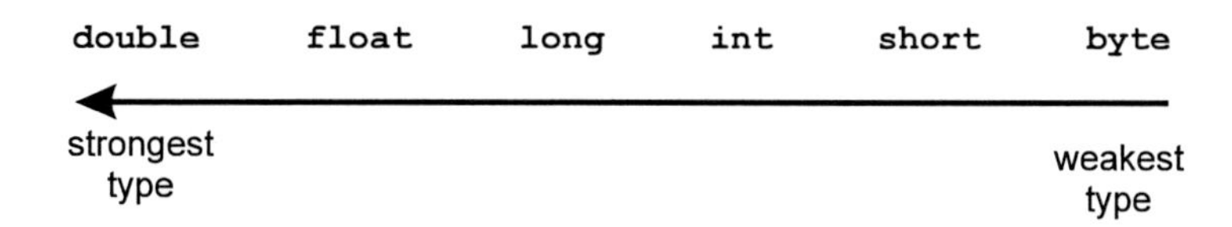

Conversion from a weak to a strong type is performed automatically. Hence, we may do such things as copy an `int` value to a `float` or a `short` to a `double`. For example, the following lines are all valid:

```
int no1 = 21;
float x = 43.12F;
double d;

d = x;      //float to double
x = no1;    //int to float
```

However, a statement such as

```
no1 = d;
```

results in the error message

```
Incompatible type for =. Explicit cast needed to convert double
to int.
```

since we are trying to convert from a strong type to a weaker one.

If the assignment is to be from a strong to a weak type, then the stronger value must be converted or **cast** to the weaker type. To perform this type of conversion, the target type is specified in parenthesis before the value being converted. Hence, to convert the `double` value *d* to an `int` we use the expression

```
(int) d
```

Therefore, to store the value of *d* in *no1*, we write

```
no1 = (int)d;
```

Of course, when transferring a value to a variable with less bytes than the original, we run the danger of having insufficient space to store that value. The problem is illustrated in FIG-2.6

FIG-2.6

Copying to a Shorter Type

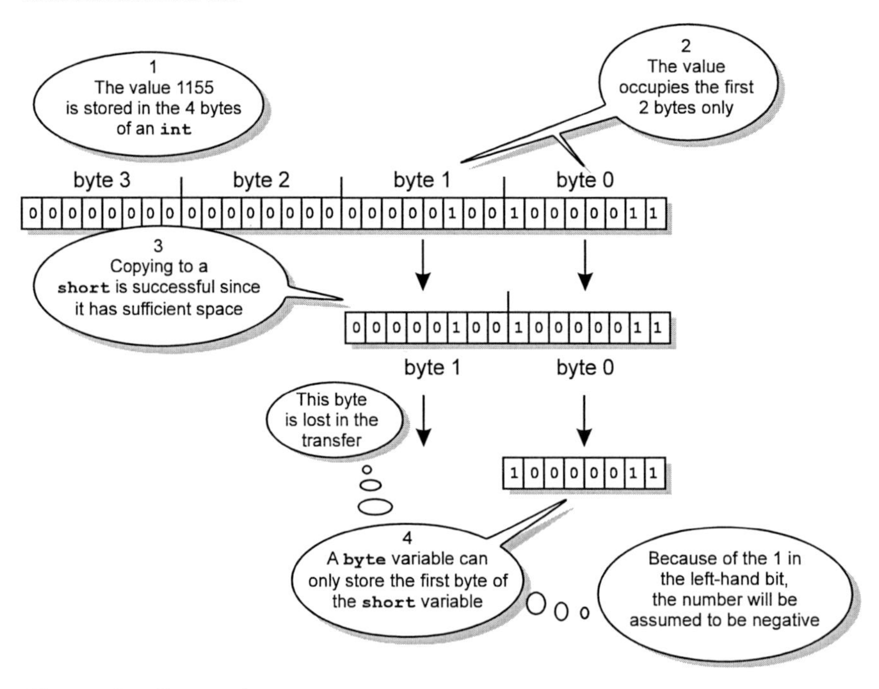

Converting Expressions

The code

```
int    no1 = 34;
double answer;
answer =  no1 * 12.3F;
```

contains three types in the final line: a `double` (*answer*), an `int` (*no1*) and a `float` (*12.3F*).

In order to evaluate any part of an expression, Java requires the values associated with an operator (such as +, - , * etc.) to be of the same type. Where this is not the case, Java converts one of the values involved to the same type as the other value. The rule is a simple one: all values in an expression are converted to the strongest type contained in that expression. In the example above, this means that the `int` value (*no1*) is converted to a `float` before the multiplication operation is performed:

$$34.0 * 12.3$$
$$= 418.2$$

Finally, this is converted to the same type as the receiving variable (`double`) before being assigned.

Activity 2.7

For each line indicated in the code given below, state what type will be used when evaluating the expression.

```
byte    cno1, cno2 = 65;
int     no1, no2 = 1452;
float   rno1, rno2 = 5.78F;


cno1    =    cno2 + 1;                line 1
no1     =    no2 + 12L;               line 2
rno1    =    rno2 + 0.5;              line 3
```

From and To boolean

No automatic or cast conversion to or from `boolean` is allowed.

From and To char

A `char` value will convert automatically to any numeric type, but numeric type must be cast to type `char`. For example:

```
char a = (char)65;
char b = (char)68.0;
```

Characters and Arithmetic Operators

Java does some rather curious conversions. For example, the term

```
'C' - 'A'
```

is accepted as valid and returns the value 2.

Java arrives at this result by converting each character to an integer based on the Unicode value of the character. Hence, since the Unicode value of 'C' is 67 and that of 'A' is 65, the above expression is resolved as

```
67 - 65
```

Activity 2.8

Enter and run the following program and observe the results:

```
public class CharToNum
{
   public static void main(String args[])
   {
       int v1 = 'C'-'A';
       int v2 = 'C'+'A';
       int v3 = 'C'*'A';
       int v4 = 'C'/'A';
       System.out.println("Values calculated were "+v1+"  "+v2
                                           ↳+"   "+v3 +"  "+v4);
   }
}
```

Arithmetic Assignment Operators:
+= -= *= /= %=

Two common instructions are adding to a count (e.g. counting cars passing a set of sensors) or adding to a total (e.g. adding the price of an item to a bill total). In Structured English we might write such statements as:

```
Add 1 to count
```
or
```
Add cost of item to total
```

Most programming languages would use statements such as:

```
count = count + 1;     // The new value of count is its current
                       // value plus one
```

and

```
total = total + cost;  // The new value of total is its current
                       // value plus cost
```

The above statements are also perfectly valid in Java (assuming the variables have been defined appropriately), but the same effects can be achieved by the briefer, but slightly less readable:

```
count += 1;
```

and

```
total += cost;
```

The overall effect of the operator += is to add the value on the right hand side to the variable on the left.

All arithmetic operators (`*`, `/`, `%`, `+` , `-`) can be used in this way. These new operators are referred to as **arithmetic assignment operators.**

All arithmetic assignment operators are given in TABLE-2.5.

TABLE-2.5

Arithmetic Assignment Operators

Operator	Description	Example	Equivalence
+=	addition assignment	`no += 6;`	`no = no + 6;`
-=	subtraction assignment	`bal -= cash;`	`bal = bal-cash;`
*=	multiplication assignment	`ans *= 5;`	`ans = ans * 5;`
/=	division assignment	`half /= 2;`	`half = half/2;`
%=	remainder assignment	`rem %= no;`	`rem = rem % no;`

Activity 2.9

Using the arithmetic assignment operators, write the equivalent of the following statements:

1. `sum = sum + no;`
2. `count = count - 6;`
3. `answer = answer * (mark / 7);`
4. `dividend = dividend / (takings - costs);`
5. `total_remainder = total_remainder % (previous*current);`

The Increment And Decrement Operators

As we have already seen, we can add one to the value of a variable in one of two ways:

```
count = count + 1;
```

or

```
count += 1;
```

But Java has an operator specifically designed to perform such an operation: ++. This **increment operator** adds one (i.e. increments) to the contents of a variable. Hence, we may add one to *count* with the statement:

```
count++;
```

It is also permissible to place the increment operator before the variable involved:

```
++count;
```

In these examples, the position of the operator has no affect on the result. But the increment operator can be used as part of a longer statement or within an arithmetic expression. Hence we may write:

```
int ans, no = 6;
ans = no++;
```

This last statement has the effect of changing the value in both *ans* and *no*. But there are two possible ways of doing this:

Copy the value in *no* into *ans* (hence *ans* = 6) then increment *no* (*no* =7)

or

Increment *no* (*no* = 7) then copy the value of *no* into *ans* (*ans* = 7)

The position of the increment operator determines which of the two alternatives is used: when ++ follows the variable (e.g. `ans = no++;`), then incrementation happens last; when ++ comes before the variable, incrementation happens first.

These options are referred to as **post-incrementing** and **pre-incrementing** respectively.

Activity 2.10

Is the statement

```
ans = no++ ;
```

pre-incrementing or post-incrementing?

Write down the coding for the alternative incremental method.

A **decrement operator** (--) is also available to subtract one from a variable. This can also be used in a pre-decrementing and post-decrementing form and as part of a larger statement. This allows statements such as:

```
int ans, no = 6;

no--;               //*** no  = 5 ***
--no;               //*** no  = 4 ***
ans = no--;         //*** ans = 4  , no  = 3 ***
ans = --no;         //*** no  = 2  , ans = 2 ***
```

Activity 2.11

Write down the intermediate and final values produced by the following code:

```
int no1 = 1, no2 = 10, answer;

answer  = ++no1 + no2--;
answer  *= no1++;
```

It is probably best not to use the increment and decrement operators in complex expressions since their effect can sometimes be hard to predict.

Multiple Assignment

If several variables are to be set to the same value, this can be done using a multiple assignment statement. As in the definition statement, it is possible to assign the same value to several variables in a single statement. For example:

```
no1 = no2 = no3 = 0;
letter1 = letter2 = 'F';
rno1 = rno2 = rno3 * 5;
```

The compiler evaluates the assignments from right to left. That is, in the first example, *no3* is given the value zero then *no2* is given the value held in *no3* then *no1* is given the value held in *no2*.

Structured English Equivalents

TABLE-2.6 lists some Structured English statements and their Java equivalent.

TABLE-2.6

Assignment Equivalents

Structured English	Java
`Set total to zero`	`int total = 0;`
`Add 1 to count`	`count++;`
`Add mark to sum`	`sum += mark;`
`Calculate dividend as 10% of total`	`dividend = total * 0.1;`
`Calculate remaining ounces as remainder of (oz1 + oz2) divided by 16`	`remoz = (oz1 + oz2) % 16;`

Summary

- **The assignment operator** is used to give a value to a variable.

  Any previous value held by the variable is overwritten by the new value.

- The simplest assignment has the form **`variable = value;`**

- **The value assigned** may be one of the following:

  a constant
  the value contained in some other variable
  the result of an expression

- **Arithmetic expressions** can use the operators:

*	Multiplication
/	Division
%	Remainder
+	Addition
-	Subtraction

- **The division operator** (/) returns an integer result when both values involved are integers, otherwise a real result is produced.

- **The remainder operator** (%) can only be used with two integer values.

- **Where the second operand is zero**, an error will occur when using the division or remainder operators (e.g. 8/0).

- **When evaluating expressions**, multiplication, division and remainder operations (*, / ,%) are performed before addition and subtraction (+, -).

  This rule is modified by the use of parentheses: expressions in parentheses being performed first.

- **Where the values used in an arithmetic operation are of mixed types** these are converted to compatible types before evaluation.

- **Assigning a value of a different type** to a variable will result in automatic conversion if conversion is from a weaker to a stronger type.

- To assign a value of a stronger type to a weaker type, the value must be cast using the form

```
(cast type) value.
```

- It is the programmer's responsibility to ensure that **the variable type being used is adequate to store the value to be placed in it.**

- **The arithmetic assignment operators** (`+=`, `-=`, `*=` , `/=` and `%=`) allow the receiving variable to be part of the right-hand-side expression without explicitly specifying it.

- **The increment operator,** `++`, is used to add 1 to the value of a variable.

  When placed before the variable, the variable is incremented before the remainder of any expression is evaluated.

  When placed after the variable, any expression is evaluated before the variable is incremented.

- **The decrement operator,- -,** is used to reduce the value of a variable by 1.

  Like `++`, it may be placed before or after the variable to be decremented.

- As in definition, **several variables may be assigned the same value in a single statement.**
  (e.g. `no1 = no2 = no3 = 12;`);

Basic Input/Output

Introduction

It is rather difficult to think of any worthwhile program which is not going to require some input from the keyboard (or other device) and produce output on the screen or paper. Strangely, this is something that basic Java isn't very good at. In fact, there are no commands within the language definition to achieve either input or output.

To perform input/output we need to use classes. At this point we'll simply state how this is done and a detailed explanation of the processes involved will be delayed until later when we have explored the concepts of object-oriented programming.

Output

System.out.println

As we saw in the two Java examples given earlier in this chapter, output is created using the phrase

```
System.out.println
```

The value to be displayed is enclosed in parentheses and this can be a literal, variable or expression:

This assumes *answer, no1* and *no2* have been declared as variables.

```
System.out.println("Hello world");
System.out.println('X');
System.out.println(17);
System.out.println(answer);
System.out.println(no1 * no2);
```

Output begins at the current cursor position and occupies as many character positions on the screen as is necessary to display the required value. The cursor will move to a new line after output is complete.

Several items can be output in a single statement. Each data item is separated by a plus (+) sign. For example, the code

```
int  no1 = 12, no2 = 5;
int answer = no1 * no2;
System.out.println("The answer is " + answer);
```

produces the output

The + operator is creating a single string from the two values

```
The answer is 60
```

> **Activity 2.12**
>
> What output do you think should be produced from the code
>
> ```
> int no1 = 12, no2 = 5;
> System.out.println(no1 + no2);
> ```

This apparent ambiguity is solved by a simple rule:

If either of the first two arguments within `println` are strings the + operator is taken to be an instruction to join other items to that string. If neither value is a string, then the plus is assumed to be part of an arithmetic expression and a calculation is performed. Hence,

```
System.out.println(no1 + no2);
```
displays ***17***

while

```
System.out.println("values are "+no1+no2);
```
displays ***values are 125***

To use the plus sign as an arithmetic operator in this situation, the expression must be enclosed in parentheses:

```
System.out.println("values are "+(no1+no2));
```

Where there are no strings, the + sign is treated as an arithmetic operator. In following this rule, characters will be converted to numbers. So while the line

```
System.out.println("The first letters are " +'A'+'B');
```

This rule is also true in an assignment statement and for other arithmetic operators. Hence, an instruction such as

no1 = 'C'-'A'
will give the result 2.
(i.e. 67-65)

will produce the output

```
The first letters are AB
```

the line

```
System.out.println('A' + 'B');
```

displays the value 131 since *A* has the value 65 and *B* the value 66 in Unicode.

Activity 2.13

What output will be produced by the following lines:

```
int no1 = 12, no2 = 5, answer=60;

System.out.println(no1 - no2);
System.out.println(no1 + '*' + no2 + '=' + answer);
System.out.println(no1 + "*"+no2+"="+answer);
```

Unicode values

* 42
= 61

Controlling the Cursor

If we need the cursor to remain on the same line after output, we can use

```
System.out.print
```

in place of `System.out.println`. This leaves the cursor immediately to the right of the last character output.

FIG-2.7

Using \t

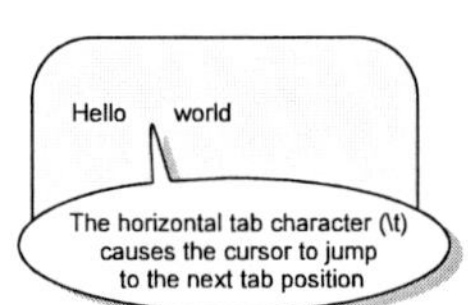

The horizontal tab character ('\t') moves the cursor to the next tab position. These are normally at columns 10, 20, 30 etc. The output produced by the statement

```
System.out.print("Hello\tworld");
```

is shown in FIG-2.7.

The cursor can be moved one space to the left using the backspace character ('\b').

Activity 2.14

1. Write a Java program to display the following shape on the screen:

```
*********
*       *
*       *
*********
```

2. Write a java program which

   Sets integer variable *no1* to 7
   Sets integer variable *no2* to 3
   Calculates *result* as *no1* / *no2*
   Displays the contents of *result*

Keyboard Input

Reading a Character

When a key is pressed on the keyboard, the code for that key is transferred to a keyboard buffer area in the main memory. A statement of the form

```
variable = System.in.read();
```

reads a character from that keyboard buffer into the named variable.

There's one more step we need to follow in order to use this method of input: the first line of `main()` must be changed to

```
public static void main(String args[]) throws
                                        ↳java.io.IOException
```

Activity 2.15

Enter the following program:

```
public class BasicInput1
{
  public static void main(String args[]) throws
                                        ↳java.io.IOException
  {
      int v = System.in.read();
      System.out.println("Value read was " + v);
  }
}
```

Run the program and enter a capital 'A' followed by the ENTER key.

Run the program a second time pressing the '7' key this time.

As you can see, the character read is returned in integer form. That is, the Unicode value of the character is returned. Hence, a capital 'A', when entered, returns the value 65 and the character '7' returns the value 55.

However, we can get the character itself by casting the returned value to a `char`:

```
char ch;
ch = (char)System.in.read();
```

Activity 2.16

Modify the program from Activity 2.15 so that a character is read and displayed.

Rename the class as *BasicInput2* and save the file accordingly.

Test your program by again entering a capital ‘A’.

Reading a Number

As we saw in Activity 2.15, if we enter a numeric digit we can either return its Unicode value as in

```
int v = System.in.read();
```

or the character itself

```
char ch = (char)System.in.read();
```

However, we can also return the number the key represents using the line

```
int v = System.in.read() - 48;
```

This derives from the fact that the numeric characters ('0' to '9') have Unicode values of 48 to 57. You saw from Activity 2.15 that pressing the character '7' on the keyboard gave a result of 55 (because ‘7’ has a Unicode value of 55). Therefore, by subtracting 48 from the result we get the numeric value of the digit (55-48 = 7) This approach works for any numeric key. In fact, we can rewrite the line as

```
int v = System.in.read() - '0'; // minus character zero
```

since zero has the Unicode value of 48 and will automatically be converted to that number when the subtraction is performed.

This is fine if you only want to read in a single digit number. However, things get more complicated with larger numbers.

If you hit several keys when inputting data from the keyboard, each key is stored, in sequence, in the keyboard buffer. Hence, if we type

```
123[Return]
```

The keyboard buffer will contain the following values

```
49 50 51 13 10
```

Notice that pressing the Enter key causes two characters to be transferred to the buffer: the return character (13) and the newline character (10) .

Unfortunately, this is not true in all environments, and sometimes only a newline character is stored when the Enter key is pressed.

We could read a two digit number using the program shown below (LISTING-2.3).

LISTING-2.3

Reading a Two-Digit Number

```
public class TwoDigitNum
{
  public static void main(String args[]) throws
                                        ↳java.io.IOException
  {
      int v1 = System.in.read()-'0';
      int v2 = System.in.read()-'0';
      int value = v1*10 + v2;
      System.out.println("Value entered was "+value);
  }
}
```

Activity 2.17

1. Enter the program shown above and test it by entering the value 26.

2. Modify the program so that a 3-digit value can be entered.

A Class to Deal with Input

Because handling input is rather awkward in Java, we'll create some code (given in LISTING-2.4) to make the job easier. At this stage, just accept the code and make use of it. Later, we'll take a second look at how it was constructed.

LISTING-2.4

Keyboard Input Methods

```
import java.io.*;

class Input
{
  public static int readInt()
  {
      byte nos[] = new byte[12];    //Stores characters read
      int noread = 0;
      int v = 0;
     //*** Read keys pressed as a set of bytes ***
     try
     {
          noread = System.in.read(nos);
     }
     catch(IOException e){}
     //*** Remove trailing newline and return characters ***
     int c = noread-1;
     while(nos[c] == 10 || nos[c] == 13)
          nos[c--] = 0;
     //*** Convert bytes to String then convert to int ***
     try
     {
          v = Integer.parseInt(new String(nos,0,++c));
     }
      //*** If not a valid integer return zero ***
     catch(NumberFormatException nfe)
     {
        v = 0;
     }
      return v;
  }

  public static float readFloat()
  {
      byte nos[] = new byte[15];
      int  noread = 0;
      float v = 0;
```

Continued on next page

LISTING-2.4
(continued)

Keyboard Input Methods

```
        //*** Read keys pressed as a set of bytes ***
        try
        {
            noread= System.in.read(nos);
        }
        catch(IOException e){}
        //*** Remove trailing newline and return characters ***
        int c = noread-1;
        while(nos[c] == 10 || nos[c] == 13)
            nos[c--] = 0;
        //*** Convert bytes to String then convert to float ***
        try
        {
            v = Float.parseFloat(new String(nos,0,++c));
        }
        //*** If string is not a valid float, return zero ***
        catch(NumberFormatException nfe)
        {
            v = 0;
        }
        return v;
    }

    public static char readChar()
    {
        byte nos[] = new byte[10];
        //*** Read keys pressed as a set of bytes ***
        try
        {
            System.in.read(nos);
        }
        catch(IOException e){}
        //*** Return the first byte as a character ***
        return (char)nos[0];
    }

    public static String readString()
    {
        byte nos[] = new byte[80];
        int  noread = 0;
        //*** Read keys pressed as a set of bytes ***
        try
        {
            noread = System.in.read(nos);
        }
        catch(IOException e){}
        //*** Remove trailing newline and return characters ***
        int c = noread - 1;
        while(nos[c] == 10 || nos[c] == 13)
            nos[c--] = 0;
        //*** Return the string constructed from remaining bytes ***
        return new String(nos,0,++c);
    }
}
```

Unlike the other programs we've created up to now, *Input.java* is not designed to be executed. Rather, it is meant to be included in other programs which need to read from the keyboard. The code it contains is not sophisticated or foolproof; it merely serves as a simple way of reading from the keyboard at this point in your learning.

The *Input* class defined above contains four methods:

```
readInt()
readFloat()
readChar()
readString()
```

By using the methods of this class in other programs we can read *int, float, char* or *String* values from the keyboard. For example, an integer can be read and assigned to a variable using statements such as:

```
int v;
v = Input.readInt();
```

Notice that when using the methods of the *Input* class, the class name must precede the method name. These are separated by a full stop. Hence, we use the term

```
Input.readInt()
```

to read an integer value.

Activity 2.18

Enter the program given in LISTING-2.4.

Save the file as *Input.java*

Compile the program.

You'll find out more about packages and how to create them in a later chapter.

We no specific package is named when saving a class, a default package is used.

Compiled classes are stored together in something called a **package**. For the moment, think of a package as doing the same type of job as a photograph album. The album contains a collection of photographs; the package contains a collection of classes.

Rather than copy the code for the *Input* class into every program that uses simple keyboard input, we can tell Java to extract the class from the package it is held in and include it in our new program. To do this we use the statement

```
import Input;
```

at the beginning of any new program. For example, LISTING-2.5 shows how we can use the new class to read in integer, real and character values.

LISTING-2.5

Using the Input Class

```
import Input;

public class TestInput
{
   public static void main (String args[])
   {
       System.out.print("Enter integer : ");
       int no1 = Input.readInt();
       System.out.print("Enter real : ");
       float r = Input.readFloat();
       System.out.print("Enter character : ");
       char ch = Input.readChar();
       System.out.println("Values entered were "+no1+" "+r
                                                 ↳+" "+ch);
   }
}
```

In fact, when an existing class and the new program using that class are held in the same package (e.g. *Input* and *TestInput* will both be held in the default package), the `import` statement is not required, but can usefully be included to act as a comment to the application programmer.

NOTE: Java v1.4 does not allow import lines for classes in the same package.

If using Java 1.4, comment out the `import` line.

Activity 2.19

Type in and test the program in LISTING-2.5.

We'll make use of this class in later examples.

You'll need to import the *Input* class to read from the keyboard.

Activity 2.20

Write programs to perform the following tasks (start a new program for each task):

1. Read in an integer value and display it. Include the text *"the value entered was"*, in your output.

2. Read in two real values. Display their sum, difference, product, and quotient.

3. Read in two times given in minutes and seconds and display their sum. Use the following logic:

```
Read in the minutes of the first time
Read in the seconds of the first time
Read in the minutes of the second time
Read in the seconds of the second time
Calculate the sum of the two times in seconds
Calculate the answer minutes as sum divided by 60
Calculate the answer seconds as sum modulus 60
Display the total minutes and total seconds
```

Summary

- `System.out.println()` produces output on the screen. The cursor moves to a new line after the output is displayed.

- `System.out.print()` does not move the cursor to a new line after output.

- **The + operator** is used as a separator when more than one value is to be displayed.

- **One of the first two values being displayed must be a string** otherwise the + operator will perform an arithmetic add operation.

- A single key can be read from the keyboard using
  `System.in.read()`

- `System.in.read()` returns the Unicode value of the key.

- **To read a character**, cast the value returned by `System.in.read()` to a `char`.
  (e.g. `char ch = (char) System.in.read();`)

- `Import` allows one class to be used within another.

- **Use the *Input* class** to read `int`, `float`, `char` and `String` values from the keyboard.

Logical and Shift Operators

Introduction

Java also contains operators to allow the logical operations AND, OR, XOR and NOT (as explained in Chapter 1).

The language also contains left and right shift operators as well as an arithmetic shift operator which retains the sign of the value being shifted.

Table 2.7 lists the operators and gives examples of their use.

TABLE-2.7

Java Logical and Shift Operators

Operator	Java Symbol	Example
AND	&	`no1 & no2`
OR	|	`no1 | no2`
XOR	^	`no1 ^ no2`
NOT	~	`~no1`
Left Shift	<<	`no1 = no2 << 3`
Right Shift (zero fills)		`no1 = no2 >>> 4`
Arithmetic Right Shift		`no1 = no2 >> 1`

The program in LISTING-2.6 demostrates the use of each operator.

LISTING-2.6

Using Logical and Shift Operators

```
public class LogicAndShift
{
  public static void main(String args[])
  {
      int no1 = 0xB6;   // 10110110
      int no2 = 0x0F;  // 00001111

      System.out.println("no1          = "+no1
          ↳+"(00000000 00000000 00000000 10110110)");
      System.out.println("no2          = "+no2
          ↳+" (00000000 00000000 00000000 00001111)");

      System.out.println("no1 AND no2 = "+(no1 & no2));
      System.out.println("no1 OR  no2 = "+(no1 | no2));
      System.out.println("no1 XOR no2 = "+(no1 ^ no2));
      System.out.println("NOT no1      = "+(~no1));
      System.out.println("no1 << 3     = "+(no1 << 3));
```

Continued on next page

LISTING-2.6
(continued)

Using Logical and Shift Operators

```
        System.out.println("no1 >> 4      = "+(no1 >> 4));

        no1=-no1;
        System.out.println("no1           = "+no1
            ↳+"(11111111 11111111 11111111 01001010)");
        System.out.println("no1 >>> 1     = "+(no1 >>> 1));
        System.out.println("no1 >> 1      = "+(no1 >> 1));
    }
}
```

Activity 2.21

Type in and test the program listed above.

Solutions

Activity 2.1

No solution required.

Activity 2.2

No solution required.

Activity 2.3

No solution required.

Activity 2.4

3no	cannot begin with a numeric digit.
try	a reserved word.
final total	no spaces are allowed.

Activity 2.5

1. Invalid. Number is too large for a byte variable.
2. Invalid. By using double quotes, "C" is a string constant. This cannot be copied into a character variable.
3. Invalid. Unless the variables *y* and *z* have previously been defined.
5. Invalid. There is no need to repeat the term int when using a comma separator.

Activity 2.6

2	0
2	1
2.25	invalid
invalid	invalid
0	0
0	2
-3	0
2	-3
-4	1

Activity 2.7

line 1	int	(1 is stored in int format)
line 2	long	
line 3	double	(0.5 is stored in double format)

Activity 2.8

No solution required.

Activity 2.9

1. sum += no;
2. count -= 6;
3. answer *= (mark / 7);
4. dividend /= (takings - costs);
5. total_remainder %= (previous*current);

Activity 2.10

Post-incrementing

```
ans = ++no;
```

Activity 2.11

	no1	no2	answer
after line 1	2	9	12
after line 2	3		24

Activity 2.12

value 17 is output.

The + sign is taken as an arithmetic operator and hence addition of the two values takes place, the result then being output.

Activity 2.13

7	(12 - 5)
180	(The characters are converted to numbers and added)
12*5=60	(The + operators cause the numeric values to be converted to strings and those strings are joined.)

Activity 2.14

1.

```
public class Rectangle
{
    public static void main(String args[])
    {
        System.out.println("*********");
        System.out.println("*       *");
        System.out.println("*       *");
        System.out.println("*********");
    }
}
```

2.

```
public class Display
{
    public static void main(String args[])
    {
        int no1 = 7, no2 = 3;
        int result = no1 / no2;
        System.out.println(result);
    }
}
```

Activity 2.15

No solution required.

Activity 2.16

No solution required.

Activity 2.17

1. No solution required.

2.

```
public class ThreeDigitNum
{
    public static void main(String args[]) throws
                                ↳java.io.IOException
    {
        int v1 = System.in.read()-'0';
        int v2 = System.in.read()-'0';
        int v3 = System.in.read()-'0';
        int value = v1*100 + v2*10 + v3;
        System.out.println("Value entered was "+value);
    }
}
```

Activity 2.18

No solution required.

Activity 2.19

No solution required.

Activity 2.20

1.

```
import Input;

public class NumberInput
{
    public static void main(String args[])
    {
        System.out.print("Enter a whole number : ");
        int v = Input.readInt();
        System.out.println("The value entered was " + v);
    }
}
```

2.

```
import Input;
public class Arithmetic
{
    public static void main(String args[])
    {
        System.out.print("Enter first value : ");
        double v1 = Input.readFloat();
        System.out.print("Enter second value : ");
        double v2 = Input.readFloat();
        double sum = v1 + v2;
        double difference = v1 - v2;
        double product = v1 * v2;
        double quotient = v1 / v2;
        System.out.println("Sum        = " + sum);
        System.out.println("Difference = " + difference);
        System.out.println("Product    = " + product);
        System.out.println("Quotient   = " + quotient);
    }
}
```

3.

```
import Input;
public class TimeTotal
{
    public static void main(String args[])
    {
        //*** Enter times ***
        System.out.print("Enter minutes : ");
        int mins1 = Input.readInt();
        System.out.print("Enter seconds : ");
        int secs1 = Input.readInt();
        System.out.print("Enter minutes : ");
        int mins2 = Input.readInt();
        System.out.print("Enter seconds : ");
        int secs2 = Input.readInt();
        //*** Calculate sum of times in seconds ***
        int sum = (mins1 + mins2 ) *60 + secs1 + secs2;
        //*** Convert sum to minutes and seconds ***
        int ansmins  = sum / 60;
        int anssecs = sum % 60;
        //*** Display total time ***
        System.out.println("Total time is "
            ↳ +ansmins+" mins "+anssecs
            ↳+" secs");
    }
}
```

Activity 2.21

No solution required.

CHAPTER 3

Control Structures

This chapter covers the following topics:

Binary Selection

Boolean Operators

Compound Statements

Iteration

Jump Statements

Multiway Selection

Nested Loops

Operator Precedence

Relational Operators

White Box Testing

Selection

Binary Selection

Binary selection allows us to choose between two alternative actions within a program. In Structured English, the simplest form of binary selection is implemented using the form:

```
IF condition THEN
    statement
        .
    statement
ENDIF
```

Java also uses an `if` statement to implement binary selection. The simplest form of this statement is:

```
if (condition)
    statement;
```

where

`condition`
: is any term which can be reduced to a *true* or *false* value.

`statement`
: is any executable Java statement. If `expression` evaluates to *true*, then `statement` will be executed, otherwise `statement` will be bypassed.

Condition

The condition must be a Boolean expression in which the relationship between two quantities is compared. For example, the expression `no < 0` will be *true* if the contents of the variable *no* is less than zero (i.e. negative). Boolean expressions have the general form:

value1 relational operator *value2*

where

value1 and *value2*
: may be literal, variables or expressions.

relational operator
: is one of the operators given in TABLE-3.1.

TABLE-3.1

Relational Operators

Relational Operators	
Symbol	**Meaning**
>	Greater than
>=	Greater than or equal to
<	Less than
<=	Less than or equal to
==	Equal to
!=	Not equal to

If *value1* and *value2* are of different types, where possible, automatic conversion takes place before the expression is evaluated.

Activity 3.1

Assuming the following definitions

```
int     no1, no2, no3;
char    let1, let2;
```

which of the following are NOT valid Boolean expressions:

1. `no1 < no2`
2. `let1 = let2`
3. `let2 >= no3`
4. `let2 == "A"`
5. `let1 != 65`

TABLE-3.2 shows some Structured English IF statements and the equivalent Java code.

TABLE-3.2

Simple Java if Statements

Structured English	Java Code

IF *no* is negative THEN
Make *no* positive
ENDIF
	`if(no < 0)`
	`no = -no;`

IF *day* is zero THEN
Display "Sunday"
ENDIF
	`if(day == 0)`
	`System.out.`
	`println("Sunday");`

IF *value* is even THEN
Subtract 1 from *value*
ENDIF
	`if(value % 2 == 0)`
	`value--;`

It's worth pointing out at this stage that one of the most common mistakes a beginner is likely to make when writing a Boolean expression, is to use the assignment operator (=) when attempting to test for equality (==).

The program below (LISTING-3.1) reads in two numbers and displays a message if the numbers are equal. It uses the following logic:

```
Get values for no1 and no2
IF no1 = no2 THEN
    Display "Numbers are equal"
ENDIF
```

LISTING-3.1

Using a Simple IF Statement

```
import Input;

public class List_3_1
{
  public static void main(String args[])
  {
      int no1, no2;
```

Continued on next page

LISTING-3.1
(continued)

Using a Simple IF Statement

```
        //*** read numbers ***
        System.out.print("Enter a number : ");
        no1 = Input.readInt();
        System.out.print("Enter a second number : ");
        no2 = Input.readInt();
        //*** IF equal display message ***
        if ( no1 == no2 )
            System.out.println("Numbers are equal");
    }
}
```

Activity 3.2

What output would be produced by the following program?

```
public class TestIf
{
  public static void main(String args[])
  {
      int no1 = 6, no2 = 2;
      int ans1 = no1 - no2;
      int ans2 = no1 + no2;
      if (ans1 == ans2)
          System.out.println("First is true");
      if (ans1 == ans2 / ans1)
          System.out.println("Second is true");
      if (ans1 * 4 > ans2 )
          System.out.println("Third is true");
  }
}
```

Activity 3.3

Write separate programs to perform the following tasks:

1. Read in an integer number and display the message *"Negative value"* if the number is less than zero.

2. Read in a real number representing the radius of a circle. If the number is greater than zero, display the area of the circle (area = 3.1416 * radius * radius)

3. Read in two numbers. Display the smaller of the two values.

4. Read in a character. If the character is 'F', display *"female"*.

Compound Conditions - the AND and OR Operators

Simple conditions or expressions, such as those used in the examples above, can be combined using the AND and OR operators to form compound relational tests. In Java, there are two ways to represent the AND operator:

```
& OR &&
```

OR can also be represented in two ways:

```
| OR ||
```

Where the AND construct is used to link expressions, then all conditions must be *true* for the overall result to be *true*. For example, if we want to test if the variable *salary* has a value of greater than 20 000 and *maritalstatus* is "s" then the required expression is:

```
if(salary > 20000 & maritialstatus == 's')
```

OR

```
if (salary > 20000 && maritialstatus == 's')
```

When a single ampersand AND (&) is used, the Boolean expression is evaluated in the following way:

1. Evaluate `salary > 20000` (we'll assume this is *false*)
2. Evaluate `maritalstatus == 's'` (we'll assume this is *true*)
3. Evaluate & (*false* & *true* gives *false*)

When the double ampersand AND (&&) is used evaluation changes to:

1. Evaluate `salary > 20000` (we'll assume this is *false*)
2. Since the first expression on an AND operation is *false*, the overall result must also be *false*.

As you can see from this example, the double ampersand operates by short-circuiting the process. It doesn't bother to evaluate the second expression (`maritalstatus == 's'`) when the first one is found to be *false,* since an AND operation needs all the expressions involved to be *true* to give an overall result of *true.*

When OR is used, at least one of the conditions must be *true* for the overall result to be *true*. The single vertical line OR (|) does a full evaluation of the expressions involved; the double vertical line OR (||) stops evaluation as soon as any expression gives a *true* result.

Activity 3.4

Type in and run the following program:

```
public class TestAnd
{
    public static void main(String args[])
    {
        int a = 0;
        if ( a!=0 & 8/a > 0 )
            System.out.println("Test");
        else
            System.out.println("This is displayed");
    }
}
```

What happens when you compile the program?

Change the code to use a double ampersand for the AND operator.

Attempt to run the program again.

What happens this time?

Almost every Java program uses the short-circuit versions of the AND and OR operator: it saves time and prevents problems.

It is also possible to construct complex expressions involving several AND and OR operators. Where this is done it may be necessary to insert additional parentheses to adjust the priority of the operators or simply to clarify the meaning of the condition. TABLE-3.3 gives several examples of structured English statements and the Java equivalent.

TABLE-3.3

Compound Expressions

Structured English	Java Code
IF *no1* = 6 AND *no2* < 0 THEN	`if(no1==6 && no2<0)`
IF *sex* = 'M' OR *sex* = 'F' THEN	`if(sex=='M' || sex=='F')`
IF letter not uppercase THEN	`if(letter<'A' || letter>'Z')`
IF *temp* in the range 15 to 20 THEN	`if(temp>=15 && temp<=20)`
IF female AND older than 59 OR male AND older than 64 THEN	`if((sex=='F'&& age>59)|| (sex=='M'&& age>64))`

Java evaluates compound expressions such as the final example in TABLE-3.3 using the following rules:

1. Evaluate `&&` operators (left to right if more than one - terminating if any expression is *false*).

2. Evaluate `||` operators (left to right if more than one - terminating if any expression is *true*).

If we assume *no1* = 5 and *no2* = *10* and *no3* = *1* in the statement

```
if (no3 == 0 && no1 > 0 || no2 == 10)
```

then the final value of the compound expression is determined by first evaluating the simple expression:

```
no3 == 0    (false)   hence && gives false result
```

This results in the expression being reduced to

```
if (false || no2 == 10)
```

The OR operator cannot short-circuit, so *no2* == *10* must be evaluated which simplifies the original statement to

```
if (false || true)
```

which is calculated to give the final result:

```
if (true)
```

If we add parentheses to the original expression, giving

```
if (no3 == 0 && ( no1 > 0 || no2 == 10))
```

then, *no1* > *0* is processed first giving

```
if (no3 == 0 && (true || no2 == 10))
```

|| short-circuits to give a *true* result

```
if (no3 == 0 && true)
```

no3 == 0 is *false* giving

```
if(false && true)
```

which finally reduces to

```
if(false)
```

Nested parentheses are allowed in expressions. Where used, the inner-most brackets are evaluated first. Parentheses of equal depth are evaluated left to right.

Activity 3.5

Write the Java equivalent for the following expressions:
(Assume any variables are already defined)

1. `IF weight > 16 THEN`
2. `IF code is not 17850 THEN`
3. `IF mark between 75 and 85 THEN`
4. `IF option = 'C' AND key = masterkey THEN`
5. `IF (command ='D' OR command ='A') AND quantity>100 THEN`

The NOT Operator

As well as using AND and OR to link simple expressions, we may negate the meaning of an expression by use of the NOT operator. In Java, NOT is implemented using the character exclamation mark (**!**).

The general structure is:

```
if ( ! (condition) )
```

The inner brackets are required because the NOT operator (!) has a higher priority than &&, ||, relational operators and assignment statements and hence would normally be evaluated first. TABLE-3.4 gives several examples of expressions involving NOT.

TABLE-3.4

Expressions using the NOT Operator

Structured English	Expression (using NOT)	Expression (without NOT)
IF *no* not equal to 10 THEN	`if(!(no == 10))`	`if(no != 10)`
IF *no1* not equal 10 AND *no2* not equal 6 THEN	`if(!(no1==10 || no2 == 6))`	`if(no1 != 10 && no2 != 6)`
IF *weight* not greater than 16 THEN	`if(!(weight > 16))`	`if(weight <= 16)`

Activity 3.6

Indicate which of the following expressions are invalid. Where an expression is valid, state its final value of the Boolean expression. Assume the definition `int no = 4;`

```
1. if (!(no == 6))
2. if (!(no = 6))
3. if (!!(no < 5))
```

Operator Precedence

We can see from the previous examples that, like arithmetic operators, relational operators (<, >, ==, etc.) and Boolean operators (&&, || and !) have an order of priority when evaluating expressions. TABLE-3.5 gives the priority of all operators we have encountered so far. This precedence list includes not only the arithmetic operators, but also conditional and assignment operators since they can be used together. Highest precedence is at the top of the table.

TABLE-3.5

Operator Precedence

Items on the same line of the table have equal priority.

Where items of equal priority exist, these are normally evaluated from left to right within the expression. However, those marked with an asterisk are processed from right to left.

Operator Precedence		
Operator	**Description**	
( )	Parentheses	
! -	Logical NOT, unary minus	*
++ --	Increment, decrement	*
* / %	Arithmetic multiply, divide, modulus	
+ -	Addition, subtraction	
< > >= <=	Inequality relational operators	
== !=	Equality relational operators	
&&	Logical AND	
||	Logical OR	
= += -= *= /= %=	Assignment	*

Activity 3.7

Write separate programs to perform the following tasks:

1. Read in the month of the year as an integer (1 to 12). If the value entered is outside this range display the message "Invalid month".

2. Read in a lowercase letter and, if it's a vowel, display the word "vowel".

Compound Statements

Where there are several statements following the expression, then they must be enclosed in braces. The general form is shown below.

```
if (condition)
{
    statement;
    statement;
        .
    statement;
}
```

For example, the Structured English statement

```
IF ozs >= 16 THEN
    Add 1 to lbs
    Subtract 16 from ozs
ENDIF
```

is coded as

```
if(ozs >= 16)
{
    lbs++;
    ozs-=16;
}
```

The position of the braces and the use of indentation should be consistent throughout your program. Although the layout is of no concern to the compiler, we humans, who have to correct programs, sometimes weeks after they have been written, will find them much easier to decipher if a clear, neat style is used.

The rule is simple: indent any code within an `if` statement (or any of the other control structures we have yet to cover).

You may come across other styles of layout but this one makes finding missing braces (a common error) easy. Whatever style you decide on, be consistent!

> **Activity 3.8**
>
> Write a program to perform the following task:
>
> Read in two real numbers (name the variables *rno1* and *rno2*). If *rno2* is not zero, calculate and display the result of *rno1/rno2*.

if else

Like Structured English, Java allows the `if` statement to be extended to include an `else` option which will be executed only if the condition specified is *false.*

Structured English uses the format

```
IF condition THEN
    statement
ELSE
    statement
ENDIF
```

Java uses

```
if (condition)
    statement;
else
    statement;
```

In LISTING-3.2, two values are read in and the smaller of the two displayed. The program employs the following logic:

```
Get values for no1 and no2
IF no1 < no2 THEN
    Display no1
ELSE
    Display no2
ENDIF
```

LISTING-3.2

Using `if..else`

```
import Input;

public class List_3_2
{
  public static void main(String args[])
  {
       int no1, no2;
       //*** read numbers ***
       System.out.print("Enter a number : ");
       no1 = Input.readInt();
       System.out.print("Enter a second number : ");
       no2 = Input.readInt();
       //*** Display smaller ***
       if ( no1 < no2 )
            System.out.println("Smaller value is " + no1);
       else
            System.out.println("Smaller value is " + no2);
  }
}
```

Activity 3.9

Write separate programs to perform the following tasks:

1. Read in two numbers and display the phrase *"The numbers are equal"* or *"The numbers are different"* as appropriate.

2. Read in a lowercase letter. If it's a vowel display *"Vowel"* otherwise display *"Consonant"*.

3. Read in an integer value. If it's an odd number display *"Odd"* otherwise display *"Even"*.

Where there is more than one statement in any section of the `if` statement, they must be enclosed in braces:

```
if (condition)
{
    statement;
        .
    statement;
}
else
{
    statement;
        .
    statement;
}
```

For example, the Structured English statement

```
IF no < 0 THEN
    Display "Negative"
    Add no to sumofnegativenumbers
ELSE
    Display "Positive"
    Add no to sumofpositivenumbers
ENDIF
```

translates in Java to

```
if (no < 0)
{
    System.out.println("Negative");
```

```
        sumofnegativenumbers += no;
}
else
{
    System.out.println("Positive");
    sumofpositivenumbers += no;
}
```

The general form of the `if` statement is shown in FIG-3.1.

FIG-3.1

The `if` Statement

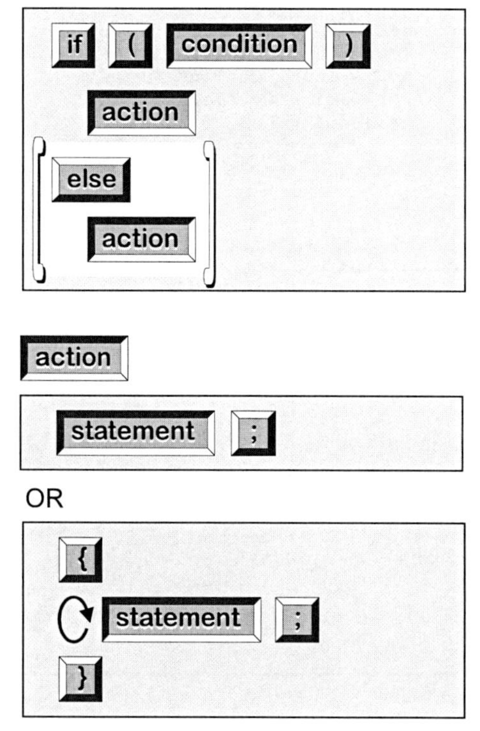

Nested `if` Statements

When dealing with more complex problems, where there are more than two alternative actions, it is sometimes necessary to place one `if` statement inside another. This is termed **nested `if`** statements. For example, we might divide males into those of working age and those of retirement age with the logic:

```
IF sex = 'M' THEN
    IF age >= 65 THEN
        Display "Retired male"
    ELSE
        Display "Working male"
    ENDIF
ELSE
    Display "Female"
ENDIF
```

which in Java is coded as:

```
if (sex == 'M')
    if (age >= 65)
        System.out.println("Retired male");
    else
        System.out.println("Working male");
else
        System.out.println("Female");
```

Activity 3.10

Write a program to perform the following task:

Read in the number of hours of overtime an employee has worked during the week (*hoursover*) and the employee's grade (*grade*). Possible values for the grade are 1 or 2.
If the employee is grade 1 then he is paid $60.00 per hour of overtime; grade 2 employees are paid $40.00.
Calculate and display the overtime payment due to the employee. If he has worked no overtime, display "No overtime payment due".

If we removed the last **`else`** option from the example shown above, giving the code

```
if (sex == 'M')
    if (age >= 65)
        System.out.println("Retired male");
    else
        System.out.println("Working male");
```

there is potential ambiguity in this structure since the `else` option could belong to the first `if` structure (`if (sex == 'M')`) rather than the second, as suggested by the indentation used. This uncertainty is avoided by applying the rule that an `else` is always assigned to the most recent `if` structure which does not already have a matching `else`.

Where the `else` statement is required to match with the first `if` rather than the second as in the logic

```
IF sex = 'M' THEN
    IF age >= 65 THEN
        Display "Retired male"
    ENDIF
ELSE
    Display "Female"
ENDIF
```

then this can be achieved by separating the second `if` statement from the `else` using braces:

Braces enclose the second `if` statement thus forcing the `else` to match with the earlier `if` statement

```
if (sex == 'M')
{
    if (age >= 65)
        System.out.println("Retired male");
}
else
    System.out.println("Female");
```

Activity 3.11

Modify and extend the above `if` statement to print one of the four following messages:

Retired male
Working male
Retired female (Females retiral age = 60)
Working female

Test your logic in a Java program which reads the *sex* and *age* from the keyboard.

Write a second version of the program using AND/OR constructs.

The `else if` Option

Although a simple `if..else` structure is ideal for choosing between two alternative actions, the nested `if` statements necessary to implement a wider range of choices can produce code which is less than easy to follow. For example, if a program requires to read in a transaction code and display one of the following messages:

Code	Message
1	CASH
2	CREDIT
3	RETURNED
other	INVALID CODE

then this requires the logic:

```
IF code = 1 THEN
    Display "CASH"
ELSE
    IF code = 2 THEN
        Display "CREDIT"
    ELSE
        IF code = 3 THEN
            Display "RETURNED"
        ELSE
            Display "INVALID CODE"
        ENDIF
    ENDIF
ENDIF
```

which, if programmed using the conventional layout, produces

```
if(code == 1)
    System.out.println("CASH");
else
    if(code == 2)
        System.out.println("CREDIT");
    else
        if(code == 3)
            System.out.println("RETURN");
        else
            System.out.println("INVALID CODE");
```

Without affecting the logic of the code, the above layout can be improved by placing each `else` and subsequent `if` expression on the same line:

```
if(code == 1)
    System.out.println("CASH");
else if(code == 2)
    System.out.println("CREDIT");
else if(code == 3)
    System.out.println("RETURN");
else
    System.out.println("INVALID CODE");
```

The effect of executing such code is to test each expression in turn until one is found to be *true*. The instruction associated with that `if` statement is then executed. If no expression is *true* then the final `else` option is executed. Where more than one statement is required after any of the options then, as usual, braces must be employed giving the general form for this structure:

```
if(condition)
{
    statement;
        .
    statement;
}
else if(condition)
```

```
{
    statement;
        .
    statement;
}
        .
else
{
    statement;
        .
    statement;
}
```

Activity 3.12

Write a program to read in the day of the week as a number (0 = Sunday; 6 = Saturday) and display the name of the corresponding day of the week.

The Conditional Assignment Operator

In most languages, if we wish to assign one of two values to a variable then a selection construct would be used. For example, we might assign the smaller of two values to a third variable with the code:

```
if (no1 < no2)
    small = no1;
else
    small = no2;
```

This is quite allowable in Java but a briefer style is available using the **conditional assignment operator**. This allows us to replace the above logic with the single statement:

```
small = (no1 < no2)? no1 : no2;
```

small is assigned the value following the question mark (i.e. the contents of *no1*) if the condition (`no1 < no2`) is *true* and assigned the value following the colon (*no2*) if the condition is *false.*

The general form of this statement is shown in FIG-3.2.

FIG-3.2

The Conditional Operator

Where

variable is assigned the value following the question mark if *expression* is *true*
variable is assigned the value following the colon if *expression* is *false.*
value is a variable, constant or expression.

Activity 3.13

Using the conditional operator, produce the equivalent of:

```
if (no < 0)
    --c;
else
    c++;
```

Multi-way Selection

Multi-way selection means choosing one option from many. Although we have already dealt with this situation using nested `if` statements and the `else if` structure, there is an alternative approach which often results in clearer code. This is the `switch` statement.

Earlier we looked at a program to read in a transaction code and display one of the following messages:

Code	Message
1	CASH
2	CREDIT
3	RETURNED
other	INVALID CODE

This could be coded in Structured English as:

```
IF
    code = 1:  Display "CASH"
    code = 2:  Display "CREDIT"
    code = 3:  Display "RETURNED"
ELSE
    Display "INVALID CODE"
ENDIF
```

Java's `switch` statement has a similar effect. One attempt at translating the Structured English to a `switch` statement might be:

```
switch (code)
{
    case 1  : System.out.println("CASH");
    case 2  : System.out.println("CREDIT);
    case 3  : System.out.println("RETURNED");
    default : System.out.println("INVALID CODE");
}
```

During execution, *code* (known as the **switch variable**) is evaluated and control jumps to the `case` statement whose value matches that of *code*. Where *code* does not match any of the `case` values, then control jumps to the `default` option.

The `switch` control structure may seem quite straight-forward, but it has an unexpected characteristic: once the appropriate `case` option has been identified, and its associated instruction executed, the instructions of succeeding `case` statements are also executed. In other words, if, in the above example, *code* has the value 2 then control jumps to `case 2 :` and the word "CREDIT" is displayed, then execution continues through `case 3 :` and `default :` resulting in the strings "RETURNED" and "INVALID CONTROL" also being displayed. This is unlike multiway branch statements implemented in other languages where only one option is executed and all other options are skipped.

> **Activity 3.14**
>
> What output would be produced by the `switch` structure given above if a value of 3 was entered?

In most circumstances we would not want the subsequent statements specified in later `case` options to be executed. These can be bypassed by using another command: `break`.

When the `break` command is executed, control jumps immediately to the end of the `switch` statement. We can now write the correct version of our code as:

```
switch (code)
{
    case 1  :   System.out.println("CASH");
                break;
    case 2  :   System.out.println("CREDIT");
                break;
    case 3  :   System.out.println("RETURNED");
                break;
    default :   System.out.println("INVALID CODE");
}
```

Using this updated version, only one of the `case` options will be executed.

The `default` section of the `switch` statement is optional and may be omitted. Where there is no `default` option and the value of the `switch` variable does not match any of those given in the `cases` which follow, then the whole `switch` structure is bypassed.

LISTING-3.3 allows the computer to be used as a simple calculator using the `switch` structure to choose the correct operation to be performed.

LISTING-3.3

Using switch

```
import Input;

public class TestSwitch1
{
  public static void main(String args[])
  {
      double   rno1, rno2, answer = 0;
      char     option;
      // *** Get expression to be evaluated
      System.out.print("Enter first number : ");
      rno1 =   Input.readFloat();
      System.out.print("Enter second number : ");
      rno2 = Input.readFloat();
      System.out.print("Enter option (+-/*): ");
      option = Input.readChar();
      // *** Execute appropriate choice ***
      boolean option_ok = true;
      switch(option)
      {
          case '+'  :   answer = rno1 + rno2 ;
                        break;
          case '-'  :   answer = rno1 - rno2;
                        break;
          case '/'  :   answer = rno1 / rno2;
                        break;
          case '*'  :   answer = rno1 * rno2;
                        break;
          default   :   System.out.println("Unknown operator");
                        option_ok = false;
      }
      // *** If a valid operator used, display result ***
      if (option_ok)
          System.out.println(""+rno1+option+rno2+'='+answer);
  }
}
```

Activity 3.15

Enter and test the program shown above.

You can see from LISTING-3.3 that the `switch` structure can be implemented using character values as well as integers; however, real and string values are not allowed.

It is also possible to have two or more `case` options relating to the same section of code.

For example, LISTING-3.3 expects the asterisk ('*') to be entered when using the multiply option but non-programmers are much more likely to enter an 'x'. Therefore, an improvement to the program would be to allow for both options. Since we already know that the `switch` statement falls through each `case` option where there is no `break` statement included, we need simply write

```
case '*'    :   ;
case 'x'    :   answer = rno1 * rno2;
                break;
```

at the appropriate point in our structure. However, Java permits a certain freedom in this situation allowing the semi-colon in the empty `case` option (`case '*':;`) to be omitted giving simply

```
case '*'    :   // *** No semi-colon required ***
case 'x'    :   answer = rno1 * rno2;
                break;
```

Activity 3.16

Make the above change to your program and test the multiplication option with both characters ('x' and '*').

Unfortunately, there is no neat way of supplying a continuous range of values to a case option. For example, if we wished to grade an exam mark as fail, pass or distinction corresponding to scores in the ranges 0 - 45, 46 - 80, 81 - 100, this would not be easily coded using the `switch` construct and we would have to revert to the `else if` format.

The general format of the `switch` statement is shown in FIG-3.3

FIG-3.3

The `switch` Statement

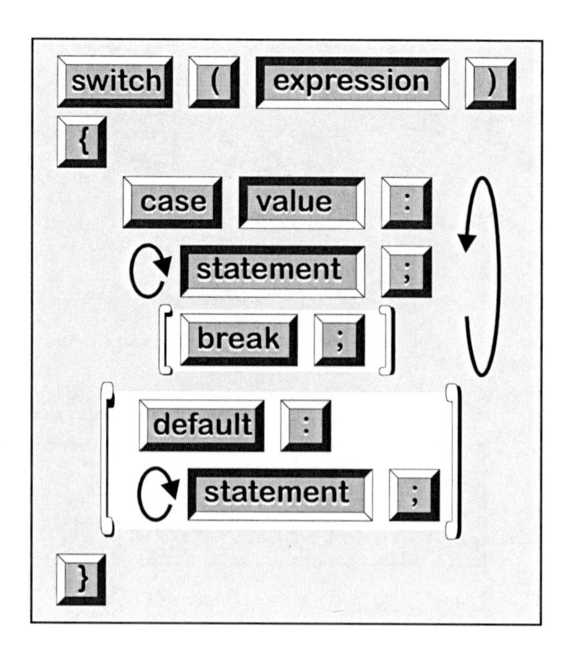

Summary

- **Boolean expressions can be linked by (AND) or (OR).**
  (e.g. `no1 < 4 && no2 > 6`)

- **The AND statement comes in two forms :** & and &&.

- **&** evaluates both Boolean expressions in an AND.

- **&&** returns *false* if the first expression is *false*. The second expression is not evaluated.

- **The OR statement comes in two forms** : | and ||.

- | evaluates both expressions in an OR.

- || returns *true* if the first expression is *true*. The second expression is not evaluated.

- **A logic value can be reversed using ! (NOT).**
  (e.g. `!(age > 18)`)

- **Nested `if` structures** can be used where a choice between more than two options has to be made.

- Where `if` statements are nested, **the `else` keyword is linked to the preceeding** `if` unless that preceeding `if` is enclosed in braces.

- The **conditional operator** allows one of two values to be assigned to a variable depending on a given condition.
  (e.g. `YC = (month <= 3) ? year - 1 :` year;)

- **The `switch` statement** can also be used when there is more than one alternative.

- **The `switch`** statement will begin execution at the first case option found to be *true*. Normally, all subsequent `case` options will also be executed.

- **Use of the `break` statement** will cause control to jump to the end of the `switch` structure.

- **Where none of the options in the `switch` statement** are appropriate, the `default` option is executed. If the `default` option is omitted, the whole `switch` structure is bypassed.

- **Values in the `case` options** may be integer or character constants; not real or string.

- **Several `case`** options can be specified together.
  (e.g.
  ```
  case 'a':
  case 'b':
  case 'c': System.out.println("A,B, or C");
  ```

- **`case`** cannot specify a range of values.
  (e.g. `case 0..45:` is not valid)

- **When `if`** statements are nested, `else` statements match with the last `if` section which is not already linked to an `else` statement.

Iteration

Java has three distinct iterative structures. However, the Java structures differ slightly in format and operation from those of Structured English and care should be taken when translating your iteration logic to Java.

The `while` Structure

The `while` structure is probably the easiest to understand, since it is identical in operation to the **while** of Structured English. This is an **entry controlled loop**; that is, the condition to be tested is at the start of the loop. If the condition is *true* the loop body is executed; if not, then the loop body is bypassed. For example, we might define the logic determining the number of times one integer divides into another as:

```
Set count to zero
WHILE dividend >= 0 DO
    Add 1 to count
    Subtract divisor from dividend
ENDWHILE
Subtract 1 from count
```

which can be coded in Java as:

```
count = 0;
while (dividend >= 0)
{
    count++;
    dividend -= divisor;
}
count--;
```

Like the `if` statement, a `while` structure requires that,where there is more than one statement in the loop body, those statements are enclosed in braces. The structure of the statement is shown in FIG-3.4.

FIG-3.4

The `while` Statement

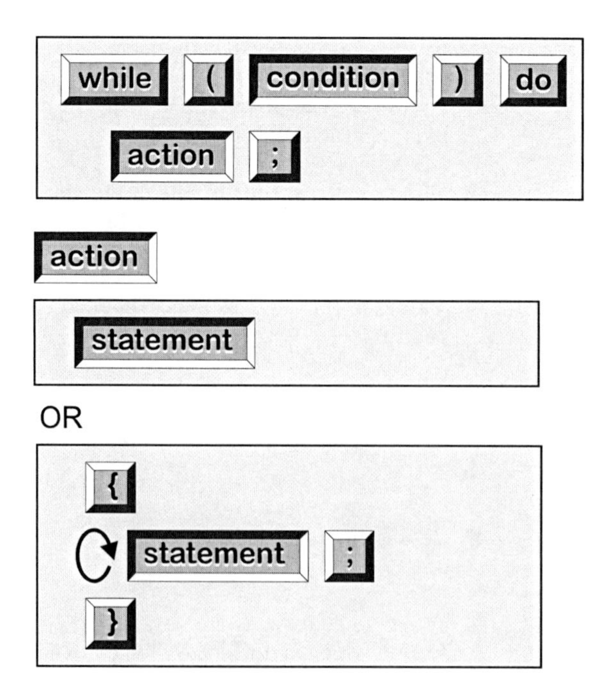

The operation of the statement is shown graphically in FIG-3.5

FIG-3.5

Executing a `while` Loop

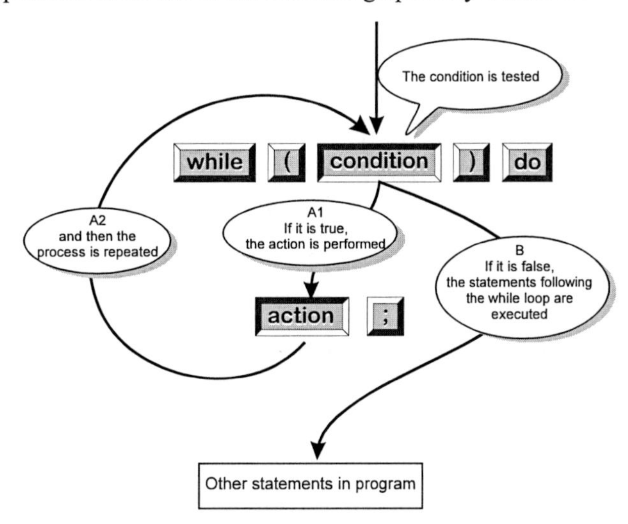

A common use for the `while` loop is validation of input. So for example, we might ensure that a positive integer is entered using the logic

```
Get value
WHILE value <= 0 DO
    Display error message
    Get value
ENDWHILE
```

which can be coded in Java as:

```
System.out.print("Enter a positive integer : ");
int value = Input.readInt();
while (value <= 0)
{
    System.out.println("You must enter a positive value");
    System.out.print("Enter a positive integer : ");
    value = Input.readInt();
}
```

TABLE-3.6 gives several examples of Structured English *while* statements and the equivalent Java code.

TABLE-3.6

`while` Structures

Structured English	Java

Get month
WHILE month outside range 1 - 12 DO
    Display "Invalid month"
    Get month
ENDWHILE
	month = Input.readInt();
	while (month < 1 || month > 12)
	{
	  System.out.println("Invalid");
	  month = Input.readInt();
	}

Get value
WHILE value not zero DO
    Add value to total
    Get value
ENDWHILE
	value = Input.readInt();
	while (value != 0)
	{
	    total += value;
	    value = Input.readInt();
	}

Activity 3.17

Write the Java equivalent of the following Structured English:

```
Get no1
Get no2
WHILE no1 not equal to no2 DO
    Set no1 equal to no2
    Get no2
ENDWHILE
```

When will the `while` loop terminate?

Activity 3.18

Write separate programs to perform each of the following tasks:

1. One method of testing if a value is divisible by 37 is to split the value into groups of 3 digits which are then added. If the resulting sum is divisible by 37 then so is the original.
   e.g. 456790086 = 456 + 790 + 086 = 1332.
   Program this test and print an appropriate message.

```
OUTLINE LOGIC:
    Set sum to zero
    Get no
    WHILE no is not zero DO
        Extract the three least significant digits of no
        Add this extracted value to sum
        Remove the three least significant digits from no
    ENDWHILE
    IF sum is exactly divisible by 37 THEN
        Display "Value divisible by 37"
    ELSE
        Display "Value not divisible by 37"
    ENDIF
```

2. The number of ways that *r* objects can be chosen from *n* objects is given by the formula
   $$^{n}C_{r} = n!/((n-r)!*r!)$$
   Write a program to read *r* and *n* (validate that $r < n$) and print the result.
   NOTE: *r!* is pronounced *r* factorial and is *r * (r-1) * (r-2) *...... *1*

```
OUTLINE LOGIC:
    Get value for n
    Get value for r
    WHILE r>= n DO
        Display error message
        Get value for n
        Get value for r
    ENDWHILE
    Set factorialn to 1
    FOR C := 2 TO n DO
        Multiply factorialn by C
    ENDFOR
```

Continued on next page

Because of the large values that may be generated, make *factorialn, factorialr* and *factorialn_r* type `double` variables.

nCr should be a `long`.

Activity 3.18 (continued)

```
Set factorialr to 1
FOR C := 2 TO r DO
    Multiply factorialr by C
ENDFOR
Set factorialn_r to 1
FOR C := 2 TO n-r DO
    Multiply factorialn_r by C
ENDFOR
Calculate nCr as Factorialn /(Factorialn_r*factorialr)
Display nCr
```

The `do..while` Structure

The `do..while` statement is as close as Java comes to supplying a **REPEAT .. UNTIL** structure.

However, the two statements differ in more than syntax, since, although both have the condition at the end of the control structure, **REPEAT .. UNTIL** exits its loop body when the given condition is *true* whereas `do .. while` exits when its condition is *false*. In other words, the `do .. while` structure is more like a `while` statement with the condition moved to the end of the loop body.

This means that the translation of a **REPEAT .. UNTIL** loop in Structured English to a `do..while` loop in Java involves inverting the condition for the Java version. For example, the logic

```
REPEAT
    Get value
    Add value to total
UNTIL value is zero
```

is coded as:

```
do
{
    value = Input.readInt();
    total += value;
}
while (!(value == 0));
```

Note that it would be quite possible to have coded the expression in the above `while` statement as

```
value != 0
```

rather than

```
!(value == 0),
```

but the latter technique of simply placing a NOT operator in front of the original Structured English condition is less prone to error, especially when the condition is a complex one.

For example, if a REPEAT loop contained the condition

```
month < 1 OR month > 12
```

this could be coded in a `do..while` structure as:

```
!(month < 1 || month > 12)
```

rather than the equally correct

```
month >= 1 && month <= 12
```

which involves more changes from the original and hence is more likely to introduce an error in translation.

The `do..while` requires additional braces when there is more than one statement in the loop body. The general form of the statement is shown in FIG-3.6.

FIG-3.6

The `do..while` Statement

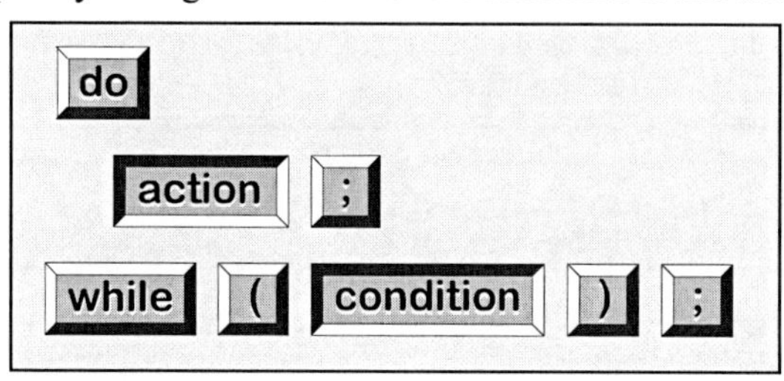

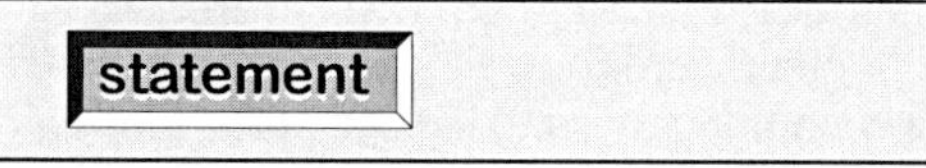

OR

TABLE-3.7 gives some examples of Structured English **REPEAT .. UNTIL** loops and the equivalent Java `do..while` structures.

TABLE-3.7

`do..while` Structures

Structured English	Java

Set target to 401
REPEAT
    Get score
    Subtract score from target
UNTIL target <= 0
	target = 401;
	do
	{
	    score=Input.readInt();
	    target -= score;
	}
	while (!(target <= 0));

Set total to zero
Set count to zero
REPEAT
    Get number
    Add number to total
    Add 1 to count
UNTIL count = 10 OR number = 0
	total = 0;
	count = 0;
	do
	{
	    number=Input.readInt();
	    total += number;
	}
	while (!(++count == 10||number ==0));

Activity 3.19

If X_i is an approximation of the cube root of N then a closer approximation is

$$X_{i+1} = (N/X_i^2 + 2X_i)/3$$

Write a program to calculate the cube root to 5 decimal places.

```
OUTLINE LOGIC:
    Get a value for N
    Set newx to N/3
    REPEAT
        Set oldx to newx
        Calculate newx as (N/(oldx*oldx)+2*oldx)/3
    UNTIL N-newx*newx*newx < 0.000005 AND
            newx*newx*newx - N < 0.000005
    Display newx
```

The `for` Structure

Like Structured English, Java contains a `for` structure. In Structured English, this control structure can perform a sequence of tasks a fixed number of times using logic such as:

```
FOR each student DO
    Get student's mark
    Add mark to total
ENDFOR
```

which, should there be 10 students, would carry out the statements

```
Get student's mark
Add mark to total
```

10 times.

When we want to perform this type of loop in Java, we usually need to define a **loop counter variable** which the `for` loop increments each time the loop body is executed. For example, the 10 students would have their marks totalled by the code:

```
int total=0,count,mark;

for(count = 1; count <= 10; count++)
{
    mark=Input.readInt();
    total += mark;
}
```

The parentheses following the word `for` contain three main components. The first of these, `count = 1`, is known as the **initialisation statement** and is executed before the loop body is entered. The second, `count <= 10`, is the condition to be tested at the start of each iteration - only if the condition is *true* will the loop body be executed. The third and final part (often called the **increment statement**), `count++`, is executed at the end of the loop body before returning to the beginning of the loop and testing the condition.

The same logic can be implemented in a `while` loop as:

```
count = 1;              // part 1 before loop body
while (count <= 10)     // part 2 condition tested at start
{                       // of loop
    mark=Input.readInt();
    total += mark;
```

```
        count++;            // part 3 executed at the end of the
    }                       // loop body
```

Like the other iteration structures, parentheses are required where there is more than one statement in the `for` loop body.

> **Activity 3.20**
>
> What output will be produced from the code below?
>
> ```
> for(no = 0; no < 5; no++)
>     System.out.println(no);
> ```

The format of the `for` statement is shown in FIG-3.7.

FIG-3.7

The `for` Statement

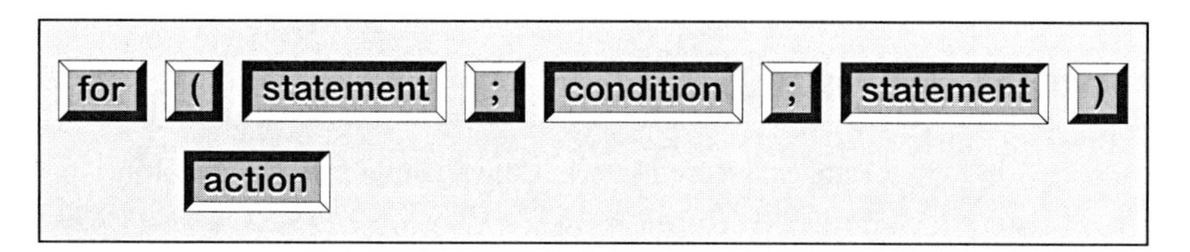

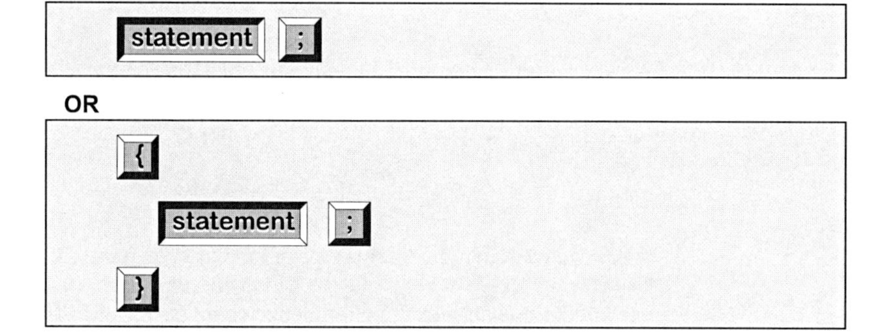

The operation of the statement is shown graphically in FIG-3.8 below.

FIG-3.8

How the `for` Statement Operates

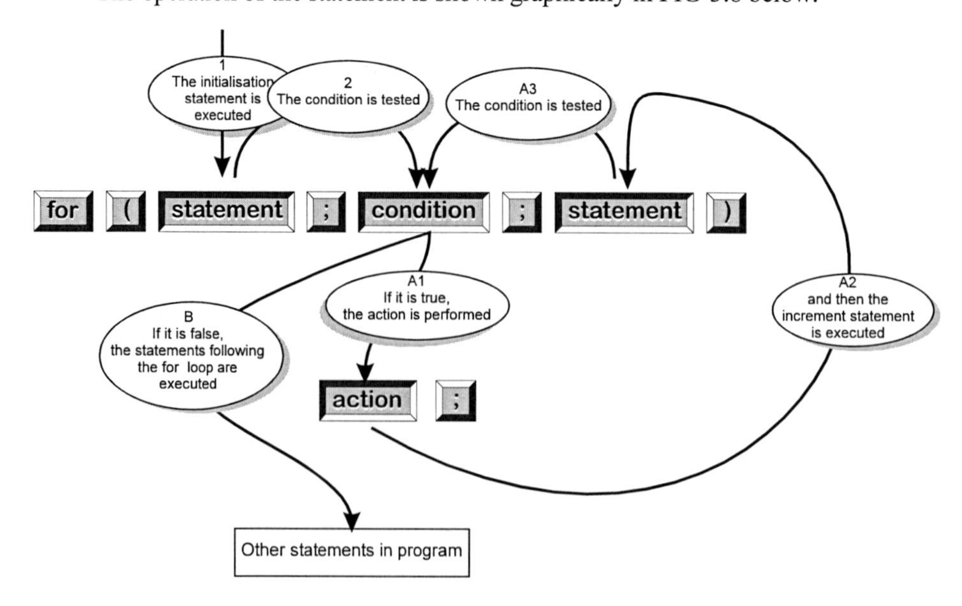

Activity 3.21

1. Write a program to display all numbers between 1 and 20 which are not divisible by 4 or 5.
   HINT: a number (*x*) is exactly divisible by some other number (*y*) when *x* divided by *y* gives no remainder.

```
OUTLINE LOGIC:
    FOR no := 1 TO 20 DO
        IF no is not divisible by 4 or 5 THEN
            Display no
        ENDIF
    ENDFOR
```

2. In ice skating, a number of judges (*N*) award marks. The highest and lowest of these are ignored and the others averaged to give a result. Write a program to input *N*, followed by *N* marks, and display the average score ignoring the highest and lowest mark. (Scores range from 0.0 to 6.0 in increments of 0.1.)

```
OUTLINE LOGIC:
    Get value for N
    Get first score
    Set highest_score to score
    Set lowest_score to score
    Set total to score
    FOR N-1 times DO
        Get score
        Add score to total
        IF score is greater than highest_score THEN
            Set highest_score to score
        ELSE
            IF score is less than lowest_score THEN
                Set lowest_score to score
            ENDIF
        ENDIF
    ENDFOR
    Subtract highest_score and lowest_score from total
    Calculate average as total/(N-2)
    Display average
```

Using `for` to Implement Other Iterative Structures

In most programming languages, the condition which must hold when iterating a counting loop is never explicitly stated. For example, in the Pascal statement

```
FOR count := 1 TO 10 DO
```

the implied loop entry condition which must hold to continue iteration is *count <=10*. As we have seen, Java requires such conditions to be stated explicitly. Hence the equivalent Java statement would be

```
for(count=1; count <= 10; count++)
```

This apparently clumsy format is, in fact, very powerful. Since there is no restriction on exactly what condition is specified, it need have nothing to do with the loop counter. For example, if we needed to count the number of values in a list of numbers which terminates with a zero, our Structured English solution might be:

```
Set count to zero
Get number
WHILE number not zero DO
    Add 1 to count
    Get number
ENDWHILE
```

Java can code this as:

```
number=Input.readInt();
for(count = 0; number != 0; count++)
    number = Input.readInt();
```

We can take this variation on the standard `for` loop a stage further and create a Java `for` loop which has no loop counter. The following code totals a list of single digit values, stopping when the total exceeds 99.

```
for(total = 0; total < 100; total += no)
    no = System.in.read() - '0';
```

The equivalent Structured English is:

```
Set total to zero
WHILE total < 100 DO
    Get no
    Add no to total
ENDWHILE
```

> **Activity 3.22**
>
> Write a program which reads in a set of numbers. No more values are read once the total of the values input passes 100. Display the average value of the numbers entered.

Omitting Parts of the `for` Statement

It is possible to omit one or more parts of the `for` statement. For example, we may remove the initialisation part as in the example below:

```
// terminate when no = -1;
int no;

//*** List each value entered ***
System.out.print("Enter number : ");
no=Input.readInt();
total = no;
for(; no != -1; total+=no)
{
    System.out.println( no);
    System.out.print("Enter number : ");
    no=Input.readInt();
}
```

Note that, although the initialisation statement has been omitted, the semicolon must remain. It is also valid to omit the post loop body statement. For example:

```
System.out.print( "Enter number : ";
no=Input.readInt();
for(total = no; no != 0;)
{
    System.out.print("Enter number : ");
    no = Input.readInt();
    total += no;
}
```

It is even possible to omit the loop condition but, of course, this would normally result in an infinite loop which is unlikely to be what you are after.

```
for( ; ; )
   System.out.println("Looping forever");
```

Using the Comma Operator

It is possible to include additional statements in any component of the `for` loop by separating these by a comma. For example, we can initialise both a count and total before entering the loop body by beginning the `for` statement with:

```
for(i = 1, total = 0;
```

These same variables can be adjusted at the end of the loop body with:

```
;i++, total += no)
```

The complete structure for summing 10 numbers would be:

```
for(i = 1, total = 0; i <= 10; i++, total += no)
{
    System.out.print("Enter number : ");
    no=Input.readInt();
}
```

This approach can be useful for initialising several variables at the start of the loop or modifying several variables at the end of the loop.

Although useful, the technique should be used sparingly since it does nothing to aid readability.

Defining Variables in the `for` Statement

Since Java allows variables to be defined at any point in a program, it is the common practice of many Java programmers to define the loop counter inside the `for` loop structure. For example:

```
for(int i = 1; i <= 10; i++)
```

This can be extended to apply to any other variables used exclusively in the loop body. For example, in the program below, two variables are declared in the `for` statement *i* and *total*

```
public class TestIf2
{
    public static void main(String args[])
    {
        int no;
        for (int i = 1, total = 0; i < 10; i++,total+=no)
        {
            no = (int)(Math.random()*10)+1;
            System.out.println(total);
        }
    }
}
```

Notice also that, by using a comma, we can execute more than one statement in the final section of the `for` statement.

Variables declared within a `for` statement exist only within that `for` loop; their space being **deallocated** when the loop is exited. TABLE-3.8 gives some examples of the `for` structure.

TABLE-3.8

for Structures

Structured English	Java

Set total to zero
FOR no := 1 TO 10 DO
    Add no to total
ENDFOR
	total = 0;
	for(no = 1; no <= 10; no++)
	    total += no;

Set total to zero
Get no of students
FOR each student DO
    Get student's mark
    Display student's mark
    Add student's mark to total
ENDFOR
Calculate average as
    total/no of students
	total = 0;
	noofstudents=Input.readInt();
	for(i=1;i<=noofstudents;i++)
	{
	    mark=Input.readInt();
	    System.out.println(mark);
	    total += mark;
	}
	average = total/noofstudents;

Jump Statements

Statements which transfer the flow of control to some other part of a program are classified as **jump statements**. There are three such statements: `break`, `continue`, and `return`. The `return` statement will be dealt with later.

The `break` Statement

The `break` statement, which we have already encountered in the `switch` structure, can be used in any of the loop structures to allow early termination of the loop. For example, where we require to read in a maximum of 10 numbers, but with the possibility of terminating sooner if a zero is entered, we can use the code:

```
for(i = 0; i < 10; i++)
{
    System.out.print("Enter value "+i+" : ");
    no=Input.readInt();
    if (no == 0)
        break; //*** for loop terminated by this statement
    total += no;
}
System.out.println("total was "+total+" after "+i+" numbers");
```

Included in the code is the conditional statement

```
if(no == 0)
    break;
```

which, when its expression `(no == 0)` is *true*, will cause control to jump to the `System.out` statement following the `for` loop body, hence terminating the execution of the loop (see FIG-3.9).

FIG-3.9

The `break` Statement

```
for (c = 0; c < 10; c++)
{
    System.out.print("Enter value : ");
    no = Input.readInt();
    if(no == 0)
        break;
    total += no;
}
System.out.println("Total was "+total+" after
"+c+" numbers");
```

In general, the use of `break` in the manner described above is not considered good technique and should be avoided by rewriting the code.

The `continue` Statement

There is another statement which can be included in any loop structure. When executed, the `continue` statement causes the remaining statements in the loop to be skipped and transfers control back to the start of the loop.

When used with `for` loops, although the loop body is skipped, the incremental statement will be executed before returning to the beginning of the loop body.

The following code accepts 10 numbers, summing those which are positive:

```
total = 0;
for(int c = 1; c <= 10; c++)
{
    System.out.print("Enter number ");
    no = Input.readInt();
    if (no <= 0)
        continue;
    total += no;
}
System.out.println("Total of positive values is "+total);
```

Where `no <= 0` is *true* the remainder of the loop body, `total += no`, will be bypassed but the incremental statement, `c++`, will be executed before returning to the beginning of the loop. Hence the for structure will terminate after 10 iterations irrespective of how often the `continue` statement is executed (see FIG-3.10).

FIG-3.10

The `continue` Statement

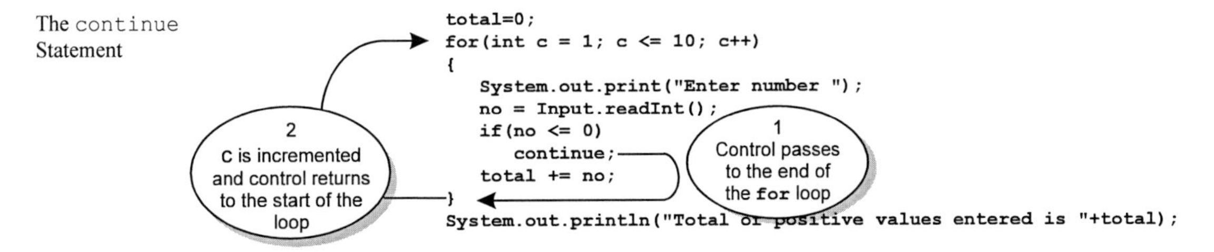

> **Activity 3.23**
>
> Write a section of Java code which makes use of the `continue` statement to read in and display up to 10 integer values. Negative values should not be displayed.

Like `break`, `continue` should be avoided since it makes a program difficult to follow and debug. For example, in the Activity above, an `if` statement could be used to create the same effect.

Nested Loops

A common requirement is to produce nested loops, that is situations where one loop control structure appears within another. For example, if we want to read in and average six exam marks, each of which needs to be in the range 0 to 100, we could describe this logic as:

```
1.  Set total to zero
2.  FOR each exam DO
3.      Get valid mark
4.      Add mark to total
5.  ENDFOR
6.  Calculate average as total/6
7.  Display average
```

This appears to have only a single loop structure beginning at statement 2 and ending at statement 5. However, if we add detail to statement 3, this gives us

```
3.  Get valid mark
    3.1 Read mark
    3.2 WHILE mark is invalid DO
    3.3     Display"Mark must be between zero and 100"
    3.4     Read mark
    3.5 ENDWHILE
```

which, if placed in the original solution, results in giving a nested loop structure, where a WHILE loop appears inside a FOR loop.

```
1.  Set total to zero
2.  FOR each exam DO
3.1     Read mark
3.2     WHILE mark is invalid DO
3.3         Display"Mark must be between zero and 100"
3.4         Read mark
3.5     ENDWHILE
4.      Add mark to total
5.  ENDFOR
6.  Calculate average as total/6
7.  Display average
```

Nested FOR Loops

Perhaps the most troublesome situation is where FOR loops are nested. The following example demonstrates the characteristics of such a structure. Consider the first two digits of a car's odometer. Initially, they are set to 00. As the car moves, the least-significant digit (units) increments while the most significant digit (tens) remains unchanged (see FIG-3.11). But when the units value reaches 9, the tens value increments and the units value is reset to zero (see FIG-3.12).

FIG-3.11 Incrementing the Inner Loop Counter **FIG-3.12** Incrementing the Outer Loop Counter

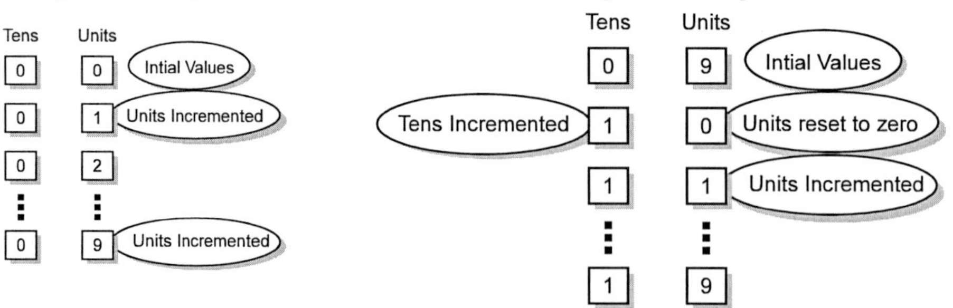

This process continues, with the tens value being incremented for every ten increments of the units.

This makes it impossible to maintain two independent counts for both the inner and outer FOR loops - leading to disastrous results.

This situation is matched exactly by the code below:

```
int     units,tens;
for(tens = 0;tens <= 9;tens++)
    for(units = 0;units <= 9;units++)
        System.out.println(tens+" "+units);
```

The tens loop is known as the outer loop, while the units loop is known as the inner loop.

A few points to note about nested for loops:

1. The inner loop increments fastest.
2. Only when the inner loop is complete does the outer loop variable increment.

Activity 3.24

What would be the output of the following code?

```
for(no1=-2;no1<=1;no1++)
    for(no2=0;no2<=6;no2+=3)
        System.out.println(no1+" "+no2);
```

Translating from Structured English

The nested iterative structures seen in the Structured English of Chapter 1 can be produced by simple translation. Where 10 students each sit six exams with a maximum possible mark of 100 for each exam, we can calculate each student's average mark using the following logic:

```
FOR each student DO
    Set total to zero
    FOR each exam DO
        Get mark
        WHILE mark is invalid DO
            Display "Mark must be in the range 0 to 100"
            Get mark
        ENDWHILE
        Add mark to total
    ENDFOR
    Calculate average as total / 6 (rounded)
    Display student number and average
ENDFOR
```

The corresponding code is

```
int student, exam,mark, total, average;

for(student = 1; student <= 10; student++)
{
    total = 0;
    for(exam = 1; exam <= 6; exam++)
    {
        System.out.print("Enter mark for exam "+exam+' ';
        mark = Input.readInt();
        while (mark < 0 || mark > 100)
        {
            System.out.println("Must be in the range 0 to 100");
            mark=Input.readInt();
        }
        total += mark;
    }
    average = total / 6.0 + 0.5;
    System.out.println("The average for student "+student
            +" was "+average);
}
```

`continue` and `break` in Nested Structures

When `continue` or `break` is used in an inner control structure, it is only that structure that is exited. For example, in the code given below:

```
for(int c = 1; c<=5; c++)
{
    System.out.println("Enter 3 numbers for student "+c);
    int total=0;
    for(int j = 1 ; j <= 3; j++)
    {
        System.out.print("Enter number "+j+" : ");
        int v = Input.readInt();
        if(v < 0)
            break;
        total+=v;
    }
    System.out.println("Total was "+total);
}
```

only the `for j` loop will be exited should the `break` statement be executed; the `for c` loop will continue as normal.

Activity 3.25

Type in and compile the following program:

```
import Input;

public class JumpOut
{
  public static void main(String args[])
  {
      for(int c = 1; c<=5; c++)
      {
          System.out.println("Enter 3 numbers for student "+c);
          int total=0;
          for(int j = 1 ; j <= 3; j++)
          {
              System.out.print("Enter number "+j+" : ");
              int v = Input.readInt();
              if(v < 0)
                  break;
              total+=v;
          }
          System.out.println("Total was "+total);
      }
  }
}
```

Run the program. Enter -1 as your fifth value (previous values being positive).

Notice that no more values are entered for student 2 when the -1 is entered (because the inner `for` loop is exited by the `break` statement) but the program then goes on to ask for the values for student 3.

Java allows the `break` (and `continue`) statement to exit both loops by making two changes to the code:

1. A label must be added at the start of the block to be exited.

2. The label name must be added to the `break` (or `continue`) statement.

LISTING-3.4 shows how to break out of both `for` loops when a negative value is entered.

LISTING-3.4

Using Labelled breaks

```
import Input;

public class JumpOut
{
    public static void main(String args[])
    {
        leave:                          //***Label***
        for(int c = 1; c<=5; c++)
        {
            System.out.println("Enter 3 numbers for student "+c);
            int total=0;
            for(int j = 1 ; j <= 3; j++)
            {
                System.out.print("Enter number "+j+" : ");
                int v = Input.readInt();
                if(v < 0)
                    break leave;        //*** break leave block***
                total+=v;
            }
            System.out.println("Total was "+total);
        }
    }
}
```

From the program you can see that a label is inserted in the line

```
leave:
```

Labels are created by creating an identifier followed by a colon. The label identifies the block that follows - in this case, the `for c` loop.

It may be necessary to insert additional braces to create the block required giving the general format:

```
label:
{
    code in block  (this includes the break statement)
}
```

Summary

■ **Iteration Structures**

```
while
        while(condition)
            action
do..while
        do
            action
        while(condition);
for
        for(statement1;condition;statement2)
            action

action :
        statement;
```

```
or
        {
            statement;
                .
            statement;
        }
```

- **The** `while` **loop body** may be iterated a minimum of zero times.
- **The** `while` **loop terminates** when *condition* is *false.*
- **On termination of the** `while` **loop**, execution jumps to the statement following the `while` structure.
- **In the** `do..while` **structure,** *condition* is evaluated after each iteration of the loop body.
- **The** `do..while` **body** may be iterated a minimum of once.
- **The** `do` **loop terminates** when *condition* is *false.*
- **On termination of the** `do` **loop**, execution jumps to the statement following the `do..while` structure.
- **In the** `for` **structure,** *condition* is evaluated before each iteration of the loop body.
- **The** `for` **loop body** may be iterated a minimum of zero times.
- **The** `for` **loop terminates** when *condition* is *false.*
- **On termination of the** `for` **loop**, execution jumps to the statement following the `for` structure.
- **The** `for` **structure,**

```
        for(statement1; condition; statement2)
            action;
```

  is exactly equivalent to

```
        statement1;
        while(condition)
        {
            action
            statement2;
        }
```

- **In the** `for` **structure,** *statement1*, *condition* and *statement2* may be omitted but the semi-colons must be retained.
- **Omitting *condition* will result in an infinite loop.**
- **In the** `for` **structure,** *condition* need not refer to a loop counter variable.
- **The comma operator** may be employed in the `for` loop structures.
- **Using** `continue` **in an iterative structure** transfers control to the end of the action defined in the loop body. However, the loop itself is not exited.
- **Using** `break` **in an iterative structure** transfers control to the first statement following the loop.

- **A variable declared within the** `for` **statement** can be accessed only within the body of that `for` loop.

- **Where loops are nested,** `break` and `continue` affect only the loop body in which they are used. That is, if they are defined in the inner loop, control will be transferred to the end of that inner loop's body (`continue`); or to the first statement following the inner loop (`break`).

- **A label can be assigned to a block of code** and a `break` or `continue` statement can be made to jump to the end of that block.

Testing Control Structures

In an ideal world we would check our programs by entering every possible value and combination of values as test data. However, this is not practical even for simple programs since the time and effort required is prohibitive. Instead, a compromise is required.

One strategy used to test a piece of code is to create test data based on the structure of that code, the aim being to pick relevant test values each of which checks differing parts of the code. This technique is called **white box** or **glass box** testing - so called, because we need to look at the internal structure of the program in order to create appropriate test values.

A minimum requirement of white box testing is that every statement in the code is executed by the test data. However, as we will see, this is a relatively poor strategy which can be improved on.

Testing Sequences

To test a sequence of statements such as

```
System.out.print("Enter a number : ");
no1 = Input.readInt();
System.out.print("Enter a number : ");
no2 = Input.readInt();
result = no1 * no2;
System.out.println(no1+" * "+no2+" = "+result);
```

we need only one set of test values (e.g. 12 and 2). This will result in all statements being executed.

Testing Selection

Simple `if` Statements

The simplest selection statement is an `if` statement without an `else` option. For example:

```
int no;

no = Input.readInt();
if(no < 0)
    System.out.println("This is a negative value");
```

Although we can ensure that all parts of this statement are executed by using any value for *no* which results in the expression `(no < 0)` evaluating to *true*, it is also important to test the structure where the expression evaluates to *false*. Why is this?

Consider the code

```
int no1,no2,ans;

no1 = Input.readInt();
no2 = Input.readInt();
if(no2 != 0)
    ans = no1 / no2;
System.out.println(ans);
```

If we test this code by entering the values 6 and 2, the result will be 3 and all the statements will have been executed.

However, if we use the values 6 and 0, *ans* will not be assigned a value and the resulting output will be unpredictable.

Obviously, we want to detect such problems while testing the code. It is therefore important that even simple `if` statements are tested with two sets of data: one which evaluates the expression as *true*; the other giving a *false* result.

`if .. else` Structures

Where an `else` is used, the need to test for both *true* and *false* situations is more obvious since this is the only way to execute all the instructions in the control structure. Hence, we might test the code

```
if(no<0)
     System.out.println("Negative");
else
     System.out.println("Positive or zero");
```

with the values *no* = -8 and *no* = 3.

Other Boolean Expressions

In Java, Boolean expressions turn up in other commands such as the conditional assignment statement:

```
discount = (total < 20)? 0.05 : 0.10;
```

Statements such as this need to be treated like `if` statements and hence should be tested with values which give both *true* and *false* results for the expression involved.

Nested `if` Statements

Since the path taken through an `if` statement is dependent on the truth of the statement's expression, where two `if` statements are nested, there are three possible paths. For example, in the code

```
if(sex == 'M')
    if(age >= 65)
        System.out.println("Retired");
    else
        System.out.println("Working");
else
     System.out.println("Female");
```

we can identify the possible truth combinations for the expressions (`sex=='M'`) and (`age>=65`) (see TABLE-3.9).

TABLE-3.9

Possible Combinations for Two Boolean Expressions

Expression	
(sex=='M')	(age>=65)
TRUE	TRUE
TRUE	FALSE
FALSE	TRUE
FALSE	FALSE

The last two combinations (*false,true* and *false,false*) execute the same section of code:

```
else
    System.out.println("Female");
```

and hence we need only three combinations of data values to test the above code.

Activity 3.26

In the code

```
if(sex=='M')
   if(age>=65)
        System.out.println("Male retired");
   else
       System.out.println("Male working");
else
    if(age>=60)
       System.out.println("Female retired");
   else
        System.out.println("Female working");
```

1. How many *true/false* combinations are possible for the expressions involved?
2. How many combinations of test data are required to test all possible paths through the code?

Complex Boolean Expressions

Where a Boolean expression is complex (i.e. contains linking AND or OR operators), as in

```
if(sex=='M' && age>=65)
     System.out.println("Male retired");
```

it is important to create test data which gives all possible combinations of *true* and *false* from the individual component of the expression. Hence, for the expression `(sex=='M' && age >= 65)`, test values resulting in each of the four possibilities shown in TABLE-3.9 are required.

Why is it important to perform all possible combinations?

Consider the situation where we had mistakenly written the above code as:

```
if(sex=='M' || age>=65)
     System.out.println("Male retired");
```

The test data *sex='M', age = 66* (*true,true*) and *sex='F',age=23* (*false,false*) would test both *true* and *false* options of the `if` statement without showing up any problems. However, by including the other combinations, for example, with the test data *sex='M',age=45* (*true,false*) and *sex='F', age=70* (*false,true*), the error in the code will be detected.

`switch` Statements

Since a `switch` statement is equivalent to a series of mutually exclusive `if` statements (assuming a `break` command ends each option), testing requires values corresponding to each of the `case` options as well as the `default` option. For example, given the code

```
switch(day)
{
    case 0:  System.out.println("Sunday");
           break;
    case 1: System.out.println("Monday");
           break;
    case 2:  System.out.println("Tuesday");
            break;
    case 3: System.out.println("Wednesday");
           break;
    case 4:  System.out.println("Thursday");
           break;
    case 5: System.out.println("Friday");
           break;
     case 6:     System.out.println("Saturday");
            break;
    default:System.out.println("Invalid value for day");
}
```

then the test values required for *day* will be 0,1,2,3,4,5,6 and some invalid value, say, -1.

As with the simple `if` statement, where we need to test both *true* and *false* options, even when no `else` section exists, so we need to include a test value for the `default` option in a `switch` statement, even when there is no explicit code for that option.

Where two or more `case` options execute the same code, each `case` value should be tested separately. Hence the section of code

```
case 'a':
case 'e':
 case 'i':
case 'o':
case 'u':    System.out.println("Vowel");
             break;
```

would require that the values 'a','e','i','o','u' are all used as part of the test data.

Testing Iteration

Infinite Loops

Iteration instructs the machine to carry out some sequence of instructions repeatedly. In order to stop this looping, the program must contain some *loop-terminating* or *loop-entry* condition. For example, in the code

```
no=Input.readInt();
while(no > 10)
    no--;
```

we have the loop-entry condition: `(no > 10)`. So iteration of the single statement, `no--`, terminates when *no* is less than or equal to 10. No matter what value we enter, iteration will eventually halt. On the other hand, the code

```
no=Input.readInt();
while(no != 10)
    no--;
```

may never exit if we give *no* a starting value of less than 10.

This situation is known as an **infinite loop**. If you are unlucky, you may have to reboot your computer to get out of this situation once your program has begun executing.

Infinite looping can occur in any of the three loop structures in Java.

We can minimise the chances of an infinite loop by checking that the loop body has an effect on the loop's exit-condition which will eventually lead to loop termination.

Testing `for` Loops

Where a `for` loop is coded for a fixed number of iterations, such as in the code

```
total = 0;
for(int c = 1; c <= 5; c++)
{
     System.out.print("Enter number : ");
    no=Input.readInt();
    total += no;
}
 System.out.println("Average is "+(total / 5));
 System.out.println("Last number entered was "+no);
```

we have no influence over the number of times the loop will be executed and hence, only the five values required to be input need be supplied as test data.

However, it is important that we check that such loops do actually execute the expected number of times since the exit condition could easily be coded wrongly. For example, writing

```
for(int c = 1; c < 5; c++)  //*** Equal sign omitted ***
```

will result in the loop iterating four, rather than five times.

Loops which iterate either one too few, or one too many times are so common that these errors are often tested for explicitly.

However, if the exit condition involves a variable as in:

```
total = 0;
System.out.println("How many values are to be entered : ");
m=Input.readInt();
 for(int c = 1; c <= m; c++)
{
    System.out.println("Enter number : ");
    no = Input.readInt();
    total += no;
}
 System.out.println("Average is "+(total / m));
 System.out.println("Last number entered was "+no);
```

we can influence the number of times the `for` loop is executed. In this situation, test data should be produced to execute the loop structure, zero, one and multiple times. For the example above, that would mean values of 0, 1 and, perhaps, 4 for the variable *m*.

Not only do such checks ensure that the loop does not execute too many or too few times, but they also highlight certain errors which only appear when a loop is executed a specific number of times. For example, the code above will result in a run-time error when $m = 0$ and hence the loop iterates zero times. This is because the expression (*total/m*) will give a division-by-zero fault.

Activity 3.27

1. Identify the error in the following code which is designed to display the average of *m* numbers and display the last number entered.

```
int total, m;
m = Input.readInt();
for(int c = 1; c <= m; c++)
{
    total = 0;
    System.out.println("Enter number : ");
    no = Input.readInt();
    total += no;
}
if(m > 0)
{
     System.out.println("Average is " +(total / m));
     System.out.println("Last number entered was "+no);
 }
```

2. In which case(s) will the above error be detected?
   a) During zero iterations test
   b) During one iteration test
   c) During multiple iteration test

Testing `while` and `do..while` Loops

The `while` loop contains an entry-condition at the beginning of the loop body and, as such, is fundamentally the same structure as a `for` loop. The two structures should therefore be tested in the same fashion with test data to perform zero, one and multiple iterations. On the other hand, the `do..while` loop has the entry-condition placed at the end of the loop structure. This means that it is normally impossible to test for zero iterations but one and multiple iterations should still be tested.

Testing Complete Programs

Most programs will consist of a combination of control structures. To test the whole program, each control structure must be identified and test data constructed.

The following design describes a program which is intended to read in 10 values in the range 1 to 100 and count how many of the values entered are divisible by exactly 3 or 4.

Program Logic:

```
Set total to zero
 FOR 10 times DO
    Read valid number
    IF number is divisible by 3 or 4 THEN
         Add 1 to total
    ENDIF
ENDFOR
 IF any values were divisible by 3 or 4 THEN
     Display total
ELSE
     Display "No values are divisible by 3 or 4"
ENDIF
```

Program Code :

LISTING-3.5

White Box Testing of a Program

```
import Input;

class Testing
{
     public static void main(String args[])
     {
          int total = 0, number;
          for(int count = 1; count <= 10; count++)
          {
               //*** Read valid number ***
               System.out.print("Enter number : ");
               number = Input.readInt();
               //***While value entered is invalid re-enter it***
               while(number < 0 || number > 100)
               {
                    System.out.print("Invalid entry. Re-enter: ");
                    number = Input.readInt();
               }
               //***If num divisible by 3 or 4 add 1 to total***
               if(number % 3 == 0 || number % 4 == 0)
                    total++;
          }
          //***Display the total numbers divisible by 3 or 4***
          if(total > 0)
               System.out.println("Number of values divisible by
                        ↳3 or 4 :" +total);
          else
               System.out.println("No values are divisible by
                        ↳3 or 4");
     }
}
```

Identifying the Test Requirements

Activity 3.28

Identify all selection and iteration control structures in LISTING-3.5.

We have two iterative and two selection structures in LISTING-3.5 to be tested.

Of these, the `for` structure is fixed to 10 iterations, hence zero and one iteration tests are not possible.

The `while` structure contains multiple conditions and therefore, as well as being tested for zero, one, and multiple iterations, should also be tested for all possible combinations of *true* and *false* within the Boolean expression itself. Note that the combination *true, true* is not possible since *number* cannot be both less than zero and greater than 100 at the same time.

There are also two selection structures, both `if`'s.

The first of these also has a complex Boolean expression and this can be tested for all four possibilities.

The second `if` statement is a simple one and needs only *true* and *false* tests.

These test requirements are summarised in TABLE-3.10.

TABLE-3.10

White Box Test Requirements

Structure to be tested	Purpose of test
`for(int count = 1;count<=10;count++)`	Test multiple iterations
`while(number<0||number>100)`	Zero iterations One iteration Multiple iterations true, false false, true false, false
`if(number%3==0||number%4==0)`	false, false false, true true, false true, true
`if(total>0)`	true false

Choosing the Test Data

One data value may test several parts of the code. For example, if we assign the value 21 to *number* then the `while` loop

```
while(number<0||number>100)
{
    System.out.println(("Invalid entry. Re-enter : ";
    Input.readInt(number;
}
```

will be iterated zero times. Not only does this value perform the zero iterations test, but, since the Boolean expressions

```
        number<0
and
        number>100
```

are both *false* when *number* is 21, this also tests the *false, false* combination for the expression `(number<0||number>100)`.

Once the `while` loop has been passed, the `if` statement

```
if(number%3==0||number%4==0)
    total++;
```

will be executed. With *number* equal to 21, the first condition, `number % 3 == 0` is *true*, while the second is *false*. Hence another of our test requirements is performed. Since all of this code is within the `for` loop which is to be executed 10 times, other values must be chosen for *number* during subsequent iterations.

Activity 3.29

Write down a value for *number* which:

a) gives a *true/false* result for `while(number<0||number>100)`
b) gives a *false/false* result for `if(number%3==0||number%4==0)`

We need to continue this process of choosing values until all the required tests will be performed by the data. Each test value, the tests they are designed to perform and the expected results should then be listed in test documentation (see TABLE-3.11).

TABLE-3.11

White Box Test Data

Run	Test Data	Reason for Test	Expected Result	Actual Result
1	number =			
	21	while iterated zero times		
		while false,false		
		if(number%3... true,false	total = 1	
	-6, 5	while iterated once	-6 rejected with error	
		while true,false	message	
		if(number%3... false,false	total unchanged	
	101,-3,8	while iterated more than once	101 and -3 rejected	
		while false,true		
		if(number%3... false,true	total= 2	
	12	if(number%3... true,true	total= 3	
	100		total= 4	
	0		total unchanged	
	1		total unchanged	
	13		total unchanged	
	31		total unchanged	
	17		total unchanged	
		for loop iterated 10 times		
		if(total>0) true	Displays	
			Number of values divisible	
			by 3 or 4 : 4	
2	number =			
	1			
	2			
	5			
	7			
	10			
	11			
	13			
	14			
	17			
	19	if(total>0) false	Displays	
			No values are divisible	
			by 3 or 4.	

There are a few points to note from TABLE-3.11 :

The RUN column refers to the program execution run number. This program will have to be run twice to test both options of the final `if` statement:

```
if(total > 0)
    System.out.println("Number of values divisible by 3 or 4 :"
                                                    ↳+total);
else
     System.out.println("No values are divisible by 3 or 4");
```

The TEST DATA column gives the values to be used when running the program. In this case, only one variable, *number*, needs to be supplied with a value. Where several variables are to be given values, the name of the variable to which a test value is to be assigned must be clearly stated in this column.

Where a single variable is given more than one value on a single line (e.g. 101,-3,8), all but the last of these represent values which will be rejected by the input validation code.

The REASON FOR TEST column states the control structure and condition being tested by that specific test value.

Where test data exercises a program condition already tested by an earlier piece of data, it need not be restated as a reason for test.

The EXPECTED RESULTS column states the expected reaction of the program to the data. This may specify the value to be taken by other variables or the output to be produced.

The ACTUAL RESULTS column is completed as the program is run. Hopefully, we may simply add an "as expected" message in this column with a reference to any printout produced during the test. But if the program should produce unexpected results, then this column should contain the following information:

- the actual results obtained.
- a reference to other documentation detailing the error that caused these unexpected results and the changes made to the program in attempting to correct that error.

If errors are detected during any test run, then all earlier test runs should be redone after corrections have been made. After all, the corrections may have introduced new errors. Where corrections have introduced new control structures or Boolean expressions, additional test data will have to be added.

Activity 3.30

Type in the program in LISTING-3.5 and run it using the test data given in TABLE-3.11.

Summary

- **White box testing** is designed to test the control structures in a program.
- **All sections of code** should be executed at least once.
- **All simple conditions** should be tested for both *true* and *false* outcomes.
- **All complex Boolean expressions** should be tested for every possible *true* and *false* combination of the component expressions.
- **All `if` statements** should be tested for both *true* and *false* outcomes.
- **Conditional assignment** and other assignments containing Boolean expressions should be tested for both *true* and *false* situations.
- **All `switch` statements** should be tested for every specified case option and the `default` option.
- **Iterative structures** should be checked for possible infinite looping before testing begins.
- **All `for` statements** should, where possible, be tested for zero, one and multiple iterations.
- **All `while`** loops should be tested for zero, one and multiple iterations.
- **All `do .. while` loops** should be tested for one and multiple iterations.

- **The test requirements for the code under test** should be identified and test data created to meet these tests.
- **A single test data value** may check several code situations.
- **The results of test runs** should be documented.
- **Where errors are discovered and corrected**, the changes made to the program code should be documented and all tests redone.

Variable Scope

A **block** is a set of statements enclosed in braces.

A variable is first allocated space in the computer's memory at the moment its definition statement is encountered during program execution. This variable continues to exist until the block in which it was defined is exited, at which point, the memory space is deallocated (the variable is **destroyed**).

The time during which a variable exists is known as the **scope** of the variable and the variable is said to be **local** to that block. Hence, in the code shown in LISTING-3.6 the variable *no2* exists only between the lines indicated.

LISTING-3.6

Variable Scope

```
import Input;
public class Scope
{
  public static void main(String args[]))
  {
      int no1;

      System.out.println(( "Enter a value : ";
      no1 = Input.readInt();
      if (no1 > 0 )
      {
          int no2;            <- Variable is created here
          no2 = no1*3;
          System.out.println("no2 is "+no2);
      }                       <- Variable is destroyed here
      System.out.println("no1 is "+no1);
  }
}
```

Activity 3.30

Enter the above program and run it.

Next, add a final line

```
System.out.println("no2 is "+no2);
```

to the code and attempt to recompile the program.

As you can see from your results, attempting to reference a variable outside its block results in a compilation error.

A variable can be recreated if it is defined in a block of code which is re-entered. This can occur in an iterative structure. For example, in LISTING-3.7 the variable *no2* is recreated on each iteration of the `for` loop.

LISTING-3.7

Recreated Variables

```
import Input;


public class Scope2
{
  public static void main(String args[])
  {
      int no1;
```

Continued on next page

LISTING-3.7
(continued)

Recreated Variables

```
    for (int i=0;i<10;i++)
    {
        System.out.println(( "Enter a value ";
        no1 = Input.readInt();
        if (no1 > 0 )
        {
            int no2;
            no2 = no1*3;
            System.out.println(("no2 is "+no2);
        }
    }
    System.out.println(("no1 is "+no1);
}
```

Summary

- **Local variables** have a lifetime extending from the point at which they are defined to the end of the block in which they are defined.

- **A variable may be reincarnated** if the block in which it is defined is re-entered.

- **The scope** of a variable defines the area of code in which it may, theoretically, be accessed. This is from definition point to the end of the definition block.

Solutions

Activity 3.1

1. Valid.
2. Invalid. A single equals sign is used for assignment. To test for equality the expression should be
   `let1 == let2`
3. Valid. Although we are comparing a `char` variable with an `int`, Java will automatically both to `int` values before testing the expression.
4. Invalid. Java cannot convert between `char` and `String` types.
5. Valid. Again, automatic conversion will deal with the two types.

Activity 3.2

The output should be *Third is true*.

Activity 3.3

```
1.
import Input;
public class Act3_3_1
{
    public static void main(String args[])
    {
        int no;

        System.out.print("Enter an integer
            ↳value : ");
        no = Input.readInt();
        if(no <= 0)
            System.out.println("Negative value");
    }
}

2.
import Input;
public class Act3_3_2
{
    public static void main(String args[])
    {
        float radius;

        System.out.print("Enter radius : ");
        radius = Input.readFloat();
        if(radius >= 0)
            System.out.println("Area of circle
                ↳ is " + 3.1416*radius*radius);
    }
}

3.
import Input;
public class Act3_3_3
{
    public static void main(String args[])
    {
        int no1, no2;
        System.out.print("Enter first number: ");
        no1 = Input.readInt();
        System.out.print("Enter second number: ");
        no2 = Input.readInt();
        if(no1 < no2)
            System.out.println("Smaller number is "
                ↳+ no1);
        if(no2 < no1)
            System.out.println("Smaller number
                ↳is " + no2);
    }
}

4.
import Input;
public class Act3_3_4
{
    public static void main(String args[])
    {
        char ch;
        System.out.print("Enter character: ");
        ch = Input.readChar();
        if(ch == 'F')
            System.out.println("Female");
    }
}
```

Activity 3.4

No solution required.

Activity 3.5

```
1.  if(weight > 16)
2.  if(code != 17850)
3.  if(mark >= 75 && mark 85)
4.  if(option == C && key == masterkey)
5.  if((command == D || command == A)
        ↳&& quantity > 100)
```

Activity 3.6

1. Valid. true
2. Invalid. Uses assignment operator.
3. Valid true

Activity 3.7

```
1.
import Input;
public class Act3_7_1
{
    public static void main(String args[])
    {
        int month;

        System.out.print("Enter a number (1-12) : ");
        month = Input.readInt();
        if(month < 1 || month > 12)
            System.out.println("Invalid month");
    }
}

2.
import Input;
public class Act3_7_2
{
    public static void main(String args[])
    {
        char letter;

        System.out.print("Enter an alphabetic
            ↳character: ");
        letter = Input.readChar();
        if(letter=='a'||letter=='e'||letter=='i'
            ↳||letter=='0'||letter=='u')
            System.out.println("vowel");
    }
}
```

Activity 3.8

```
import Input;
public class Act3_8
{
    public static void main(String args[])
    {
        double rno1, rno2;

        System.out.print("Enter first number: ");
        rno1 = Input.readFloat();
        System.out.print("Enter second number: ");
        rno2 = Input.readFloat();
        if(rno2 != 0)
        {
            double result = rno1/rno2;
            System.out.println(rno1+"/"+rno2+
                ↳"="+result);
        }
    }
}
```

Depending on the numbers you entered, you may have a display showing values to many decimal places. We'll see how to deal with this in a later chapter.

Activity 3.9

```
1.
import Input;
public class Act3_9_1
{
    public static void main(String args[])
    {
        int no1, no2;

        System.out.print("Enter first number: ");
        no1 = Input.readInt();
        System.out.print("Enter second number: ");
        no2 = Input.readInt();
        if(no1 == no2)
            System.out.println("The numbers are
                ↳equal");
        else
            System.out.println("The numbers are
                ↳different");
    }
}

2.
import Input;
public class Act3_9_2
{
    public static void main(String args[])
    {
        char letter;

        System.out.print("Enter an alphabetic
            ↳character: ");
        letter = Input.readChar();
        if(letter=='a'||letter=='e'||letter=='i'
            ↳||letter=='O'||letter=='u')
            System.out.println("Vowel");
        else
            System.out.println("Consonant");
    }
}

3.
import Input;

public class Act3_9_3
{
    public static void main(String args[])
    {
        int no;

        System.out.print("Enter integer value: ");
        no = Input.readInt();
        if(no%2 != 0)
            System.out.println("Odd");
        else
            System.out.println("Even");
    }
}
```

Activity 3.10

```
import Input;
public class Act3_10
{
    public static void main(String args[])
    {
        double hoursover, paymentdue;
        int grade;

        System.out.print("Enter hours of
            ↳overtime: ");
        hoursover = Input.readFloat();
        System.out.print("Enter employees grade
            ↳(1 or 2) : ");
        grade = Input.readInt();
        if(hoursover <= 0)
            System.out.println("No overtime
                ↳payment due");
        else
        {
            if(grade==1)
                paymentdue = 60 * hoursover;
            else
                paymentdue = 40 * hoursover;
            System.out.println("Payment due is
                ↳$"+paymentdue);
        }
    }
}
```

Activity 3.11

```
import Input;

public class Act3_11
{
    public static void main(String args[])
    {
        char sex;
        int age;

        System.out.print("Enter sex : ");
        sex = Input.readChar();
        System.out.print("Enter age : ");
        age = Input.readInt();
        if(sex == 'M')
            if(age >= 65)
                System.out.println("Retired male");
            else
                System.out.println("Working male");
        else
            if(age >= 60)
                System.out.println("Retired female");
            else
                System.out.println("Working female");
    }
}
```

Activity 3.12

```
import Input;
public class Act3_12
{
    public static void main(String args[])
    {
        int day;

        System.out.print("Enter day of week
            ↳(0 - 6) : ");
        day = Input.readInt();
        if(day == 0)
            System.out.println("Sunday");
        else if(day == 1)
            System.out.println("Monday");
        else if(day == 2)
            System.out.println("Tuesday");
        else if(day == 3)
            System.out.println("Wednesday");
        else if(day == 4)
            System.out.println("Thursday");
        else if(day == 5)
            System.out.println("Friday");
        else if(day == 6)
            System.out.println("Saturday");
        else
            System.out.println("Invalid day
                ↳entered");
    }
}
```

Activity 3.13

```
c=(no < 0)?c-1:c+1;
```

Activity 3.14

Output would be ***returned***

Activity 3.15

No solution required.

Activity 3.16

```
import Input;
public class TestSwitch1
{
    public static void main(String args[])
    {
        double      rno1, rno2, answer=0;
        char        option;
        // *** Get expression to be evaluated
        System.out.print("Enter first number: ");
        rno1 =  Input.readFloat();
        System.out.print("Enter second number: ");
        rno2 = Input.readFloat();
        System.out.print("Enter option (+-/*): ");
        option = Input.readChar();
        // *** Execute appropriate choice ***
        boolean option_ok = true;
        switch(option)
        {
            case '+' :  answer = rno1 + rno2;
                        break;
            case '-' :  answer = rno1 -rno2;
                        break;
            case '/' :  answer = rno1 / rno2;
                        break;
            case 'x' :
            case '*' :  answer = rno1 * rno2;
                        break;
            default :   System.out.println(
                            ↳"Unknown operator");
                        option_ok = false;
        }
        // *** If a valid operator used,
                ↳display result ***
        if (option_ok)
            System.out.println(""+rno1+option+
                ↳rno2+'='+answer);
    }
}
```

Activity 3.17

```
        System.out.print("Enter first number: ");
        no1 = Input.readInt();
        System.out.print("Enter second number: ");
        no2 = Input.readInt();
        while(no1 != no2)
        {
            no1 = no2;
            System.out.print("Enter number: ");
            no2 = Input.readInt();
        }
```

Activity 3.18

```
1.
import Input;
public class Act3_18_1
{
    public static void main(String args[])
    {
        int no, sum=0;

        System.out.print("Enter number:");
        no = Input.readInt();
        while (no != 0)
        {
            int leastsign = no %1000;
            sum += leastsign;
            no = no / 1000;
        }
        if(sum % 37 == 0)
            System.out.println("Value divisible
                ↳by 37");
        else
            System.out.println("Value not
                ↳divisible by 37");

    }
}

2.
import Input;
public class Act3_18_2
{
    public static void main(String args[])
    {
        int n,r;
        double factorialn=1, factorialr=1,
                ↳factorialn_r=1;
        long ncr;
        System.out.print("Enter value of n: ");
        n = Input.readInt();
        System.out.print("Enter value of r: ");
        r = Input.readInt();
        while (r >= n)
        {
            System.out.println("r must be less
                ↳than n");
            System.out.print("Enter value of n: ");
            n = Input.readInt();
            System.out.print("Enter value of r: ");
            r = Input.readInt();
        }
        for(int c = 2; c<=n; c++)
            factorialn *= c;
        for(int c = 2; c<=r; c++)
            factorialr *= c;
        for(int c = 2; c<=n-r; c++)
            factorialn_r *= c;
        ncr = (long)(factorialn/(factorialn_r *
                ↳factorialr));
        System.out.println("There are " + ncr +
                ↳" possibilities");
    }
}
```

Activity 3.19

```
import Input;

public class Act3_19
{
    public static void main(String args[])
    {
        double N, newx, oldx;

        System.out.print("Enter value: ");
        N = Input.readFloat();
        newx = N/3.0;
        do
        {
            oldx = newx;
            newx = (N/(oldx*oldx)+2*oldx)/3.0;
        }
        while(!(N-newx*newx*newx < 0.000005
            ↳&& newx*newx*newx - N < 0.000005));
        System.out.println("Cube root of "+N+
            ↳" is "+newx);
    }
}
```

We'll discover in a later chapter how to display values to a specified number of decimal places.

Activity 3.20

Output would be

```
0
1
2
3
4
```

Activity 3.21

```
1.
import Input;

public class Act3_21_1
{
    public static void main(String args[])
    {
        for(int c = 1; c <= 20; c++)
            if(c%4 != 0 && c%5 != 0)
                System.out.println(c);
    }
}

2.
import Input;
public class Act3_21_2
{
    public static void main(String args[])
    {
        int     N;
        float   score, highest_score,
                ↳lowest_score, total, average;
```

```
            System.out.print("Number of judges: ");
            N = Input.readInt();
            System.out.print("Enter first score: ");
            score = Input.readFloat();
            highest_score = score;
            lowest_score = score;
            total = score;
            for(int c = 2; c<= N; c++)
            {
                System.out.print("Next score: ");
                score = Input.readFloat();
                total += score;
                if(score < lowest_score)
                    lowest_score=score;
                else
                    if (score > highest_score)
                        highest_score = score;
            }
            total -= (highest_score + lowest_score);
            average = total / (N-2);
            System.out.println("Skater's score was "
                ↳+average);
        }
}
```

Activity 3.22

```
import Input;

public class Act3_22
{
    public static void main(String args[])
    {
        int c, no, total=0;
        float average;
        for(c = 0 ; total <= 100; c++)
        {
            System.out.print("Enter a number: ");
            no = Input.readInt();
            total += no;
        }
        average = total / (float)c;
        System.out.println("The average of the "
            ↳+c+" numbers entered is "+average);
    }
}
```

Activity 3.23

```
import Input;
public class Act3_23
{
    public static void main(String args[])
    {
        int no;

        for(int c = 1 ; c <= 10; c++)
        {
            System.out.print("Enter a number: ");
            no = Input.readInt();
            if(no < 0)
                continue;
            System.out.println(no);
        }
    }
}
```

Activity 3.24

The output would be

```
-2  0
-2  3
-2  6
-1  0
-1  3
-1  6
 0  0
 0  3
 0  6
 1  0
 1  3
 1  6
```

Activity 3.25

No solution required.

Activity 3.26

1.
There are three conditions being tested:

```
sex = 'M'
age >= 65
age >= 60
```

If the conditions were independent of each other then the possible combinations are

	sex='M'	age>=65	age>=60
	F	F	F
	F	F	T
*	F	T	F
	F	T	T
	T	F	F
	T	F	T
*	T	T	F
	T	T	T

However, the two possibilities marked with an asterisk cannot occur since *age>=65* cannot be *true* without *age>=60* also being *true*. Therefore, there are six possible combinations for the conditions specified.

2.
There are four possible paths through the code. These are reached by the combinations:

sex='M' (true)	AND	age>=65 (true)
sex='M' (true)	AND	age>=65 (false)
sex='M' (false)	AND	age>=60 (true)
sex='M' (false)	AND	age>=60 (false)

Activity 3.27

1.

The variable *total* is reset to zero on each iteration of the `for` loop. This variable should be set to zero before the loop is started.

2.

a) Not detected.
b) Not detected.
c) Detected.

Activity 3.28

Selection Structures

```
if(number % 3 == 0 || number % 4 == 0)
if(total > 0)
```

Iterative Structures

```
for(int count = 1; count <= 10; count++)
while(number < 0 || number > 100)
```

Activity 3.29

```
-7  (any negative number)
 5  (any number not divisible by 3 or 4)
```

Activity 3.30

No solution required.

Chapter 4
Functions

This chapter covers the following topics:

Black Box Testing

Calling Functions

Function Definition

Function Overloading

How Calls to a Function Operate

Mini-Specs

Parameters

Pre-conditions

Returning Values from Functions

Test Drivers

Functions

What are Functions?

Functions in Mathematics

Anyone with a basic knowledge of mathematics will have come across functions. For example, a typical statement in trigonometry might be:

x = cos(75)

This equation uses the function *cos* which calculates the cosine of an angle. The angle, in this case 75°, is known as the **argument** of the function. Mathematical functions act on the argument to produce a **result**. In the example above, the function *cos* produces the cosine of 75° which happens to be 0.25882.

We may interpret the equation

x = cos(75)

as short-hand for

x is equal to the cosine of 75°.

Functions in Java

In this text Java functions are identified by including parentheses after the function name. This makes it easy to differentiate variable names from function names.

In Java, a function is a separate piece of code which performs some specific action. Every function has an identifying name and zero or more arguments. Not all functions need to return a result.

In fact, we've already written a function, since *main()* is one. From our definition for *main()* we can see the basic structure of a function is:

```
type of value returned    function name(parameters)
{
    code
}
```

It is good practice to create a separate routine for each of the main tasks to be performed by a program. By creating a series of separate functions we construct a set of building blocks which can then be linked to produce the complete software system.

This modular approach has many benefits. It allows each function to be created and tested in isolation before being linked to others to form the final program. This tends to lead to shorter development time and more robust software.

The following example of a user-defined function displays a line of asterisks:

```
public static void line()
{
    System.out.println("****************************");
}
```

This is known as the **function definition**. Notice that we need to start all functions with the keywords `public static`. The reason for this will become clear later.

Calling a Function

With the function coded, we are now free to call that function. This is achieved in the same manner as calling standard functions. Hence our call to *line()* would be

```
line();
```

A Complete Program

LISTING-4.1 below uses *line()* to create the following output:

```
******************************
          Hello world
******************************
```

LISTING-4.1

Using Functions

```
public class UsingFunctions1
{
  public static void main(String args[])
  {
      line();
      System.out.println("     Hello world");
      line();
  }


  public static void line()
  {
      System.out.println("**********************");
  }
}
```

Activity 4.1

Enter and run the program in LISTING-4.1.

How the Program Executes

Every program instruction is stored in the computer's memory. Although these instructions are in bytecode, they are equivalent to the original Java statements. Hence, we may consider, for the purpose of this explanation, that the program is held as a sequence of Java instructions.

We can identify two main sections of code in LISTING-4.1 : the code for *main()* and that for *line()* (see FIG-4.1).

FIG-4.1

Code Held in Memory

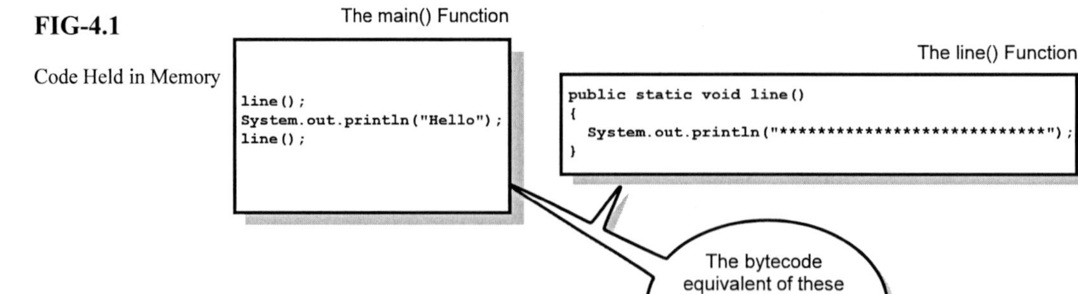

As always, execution begins in *main()*. However, the first statement in *main()* is a call to *line()* the code of which is then executed. When this is complete, the control returns to the statement in *main()* following the original function call and continues execution of *main()*.

The stages involved in the execution of LISTING-4.1 are shown in FIG-4.2.

FIG-4.2

Executing a Function

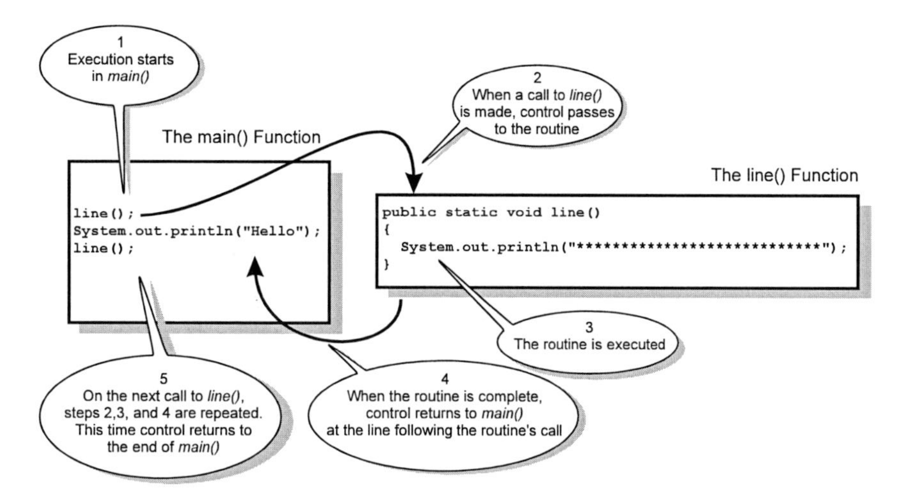

Activity 4.2

Write a new class called *TestingBox*. The class is to contain a function, *box()*, which draws a 5 by 5 square of asterisks. Your *main()* function should call the *box()* function only once.

Passing Parameters

A Single Parameter

The *line()* function is not very useful as it stands since the length of the line is predetermined. A better routine would allow us to pass the required length as a parameter. Assuming a parameter, *size*, the new version of *line()* has the logic

```
FOR length TIMES DO
    Display a single asterisk (keeping cursor on the same line)
ENDFOR
Move cursor to start of next line
```

which is coded as:

```
public static void line(int size)
{
    //*** Output a single asterisk the required number
    //*** of times
    for(int c = 1;c <= size;c++)
        System.out.print('*');
    //*** Move to a new line ***
    System.out.println();
}
```

The new version of *line()* uses a `for` loop to display a single '*' *size* times. This requires the routine to declare a variable (*c*) to be used as the loop counter. Since *c* is declared inside *line()* it is known as a **local variable** and is allocated space in the computer's memory only while *line()* is executing. This is also true for *size*, which, although a parameter to the routine, is also created as a local variable within *line()*.

When our new version of *line()* is called, a value must be supplied in the parentheses. For example, *main()* would now be written as:

```
public static void main(String args[])
{
    line(20);        //20 is the value to be assigned to size
    System.out.println("    Hello world");
    line(20);
}
```

This argument supplied is also known as the **actual parameter** of the function. When the function is called, the value of the actual parameter is copied into the formal parameter variable before execution of the function begins. In the example above, this means that the value 20 is copied to *size* (see FIG-4.3).

FIG-4.3

Passing Parameters

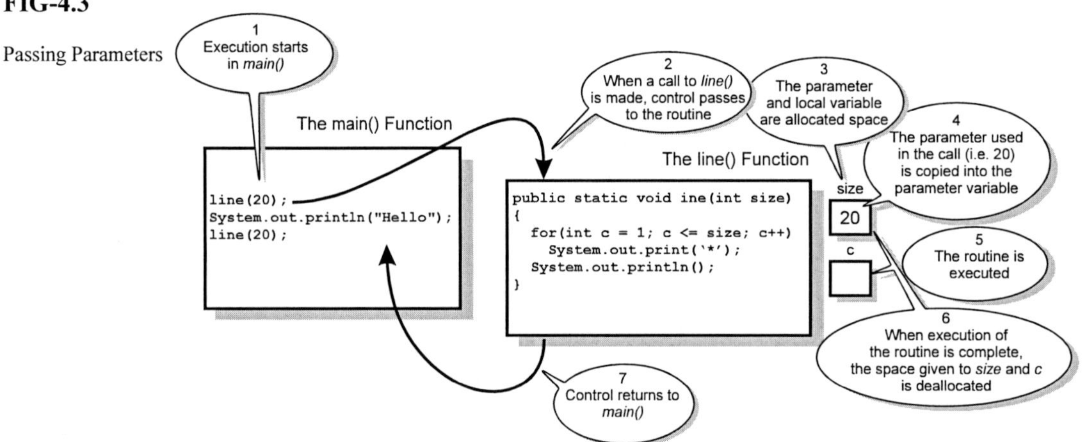

The actual parameter may be a variable or expression as well as a constant. For example:

```
int no = 12;
line(no);          // *** Variable parameter ***
line(no*2);        // *** Expression parameter ***
```

> **Activity 4.3**
>
> Modify your *box()* function to allow the height (but not the width) of the rectangle to be defined as a parameter. Name the parameter *h*.

Multiple Parameters

The function *line()* would be even more flexible if we could specify which character is to be used to create the line. This is achieved by making the character to be used in constructing the line another parameter of the function:

```
public static void line(int size, char shape)
{
```

```
        for(int c = 1; c <= size; c++)
            System.out.print(shape);
        System.out.println();
    }
```

A typical call to this new version might be:

```
line(30,'=');
```

When calling a function, it is your responsibility as the programmer to ensure that the actual parameters (30 and '=' in the call to *line()* above) are given in the correct order - integer followed by character. Failure to do so can lead to some unexpected results.

Checking a Parameter is Valid

Activity 4.4

Write a function, *month()*, which takes as a parameter an integer value, *m*, representing the month of the year and displays the corresponding month's name. For example, if *m* = 3, the word *March* should be displayed.

The parameters passed to some routines must be within a limited range. For example, in *month()* above it is important to make sure that the parameter's value lies in the range 1 to 12 - anything outside that range would be unacceptable since it would not be possible to display the corresponding month's name.

Where the value of a parameter must fall within a range, this is known as a **pre-condition** of the routine. So, in the case of function *month()*, our pre-condition is:

```
m must lie in the range 1 to 12
```

Pre-conditions are normally written as Boolean expressions, hence, the restriction on *m* would be given as:

```
1 <= m <= 12
```

We can then add this check to the function's code. Normally, pre-conditions should be checked at the start of a routine's code. When a pre-condition is not met, one option is to terminate the execution of the function. This can be done with the `return` statement.

So, the *month()* function could begin with the code

```
public static void month(int m)
{
    //*** IF pre-condition not met, exit routine ***
    if(m < 1 || m > 12 )
        return;
```

Activity 4.5

1. Make the change shown above to your copy of *month()* and test it by calling *month()* with a parameter value of 13.

2. Assuming the pre-condition for *box()* is
   `pre-condition :   3 <= h <= 22`
   modify your code for the *box()* function to reflect this pre-condition.

Returning Values from a Function

Returning a Single Value

None of the routines we have created so far return a result but simply display characters on the screen. However, most functions do return a value. For example, a routine which determines the square of a number would be coded as:

```
public static double square(double no)
{
    return no*no;
}
```

The new function has two main differences from our previous routines:

1. The term `void` (indicating that no value is returned) has been replaced by `double` (the type of value to be returned).

2. The keyword `return` is followed by the value to be returned by the function.

The term `return` can be used at several places in the code if there are alternative values to be returned. For example, the routine below returns the smaller of two numbers:

```
public static int smaller(int no1, int no2)
{
    if (no1 < no2)
        return no1;
    else
        return no2;
}
```

> **Activity 4.6**
>
> Write a function called *sum()* which takes an integer value, *v*, and returns the sum of all the numbers between 1 and *v*.
>
> The value returned should be of type `long`.

Calling the Function

It is possible to call a function that returns a value without referencing that value as in the statement

```
smaller(n1,n2);
```

Called in this way, the returned value is lost. Although this can be what is wanted on some occasions, it is more likely that we will wish the returned value to be displayed, assigned to a variable, or used in some expression. Typical calls to *smaller()* are:

```
System.out.println(smaller(n1,n2));      // *** Result displayed
charges = smaller(n1,n2)*5;     // *** Result used in expression
if (smaller(n1,n2) < 0)         // *** Result used in Boolean exp
    System.out.println("Smaller value is negative");
```

A simple example of using *smaller()* is given in LISTING-4.2 :

LISTING-4.2

Returning a Value from a Function

```
import Input;

public class Returns
{
  public static void main(String args[])
  {

      //*** Read in numbers ***
      System.out.print("Enter number : ");
      int no1 = Input.readInt();
      System.out.print("Enter number : ");
      int no2 = Input.readInt();

      //*** Display answer by calling smaller() ***
      System.out.println("Smaller value is "+smaller(no1,no2));
  }


  public static int smaller(int no1, int no2)
  {
      if(no1 < no2)
          return no1;
      else
          return no2;
  }
}
```

Activity 4.7

Write a complete class to test your *sum()* function developed in Activity 4.6

Function Results as Parameters to Other Routines

As we saw in the examples given earlier, the value returned by a function can be used in various places such as in an output statement, an arithmetic expression or within an `if` statement.

A more unusual use for the returned value is as the parameter in another function call.

For example, the line

```
line(smaller(n1,n2),'*');       // *** Result used as parameter in
                                //     other function
```

uses the smaller of *n1* and *n2* as the *size* parameter for *line()*.

Activity 4.8

Using the technique shown above, write down a single instruction involving calls to *smaller()* which displays the smallest of four values, *n1, n2, n3* and *n4*.

Activity 4.9

Write a function, *next()*, which accepts a single character argument and returns the succeeding character (HINT: Remember the + sign performs arithmetic on character values).

Most function parameters are known as **pass by value** parameters. This means that the values of the actual parameters are copied into the formal parameters (space for which is created when the function is called - as previously described in FIG-4.3).

Return Values and Pre-conditions

If a function is designed to return a value and it also has a pre-condition, we are presented with a problem of what value to return if the pre-condition isn't met.

A widely-used convention in Java when using multiple-word identifiers is to lowercase the first word and capitalise subsequent ones.

For example, a function, *areaOfCircle(double r)*, which calculates the area of a circle of radius *r* should have a pre-condition of `r >= 0`. That means its code should begin with

```
public static double areaOfCircle(double r)
{
    if(r < 0)
        return;
```

but this won't be accepted by the compiler since, according to its signature the routine must return a double value.

At this point in our knowledge of Java, we have only two choices: terminate the program or return some bogus value.

We can terminate the program using `System.exit(1)`. Hence, we can write

```
public static double areaOfCircle(double r)
{
    if(r < 0)
        System.exit(1);
    else
        return (3.1416*r*r);
}
```

Alternatively, we can return some value just to keep the compiler happy:

```
public static double areaOfCircle(double r)
{
    if(r < 0)
        return -1;
    else
        return (3.1416*r*r);
}
```

Of course, this second approach only works when it is possible to return a value that could not occur as a correct result when the parameter is valid.

If we use the first method, other programmers who make use of the *areaOfCircle()* function will find their programs terminating unexpectedly if an invalid radius is used. Of course, they should be checking the parameter's value before they call the routine in any case. For example:

```
public static void main(String args[])
{

    System.out.print("Enter radius : ");
    double r = Input.readFloat();
    if(r >= 0 )
    {
        double area = areaOfCircle(r);
        System.out.print("Circle with radius "+r+
            ↳" has an area of "+area);
    }
    else
        System.out.println("Invalid radius");
}
```

By returning a value even when an invalid parameter is used, *main()* could be written as:

```
public static void main(String args[])
{
    System.out.print("Enter radius : ");
    double r = Input.readFloat();
    double area = areaOfCircle(r);
    if(area != -1)
        System.out.print("Circle with radius "+r+
            ↳" has an area of "+area);

}
```

Designing Routines

We saw in Chapter 1 that it is necessary to design an algorithm for any program that we intend to produce. One method of doing this is to use Structured English and stepwise refinement. Often we will create routines for the main task stated in the first stages of stepwise refinement. For example, if a Structured English solution to a problem contained the line

```
Convert month number to month name
```

then we might ultimately execute that task by designing and writing the *month()* function we produced in Activity 4.4.

When we have identified the need for a routine its design takes on a fairly formal format giving the following details:

- Routine's name.

- Parameters.
  This should list each IN, OUT and IN/OUT parameter giving the parameter name and type.

- Pre-condition.
  This states as a Boolean expression what conditions must be true before the routine can execute successfully.

- Post-condition.
  This states what must be true when the routine has finished execution. Where possible this should also be written as a Boolean expression, but often this is not easily achieved.

- Description of the purpose of the routine.
  The description should contain sufficient detail to allow a programmer to create the final routine. Any error conditions and how they should be dealt with must also be stated here.

- Outline Logic.
  A Structured English overview of how the routine operates.

- Detailed Logic.
  An in-depth description of the program's logic usually written in a program description language or the target language.

These details are known as a **mini-specification** or **mini-spec** for the routine.

Below is a mini-spec for the *month()* function.

Name :	month
Parameters	
In :	m : integer
Out :	None
In/Out :	None
Pre-condition :	1 <= *m* <= 12
Post-condition:	The text representation of month *m* is displayed
Description :	The text representation of month *m* is displayed. For example, if *m* = 3 the text *March* should be displayed.
Outline Logic :	Display the name of the *m*th month of the year
Detailed Logic	

```
switch(m)
{
    case 1: System.out.println("January");
            break;
    case 2: System.out.println("February");
            break;
    case 3: System.out.println("March");
            break;
    case 4: System.out.println("April");
            break;
    case 5: System.out.println("May");
            break;
    case 6: System.out.println("June");
            break;
    case 7: System.out.println("July");
            break;
    case 8: System.out.println("August");
            break;
    case 9: System.out.println("September");
            break;
    case 10:System.out.println("October");
            break;
    case 11:System.out.println("November");
            break;
    case 12:System.out.println("December");
            break;
}
```

There are a few things to notice in the mini-spec:

The Post-condition and the Description seem similar. This is often true, but the Description will give details of what should happen on the way to achieving the final results whereas the Post-condition only gives the final results. For example, a routine which is to read in an exam mark in the range 0 to 100 would have the Post-condition:

Exam mark in the range 0 to 100 read in

whereas the Description would state

Accepts an exam mark in the range 0 to 100. If an invalid mark is entered, an error message is displayed and the user re-enters the data.

Also the Description may give examples to clarify what is required.

The Outline Logic tries to give an overview of how the routine operates. Don't put too much detail in this section.

When a routine has no pre-condition, that is when there is no restriction on the value of any parameter or other data item, use the entry

Pre-condition: *true*

If a routine returns a value, this should be treated as an Out parameter and given a name and type just as an In parameter would. For example, the smaller function would have the following mini-spec:

Name	:	smaller
Parameters		
In	:	n1, n2 : integer
Out	:	sm : integer
In/Out	:	None
Pre-condition	:	true
Post-condition	:	*sm* is set to the smaller of *n1* and *n2*
Description	:	Sets *sm* to the smaller of *n1* and *n2*. If *n1* and *n2* have the same value then *sm* is set to that value.

Outline Logic	:	IF n1 < n2 THEN
		    sm = n1
		ELSE
		    sm = n2
		ENDIF

Detailed Logic		`if(n1 < n2)`
		`    sm = n1;`
		`else`
		`    sm = n2;`

It may seem strange to ascribe a name to the returned value when the actual routine does not do so. However, the mini-spec should be created before the code is attempted and should also be independent of the target language used. Some languages allow a value to be returned by assigning it to a variable as suggested by the mini-spec.

Activity 4.10

Write a mini-spec for the *next()* function you created in Activity 4.9.

Function Overloading

Occasionally we require several functions, all of which perform similar tasks but have different parameters. For example, we might need one function to convert ounces to grams, another to convert pounds and ounces to grams and yet a third that takes a real number representing pounds and fractions of a pound (i.e. 4.5 pounds rather than 4 pounds 8 ounces). Such routines could start with the lines:

```
public static double ouncesToGrams(int oz);
public static double poundsOuncesToGrams(int lb,int oz);
public static double poundsOuncesToGrams2(double lb);
```

Anyone wishing to use these routines needs a good memory! It would be considerably easier if we could give each routine the same name since they all perform similar operations. Java allows us to do just that. Hence, the three routines above can be declared as:

```
public static double convertToGrams(int oz);
public static double convertToGrams(int lb, int oz);
public static double convertToGrams(double lb);
```

Declaring several identically named functions is called **function overloading**. The compiler doesn't have a problem with this, since it can identify each routine from the number and type of parameters supplied when the routine is called. LISTING-4.3 shows an example of the three routines described above in use.

LISTING-4.3

Overloading Functions

```
import Input;

public class List4_3
{
  public static void main(String args[])
  {
      int pounds = 12, ounces = 10;
      double pounds2 = 7.5;

      System.out.println(ounces+" oz is "
          ↳+convertToGrams(ounces)+" gms");
      System.out.println(pounds+" lbs "+ounces+
          ↳" oz is "+convertToGrams(pounds,ounces)+" gms");
      System.out.println(pounds2+
          ↳" lbs is "+convertToGrams(pounds2)+" gms");
  }


  public static double convertToGrams(int oz)
  {
      return (oz * 2.83495);
  }


  public static double convertToGrams(int lbs, int oz)
  {
      return ((lbs*16+oz) * 2.83495);
  }


  public static double convertToGrams(double lbs)
  {
      return (lbs*16 * 2.83495);
  }
}
```

Java only allows function overloading where the parameters of each function differ either in type, number or order. Hence, a function *f()* may be overloaded as follows:

```
f(int a)
f(int a, int b)     //Additional parameter
f(int a float b)    //Different parameter type
f(float a, int b)   //Different parameter order
```

However, functions which differ only by the type of value returned cannot be overloaded. For example, the following would not be allowed:

```
int f()
double f()
```

Add a pre-condition to this routine to check that the year is after 1752 when our current calendar system was adopted by Britain and its colonies. Return *false* if the pre-condition is not met.

Activity 4.11

Write and test functions to perform each of the tasks detailed below.

1. Return the second largest of four integer numbers.

```
OUTLINE LOGIC:
    IF n1> n2 THEN
        largest := n1
        second := n2
    ELSE
        largest := n2
        second := n1
    ENDIF
    IF n3 > largest THEN
        second := largest
        largest := n3
    ELSE
        IF n3 > second
            second := n3
        ENDIF
    ENDIF
    IF n4 > largest THEN
        second := largest
        largest := n4
    ELSE
        IF n4 > second
            second := n4
        ENDIF
    ENDIF
    return second
```

2. Identify a lowercase character parameter as a vowel, consonant or non-alphabetic character. (Return 1, 2 or 3 respectively).

```
OUTLINE LOGIC:
    IF ch is alphabetic THEN
        IF ch is a vowel THEN
            return 1
        ELSE
            return 2
        ENDIF
    ELSE
        return 3
    ENDIF
```

3. Return the value *true* if a specified year is a leap year, otherwise return *false*.

```
OUTLINE LOGIC:
    IF (year exactly divisible by 4 but not 100)
        OR (year exactly divisible by 400) THEN
        return true
    ELSE
        return false
    ENDIF
```

Continued on next page

Activity 4.11 (continued)

4. Return the number of days in a specified month. Ignore the possibility of leap years. Call the function *daysInMonth*

This routine has the pre-condition

1<= month <= 12

If this is not met return -1.

```
OUTLINE LOGIC:
    IF month is 4,6,9 or 11 THEN
        return 30
    ELSE
        IF month = 2 THEN
            return 28
        ELSE
            return 31
        ENDIF
    ENDIF
```

5. Write two overloaded functions (both named *convertToKilometres*) which convert imperial distances to kilometres.

   The first function accepts a `double` value representing a distance in miles and returns the equivalent distance in kilometres.
   The second function accepts two `int` values representing a distance in miles and yards and returns the equivalent distance in kilometres.
   (1 mile = 1.6 kilometres; 1 mile = 1760 yards).

   Both routines return a `double` value.

   main() should allow the user to choose which routine is being tested (enter 1 or 2) and then read in values for the routine's parameters and display the value returned.

6. Read in an integer value and return another integer whose digits are the reverse of the accepted value (e.g. 145 will return 541).

```
OUTLINE LOGIC:
      Set reversed to zero
      WHILE original != 0 DO
          Multiply reversed by 10 and add last digit of original
          Remove last digit from original
      ENDWHILE
      return reversed
```

Calling One Function from Another Function

In the examples given earlier *main()* has contained calls to the functions we have written. So, for example, *main()* called *smaller()* in LISTING-4.2.

In fact, any function can make a call to any other function. This can be very useful in reducing the amount of code and testing required by a function.

We have already created a routine which returns the number of days in a given month but took no account of leap years and a second routine that determined if a given year was a leap year.

If we now wanted to create a new routine which returns the number of days in a specified month but gives 29 days for February in a leap year we can either start from scratch to produce:

```
public static int daysInMonth(int m, int y)
{
    if(m < 1||m > 12 || y < 1753)
        return -1;
    if(m == 4|m == 6||m == 9||m == 11)
        return 30;
    if(m == 2)
        if((y%4 == 0 && y % 100 != 0)||y%400 == 0)
            return 29;
        else
            return 28;
    else
        return 31;
}
```

or, alternatively we can make use of the already created and tested routines to arrive at the same result but with much less code:

```
public static int daysInMonth(int m, int y)
{
    int days = daysInMonth(m); //Calls the simple version
    if(isLeapYear(y)&& m == 2)
        days++;
    return days;
}
```

Activity 4.12

Write a new program to implement the final version of *daysInMonth()* given above.

You will have to copy and paste the *isLeapYear()* and original *daysInMonth()* routines into your program.

Your *main()* function should read in the month and year and display the number of days in the given month.

Summary

- **A function heading** has the format

```
return-type function-name ( parameter type list);
```

- A **function definition** has the format

```
return-type function-name (named parameter list)
{
    action
}
```

- A **function call** transfers control to the function code. When the function terminates, control returns to the next statement in the calling routine.

- **When a function is called**, any input parameters are created as local variables in the routine.

- **The actual parameter values** are transferred to the formal parameters before the function is executed.

- **The term** `void` **is used** where no value is returned by a function.

- The **pre-conditions** of a function's parameter should be checked on entry to the routine.

- **When a routine's pre-conditions are not met**, the function should be exited.

- **A mini-spec** gives the design details of a function.

- The term **`System.exit(1)`** can be used to terminate a Java application.

- **Function overloading** allows two or more functions to share the same name so long as the parameter list for each is different.

- **A function can be called** from within any other function.

Testing Functions

Introduction

We've already seen in the previous chapter that test data can be created by examining the actual code of a program. This is called **white box testing**. By separating a program into several routines we can apply this technique to each routine. As long as routines are kept small and uncomplicated, then the amount of white box test data required for each should be held at a level which can be easily handled.

Black Box Testing

One problem with white box testing is that it only tests those control structures actually present in the code. If we've mistakenly omitted code from a program, then tests which should be carried out will not be generated by this approach.

Another way to test code is to create test data based on the actions that the program or routine is supposed to perform. For example, if we know a routine called *isLeapYear()* is meant to return *true* when the year given as an argument is a leap year and *false* when it is not, then we might use the values 1992 and 1995 to check that we get the expected results under both circumstances.

We have created test data without reference to the code of the routine. In fact, the test data could be generated as soon as a complete description of the purpose of the routine is given, long before any code is ever written. This approach is known as **black box testing**.

The aim of black box testing is to identify the general group of responses that may occur in a routine and, from this, to define the set of input values which should lead to each response. In the case of *isLeapYear()*, the responses are *true* or *false* and the input sets are:

1. Leap years
2. Non-Leap years
3. Years before 1753

These input sets are known as **equivalence classes** since members of a given set or class should elicit the same response from the program.

Occasionally, we may want to divide an equivalence class into sub-classes simply because we feel this might result in more rigorous testing. Hence, we might decide to identify the equivalence classes for *isLeapYear()* as:

1. Leap years
    a) Century years (i.e. 1600, 2000, 2400 etc.)
    b) Non-Century years (i.e. 1904, 1952, 1996 etc.)
2. Non-Leap years
    a) Century years (i.e. 1900, 2100, 2200 etc.)
    b) Non-Century years (i.e. 1901, 1973, 2001 etc.)
3. Years before 1753

Again, we would use a single value from each class to test the routine.

Activity 4.13

Identify the responses for *daysInMonth(int m)* which returns the number of days in a specified month. The routine accepts an integer value in the range 1 to 12 and takes no account of leap years.

Notice that invalid input also forms a valid equivalence class since the routine has a different response to such data.

Boundary Values

Some equivalence classes are linear in nature. For example, one sub-class of rejected values in *daysInMonth()* is that containing integer values of 13 or more. The boundary values for *daysInMonth()* are shown in FIG-4.4 below.

FIG-4.4

Boundary Values for *daysInMonth()*

Possible values for *daysInMonth()*

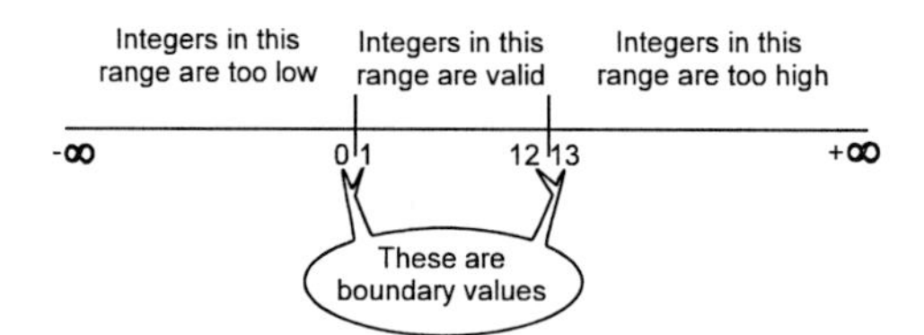

Experience has shown that with such classes the values on the boundary between one equivalence class and the next, when used as test data, often highlight problems in a piece of software. Hence, these **boundary values** should be used, along with some other value from each class, as test data.

Creating Black Box Test Data

To summarise: creating black box test data involves six steps:

Identify the differing responses of the routine to be tested.
Identify the equivalence classes for parameters or input data.
Sub-divide the main classes where thought to be useful.
Choose a value from each class as test data.
Where the values of a class are linear, add all boundary values to the test data.
Identify the expected response for each test value.

Testing *daysInMonth()*

Responses:
- -1 (Pre-condition not met)
- 28
- 30
- 31

Equivalence classes:
1. Invalid month
   a) Less than 1
   b) Greater than 12
2. 2
   (February)
3. 4,6,9,11
   (April, June, September, November)
4. 1,3,5,7,8,10,12
   (January, March, May, July, August, October, December)

Test Data is shown in TABLE-4.1.

TABLE-4.1

Black Box Test Data

Class	Test Data	Expected Result
1 a)	-7	-1
1 a) Boundary	0	-1
1 b)	20	-1
1 b) Boundary	13	-1
2	2	28
3	6	30
4	5	31

Black box testing is not an alternative to white box testing. Rather, they complement each other and increase the likelihood of discovering errors in our code. For example, once we code *daysInMonth()* we'll end up with the following control structures:

```
if (month<1||month>12)
if (month==4||month==6||month==9||month==11)
if (month == 2)
```

and these will determine the white box test data required.

As we create white box test values, we can incorporate, where possible, the values already chosen for the black box technique. The white box test data is shown in TABLE-4.2 with values extracted from the black box test data marked with an asterisk.

TABLE-4.2

White Box Test Data for *DaysInMonth()*

Run	Test Value	Reason for Test	Expected Result	Actual Result
1	month = -7*	if(month<1|| t,f	return -1	
2	month = 13*	if(month<1|| f,t	return -1	
3	month = 4	if(month<1|| f,f		
		if(month==4||t,f,f,f	return 30	
4	month = 6*	if(month==4||f,t,f,f	return 30	
5	month = 9	if(month==4||f,f,t,f	return 30	
6	month = 11	if(month==4||f,f,f,t	return 30	
7	month = 2*	if(month==4||f,f,f,f		
		if(month==2) t	return 28	
8	month = 5*	if(month==2) f	return 31	

In addition to this, the test data table has to be extended to include any test values not yet incorporated from the black box test values. In the case of *daysInMonth()*, this would require two more test runs using the values 0 and 20. These would appear on the final test data table as the test data values for runs 9 and 10.

A Test Driver

Like the components in a piece of equipment, the functions that go to make up the whole program should be tested separately. This is achieved by isolating the routine to be tested from the rest of the program and writing a small *main()* program to call up the routine and display any results it produces.

This program is known as a **test driver**. Each routine should have its own test driver.

The results produced by a test driver should be compared with the expected results and, where there are differences, these should be documented and corrections made to the routine being tested. LISTING-4.4 shows the program required to test *daysinMonth()*.

LISTING-4.4

Testing a Routine

```
import Input;

class TestingDIM
{
  public static void main(String args[])
  {

       System.out.print("Enter month : ");
       int m = Input.readInt();
       while (m != -99)
       {
            int days = daysInMonth(m);
            if(days != -1)
                 System.out.println("Month "+m+" has "+days+" days");
            else
                 System.out.println("Invalid parameter!");
            System.out.print("Enter month : ");
            m = Input.readInt();
       }

  }

  public static int daysInMonth(int m)
  {
       if(m < 1||m > 12)
            return -1;
       if(m == 4|m == 6||m == 9||m == 11)
            return 30;
       if(m == 2)
            return 28;
       else
            return 31;

  }
}
```

Summary

Black Box Testing

- **A routine's description** is used to derive test data.
- **Possible responses** are identified.
- **Reactions to invalid situations** should be included in the set of possible responses.
- **An equivalence class** is the set of data that results in an identical response.
- **Equivalence classes may be sub-divided** to generate more test data.
- **Boundary values** are that set of values in a continuous equivalence class that border some other equivalence class.
- **Test data** should consist of boundary values and some other value from within each equivalence class.

White Box Testing

- **A routine's code** is used to derive white box test data.
- `if` statements are tested for *true* and *false* situations.
- **Conditional assignment statements** are tested for true and false situations.
- `switch` statements are tested for each possible case option.
- `for, while and do` loops are tested, where possible, for zero, one and more than one iteration.
- **Complex Boolean expressions** must be tested for each possible combination of true and false conditions.

- Black box and white box data should be combined to create the final set of test data.

Solutions

Activity 4.1

No solution required.

Activity 4.2

```
public class TestingBox
{
    public static void main(String args[])
    {
        box();
    }

    public static void box()
    {
        System.out.println("*****");
        System.out.println("*   *");
        System.out.println("*   *");
        System.out.println("*   *");
        System.out.println("*****");
    }
}
```

Activity 4.3

```
public class TestingBox2
{
    public static void main(String args[])
    {
        box(8);
    }

    public static void box(int h)
    {
        System.out.println("*****");
        for(int c = 1; c <= h-2; c++)
            System.out.println("*   *");
        System.out.println("*****");
    }
}
```

Activity 4.4

```
import Input;
public class Act4_4
{
    public static void main(String args[])
    {
        System.out.print("Enter month(1-12): ");
        int mon = Input.readInt();
        month(mon);
    }

    public static void month(int m)
    {
        switch(m)
        {
            case 1: System.out.println("January");
                    break;
            case 2: System.out.println("February");
                    break;
            case 3: System.out.println("March");
                    break;
            case 4: System.out.println("April");
                    break;
            case 5: System.out.println("May");
                    break;
            case 6: System.out.println("June");
                    break;
            case 7: System.out.println("July");
                    break;
            case 8: System.out.println("August");
                    break;
            case 9: System.out.println("September");
                    break;
            case 10:System.out.println("October");
                    break;
            case 11:System.out.println("November");
                    break;
            case 12:System.out.println("December");
                    break;
        }
    }
}
```

Activity 4.5

1.
```
import Input;
public class Act4_5_1
{
    public static void main(String args[])
    {
        System.out.print("Enter month(1-12): ");
        int mon = Input.readInt();
        month(mon);
    }

    public static void month(int m)
    {
        if (m < 1 || m > 12)
            return;
        switch(m)
        {
            case 1: System.out.println("January");
                    break;
            case 2: System.out.println("February");
                    break;
            case 3: System.out.println("March");
                    break;
            case 4: System.out.println("April");
                    break;
            case 5: System.out.println("May");
                    break;
            case 6: System.out.println("June");
                    break;
            case 7: System.out.println("July");
                    break;
            case 8: System.out.println("August");
                    break;
            case 9: System.out.println("September");
                    break;
            case 10:System.out.println("October");
                    break;
            case 11:System.out.println("November");
                    break;
            case 12:System.out.println("December");
                    break;
        }
    }
}
```

2.
```
public class Act4_5_2
{
    public static void main(String args[])
    {
        System.out.print("Enter height: ");
        int height = Input.readInt();
        box(height);
    }

    public static void box(int h)
    {
        if(h <3 || h > 22)
            return;
        System.out.println("*****");
        for(int c = 1; c <= h-2; c++)
            System.out.println("*   *");
        System.out.println("*****");
    }
}
```

Activity 4.6

```
    public static long sum(int v)
    {
        int total = 0;
        for (int c = 1; c <= v ; c++)
            total += c;
        return total;
    }
```

Activity 4.7

```
import Input;
public class Act4_7
{
    public static void main(String args[])
    {
        System.out.print("Enter value: ");
        int value = Input.readInt();
        System.out.println("The sum of the values
```

```
            ↳between 1 and "+value+" is "
            ↳+sum(value));
    }

    public static long sum(int v)
    {
        int total = 0;
        for (int c = 1; c <= v ; c++)
            total += c;
        return total;
    }
}
```

Activity 4.8

```
System.out.println(smallest(smallest(
        ↳smallest(n1,n2),n3),n4));
```

Activity 4.9

```
import Input;

public class Act4_9
{
    public static void main(String args[])
    {
        System.out.print("Enter a character: ");
        char ch = Input.readChar();
        System.out.println("The character "
            ↳+ch+" is followed by "+next(ch));
    }

    public static char next(char c)
    {
        return (char)(c+1);
    }
}
```

Activity 4.10

Name : next
Parameters
In : ch : char
Out : fol : char
In/Out : None
Pre-condition : Integer value of *ch* < 127
Post-condition: *fol* is set to the character following *ch*.
Description : Returns the character following *ch*.
Outline Logic: Convert *ch* to an integer value
Add 1 to the integer value
Set *fol* to the character equivalent of the integer value.

Detailed Logic: fol = (char)(ch+1)

Activity 4.11

1.
```
import Input;
public class Act4_11_1
{
    public static void main(String args[])
    {
        System.out.print("Enter number: ");
        int n1 = Input.readInt();
        System.out.print("Enter number: ");
        int n2 = Input.readInt();
        System.out.print("Enter number: ");
        int n3 = Input.readInt();
        System.out.print("Enter number: ");
        int n4 = Input.readInt();

        System.out.println("Second largest
        ↳value is "+secondLargest(n1,n2,n3,n4));
    }

    public static int secondLargest(int n1,
                ↳int n2, int n3, int n4)
    {
        int largest, second;
        if(n1 > n2)
        {
            largest = n1;
            second = n2;
        }
        else
        {
            largest = n2;
            second = n1;
        }
        if (n3 > largest)
        {
            second = largest;
            largest = n3;
        }
        else
            if(n3 > second)
                second = n3;
        if (n4 > largest)
        {
            second = largest;
            largest = n4;
        }
        else
            if(n4 > second)
                second = n4;
        return second;
    }
}
```

2.
```
import Input;
public class Act4_11_2
{
    public static void main(String args[])
    {
        System.out.print("Enter character: ");
        char ch = Input.readChar();
        int result = charType(ch);
        switch(result)
        {
            case 1 :
                System.out.println("Vowel");
                break;
            case 2 :
                System.out.println("Consonant");
                break;
            case 3 :
                System.out.println("Non-alphabetic");
                break;
        }
    }

    public static char charType(char c)
    {
        if( c >= 'a' && c <= 'z')
            if(c =='a'||c == 'e'||c == 'i'
                ↳||c == 'o'||c == 'u')
                return 1;
            else
                return 2;
        else
            return 3;
    }
}
```

3.
```
import Input;
public class Act4_11_3
{
    public static void main(String args[])
    {
        System.out.print("Enter year: ");
        int year = Input.readInt();
        if(isLeapYear(year))
            System.out.println("This is a leap
                ↳year");
        else
            System.out.println("This is not a
                ↳leap year");
    }

    public static boolean isLeapYear(int y)
    {
        if(y < 1753)
            return false;
        if((y%4 == 0 && y % 100 != 0)||y%400 == 0)
            return true;
        else
            return false;
    }
}
```

4.
```
import Input;
public class Act4_11_4
{
    public static void main(String args[])
    {
        System.out.print("Enter month: ");
        int month = Input.readInt();
        System.out.println("That month contains
```

```
            ↳"+daysInMonth(month)+" days");
    }

    public static int daysInMonth(int m)
    {
        if(m < 1 || m > 12)
            return -1;
        if((m==4||m==6||m==9||m==11))
            return 30;
        else if (m == 2)
            return 28;
        else
            return 31;
    }
}
```

5.

```
import Input;
public class Act4_11_5
{
    public static void main(String args[])
    {
        System.out.println("Which routine is to
            ↳be used?");
        System.out.println("   Enter 1 to use the
            ↳single parameter version");
        System.out.println("   Enter 2 to use the
            ↳two parameter version");
        System.out.print("\n\nEnter your choice
            ↳now: ");
        int choice = Input.readInt();
        double kilometres=0;
        switch(choice)
        {
            case 1:
                System.out.print("Enter miles: ");
                double miles = Input.readFloat();
                kilometres =
                ↳convertToKilometres(miles);
                break;
            case 2:
                System.out.print("Enter miles: ");
                int miles2 = Input.readInt();
                System.out.print("Enter yards: ");
                int yards = Input.readInt();
                kilometres =
                ↳convertToKilometres(miles2,yards);
                break;
        }
        System.out.println("Distance is "
            ↳+kilometres+" kilometres");
    }

    public static double convertToKilometres
                                ↳(double m)
    {
        return m * 1.6;
    }

    public static double convertToKilometres
                                ↳(int m, int y)
    {
        return (m * 1.6 + y/1760 * 1.6);
    }
}
```

6.

```
import Input;
public class Act4_11_6
{
    public static void main(String args[])
    {

        System.out.print("Enter number: ");
        int no = Input.readInt();
        System.out.println(no+" reversed is "
            ↳+reverseDigits(no));
    }

    public static int reverseDigits(int v)
    {
        int reversed = 0;
        while(v != 0)
        {
            reversed = reversed*10 + v%10;
            v /= 10;
        }
        return reversed;
    }
}
```

Activity 4.12

```
import Input;
public class Act4_12
{
    public static void main(String args[])
    {

        int month, year;
        System.out.print("Enter month(1-12): ");
        month = Input.readInt();
        System.out.print("Enter year: ");
        year = Input.readInt();
        System.out.println("That month contained
            ↳"+daysInMonth(month,year)+" days");
    }

    public static int daysInMonth(int m)
    {
        if(m < 1 || m > 12)
            return -1;
        if((m==4||m==6||m==9||m==11))
            return 30;
        else if (m == 2)
            return 28;
        else
            return 31;
    }

    public static boolean isLeapYear(int y)
    {
        if(y < 1753)
            return false;
        if((y%4 == 0 && y % 100 != 0)||y%400 == 0)
            return true;
        else
            return false;
    }

    public static int daysInMonth(int m, int y)
    {
        int days = daysInMonth(m);
        if(isLeapYear(y))
            days++;
        return days;
    }
}
```

Activity 4.13

Responses:	-1	(Pre-condition not met)
	28	
	30	
	31	

Chapter 5
Arrays

This chapter covers the following topics:

Anonymous Arrays

Array Definition

Array Initialisation

Arrays as Parameters to Functions

How Java Implements Arrays

Multidimensional Arrays

One Dimensional Arrays

Passing an Array to a Function

Returning an Array from a Function

The *length* Attribute

Arrays

Problems with Simple Variables

All the variables we have encountered up to this point are known as **simple variables.** A simple variable is capable of holding only a single value. For example,

```
int no;
```

defines a simple variable *no*, which can store a single integer value.

However, there are certain problems which cannot easily be solved using this type of variable. For example, if we need to read in five numbers and then display them, the relevant code might be:

```
int no1,no2,no3,no4,no5;
System.out.print("Enter 5 numbers ");
no1=Input.readInt();
no2=Input.readInt();
no3=Input.readInt();
no4=Input.readInt();
no5=Input.readInt();
System.out.println(no1+" "+no2+" "+no3+" "+no4+" "+no5);
```

Although somewhat inelegant, this approach might be acceptable when only five values are used, but would prove more unwieldy if 50 or 100 values were involved.

Activity 5.1

Consider possible approaches to tackling the following problems:

1. Read in 20 integer values in the range 1 to 5 and print out how often each value occurred. (e.g. 1 occurred 4 times; 2 occurred 7 times etc.)

2. Read in 15 integer values. Next, read in another value and then display a message saying whether the last value is repeated anywhere in the original 15 values (display FOUND or NOT FOUND as appropriate).

Hopefully, you can see from attempting Activity 5.1 that any solution to these problems is going to be long and cumbersome if simple variables are used.

One Dimensional Arrays

What is an Array ?

An array is a collection of elements. Each of these elements can hold a single data value. That is, an element in an array performs the same role as a simple variable.

All elements of an array are of the same type (i.e. `int`, `float`, `char`, etc.).

Like other variables, an array must be given a name. Individual cells in the array are identified by a number: the first cell being 0, the second 1, etc.

Visually, we can conceive of an array as shown in FIG-5.1.

FIG-5.1

Array Characteristics

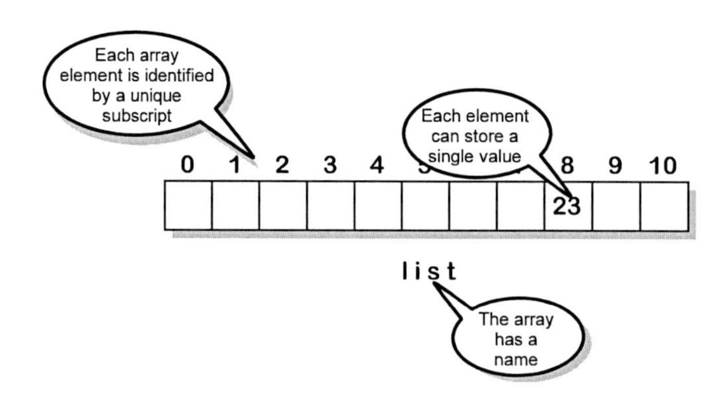

We can summarise the characteristics of an array as:

- It has an identifying name.
- It has a number of elements, the exact number being stated when the array is defined.
- It specifies the type of values which may be held within the elements of the array.

Each element in an array has :

- A unique integer value identifying its position in the array (starting at zero).
- A value assigned to it which may be changed (as with simple variables).

Defining Arrays

To set up an array in Java, we use the following format:

```
type arrayname [] = new type[number of elements];
```

Hence, we could create the 11 element integer array shown in FIG-5.1 using the statement:

```
int list[] = new int[11];
```

The elements of the array are numbered from zero, so the elements of the *list* array defined above would be identified as *list[0]* to *list[10]*. The content of each element in the array is automatically set to zero.

It's possible to separate the declaration from the definition. Hence, we can write

```
int list[];
```

and then, later in the code add

```
list = new int[11];
```

Activity 5.2

Write array definitions for the following data items:

1. An array called *results* which stores integer exam marks for 15 students.
2. A `float` array called *weights* which stores 10 weights in kilograms.

The size of the array can also be expressed using a variable or expression. For example:

```
System.out.print("How many elements? ");
int size = Input.readInt();
int list[] = new int[size];
```

Initialising Arrays

The contents of the elements of an array are initially set to zero, but it is possible to initialise them to some other value as part of the definition. Hence, the contents of an array can be initialised to required values using a statement such as:

```
int x[] = {3,7,5};
```

This creates a three element array and initialises the elements to the values 3, 7 and 5 respectively. Note that the number of elements in the array is determined by the number of values listed.

Activity 5.3

Initialise an array, *bias*, consisting of 8 elements to contain the values 6, 2, 2, 5, 1, 3, 3, 2.

Accessing Arrays

A program cannot deal with the collection of values within an array as a single entity, but must access the individual elements of the array by specifying the array name and the number of the element to be accessed. Hence, having made the declaration

```
int list[] = new int[7];
```

we can assign the value 6 to the third element of the array, using the assignment statement :

```
list[2] = 6;
```

In fact, we may use an array element in any statement where we might use a simple variable of the same type. Examples of valid statements and their effects are shown in FIG-6.2.

FIG-6.2

Using an Array

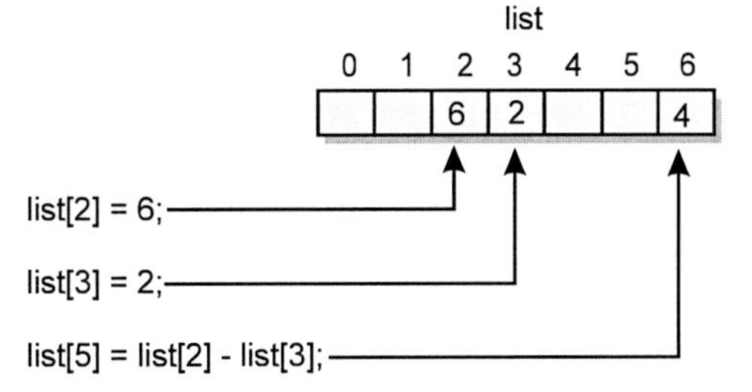

JavaScript checks that the subscript given is a valid one. If the array subscript used is out of range, as in

```
int nos[] = new int [10];
nos[12]   = 45;          //***Invalid subscript
```

then the program will terminate.

An array element can be used for any purpose that a simple variable of the same type could be used for. Some examples are:

```
list[0] = Input.readInt();
list[1] = 12;
if ( list[2] == list[3] )
    System.out.println("Last value is " + list[9]);
list[4] = list[5] + list[6];
```

If this were all that could be achieved when using arrays, their usefulness would be limited. However, the power of arrays lies in the fact that the subscript may be specified not only as an integer constant, but also as an integer variable or expression. This allows statements such as:

```
p = 3;
list[p] = 12;
```

To execute the second assignment statement above, the machine will determine the value of the array subscript variable, *p*, and use that when deciding which element of the array is to be accessed. This means that the two statements above are equivalent to

```
list[3] = 12;
```

Various examples of accessing an array using a variable subscript are shown in FIG-5.3 below.

FIG-5.3

Variable Subscripts

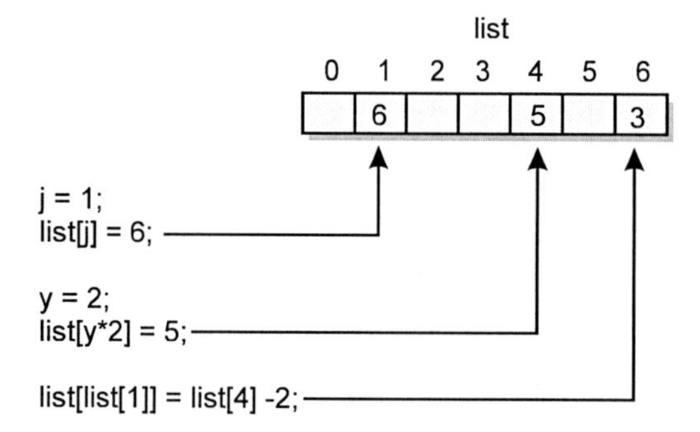

Activity 5.4

Assuming the definitions:

```
int list[]={-4,3,9,2,0,12};
int j;
```

State the contents of the array *list* and variable *j* after each of the following statements (assume effects are cumulative):

```
1.  list[2] = 7;
2.  j = list[1];
3.  list[j] = -5;
4.  list[j++] = 3;
5.  list[++j] = 8;
6.  for (j=0;j<=5;j++)
        list[j] = j*2;
```

Typically a `for` loop is used when every element of an array is to be accessed in order.

For example, the lines

```
for(int c = 0; c < 5 ; c++
    System.out.println(list[c]);
```

display the contents of *list.* As *c* changes value from 0 to 4, so the expression

```
list[c]
```

gives access to different elements of the array.

The program in LISTING-5.1 reads in and displays the five elements of the array numbers.

LISTING-5.1

Arrays for Input and Output

```
import Input;
public class UsingArrays
{
   public static void main(String args[])
   {
      //*** Declare array ***
      int numbers [] = new int[5];
      //*** Read in values into array ***
      for (int c = 0; c < 5; c++)
      {
         System.out.print("Enter a number : ");
         numbers[c] = Input.readInt();
      }
      //*** Display contents of array ***
      System.out.println("\n\n\nYour numbers were : ");
      for(int c = 0; c < 5; c++)
         System.out.print(numbers[c]+"  ");
   }

}
```

The `length` Property

Unlike many other languages, Java checks that your array subscript stays within bounds.

For example, if we mistakenly used the code

```
System.out.println(numbers[5]);
```

in line 12 of the program given above, a runtime error would be produced. The program would terminate with the message:

```
java.lang.ArrayIndexOutOfBoundsException:5 at UsingArrays.main
                                            (UsingArrays.java:12)
```

Every array keeps a record of its own size and we can determine this value with an expression of the form

```
arrayname.length
```

So, for example, if we declare an array as

```
int numbers[] = new int[5];
```

then the line

```
System.out.println(numbers.length);
```

would display the value 5.

We can make use of this feature when accessing all the elements of an array. Instead of writing

```
for(int c = 0; c < 5; c++)
    System.out.print(numbers[c]+"  ");
```

we can code this as

```
for(int c = 0; c < numbers.length; c++)
    System.out.print(numbers[c]+"  ");
```

This is a safer option since any change to the array's dimensions will automatically be compensated for in the number of iterations performed by the `for` loop.

An updated version of the program in LISTING-5.1 demonstrates this technique (see LISTING-5.2).

LISTING-5.2

Using `length`

```
import Input;

public class Arrays1
{
  public static void main(String args[])
  {
      int nos[] = new int[5];
      int p;

      // *** Read numbers into array ***
      for(p = 0 ; p < nos.length ; p++)
      {
          System.out.print("Enter number : ");
          nos[p]=Input.readInt();
      }

      // *** Display numbers ***
      for(p = 0 ; p < nos.length ; p++)
          System.out.println(nos[p]);
  }
}
```

Looking back at Activity 5.1, we can produce an equally elegant solution for each of the other problems using arrays:

Problem : Read in 20 integer values in the range 1 to 5 and display how often each value occurs.

Rather than store the 20 numbers in the array, we need to store the counts in an array.

The program employs the following logic:

```
Set five separate counters to zero
FOR 20 times DO
    Read valid number(1 to 5)
    Add 1 to the appropriate count
ENDFOR
Display counts
```

The program code is shown in LISTING-5.3.

LISTING-5.3

Counting Numbers

```
import Input;

public class Arrays2
{
  public static void main(String args[])
  {
      int counts[] ={0,0,0,0,0,0}; //*** Element zero not used
      int no,c;

      //*** Read in twenty numbers ***
      for(c = 1 ; c <= 20 ; c++)
      {
          System.out.print("Enter number : ");
          no=Input.readInt();
          //*** Check number in range 1 to 5 ***
          while (no < 1 || no > 5)
          {
              System.out.print("Must be 1 to 5. Re-enter : ");
              no=Input.readInt();
          }
          //*** Add 1 to the appropriate count ***
          counts[no] ++;
      }
      //*** Display results ***
      for(c = 1 ; c < counts.length ; c++)
          System.out.println("There are "+counts[c]+' '+c+"\'s");
  }
```

Problem: Read in 15 values followed by a final number. Search the first 15 values for one which is equal in value to the final number entered.

The logic in this case is:

```
Read all 15 values into an array
Get the value to be searched for
Starting at the first value in the array
WHILE value being examined does not match the value being
searched for AND not all values in the array have yet been
examined DO
    Move on to the next value in the array
ENDWHILE
IF a match was found THEN
    Display "Found"
ELSE
    Display "Not found"
ENDIF
```

LISTING-5.4 gives the program code.

LISTING-5.4

Counting Numbers

```
import Input;
public class Arrays3
{
  public static void main(String args[])
  {
      int list[]=new int[15];    //Values to be searched
      int no;                    // Number to be searched for
      int count;                 //*** Loop counter
```

Continued on next page

LISTING-5.4
(continued)

Counting Numbers

```
        //*** Read in 15 values ***
        for(count = 0 ; count < list.length ; count++)
        {
            System.out.print("Enter number : ");
            list[count] = Input.readInt();
        }
        //*** Read value to be searched for ***
        System.out.print("Enter search value : ");
        no=Input.readInt();
        //*** Search until match found or all numbers examined ***
        count = -1;
        while(list[++count] != no && count < list.length - 1);
        //*** Display result ***
        if(list[count] == no)
            System.out.println("FOUND at position " + count);
        else
            System.out.println("NOT FOUND");
    }
}
```

Activity 5.5

Write programs to perform the following tasks:

1. Enter six numbers; display the numbers in the same order as they were entered; display the numbers in the reverse order (i.e. last number entered displayed first).

```
OUTLINE LOGIC:
    Read numbers into an array
    Display contents of array starting at element zero
    Display contents of array starting at element five
```

2. Enter ten values and display only those in the odd-subscripted positions (i.e. subscripted positions 1,3,5,7 and 9).

The term STEP is used to specify what value is to be added to the loop counter on each iteration.

```
OUTLINE LOGIC:
    Read numbers into array
    FOR post := 1 TO 9 STEP 2 DO
            Display element post of the array
        ENDIF
    ENDFOR
```

3. Read in 10 characters and display how many E's are in the sequence. Both upper and lower case E's should be counted.

```
OUTLINE LOGIC:
    Set count to zero
    Read in 10 characters
    FOR each character DO
        IF upper case version of character is 'E' THEN
            Add 1 to count
        ENDIF
    ENDFOR
    Display count
```

Continued on next page

Activity 5.5 (continued)

4. Read in 10 numbers in the range 1 to 50 and display how many fell into each of the categories 1..10, 11..20, 21..30, 31..40, 41..50.

```
OUTLINE LOGIC:
    Set all five counts to zero
    FOR 10 times DO
        Read in a valid number
        Determine which category the number falls into
        Add 1 to the appropriate count
    ENDFOR
    Display each count
```

5. Read in 10 numbers and display the smallest number in the list.

```
OUTLINE LOGIC:
    Read in 10 numbers
    Set smallest equal to the first number
    FOR each remaining number DO
        IF it's smaller than smallest THEN
            Set smallest equal to that number
        ENDIF
    ENDFOR
    Display smallest
```

Arrays as Function Parameters

Since we can pass every other sort of value to a function, it should come as no surprise that we're allowed to pass arrays to or from functions.

To pass an array to a function we begin by specifying in the function heading that an array is to be used. For example, if we want to create a function, *smallest()*, which takes an array of numbers and returns the smallest value in that array, then the function heading might be stated as:

```
public static int smallest(int p[]);
```

Notice that the size of the array is not given within the array brackets in the heading. This is to our advantage, because it means that we are allowed to pass any size of array to the function.

To call this function, the actual parameter is given as the array name.

```
int numbers[]=new int[5];                //*** Defined in main()
    .
System.out.println("Smallest value is "+smallest(numbers));
```

A complete program defining and using this function is shown in LISTING-5.5.

LISTING-5.5

Array Parameters

```
import Input;
public class UsingArrays3
{
  public static void main(String args[])
  {
      int numbers [] = new int[5];
      for (int c = 0; c < 5; c++)
      {
          System.out.print("Enter a number : ");
          numbers[c] = Input.readInt();
      }
      System.out.println("Smallest value is "+smallest(numbers));
  }


  public static int smallest(int s[])
  {
      int smallestfound =s[0];
      for(int c = 1 ; c < s.length; c++)
          if (s[c] < smallestfound)
              smallestfound = s[c];
      return smallestfound;
  }
}
```

Activity 5.6

Write a routine, *average()*, that takes an `int` array and returns the average value of its elements. The returned value should be of type `double`.

Using `char` Arrays

It is possible to store a sequence of characters in a `char` array. For example, the line

```
char text[] = {'T','e','s','t',' ','t','h','i','s'};
```

will store the specified characters in elements 0 to 8 of *text*.

With arrays of other types, we need to display its elements one-by-one. So the code

```
for(int p = 0; p < numbers.length; p++)
    System.out.println(numbers[p]);
```

displays the values held in the array *numbers.*

However, with `char` arrays, display of the whole array can be achieved by a single output statement. To output the contents of the array *text* defined above, we would use the line

```
System.out.println(text);
```

and this would display *Test this* on the screen.

Anonymous Arrays

It's also possible to create an array constant, known as an ***anonymous array***, with a statement such as:

```
new int[]{6,3,9}
```

The above creates an unnamed three element array. One possible use of this type of array is as a parameter to some routine, so we could write:

```
System.out.println(smallest(new int[]{4,9,3,8}));
```

Even an unnamed array still has a *length* property. This allows a statement such as

```
System.out.println((new int[]{4,9,3,8}).length);
```

which would display the value 4 since that is the number of elements in the anonymous array.

Note the requirement for additional parentheses in the above example so that the `new` operation is performed before the *length* property is accessed.

Modifying Array Parameters

Normally, parameters to a function cannot be changed since the function handles only a copy of the original variable (*call by value*), but in the case of arrays it is the original array that is passed to the function (this is known as **call by reference**), so parameters may have their values changed. The following routine adds 2 to every element of the array passed to it:

```
public static void add2(int p[])
{
    for(int c = 0 ; c < p.length ; c++)
        p[c] +=2;
}
```

> **Activity 5.7**
>
> Write a program that reads 10 numbers into an array called *list*.
>
> Add the function *add2()*, given above, to your program.
>
> In your *main()* function, call *add2()*, displaying the contents of *list* both before and after the call to *add2()* is executed.

Returning an Array from a Function

Sometimes the parameters to a function will not be an array, but the result will be. For example, a function, *giveRange()*, which takes two character parameters, *c1* and *c2*, and returns a character array constructed from all the intervening characters between *c1* and *c2*, would begin with the line

```
public static char[] giveRange(char c1, char c2)
```

Notice how the return type is defined within this line: `char[]` specifies that a character array is to be returned.

The code for *giveRange()* is shown below:

```
public static char[] giveRange(char c1, char c2)
{
    char result[] = new char[c2-c1+1];
    int p=0;
    for(char j = c1; j<= c2 ; j++)
        result[p++]=j;
    return result;
}
```

Several of the lines in this function are worth a comment or two:

```
char result[] = new char[c2-c1+1];
```

This line sets up a local array, *result*. The number of elements it contains is the number of characters between *c1* and *c2*. For example, if *c1* = 'A' and *c2* = 'Z', the array would contain 26 elements.

```
for(char j = c1; j <= c2 ; j++)
```

The `for` loop counter is a character variable rather than an integer. Each increment changes the contents of *j* to the next character in the Unicode sequence.

```
result[p++] = j;
```

The character, *j*, is stored in element *p* of *result* and then *p* is incremented.

```
return result;
```

and returns the array containing the set of characters.

A complete program using *giveRange()* is shown in LISTING-5.6.

LISTING-5.6

Returning an Array

```
import Input;

public class ReturnArray
{
  public static void main(String args[])
  {
      System.out.print("Enter first letter : ");
      char c1 = Input.readChar();
      System.out.print("Enter last letter : ");
      char c2 = Input.readChar();
      char ans[]=giveRange(c1,c2);
      System.out.println(ans);
  }

  public static char[] giveRange(char c1, char c2)
  {
      char result[] = new char[c2-c1+1];
      int p=0;
      for(char j = c1; j<= c2 ; j++)
          result[p++]=j;
      return result;
  }
}
```

Activity 5.8

Type in and test the program above.

Add an appropriate pre-condition check to *giveRange()*. If the pre-condition is not met, terminate the program.

Activity 5.9

Write a function, *timesTable()* which takes an integer parameter, *v*, and returns a list of the first 12 positive values that are exactly divisible by *v*.

Include an appropriate pre-condition check in your code.

How Arrays Work

Why is it that the contents of arrays passed to a function can be changed while that of simple variables cannot?

We stated earlier that this was because arrays are *pass by reference* parameters, rather than *pass by value*: the method used on other variables. But what does this mean?

When a Java program creates an array in a single statement:

```
int numbers[] = new int[5];
```

or over two statements:

```
int numbers[];
    .
    .
numbers = new int[5];
```

three things happen:

- Java sets up a variable using the name given to the array, in this case, *numbers*. However, this variable is different from any others we have come across. It is designed, not to hold a number, character or Boolean value, but a memory address. Initially it contains no value. Its contents are said to be set to **null**. A variable of this type is known as a **reference variable**.
- A block of memory locations is now set aside ready to contain the values to be placed in the array. The amount of memory set aside depends on the type of value to be stored and the number of elements specified for the array. In *numbers* above 20 bytes would be reserved: Java `int` types occupy 4 bytes and 5 elements are required (4 * 5 = 20 bytes).
- Finally, the reference variable, *numbers*, is assigned the address of the first byte in the allocated block. For example, if the block is allocated memory locations 2001_{16} to 2014_{16}, then *numbers* would contain the value 2001_{16}.

The details of array allocation are shown in FIG-5.4 below.

FIG-5.4

An Array is Constructed Using a Reference Variable

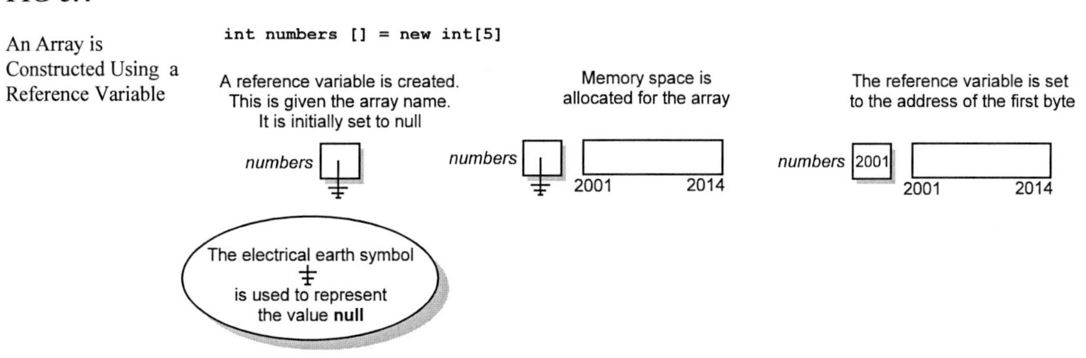

Since an `int` value occupies 4 bytes, the first value in the area will be held in addresses 2001 through 2004; the second value in locations 2005 through 2008.

Activity 5.10

Over what addresses will the fourth value in the array be held?

Notice that the block of memory where the values of the array are actually held is unnamed - only the reference variable created at the beginning of this process has a name: *numbers.*

When we write an expression such as

```
numbers[3]
```

in our subsequent code lines, Java interprets this as meaning

access the data held at the location specified by the variable numbers, *offset by three data elements - i.e. access the data at location* $2001_{16} + 0C_{16}$

Activity 5.11

Which memory address will Java access from the expression `numbers[0]`?

So how does this allow us to modify arrays used as parameters to functions?

You should recall from the previous chapter that when a function is called, a local variable is created for each parameter and the value of the actual parameter copied to it. FIG-5.5 shows the effect of this when that parameter is an array.

FIG-5.5

Reference Variables and Call by Reference

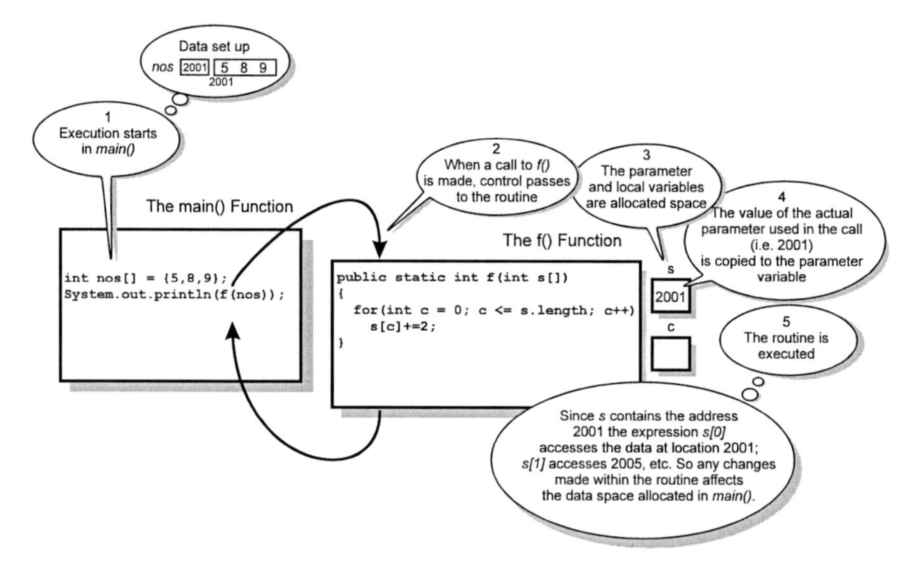

Notice that the mechanism involved is no different from the one we saw earlier. However, since the actual parameter to *f()* contains an address, that address is copied into the routine's local parameter variable (*s*) and hence terms such as *s[c]* reference the original data area defined in *main()*.

The diagrams in FIG-5.4 and FIG-5.5 show the specific addresses held in the reference variables, but in practice it is unlikely that we will know what those addresses are. It is therefore more usual for a diagram to use an arrowed line to signify that a reference variable contains the address of a data area. The two approaches are shown in FIG-5.6.

FIG-5.6

Representing a Reference Variable's Contents

Address Specific Form

numbers

2001

2001

General Form

numbers

From now, we'll use the general form to show the contents of a reference variable.

Have another look at LISTING-5.6, and the line that retrieves the result from *giveRange()*

```
char ans[]=giveRange(c1,c2);
```

From what we just learned, we can see that the first part of this line

```
char ans[]
```

creates a reference variable only, not a full array.

But equally, the routine *giveRange()* ends with the line

```
return result;
```

and, *result* is the name of an array's reference variable - not the array itself.

The end result of all this is that the contents of *result* is copied to *ans* meaning they both reference the array block created in *giveRange()*. The steps involved are shown in FIG-5.7.

FIG-5.7

Functions Return Array References

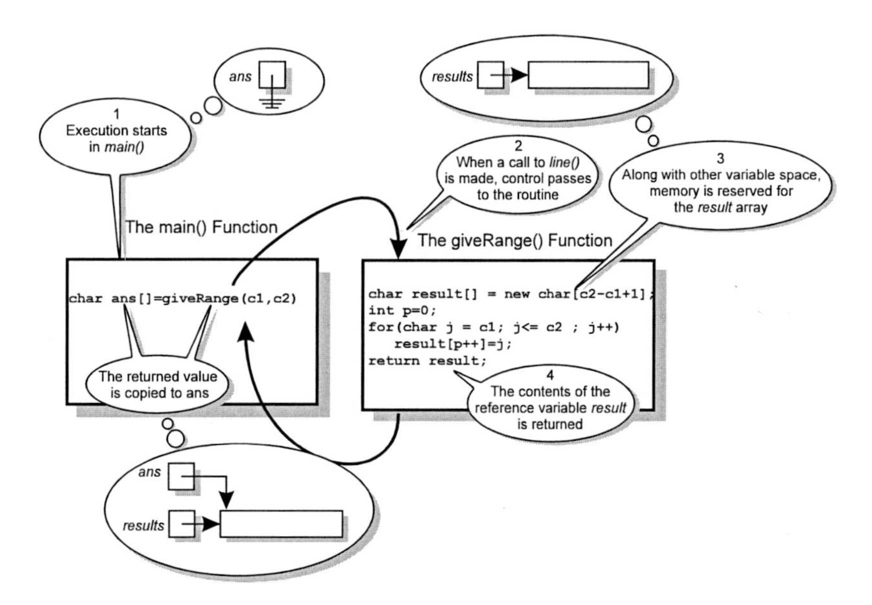

For the most part we do not need to be aware of the mechanism Java employs for manipulating arrays. However, there are occasions when we can make use of this knowledge to create more flexible structures, as we will see later.

Multi-dimensional Arrays

The Need for More Dimensions

If a student sits six exams, then an array containing 6 elements could be used to store this information:

```
int marks[] = new int[6];
```

However, if there are eight students, we would need eight such arrays in order to contain all the data. The definition for this is

```
int marks[][] = new int[8][6];
```

FIG-5.8

A 2D Array

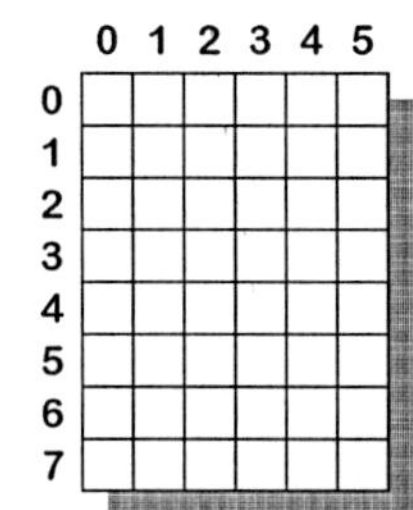

Literally, this defines 8 copies of a six element array.

The resulting data structure is a **two-dimensional array** (see FIG-5.8).

There are many situations which call for two-dimensional arrays. For example, a chess board is easily represented by an 8 by 8 array, while a class timetable could be held as a 7 by 5 array, representing seven subjects taught over five days.

These two-dimensional structures are often referred to as **matrices**.

To define a two-dimensional array, use the format

```
type identifier[][]= new type[value1][value2];
```

where

`type`	defines the type of value to be held in the elements of the array.
`identifier`	specifies the name of the array.
`value1`	specifies the number of rows in the array.
`value2`	specifies the number of columns.

Activity 5.12

Write Java definitions for the following integer arrays represented by the diagrams below. Assume, in each case, that the array is named *matrix*.

1. 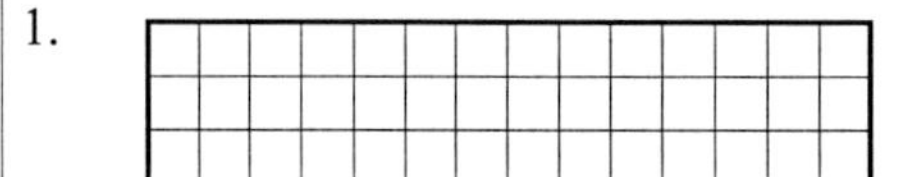

2. 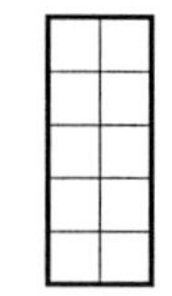

3. [diagram]

Accessing the Array

To access an individual element in the array, we must give the array name and the row and column numbers (see FIG-5.9).
To read in the six marks for each of the eight students we employ the following logic:

```
FOR each student DO
    FOR each mark DO
        Read mark into appropriate element of marks
    ENDFOR
ENDFOR
```

A more program-like logic would be

```
FOR student := 0 TO 7 DO
    FOR exam := 0 TO 5 DO
        Read valid mark into marks[student][exam]
    ENDFOR
ENDFOR
```

and the Java code for this being

```
for(int student = 0 ; student< marks.length ; student++)
{
    System.out.println("Processing student "+(student+1));
    for(exam = 0;exam <= marks[student].length ; exam++)
    {
        System.out.println("Enter mark "+(exam+1)+" : ");
        marks[student][exam]= Input.readInt();
    }
}
```

Notice that the term *marks.length* specifies the number of rows, while *marks[0].length* gives the number of columns in the first row.

FIG-5.9

Accessing Elements in a 2D Array

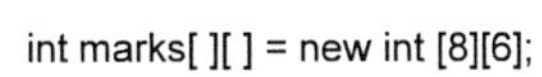

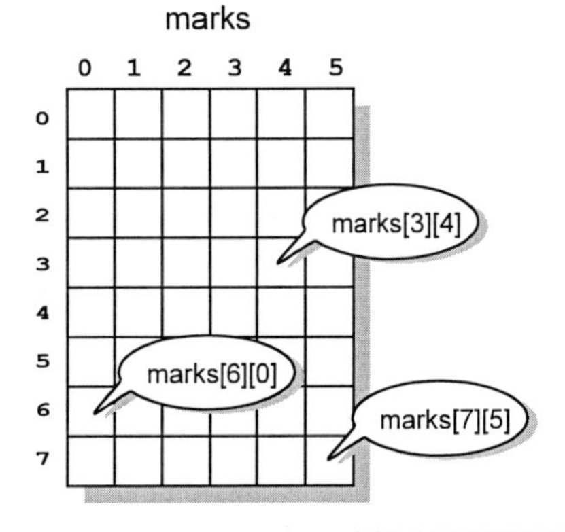

Activity 5.13

With an array, `int matrix[4][4]`, use nested `for` loops to set up the array in the following ways (in each case, insert the value 1 first; 16 last):

1	2	3	4
5	6	7	8
9	10	11	12
13	14	15	16

1	5	9	13
2	6	10	14
3	7	11	15
4	8	12	16

16	15	14	13
12	11	10	9
8	7	6	5
4	3	2	1

Initialising

To initialise the array, we bracket the values for each row in their own set of braces, separating each set of row values by a comma. For example:

```
int matrix[][]={{8,4},{1,1},{2,0},{5,5}};
```

Two-Dimensional Arrays as Parameters

Two-dimensional arrays are passed to a function in much the same way as single dimensional arrays - only an extra set of brackets is required:

```
float functname(float x[][]);
```

The program in LISTING-5.7 returns the smallest value in a two-dimensional array.

LISTING-5.7

Passing Two-Dimensional Arrays as Parameters

```
public class Arrays2D
{
    public static void main(String args[])
    {
        int list[][] = {{45,3,12},{78,7,23},{4,5,6},{7,8,9}};
        System.out.println("Smallest is "+smallest(list));
        for(int c = 0; c < list.length ; c++)
            for(int j = 0; j < list[c].length ; j++)
                System.out.println(list[c][j]);
    }

    public static int smallest(int p[][])
    {
        int small = p[0][0];
        for( int c = 1; c < p.length; c++)
            for(int j = 0; j < p[c].length; j++)
            if (p[c][j] < small)
                small = p[c][j];
        return small;
    }
}
```

Activity 5.14

Extend *Arrays2D* to include versions of *add2()* and *average()* functions which handle two-dimensional arrays.

Your *main()* function should call *smallest()*, *add2()* and *average()* before displaying the contents of the array.

Modify the way in which *list* is displayed by *main()* to give a rows and columns format.

Returning a Two-Dimensional Array from a Function

If we need to return an `int` two-dimensional array from a routine then the return type is declared as:

```
int[][]
```

For example, the routine *groupInDecades()* takes a one-dimensional array of integers between 1 and 50 and returns a two-dimensional array containing the original values separated into groups.

Each group is held in one row of the returning array. Each row contains numbers within a certain range: the first row contains values in the range 1 to 10; the second row values between 11 and 20, etc.

The heading for this function would be

```
public static int[][] groupInDecades(int v[])
```

The code for this routine and a demonstration of its use is given in LISTING-5.8 .

LISTING-5.8

Returning a Two-Dimensional Array from a Function

```
public class List5_7
{
   public static void main(String args[])
   {
        //*** Data to be arranged ***
        int values[]= {5,12,9,31,29,37,20,40,4,17,50,39,21};

        //*** Call routine and store result ***
        int result[][]= groupInDecades(values);

        //*** Display result ***
        for(int c =0; c < result.length;c++)
        {
             for(int j=0; result[c][j] != 0; j++)
                  System.out.print(result[c][j]+" ");
             System.out.println();
        }
   }

   public static int[][] groupInDecades(int v[])
   {
        //*** Set up array to contain result ***
        int temp[][]= new int[5][v.length];
        //*** Set up a count for each row to remember ***
        //*** how many numbers have been added to that row ***
        int col[] = new int[5];
        //*** Add each value to appropriate row ***
        for(int c = 0; c < v.length; c++)
        {
             int row = (v[c]-1)/10;
             temp[row][col[row]++]=v[c];
        }
        return temp;
   }
}
```

How Two-Dimensional Arrays Work

We saw with a one-dimensional array that a reference variable is created containing the address of the allocated memory block where the array's actual data is stored.

When a two-dimensional array is created as in the statement

```
int nos[][] = new int[3][5];
```

then, as before, a reference variable, *nos*, is created. But instead of referencing the data, this variable contains the address of the first of three more reference variables. These, in turn, reference the data areas reserved for each row (see FIG-5.10).

FIG-5.10

The Construction of a Two-Dimensional Array

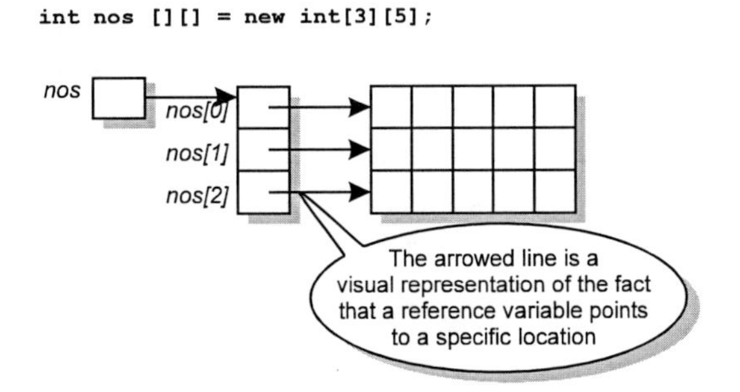

We can make use of Java's approach to two dimensional arrays to create a more flexible structure in which each row can have a different number of cells.

To do this our program needs to start by declaring the array reference variable

```
int nos[][];
```

and then create the additional reference variables for each row:

```
nos = new int[3][];
```

finally, each of these can be allocated the required number of elements. For example:

```
nos[0] = new int[6];
nos[1] = new int[4];
nos[2] = new int[7];
```

See FIG-5.11 for a visual representation of the effect of this code.

FIG-5.11

Constructing Uneven Arrays

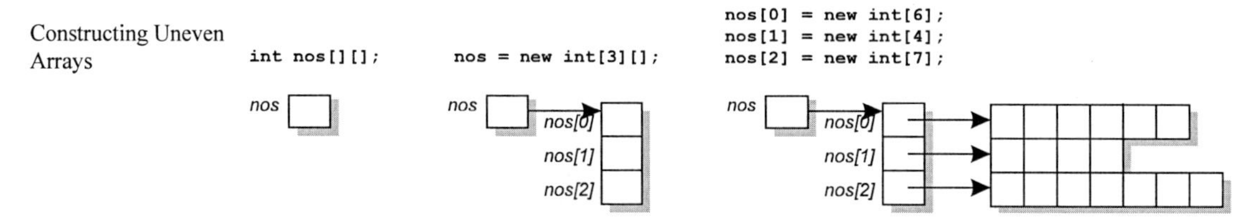

The program in LISTING-5.9 sets up such an array, assigns values to the various elements, and displays the contents of the array.

LISTING-5.9

Varying Row Lengths in a Two-Dimensional Array

```
public class ArrayRows
{
  public static void main(String args[])
  {
      int nos[][];
      nos = new int[3][];

      nos[0] = new int[6];
      nos[1] = new int[4];
      nos[2] = new int[7];
      for(int c = 0 ; c < nos.length; c++)
          for(int j=0; j < nos[c].length; j++)
              nos[c][j] = (c+1)*j;
      for(int c = 0 ; c < nos.length; c++)
          for(int j=0; j < nos[c].length; j++)
              System.out.println("nos["+c+"]["+j+"]="+nos[c][j]);
  }
}
```

Summary

- **An array is** a sequence of elements. Each element can hold a single value. Each value in an array is of the same type.

- **One-dimensional array declaration**:

  `type arrayname[]`

  `e.g. int list[];`

- **Array space is allocated using *new*.** For example, *list* can be allocated 10 elements using the statement

```
list = new int[11]
```

- **Elements in an array** are numbered from 0 to *number of elements* -1.

- **The number of elements in an array** is given by its *length* attribute. This can be accessed using the expression

```
arrayname.length
```

- **Each element is identified** by the array name followed by a subscript enclosed in square brackets.

- **Arrays can be initialised at definition time** using the format:

```
type arrayname[]={v1,v2,v3.....}
```

- **The array subscript can be given as a constant, variable or expression.**

```
e.g.    list[4];        //*** Constant
        list[no];       //*** Variable
        list[no+2];     //*** Expression
```

- **When passing an array to a function**, the prototype must contain a type followed by square brackets.

```
int myfunc( int x[] .....
```

- **The contents of an array can be changed from within a function.**

- `char` **arrays** can be treated as a single data item within the `System.out.println()` statement.

- **An anonymous array** is an unnamed array constant.

- **Construct an anonymous array** using the format

```
new type [] {value list}

e.g.   new char []{'H','e','l','p'}
```

- **Return an array** from a function using the format

```
return-type [] function-name(parameters)
```

- Create a two-dimensional array using the format

```
type array-name[][] = new type [rows][columns]

e.g. int timetable[][]= new int[5][6];
```

- Access an element of a two-dimensional array using the format

```
array-name[row][column]

e.g. timetable[2][4]
```

- **A reference variable** is used in the construction of an array.

- **The reference variable contains** the start address of the block of memory allocated to the array itself.

- **A two-dimensional array** can have varying row lengths.

Solutions

Activity 5.1

1.
Possible logic might be
Set counts1, counts2, counts3, counts4, counts5 to zero
FOR 20 times DO
    Read in a number
    IF
        number = 1:
            Add 1 to counts1
        number = 2:
            Add 1 to counts2
        number = 3:
            Add 1 to counts3
        number = 4:
            Add 1 to counts4
        number = 5:
            Add 1 to counts5
    ENDIF
ENDFOR
Display contents of counts1 to counts5

2.
Possible logic
Read in first 15 numbers to variables no1 to no15
Read in final number to no16
IF no16 = no1 THEN
    Display "Found"
ELSE IF no16 = no2 THEN
    Display "Found"
ELSE IF no16 = no3 THEN
    Display "Found"

etc

ELSE IF no16 = no15 THEN
    Display "Found"
ELSE
    Display "Not Found"

Activity 5.2

```
1.
    int results[] = new int[15];
2.
    float weights[] = new float[10];
```

Activity 5.3

```
int bias[]={6,2,2,5,1,3,3,2};
```

Activity 5.4

	list	j
Initially -	4,3,9, 2,0,12	?
1.	-4,3,7, 2,0,12	?
2.		3
3.	-4,3,7,-5,0,12	3
4.	-4,3,7, 3,0,12	4
5.	-4,3,7, 3,8,12	5
6	0,2,4, 6,8,10	6

Activity 5.5

```
1.
import Input;
public class Act5_5_1
{
    public static void main(String args[])
    {
        int nos[] = new int[6];
        for(int c = 0; c < nos.length; c++)
        {
            System.out.print("Enter number "
                ↳+(c+1)+": ");
            nos[c] = Input.readInt();
        }
        System.out.println("\nOriginal order:");
        for(int c = 0; c < nos.length; c++)
        {
            System.out.println(nos[c]);
        }
        System.out.println("\nReverse order:");
        for(int c = nos.length-1; c >= 0; c--)
        {
            System.out.println(nos[c]);
        }
    }
}
```

```
2.
import Input;
public class Act5_5_2
{
    public static void main(String args[])
    {
        int nos[] = new int[10];
        for(int c = 0; c < nos.length; c++)
        {
            System.out.print("Enter number "
                ↳+(c+1)+": ");
            nos[c] = Input.readInt();
        }
        for(int c = 1; c<nos.length; c+=2)
            System.out.println(nos[c]);
    }
}
```

```
3.
import Input;

public class Act5_5_3
{
    public static void main(String args[])
    {
        char letters[] = new char[10];
        for(int c = 0; c < letters.length; c++)
        {
            System.out.print("Enter character "
                ↳+(c+1)+": ");
            letters[c] = Input.readChar();
        }
        int count = 0;
        for(int c = 0; c < letters.length; c++)
            if(letters[c]=='E'||letters[c]=='e')
                count++;
        System.out.println(count+" Es were
                                ↳entered");
    }
}
```

```
4.
import Input;
public class Act5_5_4
{
    public static void main(String args[])
    {
        int counts[] = new int[5];
        for(int c = 1; c <= 10; c++)
        {
            System.out.print("Enter number "+c
                ↳+": ");
            int value = Input.readInt();
            counts[(value-1)/10]++;
        }

        for(int c = 0; c < counts.length; c++)
            System.out.println("Values in the
                ↳range "+(c*10+1)+"-"+((c+1)*10)
                ↳+": "+counts[c]);
    }
}
```

5.
```
import Input;
public class Act5_5_5
{
    public static void main(String args[])
    {
        int numbers[] = new int[10];
        for(int c = 0; c < numbers.length; c++)
        {
            System.out.print("Enter number "
                ↳+(c+1)+": ");
            numbers[c] = Input.readInt();
        }
        int smallest = numbers[0];
        for(int c = 1; c < numbers.length; c++)
            if(numbers[c] < smallest)
                smallest = numbers[c];
        System.out.println("Smallest value
            ↳entered was "+smallest);
    }
}
```

Activity 5.6

```
import Input;
public class Act5_6
{
    public static void main(String args[])
    {
        int numbers[] = new int[10];
        for(int c = 0; c < numbers.length; c++)
        {
            System.out.print("Enter number "
                ↳+(c+1)+": ");
            numbers[c] = Input.readInt();
        }
        System.out.println("Average of the
        ↳values entered is "+average(numbers));
    }

    public static double average(int v[])
    {
        long total = 0;
        for(int c = 0; c < v.length; c++)
            total+=v[c];
        return (total/v.length);
    }
}
```

Activity 5.7

```
import Input;
public class Act5_7
{
    public static void main(String args[])
    {
        int list[] = new int[10];
        for(int c = 0; c < list.length; c++)
        {
            System.out.print("Enter number "+
                ↳(c+1)+": ");
            list[c] = Input.readInt();
        }
        System.out.println("\nORIGINAL CONTENTS");
        for(int c = 0; c < list.length; c++)
            System.out.println("list["+c+"]="
                ↳+list[c]);
        add2(list);
        System.out.println("\nFINAL CONTENTS");
        for(int c = 0; c < list.length; c++)
            System.out.println("list["+c+"]="
                ↳+list[c]);
    }

    public static void add2(int p[])
    {
        for(int c = 0; c < p.length; c++)
            p[c]+=2;
    }
}
```

Activity 5.8

The pre-condition for *giveRange()* is

```
if(c1 > c2)
    System.exit(1);
```

Activity 5.9

```
import Input;

public class Act5_9
{
    public static void main(String args[])
    {
        System.out.print("Enter a positive
            ↳integer: ");
        int value = Input.readInt();
        int result[]= timesTable(value);
        for(int c = 0; c < result.length; c++)
        {
            System.out.println((c+1)+"*"+value
                ↳+"="+result[c]);
        }
    }

    public static int[] timesTable(int v)
    {
        int ans[] = new int[12];
        for(int c = 0; c < ans.length; c++)
            ans[c] = (c+1)*v;
        return ans;
    }
}
```

Activity 5.10

$200D_{16}$ to 2010_{16}

Activity 5.11

2001_{16}

Activity 5.12

```
1.    int matrix[][] = new int[3][14];
2.    int matrix[][] = new int[5][2];
3.    int matrix[]   = new int[8];
```

Activity 5.13

1.
```
public class Act5_13_1
{
    public static void main(String args[])
    {
        int matrix[][]=new int[4][4];

        int count = 1;
        //*** Set up values row x row***
        for(int row = 0;row < matrix.length;row++)
            for(int col = 0;col <
                    ↳matrix[row].length;col++)
                matrix[row][col]=count++;
        //*** Display matrix ***
        for(int row = 0;row < matrix.length;row++)
        {
            for(int col = 0;col <
                    ↳matrix[row].length;col++)
                System.out.print(matrix[row][col]
                    ↳+" ");
            System.out.println();
        }
    }
}
```

2.
```
public class Act5_13_2
{
    public static void main(String args[])
    {
        int matrix[][]=new int[4][4];

        int count = 1;
        //*** Set up values: column x column ***
        for(int col=0;col < matrix[0].length;col++)
            for(int row = 0;row < matrix.length;
                ↳row++)
            {
                System.out.println(row+"  "+col);
                matrix[row][col]=count++;
            }
```

```
        //*** Display matrix ***
        for(int row = 0;row < matrix.length;row++)
        {
            for(int col = 0;col <
                    ↳matrix[row].length; col++)
                System.out.print(matrix[row][col]
                    ↳+" ");
            System.out.println();
        }
    }
}
```

3.

```
public class Act5_13_3
{
    public static void main(String args[])
    {
        int matrix[][]=new int[4][4];

        int count = 1;
        //*** Set up values start bottom right***
        for(int row=matrix.length-1;row >= 0;row--)
            for(int col = matrix[row].length-1;
                    ↳col >= 0;col--)
                matrix[row][col]=count++;
        //*** Display matrix ***
        for(int row = 0;row < matrix.length;row++)
        {
            for(int col = 0;col <
                    ↳matrix[row].length;col++)
                System.out.print(matrix[row][col]
                    ↳+" ");
            System.out.println();
        }
    }
}
```

Activity 5.14

```
class Act5_14
{
    public static void main(String args[])
    {
        int list[][] =
        ↳{{45,3,12},{78,7,23},{4,5,6},{7,8,9}};

        System.out.println("Smallest is "
            ↳+smallest(list));
        add2(list);
        System.out.println("Average value is now "
            ↳+average(list));
        for(int c = 0; c < list.length ; c++)
        {
            for(int j = 0;j < list[c].length ;j++)
                System.out.print(list[c][j]+" ");
            System.out.println();
        }
    }

    public static int smallest(int p[][])
    {
        int small = p[0][0];
        for( int c = 0; c < p.length; c++)
            for(int j = 0; j < p[c].length; j++)
                if (p[c][j] < small)
                    small = p[c][j];
        return small;
    }

    public static double average(int v[][])
    {
        long total = 0;
        int noofcells = 0;
        for(int c = 0; c < v.length; c++)
        {
            noofcells+=v[c].length;
            for(int j = 0; j < v[c].length; j++)
                total+=v[c][j];
        }
        return (total/noofcells);
    }

    public static void add2(int p[][])
    {
        for(int c = 0; c < p.length; c++)
            for(int j = 0; j < p[c].length; j++)
                p[c][j]+=2;
    }
}
```

CHAPTER 6

Classes and Objects

This chapter covers the following topics:

Access Modifiers

Anonymous Objects

Basic UML Class Diagrams

Class Attributes and Methods

Class Constants

Constructors

Data Hiding

Defining Classes

Encapsulation

Method Overloading

The *finalize()* Method

The *this* Reference Variable

Using Objects

Classes and Objects

Introduction

So far we've looked at the various instructions available in Java. In many ways these are not dissimiliar to those of previous programming languages such as Pascal and Basic. However, the most fundamental aspect of Java is that, unlike Pascal and Basic, it is an object-oriented programming language.

Although object-oriented programming has been with us for over 30 years, it is still an unfamiliar concept to many - even to those who have been programming professionally for a number of years. In this chapter we'll explore the concepts of object-oriented programming and how Java implements these ideas.

What is an Object?

Real World Objects

Our lives are populated with objects: *computers, books, clouds, words, customers,* etc. Some objects have a physical existence such as *computers* and *books*; others represent roles people or things play such as *customers* or *guard dogs*; yet other objects are incidents, such as *a traffic jam* or *enrolment in a class*.

One way to describe an object is to list its characteristics and the operations which can be performed by or on the object. For example, a beach ball is round, has a diameter and colour; it can be inflated, deflated, rolled, bounced, kicked, thrown and burst.

More abstract objects, such as roles and incidents, may be defined in terms of the information required for their description and the operations which can be performed on that information. For example, a bank account might be described in terms of the *name* and *address* of the account holder and the *current balance,* while the operations likely to be performed are *make deposit*, *make withdrawal*, *change address*, and *add interest*.

Activity 6.1

List the characteristics and operations which could be used in describing:

1. a pencil
2. a date

Object Classes

We also need to differentiate between a general description of all objects of the same type and specific objects. Hence, *beach ball* is a general term for all beach balls and *Elizabeth's beach ball* refers to one specific beach ball. When we identify the attributes and operations of an item, this represents a description of all items of that type. This grouping is known as an **object class** or simply a **class**. An individual item from such a class is called an **object** or an **instance** of that class.

Activity 6.2

Identify each of the following as either a class or an object.

1. Dogs
2. Lassie
3. Galaxy class starships
4. The USS Enterprise NCC-1701-D
5. Integers
6. The value 26

Programming Objects

An object-oriented approach to software analysis and design views a system as a collection of objects and interactions between those objects. In addition, the software itself may introduce the need for additional objects which arise through implementation requirements. For example, we may need to define such objects as *drop-down menus*, *option buttons* and *scrollable data lists*.

Once the objects required in the system have been identified, the relevant characteristics and operations of the classes to which these objects belong are defined.

In the world of object-oriented design, a class's characteristics are known as its **attributes**, while the tasks it can perform are known as its **operations**. Collectively, the attributes and operations are known as the **features** or **members** of the class. For example, if a system requires an imperial weight given in pounds and ounces, the corresponding imperial weight class could be defined as in FIG-6.1.

FIG-6.1

Weight Class

The diagrams in this text use the Unified Modelling Language diagrams to represent class designs.

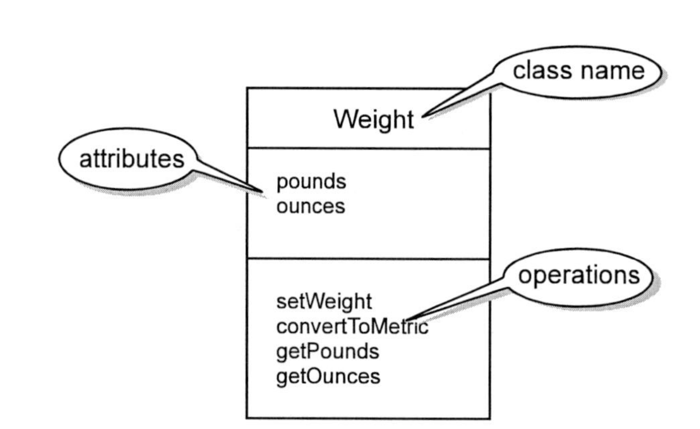

This class definition specifies the name of the class along with its attributes and operations.

FIG-6.1 states that a class *Weight* contains two attributes: *pounds* and *ounces*, and four operations: *setWeight*, *convertToMetric, getPounds* and *getOunces*.

The convention in Java, when using several words for a function name, is to start with a lowercase letter and capitalising subsequent words. That convention has also been employed here at the design stage.

Each operation requires an explanation and this can be documented in normal Mini-Spec format. Informally, the operations for the *Weight* class are:

setWeight : Sets the attributes *pounds* and *ounces* to specified values.

convertToMetric: Converts the imperial weight held in the attributes *pounds* and *ounces* to the metric equivalent in kilograms.

getPounds : Returns a copy of the value held in the *pounds* attribute.

getOunces : Returns a copy of the value held in the *ounces* attribute.

The class definition will be expanded as the design becomes more detailed to include the attribute types and the parameters of the operations. For example, the operation *setWeight()* requires, as parameters, the new values to be allocated to the class attributes, *pounds* and *ounces*. Hence the *setWeight()* function heading would be written as:

Since this is a design specification, program specific terms such as `int` and `double` are not used for the data types.

```
setWeight(newlbs, newoz : INTEGER)
```

The operation *convertToMetric*, on the other hand, has no IN parameters but does return a result and is declared as:

```
convertToMetric():REAL
```

Note that the parentheses are retained to emphasize that there are no IN parameters. These are followed by a colon and the type of value returned by the operation.

When defining operation parameters, the attributes of the class are not included since all operations of a class have automatic access to the attributes of that class (see Class Scope later in this chapter).

The more detailed definition of *Weight* class is given in FIG-6.2.

FIG-6.2

Defining a Class

NOTE: Operations of a class have global access to the attributes of that class. Hence, *pounds* and *ounces* are not parameters of the *setWeight* operation.

Weight
pounds : INTEGER ounces : INTEGER
setWeight(newlbs, newoz : INTEGER) convertToMetric():REAL getPounds():INTEGER getOunces():INTEGER

Activity 6.3

Using the box notation shown above, create a definition for a *Distance* class (attributes: *yards, feet* and *inches*) with operations *setDistance, getYards, getFeet, getInches* and *convertToMetric*.

Classes and Objects in Java

In Java, an object class is defined within the `class` statement. Although we've already made use of the class structure in our previous programs, those have not been typical of a true object-oriented design strategy. The class that contains *main()* is quite unlike the other class structures we will develop here.

A class is a blueprint for the structure of objects yet to be defined. Think of a class definition as being equivalent to the design plans a company would create for a new car before going on to build many cars based on that design.

A first attempt at a Java definition of the *Weight* class we designed earlier might be as given in LISTING-6.1.

LISTING-6.1

Defining the Weight Class

```
public class Weight
{
   int pounds;
   int ounces;

   public void setWeight(int lbs, int oz)
   {
       // *** Check parameters are valid ***
       if(lbs < 0 || oz < 0 || oz > 15)
           return;
       // *** Assign valid parameters to the attributes***
       pounds = lbs;
       ounces = oz;
   }

   public double convertToMetric()
   {
       return((pounds*16+ounces)*0.0283495);
   }

   public int getPounds()
   {
       return pounds;
   }

   public int getOunces()
   {
       return ounces;
   }
}
```

Notice that the function headings do not contain the term `static`.

Points to note:

The attributes, *pounds* and *ounces*, are defined at the start of the class and separately from the methods.

The methods make reference to the attributes without requiring them to be passed as parameters.

When an operation is finally coded it is then referred to as a **method**.

We have created a method by which the operation is implemented.

Activity 6.4

Type in and compile the *Weight* class.

Make sure it is in the same directory as your previous Java programs.

Do not try to run the program. Since this class does not contain a main() *method it cannot be executed.*

In our previous program we created variables to help in the solution to our problems. Hence, if we needed to store someone's age we created an `int` variable, for a sequence of characters we created an array of type `char`. And so, if we require to store an imperial weight for some reason, our program can create an object of the class *Weight.*

In the next program we will create a *Weight* object, set it to some user specified value and display the result in both imperial and metric values.

Our program needs to start with the statement

NOTE:

For Java 2 ver 1.4 users, the `import` statements should be omitted.

```
import Weight;
```

Unlike types such as `int` and `double`, the *Weight* class is not part of the Java language. Rather, it is something that we have created and we need to tell the Java compiler to include the *Weight.class* file when compiling our new program.

This is why we've had to use `import Input;` in many of our previous programs, so that the bytecode of the *Input* class was added.

We can now define a class containing a *main()* function in which we can create a *Weight* object:

```
import Weight;
import Input;

class TestWeight
{
    public static void main(String args[])
    {
        Weight w1;
```

We can try declaring a class object in much the same way as we declare variables:

```
Weight w1;
```

However, although this is valid code, it won't reserve space for a *Weight* object. Instead it creates a **reference variable**, *w1*. A reference variable is designed to hold the address of an area containing data (see FIG-6.3).

FIG-6.3

A Object Reference Variable

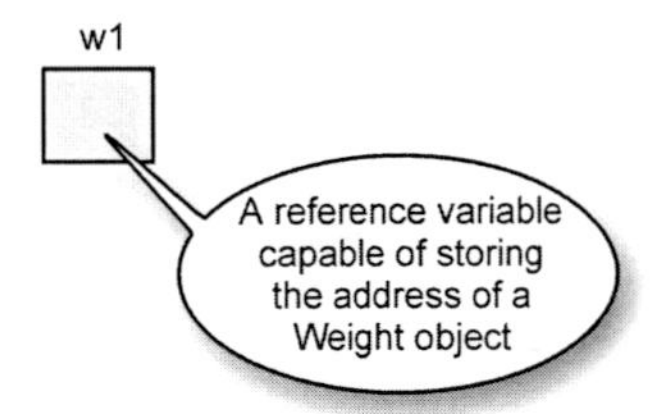

To create the object itself we need to use the `new` command:

```
w1 = new Weight();
```

which reserves space for the object and stores the address of the new object within the reference variable (see FIG-6.4).

FIG-6.4

Referencing an Object

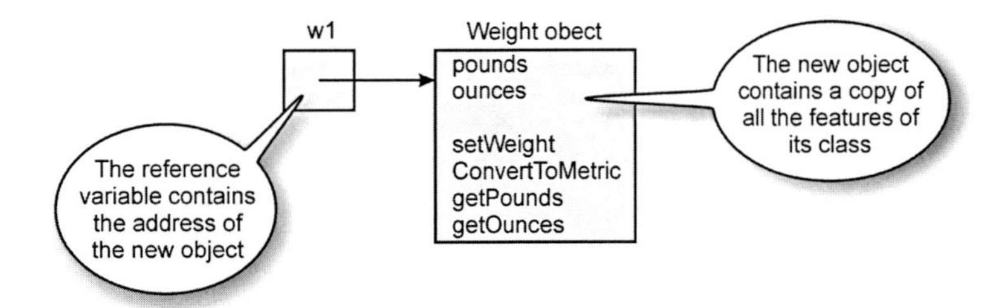

We can achieve this affect using the single statement

```
Weight w1 = new Weight();
```

The object created is known as an **instance** of the class. As you can see, this is very similar to how arrays are created.

Finally, the program needs to use the *Weight* reference variable, *w1*, to access the features of the unnamed object that has been created. The syntax for this takes the form:

```
name of the reference variable . feature to be accessed
```

In this program we only have one object whose address is stored in the reference variable *w1*, so the first part of this expression must be:

```
w1.
```

Since we'll want to start by assigning a value to our *Weight* object, the first feature we want to access is *setWeight()*. So to assign the value 7 pounds 9 ounces, we use the expression:

```
w1.setWeight(7,9)
```

Note that the expression above has the effect of dereferencing *w1* in order to access the required feature in the unnamed object.

Activity 6.5

What expression should we use to determine the value of our weight in kilogrammes?

We're now ready to attempt a complete program. The program in LISTING-6.2 employs the following logic:

```
Create Weight object
Read in the required weight value
Assign the value to the Weight object
Display the weight's value in pounds and ounces
Display the weight's value in kilogrammes
```

LISTING-6.2

Using a Weight Object

```
import Weight;
import Input;


public class UsingWeights
{
  public static void main(String args[])
  {
      //*** Create the Weight object ***
      Weight w1 = new Weight();
      //*** Read values for weight ***
      System.out.print("Enter pounds: ");
      int lbs = Input.readInt();
      System.out.print("Enter ounces: ");
      int oz = Input.readInt();
      //*** Assign value to weight object ***
      w1.setWeight(lbs, oz);
      //*** Display the weight in pounds and ounces ***
      System.out.println("The weight entered was "+w1.getPounds()
          ↳+" lbs "+w1.getOunces()+" oz");
      //*** Display the weight in kilos ***
      System.out.println("This is "+w1.convertToMetric()
          ↳+" kilos");
  }
}
```

When an object is created, its numeric attributes are automatically set to zero. In this case, that means that *pounds* and *ounces* will be zero until the *setWeight()* method is used to assign them new values.

> **Activity 6.6**
>
> Type in, compile and run this second program.

> **Activity 6.7**
>
> 1. Write a class definition for the *Distance* class you designed in Activity 6.3 (1 inch = 0.0254 metres).
>
>   Compile the program.
>
> 2. Write a second class, *UsingDistances*, which declares a *Distance* object, assigns it a value and displays the distance in imperial and metric format.
>
>   Compile and run your program.

Encapsulation

As you've experienced, there are two phases to using objects; first we design and code the class and then we create objects of that class.

Those two stages may be done separately with one person or company creating the class (the class designers) and another making use of objects of that class to produce applications (the application programmer).

These two groups may never meet or have any contact with each other. All that is required of class creators is that they produce sufficient documentation to allow the second group to manipulate the objects they wish to create.

For example, if the class designer creates the *Weight* class, then they would have to produce documentation stating the name, parameters and purpose of each operation defined for the class; the application programmer would then be in a position to make use of *Weight* objects.

You may have noticed that when designing the *setWeight()* method, pre-condition checks have been made on the parameters. If the value to be assigned to *pounds* or *ounces* is invalid then no change is made, and the routine exits.

This stops the group using *Weight* objects from creating corrupted data should they accidentally type a line such as

```
w1.setWeight(4,29);
```

because the pre-condition check will cause the *setWeight()* routine to be exited without the *pounds* and *ounces* attributes of *w1* being changed.

However, there's a problem. What if the application programmer writes

```
w1.pounds = 4;
w1.ounces = 29;
```

Because they have assigned values directly to *pounds* and *ounces* rather than used *setWeight()*, no checks are carried out and the meaningless value of 29 is assigned to the *ounces* attribute (*pounds* is also assigned the value 4).

Activity 6.8

Load up the *UsingWeights* program and, when requested, enter 4 and 29 for the pounds and ounces respectively.

The weight should display as 0 lbs 0 oz because setWeight() has exited without assigning any value.

Replace the line

```
w1.setWeight(lbs, oz);
```

with

```
w1.pounds = lbs;
w1.ounces = oz;
```

Run the program again entering 4 and 29.

This time the display reads 4 lbs 29 oz. The invalid value has been assigned.

Obviously, it would be useful if there was some way to eliminate the possibility of such a mistake occurring. In fact, that's exactly what Java allows us to do.

The solution lies in the design of the *Weight* class. By changing the lines

```
int pounds;
int ounces;
```

to

```
private int pounds;
private int ounces;
```

we restrict access to the *pounds* and *ounces* attributes of any *Weight* object.

This change has no effect on the other lines of code within the *Weight* class.

Activity 6.9

Modify the code of the *Weight* class, adding the keyword `private` to the *pounds* and *ounces* attributes as shown above.

Recompile the *Weight* class file.

Attempt to recompile the *UsingWeights* class, making sure it still contains the lines

```
w1.pounds = lbs;
w1.ounces = oz;
```

The compilation error message

Variable pounds in class Weight is not accessible from class UsingWeights

that you should have seen when completing Activity 6.9 demonstrates the effect of marking an attribute as private within a class. The creators of *UsingWeights* can no longer access the *pounds* and *ounces* attributes of *w1* directly; instead they must adjust the value of those two attributes by using *setWeight()* and hence, we ensure that only valid values can be assigned.

We can therefore make the statement that:

> *Features marked as* `private` *within a class definition cannot be directly accessed in objects of that class.*

It is equally important to remember that adding `private` to the declaration of the *pounds* and *ounces* attributes has no effect on the ability of the code within the *Weight* class to access those attributes. Hence, *setWeight()* still contains the lines

```
pounds = lbs;
ounces = oz;
```

without causing any complaint from the compiler.

Access Modifiers

In fact, any feature within a class can be marked as

```
private
public
```

or left blank

The term `public` has the opposite effect from `private` and allows full access to that feature within any objects that are created in subsequent programs.

If neither `private` nor `public` is specified, access is restricted to only those programs created in the same Java **package**. More on packages in a later chapter.

You can't fail to have noticed that we've been using the term `public` right from the first program. Just as we can specify the access to an attribute such as *pounds* or *ounces*, so we can also specify the access to the methods within a class. As a general rule, since we'll want programmers creating objects from our classes to make use of the various operations, methods are defined as having public access.

A guideline for class definitions is shown in FIG-6.5 below. Although this diagram does not reflect all possible options within a class definition, it is a good starting point for most simple classes.

FIG-6.5

Class Declaration Syntax

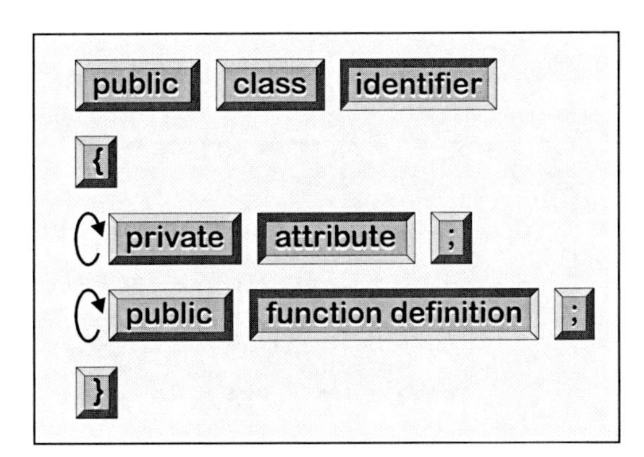

Information Hiding

The inability to access the private members of a class is the first of many advantages of an object-oriented approach to programming.

We've seen that making an attribute private forces the application programmer to use only recognised methods of access to the private attributes. However, there's another equally important reason for keeping attributes private.

Let's assume that the class designer has decided to make the attributes of the *Weight* class public since he knows that the application programmer never makes mistakes!

The application programmer can now create *Weight* objects and write statements such as

```
Weight w1 = new Weight();
w1.pounds = 8;
w1.ounces = 4;
```

Later, the class programmer has a flash of inspiration and decides that a weight can be stored as a single real value in which the ounces component is stored as a fraction of a pound. Hence, the weight 4 lbs 8 oz would be stored as 4.5.

Using this approach the attributes of the *Weight* class can be rewritten as:

```
class Weight
{
    public double value;
            .
            .
};
```

Keen to distribute the new and improved version of the code, the class designer now sends his new implementation of the *Weight* class to the application programmer in a new version of the *Weight.class* file.

The application programmer is now in big trouble! The next time he tries to compile his program containing the assignment statements

```
w1.pounds = 8;
w1.ounces = 4;
```

these will no longer be valid since the *pounds* and *ounces* attributes no longer exist within the *Weight* class.

But, by marking the attributes as private, the application programmer should not be aware of the fundamental differences between the two versions of the *Weight* class.

This alternative version of the *Weight* class is given in LISTING-6.3.

LISTING-6.3

An Alternative Implementation of the Weight Class

```
public class Weight
{
  private double value;

  public void setWeight(int lbs, int oz)
  {
      if (lbs < 0 || oz < 0 || oz > 15)
          return;
      value = lbs + oz/16.0;
  }
```

Continued on next page

LISTING-6.3
(continued)

An Alternative Implementation of the *Weight* Class

```
    public double convertToMetric()
    {
        return (value*16*0.0283495);
    }

    public int getPounds()
    {
        return (int)value;
    }

    public int getOunces()
    {
        return (int)((value - getPounds()+0.0001)*16);
    }
}
```

The 0.0001 term used in *getOunces()* compensates for possible rounding errors when converting from decimal to binary

The only constraint on the class designer is that the names and parameters of the public operations must not be changed when new versions of a class are produced.

By following these rules, the application programmer will be unaware of the actual changes implemented between one version of an object class and the next.

> **Activity 6.10**
>
> Type in and compile this new version of the *Weight* class.
>
> Return your *UsingWeights* program to the original code given in LISTING-6.2.
>
> Compile and run *UsingWeights.*

As a result of Activity 6.10 you can see that *UsingWeights* continues to execute correctly and without the need for change, even though an entirely new implementation of the *Weight* class is now being used.

This ability to conceal the details of a class implementation is known as **information hiding**. To achieve information hiding we need to restrict access to the attributes, allowing access to them through the operations of the class only. This linking of data and related operations is known as **encapsulation** (see FIG-6.6).

FIG-6.6

Encapsulation Concepts

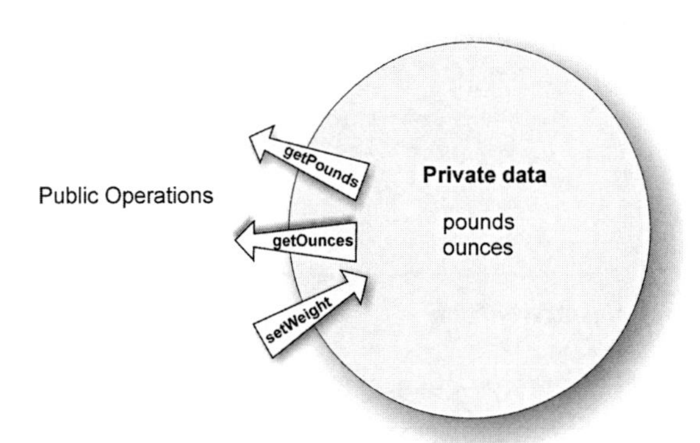

Class Scope

The attributes and methods of a class belong to that class's scope. This means that the member functions can access any other feature of the class, *private* or *public*, directly, without the need to specify them as parameters. Outside the class's scope, *public* members of the class can be accessed by objects of that class; *private* members cannot.

Multiple Objects

Just as we might need several integer variables when writing a program, so it is likely that we will need more than a single object when creating applications.

For example, let's assume we need a program to read in two weights and determine which is the larger. Our program could follow the logic:

```
Read in first weight
Read in second weight
IF first weight > second weight THEN
    Display first weight
ELSE
    Display second weight
ENDIF
```

The coding for this program is given in LISTING-6.4.

LISTING-6.4

Creating More Than One Object

For the remainder of this text, we will assume the first version of the *Weight* class is being used.

```
import Weight;
import Input;

public class List6_4
{
  public static void main(String args[])
  {
      Weight w1 = new Weight();
      Weight w2 = new Weight();

      //*** Read in First Weight ***
      System.out.print("Enter pounds: ");
      int lbs = Input.readInt();
      System.out.print("Enter ounces: ");
      int oz = Input.readInt();
      w1.setWeight(lbs, oz);
      //*** Read in second Weight ***
      System.out.print("Enter pounds: ");
      lbs = Input.readInt();
      System.out.print("Enter ounces: ");
      oz = Input.readInt();
      w2.setWeight(lbs, oz);
      //*** Display larger weight ***
      if(w1.convertToMetric() > w2.convertToMetric())
          System.out.println("Larger weight is "+w1.getPounds()
          ↳+" lbs "+w1.getOunces()+" oz");
      else
          System.out.println("Larger weight is "+w2.getPounds()
          ↳+" lbs "+w2.getOunces()+" oz");
  }
}
```

Activity 6.11

Write a program, similar to the one above, which displays the longer of two distances.

Designing a Class

The class designer has a difficult task on his hands. In creating a new class he has to attempt to predict what uses the application programmer is likely to require from the objects created. If the class designer doesn't build the correct features into the original class, then the application programmer may find it difficult or impossible to achieve the effects required.

For example, let's say the application programmer, having assigned values to two *Weight* objects (*w1* and *w2*), wishes to add *w2* to *w1*; how is this going to be achieved?

It is possible, but creates a rather complex piece of code.

We could try the line

```
w1.setWeight(w1.getPounds()+w2.getPounds(),
↳w1.getOunces()+w2.getOunces());
```

but this won't work if the expression

```
w1.getOunces()+w2.getOunces()
```

gives a total of more than 15 ounces and hence supplies an invalid parameter to *setWeight()*.

A more foolproof approach would be

```
int carrypounds = (w1.getOunces()+w2.getOunces())/16;
w1.setWeight(w1.getPounds()+w2.getPounds()+carrypounds,
↳(w1.getOunces()+w2.getOunces())%16);
```

The limited operations of the *Weight* class are making the application programmer's job difficult.

As a starting point, the class designer will often create *set* (also known as **mutator methods**) and *get* (also called **accessor methods**) methods for each attribute in a class. We already have *getPounds()* and *getOunces()* in the *Weight* class.

Occasionally, a single operation will set more than one attribute if those attributes are closely linked. For example, the *Weight* class uses *setWeight()* to set both the *pounds* and *ounces* attributes.

However, if a *Customer* class contained both *name* and *address* as attributes, the class designer would create separate *set* methods for each of these attributes since they are not closely linked.

Summary

- **A class is the blueprint** for a structure containing data and functions designed to operate on that data.
- **Using Unified Modelling Language**(UML) a class is shown in the form of a diagram.
- An **object** is an **instance** of a class.
- In Java classes are defined in a **class** statement.

- **To create an object** in Java use the following format:

```
class_name object_name = new class_name()
```

- **Java implements objects** by creating a reference variable and reserving a block of memory for the object itself.

- **All objects are unnamed** - only its reference variable is named.

- A class statement has both **private** and **public** members. **Private** members can only be accessed through public functions. **Public** members can be accessed freely.

- Variables of a class are known as **instances** of the class or class objects.

- **Access to public members** takes the form

```
instance-name.public-member-name
```

- All members of a class have **class scope**. This means all members can be accessed freely within the code defining the methods of the class.

- **As a general rule**, classes should contain methods to set and get each of its attributes.

Other Class Options

Member Functions Variations

Various categories of functions arise when writing the methods of a class. Examples of these are described below.

A Class as a Parameter Type

As we saw previously, adding one weight to another is rather difficult using the methods currently available in the *Weight* class. We can make the application programmer's job easier by adding a new method to the *Weight* class which is specifically designed to do this.

The function will take a *Weight* object as an argument and add this weight to some other named weight.

The new method (*addToWeight()*) is coded inside the *Weight* class as:

Note that the normally private attributes of object *w* can be accessed in this method because we are within a *Weight* class method.

```
public void addToWeight(Weight w)
{
    int totaloz;

    totaloz = (pounds+w.pounds)*16+ounces+w.ounces;
    pounds = totaloz/16;
    ounces = totaloz%16;
};
```

The application programmer can now use this new method to add *w2* to *w1* with the statement:

```
w1.addToWeight(w2); //*** Add w2 to w1 ***
```

Activity 6.12

Make the attributes of the *Distance* class private.

Create an *addToDistance()* method for the *Distance* class. This new method should take a *Distance* object as a parameter and add that parameter's value to a named *Distance* object.

Test your new method in a short application.

The Assignment Operator (=) and Class Objects

The assignment operator (=), when used with normal variables in code such as

```
int a = 7, b = 9;
a = b;
b = 10;
```

does the job we expect of it; copying the contents of one variable into another.

However, the same approach when using objects can give unexpected results. For example, the code

```
Weight w1 = new Weight();
Weight w2 = new Weight();
```

```
w1.setWeight(3,8);
w2 = w1;
w1.setWeight(10,9);
System.out.println("w1 contains "+w1.getPounds()+
                                    ↳" lbs "+w1.getOunces()+" oz");
System.out.println("w2 contains "+w2.getPounds()+
                                    ↳" lbs "+w2.getOunces()+" oz");
```

will not display the results

```
w1 contains 10 lbs 9 oz
w2 contains 3 lbs 8 oz
```

as you might expect. Instead the display shows

```
w1 contains 10 lbs 9 oz
w2 contains 10 lbs 9 oz
```

Activity 6.13

Using two *Distance* class objects, create code similar to that given above to duplicate the problem described.

The reason for this display lies in the statement

```
w2 = w1;
```

If you're a C++ programmer, you might expect this to copy the attributes of *w1* to the corresponding attributes in *w2*. But this ignores the fact that *w1* and *w2* are actually reference variables, holding only the address of the actual objects (see FIG-6.7).

So the assignment statement copies the address held in *w1* into *w2*. Now both contain the address of the same object (see FIG 6.8) with all contact to the second object's space being lost.

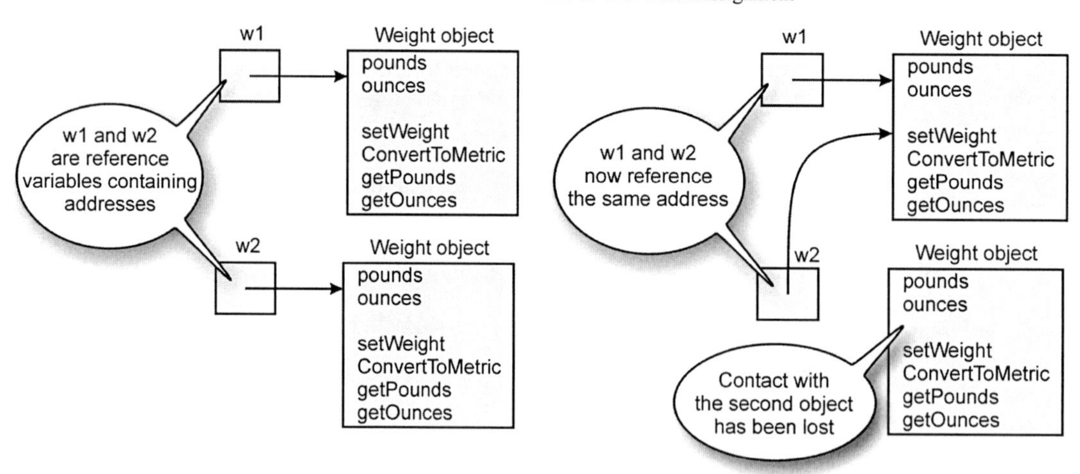

FIG-6.7 Initial Set-up

FIG-6.8 After Assignment

If we need a simple way of copying the contents of one *Weight* object into another, we can do this by adding another method to our class.

Overloading a Method

We already have a method, *setWeight()*, for assigning a value to a *Weight* object. However, that operation takes two integer values. What we need is a second *setWeight()* operation that takes a *Weight* object as a parameter.

Java is quite happy to allow two or more methods to have the same name as long as their parameters differ in type, order, or number. Hence, we can add a second *setWeight()* method coded as:

```
public void setWeight(Weight w)
{
    pounds = w.pounds;
    ounces = w.ounces;
}
```

Creating multiple methods with the same name is called **method overloading**.

When an overloaded method is called, Java determines which version of the method is to be executed by examining the parameters of the call. In the case of *setWeight()*, if two integer parameters are specified then the original version of the routine is executed; where the parameter is a *Weight* object, the new version of *setWeight()* is run.

Now we can copy the contents of *w1* to *w2* with the statement

```
w2.setWeight(w1);
```

Activity 6.14

Add a new *setDistance(Distance d)* method to your *Distance* class and modify your test program to ensure the expected results are achieved.

Returning a Class Value from a Function

Another requirement which arises in most programs is to add two values and store the result in a third variable. This situation is reflected in the statement

```
no3 = no1 + no2;
```

Although we can add one weight to another using *addToWeight()*, we have no way of adding two weights and storing the result in a third weight. To achieve this we need a new routine which returns a *Weight* value. The method, which we will call *sumWeights()*, is coded as shown below:

```
public Weight sumWeights(Weight w)
{
    Weight ans = new Weight();     //Stores result
    int temp = (pounds+w.pounds)*16 + ounces + w.ounces;
    ans.pounds = temp/16;
    ans.ounces = temp%16;
    return ans;
}
```

Now, the sum of *w1* and *w2* can be stored in *w3* using the statement:

```
w3.setWeight(w1.sumWeights(w2));
```

Alternatively, we could write

```
w3.setWeight(w2.sumWeights(w1));
```

A final possibility is that we create *w3* as a reference variable only:

```
Weight w3;
```

and assign it the address of the object created within *sumWeights()*:

```
w3 = w2.sumWeights(w1);
```

FIG-6.9

Storing a Returned Object

The difference between these two methods is highlighted in FIG-6.9.

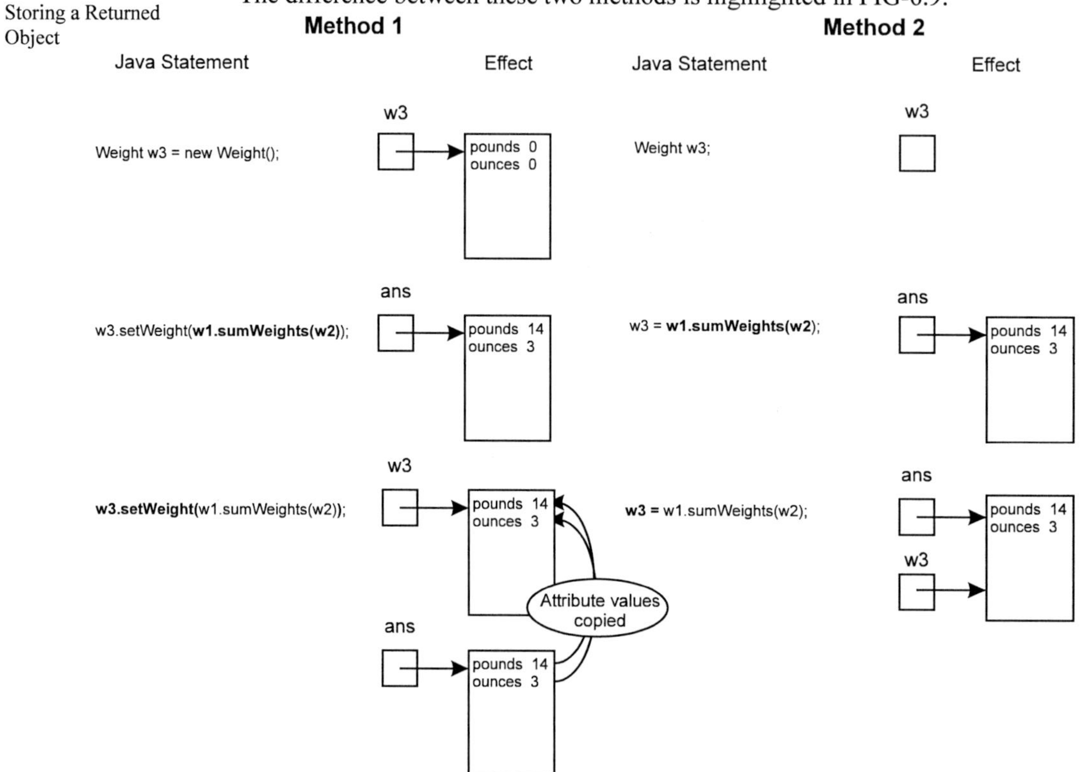

> **Activity 6.15**
>
> Add a *sumDistances()* method, which returns the sum of two distances, to the *Distance* class.
> Test your routine by storing the sum of *d1* and *d2* in a third *Distance* object, *d3*, and displaying *d3*'s contents.

Comparing Objects

With normal variables (`int, float, char`, etc) we can compare two values with statements such as:

```
if (no1 == no2)
```

However, relation operators (such as ==) can only operate on the standard variable types, so if we want to compare two *Weight* objects, we will need to add appropriate methods to the *Weight* class. For example, we could test if two *Weight* objects are equal by adding the following method to the *Weight* class:

```
public boolean same(Weight w)
{
    if (pounds == w.pounds && ounces == w.ounces)
        return true;
```

```
        else
            return false;
    }
```

This allows application programmers using *Weight* objects to write code such as:

```
if(w1.same(w2))
    System.out.println("The weights are equal");
else
    System.out.println("The weights are different");
```

The term **current object** is used to refer to the object whose routine is being executed. Hence, in the expression

`d1.isLarger(d2)`

d1 is the current object.

Activity 6.16

Add an *isLarger()* method to the *Distance* class, allowing two distances to be compared. The routine should return *true* if the current *Distance* object is longer than the parameter object, otherwise *false* should be returned.

Using this routine, modify your solution to Activity 6.11 and test that the same result is achieved.

The `this` Pointer

If we stop to take a deeper look at how objects work, we're going to discover a problem. So far we've given the impression that every object created has its own copy of all the features designed for its class (see FIG-6.7). But the truth is that this would be an unacceptably inefficient way of going about things. Of course, each object needs its own copy of any attributes specified for the class, but creating duplicates of each method serves no useful purpose and would occupy an excessive amount of memory.

Although we can continue to conceive of each object in this theoretical manner, the reality is that each method defined within a class is held only once and each object created employs a reference-type value to locate each of its methods. The setup is shown in FIG-6.10.

FIG-6.10

The Effect of Defining Objects

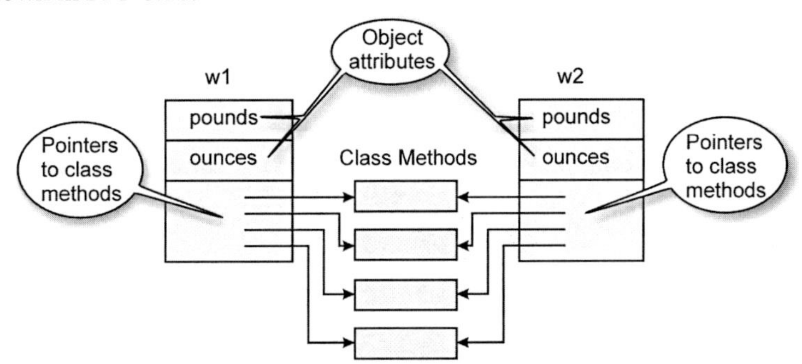

This raises a question about how a method is executed. If all objects from a given class share a common set of routines, how can the program tell which object's attributes are to be accessed?

For example, the line

```
pounds = lbs;
```

appears in the *setWeight()* method.

When this line is executed, how does the program know which object to access? Should it be *w1.pounds* that is assigned the value or *w2.pounds*?

You might be tempted to think that the line that calls the routine, such as

```
w1.setWeight(12,8);
```

supplies this information. But the object doing the calling isn't one of the parameters to *setWeight()* so that information doesn't appear to be passed to the method.

In fact, Java, like C++, employs a hidden parameter to every class method. This hidden parameter is a reference variable, specifying which object actually called the routine. The hidden parameter is called `this` and can be accessed by any of the class methods to access the calling object.

So, although a method may contain the line

```
pounds = lbs;
```

it is actually executed as

```
this.pounds = lbs;
```

and, hence, the object involved in the execution is identified and the appropriate attribute updated.

It's important to realise that `this` exists, and that you can explicitly access it within your program code. For example, let's assume we need another method in the *Weight* class which returns the smaller of two weights. Such a routine would employ the following logic:

```
IF the current weight is less than the parameter weight THEN
    return the current weight
ELSE
    return the parameter weight
ENDIF
```

This can be coded as:

```
public Weight smaller(Weight w)
{
    if ((pounds * 16 + ounces) < (w.pounds * 16 + w.ounces))
        return this;
    else
        return w;
}
```

Notice how `this` is used to return the current weight.

To assign the smaller of *w1* and *w2* to *w3* we use the code

```
w3.setWeight(w1.smaller(w2));
```

Activity 6.17

Write a *smaller()* method for the *Distance* class which returns the shorter of two distances.

Test your new method.

Another situation in which this is explicitly used is when the name used for a class method's parameter matches the name of an attribute. For example, if our original version of *setWeight()* had started with the line

```
public void setWeight(int pounds, int ounces)
```

assigning the parameter to the attribute would be a problem. After all, the line

```
pounds = pounds;
```

doesn't make a lot of sense! However, we can write

```
this.pounds = pounds;
```

in which case, the *pounds* parameter has its value copied to the *pounds* attribute.

Private Methods

Some of the methods of *Weight* class make use of the expression `pounds*16+ounces;` which calculates the total number of ounces in a weight. It may be useful to create a method, *toOunces()*, to perform this operation. Yet, *toOunces()* is not a basic operation of the class, rather it is a subsidiary function which comes in useful in coding the main methods of the class. As such, we would not want the application programmer to have access to the *toOunces()* function.

To achieve this, we declare *toOunces()* as a `private` method of *Weight*. This prevents programmers using *Weight* objects from accessing the routine, yet still allows it to be used in coding other methods in the *Weight* class.

The new method is coded as:

```
private int toOunces()
{
    return pounds * 16 + ounces;
}
```

We can now use the function in the definition of the other *Weight* methods. For example, *convertToMetric()* could now be coded as:

```
public double convertToMetric()
{
    return toOunces()*0.0283495;
};
```

The code for the *addToWeight()* operation would become

```
public void addToWeight(Weight w)
{
    int temp = toOunces() + w.toOunces();
    pounds = temp / 16;
    ounces = temp%16;
}
```

Activity 6.18

Create a private *toInches()* method for the *Distance* class which converts the distance held within the object from yards, feet, and inches to inches.

Using this new method, write an *addToDistance(Distance d)* method for the *Distance* class that adds distance *d* to the existing object.

Constructors

If we were to call the *getPounds()* for some object before using its *setWeight()* method, we would get the value zero returned. This is because the attributes, *pounds* and *ounces,* are automatically set to zero.

Although this action might be appropriate in the case of a *Weight* object, there will be other classes where we might want the attributes to start with other values.

Let's assume we want to be able to specify the initial value of all *Weight* objects. To achieve the results we require, we have to add a new type of method, known as a **constructor**, to our class.

Unlike other methods, a constructor is executed by the program at the instant an object variable's space is allocated.

A constructor method is used to initialise class objects. A constructor always has the same name as the class itself. Although a constructor can have any number of parameters, it cannot return a value; even the term `void` is not allowed as a return type. Instead any mention of a return type is omitted.

To create a constructor, we begin by adding the constructor method to the class declaration:

```
public Weight(int lbs, int oz)
{
    if (lbs < 0 || oz < 0 || oz > 15)
    {
        pounds = 0;
        ounces = 0;
    }
    else
    {
        pounds = lbs;
        ounces = oz;
    }
};
```

Objects of the class can now be declared with statements such as

```
Weight w1 = new Weight(5,0);
```

which sets *w1* to 5 lbs 0 oz.

Now we have the full picture of what is happening when we create an object. We begin by creating a reference variable:

```
Weight w1 = new Weight(5,0);
```

then reserve space for the object and assign its start address to the reference variable:

```
Weight w1 = new Weight(5,0);
```

and finally initialise the contents of the object by executing its constructor:

```
Weight w1 = new Weight(5,0);
```

Of course, we won't want to initialise every variable to a specific value, and so we might still want to use statements such as:

```
Weight totalweight = new Weight();
```

It will, therefore, come as a bit of a shock to discover that this no longer works! Instead, we get the error message

```
No constructor matching Weight() found in class Weight
```

Why did this work fine before we added a constructor? The truth is that the Java always calls a constructor when a class object is defined. After all, we now know that the final part of the statement

```
Weight totalweight = new Weight();
```

is a call to a constructor. The only difference is that this time the constructor takes no arguments.

Where no constructor has been defined with the class, the compiler generates a default constructor with no parameters and this is called at the start of the class object's lifetime. When a constructor is explicitly defined by the programmer, no default constructor is created. In the case of *Weight* class, this means that we now have only one constructor (as defined above) which requires two parameters and it is not possible to define an object of class *Weight* without supplying the parameters required by that constructor.

To overcome this problem, we need to overload the constructor with a second version which requires no parameters

Actually, since the attributes would be set to zero automatically, we could achieve the same result by just creating an empty constructor

```
public Weight(){}
```

```
public Weight()
{
    pounds = 0;
    ounces = 0;
};
```

to define the second version of the constructor.

Now, object definitions with or without parameters are acceptable.

Activity 6.19

Write two constructors for the *Distance* class.

The first of these should take no parameters and set each attribute to zero.

The second should take three integer parameters and use these to set the value of yards, feet and inches. If any of the parameters are invalid, all attributes should be set to zero.

It may appear that a constructor that sets attributes to zero is unnecessary since numeric attributes will automatically be set to zero in any case. However, if we've created any other constructor, then we will have lost the automatic zero-argument constructor created by Java and only by replacing it can we continue to write lines such as

```
Weight w3 = new Weight();
```

Rather than use a constructor, we can initialise the attributes of every new object of a class by assigning values to the attributes:

```
public class Weight
{
    private int pounds = 1;
    private int ounces = 0;
```

And if we want to continue with a zero-argument constructor we can create an empty constructor

```
public Weight(){};
```

which is quite valid. Now the statement

```
Weight w3 = new Weight();
```

will initialise *w3* to 1 lb 0 oz.

Another useful form of the constructor is one which takes an object of its own class as an argument. For example, having created the following *Weight* constructor

```
public Weight(Weight w)
{
    pounds = w.pounds;
    ounces = w.ounces;
}
```

we can then assign the contents of an earlier *Weight* object to one being created:

```
Weight w1 = new Weight(5,3);
Weight w2 = new Weight(w1);    // w1 copied to w2 as it's created
```

Having written one constructor, we may find it useful to implement a second by calling the original constructor. For example, we now have three constructors for the *Weight* class:

```
public Weight(int lbs, int oz)
{
    if (lbs < 0 || oz < 0 || oz > 15)
    {
        pounds = 0;
        ounces = 0;
    }
    else
    {
        pounds = lbs;
        ounces = oz;
    }
};

public Weight(){};
```

and

```
public Weight(Weight w)
{
    pounds = w.pounds;
    ounces = w.ounces;
}
```

But the third constructor could be implemented by calling the first with the arguments *w.pounds* and *w.ounces*. Possibly we could re-code this third constructor as

```
public Weight(Weight w)
{
    Weight(w.pounds, w.ounces);
}
```

In fact, Java won't let us use this syntax. Instead, a constructor may call another constructor from the same class by using the term `this` as the function name. Hence, we have to write the third constructor as

```
public Weight(Weight w)
{
    this(w.pounds, w.ounces);
}
```

As with the previous version of this routine, it's still only the address of the object that is returned.

Activity 6.20

Create a similar constructor for the *Distance* class which takes a *Distance* object as its parameter.

Implement this new constructor by calling the original three integer version of the *Distance* constructor.

Creating Anonymous Objects

We can make use of the class constructor and the `new` keyword to create anonymous objects. One possible use of this could be as the parameter to a method that takes an object parameter. Hence, we could add 3 lbs 7 oz to the *Weight* object *w1* using the statement:

```
w1.addToWeight(new Weight(3,7));
```

where the term

```
new Weight(3,7)
```

creates an anonymous *Weight* object.

Alternatively, we could use an anonymous object as the return value for a method. Below is an alternative way of writing the *Weight* class method *sumWeight()* described earlier:

```
public Weight sumWeights(Weight w)
{
    int temp = toOunces() + w.toOunces();
    return (new Weight(temp/16,temp%16));
}
```

finalize() Method

As at the start of an object's life its constructor is called, so, at the end of its life (when its space is deallocated), a method called *finalize()* is executed.

Like the constructor, Java will provide a *finalize()* method if none is explicitly defined in the class. The default version of this method doesn't actually do anything, so a class needs to override it in order to do something useful.

However, since Java does all the hard work of tidying up memory after an object's space is deallocated (this process is known as **garbage collection**), the *finalize()* methods are only really needed when a class has to make sure some other part of the system is correctly shut down. For example, a class might have an explicit *finalize()* method if a file needs to be closed, or some terminating message needs to be transmitted over a network. Unfortunately, there is no guarantee that a *finalize()* method will be automatically executed before the program terminates. However, as with other methods of a class, you are at liberty to make an explicit call to the routine from your code.

Constants

For some classes there are certain fixed values that it seems sensible to associate with that class. For example, if we implemented a *Date* class we might want to associate the term *NewYear* with 1st of January; in the *Math* class the term *pi* is associated with the value 3.1415 (but to more decimal places).

We can set up such constants as class attributes by preceding them with the term `final`. For example, if we had designed the *Weight* class for a program involving postage, we might want to set the various weight limits on letters, packages and parcels.

This can be done as shown below:

```
class Weight
{
    //*** Maximum weights in ounces for each type ***
    public final int letter   = 2;
    public final int package  = 16;
    public final int parcel   = 160;

    private int pounds;
    private int ounces;
        .
        .
```

Any feature of a class that uses the term `final` cannot have its value modified. So, although we have defined *letter, package* and *parcel* as `public`, there is no danger of the application programmer modifying their values.

These constants can be used anywhere in the methods of the class or in any other code where objects of the *Weight* class are used. Hence, *main()* might contain the line:

```
System.out.println("Upper limit for 19p letters is "
                                        ↳+w1.letter+" ounces");
```

There is one aspect of this feature that has to be questioned - *if the value held in a constant is fixed, why do we need a copy of that value in every single object that is created when one copy would be sufficient?*

The answer is - we don't. But as things stand, any attribute defined within a class is duplicated in every object of that class. (see FIG-6.11)

FIG-6.11

Normal Attributes are Duplicated in each

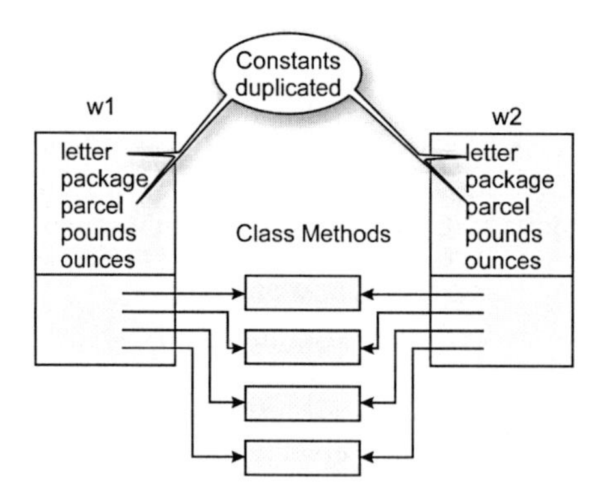

However, there's a way round that - we can declare an attribute as `static`.

Static Attributes

If we use the term `static` beside any feature of a class it means that only a single copy of that feature is ever allocated space and that all objects of the class access that single copy. Therefore, by changing the definition of the *Weight* constants to

```
public static final int letter = 2;
public static final int package = 16;
public static final int parcel = 160;
```

there is now only a single copy of each attribute (see FIG-6.12).

FIG-6.12

Sharing static Attributes

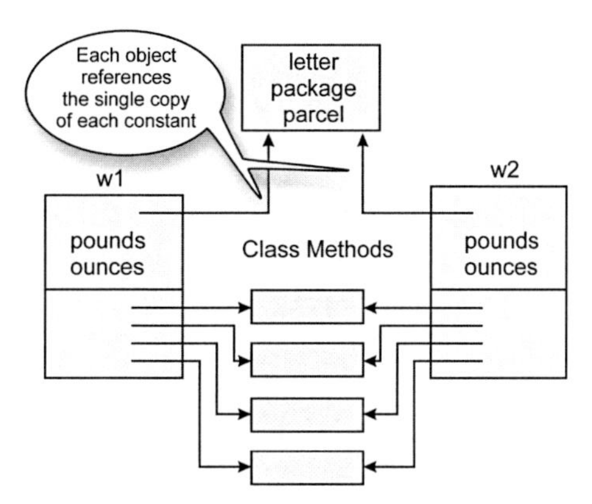

Another characteristic of a `static` feature is that those features exist even when no objects of that class have been created. When you want to access `static` attributes before any objects are created, you need to use the class name. Hence, we can access the constant *letter* with the term

```
Weight.letter
```

allowing statements such as:

```
System.out.println("Upper limit for 19p letters is "
➥+Weight.letter+" ounces");
```

Of course, it is also still possible to access the constants through any objects that are created, so we can still write *w1.letter* within our code after *w1* has been defined.

Activity 6.21

Add two `static` constants to the *Distance* class:

metre = 39
centimetre = 0.3937

Test accessing these values by using both the class name and object name approaches. That is, *Distance.metre* and *d1.centimetre.*

Static attributes need not be constants. It is also possible to create static variable attributes simply by including the term `static`.

It's not often that we'll want to do this, but one simple example might be to keep a count of how many objects of a given class are in existence. For example, if we define the attributes of the *Weight* class as

```
public class Weight
{
    public static final int letter = 2;
    public static final int package = 16;
    public static final int parcel = 160;
    public static int count = 0;          //Object count
    private int pounds;
    private int ounces;
```

and increment *count* each time an object is created (by adding the appropriate statement to each constructor).

```
public Weight(int lbs, int oz)
{
    if (lbs < 0 || oz < 0 || oz > 15)
    {
        pounds = 0;
        ounces = 0;
    }
    else
    {
        pounds = lbs;
        ounces = oz;
    }
    count++;
}

public Weight()
{
    pounds = 0;
    ounces = 0;
    count++;
}

public Weight (double v)
{
    if (v < 0)
    {
        pounds = 0;
        ounces = 0;
    }
    else
    {
        pounds = (int)v;
        ounces = (int)((v - (int)v)*16);
    }
    count++;
}
```

then we can find out how many objects are in existence at any time by accessing *count:*

```
public class TestWeight7
{
    public static void main(String args[])
    {
        System.out.println("There are "+Weight.count
        ↳+" Weight objects");
        Weight w1 = new Weight(4,2);
        System.out.println("There are "+Weight.count
        ↳+" Weight objects");
        Weight w2 = new Weight(6.8);
        System.out.println("There are "+Weight.count
        ↳+" Weight objects");
    }
}
```

Activity 6.22

Add a *count* to the *Distance* class and test it as in *main()* above.

To differentiate between attributes which are created in every object of a given class and those that are created only once and shared between the objects, the terms **instance attribute** (occurs in every object) and **class attribute** (shared by objects) are used. Hence, *pounds* is a instance attribute of the *Weight* class, while *letter* is a class attribute.

Class Methods

It's not only attributes that can be declared static, methods can also be static. Such routines are known as **class methods**. And, as with attributes, class methods are available even when an object of the class has not yet been defined.

There are two main reasons for having static methods.

You'll see in the example above that *count* has been declared as `public`. If it were `private` the statement

```
System.out.println("There are "+Weight.count+" Weight objects");
```

would produce an error message, since we cannot access `private` methods of a class - even if they are static.

But we also know it's good policy to keep attributes private, for as things stand, it is possible to write

```
Weight.count = 23;
```

inside *main()* and destroy the purpose of *count.*

However, if we make *count* `private`, we are going to have to write a new method, *getCount(),* in order to access the new attribute.

Now, although we declare these methods like any others, that would mean the methods can't be accessed until an object of the *Weight* class is declared. This leads to the situation where, when no *Weight* objects have been defined, *count* exists but it cannot be accessed. However, if we declare a method to be `static` it will exist independently of objects of the class.

To summarise, it is best to make methods which are designed solely to access static attributes static themselves.The relevant code for the *Weight* class is given below

```
public class Weight
{
    public static final int letter = 2;
    public static final int package = 16;
    public static final int parcel = 160;
    private static int count = 0;
              .
              .
    public static int getCount()
    {
        return count;
    }
              .
              .
public class TestWeight7
{
    public static void main(String args[])
    {
        System.out.println("There are "+Weight.getCount()
        ↳+" Weight objects");
        Weight w1 = new Weight(4,2);
        System.out.println("There are "+Weight.getCount()
        ↳+" Weight objects");
        Weight w2 = new Weight(6.8);
        System.out.println("There are "+Weight.getCount()
        ↳+" Weight objects");
    }
}
```

Activity 6.23

Make a similar change to the *Distance* class, so that its *count* property is private and accessed through a static *getCount()* method.

Modify your test program to make use of this new method.

We'll look at the *Math* class in a later chapter.

A second reason for creating class methods is when a set of methods have a tight commonality but do not require specific objects. A good example of this is Java's own *Math* class which contains class methods such as *sqrt(), sin(), cos(),* etc.

These routines obviously belong together and yet do not involve *Math* objects in their results. Rather, results will tend to be of type `double` or `int`.

By including related functions in a single class the application programmer can write statements such as:

```
double x = Math.sin(1.3);
```

Items of a class which are declared as `static` are usually referred to as **class** features. Hence, *letter* is a **class constant**, *count* is a **class variable**, and *getCount()* is a **class method**.

Summary

- **A class object may appear as a parameter** to a function.
- **A class object may be returned** by a function.
- **Methods may be private,** in which case they can only be called from within other member methods of the class.
- A **constructor** is a method which is called automatically when a class object is created.
- If no constructor is created by the programmer, a **default constructor** is created automatically.
- A **constructor** must have the same name as the class and may return no value.
- **Constructors** can be overloaded.
- **Only a single copy of static data members is created** no matter how many objects from that class exist.
- A static, variable, data item is often known as a **class variable.**
- Each object accesses the same copy of the **static item.**
- **Static items exist even when no object of that class exists.**
- **To access a public static attribute** when no object exists, use the format

```
Class-name.static-data-name
```

- **To access a private static attribute** when no object exists, a public class method is required

```
public static return-type function-name(parameter list);
```

to declare the function.

Designing Classes

Introduction

At the beginning of this chapter we saw that one tool for helping with the design of an object-oriented system is the Unified Modelling Language (UML). The complete UML system and object-oriented design as a whole is outside the scope of this text. However, it will be useful to explore UML class diagrams in some more detail by showing how the *Weight* class would be represented in this system.

We've already seen that the basic diagram is a rectangle split into three areas. These areas contain:

the class name
the attributes of the class
the operations of the class

In addition, the access modifier information can be added to the diagram: private items are started with a minus (-) sign; public features begin with a plus (+) sign.

The modified version of the *Weight* class is shown in FIG-6.13.

FIG-6.13

A UML Class Diagram

Weight
- pounds:integer - ounces:integer + letter:integer = 2 + package:integer=16 + parcel:integer=160
+ create():Weight + create(lbs, oz:integer):Weight + create(w:Weight) : Weight + setWeight(newlbs, newoz:integer) + setWeight(w:Weight) + convertToMetric():real + getPounds():integer + getOunces():integer + addToWeight(w:Weight) + sumWeights(w:Weight):Weight + same(w:Weight):boolean - toOunces():integer

Notice that constructor operations are named *create* and return an object of the class being defined. This is a useful convention to follow with all classes. Of course, in the implementation, Java requires that the constructors are named after the class.

Any class attributes or methods (only the constant class attributes *letter, package* and *parcel* are shown above) are underlined.

The initial value of an attribute is shown by adding an equals sign followed by the required initial value, but there is no specific method for signifying a constant attribute.

Other documentation in the form of mini-specs will be required for each operation. In addition to the information given in previously discussed mini-specs, we'll need to add access details and which attributes are accessed by an operation. For example, the mini-spec for *setWeight(newlbs, newoz : integer)* would be as shown below:

```
Operation      :  setWeight
Access         :  public
Parameters
    In         :  newlbs : integer
                  newoz  : integer
    Out:       :  None
    In/Out     :  None
Attributes Accessed
    read       :  None
    written    :  pounds
                  ounces
Pre-condition  :  newlbs >= 0 AND newoz >= 0 AND newoz <= 15
Post-condition :  pounds = newlbs AND ounces = newoz
Description    :  newlbs copied to pounds and newoz copied to ounces.
Outline Logic  :  Set pounds to newlbs
                  Set ounces to newoz
```

Activity 6.24

Create and test new classes for each of the following:

1.

Clock : Objects of this class are set to a specific time and made to increment by one second each time the *tick()* method is executed.

Attributes:

hours : integer
minutes : integer
seconds : integer

Operations:

create()
    Creates a *Clock* object with the time set to midnight (0,0,0)

create(h,m,s:integer)
    Creates an *Clock* object set to time *h:m:s*. If the parameters are invalid, the time is set to midnight.

setTime(h,m,s:integer)
    Sets time to *h:m:s*. If the parameters are invalid, the time is unchanged.

tick()
    Adds one second to the current time.

displayTime()
    Displays the values of the *hours, minutes* and *seconds* attributes using the format hh:mm:ss

getHours():integer
    Returns a copy of the *hours* attribute.

getMinutes():integer
    Returns a copy of the *minutes* attribute.

getSeconds():integer
    Returns a copy of the *seconds* attribute.

Activity 6.24 (continued)

2.

ChangeDispenser: This represents the type of mechanism found inside a drinks machine. Money is added to its store and change is returned. This class will accept the price of an item, insertion of coins and return a set of coins as change.

Attributes:

coins[2][5] : integer = {5,10,20,50,100}{3,3,3,3,0} -coin values:no. of coins in machine
moneyinserted : integer - all values are in pence
costofitem : integer

Operations:

create()
Creates an object with default number of coins(as shown above); *moneyinserted* = 0 and *costofitem*=0.

create(coincount[5]:integer)
Creates an object with number of coins specified by *coincount[]* parameter. If the parameter is invalid, then the default number of coins is used.

setCostOfItem(cost:integer)
Sets *costofitem* to *cost*. If *cost* is invalid no change is made.(0 to 500 and some multiple of the coin values)

addMoney(coin:integer)
Adds *coin* to *moneyinserted*. Adds 1 to appropriate element of *coins[][]*. If parameter does not match known coin values then exit routine.

refund():integer[]
Returns a set of coins to the value of *moneyinserted*. *moneyinserted* is reset to zero. Appropriate elements of *coins[1][]* are decremented to reflect the coins returned.

buy():integer[]
Returns change due after purchase. If *moneyinserted* is less than *costofitem* or *costofitem* is zero, then coins to the value of *moneyinserted* are returned.

isSufficient():boolean
Returns *true* if *moneyinserted* > *costofitem*, otherwise *false* is returned.

empty():integer[]
Returns the coins held in the machine. *coins[1][0..4]* are set to zero.

addChange(cash:integer[])
adds set of coins specified in *cash[]* to *coins[1][]*. If any elements of cash are invalid no coins of that particular value are added.

getCoins():integer[]
Returns the number of coins of each denomination held. The contents of *coins[][]* are unchanged.

getCoinValues:integer[]
Returns the denomination of each coin type.

getMoneyInserted():integer
Returns the value of *moneyinserted*.

getCostOfItem():integer
Returns the value of *costofitem*.

Summary

UML

- Private features are marked with a minus sign.
- Public features are marked with a plus sign.
- Class features are shown using an underline.
- The initial value of items can be shown in the diagram.
- Array attributes or parameters should be shown with square brackets and where appropriate these should enclose the number of elements.

Mini-specs

- Should include access modifier details.
- Should identify which attributes are accessed by the method.
- Attributes that will be changed should be marked as written.
- Attributes that are not changed should be marked as read.

Solutions

Activity 6.1

Characteristics
- length
- diameter
- colour of lead
- lead hardness

Operations:
- Sharpen
- Write

Characteristics
- day
- month
- year

Operations

setDate	Sets to a given date
getDate	Finds out what the date is currently set to
isLeapYear	Returns *true* if the date is in a leap year
DayOfWeek	Returns the name of the day of the week on which the date falls.

Activity 6.2

1.	Dogs	Class
2.	Lassie	Object
3.	Galaxy class starships	Class
4.	The USS Enterprise NCC-1701-D	Object
5.	Integers	Class
6.	The value 26	Object

Activity 6.3

Distance
yards : INTEGER feet : INTEGER inches : INTEGER
setDistance(y,f,i : INTEGER) convertToMetric():REAL getYards() :INTEGER getFeet() :INTEGER getInches() :INTEGER

Activity 6.4

No solution required.

Activity 6.5

```
w1.convertToMetric()
```

Activity 6.6

No solution required.

Activity 6.7

```
public class Distance
{
    private int yards;
    private int feet;
    private int inches;

    public void setDistance(int y, int f, int i)
    {
        if(y<0||f<0||f>2||i<0||i>11)
            return;
        yards = y;
        feet = f;
        inches = i;
    }

    public double convertToMetric()
    {
        return(yards*36+feet*12+inches)*0.0254;
    }

    public int getYards()
    {
        return yards;
    }

    public int getFeet()
    {
        return feet;
    }

    public int getInches()
    {
        return inches;
    }
}
```

```
import Distance;
import Input;

public class UsingDistances
{
    public static void main(String args[])
    {
        Distance d1 = new Distance();
        System.out.print("Enter yards: ");
        int y = Input.readInt();
        System.out.print("Enter feet: ");
        int f = Input.readInt();
        System.out.print("Enter inches: ");
        int i = Input.readInt();
        d1.setDistance(y,f,i);
        System.out.println("The distance "
            ↳+d1.getYards()+" yds "+d1.getFeet()
            ↳+" ft "+d1.getInches()+" in is "
            ↳+d1.convertToMetric()+" metres");
    }
}
```

Activity 6.8

No solution required.

Activity 6.9

No solution required.

Activity 6.10

No solution required.

Activity 6.11

```
import Distance;
import Input;
public class Act6_11
{
    public static void main(String args[])
    {
        Distance d1 = new Distance();
        Distance d2 = new Distance();
        //*** Read in First Distance ***
        System.out.print("Enter yards: ");
        int y = Input.readInt();
        System.out.print("Enter feet: ");
        int f = Input.readInt();
        System.out.print("Enter inches: ");
        int i = Input.readInt();
        d1.setDistance(f,y,i);
        //*** Read in second Distance ***
        System.out.print("Enter yards: ");
        y = Input.readInt();
        System.out.print("Enter feet: ");
        f = Input.readInt();
        System.out.print("Enter inches: ");
        i = Input.readInt();
        d2.setDistance(f,y,i);
        //*** Display larger Distance ***
        if(d1.convertToMetric() >
                    ↳d2.convertToMetric())
            System.out.println("Larger distance
                ↳is "+d1.getYards()+" yds "
                ↳+d1.getFeet()+" ft "
                ↳+d1.getInches()+" in");
        else
            System.out.println("Larger distance
                ↳is "+d2.getYards()+" yds "
                ↳+d2.getFeet()+" ft "
                ↳+d2.getInches()+" in");
    }
}
```

Activity 6.12

```
public class Distance
{
    private int yards;
    private int feet;
    private int inches;

    public void setDistance(int y, int f, int i)
    {
        if(y<0||f<0||f>2||i<0||i>11)
            return;
        yards = y;
        feet = f;
        inches = i;
    }

    public double convertToMetric()
    {
        return(yards*36+feet*12+inches)*0.0254;
    }

    public int getYards()
    {
        return yards;
    }

    public int getFeet()
    {
        return feet;
    }

    public int getInches()
    {
        return inches;
    }

    public void addToDistance(Distance d)
    {
        int totalinches =
            ↳(yards+d.yards)*36+(feet+d.feet)*12
            ↳+inches+d.inches;
        yards = totalinches/36;
        feet = totalinches%36/12;
        inches = totalinches%12;
    }
}
```

```
import Distance;
import Input;
public class Act6_12
{
    public static void main(String args[])
    {
        Distance d1 = new Distance();
        Distance d2 = new Distance();
        //*** Read in First Distance ***
        System.out.print("Enter yards: ");
        int y = Input.readInt();
        System.out.print("Enter feet: ");
        int f = Input.readInt();
        System.out.print("Enter inches: ");
        int i = Input.readInt();
        d1.setDistance(y,f,i);
        //*** Read in second Distance ***
        System.out.print("Enter yards: ");
        y = Input.readInt();
        System.out.print("Enter feet: ");
        f = Input.readInt();
        System.out.print("Enter inches: ");
        i = Input.readInt();
        d2.setDistance(y,f,i);
        //*** Add d2 to d1 ***
        d1.addToDistance(d2);
        //*** Display total distance ***
        System.out.println("Total distance
            ↳is "+d1.getYards()+" yds "
            ↳+d1.getFeet()+" ft "+d1.getInches()
            ↳+" in");
    }
}
```

Activity 6.13

The program uses the following logic:

```
Read a value for d1
Read a value for d2
Copy d1 to d2 using the line d2 = d1
Set d1 to 1yd 1ft 1in
Display d1 and d2
```

```
import Distance;
import Input;
public class Act6_13
{
    public static void main(String args[])
    {
        Distance d1 = new Distance();
        Distance d2 = new Distance();
        //*** Read in First Distance ***
        System.out.print("Enter yards: ");
        int y = Input.readInt();
        System.out.print("Enter feet: ");
        int f = Input.readInt();
        System.out.print("Enter inches: ");
        int i = Input.readInt();
        d1.setDistance(y,f,i);
        //*** Read in second Distance ***
        System.out.print("Enter yards: ");
        y = Input.readInt();
        System.out.print("Enter feet: ");
        f = Input.readInt();
        System.out.print("Enter inches: ");
        i = Input.readInt();
        d2.setDistance(y,f,i);
        //*** Attempt to copy d1 to d2 ***
        d2 = d1;
        //*** Change d1 only ***
        d1.setDistance(1,1,1);
        //*** Display d1 and d2 ***
        System.out.println("d1 is "+d1.getYards()
            ↳+" yds "+d1.getFeet()+" ft "
            ↳+d1.getInches()+" in");
        System.out.println("d2 is "+d2.getYards()
            ↳+" yds "+d2.getFeet()+" ft "
            ↳+d2.getInches()+" in");
    }
}
```

d1 and *d2* both display 1 yd 1ft 1in.

Activity 6.14

```
public class Distance
{
    private int yards;
    private int feet;
    private int inches;

    public void setDistance(int y,int f,int
i)
    {
        if(y<0||f<0||f>2||i<0||i>11)
            return;
        yards = y;
        feet = f;
        inches = i;
    }

    public void setDistance(Distance d)
    {
        yards = d.yards;
        feet = d.feet;
        inches = d.inches;
    }

    public double convertToMetric()
    {
        return(yards*36+feet*12+inches)*0.0254;
    }

    public int getYards()
    {
        return yards;
    }

    public int getFeet()
    {
        return feet;
    }

    public int getInches()
    {
        return inches;
    }

    public void addToDistance(Distance d)
    {
        int totalinches =
(yards+d.yards)*36+(feet+d.feet)*12+inche
s+d.inches;
        yards = totalinches/36;
        feet = totalinches%36/12;
        inches = totalinches%12;
    }
}

import Distance;
import Input;
public class Act6_14
{
    public static void main(String args[])
    {
        Distance d1 = new Distance();
        Distance d2 = new Distance();
        //*** Read in First Distance ***
        System.out.print("Enter yards: ");
        int y = Input.readInt();
        System.out.print("Enter feet: ");
        int f = Input.readInt();
        System.out.print("Enter inches: ");
        int i = Input.readInt();
        d1.setDistance(y,f,i);
        //*** Read in second Distance ***
        System.out.print("Enter yards: ");
        y = Input.readInt();
        System.out.print("Enter feet: ");
        f = Input.readInt();
        System.out.print("Enter inches: ");
        i = Input.readInt();
        d2.setDistance(y,f,i);
        //*** Attempt to copy d1 to d2 ***
        d2.setDistance(d1);
        //*** Change d1 only ***
        d1.setDistance(1,1,1);
        //*** Display d1 and d2 ***
        System.out.println("d1 is
"+d1.getYards()
            ↳+" yds "+d1.getFeet()+" ft "
            ↳+d1.getInches()+" in");
        System.out.println("d2 is
"+d2.getYards()
            ↳+" yds "+d2.getFeet()+" ft "
            ↳+d2.getInches()+" in");
    }
}
```

Activity 6.15

```
public class Distance
{
    private int yards;
    private int feet;
    private int inches;

    public void setDistance(int y, int f, int i)
    {
        if(y<0||f<0||f>2||i<0||i>11)
            return;
        yards = y;
        feet = f;
        inches = i;
    }

    public void setDistance(Distance d)
    {
        yards = d.yards;
        feet = d.feet;
        inches = d.inches;
    }

    public double convertToMetric()
    {
        return(yards*36+feet*12+inches)*0.0254;
    }

    public int getYards()
    {
        return yards;
    }

    public int getFeet()
    {
        return feet;
    }

    public int getInches()
    {
        return inches;
    }

    public void addToDistance(Distance d)
    {
        int totalinches =
            ↳(yards+d.yards)*36+(feet+d.feet)*12
            ↳+inches+d.inches;
        yards = totalinches/36;
        feet = totalinches%36/12;
        inches = totalinches%12;
    }

    public Distance sumDistances(Distance d)
    {
        Distance total = new Distance();
        int totalinches =
            ↳(yards+d.yards)*36+(feet+d.feet)*12
            ↳+inches+d.inches;
        total.yards = totalinches/36;
        total.feet = totalinches%36/12;
        total.inches = totalinches%12;
        return total;
    }
}

import Distance;
import Input;
public class Act6_15
{
    public static void main(String args[])
    {
        Distance d1 = new Distance();
        Distance d2 = new Distance();
        //*** Read in First Distance ***
        System.out.print("Enter yards: ");
        int y = Input.readInt();
        System.out.print("Enter feet: ");
        int f = Input.readInt();
        System.out.print("Enter inches: ");
        int i = Input.readInt();
        d1.setDistance(y,f,i);
        //*** Read in second Distance ***
        System.out.print("Enter yards: ");
        y = Input.readInt();
        System.out.print("Enter feet: ");
        f = Input.readInt();
        System.out.print("Enter inches: ");
        i = Input.readInt();
        d2.setDistance(y,f,i);
        //*** Add d1 + d2 giving d3 ***
        Distance d3 = d1.sumDistances(d2);
        //*** Display d1 and d2 ***
        System.out.print(d1.getYards()+" yds "
            ↳+d1.getFeet()+" ft "+d1.getInches()
            ↳+" in");
```

```
            System.out.print("+ "+d2.getYards()
                ⤷+" yds "+d2.getFeet()+" ft "
                ⤷+d2.getInches()+" in");
            System.out.print(" = "+d3.getYards()
                ⤷+" yds "+d3.getFeet()+" ft "
                ⤷+d3.getInches()+" in");
        }
}
```

Activity 6.16

The new version of *Distance* class is

```
public class Distance
{
    private int yards;
    private int feet;
    private int inches;

    public void setDistance(int y, int f, int i)
    {
        if(y<0||f<0||f>2||i<0||i>11)
            return;
        yards = y;
        feet = f;
        inches = i;
    }

    public void setDistance(Distance d)
    {
        yards = d.yards;
        feet = d.feet;
        inches = d.inches;
    }

    public double convertToMetric()
    {
        return(yards*36+feet*12+inches)*0.0254;
    }

    public int getYards()
    {
        return yards;
    }

    public int getFeet()
    {
        return feet;
    }

    public int getInches()
    {
        return inches;
    }

    public void addToDistance(Distance d)
    {
        int totalinches =
            ⤷(yards+d.yards)*36+(feet+d.feet)*12
            ⤷+inches+d.inches;
        yards = totalinches/36;
        feet = totalinches%36/12;
        inches = totalinches%12;
    }

    public Distance sumDistance(Distance d)
    {
        Distance total = new Distance();
        int totalinches =
            ⤷(yards+d.yards)*36+(feet+d.feet)*12
            ⤷+inches+d.inches;
        total.yards = totalinches/36;
        total.feet = totalinches%36/12;
        total.inches = totalinches%12;
        return total;
    }

    public boolean isLarger(Distance d)
    {
        if(convertToMetric()>d.convertToMetric())
            return true;
        else
            return false;
    }
}
```

The new version of the application program is

```
import Distance;
import Input;
public class Act6_16
{
    public static void main(String args[])
    {
        Distance d1 = new Distance();
        Distance d2 = new Distance();
        //*** Read in First Distance ***
        System.out.print("Enter yards: ");
        int y = Input.readInt();
        System.out.print("Enter feet: ");
        int f = Input.readInt();
        System.out.print("Enter inches: ");
        int i = Input.readInt();
        d1.setDistance(f,y,i);
        //*** Read in second Distance ***
        System.out.print("Enter yards: ");
        y = Input.readInt();
        System.out.print("Enter feet: ");
        f = Input.readInt();
        System.out.print("Enter inches: ");
        i = Input.readInt();
        d2.setDistance(f,y,i);
        //*** Display larger Distance ***
        if(d1.isLarger(d2))
            System.out.println("Larger distance
                ⤷is "+d1.getYards()+" yds "
                ⤷+d1.getFeet()+" ft "
                ⤷+d1.getInches()+" in");
        else
            System.out.println("Larger distance
                ⤷is "+d2.getYards()+" yds "
                ⤷+d2.getFeet()+" ft "
                ⤷+d2.getInches()+" in");
    }
}
```

Activity 6.17

The new version of *Distance* class is

```
public class Distance
{
    private int yards;
    private int feet;
    private int inches;

    public void setDistance(int y, int f, int i)
    {
        if(y<0||f<0||f>2||i<0||i>11)
            return;
        yards = y;
        feet = f;
        inches = i;
    }

    public void setDistance(Distance d)
    {
        yards = d.yards;
        feet = d.feet;
        inches = d.inches;
    }

    public double convertToMetric()
    {
        return(yards*36+feet*12+inches)*0.0254;
    }

    public int getYards()
    {
        return yards;
    }

    public int getFeet()
    {
        return feet;
    }

    public int getInches()
    {
        return inches;
    }

    public void addToDistance(Distance d)
    {
        int totalinches =
            ⤷(yards+d.yards)*36+(feet+d.feet)*12
            ⤷+inches+d.inches;
        yards = totalinches/36;
        feet = totalinches%36/12;
        inches = totalinches%12;
    }

    public Distance sumDistances(Distance d)
    {
        Distance total = new Distance();
        int totalinches =
            ⤷(yards+d.yards)*36+(feet+d.feet)*12
            ⤷+inches+d.inches;
```

```
            total.yards = totalinches/36;
            total.feet = totalinches%36/12;
            total.inches = totalinches%12;
            return total;
        }

        public boolean isLarger(Distance d)
        {
            if(convertToMetric()>d.convertToMetric())
                return true;
            else
                return false;
        }

        public Distance smaller(Distance d)
        {
            if(isLarger(d))
                return d;
            else
                return this;    }
    }
```

```
import Distance;
import Input;
public class Act6_17
{
    public static void main(String args[])
    {
        Distance d1 = new Distance();
        Distance d2 = new Distance();
        //*** Read in First Distance ***
        System.out.print("Enter yards: ");
        int y = Input.readInt();
        System.out.print("Enter feet: ");
        int f = Input.readInt();
        System.out.print("Enter inches: ");
        int i = Input.readInt();
        d1.setDistance(y,f,i);
        //*** Read in second Distance ***
        System.out.print("Enter yards: ");
        y = Input.readInt();
        System.out.print("Enter feet: ");
        f = Input.readInt();
        System.out.print("Enter inches: ");
        i = Input.readInt();
        d2.setDistance(y,f,i);
        //*** Get shorter***
        Distance d3 = new Distance();
        d3 = d1.smaller(d2);
        //*** Display d3 ***
        System.out.print(" Shorter distance is "
            ↳+d3.getYards()+" yds "+d3.getFeet()
            ↳+" ft "+d3.getInches()+" in");
    }
}
```

Activity 6.18

The routines to be added to the *Distance* class are shown below:

```
private int toInches()
{
    return (yards*36 + feet*12 + inches);
}


    public void addToDistance(Distance d)
    {
        int totalinches = toInches()
                                ↳+ d.toInches();
        yards = totalinches/36;
        feet = totalinches%36/12;
        inches = totalinches%12;
    }
```

Activity 6.19

The constructors for the *Distance* class are

```
public Distance()
{
    yards = 0;
    feet = 0;
    inches = 0;
};
```

```
public Distance(int y, int f, int i)
{
    if(y<0 || f<0 || f > 2 || i < 0 || i > 11)
    {
        yards = 0;
        feet = 0;
        inches = 0;
    }
    else
    {
        yards = y;
        feet = f;
        inches = i;
    };
}
```

Activity 6.20

```
public Distance (Distance d)
{
    this(d.yards, d.feet, d.inches);
}
```

Activity 6.21

The *Distance* class should now begin with the attributes set as follows:

```
public class Distance
{
    private int yards;
    private int feet;
    private int inches;

    public static final int metre = 39;
    public static final double centimetre = 0.3937;
```

Activity 6.22

Distance class now begins with the lines

```
public class Distance
{
    private int yards;
    private int feet;
    private int inches;

    public static final int metre = 39;
    public static final double centimetre = 0.3937;

    public static int count = 0;
```

Test program:

```
import Distance;
public class TestDistanceCount
{
    public static void main(String args[])
    {
        System.out.println("There are "
            ↳+Distance.count+" Distance objects");
        Distance d1 = new Distance(4,2,10);
        System.out.println("There are "
            ↳+Distance.count+" Distance objects");
        Distance d2 = new Distance(6,1,1);
        System.out.println("There are "
            ↳+Distance.count+" Distance objects");
    }
}
```

Activity 6.23

Distance now begins

```
public class Distance
{
    private int yards;
    private int feet;
    private int inches;

    public static final int metre = 39;
    public static final double centimetre = 0.3937;

    private static int count = 0;
```

```
    public static int getCount()
    {
        return count;
    }
```

The test program changes to

```
import Distance;
public class TestDistanceCount
{
    public static void main(String args[])
    {
        System.out.println("There are "
        ↳+Distance.getCount()+" Distance objects");
        Distance d1 = new Distance(4,2,10);
        System.out.println("There are "
        ↳+Distance.getCount()+" Distance objects");
        Distance d2 = new Distance(6,1,1);
        System.out.println("There are "
        ↳+Distance.getCount()+" Distance objects");
    }
}
```

Activity 6.24

```
1.

public class Clock
{
    private int hours;
    private int minutes;
    private int seconds;

    public Clock()
    {
        hours = 0;
        minutes = 0;
        seconds = 0;
    }

    public Clock(int h, int m, int s)
    {
        if(h>23||h<0||m<0||m>59||s<0||s>59)
        {
            hours = 0;
            minutes = 0;
            seconds = 0;
        }
        else
        {
            hours = h;
            minutes = m;
            seconds = s;
        }
    }

    public void setTime(int h, int m, int s)
    {
        if(h>23||h<0||m<0||m>59||s<0||s>59)
            return;
        hours = h;
        minutes = m;
        seconds = s;
    }

    public void tick()
    {
        int totalsecs = hours*3600+minutes*60
                    ↳+seconds + 1;
        hours = (totalsecs /3600)%24;
        minutes = (totalsecs % 3600 / 60);
        seconds = totalsecs % 60;
    }

    public void displayTime()
    {
        System.out.println(hours+":"+minutes+":"
            ↳+seconds);
    }

    public int getHours()
    {
        return hours;
    }

    public int getMinutes()
    {
        return minutes;
    }

    public int getSeconds()
    {
        return seconds;
    }
}

import Clock;
public class TestingClock
{
    public static void main(String args[])
    {
        Clock c1=new Clock(1,2,3);
        c1.displayTime();
        c1.tick();
        System.out.println(c1.getHours()+":"
        ↳+c1.getMinutes()+":"+c1.getSeconds());
        c1.setTime(2,3,4);
        c1.displayTime();
    }
}

2.

public class ChangeDispenser
{
    private int coins[][] =
                ↳{{5,10,20,50,100},{3,3,3,3,0}};
    private int moneyinserted;
    private int costofitem;

    public ChangeDispenser(){};

    public ChangeDispenser(int coincount[])
    {
        if(coincount.length != coins[1].length)
            return;
        for(int c = 0; c < coins[1].length; c++)
            coins[1][c]=coincount[c];
    }

    public void setCostOfItem(int cost)
    {
        if(cost < 0 || cost > 500
                ↳|| cost % coins[0][0] != 0)
            return;
        costofitem = cost;
    }

    private int matchCoin(int coin)
    {
        for(int c = 0; c < coins[0].length; c++)
            if (coin == coins[0][c])
                return c;
        return -1;
    }

    public void addMoney(int coin)
    {
        int foundat = matchCoin(coin);
        if (foundat == -1)
            return;
        coins[1][foundat]++;
        moneyinserted+=coin;
    }


    public int[] refund()
    {
        int moneyreturned[] = new int[5];
        int insertedcopy = moneyinserted;
        int position = coins[0].length-1;
        while (insertedcopy!=0 && position>=0)
        {
            moneyreturned[position] =
            ↳insertedcopy / coins[0][position];
            if (coins[1][position] <
                ↳moneyreturned[position])
                moneyreturned[position] =
                ↳coins[1][position];
            insertedcopy -=
                ↳moneyreturned[position]*
                ↳coins[0][position];
            coins[1][position] -=
                ↳moneyreturned[position];
            position--;
        }
        moneyinserted = 0;
        return moneyreturned;
    }

    public int[] buy()
    {
        if(!isSufficient())
            return refund();
        moneyinserted -=costofitem;
        int result[]= refund();
        moneyinserted = 0;
        return result;
    }
```

```
    public boolean isSufficient()
    {
        return (moneyinserted >= costofitem);
    }

    public int[] empty()
    {
        int copy[] = new int[coins[1].length];
        for(int c = 0; c < copy.length; c++)
        {
            copy[c] = coins[1][c];
            coins[1][c]=0;
        }
        return copy;
    }

    public void addChange(int cash[])
    {
        if(cash.length != coins[1].length)
            return;
        for(int c = 0; c < cash.length; c++)
            coins[1][c]+=cash[c];
    }

    public int[] getCoins()
    {
        int coinscopy[]=new int[coins[1].length];
        for(int c = 0; c < coinscopy.length; c++)
            coinscopy[c] = coins[1][c];
        return coinscopy;
    }

    public int[] getCoinValues()
    {
        int coinscopy[]=new int[coins[0].length];
        for(int c = 0; c < coinscopy.length; c++)
            coinscopy[c] = coins[0][c];
        return coinscopy;
    }

    public int getMoneyInserted()
    {
        return moneyinserted;
    }

    public int getCostOfItem()
    {
        return costofitem;
    }
}

import ChangeDispenser;
import Input;
public class UsingChangeDispenser
{
    public static void main(String args[])
    {
        int op;
        ChangeDispenser cd = new ChangeDispenser();
        do
        {
            op = displayMenu();
            executeOption(op,cd);
        }
        while (op != 8);
    }

    public static int displayMenu()
    {
        System.out.println("\n\n Menu \n\n");
        System.out.println("1  - SetCost");
        System.out.println("2  - Add Money");
        System.out.println("3  - refund");
        System.out.println("4  - buy");
        System.out.println("5  - empty");
        System.out.println("6  - Add Change");
        System.out.println("7  - getCoins");
        System.out.println("8  - QUIT");

        System.out.print("Enter option(1-8): ");
        int op = Input.readInt();
        return op;
    }

    public static void executeOption(int op,
        ↳ChangeDispenser cd)
    {
        int money[], denom[];
        switch(op)
        {
            case 1:
                System.out.print("Enter cost of
                    ↳item(in pence): ");
                int cost = Input.readInt();
                cd.setCostOfItem(cost);
                break;
            case 2:
                System.out.print("Insert coins
                    ↳(value in pence)");
                System.out.println("Enter -1
                    ↳after last coin");
                System.out.print("Coin value: ");
                int coin = Input.readInt();
                while(coin != -1)
                {
                    cd.addMoney(coin);
                    System.out.print("Coin
                        ↳value: ");
                    coin = Input.readInt();
                }
                break;
            case 3:
                System.out.println("Your refund
                    ↳is "+cd.getMoneyInserted());
                System.out.println("Coins returned");
                money=cd.refund();
                denom=cd.getCoinValues();
                for(int c = 0;c < money.length;c++)
                    if(money[c] > 0)
                        System.out.println(money[c]
                        ↳+" "+denom[c]+"p coins");
                break;
            case 4:
                System.out.println("Your item
                ↳cost " +cd.getCostOfItem()+"p");
                System.out.println("Your inserted "
                ↳+cd.getMoneyInserted()+"p");
                System.out.println("Coins returned");
                money=cd.buy();
                denom=cd.getCoinValues();
                for(int c = 0;c < money.length;c++)
                    if(money[c] > 0)
                        System.out.println(money[c]
                        ↳+" "+denom[c]+"p coins");
                break;
            case 5:
                System.out.println("The machine
                    ↳contained ");
                money=cd.empty();
                denom=cd.getCoinValues();
                for(int c = 0;c < money.length;c++)
                    System.out.println(money[c]+
                    ↳" "+denom[c]+"p coins");
                break;
            case 6:
                denom = cd.getCoinValues();
                money = new int[denom.length];
                for(int j = 0;j < denom.length;j++)
                {

                    System.out.print("How many "
                    ↳+denom[j]+"p coins? ");
                    money[j] = Input.readInt();
                }
                cd.addChange(money);
                break;
            case 7:
                System.out.println("The machine
                ↳contains ");
                money=cd.getCoins();
                denom=cd.getCoinValues();
                for(int c = 0;c < money.length;c++)
                    System.out.println(money[c]
                    ↳+" "+denom[c]+"p coins");
                break;
            case 8:
                System.out.println("Program
                ↳terminated");
        }
    }
}
```

CHAPTER 7
Class Relationships

This chapter covers the following topics:

Implementing Derived Classes

Inheritance

Parameters and Descendant Classes

Polymorphism

Protected Features

The Object Class

Inheritance

Relationships

Introduction

We all have ancestors. From these ancestors we have inherited our features and basic abilities through our DNA. Although this DNA comes from both our parents, in asexual species the DNA is an exact copy of the parent. Nevertheless, even asexual species can adapt and modify inherited traits from generation to generation.

Inheriting what has gone before and adapting it to the current environment is not limited to the animal kingdom; for example, widescreen high-definition stereo television also has an ancestry which can be traced through radio; black-and-white TV; colour TV; stereo, colour TV; and 16:9 widescreen TV. At each step in the process the features of its immediate predecessor were incorporated in the latest advance, but these were then added to and modified where necessary to create the new product.

This approach of building on what has gone before is one of the main goals of object-oriented programming. By adopting this technique it is hoped that classes can be reused in other applications, or modified to create new classes with a minimum amount of development time and a reduction in errors.

Class Relationships

If we were to create UML class diagrams for radio and black-and-white television we might come up with the diagrams shown in FIG-7.1

FIG-7.1

Radio and B&W TV Classes

The diagrams have been kept brief, hence, types and parameters are omitted.

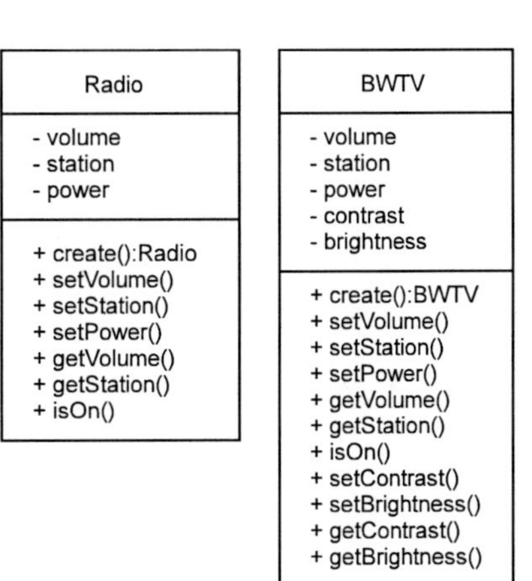

We can see that the television class (BWTV) is simply an extension of the *Radio* class with extra attributes and operations. That isn't surprising since, as we have already inferred, television is simply a radio with pictures.

UML uses a diagram somewhat akin to a family tree, to represent this relationship (see FIG-7.2).

The diagram with the arrowed line shows that *BWTV* is a class which is descended from the *Radio* class. Notice also that only the features new to the *BWTV* class are included in its rectangle. This is because, in object-oriented design, any new class is automatically assumed to have inherited all its parent's features. The new class can then have additional features added and only these new features are shown in the diagram.

FIG-7.2

A Class Relationship Diagram

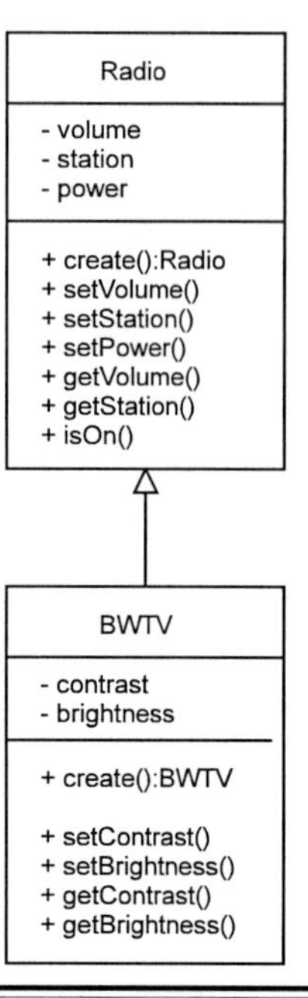

> **Activity 7.1**
>
> From the diagram above, list the attributes of the *BWTV* class.

If these two classes were to become part of a computer program (perhaps as part of a simulation game), then the traditional program approach would require each to be coded separately. Since both items have many things in common, the resulting code would contain a great deal of duplication. However, using an object-oriented approach, this duplication can be avoided.

There are a few terms to note from FIG-7.2:

- The terms **base class**, **superclass** or **parent class** are used to describe the class from which another class is derived. In the diagram above, Radio is the super class.

Java uses the terms *superclass* and *subclass.*

- The terms **derived class**, **subclass** or **child class** are used to describe a descendant class.

There are no restrictions on the number of generations of derived classes that may be created or the number of child classes that can be derived from a single class.

> **Activity 7.2**
>
> Draw the UML diagram above.
>
> Add a new class, *ColourTV*, which is derived from *BWTV* class.
>
> The new class has the attributes:
> *volume, station, power, contrast, brightness,* and *colour intensity*
> It has the same operations as the *BWTV* class but adds *setColourIntensity()* and *getColourIntensity()* operations.

balance sets the relative difference in volume between the left and right loudspeakers.

> **Activity 7.3**
>
> Add a fourth class to your diagram: *StereoRadio.*
> This class is derived from the *Radio* class but has an additional *balance* attribute and *setBalance()* and *getBalance()* methods.

Implementing Derived Classes

In the previous chapter we created a *Clock* class. The code for the class is given below:

```
public class Clock
{
    private int hours;
    private int minutes;
    private int seconds;

    public Clock()
    {
            hours = 0;
            minutes = 0;
            seconds = 0;
    }

    public Clock(int h, int m, int s)
    {
        if(h < 0 || h > 23 || m < 0 || m > 59 || s < 0 || s > 59)
        {
            hours = 0;
            minutes = 0;
            seconds = 0;
        }
        else
        {
            hours = h;
            minutes = m;
            seconds = s;
        }
    }

    public void setTime(int h, int m, int s)
    {
        if(h > 23 || h < 0 || m < 0 || m > 59 || s < 0 || s > 59)
            return;
        hours = h;
        minutes = m;
        seconds = s;
    }

    public int getHours()
    {
        return hours;
    }

    public int getMinutes()
    {
        return minutes;
    }

    public int getSeconds()
    {
        return seconds;
    }

    public void tick()
    {
        int totalsecs = hours *3600 + minutes * 60 + seconds + 1;
        hours = (totalsecs /3600)%24;
```

```
        minutes = (totalsecs % 3600 / 60);
        seconds = totalsecs % 60;
    }

    public void displayTime()
    {
        System.out.println(hours+":"+minutes+":"+seconds);
    }
}
```

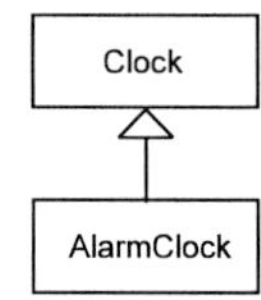

If we assume we now require a new class (*AlarmClock*) which displays an alarm message whenever a set time is reached, then we could create this new class by making it a descendant of the original *Clock* class. To do this, our program would begin with the statements

```
//import Clock;
public class AlarmClock extends Clock
```

This imports the existing *Clock* class and then defines *AlarmClock* as a descendant of *Clock* (Java uses the term `extends` to achieve this).

As a subclass of *Clock, AlarmClock* inherits all the features of *Clock*. This means our code only requires to specify the additional features of the new class. We need new attributes to record the time at which the alarm is to go off:

```
//import Clock;

public class AlarmClock extends Clock
{
    private int ahours;
    private int aminutes;
    private int aseconds;
```

We also need new methods to set and get these new attributes:

```
public void setAlarm(int h, int m, int s)
{
    if(h < 0 || h > 23 || m < 0 || m > 59 || s < 0 || s > 59)
        return;
    ahours = h;
    aminutes = m;
    aseconds = s;
}

public int getAlarmHours()
{
    return ahours;
}

public int getAlarmMinutes()
{
    return aminutes;
}

public int getAlarmSeconds()
{
    return aseconds;
}
```

Finally, a new operation to check if the actual time and alarm activation time are equal:

```
public boolean isAlarmTime()
{
    if(hours==ahours && minutes==aminutes && seconds==aseconds)
        return true;
    else
        return false;
}
```

> **Activity 7.4**
>
> Type in the code for the *AlarmClock* class and attempt to compile it.

If we try compiling this, we'll get error messages such as:

```
AlarmClock.java:96: Undefined variable: hours
```

The reason for this is that *hours, minutes* and *seconds* are declared as private within the superclass, *Clock*. We've already seen that an attribute that is declared as private cannot be accessed by an application program which defines objects of that class. Now a further restriction has become apparent: private attributes inherited by a descendent class cannot be accessed from the methods added to that new class. To get round this we could rewrite *isAlarmTime()* using *getHours(), getMinutes()* and *getSeconds()*:

```
public boolean isAlarmTime()
{
    if(getHours() == ahours && getMinutes() == aminutes
    ↳&& getSeconds() == aseconds)
        return true;
    else
        return false;
}
```

Protected Attributes

Alternatively, since we have access to the *Clock* source code, we could replace the term `private` with the keyword `protected`.

An attribute labelled as `protected` is still inaccessible to the application programs that create objects of that class, but descendent classes have free access. Hence, if we re-code the *Clock* class to begin

In UML class diagrams a protected feature is marked with a hash (#) symbol.

```
public class Clock
{
    protected int hours;
    protected int minutes;
    protected int seconds;
                  .
                  .
```

we can use our original version *isAlarmTime()*.

> **Activity 7.5**
>
> Load your original *Clock* class file.
> Change the attributes of the class from `private` to `protected`.
> Recompile the class.
> Mark the attributes of the *AlarmClock* class as `protected`.
> Recompile the *AlarmClock* class.

Constructors in Descendant Classes

The one feature that a class does not inherit from its parent class is its constructor. After all, a constructor must have the same name as the class to which it belongs, so it would not be appropriate for *AlarmClock* to inherit a constructor called *Clock()*.

So, we could include a constructor for *AlarmClock* which contains the code:

```
public AlarmClock(int h, int m, int s, int ah, int am, int as)
{
    if(h<0||h>23||m<0||m>59||s<0||s>59||ah<0||ah>23||am<0
    ↳||am>59||as<0||as>59)
    {
        hours = 0;
        minutes = 0;
        seconds = 0;
        ahours = 0;
        aminutes = 0;
        aseconds = 0;
    }
    else
    {
        hours = h;
        minutes = m;
        seconds = s;
        ahours = ah;
        aminutes = am;
        aseconds = as;
    }
}
```

This code assumes we have declared *hours, minutes* and *seconds* as protected within the *Clock* class.

Calling the Base Class Constructor

If you compare the code for the *Clock* class constructor with that of the *AlarmClock*'s constructor, you'll see that both contain similar code for assigning values to *hours, minutes* and *seconds.*

We can save many lines of coding within the *AlarmClock* constructor by getting it to execute the code of the *Clock* constructor. Luckily, this is possible. A descendant class can execute its parent's constructor within its own constructor by using the instruction `super()`. The term used refers to the fact that a parent class is also known as the **superclass**, while the descendant class is called the **subclass**.

So we might try rewriting the *AlarmClock* constructor as:

```
public AlarmClock(int h, int m, int s, int ah, int am, int as)
    {
        if(h<0||h>23||m<0||m>59||s<0||s>59||ah<0||ah>23||am<0
        ↳||am>59||as<0||as>59)
        {
            super(0,0,0);
            ahours = 0;
            aminutes = 0;
            aseconds = 0;
        }
        else
        {
            super(h,m,s);
            ahours = ah;
            aminutes = am;
            aseconds = as;
        }
    }
```

Call to the base class's constructor

Call to the base class's constructor

Unfortunately, this code won't work! Java insists that, when a call is made to the constructor in the superclass, it appears as the first line in the new constructor. However, we could recode the constructor as:

```
public AlarmClock(int h, int m, int s, int ah, int am, int as)
{
    super(h,m,s);
    if(ah < 0 || ah > 23 || am < 0 || am > 59 || as < 0 || as>59)
    {
        ahours = 0;
        aminutes = 0;
        aseconds = 0;
```

Call to the base class's constructor

```
        }
        else
        {
            ahours = ah;
            aminutes = am;
            aseconds = as;
        }
    }
```

In fact, the constructor of a new class MUST call the constructor of its parent class Where the parent class has a zero-argument constructor, that constructor will be called automatically, but when this is not the case, there must be an explicit call (using *super()*) to the parent constructor as the first line in the constructor of the new class.

Activity 7.6

Add the constructor given above to the *AlarmClock* class and recompile your file.

Write an application program which uses the following logic:

```
Create an alarm clock set to 12:29:59
Set the alarmTime to 12:30:00
Add 1 second to the time (Using tick())
IF alarm time reached THEN
    Display "Time to get up "
ENDIF
```

Overriding Methods

Of course, there will be times when an inherited method is not appropriate for a new class. For example, looking at the code for *tick()*:

```
public void tick()
{
    int totalsecs = hours *3600 + minutes * 60 + seconds + 1;
    hours = (totalsecs /3600)%24;
    minutes = (totalsecs % 3600 / 60);
    seconds = totalsecs % 60;
}
```

We can see that it does not react to reaching the specified alarm time. Because of this, the solution to Activity 7.6 contained code such as:

```
ac.tick();
if (ac.isAlarmTime())
    System.out.println("Time to get up");
```

However, it might suit our purposes if this message was displayed by *tick()* itself when the appropriate time was reached.

To achieve this, the *AlarmClock* class needs a new version of the *tick()* method. To create the new routine, we simply include the code for the new method within the *AlarmClock* class.

This is known as **overriding** the inherited method. To overwrite an inherited method the new version must have the same name and parameters as the original inherited method.

The code is:

```
public void tick()
{
    int totalsecs = hours *3600 + minutes * 60 + seconds + 1;
    hours = (totalsecs / 3600) % 24;
    minutes = (totalsecs % 3600 / 60);
    seconds = totalsecs % 60;
    if (isAlarmTime())
        System.out.println("Time to get up");
}
```

Notice, as in the constructor, we're using code that duplicates all the lines given in the original version of *tick()*. Again, we can get the new routine to call the old one and save the extra typing and testing. This time, however, the line required to do this is

```
super.tick();
```

which executes the *tick()* method used in the superclass.

This gives us the final code for the new version of *tick()* in the *AlarmClock* class:

```
public void tick()
{
    super.tick();
    if(isAlarmTime())
        System.out.println("Time to get up");
}
```

Activity 7.7

Add the overridden version of *tick()* to *AlarmClock* and test the class.

If the parameters of the new method were different, then the method would have been overloaded, giving multiple versions of *tick()* within the *AlarmClock* class. So, the *AlarmClock* version of *tick()* is coded as

```
public void tick(String s)
{
    super.tick();
    if(isAlarmTime())
        System.out.println(s);
}
```

which allows the message displayed to be passed as a parameter, then we would have two versions of *tick()* within the *AlarmClock* class; the one inherited from *Clock* (which takes no parameters) and this new one defined within *AlarmClock* (which takes a *String* parameter).

Activity 7.8

Create a new class, *CountdownClock*, which is a descendant of the *Clock* class, but differs from that class in that the *tick()* method reduces the time by one second.

Add two constructors to the class. The first of these should be a zero-argument constructor which sets the time to midnight; the second has three parameters representing the time (hours, minutes and seconds) to which the clock is to be set.

Compile the file.

Polymorphism

> **Activity 7.9**
>
> Create an application program containing both a *Clock* object and a *CountdownClock* object.
>
> Set both objects to the time 12:00:00.
>
> Execute the *tick()* methods of both objects and display the time of each.

From the results of Activity 7.9 we can see that each object executes its own version of *tick()*. So the *Clock* object moves on to 12:00:01 while the *CountdownClock* object moves back to 11:59:59. This ability to execute the version of a routine appropriate to the type of object involved is known as **polymorphism** and, as we will see, is a cornerstone of object-oriented programming.

With Overridden Methods

Descendant classes have another unexpected feature; when we define a class reference variable, as in the statement

```
Clock cl;
```

we can use that variable to reference an object of the stated class OR ANY DESCENDANT CLASS. This last statement is important since it means, as well as being able to write

```
cl = new Clock(1,2,3);
```

it is equally valid to write

```
cl = new AlarmClock(1,2,3,1,2,4)
```

and *cl* will quite happily reference an *AlarmClock* object.

What's more, if we use a statement such as

```
cl.tick();
```

Java will execute the version of *tick()* appropriate to the actual class of object that *cl* is referencing. Hence, the combination

```
Clock cl = new Clock(1,2,3);
cl.tick();
```

will execute the code

The version of *tick()* defined in the *Clock* class.

```
public void tick()
{
    int totalsecs = hours *3600 + minutes * 60 + seconds + 1;
    hours = (totalsecs /3600)%24;
    minutes = (totalsecs % 3600 / 60);
    seconds = totalsecs % 60;
}
```

while the lines

```
Clock cl = new AlarmClock(1,2,3,1,2,4);
cl.tick();
```

will execute

The version of *tick()* defined in the *AlarmClock* class.

```
public void tick()
{
    super.tick();
    if (isAlarmTime())
        System.out.println("Time to get up");
}
```

This ability to call the correct method, depending on the object's class, is known as **polymorphism**.

> **Activity 7.10**
>
> Create a new test program for the *Clock* classes. Within *main()* begin with the line
>
> ```
> Clock time;
> ```
>
> and then make this variable reference an *AlarmClock* object:
>
> ```
> time = new AlarmClock(1,2,3,1,2,4);
> ```
>
> and check that the *AlarmClock* version of *tick()* is executed by the statement
>
> ```
> time.tick()
> ```
>
> Modify the program to check that the *CountdownClock* version of *tick()* is executed when *time* references a *CountdownClock* object.

With Inherited Routines

The *Clock* class isn't very useful yet; it would take anyone using an object of the class some trouble to get a clock on the screen that updated each second. The *Clock* class designer could make life easier for the application programmer by adding a *runTime()* method to the class that actually showed the changing time.

We might code the new routine as:

```
public void runTime(int v)
{
    for(int c = 0; c<=v; c++)
    {
        System.out.print(hours+":"+minutes+":"+seconds+"    \r");
        tick();
    }
}
```

The routine is designed to display the clock time as it moves through *v* seconds. Actually, if we leave the code like this, the `for` loop will execute so quickly that we won't see the changing time. So, to overcome this, we need to add some code just to keep the processor busy for approximately one second between ticks. The second version of the routine does this by executing thousands of meaningless calculations:

```
public void runTime(int v)
{
    double x;
    for(int c = 0; c<=v; c++)
    {
        System.out.print(hours+":"+minutes+":"+seconds+"    \r");
        tick();
        //***Do something that takes about 1 second ***
```

```
            for(int k=0; k<500000; k++)
                x = Math.sin(k/1000)/Math.tan(k/1000);
        }
    }
```

Notice that the new routine calls *tick()*. Now if we create a *Clock* class object in our program, then when *main()* contains the lines

```
Clock time = new Clock(1,2,3);
time.runTime(20);
```

we should see the clock count though the time interval 1:2:3 to 1:2:22.

Activity 7.11

Create a new application program using the *Clock* reference variable *time*. Make *time* reference a *Clock* object and call *runTime()* to display for 20 seconds.

Now, change *time* to reference a *CountdownClock* object and execute the program again.

What effect does this have on the statement

`time.runTime(20);` ?

This is polymorphism at work again. The *runTime()* routine is smart enough to use the version of *tick()* belonging to the current object's class. This means that the line

```
time.runTime(20);
```

makes the clock count forwards when *time* references a *Clock* object, but backwards when a *CountdownClock* object is involved.

Limitations

However, there are limitations in making an object variable reference a descendant class; methods not named in the original class cannot be accessed directly.

Hence, having written

```
Clock cl = new AlarmClock(1,2,3,1,2,4);
```

the term

```
cl.getAlarmHours()
```

is invalid because *getAlarmHours()* is not defined in the *Clock* class which *cl* is primarily designed to reference. To access methods named for the first time in the *AlarmClock* class, we need to cast *cl* to a *AlarmClock* type using the expression

```
((AlarmClock)cl).getAlarmHours()
```

This allows code such as:

```
System.out.println("Alarm hour is" +
    ((AlarmClock)cl).getAlarmHours());
```

Activity 7.12

If a program contains the line

```
Clock cl = new CountdownClock(1,2,3);
```

what methods of the *CountdownClock* class would necessitate the casting of *cl* to a *CountdownClock* object?

There are some situations where the programmer might not know the type of object that is being referenced. For example, the program in LISTING-7.1 has the following logic:

```
Ask user what type of clock is to be created
Create requested clock type
Display time
Make clock tick for 1 second
Display clock time
```

LISTING-7.1

Referencing Descendant Objects

Note that *c1* is initially set to `null` to show that it does not reference any object at the start of the program.

```
import Input;
import Clock;
import AlarmClock;
import CountdownClock;

public class TestingClocks
{
  public static void main(String args[])
  {
      Clock c1=null;
      System.out.println("Which type of clock?");
      System.out.println("1  - Clock");
      System.out.println("2  - AlarmClock");
      System.out.println("3  - CountdownClock");
      System.out.print("Enter choice (1,2,3): ");
      int choice = Input.readInt();
      switch(choice)
      {
          case 1:
              c1 = new Clock(1,2,3);
              break;
          case 2:
              c1 = new AlarmClock(1,2,3,4,5,6);
              break;
          case 3:
              c1 = new CountdownClock(1,2,3);
              break;
      }
      c1.displayTime();
      c1.tick();
      c1.displayTime();
  }
}
```

Activity 7.13

Type in and run the program in LISTING-7.1

As you can see, the programmer cannot know which type of object will be created. For the most part that doesn't matter since the correct version of *tick()* will be automatically chosen and executed. But what if we wanted to allow the user to set the alarm time when an *AlarmClock* object is created?

Since *setAlarm()* is a method only defined within the *AlarmClock* class we need to add the following logic to our program:

```
IF alarm clock created THEN
    Set Alarm time
ENDIF
```

Java allows us to find out exactly the type of object referenced by using the keyword

```
instanceof
```

in a Boolean expression. This gives us the ability to check for an alarm clock with the statement

```
if(c1 instanceof AlarmClock)
```

If the result is true, then we can cast *c1* to an *AlarmClock* reference type and access the *setAlarm()* method:

```
if(c1 instanceof AlarmClock)
    ((AlarmClock)c1).setAlarm(1,1,1);
```

Activity 7.14

Modify the program you created in Activity 7.13 so that the user can choose the alarm time if an alarm clock is created..

Insert your code after the end of the `switch` statement.

The `instanceof` test will give a compilation error if you test for a class that is not the original class stated or a descendant class. For example, if *c1* is originally defined as

```
Clock c1;
```

then we can use `instanceof` to test for *Clock, AlarmClock* or *CountdownClock* but not for *Weight*, *Distance* or *Input.*

Parameters and Descendant Classes

As demonstrated above, we can create a reference variable designed to contain the address of an object of one class and end up using it to reference an object of a descendant class. The same rules apply to parameters; if a routine begins with the heading

```
public void myfunction(Clock c)
```

then it can be called using a *Clock* object as the actual parameter or an object from any descendant class. For example, assuming the declarations

```
Clock c1 = new Clock(1,2,3);
CountdownClock c2 = new CountdownClock(1,2,3);
AlarmClock c3 = new AlarmClock(1,2,3,4,5,6);
```

each of the following expressions would be valid as part of a statement:

```
myfunction(c1)
myfunction(c2)
myfunction(c3)
```

Within the routine itself the `instanceof` keyword could be used, where necessary to discover the type of object actually passed.

The Object Class

We've seen that a new class can inherit features from a super class. This whole process can be extended so that we have a whole family of classes, each descendant from some other class.

Of course, some class has to start off this whole process and it will have no ancestor class. For example, we might reasonably assume that the *Weight*, *Distance* and *Clock* classes are such basic classes since we did not define them as extending any existing class.

Activity 7.15

Type in and run the following program:

```
import Distance;

public class TestInherited
{
    public static void main(String args[])
    {
        Distance d1 = new Distance(1,2,3);
        System.out.println(d1.toString())
    }
}
```

So where did this *toString()* method come from?

In Java, all classes that are not explicitly stated as extending some existing class are assumed to be descendants of the *Object* class. This means that the *Object* class's features are inherited by every class in Java. The two operations of the *Object* class that are most often used have the headings

```
public String toString();
public boolean equals(Object obj);
```

public String toString()

The method *toString()* is designed to be used in descendant classes to return a string representing the value of the object to which it is attached. The *toString()* method defined by class *Object* returns a string consisting of the name of the class of which the object is an instance, an'@' character, and an unsigned hexadecimal value. You can see this format in the output produced by Activity 7.15.

public boolean equals(Object obj)

This method indicates whether some other object is "equal to" this one. Don't be fooled by the parameter to this method - remember, in practice, any class which is descendant from the specified class can be used instead.

The *equals()* method defined by class *Object* implements returns true only if the current object and *obj* have the same reference address (i.e. are the same object). However, *equals()* should be overridden in every new class created so that it tests to check the equality of relevant attributes. For example, in the *Clock* class we could override *equals()* to check if the hours, minutes and seconds properties of two *Clock* objects are equal.

toString() and equals() in the Weight Class

To make use of the *toString()* and *equals()* inherited by *Weight* class, we'll need to override them. For example, it would be useful if the *toString()* method returned a string of the form

```
x lbs y oz
```

To do this the *Weight*'s *toString()* method is coded as

```
public String toString()
{
    return (pounds+" lbs "+ounces+" oz");
}
```

equals(), on the other hand, should return *true* if two weights have the same numeric value.

The code for this is:

```
public boolean equals(Object obj)
{
    if (toOunces() == ((Weight)obj).toOunces())
        return true;
    else
        return false;
}
```

Notice that the parameter type must remain as *Object* class otherwise we would not be overriding the inherited method.

Within the code, we need to cast the parameter to its actual class in order to access the *toOunces()* method of the *Weight* class.

We can test our changes with the following code:

```
Weight w = new Weight(3,10);
Weight w2 = new Weight (3,10);
System.out.println(w.toString());
if (w.equals(w2))
    System.out.println("Equal");
else
    System.out.println("Not equal");
```

> **Activity 7.16**
>
> Add a *toString()* and *equals()* to the *Clock* class.
>
> Modify the program from Activity 7.14 so that *toString()* is used to display the clock time.

If you're using the *toString()* method in a `System.out.println()` statement, you need only give the name of the object involved and the *toString()* method will be executed automatically. So, although we may write

```
System.out.println(time.toString());
                              ↳//time references a Clock object
```

it's also valid to write only

```
System.out.println(time);
```

and still achieve the same effect.

Input and Output Operations

You may have noticed that, with one exception, none of the classes we have created contain operations to read information from the keyboard or display information on the screen. The reason for this is simply that such routines are of very limited use. If we add a *readWeight()* method to the *Weight* class that reads the value for pounds and ounces from the keyboard, it will be of little use to the application programmer if he needs to read the information from a disk file or from an item selected in a menu. An output method that displays on the screen is no use if we want to output to a printer or a file.

So our alternative, as the class designer is to produce set and get methods which the application programmer can use as required.

The one exception to this has been the *displayTime()* method defined in the *Clock* class. But this can be removed without affecting the usability of the class since the application programmer can still write

```
System.out.println(c1.getHours()+":"+c1.getMinutes()+":"
    ↳+c1.getSeconds());
```

or

```
System.out.println(c1.toString());
```

Of course, there are exceptions to this rule. For example, a set of graphics classes designed to create circles, polygons, lines etc. will require a method to display the shape on the screen.

Static Attributes and Derived Classes

We already know that a `static` attribute of a class has only one occurrence irrespective of the number of objects of that class created.

This rule extends to classes derived from a class containing a `static` attribute. Hence, if *Clock* were to contain a `static` attribute, there would only be one occurrence of this attribute, no matter how many *Clock, AlarmClock* or *CountdownClock* objects are defined.

Summary

- **New classes can be created as descendants** of existing classes.
- **Superclass** is the term used for the parent class.
- **Subclass** is the term used for the descendant class.
- **A subclass inherits** all the features of its superclass.

- **Only constructors are not inherited**
- **Private features of the superclass** cannot be accessed in the subclass.
- **Protected features of a superclass** can be accessed in the subclass.
- **Constructors in the subclass** must call the constructor of the superclass.
- **Superclass constructor calls are automatic if** the superclass's constructor has no arguments.
- `super()` makes an explicit call to a superclass's constructor.
- **Inherited methods can be overridden** in the subclass.
- **Overridden methods** must have the same heading as the original, inherited method.
- **A reference variable** can hold the address of an object from the specified class or any descendant class.
- **The correct version of an overridden routine** is automatically selected.
- **When a reference variable contains the address of a descendant class object**, only methods named in the original class can be accessed.
- **When a referencing a subclass,** methods not named in the reference variable's class can be accessed by casting the reference variable to the appropriate class.
- **The** `instanceof` **keyword** returns true if a reference variable contains the address of an object of the specified type.
- **The actual parameter to a routine** can be of the class specified or any descendant class.
- **The *Object* class** is an ancestor of all classes in Java.
- **The *Object* class contains *toString()* and e*quals()*** which should be overridden in descendant classes.
- **Input and output operations should be avoid** within a class.
- **Any static feature** in an ancestral class has only a single occurrence irrespective of the number of objects or their classes.

Solutions

Activity 7.1

The attributes of the BWTV are

volume
station
power
contrast
brightness

Activity 7.2

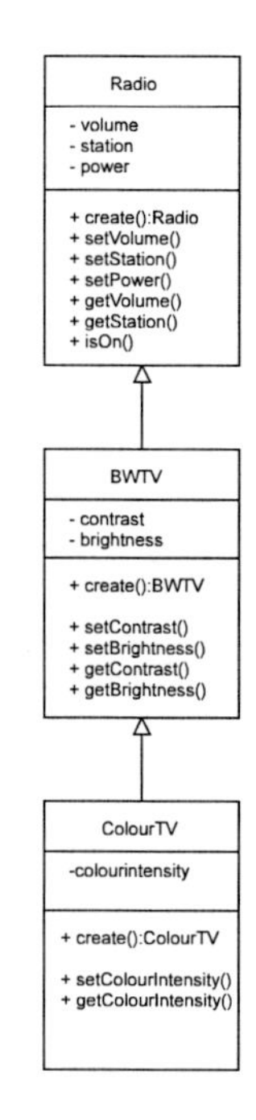

Activity 7.3

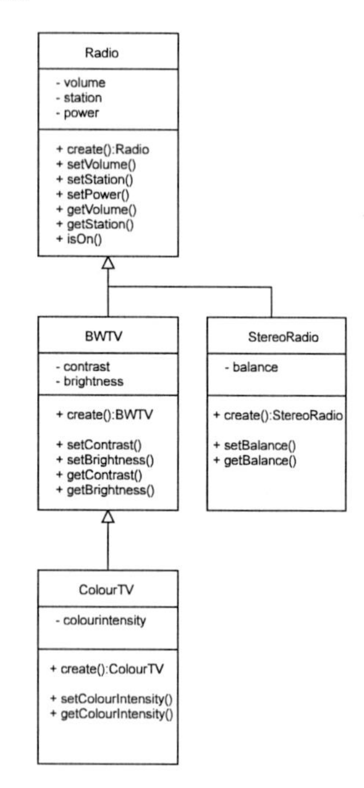

Activity 7.4

No solution required.

Activity 7.5

No solution required.

Activity 7.6

Latest version of *AlarmClock* class is

```
import Clock;
public class AlarmClock extends Clock
{
     protected int ahours;
     protected int aminutes;
     protected int aseconds;

     public AlarmClock(int h, int m, int s,
     ↳int ah, int am, int as)
     {
          if(h<0||h>23||m<0||m>59||s<0||s>59||
          ↳ah<0||ah>23||am<0||am>59||as<0||as>59)
          {
               ahours = 0;
               aminutes = 0;
               aseconds = 0;
          }
          else
          {
               hours = h;
               minutes = m;
               seconds = s;
               ahours = ah;
               aminutes = am;
               aseconds = as;
          }
     }

     public void setAlarm(int h, int m, int s)
     {
          if(h>23||h<0||m<0||m>59||s<0||s>59)
               return;
          ahours = h;
          aminutes = m;
          aseconds = s;
     }

     public int getAlarmHours()
     {
          return ahours;
     }
     public int getAlarmMinutes()
     {
          return aminutes;
     }
     public int getAlarmSeconds()
     {
          return aseconds;
     }
     public boolean isAlarmTime()
     {
          if(hours == ahours && minutes == aminutes
          ↳&& seconds == aseconds)
               return true;
          else
               return false;
     }
}
```

The code for the test program is:

```
import AlarmClock;
public class Act7_6
{
     public static void main(String args[])
     {
          AlarmClock ac = new AlarmClock(12,29,59,
                                        ↳12,30,0);
          ac.tick();
          if(ac.isAlarmTime())
               System.out.println("Time to get up");
     }
}
```

Activity 7.7

No solution required.

Activity 7.8

```
import Clock;
class CountdownClock extends Clock
{
    public CountdownClock()
    {
        super();
    }
    public CountdownClock(int h, int m, int s)
    {
        super(h,m,s);
    }
    public void tick()
    {
        int totalsecs = hours*3600 + minutes*60
                        ↳+ seconds - 1;
        if (totalsecs < 0)
            totalsecs = 24*36000-1;
        hours = (totalsecs /3600)%24;
        minutes = (totalsecs % 3600 / 60);
        seconds = totalsecs % 60;
    }
}
```

Activity 7.9

```
import Clock;
import CountdownClock;
public class Act7_9
{
    public static void main(String args[])
    {
        Clock cl = new Clock(12,0,0);
        CountdownClock cd =
                        ↳new CountdownClock(12,0,0);
        cl.tick();
        cd.tick();
        System.out.println("Clock          :"
            ↳+cl.getHours()+":"+cl.getMinutes()
            ↳+":"+cl.getSeconds());
        System.out.println("CountdownClock:"
            ↳+cd.getHours()+":"+cd.getMinutes()
            ↳+":"+cd.getSeconds());
    }
}
```

Activity 7.10

Version 1 produces the message "Time to get up".

```
import AlarmClock;
import Clock;
import CountdownClock;

public class Act7_10
{
    public static void main(String args[])
    {
        Clock time;
        time = new AlarmClock(1,2,3,1,2,4);
        time.tick();
    }
}
```

Version 2 decrements the clock's time by 1 second.

```
import AlarmClock;
import Clock;
import CountdownClock;

public class Act7_10
{
    public static void main(String args[])
    {
        Clock time;
        time = new CountdownClock(1,2,3);
        time.tick();
        System.out.println("Time :"
            ↳+time.getHours()+":"
            ↳+time.getMinutes()+":"
            ↳+time.getSeconds());
    }
}
```

Activity 7.11

Begin by adding the *runTime()* routine to the *Clock* class and saving the file.

Version 1 runs forward for 20 seconds

```
import AlarmClock;
import Clock;
import CountdownClock;

public class Act7_11
{
    public static void main(String args[])
    {
        Clock time;
        time = new Clock(1,2,3);
        time.runTime(20);
    }
}
```

This shows that the *Clock* version of *tick()* has been executed by *runTime()*.

Version 2 runs backwards for 20 seconds.

```
import AlarmClock;
import Clock;
import CountdownClock;

public class Act7_11
{
    public static void main(String args[])
    {
        Clock time;
        time = new CountdownClock(1,2,3);
        time.runTime(20);
    }
}
```

This shows that the *CountdownClock* version of *tick()* is being executed by *runTime()*.

Activity 7.12

Since the *CountdownClock* class contains no newly named methods, no casting will be required.

The only method coded within the *CountdownClock* class is *tick()*. Since a method of this name already exists in the *Clock* class, no casting will be required when running a method in the *CountdownClock*. The *CountdownClock* version of *tick()* will automatically be executed when using a *CountdownClock* object.

Activity 7.13

No solution required.

Activity 7.14

```
import Input;
import Clock;
import AlarmClock;
import CountdownClock;

public class Act7_14
{
    public static void main(String args[])
    {
        Clock cl=null;
        System.out.println("Which type?");
        System.out.println("1  - Clock");

        System.out.println("2  - AlarmClock");
        System.out.println("3  - CountdownClock");
        System.out.print("Enter choice(1,2,3): ");
```

```
            int choice = Input.readInt();
            switch(choice)
            {
                case 1:
                    c1 = new Clock(1,2,3);
                    break;
                case 2:
                    c1 = new AlarmClock(1,2,3,4,5,6);
                    break;
                case 3:
                    c1 = new CountdownClock(1,2,3);
                    break;
            }
            if(c1 instanceof AlarmClock)
            {
                System.out.println("Enter alarm time");
                System.out.print("Enter hour: ");
                int h = Input.readInt();
                System.out.print("Enter minute: ");
                int m = Input.readInt();
                System.out.print("Enter second: ");
                int s = Input.readInt();
                ((AlarmClock)c1).setAlarm(h,m,s);
            }
            c1.displayTime();
            c1.tick();
            c1.displayTime();
        }
    }
```

Activity 7.15

No solution required.

Activity 7.16

The *Clock* class should have the following method added

```
public String toString()
{
    return(hours+":"+minutes+":"+seconds);
}
```

Only two of the last three lines of the application program needs to be changed to

```
System.out.println(c1.toString());
c1.tick();
System.out.println(c1.toString());
```

CHAPTER 8

Basic Java Classes

This chapter covers the following topics:

Accessing Java Class Documentation

Arrays Class

Class Class

Date Class

DecimalFormat Class

GregorianCalendar Class

Java Packages

Math Class

String Class

StringBuffer Class

Wrapper Classes

Some Basic Classes In Java

Introduction

As well as creating classes of our own, Java has many built-in classes which we can use. In fact, Java 2 comes with over 1500 built-in classes. You'll find that mastering the basics of Java is relatively straightforward; it's getting to know all the classes that takes time and effort.

These classes are grouped into **packages**. A package is simply a collection of classes that usually have some common features. For example, although we won't be looking at it yet, the *Button* class is held in a package indentified as *java.awt*. This package contains many of the Graphical User Interface (GUI) classes that we would expect such as buttons, edit boxes, menus, etc.

To make use of a class defined within a package we need to use the `import` statement (as we have already for our own classes) but this time we need to include the package name. So to make use of a *Button* object we would need to include the line

```
import java.awt.Button;
```

at the beginning of our program. We can then use statements such as

```
Button press = new Button();
```

to declare a *Button* object in the code that follows.

If we are going to use several classes from a single package, rather than name each class individually, we can use a statement such as:

```
import java.awt.*;
```

The compiler recognises the asterisk in the line above as a request to use an indeterminate number of classes from the *awt* package. It will then automatically load all *awt* classes referenced in your program.

Alternatively, the `import` statement can be omitted entirely and full details of where to find a class can be given whenever an object is created. For example, without an appropriate `import` statement, creating a *Button* object would require the line

```
java.awt.Button press = new java.awt.Button();
```

The classes of one standard package, *java.lang* are automatically available in every Java program, so no import statement is required with these classes.

Here we're going to look at a few of those classes, just to get a feel for what they look like and how they are used. Unless stated otherwise these classes are contained in the *java.lang* package.

The String Class

The *String* class is treated as a special case in Java. Because strings are so widely used in programming, Java allows objects of this class to be used in a slightly unconventional way.

For example, we can declare a *String* reference variable in the conventional way:

```
String s1;
```

but then we write a line such as:

```
s1 = "Hello world";
```

Shouldn't we have written

```
s1 = new String();    ?
```

We can get away with the first statement because the term *"Hello world"* is in fact stored as an anonymous *String* object and the line

```
s1 = "Hello world";
```

results in the reference variable *s1* referencing the anonymous *String* object as shown in FIG-8.1.

FIG-8.1

Referencing a String Object

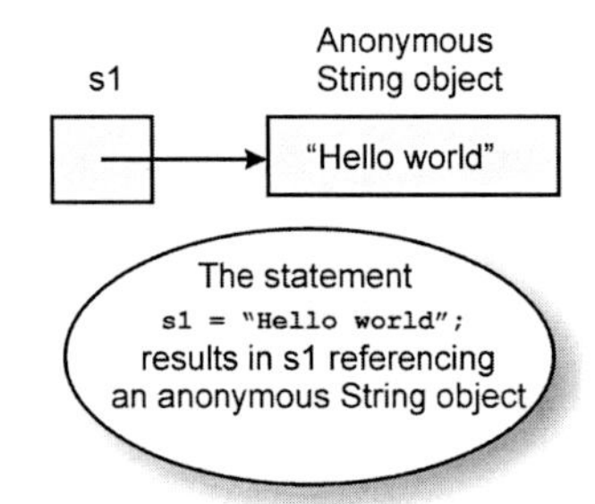

If we create a second *String* reference variable

```
String s2;
```

and assign it the same value as *s1*:

```
s2 = "Hello world";
```

then both reference variables point to the same anonymous object (FIG-8.2).

FIG-8.2

Identical Strings reference the same

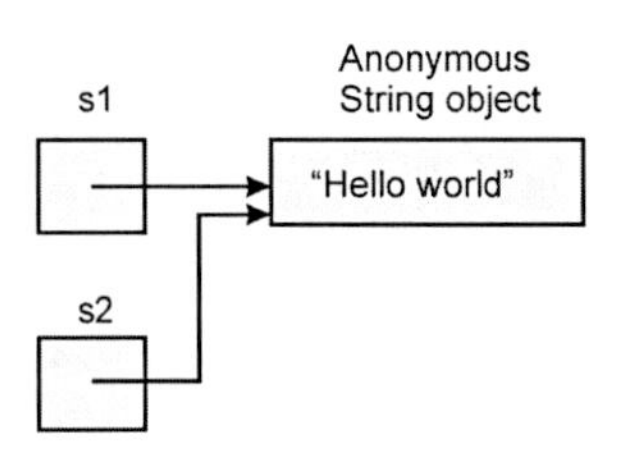

This seems a dangerous thing to do. What if we try to change *s2*? For example:

```
s2 = "Goodbye";
```

Will the contents of *s1* change as well? No, because the above statement tells *s2* to reference a *String* object containing the text *"Goodbye"*, so once the above statement is executed, we get the situation shown in FIG-8.3.

FIG-8.3

Changing References

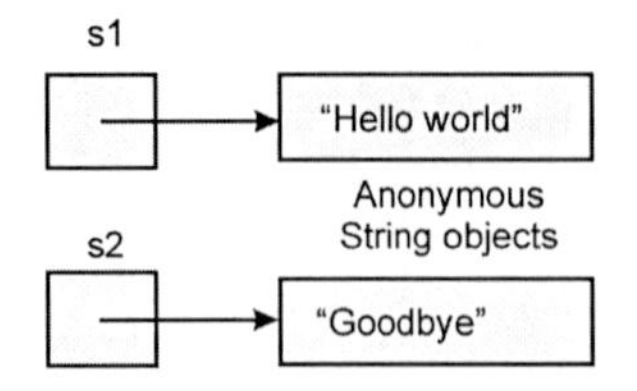

But what if, when *s1* and *s2* referenced the same anonymous string, we changed the contents of that string via *s1*, wouldn't that change be reflected in *s2* if we displayed its contents?

Java gets round that problem by implementing a simple rule: **String objects cannot have their values changed.**

At first glance this may seem a very restricting rule, but it isn't. The rule means that we cannot change the contents of the anonymous string *"Hello world"* to read *"HELLO WORLD"* but we could create a new string containing *"HELLO WORLD"* and then make *s1* (or *s2*) reference that new string.

In fact, the *String* class allows us to do just that. The *toUpperCase()* method (which the *String* class contains) can be used to create a new string which is the uppercase equivalent of the current string. This method returns a *String* object, which can then be pointed to by a *String* reference variable.

For example, the lines

```
String s1 = "Hello world";
String s2 = s1;
s1 = s1.toUpperCase();
```

have the effect shown in FIG-8.4

FIG-8.4

Creating new Strings

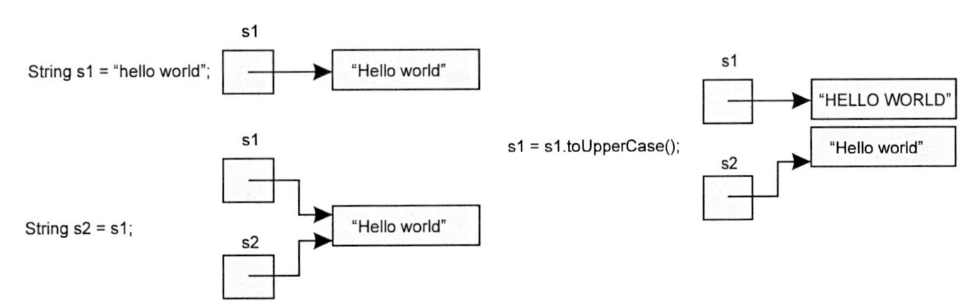

Of course, it is possible to create a *String* object in a more conventional way with a statement such as

```
String s1 = new String();
```

The above statement would be a bit pointless since *s1* would then reference an empty string and could only be changed by referencing a different string.

Luckily the *String* class constructor is overloaded. A second more useful alternative would be:

```
String s1 = new String("Hello");
```

By using this approach we could create two *String* objects that hold the same string value but do not reference the same object:

```
String s1 = new String("Hello");
String s2 = new String("Hello");
```

The results of the above statements are represented in FIG-8.5

FIG-8.5

Different Objects with the same Value

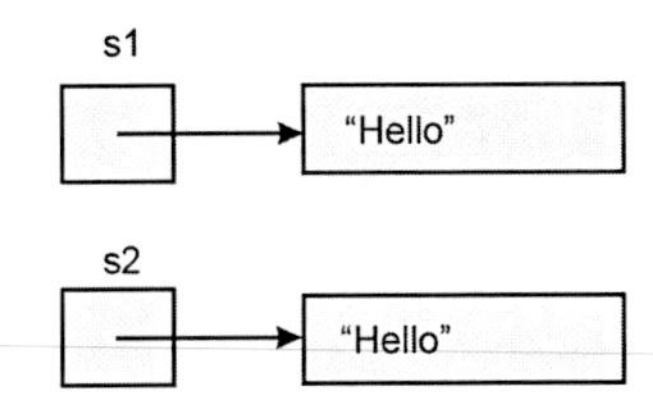

As we saw in `System.out.println()`, a new string can be created by joining existing strings using the plus (+) symbols. For example:

```
String s3 = s1 + s2;
String s4 = new String(s1+" world");
```

FIG-8.6 shows the effects of the two statements above.

FIG-8.6

Joining Strings

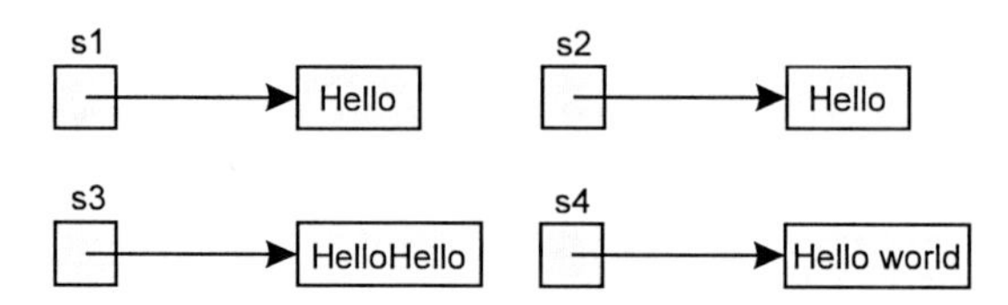

Notice that no string is changed by any of these operations; instead, new ones are created.

Details of the methods available in the *String* class are given below.

Constructor Methods

String() — This method creates a string object containing no characters.

String(byte w[]) — Creates a *String* object. The contents of array *w* are converted to characters and stored in the *String*. (See FIG-8.7)

FIG-8.7

String(byte [])

65 converts to a capital 'A'; 66 to a capital 'B', etc.

```
class StringConstructors1
{
  public static void main(String args[])
  {
    byte text[] = {65,66,67,68,69,70};
    String s = new String(text);
    System.out.println(s);
  }
}
```

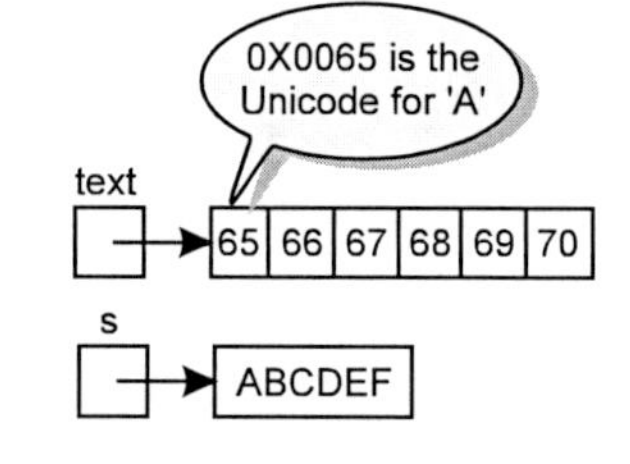

String(byte w[], int st, int num) — *num* elements of *w*, starting from *w[st]*, are converted to characters and stored in *s*. (See FIG-8.8)

FIG-8.8

String(byte [], int, int)

```
class StringConstructors1
{
  public static void main(String args[])
  {
    byte text[] = {65,66,67,68,69,70};
    String s = new String(text,2,4);
    System.out.println(s);
  }
}
```

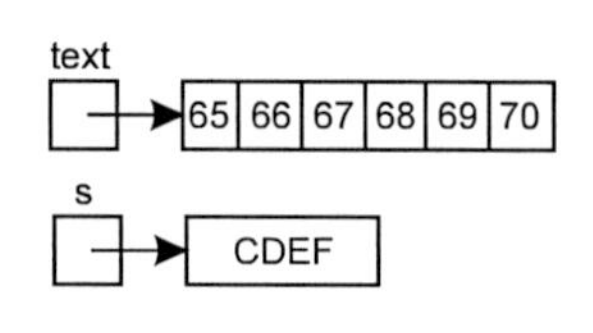

String (char c[]) — Assigns the characters in array *c* to the string. (See FIG-8.9)

FIG-8.9

String(char [])

```
class StringConstructors1
{
  public static void main(String args[])
  {
    char text[] = {'A','B','C','D','E','F'};
    String s = new String(text);
    System.out.println(s);
  }
}
```

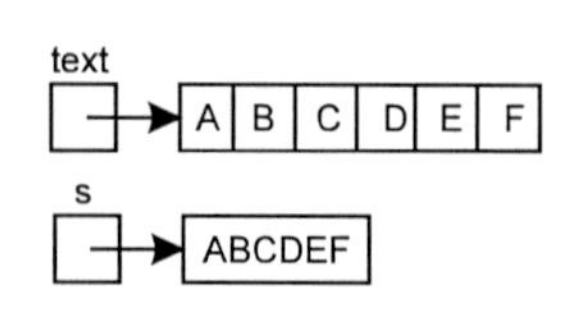

String (char c[], int st, int num) — Assigns *num* characters from *c*, starting at *c[st]* to the string (see FIG-8.10).

FIG-8.10

String(char [], int, int)

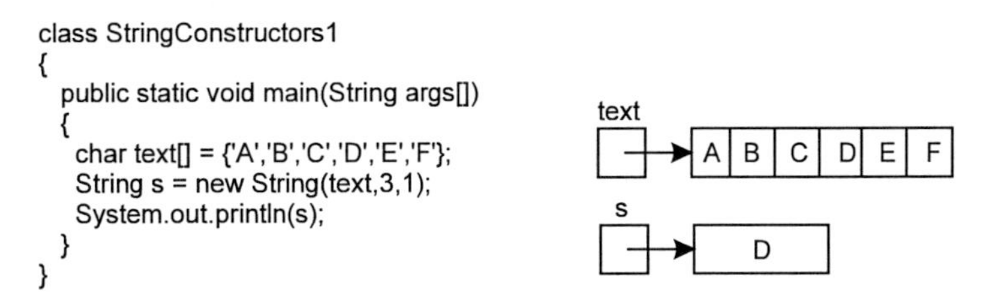

String (String s2) — Copies the characters held in *s2* to the new *String* object (see FIG-8.11).

FIG-8.11

String(char [], int, int)

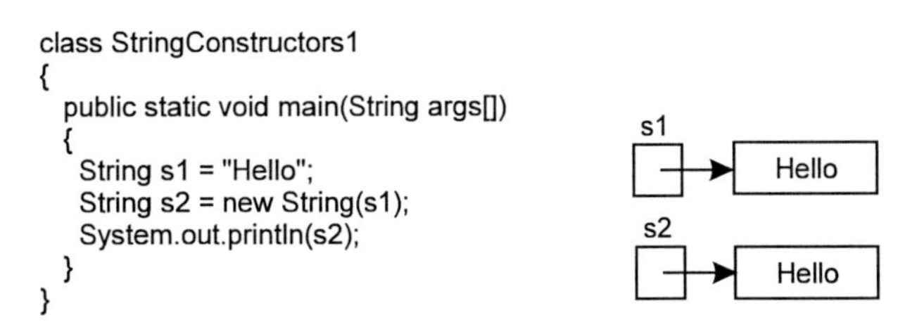

String (StringBuffer sb) — Copies the characters in *sb* to the new *String* object (see *StringBuffer* class later in this chapter).

Extraction Methods

The following methods extract one or more characters from a *String* object.

char charAt(int post) — Returns the character at position *post* within the string (see FIG-8.12).

FIG-8.12

char charAt(int)

void getChars(int st, int fin, char res[], int insertat)

Copies charcters from the string to *res*. The characters between positions *st* and *fin-1* are copied The characters are placed in *res* starting at element number *insertat* (see FIG-8.13).

FIG-8.13

void getChars(int,int, char[], int)

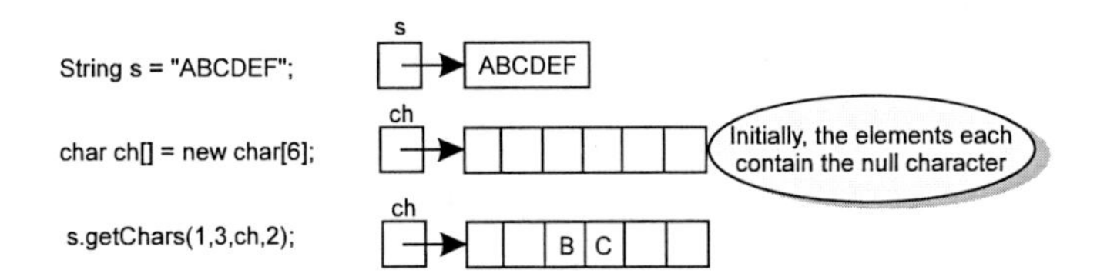

This routine is unusual in that the result is returned within a parameter of the routine. Because of this, the array used must have been allocated space before the call is made.

byte[] getBytes() Returns a byte array containing the integer values of the characters in the string (see FIG-8.14).

FIG-8.14

byte[] getBytes()

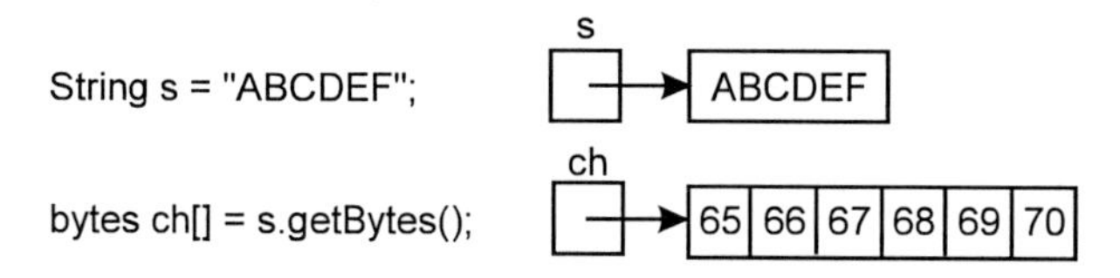

Notice that, unlike the *getChars()* method, the result is returned in the traditional way and that the array *ch[]* does not have to have allocated space previously.

String substring(int st) Returns a substring consisting of characters *st* to the end of the original string (see FIG-8.15).

FIG-8.15

String substring(int)

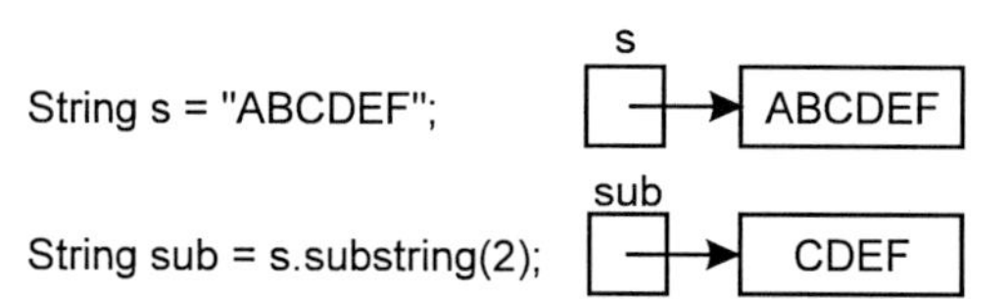

String substring(int st, int fin) Returns a *String* object constructed from characters *st* to *fin-1* of the original string (see FIG-8.16).

FIG-8.16

String substring(int,int)

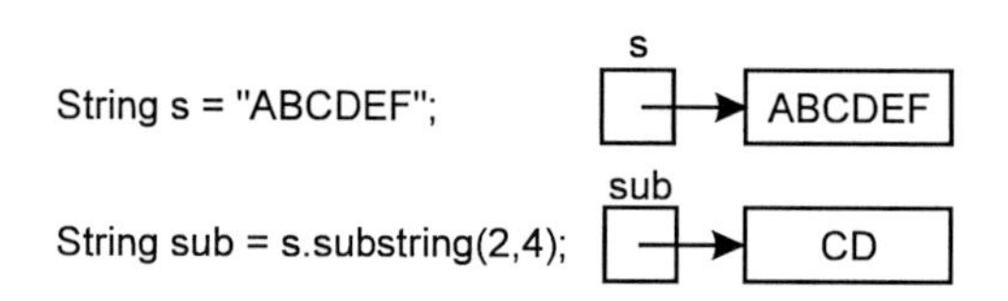

char[] toCharArray() Returns the contents of the string as an array of characters (see FIG-8.17)

FIG-8.17

char[] toCharArray()

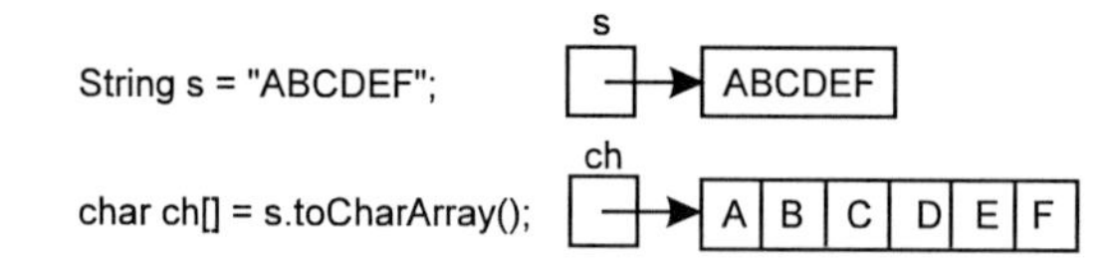

Comparison Methods

The following methods compare the current string with some other value, usually a string or a character.

int compareTo(String s2) Compares the current string to *s2*. There are three possible results:

0	returned if current string = *s2*
-ve value	returned if current string < *s2*
+ve value	returned if current string > *s2*

The result from the following code

```
String s = new String("ABCDEF");
int result = s.compareTo("ABC");
if (result == 0)
    System.out.println("Strings are identical");
else if (result < 0)
    System.out.println("String is less than ABC");
else if (result > 0)
    System.out.println("String is greater than ABC");
```

is *String is greater than ABC.*

boolean equalsIgnoreCase(String s2) Returns *true* if *s2* contains the same sequence of characters as the current string, ignoring case differences.

For example, the `if` statement below would give the result *true*:

```
String s = new String("ABCDEF");
if(s.equalsIgnoreCase("aBcdeF"))
    System.out.println("Strings are equal");
```

boolean endsWith(String s2) Returns *true* if the current string ends with the substring *s2*.

The code

```
String s = new String("www.kirkman.co.uk");
if(s.endsWith(".uk"))
    System.out.println("This is a British site");
else
    System.out.println("This is not a British site");
```

displays the message *This is a British site.*

boolean startsWith(String s2) Returns *true* if the current string starts with the substring *s2*.

boolean equals(Object obj) Returns *true* if the current string and *obj* have the same value; otherwise *false* is returned.
This is an overridden version of the operation inherited from the *Object* class.
In the example below, the first message is displayed.

```
public class TestingStrings
{
    public static void main(String args[])
    {
        String s1 = new String("Hello");
        String s2 = new String("Hello");
        if(s1.equals(s2))
            System.out .println("Strings contain the
            ↳same value");
        if(s1 == s2)
            System.out.println("s1 and s2 contain the
            ↳same address");
    }
}
```

If the parameter *obj* is not a *String* object only *false* will be returned.

Search Methods

The following routines search the string for specified charcters or substrings.

int indexOf(int ch) Returns the position in the current string of the first occurrence of *ch*. If *ch* does not appear in the string, -1 is returned. *ch* can be specified as a `char` or `int` type. Hence, assuming the definition

```
String s = new String("ABCDEF");
```

both of the following lines are valid

```
System.out.println("C is at position "+s.indexOf('C'));
System.out.println("C is at position "+s.indexOf(67));
```

and will display the message *C is at position 2*

int indexOf(int ch, int st) Returns the position in the current string of the first occurrence of *ch*. If *ch* does not appear in the string, -1 is returned. Searching begins at position *st* in the string.

Assuming the definition:

```
String s = new String("ABCDEF");
```

The line

```
System.out.println("D is at position "+s.indexOf('D',1));
```

displays *D is at postion 3*

while the line

```
System.out.println("D is at position "+s.indexOf('D',4));
```

will display *D is at position -1*

int indexOf(String s2) Returns the position in the current string of the first occurrence of the substring *s2*. If *s2* does not appear in the string, -1 is returned.

int indexOf(String s2, int st) Returns the position in the current string of the first occurrence of the substring *s2*. If *s2* does not appear in the string, -1 is returned. Searching begins at position *st* in the string.

int lastIndexOf(int ch) Returns the position in the current string of the last occurrence of *ch*. If *ch* does not appear in the string, -1 is returned. *ch* can be specified as a `char` or `int` type.

Assuming the definition

```
String s = new String("ABCDEFFEDCBA");
```

both of the following lines are valid

```
System.out.println("C is at position "+s.lastIndexOf('C'));
System.out.println("C is at position "+s.lastIndexOf(67));
```

and will display the message *C occurs at position 9*

int lastIndexOf(int ch, int st) Returns the position in the current string of the last occurrence of *ch*. If *ch* does not appear in the string, -1 is returned. Searching begins at position *st* in the string.

Assuming the definition

```
String s = new String("ABCDEFFEDCBA");
```

the line

```
System.out.println("D is at position "+s.lastIndexOf
↳('D',6));
```

displays *D is at postion 8*

int lastIndexOf(String s2) Returns the position in the current string of the last occurrence of the substring *s2*. If *s2* does not appear in the string, -1 is returned.

int lastIndexOf(String s2, int st) Returns the position in the current string of the last occurrence of the substring *s2*. If *s2* does not appear in the string, -1 is returned. Searching begins at position *st* in the string.

Modifying Methods

The following methods create a new string based on some modification of the original string.

String concat(String s2) Creates a new string by joining *s2* to the end of the current string (see FIG-8.18).

FIG-8.18

String concat(String)

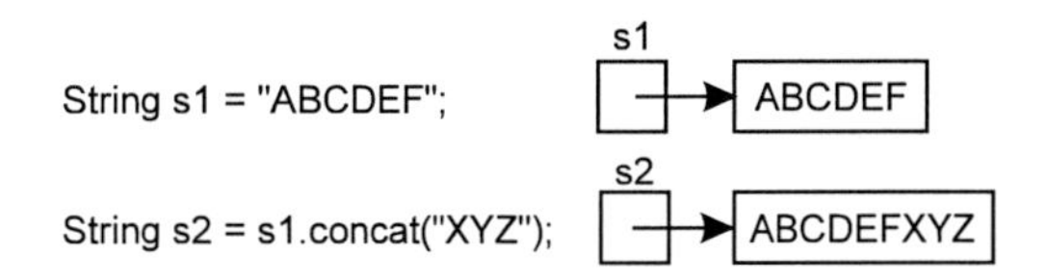

String replace(char oldch, char newch) Creates a new string which is identical to the current string except for the fact that all occurrences of charcater *oldch* have been replaced by *newch* (see FIG-8.19)

FIG-8.19

String replace(char,char)

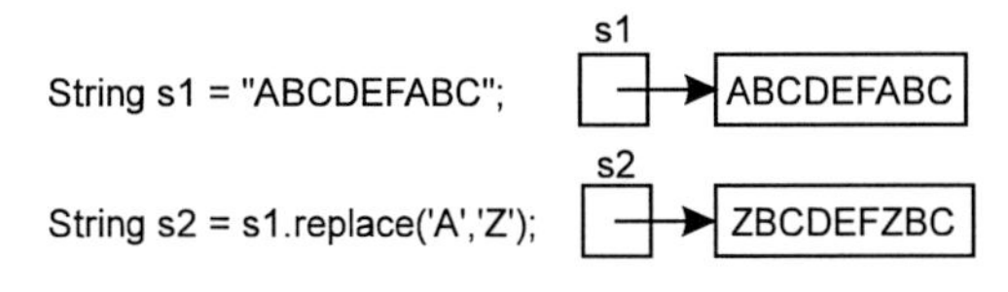

String toLowerCase() Returns a string identical to the original but all capital letters are replaced by the lowercase equivalent.

String toUpperCase() Returns a string identical to the original but all lowercase letters are replaced by the uppercase equivalent.

String trim() Returns a string which is a copy of the current string with all leading and trailing spaces removed.

Convertion Methods

The following methods convert values of some other type (such as `int`, `float`, etc) to a *String* object. All of these methods are static.

String valueOf(boolean b) Converts a boolean value to the string equivalent.

For example, the code

```
boolean b = true;
String ss = String.valueOf(b);
System.out.println("b contains "+s);
```

displays the message *b contains true.*

String valueOf(...) This method is also overloaded for each of the following types: *char, int, long, float,* and *double*.

This allows statements such as:

```
s = String.valueOf('B');        //char conversion
s = String.valueOf(123);        //int
s = String.valueOf(3.1415);     //double
```

String valueOf(char chs[]) Creates a *String* object containing the characters held in *chs*.

String valueOf(char chs[], int st, int cnt) Creates a *String* object containing the *cnt* characters. The first character is extracted from *chs[st]* (see FIG-8.20)

FIG-8.20

String valueOf(char[],int,int)

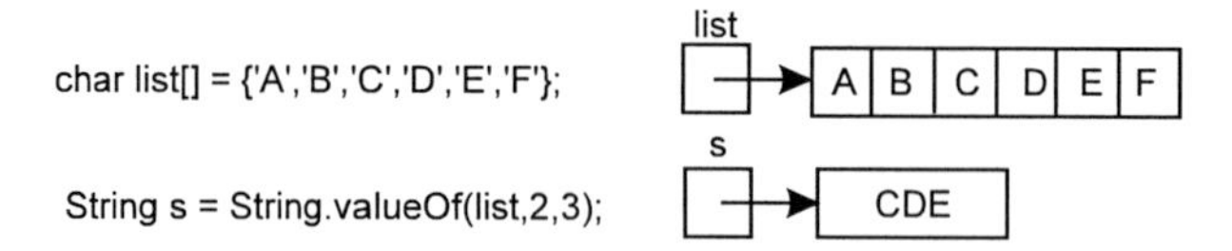

Other String Methods

int length() Returns the number of characters in the current string. Notice that this is a function call and requires the parentheses. Do not confuse it with the *length* property of an array where no parentheses are involved.

Using Strings

The program in LISTING-8.1 sorts an array of *String* objects using the Bubble sort.

LISTING-8.1

Sorting Strings

```
public class StringSort
{
  public static void main(String args[])
  {
      String s[] = {"Heron, Liz", "Tait, Avril",
                    "Taylor, Sandra", "Ferguson, Jackie",
                    "Garry, Lynn", "Bell, Gillian"};
      for (int pass = 1; pass < s.length; pass++)
          for(int c = 0; c < s.length-pass; c++)
              if(s[c].compareTo(s[c+1]) > 0)
              {
                  String temp = s[c];
                  s[c] = s[c+1];
                  s[c+1] = temp;
              }
      for(int c = 0; c < s.length; c++)
          System.out.println(s[c]);
  }
}
```

Activity 8.1

Write a Java program which displays the average number of characters in the strings given in the example above.

A fact that can easily be overlooked is that since all string constants are stored as anonymous string objects, they have all the methods of that class. This means that an expression such as

```
"Hello world".length()
```

is perfectly valid.

Activity 8.2

Create a short program containing the line

```
System.out.println("Hello  world contains "+
↳"Hello world".length()+" characters. In upper case it is "
↳+ "Hello world".toUpperCase());
```

Run the program.

Use *Input.readString()* to read in a string value.

Activity 8.3

Write a program to read in a sentence of up to 10 words, extract the words within the sentence and list them. You may assume there is exactly one space between each word and that there are no punctuation characters.

Strings and *main()*

The method *main()* always begins with the line

```
public static void main(String args[])
```

and, at last, we have enough knowledge to know the meaning of the line:

`public`	*main()* is a public method
`static`	*main()* is a class method
`void`	*main()* does not return a value
`String args[]`	*main()* takes an array of *Strings* as a parameter

But what is the purpose of the *String* array? It allows arguments to be passed from the command line to the program as part of the execution instruction. For example, if a class *Test* is executed with the line

```
java Test one two three
```

then the *args[]* parameter of *main()* will have the following contents:

```
args[0] = "one"
args[1] = "two"
args[2] = "three"
```

args will contain exactly the number of elements required to store all the values passed from the command line. For the above example *args.length* would have the value 3.

This can be useful, particularly when writing utility programs where the arguments could be used to pass file or directory names.

> **Activty 8.4**
>
> Write a program which displays any arguments passed to it from the command line.

The StringBuffer Class

If you need a string whose contents can be changed, a *StringBuffer* object can be used. This class stores the string in a `char` array which can be lengthened automatically if the string grows larger. Also individual characters can be accessed and modified.

This is a more conventional class than *String*. We need to start by creating an object of the class with a statement such as:

```
StringBuffer sb1 = new StringBuffer();
```

The length of the string held in a *StringBuffer* object can be determined using the *length()* method. For example:

```
System.out.println(sb1.length());
```

The number of elements within the array used to store the string can be determined by the *capacity()* method. For example:

```
System.out.println(sb1.capacity());
```

> **Actvity 8.5**
>
> Create a Java program containing the three lines given above and execute it.

As you can see from the results of Activity 8.5 above, if an empty object is created it has a length of zero and can hold up to 14 characters.

Constructor Methods

StringBuffer() — Creates an empty object as shown in the example above.

StringBuffer(int size) — Creates an object with a capacity for *size* characters.

Actvity 8.6

Change the constructor call in your previous program to read

```
StringBuffer sb1 = new StringBuffer(30);
```

Test the program.

StringBuffer(String s) — Stores the characters of *s* within the new object.

Activity 8.7

Change the constructor call in your program to

```
StringBuffer s1 = new StringBuffer("Hello world");
```

Run the program.

You'll see from the above examples that, unless stated otherwise, *StringBuffer* objects are created with space for an additional 16 characters over and above those stored within it at creation.

Extraction Methods

The following methods extract part of the *StringBuffer* object.

char charAt(int post) — Returns the character at element *post*. To return the first character *post* should have the value zero.

void getChars(int st, int fin, char result[], int insertat) — Extracts elements [*st*] to [*fin*-1] from the current object. These characters are then stored in the *result* character array. The first character is copied into position *result[insertat]*.

String substring(int st) — Returns the characters from [*st*] to the end of text as a *String* object.

String substring(int st, int fin) — Returns the characters from [*st*] to [*fin*-1] as a *String* object.

Modifying Methods

StringBuffer append(...)

This method adds the specified characters to the end of the string held in the object (see FIG-8.21).
It is overloaded to accept the following types as its parameter:

```
char[]
boolean
int
long
float
double
Object
String
```

FIG-8.21

StringBuffer(String)

StringBuffer sb = new StringBuffer("ABCDEF"); sb → ABCDEF

boolean b = true; b: true

sb.append(b); sb → ABCDEFtrue

Activity 8.8

Modify your program to read

```
StringBuffer sb1 = new StringBuffer("Hello world");
sb1.append(" - Mars calling");
System.out.println(sb1.length());
System.out.println(sb1.capacity());
System.out.println(sb1);
```

Test your program.

As you can see, the extra text is added to the object. However, you should also have noticed that the *append()* method returns a *StringBuffer* object. This allows us to copy the result to another object of this class.

Activity 8.9

Change the *append()* line in your previous program to

```
StringBuffer sb2 = sb1.append(" - Mars calling");
```

Modify the output statement to display both *sb1* and *sb2*.

Run your program.

Unlike *String* objects, *sb1* and *sb2* reference two different objects in the above program.

Notice that the *append()* method is overloaded to take an *Object* class object. You will recall that the actual parameter to routines such as these can be of the specified class, or any descendant class. *append()* creates a string from an object by executing that object's *toString()* method. In the next Activity we will use the feature to append a *Distance* object to the string.

Activity 8.10

Make sure you have overridden the *toString()* method which your *Distance* class inherited from the *Object* class.

It should be designed to return a value such as "3 yds 2 ft 1 in".

Enter and run the following program

```
import Distance;

public class TestStringBuf
{
  public static void main(String args[])
  {
      StringBuffer sb1 =
          ↳new StringBuffer("On the moon you can jump ");
      Distance d = new Distance(4,1,0);
      sb1.append(d);
      System.out.println(sb1);
  }
}
```

StringBuffer append(char s[] , int startat, int noofchars)

This final version of *append()* allows part of a character array to be copied to the end of the *StringBuffer* object. Starting at position *startat* in *s*, *noofchars* characters are copied into the *StringBuffer* object.

The lines

```
StringBuffer sb1 = new StringBuffer("Hello world");
char letter[] = {'A','B','C','D','E','F'};
sb1.append(letter,1,3);
System.out.println(sb1);
```

create the output *Hello worldBCD*

StringBuffer insert(int post, ...)

This routine allows characters to be inserted at element *post* within the current object. The method is overloaded so that the second parameter can be any of the following:

```
char[]
boolean
Object
String
char
int
long
float
double
```

The code

```
StringBuffer sb1 = new StringBuffer("ABCDEF");
sb1.insert(2,123);
System.out.println(sb1);
```

creates the output

```
AB123CDEF
```

StringBuffer insert(int post, char s[], int startat, int noofchars)
Inserts part of array *s* into the current object starting at element post. Elements *s[startat]* to *s[start+noofchars-1]* are copied into the current object (see FIG-8.22).

FIG-8.22

StringBuffer insert(int,char[],int,int)

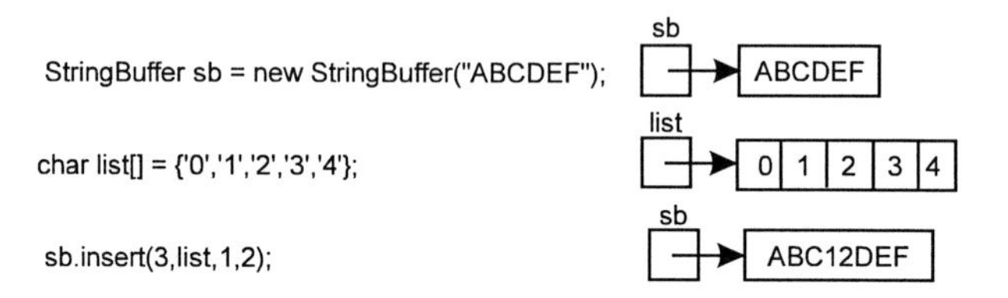

StringBuffer delete(int st, int fin) Deletes the characters from elements [*st*] to [*fin*-1] (see FIG-8.23).

FIG-8.23

StringBuffer delete(int,int)

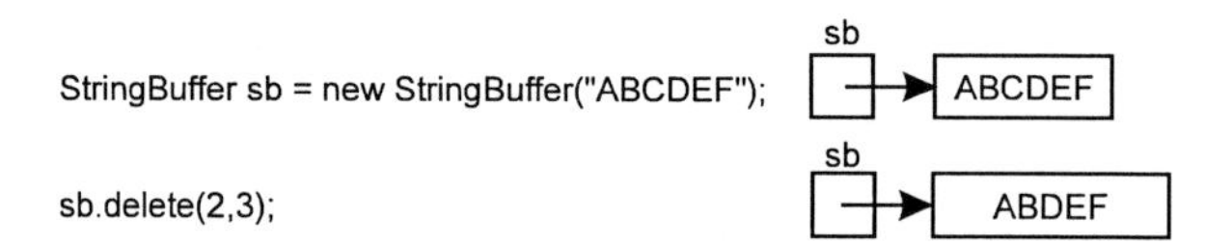

StringBuffer deleteCharAt(int post) Deletes the character at [*post*] w(see FIG-8.24)

FIG-8.24

StringBuffer delete(int,int)

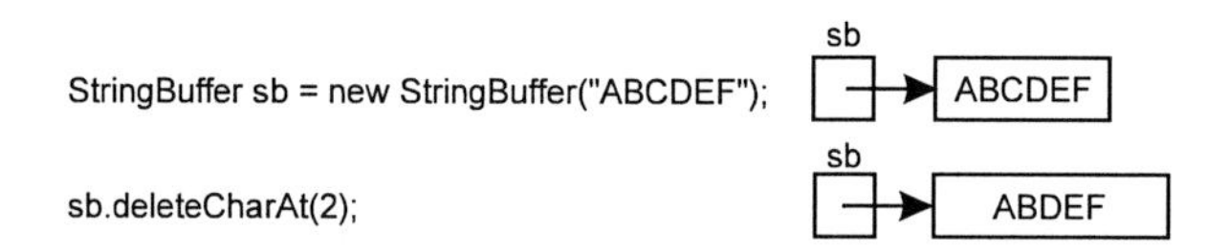

StringBuffer replace(int st, int fin, String s)
The characters between positions [*st*] to [*fin*-1] are deleted from the *StringBuffer* object and the contents of *s* inserted starting at position [*st*] (see FIG-8.25).

FIG-8.25

StringBuffer delete(int,int)

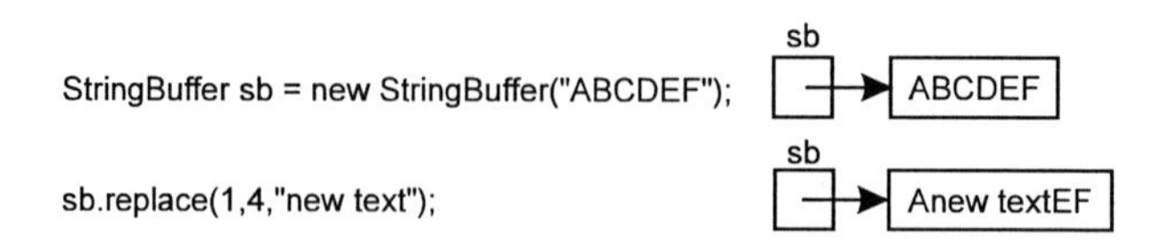

StringBuffer reverse() — Reverses the contents of the *StringBuffer* object.

StringBuffer setCharAt(int post, char ch) — Sets the character at element [*post*] to character *ch*.

String toString() — The inherited method is overridden to return a *String* equivalent to the contents of the *StringBuffer* object.

Using StringBuffer Objects

You may have noticed that there are no methods for searching or comparing within the *StringBuffer* class. The inherited *equals()* method has not been overridden, so the code

```
StringBuffer sb1 = new StringBuffer("ABCDEF");
StringBuffer sb2 = new StringBuffer("ABCDEF");
if (sb1.equals(sb2))
    System.out.println("Equal");
else
    System.out.println("Not equal");
```

produces the output

```
Not equal
```

However, we can convert the *StringBuffer* objects to *String* objects for such tests. Hence, if we use the line

```
if (sb1.toString().equals(sb2.toString()))
```

in the program above, then the output will be

```
Equal
```

> **Activity 8.11**
>
> Write a program to read in a sentence, change all 'e's to 'a's, and display the final result.

The Math Class

This class contains a set of mathematical functions and constants. Every operation is a class method, hence there is no requirement to create objects of this class.

Math Constants

The class defines the following class constants (i.e. static values):

E
PI

These can be accessed with expressions such as `Math.PI`

Trigometric Methods

double acos(double v)	Returns the arcosine of *v* in the range 0 to PI.
double asin(double v)	Returns the arcsine of *v* in the range -PI/2 to PI/2.
double atan(double v)	Returns the arctangent of *v* in the range -PI/2 to PI/2.
double cos(double v)	Returns the sine of angle *v* (angle given in radians).
double sin(double v)	Returns the sine of angle *v* radians.
double tan(double v)	Returns the tangent of angle *v* radians.
double toDegrees(double rad)	Coverts *rad* radians to degrees.
double toRadians(double deg)	Converts *deg* degrees to radians.

Arithmetic Methods

... abs(... v)	Returns the absolute value of *v*. Overloaded for
	`int`
	`long`
	`float`
	`double`

double ceil(double v)	Returns the smallest whole number not less than *v*.
double exp(double v)	Returns e^v.
double floor(double v)	Returns the largest whole number not greater than *v*.
double log(double v)	Returns the natural log of *v* (i.e. $\log_e v$)

... max(... a, ... b)	Returns the either *a* or *b*, whichever is the greater. Overloaded for
	`int`
	`long`
	`float`
	`double`

... min(...a, ... b)	Returns either *a* or *b*, whichever is the smaller. Overloaded for
	`int`
	`long`
	`float`
	`double`

double pow (double a, double b)	Returns a^b.

double random()	Returns a random value between 0 and 1. The value will never quite reach 0 or 1.
double rint(double v)	Rounds *v* to the nearest whole number.
int round(float v) *long round(double v)*	Rounds *v* to the nearest whole number. This is similar to *rint()*, but the type returned is different.
double sqrt(double v)	Returns the square root of *v*.

Using Math Class Features

The program in LISTING-8.2 displays the square root of all numbers between 1 and 20.

LISTING-8.2

Using the Math Class

```
public class UsingMath
{
  public static void main(String args[])
  {
      System.out.println("SQUARE ROOTS");
      for(int c = 1; c <= 20; c++)
          System.out.println("The square root of "+c
              ↳+" is "+Math.sqrt(c));
  }
}
```

Activity 8.12

Type in and run the program above.

Activity 8.13

Write a game in which the computer generates a number in the range 1 to 100 and allows the player up to 6 attempts to guess the value. The computer should respond with the messages

Correct
Too high
Too low

as appropriate.

At the end of the game the computer should display the number it had generated.

The DecimalFormat Class

You will have seen from the output of the program in LISTING-8.2 that having no control over the format of our output can result in untidy displays. The *DecimalFormat* class allows us to define how numeric values are to be output.

We need to start by creating a *DecimalFormat* object. The most useful constructor for this class takes a single *String* argument. This string gives details of how the number is to be displayed. Only a limited range of characters is allowed in this string. For example, if we wanted the square root values to be displayed with 1 digit before the decimal point and exactly three digits after the decimal point we would create a *DecimalFormat* object using the following line:

```
DecimalFormat df = new DecimalFormat("#.###");
```

DecimalFormat's *format()* operation is then used to convert the value we wish displayed to a string of the required layout format and this can then be displayed:

```
System.out.println(df.format(value));
```

The program in LISTING-8.3 demonstrates the use of this technique:

LISTING-8.3

Formatted Output

```
import java.text.*;

public class TestFormatting
{
  public static void main(String args[])
  {
      DecimalFormat df = new DecimalFormat("#.###");
      System.out.println("SQUARE ROOTS");
      for(int c = 0; c <= 20; c++)
          System.out.println(df.format(Math.sqrt(c)));
  }
}
```

This program gives the output shown below.

SQUARE ROOTS
0
1
1.414
1.732
2
2.236
2.449
2.646
2.828
3
3.162
3.317
3.464
3.606
3.742
3.873
4
4.123
4.243
4.359
4.472

Notice that the value zero disobeys this rule otherwise it would be totally invisible!

When the '#' symbol is used in the formatting string, leading zeros in the integral part of the number and trailing zeros in the fractional part are not allocated space in the display.

We can force these zeros to be displayed by replacing the '#' character with a '0'. So using the constructor call

```
DecimalFormat df = new DecimalFormat("#.0##");
```

the value 1 would be displayed as 1.0 and 2 as 2.0, etc.

Activity 8.14

Modify the program in LISTING-8.3 to show all results to 4 decimal places.

Re-run the program.

Activity 8.15

Write a program which performs a money conversion.

The program should have the following logic:

```
Read in an amount of money in pounds sterling
Convert to dollars ($1.42 = £1.00)
Format the output to 2 decimal places
Output original amount and equivalent dollar amount
```

The Arrays Class

This class is in the package *java.util.*

We've looked at arrays in a previous chapter, but there is also an *Array* class which can be used to manipulate the contents of existing arrays.

All the methods mentioned here are class methods.

The other methods of this class also take arrays of any of the types listed.

void sort(type arr[])

The array *arr,* can be any of the following types:

```
byte
short
int
long
float
double
char
boolean
```

The contents of the array are sorted into ascending order by this method. The program in LISTING-8.4 displays an arrays contents before and after a call to *Arrays.sort()*.

LISTING-8.4

The *sort()* Method

```
import java.util.Arrays;

public class UsingArraysClass
{
  public static void main(String args[])
  {
      int nos[]={7,1,9,5,2,7,4};

      for(int c = 0; c < nos.length; c++)
          System.out.print(nos[c]+ " ");
      System.out.println();
      Arrays.sort(nos);
      for(int c = 0; c < nos.length; c++)
          System.out.print(nos[c]+ " ");
  }
}
```

> **Activity 8.16**
>
> Type in and run the program above.

int binarysearch(type arr[], type v) — This method will search array *arr* for value *v*. If *v* is found in *arr*, then the position at which a match was found is returned. If no match is found, a negative value, *p*, is returned. The absolute value of *p*, -1 is where the value *v* should have appeared in the array. The search uses the binary search method.

We need not concern ourselves with the mechanics of this technique other than to state that it is a pre-condition of the operation that the contents of the array be sorted.

> **Activity 8.17**
>
> Return to the program you entered in Activity 8.16 and add the following logic, in Java, to the end of *main()*:
>
> ```
> Read value from keyboard
> Search for value in array
> IF found THEN
>     Display its position
> ELSE
>     Display "Not found"
> ENDIF
> ```
>
> Re-run the program and observe the results.

void fill(type arr[], type v) — Every element of *arr* is assigned the value *v*.

arr[] and *v* should be of the same type.

boolean equals(type arr[], Object v) — Returns *true* if *v* is an exact match for *arr*. There is a match if both are arrays of the same type, contain the same number of elements and the contents of every element matches.

The Date Class

Objects of the *Date* class can be used to hold a specific date and time down to a millisecond.

Constructors

Date() — Creates a *Date* object. Its initial value is taken from the system clock

Date(long milli) — Sets the date and time to *milli* milliseconds after midnight 31 Dec 1969.

Other Methods

long getTime()	Returns the number of milliseconds since midnight 31/12/1969.
setTime(long milli)	Sets the date and time to *milli* milliseconds after midnight 31 Dec 1969.
boolean after(Date d)	Returns *true* if the current date is after *d*; otherwise *false* is returned.
boolean before(Date d)	Returns *true* if the current date is before d; otherwise *false* is returned.
int compareTo(Date d)	Compares the current date to *d*. There are three possible results: 0 returned if current date = *d* -ve value returned if current date < *d* +ve value returned if current date > *d*
boolean equals(Object obj)	Returns *true* if the current date is equal to *obj*. *true* will only be returned if obj is a *Date*-based object containing exactly the same date and time as the current date.
Object clone()	Creates a copy of the current *Date* object.

The program in LISTING-8.5 demonstrates the use of a *Date* object.

LISTING-8.5

The *Date* Class

```
import java.util.Date;

public class TestDate
{
  public static void main(String args[])
  {
      Date d = new Date();
      System.out.println(d);
  }
}
```

The GregorianCalendar Class

The *Date* class is probably of limited use for most applications. A more comprehensive class is the *GregorianCalendar* class which offers many more operations for handling dates and time.

Class Constants

int ERA
int YEAR
int MONTH
int WEEK_OF_YEAR
int WEEK_OF_MONTH
int DATE
int DAY_OF_MONTH
int DAY_OF_YEAR
int DAY_OF_WEEK
int DAY_OF_WEEK_IN_MONTH

int AM_PM
int HOUR
int HOUR_OF_DAY
int MINUTE
int SECOND
int MILLISECOND

int ZONE_OFFSET
int DST_OFFSET
int FIELD_COUNT

int SUNDAY
int MONDAY
int TUESDAY
int WEDNESDAY
int THURSDAY
int FRIDAY
int SATURDAY

int JANUARY
int FEBRUARY
int MARCH
int APRIL
int MAY
int JUNE
int JULY
int AUGUST
int SEPTEMBER
int OCTOBER
int NOVEMBER
int DECEMBER

int UNDECIMBER
int AM
int PM
int BC
int AD;

Constructors

GregorianCalendar() — Creates a *GregorianCalendar* object set to the current date and time.

GregorianCalendar(int y, int m, int d) — Creates a *GregorianCalendar* object set to the date (*d/m*+1/*y*). Note that *m* = 0 sets the month to January. Time is set to zero.

GregorianCalendar(int y, int m, int d, int hrs, int mins)
Creates a *GregorianCalendar* object set to the date (*d/m*+1/*y*). Note that *m* = 0 sets the month to January. Time is set to *hrs* hours, *mins* minutes and zero seconds.

GregorianCalendar(int y, int m, int d, int hrs, int mins, int secs)
Creates a *GregorianCalendar* object set to the date (*d/m*+1/*y*). Note that *m* = 0 sets the month to January. Time is set to *hrs* hours, *mins* minutes and *secs* seconds.

Other Methods

add(int f, int v)

Adds *v* to field *f*. Use a named constant to identify the field to be updated. That is, *f* should be one of the following.

```
DAY_OF_MONTH
MONTH
YEAR
HOUR
MINUTE
SECOND
```

Adding may cause rollover of subsequent fields. For example, if we add 12 days to the 30 Dec 2001, the calendar's value will change to 11 Jan 2002.

roll(int f, boolean b)

If *b* is *true*, field *f* is incremented. If *b* is *false*, field *f* is decremented. No other field is affected, so if incrementing a field takes it beyond its highest allowed value, it returns to its lowest value.

roll(int f, int v)

Adds *v* to field *f*. No other field is affected. For example, the month field must be in the range 0-11. If it currently contains the value 10 and we use roll() to add 5 to the month it will change to 3, but the year value will remain unchanged.

int getMinimum(int f)

Returns the minimum value for field *f*.

int getMaximum(int f)

Returns the maximum value for field *f*.

void set(int y, int m, int d)

Sets the date (*d/m*+1/*y*). Time remains unchanged.

void set(int y, int m, int d, int hrs, int mins)

Sets the date (*d/m*+1/*y*). Time is set to *hrs* hours, *mins* minutes. Seconds remain unchanged.

void set(int y, int m, int d, int hrs, int mins, int secs)

Sets the date (*d/m*+1/*y*). Time is set to *hrs* hours, *mins* minutes and *secs* seconds.

boolean after(Object d)

Returns *true* if the current date is after *d*; otherwise *false* is returned.

boolean before(Object d)

Returns *true* if the current date is before d; otherwise *false* is returned.

boolean equals(Object obj)

Returns *true* if the current date is equal to *obj*. *true* will only be returned if *obj* is a *GregorianCalendar*-based object containing exactly the same date and time as the current object.

Object clone()

Creates a copy of the current *GregorianCalendar* object.

The Class Class

When a Java program is running the Java Virtual Machine maintains runtime type information (RTTI) about every class and variable type in use. Each variable or object in the program is then linked to this information. So, if in your program you create two *Weight* objects and a *Clock* object, Java will maintain information about the *Weight* and *Clock* class and link this information to the objects (see FIG-8.26).

FIG-8.26

Runtime Type Information

Program code segment

```
Weight w1 = new Weight();
Weight w2 = new Weight();
Clock cd = new Clock(1,2,3);
```

Java creates the necessary data items

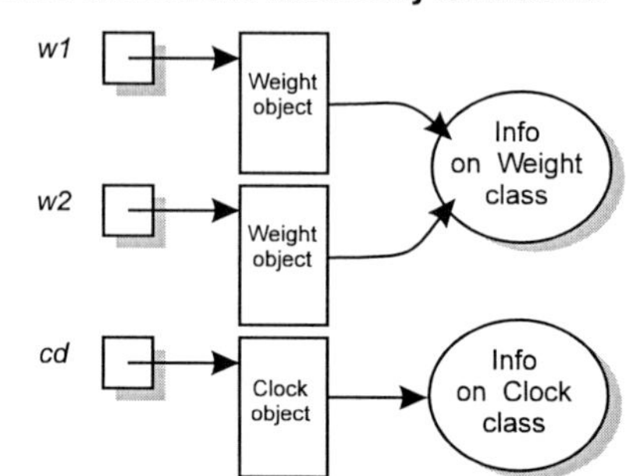

Java uses this information to make sure that the correct version of a method is executed.

We can gain access to this information by creating a *Class* class reference variable and storing within it the address of the RTTI for that object's class.

The *Object* class, which we discussed earlier, contains a method called *getClass()* which returns a reference to a *Class* object which in turn gives us access to the RTTI. Since the *Object* class is an ancestor of every other class, the *getClass()* method is inherited by every class. Once we have this reference set up, we can use the methods of the *Class* object to access the RTTI data.

Instance Methods

String getName()	Returns the name of the object's class.
String getSuperclass()	Returns the parental class of the referenced object.

The program in LISTING-8.6 demonstrates the use of these two methods by linking to the RTTI of an *AlarmClock* object and displaying its class name and its superclass.

LISTING-8.6

Accessing RTTI

```
import AlarmClock;

public class UsingClass
{
  public static void main(String args[])
  {
      AlarmClock ac = new AlarmClock(1,2,3,1,2,4);
      Class cl = ac.getClass();

      System.out.println("ac is of class "+cl.getName());
      System.out.println(cl.getName()+" is a subclass of "
          ↳+cl.getSuperclass());
  }
}
```

The *Class* class contains many more methods. These allow, amongst other things, the methods and attributes of an object's class to be discovered.

However, *Class* objects are rarely used in normal Java applications and so no more details will be covered here. It is simply useful to know that this class exists and to have some idea of its purpose.

Other Java Classes

There are far too many Java classes to describe each of them in a text designed to give you a start in the language. However, those classes are stored in a handful of packages each of which contain classes with a common theme. As we've seen already, these classes can be used in your programs by including the appropriate `import` statement.

Some of these packages and the type of classes it holds is described below:

Package Name	***Type of Classes***	***Class Examples***
java.io	Data streams, files	File InputStream OutputStream Writer (see Chapter 11)
java.lang	Basic Classes	Object Class Math String (Classes from this package are included automatically without the need for an import statement.)
java.net	Network applications	InetAddress Socket URL Authticator (Network programming is not covered in this text.)
java.text	Handling and formatting text, dates and numbers	DecimalFormat DateFormat
java.util	Collection classes date and time	Arrays ArrayList Hashtable Calendar Date Random

Accessing Java's Documentation

So, what if you'd like to find out more about the *Class* class, or some other class not covered in this text? After all, there are over 1500 classes in the various Java packages,

Luckily, java helps with built-in documentation. If you know the name of a class, and the package in which it is held, you can use the **javap** utility program to have the details of any class listed. For example, if you'd like to discover all of the methods available in the *Object* class, type the following line at the command line prompt:

```
javap java.lang.Object
```

This will result in the following display:

Some of the terms here will be unfamilair to you.

native means that the method is written in some langauge other than Java and is compiled to machine code for the specific hardware and operating system being used.

final is used with a method to stop it being overridden in any descendant class.

```
Compiled from Object.java
public class java.lang.Object {
    static {};
    public java.lang.Object();
    protected native java.lang.Object clone() throws
                          java.lang.CloneNotSupportedException;
    public boolean equals(java.lang.Object);
    protected void finalize() throws java.lang.Throwable;
    public final native java.lang.Class getClass();
    public native int hashCode();
    public final native void notify();
    public final native void notifyAll();
    public java.lang.String toString();
    public final void wait() throws java.lang.InterruptedException;
    public final native void wait(long) throws
java.lang.InterruptedException;
    public final void wait(long, int) throws
java.lang.InterruptedException;
}
```

As you can see, there is little detail, but all public and protected features of the class are displayed.

If there's too much detail to fit on a single screen, or you want to retain the information for later, you can redirect the output to a text file. From MSDOS prompt, for example, you could enter

```
javap java.lang.Object > Object.txt
```

and this would redirect the output to the file *Object.txt* in the current directory. The file can then be opened in an editor.

> **Activity 8.18**
>
> Use *javap* to list the details of the *Class* class and save the details to the file *Class.txt*.
>
> Examine the details listed.

Java Class Documentation

If you have a complete installation of the Java Development Kit you should find a folder called *docs*. This contains a set of *html* files documenting all Java classes. To access the information, load a browser and search for the class whose details you require.

If there is no *docs* folder, the necessary files may be downloaded from the Sun web site. The zipped file is about 22Mbytes!

Wrapper Classes

Introduction

Java is primarily an object-oriented programming language. No code can be written without including it within a class of some type. And yet it also allows non-object data items such as `int`, `long`, `float`, `double`, `char` and `boolean`. There are times when this can be a problem. For example, if we write a function with an Object class parameter, we know that we can pass an object of any class to that function. However, we wouldn't be able to pass an `int` or `float` value since these are variable types, not class objects.

Java gets round this problem by creating a set of classes corresponding to the basic types. Hence, we can use an Integer class object rather than an `int` value. Most of the time its not worth the overheads involved and hence we stick with normal variable types, but on occassion it can be useful to cast a variable to its corresponding class type.

However, Java has placed many useful class methods in the **wrapper classes** and it is these that are most often used in simple programs.

The collective title of **wrapper classes** comes from the idea that a class structure encloses the basic data type.

The Integer Class

Use an *Integer* class object to treat an `int` value as an object.

There are two numeric constants in this class: MIN_VALUE and MAX_VALUE. These can be used to determine the largest and smallest (most negative) value that can be placed in a normal integer.

The program in LISTING-8.7 displays this range of values:

LISTING-8.7

Integer Class Constants

```
public class UsingInteger
{
    public static void main(String args[])
    {
        System.out.println("The smallest possible number is "
        ⇘+Integer.MIN_VALUE);
        System.out.println("The largest possible number is "
        ⇘+Integer.MAX_VALUE);
    }
}
```

The following are all class methods:

String toString(int no) — Returns *no* as a string. The value is shown in base 10.

For example,

`Integer.toString(255)`

returns the string "255".

String toString(int no, int base)

Returns *no* as a string. The string shows *no* is shown as a number to the base *base.*

For example:

```
Integer.toString(255,16)
```

returns "FF"

The program in LISTING-8.8 lists the value input in decimal, hex, octal and binary:

LISTING-8.8

`int` to `String`

```
import Input;
public class UsingInteger
{
   public static void main(String args[])
   {
        System.out.print("Enter a number:");
        int val = Input.readInt();
        System.out.println("In Decimal: "+Integer.toString(val));
        System.out.println("In Hex     : "+Integer.toString(val,16));
        System.out.println("In Octal   : "+Integer.toString(val,8));
        System.out.println("In Binary  : "+Integer.toString(val,2));
   }
}
```

int parseInt(String)

Converts string *st* to an integer. The string is assumed to represent a base 10 number.

int parseInt(String st, int base)

Converts string *st* to an integer. The string is assumed to represent a base *base* number.

Integer valueOf(String st)

Converts string *st* to an *Integer* class object. The string is assumed to represent a base 10 number.

Integer valueOf(String st, int base)

Converts string *st* to an Integer class object. The string is assumed to represent a base *base* number.

Constructors

Integer(int v)

Creates an *Integer* object with the initial value *v.*

Integer(String st)

Creates an *Integer* object with the initial value equivalent to the numeric value of *st*.

Instance Methods

byte byteValue()
short shortValue()
int intValue()
long longValue()
float floatValue()
double doubleValue()

These routines convert the value of the current object to the return type of the method.

For example, the code

```
Integer c = new Integer("15");
double x = c.doubleValue();
```

assigns a `double` value equivalent to that held in *c,* to *x*.

int compareTo(Integer v)	Compares the current object to *v*. There are three possible results: 0 returned if current object = *v* -ve value returned if current object < *v* +ve value returned if current object > *v*

The Byte Class

This is a wrapper class for the `byte` type.

Constants

MIN_VALUE *MAX_VALUE*	Hold the minimum and maximum values that can be held in a *byte* variable.

Constructors

Byte(byte v)	Creates a *Byte* object with the initial value *v*.
Byte(String st)	Creates a *Byte* object with the intial value equivalent to the numeric value of *st*.

Class Methods

String toString(byte no)	Converts *no* to a string.
byte parseByte(String st)	Converts *st* to a `byte` value.
byte parseByte(String st, int base)	Converts *st* to a `byte`. *st* is assumed to be to the base *base.*
Byte valueOf(String st)	Converts *st* to a *Byte* object.
Byte valueOf(String st, int base)	Converts *st* to a *Byte* object. *st* is assumed to be to the base *base.*

Instance Methods

byte byteValue() *short shortValue()* *int intValue()* *longValue()* *float floatValue()* *double doubleValue()*	These routines convert the value of the current object to the return type of the method.

int compareTo(Byte v)	Compares the current object to *v*. There are three possible results: 0 returned if current object = *v* -ve value returned if current object < *v* +ve value returned if current object > *v*

The Long Class

This is a wrapper class for the `long` type.

Constants

MIN_VALUE *MAX_VALUE*	Hold the minimum and maximum values that can be held in a `long` variable.

Constructors

Long(long v)	Creates a *Long* object with the initial value *v*.
Long(String st)	Creates a *Long* object with the intial value equivalent to the numeric value of *st*.

Class Methods

String toString(long no)	Converts *no* to a string.
String toString(long no, int base)	Converts *no* to a string. The string shows *no* as a number to the base *base.*
long parseLong(String st)	Converts *st* to a *long* value.
long parseLong(String st, int base)	Converts *st* to a *long*. *st* is assumed to be to the base *base.*
Long valueOf(String st)	Converts *st* to a *Long* object.
Long valueOf(String st, int base)	Converts *st* to a *Long* object. *st* is assumed to be to the base *base.*

Instance Methods

byte byteValue() *short shortValue()* *int intValue()* *long longValue()* *float floatValue()* *double doubleValue()*	These routines convert the value of the current object to the return type of the method.
int compareTo(Long v)	Compares the current object to *v*. There are three possible results: 0 returned if current object = *v* -ve value returned if current object < *v* +ve value returned if current object > *v*

The Float Class

This is a wrapper class for the `float` type.

Constants

POSITIVE_INFINITY	Represents negative infinity in `float` format.
NEGATIVE_INFINITY	Represents positive infinity in `float` format.
NaN	Not-a-number.
MAX_VALUE	The maximum value a `float` can hold.
MIN_VALUE	The smallest positive value a `float` can hold.

One way of ending up with a POSITIVE_INFINITY value is to divide a `float` value by zero. For example, the code fragment

```
float x = 9;
if(x/0 == Float.POSITIVE_INFINITY)
    System.out.println("Positive infinity");
```

when executed as part of a program will display the message "Positive infinity".

If *x* had the value -9 the x/0 would equal `Float.NEGATIVE_INFINITY.`

`Float.Nan` can be assigned to a `float` variable as the result of some impossible calculation. For example:

```
float y = (float)Math.sqrt(-9);
```

Constructors

Float(float v)	Creates a *Float* object from the intial value *v*.
Float(double v)	Creates a *Float* object from the intial value *v*.
Float(String st)	Creates an *Float* object with the intial value equivalent to the numeric value of *st*.

Class Methods

String toString(float no)	Converts *no* to a string.
float parseFloat(String v)	Converts *st* to a `float` value.
Float valueOf(String st)	Converts *st* to a *Float* object.
boolean isNaN(float no)	Returns *true* if *no* contains an invalid value.

For example, the code

```
float y = (float)Math.sqrt(-9);
if(Float.isNaN(y))
    System.out.println("Invalid operation");
```

would display the message "*Invalid operation*".

boolean isInfinite(float no)	Returns *true* if *no* has an infinite value, positive or negative; otherwise *false* is returned.

Instance Methods

boolean isNaN()	Returns *true* if the current *Float* object contains an invalid value; otherwise *false* is returned.

For example, the code

```
Float y = new Float(Math.sqrt(-9));
if(y.isNaN())
    System.out.println("Invalid operation");
```

would display the message "*Invalid operation*".

boolean isInfinite()	Returns *true* if the current *Float* object has an infinite value, positive or negative; otherwise *false* is returned.
byte byteValue() *short shortValue()* *int intValue()* *long longValue()* *float floatValue()* *double doubleValue()*	These routines convert the value of the current object to the return type of the method.
int compareTo(Float v)	Compares the current object to *v*. There are three possible results: 0 returned if current object = *v* -ve value returned if current object < *v* +ve value returned if current object > *v*

The Double Class

This is a wrapper class for the `double` type.

Constants

POSITIVE_INFINITY
NEGATIVE_INFINITY
NaN
MAX_VALUE
MIN_VALUE

These have the same purpose as the named constants of the *Float* class.

Constructors

Double(double v)	Creates a *Double* object from the initial value *v*.

Double(String st)	Creates a *Double* object with the initial value equivalent to the numeric value of *st*.

Class Methods

String toString(double no)	Converts *no* to a string.
Double valueOf(String st)	Converts *st* to a *Double* object.
double parseDouble(String st)	Converts *st* to a `double` value.
boolean isNaN(double no)	Returns *true* if *no* contains an invalid value; otherwise *false* is returned.
isInfinite(double no)	Returns *true* if *no* has an infinite value, positive or negative; otherwise *false* is returned.

Instance Methods

boolean isNaN()	Returns *true* if the current *Double* object contains an invalid value; otherwise *false* is returned.
boolean isInfinite()	Returns *true* if the current *Double* object has an infinite value, positive or negative; otherwise *false* is returned.
byte byteValue() *short shortValue()* *int intValue()* *long longValue()* *float floatValue()* *double doubleValue()*	These routines convert the value of the current object to the return type of the method.
int compareTo(Double v)	Compares the current object to *v*. There are three possible results: 0 returned if current object = *v* -ve value returned if current object < *v* +ve value returned if current wobject > *v*

The Character Class

This is a wrapper class for the *char* type. Because Unicode can represent characters from around the world, some of the methods do more than you might assume from their name. For example, the method *isLowerCase(ch)* returns *true* if *ch* is a lowercase character. For English speaking countries the assumption is that the method will return *true* only if *ch* lies between 'a' and 'z', but other countries have other symbols that they would consider lowercase and these characters also return *true* when used as arguments to *isLowerCase()*. However, for the most part we will restrict the discussion here to the English alphabet.

Constants

int MIN_RADIX
int MAX_RADIX

The minimum and maximum values allowed when converting a character to or from a number. See *digit()* and *forDigit()* below.

char MIN_VALUE
char MAX_VALUE

The minumum and maximum value that can be assigned to a character.

byte UNASSIGNED
byte UPPERCASE_LETTER
byte LOWERCASE_LETTER
byte TITLECASE_LETTER
byte MODIFIER_LETTER
byte OTHER_LETTER
byte NON_SPACING_MARK
byte ENCLOSING_MARK
byte COMBINING_SPACING_MARK
byte DECIMAL_DIGIT_NUMBER
byte LETTER_NUMBER
byte OTHER_NUMBER
byte SPACE_SEPARATOR
byte LINE_SEPARATOR
byte PARAGRAPH_SEPARATOR
byte CONTROL
byte FORMAT
byte PRIVATE_USE
byte SURROGATE
byte DASH_PUNCTUATION
byte START_PUNCTUATION
byte END_PUNCTUATION
byte CONNECTOR_PUNCTUATION
byte OTHER_PUNCTUATION
byte MATH_SYMBOL
byte CURRENCY_SYMBOL
byte MODIFIER_SYMBOL
byte OTHER_SYMBOL

Possible values returned by the *getType()* method (see next page)

Constructor

Character(char ch)	Creates a *Character* object from the intial value *ch*.

Class methods

boolean isLowerCase(char ch)	Returns *true* if *ch* is a lowercase character; otherwise *false* is returned.
boolean isUpperCase(char ch)	Returns *true* if *ch* is a uppercase character; otherwise *false* is returned.

boolean isDigit(char ch)	Returns *true* if *ch* is a numeric digit (0 to 9); otherwise *false* is returned.
boolean isDefined(char ch)	Returns *true* if *ch* is a valid Unicode character; otherwise *false* is returned.
boolean isLetter(char ch)	Returns *true* if *ch* is a letter; otherwise *false* is returned.
boolean isLetterOrDigit(char ch)	Returns *true* if *ch* is a letter or numeric digit character; otherwise *false* is returned.
boolean isJavaIdentifierStart(char ch)	Returns *true* if *ch* is a valid first character of a Java identifier; otherwise *false* is returned.
boolean isJavaIdentifierPart(char ch)	Returns *true* if *ch* is a valid second or subsequent character of a Java identifier; otherwise *false* is returned.
char toLowerCase(char ch)	Returns the lowercase equivalent of *ch*.
char toUpperCase(char ch)	Returns the uppercase equivalent of *ch*.
int digit(char ch, int rdx)	Returns the numeric value of *ch* assuming *ch* is a valid digit in the number system of base *rdx*.
int getNumericValue(char ch)	Returns the Unicode value of *ch* as an integer.
boolean isSpaceChar(char ch)	Returns true if *ch* is a space character in Unicode.
boolean isWhitespace(char ch)	Returns true if *ch* is a space character in ISO-LATIN-1
boolean isISOControl(char ch)	Returns true if *ch* is a ISO control character.
int getType(char ch)	Returns an integer value categorising *ch*. Possible return values are defined in the *Character* class constants.
char forDigit(int v, int rdx)	Returns the char value of the numeric value *v* which is assumed to be of the radix *rdx*.

ISO-LATIN-1 is the normal European character set.

Instance Methods

char charValue()	Returns the char equivalent of the current *Character* object.

The Boolean Class

Constants

TRUE
FALSE

Constructors

Boolean(boolean b)	Creates a *Boolean* object from the intial value *b*.
Boolean(String st)	Creates a *Boolean* object from the intial value *st*. If *st* is any value other than "true" then the *Boolean* object is set to *false.* The value of *st* is not case-sensitive.

Class Methods

Boolean valueOf(String st)	Returns a *Boolean* object whose value is determined by *st*.
boolean getBoolean(String st)	Returns a boolean type whose value is determined by *st*.

Instance Methods

boolean booleanValue()	Returns the boolean value of the current object

Solutions

Activity 8.1

```
public class Act8_1
{
    public static void main(String args[])
    {
        String s[] = {"Heron, Liz", "Tait, Avril",
            ↳"Taylor, Sandra", "Ferguson, Jackie",
            ↳"Garry, Lynn", "Bell, Gillian"};
        int total = 0;
        for(int c = 0; c < s.length; c++)
            total += s[c].length();
        System.out.println("Average length of
            ↳the names is "+total/s.length);
    }
}
```

Activity 8.2

```
public class Act8_2
{
    public static void main(String args[])
    {
        System.out.println("Hello world contains "
        ↳+"Hello world".length()
        ↳+" characters. In upper case it is "
        ↳+"Hello world".toUpperCase());
    }
}
```

Activity 8.3

```
import Input;

public class Act8_3
{
    public static void main(String args[])
    {
        String words[] = new String[10];
        System.out.print("Enter sentence: ");
        String sentence = Input.readString();
        System.out.println(sentence);
        sentence = sentence+" ";
        int index = 0;
        int startat = 0;
        int endofword =
            ↳sentence.indexOf(" ",startat);
        while (endofword != -1)
        {
            words[index++] =
            ↳sentence.substring(startat,endofword);
            startat = endofword+1;
            endofword =
                ↳sentence.indexOf(" ",startat);
        }
        for(int c = 0; c < index; c++)
            System.out.println(words[c]);
    }
}
```

Activity 8.4

```
public class Act8_4
{
    public static void main(String args[])
    {
        for(int c=0; c < args.length; c++)
            System.out.println(args[c]);
    }
}
```

Activity 8.5

```
public class Act8_5
{
    public static void main(String args[])
    {
        StringBuffer sb1 = new StringBuffer();
        System.out.println(sb1.length());
        System.out.println(sb1.capacity());
    }
}
```

Activity 8.6

```
public class Act8_6
{
    public static void main(String args[])
    {
        StringBuffer sb1 = new StringBuffer(30);
        System.out.println(sb1.length());
        System.out.println(sb1.capacity());
    }
}
```

The string buffer now has a capacity of 30.

Activity 8.7

```
public class Act8_7
{
    public static void main(String args[])
    {
        StringBuffer sb1 = new StringBuffer("Hello
world");
        System.out.println(sb1.length());
        System.out.println(sb1.capacity());
    }
}
```

The string buffer is created with capacity of its initial value + 16.

Activity 8.8

No solution required.

Activity 8.9

```
public class Act8_9
{
    public static void main(String args[])
    {
        StringBuffer sb1 =
            ↳new StringBuffer("Hello world");
        StringBuffer sb2 =
            ↳sb1.append(" - Mars calling");
        System.out.println(sb1.length());
        System.out.println(sb1.capacity());
        System.out.println(sb1+"\n"+sb2);
    }
}
```

Activity 8.10

No solution required.

Activity 8.11

```
import Input;

public class Act8_11
{
    public static void main(String args[])
    {
        System.out.print("Enter sentence: ");
        StringBuffer sentence =
        ↳new StringBuffer(Input.readString());
        for(int c = 0;c < sentence.length()-1;c++)
            if(sentence.charAt(c)=='e')
                sentence.setCharAt(c,'a');
        System.out.println(sentence);
    }
}
```

Activity 8.12

No solution required.

Activity 8.13

```
import Input;

public class Act8_13
{
    public static void main(String args[])
    {
        int number = (int)(Math.random()*100)+1;
        for(int c = 1; c <= 6; c++)
        {
            System.out.print("Enter guess: ");
            int guess = Input.readInt();
            if(guess == number)
            {
                System.out.println("Correct");
                break;
            }
            if(guess < number)
                System.out.println("Too low");
            else
                System.out.println("Too high");
        }
        System.out.println("The number was "+number);
    }
}
```

Activity 8.14

```
import java.text.*;

public class TestFormatting
{
    public static void main(String args[])
    {
        DecimalFormat df = new DecimalFormat
        ↳("#.0000");
        System.out.println("SQUARE ROOTS");
        for(int c = 0; c <= 20; c++)
            System.out.println(df.format
            ↳(Math.sqrt(c)));
    }
}
```

Activity 8.15

```
import java.text.DecimalFormat;
import Input;

public class Act8_15
{
    public static void main(String args[])
    {
        DecimalFormat df = new
        ↳DecimalFormat("##0.00");
        System.out.print("Enter amount :");
        double pounds = Input.readFloat();
        double dollars = pounds *1.42;
        System.out.println(df.format(pounds)+
        ↳"GBP converts to $"+df.format(dollars));
    }
}
```

Activity 8.16

No solution required.

Activity 8.17

```
import java.util.Arrays;

public class Act8_17
{
    public static void main(String args[])
    {
        int nos[]={7,1,9,5,2,7,4};
        for(int c=0; c < nos.length; c++)
            System.out.print(nos[c]+ " ");
        System.out.println();
        Arrays.sort(nos);
        for(int c=0; c < nos.length; c++)
            System.out.print(nos[c]+ " ");
        System.out.print("Enter value: ");
        int value = Input.readInt();
        int position =
            ↳Arrays.binarySearch(nos,value);
        if(position > -1 )
            System.out.println("Found at position "
                ↳+position);
        else
            System.out.println("Not found");
    }
}
```

Activity 8.18

Requires the DOS command:

```
javap java.lang.Class > Class.txt
```

CHAPTER 9

Advanced Features

This chapter covers the following topics:

Abstract Classes

Aggregate Classes

Anonymous Derived Classes

Arrays of Objects

Container Classes

Inner Classes

Interfaces

JavaDoc

List

Packages

Queue

Stack

Advanced Class Features

Arrays of Objects

As well as individual objects, we can create arrays of objects. To set up an array of *Weight* objects we use the declaration

```
Weight list[];
```

Later in the program we can set the size of the array. For example, a 3 element array would be constructed using the statement.

```
list = new Weight[3];
```

As with arrays of variables, we can combine these two statements:

```
Weight list [] = new Weight[3];
```

Since we are dealing with objects, the array contains only object references, not the actual objects themselves. To create the objects we have to use the `new` statement on each element of the array:

```
for(int c = 0; c < list.length; c++)
    list[c] = new Weight();
```

The effects of these statements are shown in FIG-9.1.

FIG-9.1

Arrays of Objects

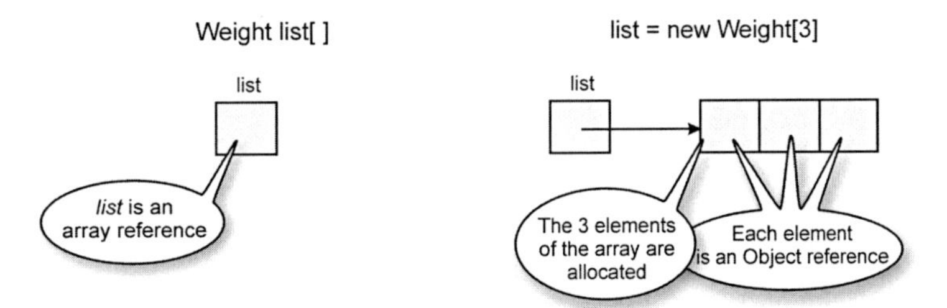

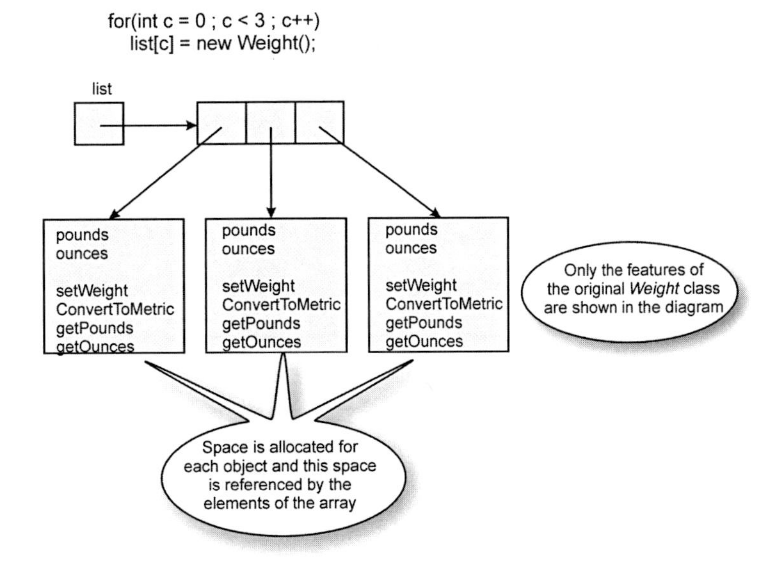

Alternatively, we can construct the array and its objects using a statement such as:

```
Weight list[]={new Weight(2,3),new Weight(1,1),new Weight(2,3)};
```

Access to the array elements and the corresponding methods uses a combination of the array subscript syntax and object method access. For example, to execute the *setWeight()* method of the object in *list[0]* we write a statement such as

```
list[0].setWeight(6,3);
```

And to display each *Weight* object in the array we use

```
for(int c = 0; c < list.length; c++)
    System.out.println(list[c].getPounds()+" lbs "
    ↳+list[c].getOunces() + " oz");
```

Activity 9.1

Create an array containing 4 *Distance* objects, initialising each object to a non-zero value.

Display the total of the four distances and the longest distance held.

If we create an array of some base class, then objects of derived classes can be referenced. For example, the code

```
Clock list[] = new Clock[3];
```

creates an array in which we can store references to *Clock, AlarmClock* or *CountdownClock* objects. The program in LISTING-9.1 demonstrates this technique by creating one clock of each type, applying the *tick()* method to these objects and then displaying the time on each.

LISTING-9.1

Array of Class and Subclass Objects

```
import Clock;
import AlarmClock;
import CountdownClock;

public class List9_1
{
  public static void main(String args[])
  {
      Clock list[] = {new Clock(1,2,3),
      ↳new AlarmClock(1,2,3,2,2,2), new CountdownClock(1,2,3)};
      for(int c = 0; c < list.length; c++)
          list[c].tick();
      for(int c = 0; c < list.length; c++)
          System.out.println(list[c]);
  }
}
```

Abstract Classes

Dogs, cats and mice are different, but we can link them by saying that they are all types of mammal. We can make use of this idea to link seemingly incompatible classes in an object-oriented system.

Imagine a software system in which we want to create the classes shown in FIG-9.2

FIG-9.2

Types of Worker

PartTimeWorker	FullTimeWorker	ContractWorker
name address salary hoursthisweek	name address salary pensioncontr	name address salary contractperiod
setName() setAddress() setSalary() setHours() getName() getAddress() getSalary() getHours()	setName() setAddress() setSalary() setPension() getName() getAddress() getSalary() getPension()	setName() setAddress() setSalary() setContract() getName() getAddress() getSalary() getContract()

Each is a different class and yet they are related in that all three are types of worker.

We can emphasis this relationship by defining a *Worker* class and then creating *FullTimeWorker, PartTimeWorker* and *ContractWorker* as classes descendent from the *Worker* class (see FIG-9.3)

FIG-9.3

Creating an Abstract Class

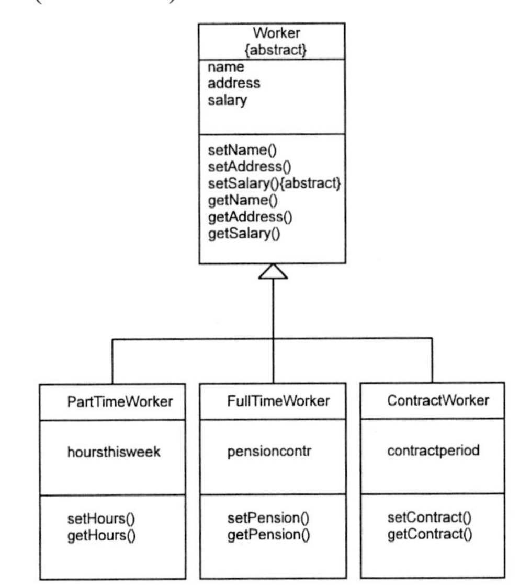

Note that the *Worker* class is marked as abstract. Routines in that class that are not coded are also marked as abstract.

What advantages are there in doing this? To start with, the attributes and methods common to all three of the original classes need only be defined once - in the *Worker* class; these will then be inherited by the descendant classes where only new and updated features need be coded.

Of course, defining the *Worker* class is only a ploy to connect the other three classes together. When we create objects using these classes in subsequent application programs, none of those objects will be of type *Worker*, but of one of its descendant classes. In the same way, no animal can be described solely as a mammal, but is always one of the descendant types (cat, dog or mice, etc.)

When we define a class like the *Worker* class, where we have no intention of creating an actual object of that classes but simply employ the class as a common ancestor to more practical classes, that class is known as an **abstract class.** Normal classes - those from which we can create objects - are known as **concrete classes.**

To define an abstract class in Java we need to use the `abstract` keyword in the class definition:

```
public abstract class Worker
{
    protected String name;
    protected String address;
    protected float salary;

    public void setName(String s)~
    {
        name = s;
    }

    public void setAddress(String s)
    {
        address = s;
    }

    public String getName()
    {
        return name;
    }

    public String getAddress()
    {
        return address;
    }

    public float getSalary()
    {
        return salary;
    }
}
```

If you want to include the name of a method within an abstract class but not its code (because it is to be coded with differing logic in each of the descendant classes) then we can define the method as abstract as well:

```
    public abstract void setSalary(int v);
```

We can then go on and define the descendant classes. It is possible, in a complex situation that some of these descendant classes could themselves be abstract. But, more often, we will create concrete descendant classes. These concrete sub-classes must include code for any methods defined as abstract within the super-class. Of course, new methods can be added as required in the descendant class.

For example, the code for the *PartTimeWorker* class might be defined as:

```
    public class PartTimeWorker extends Worker
    {
        protected double hoursthisweek;

        public void setSalary(int v)
        {
            salary = (int)(v *0.5);
        }

        public  void setHours(double h)
        {
            if (h < 0 || h > 168)
                return;
            hoursthisweek = h;
        }

        public double getHours()
        {
            return hoursthisweek;
        }
    }
```

Activity 9.2

Type in the code for both classes above *(Worker* and *PartTimeWorker)*.

Add the *FullTimeWorker* class. Its *setSalary(int v)* assigns *v* to *salary*. *pensioncntr* is a `double` value representing an cash paid to pension fund.
Add the *ContractWorker* class. Its *setSalary(int v)* assigns *v* * 2 to *salary*. *contractperiod* is the number of weeks a contract is to last.

Because each of the worker classes has a common ancestor in the abstract *Worker* class, we can create an array of workers using the same idea as we did with the array of clocks earlier:

```
Worker employees[] = new Worker[10];
```

You might think, at first glance, that the above line creates objects of the *Worker* class; something we are not allowed to do because the *Worker* class is abstract. But, of course, all that has been created is an array of reference variables; no actual objects have yet been produced.

The new array can then have workers of any of the descendant types added. For example:

```
employees[0] = new FullTimeWorker();
employees[1] = new PartTimeWorker();
employees[2] = new ContractWorker();
```

We can then cycle through each element of the array and set the salaries:

```
for(int c = 0; c < employees.length; c++)
    employees[c].setSalary(35000);
```

Aggregate Classes

In the simple classes we have examined so far the attributes of the class have been simple variables, but a class attribute can also be an object from a second class type. To illustrate this idea, let's assume we require a class containing the name, handicap weight and winning distance of a race horse. We could define the attributes of such such a class as

```
public class Horse
{
    private String name;
    private Weight handicap;
    private Distance length;
```

Because each attribute of the class is itself an object, declaring a *Horse* object with the statement

```
Horse h = new Horse()
```

will only create reference fields within the object (see FIG-8.4)

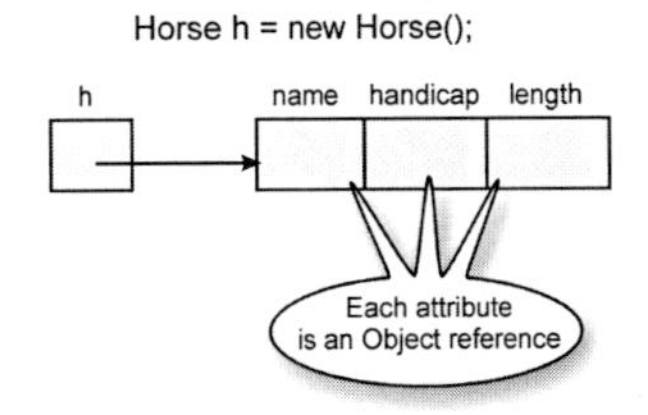

FIG-9.4

Creating an Object containing Class Attributes

There are two ways to solve this problem:

The first is to include the object creation within the declaration:

```
public class Horse
{
    private String name = new String();
    private Weight handicap = new Weight();
    private Distance length = new Distance();
```

Alternatively, we can write a constructor which will allocate the required inner objects:

```
    public Horse()
    {
        name = new String();
        handicap = new Weight();
        length = new Distance();
    }

    Horse h = new Horse();
```

In either case *h* is now constructed as shown in FIG-9.5.

FIG-9.5

Making the Constructor Allocate Space for the Objects

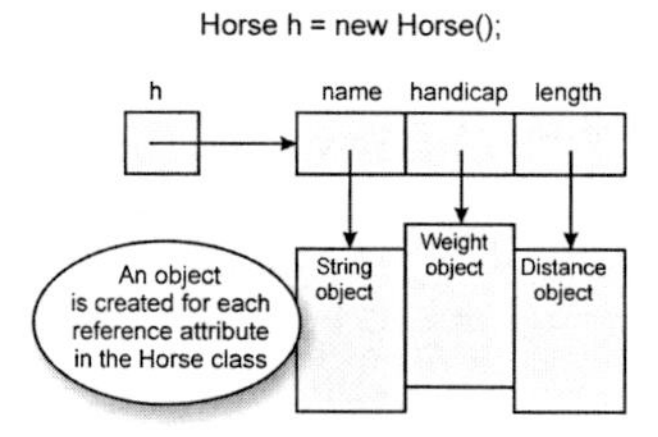

If we want to initialise the new object with specified values then we need a second version of the constructor that takes parameters:

```
    public Horse(String s, Weight w, Distance d)
    {
        name = new String(s);
        handicap = new Weight(w);
        length = new Distance(d);
    }
```

Activity 9.3

Create a third constructor for the *Horse* class which takes a *Horse* object as a parameter. That is, the signature of the new constructor should be

```
public Horse(Horse h)
```

A class in which one or more of the attributes are themselves objects are sometimes known as **aggregate classes**.

Like other classes, we'll need to create get and set methods for the private attributes of the class.
The *setName()* and *getName()* routines would be coded as

```
    public void setName(String s)
    {
        name = s;
    }

    public String getName()
    {
```

```
        return name;
    }
```

When setting the other attributes, we need to make use of the *setWeight(Weight w)* and *setDistance(Distance d)* methods. Hence, setting and getting *handicap* is coded as

```
public void setHandicap(Weight w)
{
    handicap.setWeight(w);
}

public Weight getHandicap()
{
    return handicap;
}
```

Activity 9.4

Write the code necessary to get and set *length* in the *Horse* class.

UML shows aggregate classes using a diamond-tipped line between the various classes involved. The UML class diagram for the *Horse* class is shown in FIG-9.6.

FIG-9.6

UML Aggregation

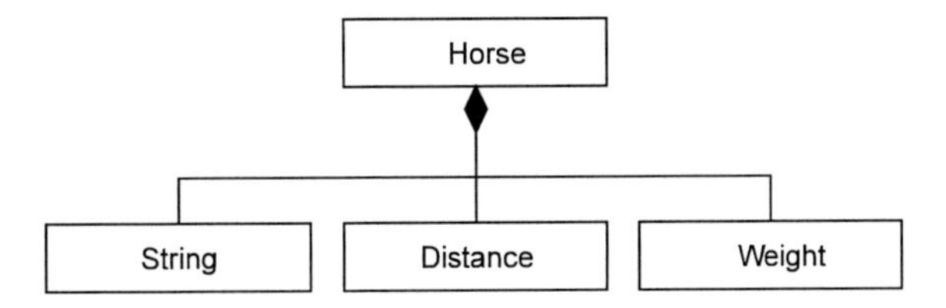

Activity 9.5

Type in and compile the *Horse* class.

Write a test program in which two *Horse* objects are created. Initialise the first of these using a constructor call with the values

```
"Red Rum",new Weight(12,7),new Distance(0,2,1)
```

Create a second horse object and assign its attributes values using the appropriate set methods.

Overriding toString()

Unlike previous classes, the *Horse* class has attributes that are not as closely tied as those of the *Weight, Distance* and *Clock* classes. It is therefore no longer as obvious how to deal with the *toString()* method for this class. A widely used convention is to create a string containing the name of the class followed by braces enclosing attribute names and values. Using this approach the *toString()* method in the *Horse* class would be

This requires the *toString()* method of the *Weight* and *Distance* classes to have been overridden as described earlier.

```
public String toString()
{
    return("Horse[name="+name+"handicap="+handicap+"length="
    ↳+length+"]");
}
```

Inner Classes

In the last example, we saw that it is possible to create a class in which some or all the attributes are themselves objects. It is also possible to construct a class within a class. This shouldn't be too strange an idea if you've every used record structures. We might define a student's details as containing the name and date of birth of a student. But *date of birth* is itself a record structure containing *day, month* and *year*. So, in some hypothetical language, we might define a variable of this type as

```
Student:
RECORD
    name : string
    dateofbirth :
        RECORD
            day : integer
            month : integer
            year : integer
        ENDRECORD
ENDRECORD
```

The same sort of structure can be created in Java.

The top level class starts here

The inner class starts here

This attribute is of the type defined in the inner class

```
public class Student
{
    private String name;
    public Date dateofbirth;

    class Date
    {
        private int day;
        private int month;
        private int year;

        public Date()
        {
            day = 1;
            month = 1;
            year = 2001;
        }


        public Date (int d, int m, int y)
        {
            day = d;
            month = m;
            year = y;
        }

        public void setDate(int d, int m, int y)
        {
            day = d;
            month = m;
            year = y;
        }


        public int getDay()
        {
            return day;
        }


        public int getMonth()
        {
            return month;
        }
```

```
        public int getYear()
        {
            return year;
        }
    }

    Student()
    {
        dateofbirth = new Date();
    }

    public void setName(String s)
    {
        name = s;
    }

    public String getName()
    {
        return name;
    }

    public void setDOB(int d, int  m, int y)
    {
        dateofbirth.setDate(d,m,y);
    }
}
```

We could then use objects of this class in code such as

```
class TestInner
{
    public static void main(String args[])
    {
        Student s = new Student();
        s.setName("Liz Heron");
        s.setDOB(9,9,1999);
        System.out.println(s.getName());
        System.out.println(s.dateofbirth.getDay()+"/"
        +s.dateofbirth.getMonth()+"/"+s.dateofbirth.getYear());
    }
}
```

The ability to use inner classes was introduced in Java 1.1. The technique is actually helpful in a few specialised situations, one of which we will examine in a later chapter. As a general rule, don't use inner classes.

Anonymous Derived Classes

We have already seen that it can be useful to create anonymous objects, perhaps as a parameter to some routine. For example, look at the program in LISTING-9.2

LISTING-9.2

An Anonymous Object as an Parameter

```
import Weight;

public class ADC
{
  public static void main(String args[])
  {
      displayObject(new Weight());
  }

  public static void displayObject(Object v)
  {
      System.out.println(v);
  }
}
```

This program contains a method called *displayObject()* which displays the contents of an object (Recall that *println()* calls the *toString()* method of the object to create the string to be output).

An anonymous *Weight* object is created as the argument to the routine.

> **Activity 9.6**
>
> What value should be displayed from the above program?
>
> Type in and run the program.

What if we want to create a derivative of the *Weight* class in order to override the *toString()* method and achieve a different effect when an object of this new class is passed to *displayObject()*? One way to do this is to define a new class:

Ensure that all the classes you have created up to this point have *toString()* methods.

```
public class WeightA extends Weight
{
    public String toString()
    {
        return "Hello";
    }
}
```

And then use an object of this class as the argument to *displayObject()*:

```
displayObject(new WeightA());
```

But a second alternative is to combine the creation of the required object and the definition of its class:

```
displayObject(new Weight(){public String toString()
                                        ➥{return"Hello";}});
```

The syntax of this second approach does not make it clear that an object of a new class which extends the *Weight* class is being created. Neither the class nor the object created are named. Unfortunately, this is a technique that is widely used by some programmers as we will see in a later chapter.

> **Activity 9.7**
>
> Add the line
>
> ```
> displayObject(new Weight(){public String toString()
>                                         ➥{return"Hello";}});
> ```
>
> to your previous program's *main()* method and execute the code.

Summary

- **Declaring a class array** creates an array of reference variables.
- **The references variables in a class array** must be assigned the address of an object or set to null.
- **A class array can be initialised** using the format

```
Class_name array_name[] = { new Constructor(),....};
```

- **Declaring a class as abstract** means no objects of that class can be created.
- **A class is abstract if** one or more of its operations are defined as abstract and contain no code.
- **Abstract class are often created to serve as a common ancestor** to other classes.
- **Any descendant class will also be abstract** unless it overrides the abstract class of its parent.
- **A abstract class reference variable** may be created but it must reference a non-abstract descendant class.
- **An aggregate class** is one in which one or more of the attributes are objects of some other class.
- **Use the `new` command** within the attribute section or the constructor of the aggregate class to create the required attribute objects.
- **An inner class** is a class defined within an existing class.
- **Only the outer class** can create objects of the inner class.
- **The inner class has full access** to the attributes of the outer class.
- **An anonymous derived class** creates a one-off object which overrides methods in an existing class.

Container Classes

Introduction

An important category of class structures is the **container classes**. A container class is designed to contain a collection of values. For example, we earlier designed the *Weight* class to contain a single imperial weight value. If we required several weights within a program then we had to create several *Weight* objects or an array of *Weights*. However, by creating a *Weight* container class we could store several weights within a single object. Typically, container classes supply methods of inserting, deleting, retrieving and modifying the items it contains.

The IntList Class

One of the simplest container structures is the **List**. This, as the name suggests, simply contains a list of values held one after the other. The obvious way to implement this is within an array. So, as items are added the array begins to fill Since it will be useful to know how much of the array is occupied, we can add a second attribute, *count*, to record this information(see FIG-9.6).

FIG-9.6

The List Attributes

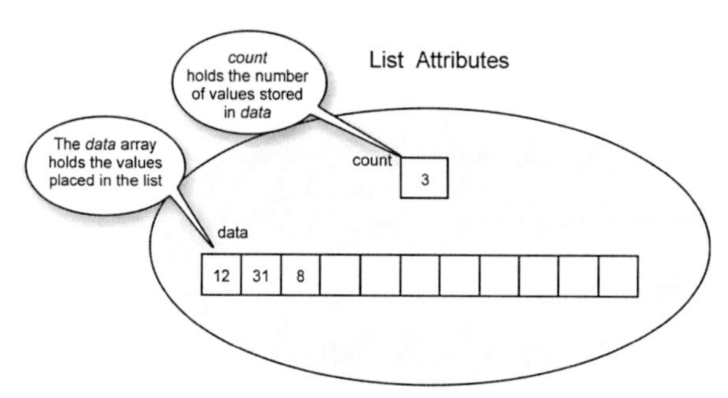

Since Java actually contains a class called *List*, we'll call our implementation *IntList* since our list is restricted to holding `int` values.

The *IntList* class can have many operations. These are described informally below:

`create()` methods will be implemented as constructors.

NOTE: The first item in the list is considered to be at position 1.

create()	Creates an empty list with 10 elements.
create(int sz)	Creates a list with *sz* elements.
create(IntList s)	Creates a new list which is an exact copy of *s*.
boolean isFull()	Returns *true* if the list is full, otherwise returns *false*.
boolean isEmpty()	Returns *true* if the list is empty, otherwise returns *false*.
void clear()	Clears the contents of the list.
int indexOf(int v)	Returns the position at which *v* is found in the list. This will range from 1 to *count*. If the value is not found, zero is returned.
int get(int p)	Returns the value at position *p*. If *p* is outside the range 1 to *count*, the program terminates.
int occupied()	Returns the number of values held in the list.

int free() Returns the number of empty elements in the list.

void add(int v, int p) Adds *v* at position *p*.
If *p* is outside the range 1 to *count*+1 or the list is full, the value is not added.

void add(int v) Adds *v* to the end of the list.
If the list is full, the value is not added.

void delete(int p) Deletes the item at position *p* in the list.
If *p* is outside the range 1 to *count* or the list is empty, no value is deleted.

void delete() Deletes the first item in the list.
There is no change if the list is empty.

int head() Returns the first value in the list.
If the list is empty, the program terminates.

IntList tail() Removes the first item from the list and returns this reduced list.
If the list is empty, the program terminates.

String toString() Returns the values held in the list as a string.
Each value is separated from the next by a newline character.

boolean equals(Object obj) Returns *true* if *obj* (which should be another list) contains exactly the same values in the same order as the current list.

The code for the *IntList* class is given below in LISTING-9.3.

LISTING-9.3

The IntList Class

```
public class IntList
{
  protected int data[];
  protected int count;

  public IntList()
  {
      data = new int[10];
      count = 0;
  }

  public IntList(int sz)
  {
      if (sz>1)
          data = new int [sz];
      else
          data = new int[10];
      count = 0;
  }

  public IntList(IntList l)
  {
      data = new int[l.data.length];
      for(int p = 0; p < l.data.length; p++)
          data[p]=l.data[p];
      count = l.count;
  }

  public boolean isFull()
  {
      if(count==data.length)
          return true;
      else
          return false;
   }
```

Continued on next page

LISTING-9.3
(continued)

The IntList Class

```
public void clear()
{
    count = 0;
}

public boolean isEmpty()
{
    if(count == 0)
        return true;
    else
        return false;
}

public int indexOf(int v)
{
    for (int c = 0 ; c < count ; c++)
    if (data[c] == v)
        return c+1;
    return 0;
}

public int get(int p)
{
    if (p < 1 || p > count)
        System.exit(0);
    return data[p-1];
}

public int occupied()
{
    return count;
}

public int free()
{
    return (data.length - count);
}

public void add(int v, int p)
{
    if(isFull()||p<1||p>count+1)
        return;
    for(int c = count-1;c >= p-1 ;c--)
        data[c+1]=data[c];
    data[p-1] = v;
    count++;
}

public void add(int v)
{
    if(isFull())
        return;
    data[count++] = v;
}

public void delete(int p)
{
    if (p<1 || p>count)
        return;
    for(int c = p; c<=count-1; c++)
        data[c-1]=data[c];
    count--;
}

public void delete()
{
    tail();
}
```

Continued on next page

LISTING-9.3
(continued)

The IntList Class

```
  public int head()
  {
       if (isEmpty())
            System.exit(0);
       return data[0];
  }

  public IntList tail()
  {
       if (isEmpty())
            System.exit(0);
       else
       {
            for(int p = 1 ; p < count ; p++)
                 data[p-1]=data[p];
            count--;
       }
       return this;
  }

  public String toString()
  {
       StringBuffer s = new StringBuffer();
       for(int p = 0; p <= count-1; p++)
       {
            s.append(data[p]);
            s.append('\n');
       }
       return s.toString();
   }

  public boolean equals(Object l)
  {
       if(!(l instanceof IntList)
            return false;
       IntList temp = (IntList)l;
       if(count != temp.count)
            return false;
       for(int c = 0; c < count ; c++)
            if(data[c] != temp.data[c])
                 return false;
       return true;
  }
}
```

The program in LISTING-9.4 tests the various features of the *IntList* class.

LISTING-9.4

Testing the IntList Class

```
import IntList;
import Input;


public class TestList
{
  public static void main(String args[])
  {
       IntList info = new IntList();
       int option = displayMenu();
       while (option != 11)
       {
            executeOption(info,option);
            option = displayMenu();
       }
  }
```

continued on next page

LISTING-9.4
(continued)

Testing the IntList

```
public static int displayMenu()
{
     System.out.println(" 1. Add item at position \n"+
     ↪" 2. Add item at end\n"+
     ↪" 3. Delete item from specified position\n"+
     ↪" 4. Delete first item\n"+
     ↪" 5. List\n"+
     ↪" 6. No. of items in list\n"+
     ↪" 7. Empty?\n"+
     ↪" 8. Full?\n"+
     ↪" 9. Head\n"+
     ↪"10. Tail\n"+
     ↪"11. Quit");
     System.out.print("Enter option : ");
     int option = Input.readInt();
     return option;
}

public static void executeOption(IntList info, int op)
{
     int p, v;
     switch(op)
     {
          case 1:
               System.out.print("Enter new value : ");
               v = Input.readInt();
               System.out.print("Enter position 1 to "
               ↪+(info.occupied()+1)+" ");
               p = Input.readInt();
               info.add(v,p);
               break;
          case 2:
               System.out.print("Enter new value : ");
               v = Input.readInt();
               info.add(v);
               break;
          case 3:
               System.out.print("Position of item to delete ");
               System.out.print(" 1 to "+info.occupied());
               p = Input.readInt();
               info.delete(p);
               break;
          case 4:
               info.delete();
               break;
          case 5:
               System.out.println(info.toString());
               break;
          case 6:
               System.out.println("The list contains "
               ↪+info.occupied()+" items");
               break;
          case 7:
               if (info.isEmpty())
                    System.out.println("List is empty");
               else
                    System.out.println("List is not empty");
               break;
          case 8:
               if (info.isFull())
                    System.out.println("List is full");
               else
                    System.out.println("List is not full");
               break;
          case 9:
               System.out.println("First in list:"+info.head());
               break;
```

Continued on next page

LISTING-9.4
(continued)

Testing the IntList

```
            case 10:
                System.out.println("Tail is "
                ↳+info.tail().toString());
               break;
            case 11:
                System.out.println("Program terminated");
                break;
            default:
                System.out.println("Invalid code");
        }
    }
}
```

Activity 9.8

Type in and test the *IntList* class programs.

You should have noticed that not all the *IntList* class operations are offered in the menu.

Add the missing items to the test program.

Activity 9.9

The *IntList* class is of limited use since it can only hold integer values. How could we create a new *ObjList* class capable of holding objects of any type (e.g. *Weight, Distance, Clock*, etc.)

Implement and test this new *ObjList* class. The contents of the list should be displayed by calling the *toString()* methods of each class.

The Stack

A pile of books lying on a table is an pratical example of a **stack** (see FIG-9.7). Books are placed only on top of the stack or removed from the top of the stack.

This can be considered as a restricted form of list. In a list items can be added or removed from any position; in a stack items can only be added at one end and can only be removed from the same end.

FIG-9.7

The Stack Concept

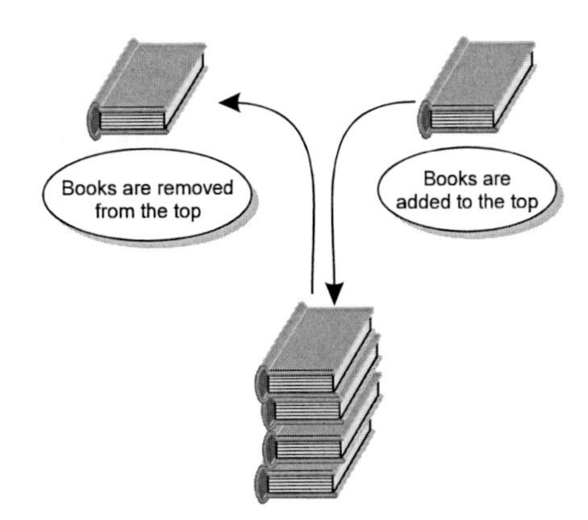

The attributes of the *Stack* class are shown in FIG-9.8.

FIG-9.8

The Stack Attributes

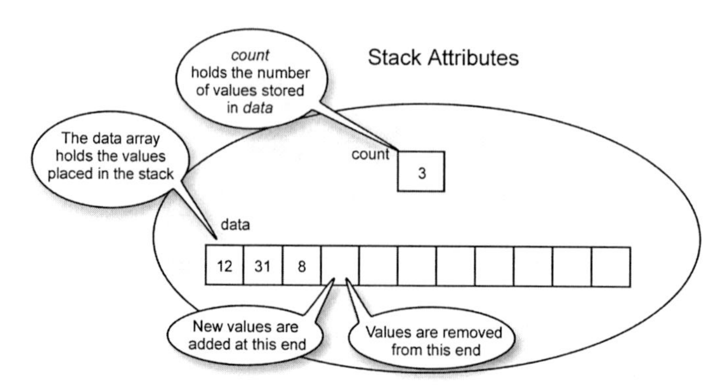

The operations required are given below. Note that they are similar, but not identical to that of the *IntList* class.

create()	Creates an empty stack with 10 elements.
create(int sz)	Creates a new stack with *sz* elements.
create(Stack s)	Creates a new stack which is an exact copy of *s*.
boolean isFull()	Returns *true* if the stack is full, otherwise returns *false*.
boolean isEmpty()	Returns *true* if the stack is empty, otherwise returns *false*.
void clear()	Clears the contents of the stack.
int occupied()	Returns the number of values held in the stack.
int free()	Returns the number of empty elements in the stack.
void add(int v)	Adds *v* to the top of the stack. If the stack is full, the value is not added.
void delete()	Deletes the top (last) item in the stack. There is no change if the stack is empty.
int top()	Returns the top (last) item in the stack. The contents of the stack are not changed by this operation.
String toString()	Returns the values held in the stack as a string. Each value is separated from the next by a newline character. The top value should be first in the string.
boolean equals(Object obj)	Returns *true* if *obj* (which should be another stack) contains exactly the same values in the same order as the current stack.

> **Activity 9.10**
>
> Write a definition of the *Stack* class (do not make it a descendant of the *IntList* class).
>
> Test the operations of the *Stack* class using a program similar to that in LISTING-9.4.

Interfaces

There are occasions when an abstract class contains neither attributes nor the code for any of the routines it declares. Although Java would allow us to create such a structure using the `class` keyword, there is another option available to us in such circumstances: we can declare the class as an **interface.**

For example, we can see that there are many common operations within the *IntList* and *Stack* classes. Some or all of these could be extracted and defined within an interface class as shown below:

In this example only a few of the common operations have been defined within the interface class.

```
public interface ContainerOps
{
    public void add(int v);
    public void delete();
    public boolean isEmpty();
    public boolean isFull();
}
```

All methods in an interface are assumed to be `public` and `abstract`, so the term `public` could be omitted from the above example. In fact, it is illegal to place any coding in an interface.

It is possible to add attributes to an interface, but these are automatically assumed to be `public`, `static` and `final`.

In UML an interface class is identified by including the term <<interface>> in the heading as shown in FIG-9.9.

FIG-9.9

Specifying an Interface in UML

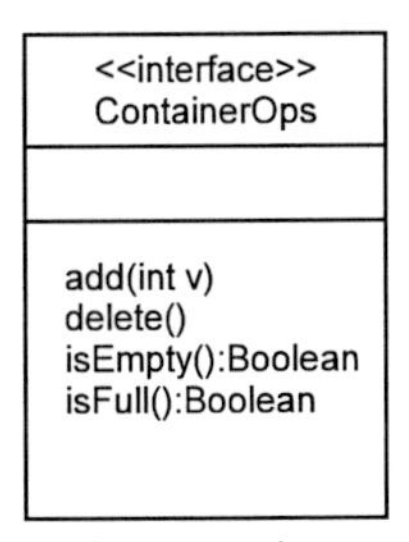

Once the interface has been written, normally classes can be defined as **implementing** an interface class. For example, we can state that the *IntList* class implements the *ContainerOps* interface by starting the definition of the *IntList* class with the line

```
public class IntList implements ContainerOps
```

The *IntList* class is now committed to containing coded versions of all the operations defined within the *ContainerOps* interface. This is something *IntList* already does, so no other changes are required to the class.

In UML we show that a class implements an interface in the manner shown in FIG-9.10.

FIG-9.10

A Class Implementing an Interface in UML

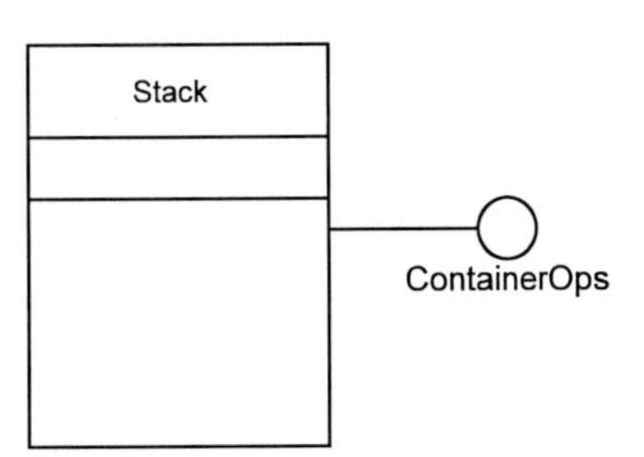

Notice that the interface is shown as a circle and named. It is joined by a line to the class implementing the interface.

> **Activity 9.11**
>
> Code and compile the *ContainerOps* interface.
>
> Modify the first line of your *IntList* and *Stack* classes to implement the *ContainerOps* interface.

But what advantage have we gained from creating this interface class? Well, since both the *IntList* and *Stack* classes implement the same interface, they are now related through this common parent class - *ContainerOps.*

And, just as we could create a *Clock* reference variable and actually use it to reference a *Clock*, *AlarmClock* or *CountDownClock* object, so we can create a *ContainerOps* reference variable and use it to reference an *IntList* or *Stack* object.

The program in LISTING-9.5 shows this technique being used. The user gets to choose between creating an *IntList* or *Stack* object. The options allowed in the menu are those defined within the *ContainerOps* interface. There is one exception to this: the display option. To achieve a display we need to call the *toString()* method - something not defined within the interface class, but rather in the *IntList* and *Stack* classes. To call the *toString()* method we need to cast the reference variable to the actual class being used. This is done with the statement

```
if(info instanceof IntList)
    System.out.println(((IntList)info).toString());
else
    System.out.println(((Stack)info).toString());
```

LISTING-9.5

Using an Interface

```
import IntList;
import Stack;
import Input;

public class TestListOps
{
   public static void main(String args[])
   {
       ContainerOps info;
       System.out.println("List or Stack (L or S) : ");
       char ch = Input.readChar();
       if(ch=='L')
           info = new IntList();
       else
           info = new Stack();
       int option = displayMenu();
       while (option != 6)
       {
           executeOption(info,option);
           option = displayMenu();
       }
   }

   public static int displayMenu()
   {
       System.out.println("1. Add item\n2. Delete item\n3. List\n"
       ↳+"4. Empty?\n5. Full?\n"+"6. Quit");
       System.out.print("Enter option : ");
       int option = Input.readInt();
           return option;
   }
```

continued on next page

LISTING-9.5
(continued)

Using an Interface

```
public static void executeOption(ContainerOps info, int op)
{
    int p, v;
    switch(op)
    {
        case 1:
            System.out.print("Enter new value : ");
            v=Input.readInt();
            info.add(v);
            break;
        case 2:
            info.delete();
            break;
        case 3:
            if(info instanceof IntList)
                System.out.println(((IntList)info).toString());
            else
                System.out.println(((Stack)info).toString());
            break;
        case 4:
            if (info.isEmpty())
                System.out.println("Container is empty");
            else
                System.out.println("Container is not empty");
            break;
        case 5:
            if (info.isFull())
                System.out.println("Container is full");
            else
                System.out.println("Container is not full");
            break;
        case 6:
            System.out.println("Program terminated");
            break;
        default:
            System.out.println("Invalid code");
    }
  }
}
```

Activity 9.12

Type in and test the program.

What differences are there when deleting items and displaying the contents of each on the container types?

An interface class can even be completely empty:

```
public interface FalseClass{};
```

Even this has a purpose, since all the classes that implement this interface will then be related through this common ancestor. Empty interfaces are often referred to as **tagging interfaces**.

Although a class can extend only one other class, it can implement as many interfaces as required.

If a class states that it implements an interface but does not contain code for every operation of that interface it must be declared as an abstract class. All descendant classes must also be abstract until every operation of the interface has been coded.

Interfaces can be declared as extending existing interfaces. There are no limits on the number of interfaces it may extend. For example, if Interface A is defined as

```
public interface A
{
    void f1();
    void f2();
}
```

and Interface B as

```
public interface B
{
    int f3();
    int f4();
}
```

and if Interface C extends both of these with the lines

```
public interface C extends A, B
{
    int f5();
    int f6();
}
```

then when a class implements Interface C:

```
public class D implements C
```

then class D must contain code for operations f1(), f2(), f3(), f4(), f5() and f6().

Queues

In many ways a **queue** is like a stack. It contains a collection of values and new values are added to the end of the list. The main difference in a queue is that values are removed from the opposite end to which they are added.

This makes the attributes of the class and algorithms required when adding and removing values a little different from those in the stack. The changes to the attributes are shown in FIG-9.11.

FIG-9.11

A Queue Class

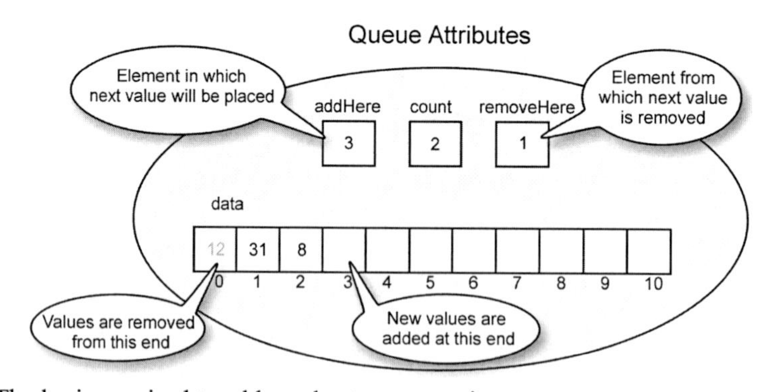

The logic required to add a value to a queue is

```
IF full THEN
    exit
ENDIF
data[addHere]=v
addHere := (addHere + 1) modulus (no. of elements in data)
Increment count
```

and for remove

```
IF empty THEN
    exit
ENDIF
removeHere := (removeHere + 1 ) mod MAXSIZE
Decrement count
```

Activity 9.13

Identify other methods described in the *Stack* class which will require different algorithms when implemented in the *Queue* class. Omit the *top()* method which will not be used in the *Queue* class.

Activity 9.14

Implement and test the *Queue* class. Add a *front()* operation which returns the first value in the queue. Like the *Stack* class, *Queue* should implement the *ContainerOps* interface.
Use an expanded version of the program in LISTING-9.5 to test your code.

Summary

- **A container class** is one which contains a collection of values
- **A List container** can have value inserted and removed from any position in the list.
- **A Stack** has values inserted and removed from the *top* only.
- **A Queue** has values inserted at one end and removed from the other.

Interfaces

- **An interface** is an abstract collection of named operations.
- **All operations of an interface** are assumed to be public.
- **No operation can contain code.**
- **There can be no instance attributes.**
- **Named constants may be included.**
- **A class may implement** one or more interfaces.
- **If a class implements an interface** it must contain code for all the operations of the interface, otherwise the class must be declared as abstract.
- **Interface reference variables** may be created.
- **These reference variables** must reference an object from a class that implements the interface.

Packages

Introduction

Most programming languages supply a variety of software routines. These are held in libraries which contain groups of similar subroutines.

In Java such libraries are known as **packages** and each package holds a set of related classes. So just as we might store our word processing documents within a single folder in our hard disk, so we can store a related set of classes in a package.

To use a class held in a package we must import that class from the relevant package.

Creating a Package

To create a package we must begin by creating the folder in which the package is to be held.

> **Activity 9.15**
>
> Within your Java directory create a sub-directory called *myclasses.*
>
> Within *myclasses* create a sub-directory called *containers.*
>
> The complete path to this new folder should be
> `C:\Javaxxx\myclasses\containers`
> (where xxx represents your forename)

This directory now acts as the depository for the package.

Next we need to add classes to the package.

Adding Classes to a Package

To add a class to a package you must insert a line within the Java source code. To add the *IntList* class to our new *containers* package we need to insert the code

```
package myclasses.containers;
```

as the first line in *IntList.java.*

> **Activity 9.16**
>
> Add the above line to your *IntList* class and recompile.

In addition, during compilation you need to use the -d option to specify where these subdirectories are held. For example, if the full path information is

```
c:\javaElizabeth\myclasses\containers
```

then the compilation statement for *IntList.java* would be

```
javac -d c:\javaElizabeth IntList.java
```

So the combination of information given by the line above (`c:\javaElizabeth`) and that in the `package` statement (`package myclasses.containers`) gives full information on where the compiled file is to be stored.

If the subdirectories mentioned in the `package` statement do not exist, they will be created automatically. This is not true of the directories specified at the prompt (i.e. if *javaElizabeth* does not exist an error message will be given.

Note that none of this affects the location of the source file (*IntList.java*).

If you don't specify a specific package in which to store your class, Java places it in a default package.

Activity 9.17

Compile your *IntList.java* program again using the command line

```
javac  -d c:\javaxxx IntList.java
```

where xxx represents end text of your Java directory.

Activity 9.18

Insert the appropriate lines and recompile the files for *ContainerOps.java, Stack.java* and *Queue.java* so that all of these are included in the *containers* package.

Importing a Class from a Package

All compiled Java classes are placed in some package. If you haven't specified a package then a default one is used. Any new classes placed in the same package have automatic access to all the classes already held in that package. For example, the *TestListOps* program in LISTING-9.5 begins with the lines

```
import IntList;
import Stack;
import Input;
```

but, in fact, these can be omitted since all of the files involved will be placed in the same default package giving *TestListOps.java* full access to the other classes.

However, if we create a class, store it in a specific package, and expect it to be used outside that package, then we must begin the class definition with the term `public`.

To use an existing class in a new program, begin with the import statement at the start of your program. This states the path and class name. To import the *Stack* class into some other file not compiled into the *containers* package we'd start with the line

```
import myclasses.containers.Stack;
```

However, since this only specifies part of the path information (*C:\JavaElizabeth* is missing), the compiler needs to be given this additional information. This is done by setting the CLASSPATH system variable within the AUTOEXEC.BAT file.

Your AUTOEXEC.BAT file will almost certainly already contain a line such as

```
SET CLASSPATH=E:\VENTURA8\TRUEDOC;
```

you need to add to this to include your initial path information:

```
SET CLASSPATH=E:\VENTURA8\TRUEDOC;C:\JavaElizabeth
```

There's just one last problem that might catch you out; the constructors of imported classes must be marked as `public` or you won't be able to access them when writing classes which are to be stored outside the original package.

Activity 9.19

If possible modify your *C:\autoexec.bat* file so that the CLASSPATH variable specifies the location of your initial Java directory.

Create a new subdirectory, *Importing,* off your *Javaxxx* directory.

Copy your *TestListOps.java* file to this location.

Add the correct import lines to this program so that the various container classes can be access from the containers package.

Creating Documentation

The javadoc Tool

All software needs accompanying documentation. Some of that documentation can be produced automatically from your source code using the **javadoc** tool.

Activity 9.20

Open a DOS window and move to your java folder.

Open your *Distance.java* file and make sure the *Distance* class is marked as public.

Type the command

```
javadoc Distance.java
```

This will create a set of html documents containing details about the *Distance* class.

Load Internet Explorer or some other browser and open the file called *Distance.html.*

Part of the page you should see is given below:

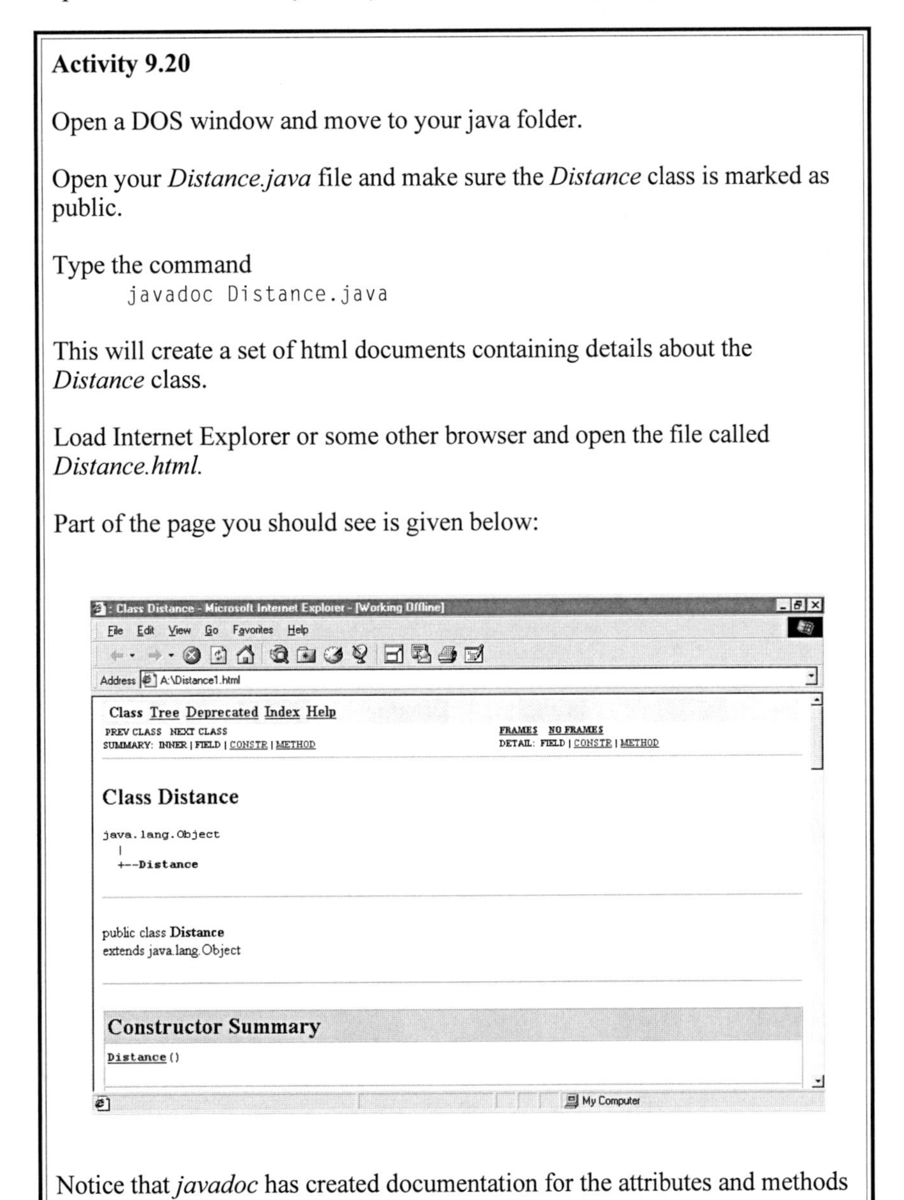

Notice that *javadoc* has created documentation for the attributes and methods of the class. Try out the various links on the page.

Adding Details

We can get *javadoc* to add more details to the documentation produced by adding a special type of comment.

These comments begin with the symbols /**. They may span an unlimited number of lines and end with */

These are known as **doc comments** and should be placed before the item they refer to. Typically at the start of the class, before each attribute and before each method.

These comments will then be added to documentation produced by javadoc.

Activity 9.21

Add a comment to the zero argument constructor in *Distance.java*:

```
/** Zero argument constructor - sets yards,feet and inches to
      ↳zero */
```

Save this new version of *Distance.java*.

Rerun *javadoc* on *Distance.java* (you don't need to compile the class again).

View *Distance.html*. The comment should have been added to the documentation.

Adding HTML Tags

You can gain more control over the look of the comments within the generated page by adding HTML tags within your comments.

The most obvious tags to add are <br/> tags to force a new line. For example:

```
/** Zero argument constructor <br/> Sets yards, feet and
    ↳inches to zero */
```

You can also mark paragraphs using <p> </p>.

Comment Contents

Begin with a single sentence giving an overview of the purpose of the class or method. For methods, add more detail of what the method does. State possible responses. Where limitations apply or errors may occur, these should be documented. State equivalence class limits where necessary.

Javadoc Tags

Javadoc also allows you to add specific tags within your comments. These have the form

```
@tagname comment.
```

@author

This tag should be added at the start of your file giving the programmer's name. For example:

```
@author Alistair Stewart
```

@version

Used to state the version number of the program. For example:

```
@version 1.0
```

@param

Gives details of a parameter to a routine. For example:

```
@param y Assigned to the <code>yards</code> attribute.<br/>
Must not be negative.
```

@return

Details the value returned by the method. For example:

```
@return distance in centimetres
```

@throws

Details any exception thrown by a method

```
@throws IOException if file not found
```

The author and version details will only be included in the generated documentation if javadoc is called with the appropriate arguments.

To generate author details use -author

To generate version details use - version.

So, for example, to generate both author and version details for *Stack.java* (assuming the tags have been added to the source file), use the line

```
javadoc -author -version Stack.java
```

A section of a commented version of the *Stack* class is shown in LISTING-9.6 below.

LISTING-9.6

Comments for javadoc

```
import ContainerOps;

/** The Stack class. Creates a last-in first-out data structure
*@author Alistair Stewart
*@version 0.1
*<b> Date </b> 17/8/2001
*/
public class Stack implements ContainerOps
{ /** Contains the values held in the stack */
  protected int data[];
  /** Contains a count of how many items are currently held
  ↳in the stack */
  protected int count;

  /** Creates an empty stack with 10 elements */
  public Stack()
  {
      data = new int[10];
      count = 0;
  }
```

LISTING-9.6
(continued)

Comments for javadoc

```
/** Creates an empty stack with sz elements */
  public Stack(int sz)
  {
  if (sz>1)
      data = new int [sz];
  else
      data = new int[10];
  count = 0;
  }

  /** Creates a stack which is an exact copy of l */
  public Stack(Stack l)
  {
      data = new int[l.data.length];
      for(int p = 0; p<=l.count-1; p++)
          data[p]=l.data[p];
      count = l.count;
  }

  /** Returns true if the stack is full */
  public boolean isFull()
  {
      if(count==data.length)
          return true;
      else
          return false;
  }
  /** Returns true if the stack is empty */
       public boolean isEmpty()
  {
      if(count == 0)
          return true;
      else
          return false;
  }

  /** Removes all values from the stack and resets the count to
zero */
  public void clear()
  {
      count = 0;
  }

  /** Returns the number of occupied positions in the stack */
  public int occupied()
  {
      return count;
  }

  /** Returns the number of unoccupied positions in the stack */
  public int free()
  {
      return (data.length - count);
  }

  /** Adds v to the top of the stack
  *<br/><b>pre-condition:</b> stack not full */
  public void add(int v)
  {
      if(isFull())
          return;
      data[count++] = v;
  }
```

Solutions

Activity 9.1

```
import Distance;

public class Act9_1
{
    public static void main(String args[])
    {
        Distance list[] = {new Distance(1,2,3),
        ↳new Distance(2,1,11),new Distance(1,1,8)
        ↳,new Distance(2,0,0)};
        Distance total = new Distance(list[0]);
        Distance longest = list[0];
        for(int c = 0; c < list.length; c++)
        {
            total.addToDistance(list[c]);
            if(list[c].isLarger(longest))
                longest = list[c];
        }
        System.out.println("Total distance is "
            ↳+total);
        System.out.println("Longest distance is "
            ↳+longest);
    }
}
```

Activity 9.2

The *Worker* class is defined as

```
public abstract class Worker
{
    protected String name;
    protected String address;
    protected float salary;

    public void setName(String s)
    {
        name = s;
    }

    public void setAddress(String s)
    {
        address = s;
    }

    public abstract void setSalary (int v);
}
```

The *PartTimeWorker* class is defined as

```
public class PartTimeWorker extends Worker
{
   public void setSalary(int v)
   {
      salary = (int)(v *0.5);
   }
}
```

The *FullTimeWorker* class is defined as

```
public class FullTimeWorker extends Worker
{
    protected double pensioncontr;

    public void setSalary(int v)
    {
            salary = v;
    }

    public double getPension()
    {
        return pensioncontr;
    }

    public double setPension(double v)
    {
        pensioncontr = v;
    }
}
```

The *ContractWorker* class is defined as

```
public class ContractWorker extends Worker
{
    protected int contractperiod;

    public void setSalary(int v)
    {
            salary = (int)(v *0.5);
    }

    public void setContractPeriod(int v)
    {
        if (v < 0 )
            return;
        contractperiod = v;
    }

    public int getContractPeriod()
    {
        return contractperiod;
    }
}
```

Activity 9.3

```
public Horse(Horse h)
{
    name = new String(h.name);
    handicap = new Weight(h.handicap);
    length = new Distance(h.length);
}
```

Activity 9.4

```
public void setLength(Distance d)
{
    length.setDistance(d);
}

public Distance getLength()
{
    return length;
}
```

Activity 9.5

```
import Weight;
import Distance;

public class Horse
{
    private String name;
    private Weight handicap;
    private Distance length;

    public Horse()
    {
        name = new String();
        handicap = new Weight();
        length = new Distance();
    }

    public Horse(String s, Weight w, Distance d)
    {
        name = new String(s);
        handicap = new Weight(w);
        length = new Distance(d);
    }

    public Horse(Horse h)
    {
        name = new String(h.name);
        handicap = new Weight(h.handicap);
        length = new Distance(h.length);
    }

    public void setName(String s)
    {
        name = s;
    }

    public void setHandicap(Weight w)
    {
        handicap.setWeight(w);
    }

    public void setLength(Distance d)
    {
        length.setDistance(d);
    }
```

```
        public String getName()
        {
            return name;
        }

        public Weight getHandicap()
        {
            return handicap;
        }

        public Distance getLength()
        {
            return length;
        }
    }


    public class TestHorse
    {
        public static void main(String args[])
        {
            Horse h1 = new Horse("Red Rum",
                ↳new Weight(12,7),new Distance(0,2,1));
            Horse h2 = new Horse();
            System.out.println(h1.getName()+"    "
            ↳+h1.getHandicap().getPounds()+" lbs "
            ↳+h1.getHandicap().getOunces()+" oz");
            h2.setName("Red Rooster");
            h2.setHandicap(new Weight(12,0));
            h2.setLength(new Distance(3,1,5));
            System.out.println(h2.getName()+"    "
            ↳+h2.getHandicap().getPounds()+" lbs "
            ↳+h2.getHandicap().getOunces()+" oz");
        }
    }
```

Activity 9.6

The output should be

0 lbs 0 oz

as delivered by Weight.toString().

Activity 9.7

No solution required.

Activity 9.8

Menu options for the following operations are required:

```
indexOf()
get()
free()
equals()
```

The updated code for the *TestList* class is shown below.

```
import IntList;
import Input;
public class TestList2
{
    public static void main(String args[])
    {
        IntList info = new IntList();
        int option=displayMenu();
        while (option != 16)
        {
            executeOption(info,option);
            option = displayMenu();
        }
    }

    public static int displayMenu()
    {
        System.out.println("1. Add item at position
        ↳\n2. Add item at end\n3. Delete item from
        ↳specified position\n4. Delete first item\n5.
        ↳List\n"+
        ↳"6. No. of items in list\n7. Empty?\n
        ↳8. Full?\n"+"9. Head\n10. Tail\n
        ↳11. Clear\n12. IndexOf\n13. get\n14. free
        ↳\n15. Equals\n16. Quit");
        System.out.print("Enter option : ");
        int option = Input.readInt();
        return option;
    }

    public static void executeOption(IntList info
    ↳, int op)
    {
        int p, v, result;
        switch(op)
        {
            case 1:
                System.out.print
                ↳("Enter new value : ");
                v=Input.readInt();
                System.out.print
                ↳("Enter position 1 to "
                ↳+(info.occupied()+1)+" ");
                p = Input.readInt();
                info.add(v,p);
                break;
            case 2:
                System.out.print
                ↳("Enter new value : ");
                v=Input.readInt();
                info.add(v);
                break;
            case 3:
                System.out.print
                ↳("Enter position of item to be
                ↳deleted ");
                System.out.print(" 1 to "
                ↳+info.occupied());
                p = Input.readInt();
                info.delete(p);
                break;
            case 4:
                info.delete();
                break;
            case 5:
                System.out.println(info.toString());
                break;
            case 6:
                System.out.println
                ↳("The list contains "
                ↳+info.occupied()+" items");
                break;
            case 7:
                if (info.isEmpty())
                    System.out.println
                    ↳("List is empty");
                else
                    System.out.println
                    ↳("List is not empty");
                break;
            case 8:
                if (info.isFull())
                    System.out.println
                    ↳("List is full");
                else
                    System.out.println
                    ↳("List is not full");
                break;
            case 9:
                System.out.println
                ↳("First item in the list is "
                ↳+info.head());
                break;
            case 10:
                System.out.println("Tail is "
                ↳+info.tail().toString());
                break;
            case 11:
                info.clear();
                break;
            case 12:
                System.out.print
                ↳("Enter value to be found: ");
                p = Input.readInt();
                result = info.indexOf(p);
                if(result == 0)
                    System.out.println("not found");
                else
                    System.out.println
                    ↳(p+" found at "+result);
                break;
            case 13:
                System.out.print
                ↳("Enter position of value to be
                ↳retrieved");
                System.out.print(" 1 to "
                ↳+info.occupied()+": ");
                p = Input.readInt();
                result = info.get(p);
                System.out.println
                ↳("Value at position "+p+" is "
                ↳+result);
                break;
            case 14:
```

```
                    System.out.println("There are "
                    ↳+info.free()+" free positions");
                    break;
                case 15:
                    IntList temp = new IntList();
                    if(info.equals(temp))
                        System.out.println
                        ↳("Info has 10 elements and
                        ↳is empty");
                    else
                        System.out.println
                        ↳("Info does not have 10
                        ↳elements and/or is not empty");
                    break;
                case 16:
                    System.out.println
                    ↳("Program terminated");
                    break;
                default:
                    System.out.println("Invalid code");
            }
        }
    }
```

Activity 9.9

If *Weight*, *Distance* and *Clock* objects are to be added to an *ObjList* container, then those classes must override the inherited *toString()* and *equals()* methods since they will be called by code in the *ObjList* class.

Weight Overrides:

```
public String toString()
{
    return (pounds+" lbs "+ounces+" oz");
}

public boolean equals(Object o)
{
    if(!(o instanceof Weight))
        return false;
    Weight temp = (Weight)o;
    if(temp.pounds != pounds ||
    ↳temp.ounces != ounces)
        return false;
    return true;
}
```

Distance Overrides:

```
public String toString()
{
    return yards+" yds "+feet+" ft "+inches+" in";
}

public boolean equals(Object o)
{
    if(!(o instanceof Distance))
        return false;
    Distance temp = (Distance)o;
    if(temp.yards != yards || temp.feet != feet
    ↳|| temp.inches != inches)
        return false;
    return true;
}
```

Clock Overrides:

```
public String toString()
{
    return(hours+":"+minutes+":"+seconds);
}

public boolean equals(Object o)
{
    if(!(o instanceof Clock))
        return false;
    Clock temp = (Clock)o;
    if(temp.hours != hours ||
    ↳temp.minutes != minutes ||
    ↳temp.seconds != seconds)
        return false;
    return true;
}
```

The *ObjList* class has relatively few changes from the original *IntList*.

The *data* attribute is now an array of *Object* reference variables.

The parameter and return types for some methods are changed to *Object* from `int`.

Tests for equality are done using the *equals()* methods rather than the == operator.

```
public class ObjList
{
    protected Object data[];
    protected int count;

    public ObjList()
    {
        data = new Object[10];
                count = 0;
    }

    public ObjList(int sz)
    {
        if (sz>1)
            data = new Object [sz];
        else
            data = new Object [10];
            count=0;
    }

    public boolean isFull()
    {
        if(count==data.length)
            return true;
        else
            return false;
    }

    public void clear()
    {
        count = 0;
    }

public boolean isEmpty()
    {
        if(count == 0)
            return true;
        else
            return false;
    }

    public int indexOf(Object v)
    {
        for (int c = 0 ; c < count ; c++)
        if (data[c].equals(v))
            return c+1;
        return 0;
    }

    public Object get(int p)
    {
        if (p < 1 || p > count)
            System.exit(0);
        return data[p-1];
    }

    public int occupied()
    {
        return count;
    }

    public int free()
    {
        return (data.length - count);
    }

    public void add(Object v, int p)
    {
        if(isFull()||p<1||p>count+1)
            return;
        for(int c = count-1;c >= p-1 ;c--)
            data[c+1]=data[c];
        data[p-1] = v;
        count++;
    }

    public void add(Object v)
    {
        if(isFull())
            return;
```

```
        data[count++] = v;
    }
    public void delete(int p)
    {
        if (p<1 || p>count)
            return;
        for(int c = p; c<=count-1; c++)
            data[c-1]=data[c];
        count--;
    }

    public void delete()
    {
        tail();
    }

    public Object head()
    {
        if (isEmpty())
            System.exit(0);
        return data[0];
    }

    public ObjList tail()
    {
        if (isEmpty())
            System.exit(0);
        else
        {
            for(int p = 1 ; p < count; p++)
                data[p-1]=data[p];
            count--;
        }
        return this;
    }

    public String toString()
    {
        StringBuffer s = new StringBuffer();
        for(int p = 0; p <= count-1 ; p++)
        {
            s.append(data[p].toString());
            s.append('\n');
        }
        return s.toString();
    }

    public boolean equals(Object l)
    {
        if(!(l instanceof ObjList))
            return false;
        ObjList temp = (ObjList)l;
        if(count != temp.count)
            return false;
        for(int c = 0; c < count ; c++)
            if(!(data[c].equals(temp.data[c])))
                return false;
        return true;
    }
}
```

The largest change to the test program is the requirement to let the user choose which type of object is to be inserted and then to read values for it. This is done by the *readObject()* method which calls other routines for reading specific object types.

```
import ObjList;
import Input;
import Weight;
import Distance;

public class TestList2
{
    public static void main(String args[])
    {
        ObjList info = new ObjList();
        int option=displayMenu();
        while (option != 16)
        {
            executeOption(info,option);
            option = displayMenu();
        }
    }

    public static int displayMenu()
    {
        System.out.println("1. Add item at
        ↳position \n2. Add item at end\n
        ↳3. Delete item from specified position\n
        ↳4. Delete first item\n5. List\n"+
        ↳"6. No. of items in list\n7. Empty?\n
        ↳8. Full?\n"+"9. Head\n10. Tail\n
        ↳11. Clear\n12. IndexOf\n13. get\n
        ↳14. free\n15. Equals\n16. Quit");
        System.out.print("Enter option : ");
        int option = Input.readInt();
        return option;
    }

    public static int getObjectType()
    {
        System.out.println("\n1. Weight Object\n
        ↳2. Distance Object\n3. Clock Object\n");
        int result = Input.readInt();
        return result;
    }

    public static Weight readWeight()
    {
        System.out.print("Pounds : ");
        int lb = Input.readInt();
        System.out.print("Ounces : ");
        int oz = Input.readInt();
        return new Weight(lb,oz);
    }

    public static Distance readDistance()
    {
        System.out.print("Yards : ");
        int yd = Input.readInt();
        System.out.print("Feet : ");
        int ft = Input.readInt();
        System.out.print("Inches : ");
        int in = Input.readInt();
        return new Distance(yd,ft,in);
    }

    public static Clock readClock()
    {
        System.out.print("Hours : ");
        int hr = Input.readInt();
        System.out.print("Minutes : ");
        int min = Input.readInt();
        System.out.print("Seconds : ");
        int sec = Input.readInt();
        return new Clock(hr,min,sec);
    }

    public static Object readObject()
    {
        int obtype = getObjectType();
        Object result=null;
        switch(obtype)
        {
            case 1:
                result = readWeight();
                break;
            case 2:
                result = readDistance();
                break;
            case 3:
                result = readClock();
        }
        return result;
    }

    public static void executeOption(ObjList info,
int op)
    {
        int p, result;
        Object v;
        switch(op)
        {
            case 1:
                v = readObject();
                System.out.print("Enter position
                ↳1 to "+(info.occupied()+1)+" ");
                p = Input.readInt();
                info.add(v,p);
                break;
            case 2:
                v=readObject();
                info.add(v);
                break;
            case 3:
                System.out.print("Enter position
                ↳of item to be deleted ");
                System.out.print(" 1 to "
                ↳+info.occupied());
                p = Input.readInt();
                info.delete(p);
                break;
            case 4:
                info.delete();
                break;
            case 5:
                System.out.println(info.toString());
                break;
            case 6:
                System.out.println("The list
                ↳contains "+info.occupied()
```

```
                    ↳+" items");
                    break;
                case 7:
                    if (info.isEmpty())
                        System.out.println
                        ↳("List is empty");
                    else
                        System.out.println
                        ↳("List is not empty");
                    break;
                case 8:
                    if (info.isFull())
                        System.out.println
                        ↳("List is full");
                    else
                        System.out.println
                        ↳("List is not full");
                    break;
                case 9:
                    System.out.println
                    ↳("The first item in the list is "
                    ↳+info.head());
                    break;
                case 10:
                    System.out.println
                    ↳("Tail is "+info.tail().toString());
                    break;
                case 11:
                    info.clear();
                    break;
                case 12:
                    System.out.println
                    ↳("Enter value to be found: ");
                    v = readObject();
                    result = info.indexOf(v);
                    if(result == 0)
                        System.out.println("not found");
                    else
                        System.out.println
                        ↳(v+" found at "+result);
                    break;
                case 13:
                    System.out.print
                    ↳("Enter position of value to be
                    ↳retrieved");
                    System.out.print(" 1 to "
                    ↳+info.occupied()+": ");
                    p = Input.readInt();
                    v = info.get(p);
                    System.out.println
                    ↳("Value at position "+p+" is "+v);
                    break;
                case 14:
                    System.out.println
                    ↳("There are "+info.free()+
                    ↳" free positions");
                    break;
                case 15:
                    ObjList temp = new ObjList();
                    if(info.equals(temp))
                        System.out.println
                        ↳("Info has 10 elements and
                        ↳is empty");
                    else
                        System.out.println
                        ↳("Info does not have 10
                        ↳elements and/or is not empty");
                    break;
                case 16:
                    System.out.println
                    ↳("Program terminated");
                    break;
                default:
                    System.out.println("Invalid code");
            }
        }
    }
```

Activity 9.10

The code for the *Stack* class is

```
public class Stack
{
    protected int data[];
    protected int count;

    public Stack()
    {
        data = new int[10];
        count = 0;
    }

    public Stack(int sz)
    {
    if (sz>1)
        data = new int [sz];
    else
        data = new int[10];
    count = 0;
    }

    public Stack(Stack l)
    {
        data = new int[l.data.length];
        for(int p = 0; p<=l.count-1; p++)
            data[p]=l.data[p];
        count = l.count;
    }

    public boolean isFull()
    {
        if(count==data.length)
            return true;
        else
            return false;
    }

        public boolean isEmpty()
    {
        if(count == 0)
            return true;
        else
            return false;
    }

    public void clear()
    {
        count = 0;
    }


    public int occupied()
    {
        return count;
    }

    public int free()
    {
        return (data.length - count);
    }

    public void add(int v)
    {
        if(isFull())
            return;
        data[count++] = v;
    }

    public void delete()
    {
        if(isEmpty())
            System.exit(0);
        count--;
    }

    public int top()
    {
        if(isEmpty())
            System.exit(0);
        return data[count-1];
    }

    public String toString()
    {
        StringBuffer s = new StringBuffer();
        for(int p = count-1; p>=0 ; p--)
        {
            s.append(data[p]);
            s.append('\n');
        }
        return s.toString();
    }

    public boolean equals(Object l)
    {
        if(!(l instanceof Stack))
            return false;
        Stack temp = (Stack)l;
        if(count != temp.count)
            return false;
        for(int c = 0; c < count ; c++)
            if(data[c] != temp.data[c])
                return false;
        return true;
    }
}
```

The test program is coded as

```
import Stack;
import Input;

public class TestStack
{
    public static void main(String args[])
    {
        Stack info = new Stack();
        int option=displayMenu();
        while (option != 10)
        {
            executeOption(info,option);
            option = displayMenu();
        }
    }

    public static int displayMenu()
    {
        System.out.println("1. Add item\n2.
        ↳Delete item\n3. Display top item\n
        ↳4. List\n5. No. of items in list\n
        ↳6. Empty?\n7. Full?\n8. Clear\n9. Free\n
        ↳10. Quit");
        System.out.print("Enter option : ");
        int option = Input.readInt();
        return option;
    }

    public static void executeOption(Stack info,
    ↳int op)
    {
       int p, v;
    switch(op)
        {
            case 1:
                System.out.print
                ↳("Enter new value : ");
                v=Input.readInt();
                info.add(v);
                break;
            case 2:
                info.delete();
                break;
            case 3:
                System.out.println
                ↳("Top value in stack is "
                ↳+info.top());
                break;
            case 4:
                System.out.println
                ↳(info.toString());
                break;
            case 5:
                System.out.println
                ↳("The stack contains "
                ↳+info.occupied()+" items");
                break;
            case 6:
                if (info.isEmpty())
                    System.out.println
                    ↳("Stack is empty");
                else
                    System.out.println
                    ↳("Stack is not empty");
                break;
            case 7:
                if (info.isFull())
                    System.out.println
                    ↳("Stack is full");
                else
                    System.out.println
                    ↳("Stack is not full");
                break;
            case 8:
                info.clear();
                break;
            case 9:
                System.out.println
                ↳("The stack contains "
                ↳+info.free()+" empty positions");
                break;
            case 10:
                System.out.println
                ↳("Program terminated");
                break;
            default:
                System.out.println("Invalid code");
        }
    }
}
```

Activity 9.11

Type in the *ContainerOps* code.
Save it as *ContainerOps.java*
Compile the file with the statement

```
javac ContainerOps.java
```

The first two lines of the *IntList* class should become

```
import ContainerOps;
public class IntList implements ContainerOps
```

The first two lines of the *Stack* class should become

```
import ContainerOps;
public class Stack implements ContainerOps
```

Compile both the *Stack* and *IntList* classes.

Activity 9.12

Deleted items are removed from opposite ends in the *Stack* and *IntList* classes.

The *Stack* class displays the most recently entered value at the top of the list.

The *IntList* class displays the oldest entry at the top of the list.

Activity 9.13

Other than the constructors, which will be different for a new class, the *toString()* and *clear()*operations will change. The *Queue*'s *toString()* method must reverse the order of the value from that used in the *Stack* class.
The clear() operation must reset the *count, addHere* and *removeHere* attributes to zero.

Activity 9.14

The code for the *Queue* class is

```
import ContainerOps;

public class Queue implements ContainerOps
{
    protected int data[];
    protected int count;
    protected int addHere;
    protected int removeHere;

    public Queue()
    {
        data = new int[10];
        count = 0;
        addHere = 0;
        removeHere = 0;
    }

    public Queue(int sz)
    {
        if (sz>1)
            data = new int [sz];
        else
            data = new int[10];
        count = 0;
        addHere = 0;
        removeHere = 0;
    }

    public Queue(Queue l)
    {
        data = new int[l.data.length];
        for(int p = 0; p<=l.count-1; p++)
            data[p]=l.data[p];
        count = l.count;
```

```
        addHere = l.addHere;
        removeHere = l.removeHere;
    }

    public boolean isFull()
    {
        if(count==data.length)
            return true;
        else
            return false;
    }

    public boolean isEmpty()
    {
        if(count == 0)
            return true;
        else
            return false;
    }

    public void clear()
    {
        count = 0;
        addHere=0;
        removeHere = 0;
    }

    public int occupied()
    {
        return count;
    }

    public int free()
    {
        return (data.length - count);
    }

    public void add(int v)
    {
        if(isFull())
            return;
        data[addHere] = v;
        addHere = (addHere+1) % data.length;
        count++;
    }


    public void delete()
    {
        if(isEmpty())
            System.exit(0);
        removeHere = (removeHere+1) % data.length;
        count--;
    }

    public int front()
    {
        if(isEmpty())
            System.exit(0);
        return data[removeHere];
    }

    public String toString()
    {
        StringBuffer s = new StringBuffer();
        int p = removeHere;
        for(int c = 1; c <= count; c++)
        {
            s.append(data[p]);
            s.append("   ");
            p=(p+1)%data.length;
        }
        return s.toString();
    }

    public boolean equals(Object l)
    {
        if(!(l instanceof Queue))
            return false;
        Queue temp = (Queue)l;
        if(count != temp.count)
            return false;
        for(int c = removeHere; c != addHere ;
        ↳c = (c + 1) % data.length)
            if(data[c] != temp.data[c])
                return false;
        return true;
    }
}
```

The code for testing the *Queue* class is:

```
import IntList;
import Stack;
import Queue;
import Input;

class TestListOps
{
    public static void main(String args[])
    {
        ContainerOps info;
        System.out.print("List, Stack or Queue(L,S, or
Q) : ");
        char ch = Input.readChar();
        if(ch=='L')
            info = new IntList();
        else if(ch == 'S')
            info = new Stack();
        else
            info = new Queue();
        int option=displayMenu();
        while (option != 6)
        {
            executeOption(info,option);
            option = displayMenu();
        }
    }

    public static int displayMenu()
    {
        System.out.println("1. Add item\n2. Delete
item\n3. List\n"+
            "4. Empty?\n5. Full?\n"+
            "6. Quit");
        System.out.print("Enter option : ");
        int option = Input.readInt();
        return option;
    }

    public static void executeOption(ContainerOps
info, int op)
    {
    int p, v;
    switch(op)
        {
            case 1:
                System.out.print
                ↳("Enter new value : ");
                v=Input.readInt();
                info.add(v);
                break;
            case 2:
                info.delete();
                break;
            case 3:
                if(info instanceof IntList)
                    System.out.println
                    ↳(((IntList)info).toString());
                else if (info instanceof Stack)
                    System.out.println
                    ↳(((Stack)info).toString());
                else
                    System.out.println
                    ↳(((Queue)info).toString());
                break;
            case 4:
                if (info.isEmpty())
                    System.out.println
                    ↳("Container is empty");
                else
                    System.out.println
                    ↳("Container is not empty");
                break;
            case 5:
                if (info.isFull())
                    System.out.println
                    ↳("Container is full");
                else
                    System.out.println
                    ↳("Container is not full");
                break;
            case 6:
                System.out.println
                ↳("Program terminated");
                break;
            default:
                System.out.println("Invalid code");
        }
    }
}
```

Activity 9.15

No solution required.

Activity 9.16

No solution required.

Activity 9.17

No solution required.

Activity 9.18

No solution required.

Activity 9.19

No solution required.

Activity 9.20

No solution required.

Activity 9.21

No solution required.

CHAPTER 10

Error Handling

This chapter covers the following topics:

Checked and Unchecked Exceptions

Creating New Exception Classes

Exception Handling Concepts

Java's Exception Classes

Tranditional Error Handling Methods

try .. catch .. finally Keywords

Traditional Error Handling

Every line of code we write introduces the possibility of error. Some errors are due to incorrect syntax, others to faulty or incomplete logic, yet others may be caused by accepting invalid input. While it may not be possible to eliminate all errors from a program, if we are to be taken seriously as software engineers, this is a task we must attempt.

Some errors, such as syntax errors are easily detected by the compiler, while the more trivial logic errors are often highlighted using black and white box testing methods. However, some error situations may arise infrequently and be more difficult to detect. For example, we might run into insufficient storage space problems when attempting to store a large number of records in a dynamically created linked list or on a disk file. Such a problem is less likely to be detected during program testing.

By necessity, the amount of error detection included in the examples in this text has been limited. If this had not been the case, the methods and techniques being demonstrated would have been obscured under a blanket of error detection code. However, we have already covered the main traditional methods of error detection:

- **User input validation.** If we create code to examine each character as it is read from the keyboard then we can gain considerable control over what characters are accepted and rejected by a program. More simply, we could use a `while` loop to make sure that a variable contains a value within an acceptable range:

```
int month = Input.readInt();
while(month < 1 || month > 12)
{
    System.out.println("Invalid month must be 1-12");
    month = Input.readInt();
}
```

- **Function pre-conditions.** Placing a pre-condition check at the start of every applicable function has ensured that the parameters supplied to the function are within an acceptable range.

```
public static void add(int v)
{
    if (isFull())
        return;
          .
```

- **Function result indicators**. By returning a result indicator from a function, we have allowed the function user to check on the success or failure of calls to a routine.

```
public static boolean add(int v)
{
    if (isFull())
        return false;
          .
```

- **Termination of program**. If we feel that an error is too serious to allow a program to continue we can terminate the program.

```
public static boolean add(int v)
{
    if (isFull())
        System.exit(1);
          .
```

Exception Handling

Introduction

Java has an alternative way of handling certain types of error conditions. Generally, it is used by functions to allow them to terminate early and return an indication of the error which has occurred; this error is then handled by some piece of code in the routine which called the offending function.

Typical errors which might be detected in this way are such things as running out of memory, an out-of-bounds array subscript error, or failing the pre-condition of a function.

Using this approach, when a function detects an error it is unable to handle it **throws** (or **raises**) an **exception**. This should then be received and dealt with by an **exception handler**. If no appropriate exception handler exists the program terminates.

Activity 10.1

The following program sets up a small array and then displays the contents of the element specified by the user. The program continues until -99 is entered.

```
import Input;

public class Errors1
{
   public static void main(String args[])
   {
       int list[] = {3,6,9,12,15,18,21};
       System.out.print("Which element: ");
       int post = Input.readInt();
       while(post != -99)
       {
           System.out.println("list["+post+"]="+list[post]);
           System.out.print("Which element: ");
           post = Input.readInt();
       }
   }
}
```

Type in the program and run it.

Enter the values 3, 1 and 10 when prompted for the element number

The program terminated when 10 was entered and an error message was displayed on the screen:

```
Exception in thread "main" java.lang.ArrayIndexOutOfBoundsException
        at Errors1.main(Errors1.java:12)
```

This is the result of Java throwing an exception when you attempted to access an element of the array that didn't exist. The message also specifies which routine was being executed (*main()*), file name containing the source code (*Errors1.java*) and the line at which the problem occurred (12). Notice the term

ArrayIndexOutOfBoundsException in the message. This is a class name. Java defines a large family of classes associated with error conditions. An object of one of these classes is thrown when an exception occurs. In this case, an object of the *ArrayIndexOutOfBoundsException* class is thrown. As you can see, the classes are given very descriptive names.

If we don't want the program to terminate we can write an exception handler block of code specifically to deal with *ArrayIndexOutOfBoundsException* objects which have been thrown by an exception condition. For this example, we'll create an exception handler which displays the message *"Subscript out of bounds"*. The code for this block is

```
catch(ArrayIndexOutOfBoundsException err)
{
    System.out.println("Subscript out of bounds");
}
```

However, this in itself is not enough to deal with exceptions. The line of code which may cause an exception to be thrown must be placed inside a block beginning with the keyword `try`:

```
try
{
    System.out.println("list["+post+"]="+list[post]);
}
```

The final rule we must obey is that the `catch` block must come immediately after the `try` block, so our final code is:

```
import Input;

public class Errors1
{
    public static void main(String args[])
    {
        int list[] = {3,6,9,12,15,18,21};
        System.out.print("which element: ");
        int post = Input.readInt();
        while(post != -99)
        {
            try
            {
                System.out.println("list["+post+"]="+list[post]);
            }
            catch(ArrayIndexOutOfBoundsException err)
            {
                System.out.println("Subscript out of bounds");
            }
            System.out.print("which element: ");
            post = Input.readInt();
        }
    }
}
```

Activity 10.2

Make the modifications necessary to your program to produce the code given above.

Compile and run the program.

What happens when invalid subscript values are entered this time?

How the Program Executes

When you run the program given earlier with a valid subscript it responds in the same way as before. The code within the `catch` block is completely ignored. However, if an invalid subscript is entered, an attempt to execute the line

```
System.out.println("list["+post+"]="+list[post]);
```

causes an exception to be thrown. This in turn results in control jumping from the `try` block to the `catch` block which is then executed. After the catch block is executed, the program continues with the lines immediately following the `catch` block.

Creating a try block is an indication to Java that there may be problems in that part of the code. If a problem does occur any remaining lines within the try block are bypassed as a jump is made to the catch block.

Activity 10.3

Add the line

```
System.out.println("***************");
```

as the last line in the `try` block.

Re-run the program and enter the values 3,1, and 10.

You should see that this new line is not executed when the exception is thrown.

When an error is generated by one of the lines in a try block, the remainder of the `try` block is ignored as the program jumps to the `catch` block.

Checked and Unchecked Exceptions

Unchecked exceptions are those that can happen at any point in a program and are unpredictable. For example, we can never know when an array subscript might become out-of-bounds or when we might run out of available memory.

Since this type of problem can arise almost anywhere in your code Java does not demand that you use `try` and `catch` blocks to deal with them. Where there is no `try` or `catch` block the program simply terminates with an error message giving some indication of where the problem occurred.

The *ArrayIndexOutOfBoundsException* error is an unchecked exception.

Other exceptions can only be thrown at specific areas in a program. So, for example, the *FileNotFoundException* error will only happen when you try to open a file. This type of problem is much more predictable and hence Java insists that your code explicitly deals with these exceptions in some way. These are known as **checked exceptions**.

Back in Chapter 2 we looked at keyboard input. A single key's integer value can be retrieved using `System.in.read()`. But if we write a simple program using this statement such as

```
public class BasicInput
{
    public static void main(String args[])
    {
        int v = System.in.read();
        System.out.println("Value read was " + v);
    }
}
```

when we try to compile the program we get the error message

```
basicInput.java:7: unreported exception java.io.IOException; must
be caught or declared to be thrown
                int v = System.in.read();
                                 ^
```

Unfortunately, the *read()* method may throw an *IOException* error. This exception is a checked exception, so the program must deal with it in some way. From what we've said before, that means we should write `try` and `catch` blocks in the program. If we do that, the new version of the program is:

```
import java.io.IOException;

public class BasicInput1
{
    public static void main(String args[])
    {
        try
        {
            int v = System.in.read();
            System.out.println("Value read was " + v);
        }
        catch(IOException ioe)
        {
            System.out.println("Input problems");
        }
    }
}
```

This time the program will compile successfully.

However, a second option is available to us. Instead of write a `try` and `catch` block within our routine to deal with the *IOException* error, the routine can pass the problem back to wherever it was called from.

You can compare the concept to that of an irate customer coming to complain about faulty goods. Instead of the sales assistant dealing with the complaint he can call the manager over and get him to deal with the customer. In the same way, if routine A calls routine B and routine B calls a method that throws an exception, instead of writing the `try` and `catch` blocks in routine B; it may pass the problem back to routine A which will contain the `try` and `catch` blocks. To do this a routine simply states, in its heading, that it will throw the exception.

In the case of the example above, we can remove the `try` and `catch` blocks by starting *main()* with the heading

```
public static void main(String args[]) throws IOException
```

The whole program now becomes

```
import java.io.IOException;
public class BasicInput
{
    public static void main(String args[]) throws IOException
    {
        int v = System.in.read();
        System.out.println("Value read was " + v);
```

```
        }
    }
```

Since *main()* is called directly by the Java interpreter, there is no calling routine in which to write our `try` and `catch` blocks, so if the error occurs the program will terminate with a message describing the exception thrown in the same style as we saw earlier with the arrays problem.

Catching Multiple Exceptions

The program in LISTING-10.1 employs the following logic:

```
Get size of array from user
Create array of specified size
Read values into each element of the array
Get element to be accessed
WHILE not -99 DO
    Display element's contents
    Get element to be accessed
ENDWHILE
```

There are two possible exceptions that can be thrown:

NegativeArraySizeException	If the user wants the array to have, say, -9 elements.
ArrayOutOfBoundsEcxeption	If the user specifies an invalid element number.

The program contains a separate `catch` block for each potential problem.

LISTING-10.1

Multiple `catch` Blocks

```
import Input;
public class Errors2
{
    static void main(String args[])
    {
        System.out.print("How many numbers ? ");
        int size = Input.readInt();
        try
        {
            int list[] = new int[size];
            for(int c = 0; c < list.length; c++)
            {
                System.out.print("Enter value : ");
                list[c] = Input.readInt();
            }
            System.out.print("which element: ");
            int post = Input.readInt();
            while(post != -99)
            {
                System.out.println("list["+post+"]="+list[post]);
                System.out.println("**************");
                System.out.print("which element: ");
                post = Input.readInt();
            }
        }
        catch(ArrayIndexOutOfBoundsException err)
        {
            System.out.println("Subscript out of bounds");
        }
        catch(NegativeArraySizeException nas)
        {
            System.out.println("Array size negative");
        }
    }
}
```

The exceptions thrown from a piece of code are actually objects from one of the many classes derived from the base class *Throwable*. Some of these classes are shown in FIG-10.1.

FIG-10.1

Exceptions Family Tree

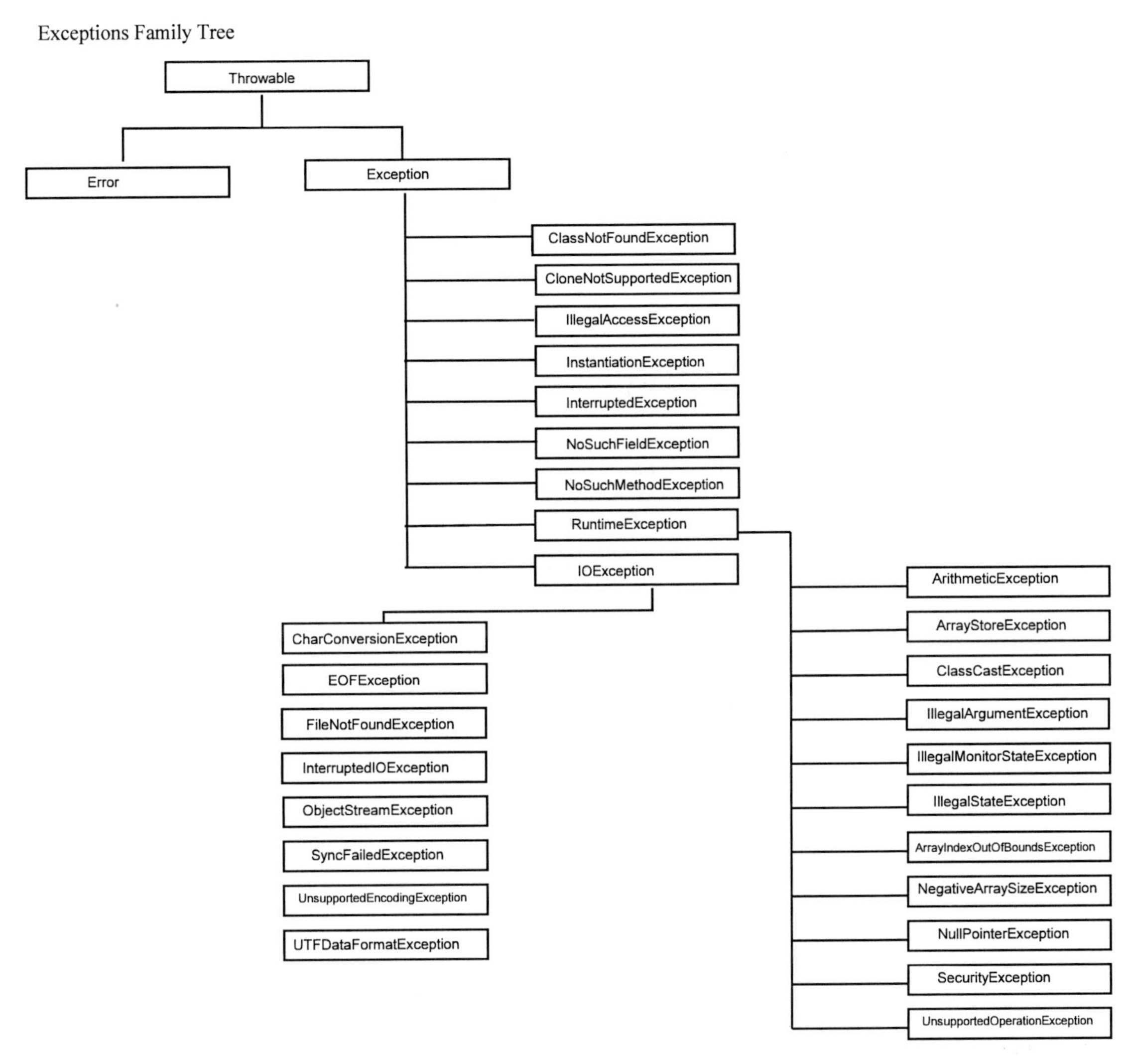

Error class derivatives may be ignored since these errors are severe and cannot be handled by the application program. *Exception* classes derived from *RuntimeException* are unchecked and so need not be caught; others are checked and hence require `try` and `catch` blocks or must be thrown to a higher level routine.

When an exception is thrown, Java searches for an appropriate `catch` block. When an exception is thrown, the first acceptable `catch` block is executed, all other `catch` blocks are ignored. An acceptable `catch` block is one defined for the type of exception thrown or for any superclass exception type. Hence, if a single catch block is defined as

```
catch(RuntimeException err)
{
    System.out.println("Subscript out of bounds
        ↳or Array size negative");
}
```

then it will catch every type of exception that might be thrown.

Knowing this we could rewrite the program in LISTING-10.1 with a single `catch` block designed to catch *RuntimeException* errors - a class from which both of the possible exceptions are derived. A new version of the program is shown in LISTING-10.2

LISTING-10.2

A Superclass `catch` Block

```
import Input;

public class Errors2
{
   static void main(String args[])
   {
       System.out.print("How many numbers ? ");
       int size = Input.readInt();
       try
       {
           int list[] = new int[size];
           for(int c = 0; c < list.length; c++)
           {
               System.out.print("Enter value : ");
               list[c] = Input.readInt();
           }
           System.out.print("which element: ");
           int post = Input.readInt();
           while(post != -99)
           {
               System.out.println("list["+post+"]="+list[post]);
               System.out.println("**************");
               System.out.print("which element: ");
               post = Input.readInt();
           }
       }
       catch(RuntimeException err)
       {
           System.out.println("Subscript out of bounds or
               ↳Array size negative");
       }
   }
}
```

Since only one `catch` block will be executed - even if a later block matches the exception thrown - you have to make sure catch blocks are placed in the correct order: subclass types before superclass types. So, if a program contained a *RuntimeException* `catch` block and a *ArrayIndexOutOfBounds* block, the *RuntimeException* block must come last in the actual coding.

Throwing Exceptions

In the *IntList* class we created earlier, the *head()* and *tail()* operations cannot function properly on an empty list. In the case of the *head()* operation our code for that method was:

```
public int head()
{
    if (isEmpty())
        System.exit(0);
    return data[0];
}
```

This approach isn't very satisfactory: we are forced to return some value since the method is defined as returning an int and we have no choice but to do that. However, the value we return, -1, might match the value held in *data[0]* of the array and, in that case, there would be no way of telling if the -1 represented failure or the head of the list.

An alternative approach is to use exceptions. When a problem is encountered (such as failure to meet an important pre-condition) a method can throw an exception.

Before we can throw exceptions in our own programs, we need to know a little of the methods available. In fact, although there are a large number of *Exception* derived classes, most contain only the methods inherited from *Throwable*. These are described below:

Throwable(String s)	Creates a *Throwable* object containing the string *s*. The contents of this string can be accessed by other methods. All descendant class have a constructor of a similar nature.
String getMessage()	Returns the string stored by the constructor.
void printStackTrace()	Displays details of where in the program execution had reached when the exception was thrown. There are examples of this later.

Java defines an *IllegalStateException* class. An object of this class should be thrown when an object is in a state where the method being attempted cannot be performed. For example, when we try to find the head of an empty list.

An anonymous object of this class is thrown when an object is not in an appropriate state for the operation that is being attempted. Using this approach we can rewrite the *IntList*'s *head()* method as:

```
public int head()
{
    if (isEmpty())
        throw new IllegalStateException("List is empty");
    return data[0];
}
```

Notice that we've managed to avoid returning an `int` value when the error occurs. Throwing an exception overrides the normal return mechanism for a method. In this case, that means that the routine is terminated immediately and control returned to the calling routine.

Activity 10.4

Make the modification given above to the *IntList* class *head()* method.

Also modify the *tail()* method so it throws the same exception if the list is empty.

Run the test program.

Attempt to perform the *head()* method as your first choice.

Your program should have terminated with a message such as:

```
java.lang.IllegalStateException: List is empty
    at List.head(List.java:68)
    at TestList.executeOption(TestList.java:63)
    at TestList.main(TestList.java:11)
```

To deal with the exception thrown by *head()* we might write the code:

```
catch(IllegalStateException e)
{
    System.out.println(e.getMessage());
    System.out.println("Choose another option");
}
```

We could then place this code beside the call to *head()* within *executeOption()*:

```
case 9:
    System.out.println("The first item in the list is "
                                        +info.head());
    catch(IllegalStateException e)
    {
        System.out.println(e.getMessage());
        System.out.println("Choose another option");
    }
```

We also need to place the call to *head()* within a `try` block. This means that the above lines are changed to:

```
case 9:
            // an exception may be thrown by code executed in
    try     // this block
    {
        System.out.println("The first item in the list is "
                                        +info.head());
    }
    catch(IllegalStateException e)
    {
        System.out.println(e.getMessage());
        System.out.println("Choose another option");
    }
```

We can generalise this to:

Arrange `catch` blocks for subclass objects before superclass objects.

```
try
{
    instructions that might cause an exception
    (other instructions may be included here)
}

catch(exception_classname exception_object)
{
    code to deal with exception of a specified class
}

catch(exception_classname exception_object)
{
    code
}
```

Activity 10.5

Modify your *TestList* class as shown above to deal with the exception thrown by *head()*.

Use a similar approach to deal with attempting to perform the *tail()* method on an empty list.

What happens when these exceptions are thrown?

How Java Handles Exceptions

The `try` and `catch` blocks can be placed at any level within your program. For example, we could have placed them within the *head()* method itself:

```
public int head()//throws IllegalStateException
{
    try
    {
        if (isEmpty())
            throw new IllegalStateException("List is empty");
    }
    catch(IllegalStateExceptions e)
    {
        System.out.println(e.getMessage();
    }
    return data[1];
}
```

However, this isn't really an effective approach in most cases (it isn't in the above example). Alternatively, the routine can throw an exception and the code which calls the routine throwing the error can catch the exception. That's the approach we used earlier:

```
try
{
    System.out.println("The first item in the list is "
                                        +info.head());
}
catch(IllegalStateException e)
{
    System.out.println(e.getMessage());
    System.out.println("Choose another option");
}
```

In fact, we can catch the exception at any level within a program. In our program, *head()* is called by *executeOption()* which is itself called from *main()* within *TestList*. So rather than catch the exception in *executeOption()* we could catch it in *main()*:

```
public static void main(String args[])
{
    IntList info = new IntList();
    int option=displayMenu();
    while (option != 9)
    {
        try
        {
            executeOption(info,option);
        }
        catch (IllegalStateException e)
        {
            System.out.println(e.getMessage());
        }
        option = displayMenu();
    }
}
```

When an exception is thrown, Java ignores the remaining code within the `try` block. Instead it now looks for a `catch` block which handles the type of exception it has thrown. The `catch` block, if it exists is, then executed. If no appropriate `catch` block exists the program exits. FIG-10.2 below shows what happens when an exception is thrown by a routine which is called indirectly:

FIG-10.2

Unwinding the Stack

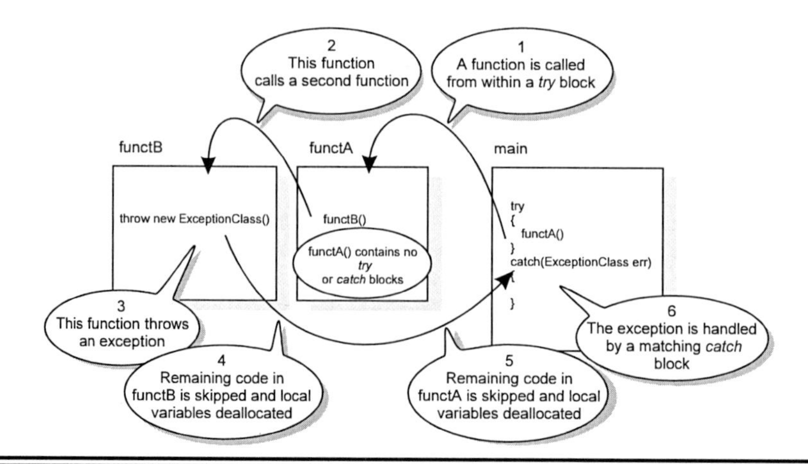

> **Activity 10.6**
>
> Modify *TestList.java* so that the `case` statements for *head()* and *tail()* revert to their original form and the *main()* method is coded as shown above.
>
> Test the effect by beginning with a request for the head of the list.

We can enclose as much of our code as we require within the `try` block. For example, in the code below, the `while` loop is included:

```
public static void main(String args[])
{
    List info = new List();
    int option=displayMenu();
    try
    {
        while (option != 9)
        {
            executeOption(info,option);
            option = displayMenu();
        }
    }
    catch(IllegalStateException e)
    {
        System.out.println(e.getMessage());
    }
}
```

> **Activity 10.7**
>
> Modify your code as shown above and test the code by selecting the *tail()* option.

It's possible to catch an exception, deal with it in some way, and then throw the same exception to a higher level routine. For example, we might catch the *IllegalStateException* in *executeOption()* and throw it again so that *main()* can also catch and deal with the same exception.

We make a `catch` block throw the exception it is handling by adding another `throw` statement within the `catch` block. For example, by using the code

```
case 7:
    try
    {
        System.out.println("The first item in the list is "
                                              +info.head());
```

```
        }
        catch(IllegalStateException e)
        {
            System.out.println(e.getMessage());
            System.out.println("Problem in class");
            throw e;
        }
```

The `finally` Block

As well as using `try` and `catch` blocks, we can also add a `finally` block. Such a block of code will always be executed whether or not an exception is thrown. Often the `finally` block is used to close a file or clear some resource before a program terminates.

For example, we might rewrite the *main()* method for the *TestList* class as:

```
public static void main(String args[])
{
    IntList info = new IntList();
    int option=displayMenu();
    try
    {
        while (option != 9)
        {
            executeOption(info,option);
            option = displayMenu();
        }
    }
    catch(IllegalStateException e)
    {
        System.out.println(e.getMessage());
    }
    finally
    {
        System.out.println(info.toString());
    }
}
```

This ensures that the contents of the *IntList* object are displayed even if an exception is thrown.

Summary

- **An exception** is an error indicator thrown by a section of code to indicate some error or unexpected condition has occurred.

- **Typical uses of an exception**: Invalid function parameters, array subscripts out of bounds, division by zero, etc. where error handling is to be dealt with in another function from the one in which the error was detected.

- **Exceptions should not be used** where normal error handling methods are sufficient.

- **The format for a `throw` statement is**

```
throw object;
```

- **An exception can be thrown from**

a) code within a `try` block
b) a function called directly by the `try` block
c) a function called indirectly from the `try` block

- **Once thrown, an exception causes** the remaining code in its function to be ignored. Any local variables are deallocated; any local objects are destroyed.

- **The remainder of the `try` block is bypassed** when an exception is thrown.

- **The general format for an exception handler is:**

```
try
{
    actions
}
catch( classname objectname)
{
    actions
}
```

  There may be many `catch` blocks

- **A `catch` block which catches all exceptions has the format**

```
catch(Exception e)
{
    actions
}
```

- **When an object is thrown**, the first `catch` specifying that class or an ancestor of that class is executed; other `catch` blocks are ignored.

- **An unchecked exception** is one which Java does not require your code to handle.

- **If an unchecked exception is thrown** and not handled, the program will terminate giving details of where the exception occurred.

- **Unchecked exceptions are derived** from the *RuntimeException* class.

- **A checked exception** must be handled by your program.

- **Checked exceptions can be handled** by including `try` and `catch` blocks or by throwing the exception to a higher level without defining `try` and `catch` blocks.

- **A `finally` block** may be included following the `catch` blocks.

- **A `finally` block will be executed** whether or not an exception is thrown.

Solutions

Activity 10.1

No solution required.

Activity 10.2

The `catch` block is executed and hence the error message is displayed. The program continues to execute as normal.

Activity 10.3

No solution required.

Activity 10.4

The routines *head()* and *tail()* in your *IntList* class should now read:

```
public int head()
{
    if (isEmpty())
        throw new
        ↪IllegalStateException("List is empty");
    else
        return data[0];
}

public IntList tail()
{
    if (isEmpty())
        throw new
        ↪IllegalStateException("List is empty");
    else
    {
        for(int p = 1 ; p < count ; p++)
            data[p-1]=data[p];
        count--;
    }
    return this;
}
```

You need to recompile *IntList.java* and *TestList2.java*.

Activity 10.5

The relevant `case` statements in the *executeOption()* method should be

```
case 9:
    try
    {
        System.out.println("The first item in
        ↪the list is "+info.head());
    }
    catch(IllegalStateException e)
    {
        System.out.println(e.getMessage());
        System.out.println("Choose another option");
    }
    break;
case 10:
    try
    {
        System.out.println("Tail is "
        ↪+info.tail().toString());
    }
    catch(IllegalStateException e)
    {
        System.out.println(e.getMessage());
        System.out.println("Choose another option");
    }
    break;
```

When *head()* and *tail()* throw exceptions both will display the message *List is empty* and *Choose another option*. The program will then return to the menu.

Activity 10.6

The *List is empty* message displays for exceptions thrown by *head()* and *tail()* just as before. Otherwise the program continues as normal.

Activity 10.7

The *List is empty* message displays but the program terminates. This is because the while loop is within the `try` block

Chapter 11
Streams

This chapter covers the following topics:

Buffered Files

Byte Streams

Character Streams

Data Files

File Class

FileInputStream Class

FileOutputStream Class

InputStream Class

OutputStream Class

Outputting to a File

Random Access

RandomAccessFile Class

Reading From a File

Streaming Objects

Using Debug

Streams

Introduction

Data held exclusively in the variables of a program is going to be lost when that program is terminated. Hence, it is normal to store important data which is likely to be required at a later date in a more permanent form. This means using disk files in which information can be held indefinitely.

We need to begin by looking at the way in which Java views the transfer of information to and from peripheral devices. The philosophy of the language is to make this transfer of information independent from the physical devices which may be linked to your computer. This is achieved by doing all input/output (I/O) via a **stream**.

We can consider a stream as a store of sequential characters or bytes. To use a stream, we must, normally, link it to a physical device. The devices themselves are called **files**. In Java there is no basic difference between linking a stream to a disk file or some other peripheral such as a printer - all are considered to be files (see FIG-11.1).

FIG-11.1

Streams are Linked to Devices

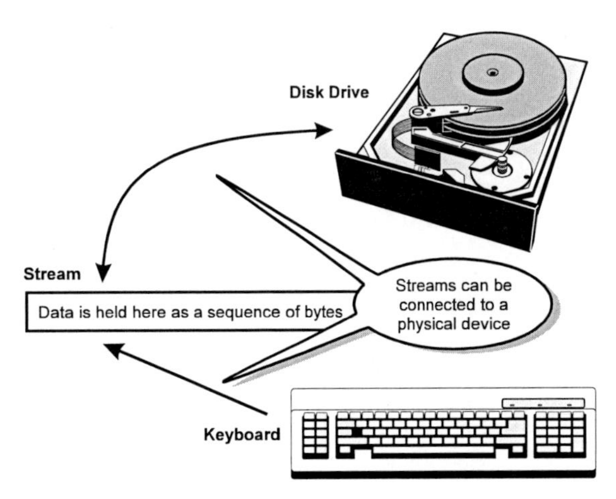

A stream can even be linked to an array in memory, but we will not deal with streams of that type here.

Transferring data to and from streams is handled by a series of Java classes held in the *java.io* package. Each of these classes offers different operations.

There are two main types of streams:

- **byte streams** in which data is held as a series of bytes ranging in value from 0 to 255. Other languages refer to data in this format as a **binary file**.
- **character streams** in which all information is held as a sequence of 16 bit characters.

As a general rule we need to follow three steps when handling a stream:

```
Open the stream. This associates the device or disk file with an
    appropriate stream object.
Read from or write to the stream.
Close the stream.
```

The Byte Stream Classes

Sound, image, and executable files are typical examples of formats where the data is organised as a sequence of bytes. However, simple text files may also be held in byte format. In this section we'll look at some of the stream classes designed for handling byte input/output.

Since we have to create a file before we can read from it, we'll start with byte output classes.

The OutputStream Class

The *OutputStream* class is an abstract class, which means we cannot create object from this class. However, it does define many of the methods inherited by later classes, so it's worth looking at it in some detail.

close()	Closes the stream.
flush()	Forces any data held in the stream buffer to be output to the device or file used. The *close()* method also causes the stream buffer to be flushed.
write(int v)	Writes the least-significant byte of *v* to the stream.
write(byte[] b)	Writes the contents of *b* to the stream.
write(byte[] b, int st, int fin)	Writes a section of *b* to the stream. Elements *b[st]* to *b[fin-1]* are written.

Most of these are overridden in descendant classes.

The FileOutputStream Class

It's from this class (a descendant of the *OutputStream* class) that we can create real stream objects and hence our aim of outputting data. The class contains the constructors necessary for creating byte stream objects:

FileOutputStream(String f) Creates a byte stream object and links it to the file whose name is given by *f*. Path information may be included in *f*.
If the file specified does not exist, it is created.
If the file exists, its current contents are destroyed.

FileOutputStream(String f, boolean b)
Creates a byte stream object and links it to the file *f*. If *b* is *true*, new data is appended to existing file data. If *b* is *false*, new data overwrites existing data.

Outputting to a File

In the next program the details of a single student (*idcode, name* and *sex*) are read from the keyboard and written to a file. The program employs the following logic:

The file is named mydata.dat and is to be created in the current directory.

```
Read student details from the keyboard
Open the file using a FileOutputStream object
Write the student's details to the file
Close the file
```

The first version of the program, given below (see LISTING-11.1), only writes the student's *idcode* to the file.

LISTING-11.1

Writing to a Basic Byte Stream.

```
import Input;
import java.io.*;

public class TestFiles1
{
  public static void main(String args[])
  {
      int idcode;
      String name;
      char sex;

      //*** Read data from the keyboard ***
      System.out.println("Enter idcode : ");
      idcode = Input.readInt();
      System.out.print("Enter name : ");
      name = Input.readString();
      System.out.print("Enter sex : ");
      sex = Input.readChar();

      //*** Create a FileOutpuStream object ***
      FileOutputStream myfile;
      try
      {
          //*** Link the object to the actual file ***
          myfile = new FileOutputStream("mydata.dat");
          //*** Write idcode to the file ***
          myfile.write(idcode);
          //*** Close the file ***
          myfile.close();
      }
      catch(IOException e)
      {
          System.out.println(e.getMessage());
          System.exit(0);
      }
  }
}
```

As you can see, the file handling methods are all enclosed in a `try` block since streams and file handling methods can cause many problems.

Activity 11.1

Type in and test the program.

Enter the following values when prompted:

idcode	255
name	Liz Heron
sex	F

Activity 11.2

The DOS DEBUG program will display the contents of the file in both hexadecimal and character formats. To use DEBUG type

DEBUG C:\MYDATA.DAT

The DEBUG prompt is the hyphen. When this appears type

D

to display the contents of the file. A typical display from DEBUG is shown below.

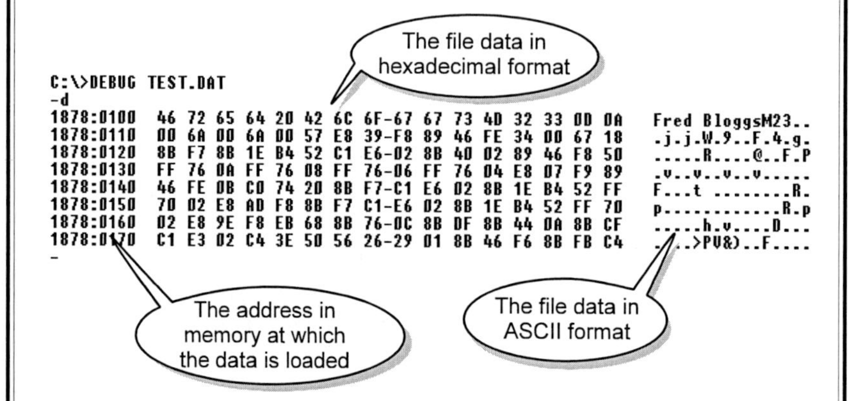

DEBUG displays a block of main memory into which MYDATA.DAT has been loaded. Since the file's contents are much smaller than the block displayed, much of what appears in the display is of no interest to us.

Use Q to quit DEBUG.

The first byte of the display should be FF (255 decimal) - the value given to the idcode variable.

Activity 11.3

Run the program again.

Enter 254 for the *idcode* (enter other values as before).

Examine the contents of the file using DEBUG.

It should now start with FE (254).

From the inherited methods we can see that the abilities of the *FileOutputStream* are somewhat limited since all the data we intend to write to the file must be held in a single byte or an array of bytes. Luckily, we can convert the *name* string to an array of bytes using the expression:

```
name.getBytes ()    //*** Method of the String class
```

To write the name to the stream we use the line:

```
myfile.write(name.getBytes());
```

The *sex* value can be output in the same way as the *idcode* since `char` value will automatically be converted to a `byte` value.

The completed program is shown in LISTING-11.2 below.

LISTING-11.2

Writing All the Data

```
import Input;
import java.io.*;

public class TestFiles1
{
  public static void main(String args[])
  {
      int idcode;
      String name;
      char sex;

      System.out.println("Enter idcode : ");
      idcode = Input.readInt();
      System.out.print("Enter name : ");
      name = Input.readString();
      System.out.print("Enter sex : ");
      sex = Input.readChar();

      FileOutputStream myfile;
      try
      {
          myfile = new FileOutputStream("mydata.dat");
          myfile.write(idcode);
          myfile.write(name.getBytes());
          myfile.write(sex);
          myfile.close();
      }
      catch(IOException e)
      {
          System.out.println(e.getMessage());
          System.exit(0);
      }
  }
}
```

> **Activity 11.4**
>
> Complete the program and test it (use the data "255, Liz Heron,F").
>
> Use DEBUG to check the contents of the file.

If we look at the contents of the file we've created using DEBUG, we'll see that the data is held as a continuous sequence of characters:

```
.Liz HeronF          (FF 4C 69 7A 20 48 65 72 6F 6E 46)
```

Holding information in this way can make reading the data back later rather difficult since there is no way to tell where one piece of information ends and another begins.

Activity 11.5

Write a program which accepts one student's details from the keyboard and saves this information to disk file.

The student's information is defined as:

```
byte idcode;
String name;
char sex;
byte scores[] = new byte[3];
```

The file should be named "STUDENT.DAT".

Once we have a file containing data then we can use some input classes to access that data.

The InputStream Class

The *InputStream* class is also an abstract class. Like the *OutputStream* class, it defines many of the methods inherited by latter classes:

Threads are explained in the next chapter.

available()	Checks the number of bytes that can be read from the file without the thread in which the file handling operation is being run entering a *Blocked* state. The *Blocked* state would be entered when no more bytes were immediately available for reading.
boolean markSupported()	Returns *true* if the stream supports *mark()* and *reset()*(see below).
mark(int v)	Marks the current position in the file. The *reset()* method returns to this marked position as long as no more than *v* bytes have been read since the *mark()* was put in place.
reset()	Returns to the marked position in the file as long as the current position is no more than *v* bytes from the marked position.
skip(long v)	Bypasses the next *v* bytes in the input stream.
int read()	Reads a single byte from the input stream.
int read(byte [] b)	Fills *b* with bytes read from the input stream. Returns the number of bytes read. If no bytes are read, -1 is returned.
int read(byte [] b, int st, int count)	Reads *count* bytes from the file the array *b*. The first byte is placed in *b[st]*. Returns the number of bytes read or -1 if no bytes are read.

The FileInputStream Class

This is the first class we can use to basic input. It inherits the features of the InputStream class and adds only a constructor:

FileInputStream(String f)	Creates a byte stream object and links it to the file whose name is given by *f*. Path information may be included in *f*.

Reading from a File

Using a *FileInputStream* object we can read back the data we saved in the earlier program.

The program in LISTING-11.3 uses the following logic:

```
Open the file
Read one byte
Display the byte read
Close the file
```

LISTING-11.3

Reading a Single Byte

```
import java.io.*;

class TestFiles2
{
  public static void main(String args[])
  {
       int idcode;
       FileInputStream myfile;

       try
       {
            myfile = new FileInputStream("mydata.dat");
            idcode = myfile.read();
            System.out.println(idcode);
            myfile.close();
       }
       catch(IOException e)
       {
            System.out.println(e.getMessage());
            System.exit(0);
       }
  }
}
```

Activity 11.6

Type in and test the program above.

Of course, we'll want to read the complete contents of the file. To do that we'll need to put the *read()* and *println()* statements in a `while` loop. When the value -1 is returned the end of file will have been reached.

The new program uses the following logic:

```
Open file
read a byte from the file
WHILE byte not -1 DO
    display byte
    read a byte from the file
ENDWHILE
Close file
```

Its code is shown in LISTING-11.4.

LISTING-11.4

Reading Every Byte from a Stream

```
import java.io.*;

class TestFiles3
{
   public static void main(String args[])
   {
        int value;

        FileInputStream myfile;
        try
        {
             myfile = new FileInputStream("mydata.dat");
             value = myfile.read();
             while(value != -1)
             {
                  System.out.print(value);
                  value = myfile.read();
             }
             myfile.close();
        }
        catch(IOException e)
        {
             System.out.println(e.getMessage());
             System.exit(0);
        }
   }
}
```

Activity 11.7

Type in the program and run it.

You'll see that all the values are displayed as integers even though most of the bytes in the file represent characters from the name. There is no easy way to determine where each data item starts and stops.

Buffered Files

Reading or writing directly to a file can be very inefficient. The time taken to access data held on a backing store device (such as a hard disk) is very slow compared to the speed of the processor. We can reduce this need for access by using buffering. In a buffered system data is transferred to a buffer. A buffer is simply a reserved area of main memory. When writing to a buffered stream, information destined for the hard disk is actually copied to a buffer area. Only when this area is full does the data actually get transferred to the disk. This approach reduces the number of times the disk needs to be accessed and hence speeds up the whole process.

Reading works in much the same way. Instead of reading a single value from a disk, many values are read and placed in a buffer. When a *read()* method is then executed the required information is picked up from the buffer area rather than the disk itself. When all the data in the buffer has been read, more data is transferred there from the hard disk.

Buffered Output

The *BufferedOutputStream* class defines a buffered output stream. This class has the same methods as the *FileOutputStream* class but the constructors are a little different. Instead of a string argument giving the name of the file to be used the parameter must be an object of a class descended from the *OutStream* class. The two constructors are:

BufferedOutputStream(OutputStream os)	Creates a buffered output stream with a default buffer size.
BufferedOutputStream(OutputStream os, int sz)	Creates a buffered output stream object . The buffer has space for *sz* bytes.

We could create the buffered stream equivalent of the program in LISTING-11.2 by creating an *OutputFile* object

```
FileOutputStream file = new FileOutputStream("mydata.dat");
```

and using this as the argument for the *BufferedOutputStream* object:

```
BufferedOutputStream myfile = new BufferedOutputStream(file);
```

Alternatively, we could just combine both statements:

```
BufferedOutputStream myfile = new BufferedOutputStream
    ↳(new FileOutputStream("mydata.dat"));
```

Activity 11.8

Rewrite the program in LISTING-11.2 using a buffered output file.

Buffered Input

Again, we would use a *BufferedInputStream* in preference to an *InputFileStream* to make use of the greater efficiency of the buffered approach when reading from an existing file.

Like the *BufferedOutputStream*, there are two versions of the constructor:

BufferedInputStream(InputStream os)	Creates a buffered input stream with a default buffer size.
BufferedInputStream(InputStream os, int sz)	Creates a buffered input stream object. The buffer has space for *sz* bytes.

Data Files

Output

Byte-based data is an important format. For example, image and sound files will be in this basic format. However, in a more mundane vein, we will need to store things like names, dates, prices, etc. We can do this using a stream based on the *DataOutputStream* class. Objects of this class can be used to write the basic primitive types such as `int` and `float` values to a file.

Data is output to the file in exactly the same format as it is held in memory.

The *DataOutputStream* class contains the following methods:

DataOutputStream(OutputStream os)	Creates a *DataOutputStream* object.
void write(int v)	Writes the least-significant byte of *v* to the stream.
void write(byte[] b)	Writes the contents of *b* to the stream.
void write(byte[] b, int st, int fin)	Writes a section of *b* to the stream. Elements *b[st]* to *b[fin-1]* are written.
void flush()	Forces the any data held in the stream buffer to be output to the device or file.
void writeBoolean(boolean b)	Writes the Boolean value *b* to the stream.
void writeByte(int b)	Writes the least-significant byte of *v* to the stream.
void writeShort(int v)	Writes the value of *v* in `short` format.
void writeChar(int v)	Writes the value of *v* as a `char`.
void writeInt(int v)	Writes *v* in `int` format.
void writeLong(long v)	Writes *v* in `long` format.
void writeFloat(float f)	Writes *v* in `float` format.
void writeDouble(double v)	Writes *v* in `double` format.
void writeBytes(String s)	Writes the contents of *s* as a sequence of bytes.
void writeChars(String s)	Writes the contents of *s* as a sequence of characters.
void writeUTF(String s)	Writes the contents of *s* as a sequence of single byte characters.
int size()	Returns the number of bytes written so far.

Notice that the constructor requires an object from an *OutputStream* subclass as an argument. As we saw earlier it is best to use a buffered stream when dealing with peripheral devices. Such a buffered stream is defined with the line:

```
myfile = new DataOutputStream(new BufferedOutputStream
    ↳(new FileOutputStream("mydata.dat")));
```

The program in LISTING-11.5 reads the idcode, name and sex of a student and writes each component to a file using the appropriate *write()* method.

LISTING-11.5

Using DataOutputStream

```
import java.io.*;

public class TestFiles4
{
  public static void main(String args[])
  {
      int idcode;
      String name;
      char sex;

      System.out.print("Enter idcode : ");
      idcode = Input.readInt();
      System.out.print("Enter name : ");
      name = Input.readString();
      System.out.print("Enter sex : ");
      sex = Input.readChar();

      DataOutputStream myfile;
      try
      {
          myfile = new DataOutputStream
                ↳(new FileOutputStream("mydata.dat"));
          myfile.writeInt(idcode);
          myfile.writeChars(name);
          myfile.writeChar(sex);
          myfile.close();
      }
      catch(IOException e)
      {
          System.out.println(e.getMessage());
          System.exit(0);
      }
  }
}
```

Activity 11.9

Enter and run the program above.

use the data

```
255 Liz Heron F
```

Modify the program so that the instruction

```
myfile.writeUTF(name);
```

is used to write the name to the file.

Use DEBUG to examine the differing effects on the contents of the file of each output method.

Input

The *DataInputStream* has, for the most part, a matching set of *read()* methods to extract data. These methods of the class are:

DataInputStream(InputStream os)	Creates a *DataInputStream* object.
int read(byte[] b)	Fills *b* with bytes read from the input stream. Returns the number of bytes read. If no bytes are read, -1 is returned.

int read(byte[] b, int st, int count)	Reads *count* bytes from the file into the array *b*. The first byte is placed as *b[st]*. Returns the number of bytes read or -1.
void readFully(byte[] b)	Reads the complete contents of the stream into *b*.
void readFully(byte[] b, int st, int count)	
int skipBytes(int v)	Skips *v* bytes passed the current position in the stream.
boolean readBoolean()	Reads a `boolean` value from the stream.
byte readByte()	Reads a `byte` value from the stream.
short readShort()	Reads a `short` value from the stream.
char readChar()	Reads a `char` value from the stream.
int readInt()	Reads an `int` value from the stream.
long readLong()	Reads a `long` value from the stream.
float readFloat()	Reads a `float` value from the stream.
double readDouble()	Reads a `double` value from the stream.
String readUTF()	Reads a string stored in UTF format from the stream. UTF strings start with a character count and this is used to determine how many characters should be read from the stream. The count is not included in the returned string.

This class has the read equivalent of many of the write methods we have already met in the *DataOutputStream* class. However, notice that there is no *readString()* method. This is simply because there is no way to know how many bytes a string will occupy in the file and hence it cannot be extracted by a single instruction from the stream. For example, when we wrote the contents of *name* using *writeString()* or *writeBytes()* no information was recorded in the file about the length of the string.

However, if we wrote data using the *writeUTF()* method a character count was included and this extra information allows the string to be extracted from the file using *readUTF()*.

Activity 11.10

Write a program using a *DataInputStream* object to extract and display the *idcode, name* and *sex* data that was written to *mydata.dat* in the previous Activity.

Make sure that the name was written using *writeUTF()*.

Character Streams

Writing data to a stream in the same format as it is held within the basic data types can be useful but there are occasions when writing the character equivalent of a value is more useful. For example, the int value 12 would be written as 00 00 00 0C to a byte-oriented file, but in a character file the output would be 00 31 00 32 (the Unicode values for the characters '1' and '2'). Since little software, other than Java, stores characters in Unicode format, these streams can automatically convert characters to ASCII format (the value 12 would now be stored as 31 32).

Character output can be achieved using a character stream object.

Writing

The starting class for an output character stream is the abstract *Writer* class which declares the following operations:

void write(int v)	Writes the least significant byte of *v* to the stream.
void write(char[] ch)	Writes the contents of the char array *ch* to the stream.
void write(char[] ch, int st, int count)	Writes a portion of *ch* to the stream. The section written starts at *ch[st]* and is *count* characters in length
void write(String s)	Writes the contents of the String *ch* to the stream.
void write(String s, int st, int count)	Writes a portion of *s* to the stream. The section written starts at *s[st]* and is *count* characters in length
void flush()	Flushes the stream.
void close()	Closes the stream.

ASCII is the default encoding assumed but other character codes can be output.

This is determined by the value of parameter *s* in the first class constructor.

Writer is the super class for *OutputStreamWriter*. Objects of this class automatically convert the 2-byte Unicode characters held in Java variables and constants to single byte ASCII characters which are then written to the stream.

The class defines the following constructors:

OutputStreamWriter(OutputStream os, String s)

Creates an *OutputStreamWriter* object. Characters are output in the code specified by *s* Examine the documentation for this class to determine possible values for this parameter.

OutputStreamWriter(OutputStream os)

Creates an *OutputStreamWriter* object. Characters are output in ASCII format.

Another class, *FileWriter* is a subclass of *OutputStreamWriter* and serves only the single purpose of allowing a simpler constructor to be used. It has two constructors:

FileWriter(String f)	Creates a *FileWriter* object linked to the file named *f*.
FileWriter(String f, boolean s)	Creates a *FileWriter* object linked to the file named *f*. Characters are output in the format specified by *s*.

If we create an *OutputStreamWriter* object then we need a line such as

```
OutputStreamWriter myfile = new OutputStreamWriter
    ↳(new FileOutputStream(mydata.txt"));
```

but by using a *FileWriter* object we can use the shorter

```
FileWriter myfile = new FileWriter("mydata.txt");
```

The class designed to do all the hard work of writing characters to a stream is *PrintWriter*. Use an object of this class if you want to create a file that can be read into a text editor or sent to the screen or printer.

Writer is also the superclass for *PrintWriter*. This class has four constructors:

PrintWriter(Writer wr)	Creates a *PrintWriter* object.
PrintWriter(Writer wr, boolean af)	Creates a *PrintWriter* object. If *af* is *true* line flushing is automatic.
PrintWriter(OutputStream os)	Creates a *PrintWriter* object linked to *os*. An intermediate *OutputStreamWriter* object is automatically created. Line flushing is not automatic
PrintWriter(OutputStream os,boolean af)	Creates a *PrintWriter* object linked to *os*. An intermediate *OutputStreamWriter* object is automatically created. If *af* is *true,* line flushing is automatic.

void print(boolean)
void print(char)
void print(int)
void print(long)
void print(float)
void print(double)
void print(char[])
void print(String)
void print(Object)

These routines take a value of the type specified and output the equivalent set of ASCII characters to the stream *Object* types are converted to characters using the *toString()* method of the relevant class.

void println()	Outputs the end-of-line character for the current operating environment. In Microsoft Windows this is "\r\n"

void println(boolean)
void println(char)
void println(int)
void println(long)
void println(float)
void println(double)
void println(char[])
void println(String)
void println(Object)

These routines take a value of the type specified and output the equivalent set of ASCII characters to the stream. The value output is followed by the end-of-line character.

The program in LISTING-11.6 writes the details of a student to the file *mydata.txt.*

LISTING-11.6

Outputting Text

```
import java.io.*;

class TestFiles6
{
  public static void main(String args[])
  {
      int idcode=255;
      String name="Liz Heron";
      char sex='F';
      try
      {
          PrintWriter myfile = new PrintWriter(new FileWriter
          ↳("mydata.txt"));
          myfile.print(idcode);
          myfile.print(name);
          myfile.print(sex);
          myfile.close();
      }
      catch(IOException e)
      {
          System.out.println(e.getMessage());
          System.exit(1);
      }
  }
}
```

Activity 11.11

Type in and run the program above.

use DEBUG to examine the contents of the file.

Modify the program so that an end-of-line character is inserted between each data item.

From the results of the above activity we can see that one of the main features of character streams is to convert numeric values to ASCII characters and to convert Unicode characters to ASCII.

Reading

There is a similar set of classes for reading from a character stream. The abstract *Reader* class declares the following methods:

boolean markSupported()	Returns *true* if the stream supports *mark()* and *reset()*.(see below)
mark(int v)	Marks the current position in the file. The *reset()* method returns to this marked position as long as no more than *v* bytes have been read since the *mark()* was put in place.
reset()	Returns to the marked position in the file as long as the current position is no more than *v* bytes from the marked position.
skip(long v)	Bypasses the next *v* bytes in the input stream.
int read()	Reads a single byte from the input stream.
int read(char [] b)	Fills *b* with characters read from the input stream. Returns the number of characters read. If no bytes are read, -1 is returned.
int read(char [] n, int st, int count)	Reads *count* characters from the file into the array *b*. The first character is placed in *b[st]*. Returns the number of characters read or -1 if no characters are read.

Reader is the super class for *InputStreamReader.* Objects of this class automatically convert the single byte characters held in a file to 2-byte Unicode characters.

The class defines the following constructors:

InputStreamReader(InputStream is, String s)	Creates a *InputStreamReader* object. Characters from the stream are assumed to be in the format specified by *s* Examine the documentation for this class to determine possible values for this parameter.
InputStreamReader(InputStream is)	Creates an *InputStreamReader* object. Characters are assumed to be held in ASCII format.

Another class, *FileReader*, is a subclass of *InputStreamReader* and serves only the single purpose of allowing a simpler constructor to be used. It has two constructors:

FileReader(String f)	Creates a *FileReader* object linked to the file named *f.*
FileReader(String f, boolean s)	Creates a *FileReader* object linked to the file named *f.* Characters in the file

are assumed to be in the format specified by *s*.

If we create an *InputStreamReader* object then we need a line such as

```
InputStreamReader myfile = new InputStreamReader
    ↳(new FileInputStream(mydata.txt"));
```

but by using a *FileReader* object we can use the shorter

```
FileReader myfile = new FileReader("mydata.txt");
```

At this point you should be expecting a *PrintReader* class to read back the text created by a *PrintWriter* object. However, no such class exists. Since the characters written to a file cannot easily be separated into the original data types from which they were created, such a class is not part of Java.

Instead we have to content ourselves with the *BufferedReader* class which can be used to read a line of text from the stream. If possible the string retrieved in this way can then be converted to an appropriate type.

BufferedReader(Reader rs, int bs)	Creates a *BufferedReader* object linked to *rs*. The buffer is *bs* bytes long.
BufferedReader(Reader rs)	Creates a *BufferedReader* object linked to *rs*. The buffer is the default size.
String readLine()	Returns a string of all the characters in the stream up to the next end-of-line marker. `null` is returned if the end of file is reached.
boolean markSupported()	Returns *true* if the stream supports *mark()* and *reset()*(see below).
mark(int v)	Marks the current position in the file. The *reset()* method returns to this marked position as long as no more than *v* bytes have been read since the *mark()* was put in place.
reset()	Returns to the marked position in the file as long as the current position is no more than *v* bytes from the marked position.
skip(long v)	Bypasses the next *v* bytes in the input stream.
int read()	Reads a single byte from the input stream.
int read(byte [] n,. int st, int count)	Reads *count* bytes from the file into the array *b*. The first byte is placed in *b[st]*. Returns the number of bytes read or -1 if no bytes are read.

void close() Closes the stream.

The program in LISTING-11.7 uses a *BufferedReader* object and the *readLine()* method to retrieve the student details written by the previous program.

LISTING-11.7

Reading Text

```
import java.io.*;

public class ReadingText
{
  public static void main(String args[]) throws IOException
  {
      BufferedReader myfile = new BufferedReader(new FileReader
      ↳("mydata.txt"));
      String textread = myfile.readLine();
      while(textread != null)
      {
          System.out.println(textread);
          textread = myfile.readLine();
      }
      myfile.close();
  }
}
```

Notice that there is no `try` or `catch` block in the program above. Rather than handle an exception, *main()* throws any exception to a higher level. This is stated in the line

```
public static void main(String args[]) throws IOException
```

Since *main()* is not called by any routine, if an exception is thrown, the JVM would handle the error.

The `while` loop in the program reads each line of text from the file until there are no more lines at which time text read will have the value `null`.

Summary

- **Use a PrintWriter object** to output all values as characters.
- **Values are written using ASCII** format by default.
- **Use a BufferedReader object** to read back text formatted files.
- **The ASCII coded characters in the file are automatically converted to Unicode.**

Random Access

Introduction

Often files are used to store hundreds, thousands and even millions of records. A company selling airline tickets needs to retain information of thousands of flights. That information needs to be searched (for example, when a customer asks if a seat is available on a specific flight) and to be updated (when a seat is booked) and deleted (when a flight has occurred and can be removed from the system).

The term **sequential access** is used to describe how the records of a file are accessed one after the other, starting at the first record and ending at the last. This type of access is inappropriate where we need to read only a single, but specific record in a file containing thousands of records. Direct access to a required record is known as **random access**.

Java offers random access through the *RandomAccessFile* class.

The RandomAccessFile Class

Unlike other stream classes we have encountered so far a *RandomAccessFile* object allows us to read and write to a file. This means we can read a record, modify its contents, and then rewrite the updated record back to the file.

Because there is a requirement to jump to various points within the file, a *RandomAccessFile* object maintains a file pointer which indicates the current position within the file. You can think of the file pointer as something similar to the edit cursor you see in a word processor document which shows you where you are in the current document. The file pointer contains the byte number of the current position in the file. So when a *RandomAccessFile* object is first opened the file pointer will contain the value zero indicating that it is currently at the start of the file. As data is read from or written to the file the value of the file pointer is updated.

The class's methods are given below:

RandomAccessFile(String f, String ac)	Creates a *RandomAccessFile* object. The file name is specified by *f* and the access mode by *ac*. Possible values for *ac* are "r" which allows read only access to the file, and "rw" which allows read/write access.
long getFilePointer()	Returns the current value of the file pointer.
void seek(long p)	Moves the file pointer to byte *p* in the file. The first byte is byte 0.
int skipBytes(int sk)	The file pointer is moved by *sk* bytes. It is possible that an invalid number of bytes is specified. For example, trying to skip 100 bytes when only 50 remain before the end of the file is reached. In this case, only the

number of bytes possible is skipped The actual number of bytes skipped is returned.

The other methods of the class we have met before:

void write(int v)	Writes the least-significant byte of *v* to the stream.
void write(byte[] b)	Writes the contents of *b* to the stream.
void write(byte[] b, int st, int fin)	Writes a section of *b* to the stream. Elements *b[st]* to *b[fin-1]* are written.
void flush()	Forces the any data held in the stream buffer to be output to the device or file.
void writeBoolean(boolean b)	Writes the Boolean value *b* to the stream.
void writeByte(int b)	Writes the least-significant byte of *v* to the stream.
void writeShort(int v)	Writes the value of *v* in `short` format.
void writeChar(int v)	Writes the value of *v* as a `char`.
void writeInt(int v)	Writes *v* in `int` format.
void writeLong(long v)	Writes *v* in `long` format.
void writeFloat(float f)	Writes *v* in `float` format.
void writeDouble(double v)	Writes *v* in `double` format.
void writeBytes(String s)	Writes the contents of *s* as a sequence of bytes.
void writeChars(String s)	Writes the contents of *s* as a sequence of characters.
void writeUTF(String s)	Writes the contents of *s* as a sequence of single byte characters.
int length()	Returns the number of bytes in the file.
int read(byte[] b)	Fills *b* with bytes read from the input stream. Returns the number of bytes read. If no bytes are read, -1 is returned.
int read(byte[] b, int st, int count)	Reads *count* bytes from the file into the array *b*. The first byte is placed as *b[st]*. returns the number of bytes read or -1.
void readFully(byte[] b)	Reads the complete contents of the stream into *b*.

int skipBytes(int v)	Skips *v* bytes past the current position in the stream.
boolean readBoolean()	Reads a `boolean` value from the stream.
byte readByte()	Reads a `byte` value from the stream.
short readShort()	Reads a `short` value from the stream.
char readChar()	Reads a `char` value from the stream.
int readInt()	Reads an `int` value from the stream.
long readLong()	Reads a `long` value from the stream.
float readFloat()	Reads a `float` value from the stream.
double readDouble()	Reads a `double` value from the stream.
String readUTF()	Reads a string stored in UTF format from the stream.

The sample program in LISTING-11.8 demonstrates a simple application of a random access file. The program has the following logic:

```
Open random access file for reading and writing
Write 10 random integers to the file
Display the size of the file
Display the values written
Display values chosen by user
Close file
```

LISTING-11.8

Using Random Access

```
import java.io.*;
import Input;

public class UsingRandomFiles
{
  public static void main(String args[])
  {
      int num;
      RandomAccessFile myfile;
      try
      {
          //*** Open random access file ***
          myfile = new RandomAccessFile("mynumbers.dat","rw");
          myfile.seek(0);
          //*** Write 10 random numbers to file ***
          for(int j = 0; j < 10 ; j++)
          {
              num = (int)(Math.random()*100)+1;
              myfile.writeInt(num);
          }
          //*** Display the size of the file ***
          System.out.println("The file contains "+myfile.length()
          ↳+" bytes");
          //*** Display the contents of the file ***
          myfile.seek(0);
          for(int j = 1; j <= 10 ; j++)
          {
              num = myfile.readInt();
              System.out.println(j+" = "+num);
          }
```

continued on next page

LISTING-11.8
(continued)

Using Random Access

```
            //*** Display values chosen by user ***
            System.out.print("Which number (1 - 10):");
            int p = Input.readInt();
            while(p >= 1 && p <= 10)
            {
                myfile.seek((p-1)*4); // 4 bytes per int value
                num = myfile.readInt();
                System.out.println(num);
                System.out.print("Which number (1 - 10):");
                p = Input.readInt();
            }
            //*** Close file ***
            myfile.close();
        }
        catch(IOException e)
        {
            System.out.println(e.getMessage());
            System.exit(0);
        }
    }
}
```

Notice that the program above makes use of the *seek()* method to reposition the file pointer. Hence, the line

```
myfile.seek(0);
```

moves the file pointer back to the start of the file.

The line

```
myfile.seek((p-1)*4);
```

positions the file pointer at the start of the value requested by the user. An `int` value occupies 4 bytes and the first value in the file starts at position zero, the second at position 4, the third at position 8 and so on. If the user wants to display the third value in the file (i.e. p = 3) then the *seek()* line evaluates to

```
(3-1)*4 = 8
```

which positions the file pointer at the start of the third value which is then extracted from the stream by the subsequent *readInt()* statement.

Activity 11.12

Type in and run the file above.

Change the program so that 10 `double` values are written to the file.

A more realistic use of a random access file is to store and retrieve records. For example, a college might store details of thousands of students.

As we saw with the previous example, we need to be able to calculate the start position of a data item and then use the *seek()* method to position the file pointer at the desired position in the file. So if we want to store student records in our random access file, we need to make sure that every record contains exactly the same number of bytes. Where a record contains only primitive types this isn't a problem since they are all of fixed size, but where strings are held there's a complication. Strings vary in length depending on the number of characters they contain; if we were to write strings as part of a student's record the ability to jump directly to a specific record would be lost. We can get round this by converting every string to a fixed size array of characters. Obviously this array must be large enough to contain the longest string; where a string has less characters than the array, the extra positions in the array can be space filled.

The next program (LISTING-11.9) writes the *idcode, name* and *sex* of students to a random access file and allows the user to retrieve any record.

The string is handled by writing a UTF string to the file and then writing additional bytes to pad the string out to 30 characters. The total number of bytes written per record are:

idcode	int	4 bytes
name	UTF	32 bytes (2 byte count; characters in *name*; padding)
sex	char	2 bytes
	TOTAL	38 bytes

LISTING-11.9

Writing Records to Random Access Files

```
import java.io.*;
import Input;

public class RandomRecords
{
  public static void main(String args[])
  {
       int idcode;
       String name;
       char sex;
       try
       {
            RandomAccessFile myfile = new RandomAccessFile
            ↳("mydata.dat","rw");
            myfile.seek(0);

            System.out.print("Enter idcode : ");
            idcode = Input.readInt();
            while(idcode != -99)
            {
                 System.out.print("Enter name : ");
                 name = Input.readString();
                 System.out.print("Enter sex : ");
                 sex = Input.readChar();
                 myfile.writeInt(idcode);
                 myfile.writeUTF(name);
                 for(int c = 1; c <= 30 - name.length(); c++)
                      myfile.writeByte(32);
                 myfile.writeChar(sex);
                 System.out.print("Enter idcode : ");
                 idcode = Input.readInt();
            }
            myfile.close();
       }
       catch(IOException e)
       {
            System.out.println(e.getMessage());
            System.exit(0);
       }
  }
}
```

Activity 11.13

Modify the above program so that as well as *idcode, name* and *sex* values, three byte-sized exam marks are also stored for each record.
Enter the following record details:

```
1 Liz Heron    F   98 79 82
2 Avril Tait   F   78 69 34
3 John Farrell M   85 89 93
```

The program in LISTING-11.10 reads back the information in the file, displays the number of records held, and allows the user to choose which record is to be displayed.

LISTING-11.10

Retrieving Records from Random Access Files

```
import java.io.*;
import Input;
public class Random3
{
  public static void main(String args[])
  {
      int idcode;
      String name;
      char namechars[] = new char[30];
      char sex;
      byte temp;
      RandomAccessFile myfile;
      try
      {
          myfile = new RandomAccessFile("mydata.dat","r");
          myfile.seek(0);
          for(int j = 0; j < 3 ; j++)
          {
              idcode = myfile.readInt();
              name = myfile.readUTF();
              for(int c = 1; c <= 30-name.length(); c++)
                  temp = myfile.readByte();
              sex = myfile.readChar();
              System.out.println("id:"+idcode+" name:"+name+
              ↳" sex:"+sex);
          }
          System.out.println("File contains " +myfile.length()/38
          ↳ + " records");
          System.out.print("Which number (1 - 3):");
          int p = Input.readInt();
          while(p >= 1 && p <= 3)
          {
              myfile.seek((p-1)*38);
              idcode = myfile.readInt();
              name = myfile.readUTF();
              for(int c = 1; c <= 30-name.length(); c++)
                  temp = myfile.readByte();
              sex = myfile.readChar();
              System.out.println("id:"+idcode+" name:"+name+
              ↳" sex:"+sex);
              System.out.print("Which number (1 - 3):");
              p = Input.readInt();
          }
          myfile.close();
      }
      catch(IOException e)
      {
          System.out.println(e.getMessage());
          System.exit(0);
      }
  }
}
```

> **Activity 11.14**
>
> Write a program, similar to that above, which displays at the user's request any record in your own file which also includes scores.
>
> Notice that the blank characters used to pad out the name are passed over using a `for` loop. In your own program use the *skipBytes()* method to achieve the same effect.

Summary

- **The *RandomAccessFile* class** allows random access files to be employed in a Java application.
- **Random access files use a file pointer** to indicate the current position in the file.
- **Any reading or writing will begin at the current file pointer position.**
- **The file pointer's position moves on** when reading or writing takes place.
- **To use random access each record most contain exactly the same number of bytes.**

Streamable Objects

Introduction

As well as reading and writing primitive data types such as `int` and `float`, there will be times when we want to save and load complete objects. For example, we might want to write a complete *Weight* object to a file. Although we could save an object by writing each attribute separately to a file this would be a rather tedious task. Instead, we can create stream objects specifically designed to do this job.

Writing an Object to a Stream

The *ObjectOutputStream* class defines a set of operations each of which throw *IOException* errors. Since this is a checked exception any code you create must handle the exception in some way. The main operations are defined below:

ObjectOutputStream(OutputStream os) Creates an *ObjectOutputStream* object linked to *os*.

void writeObject(Object obj) Writes the attributes of *obj* to the stream.

void writeBoolean(boolean)
void writeByte(int)
void writeShort(int)
void writeChar(int)
void writeInt(int)
void writeLong(long)
void writeFloat(float)
void writeDouble(double) Each of the above take a primitive data value and output it to the stream.

void writeBytes(String)
void writeChars(String)
void writeUTF(String) Each routine takes a String and outputs to the stream in the specified format.

void flush() Flushes the stream's contents to the device.

close() Closes the stream. This causes the stream to be flushed.

There's one more task that needs to be performed before we can use an *ObjectOutputStream* object to save a *Weight* object: only classes that implement the *Serializable* interface can be written to such a stream.

Serializable is defined in the package java.io.

However, this isn't too great a hardship since the *Serializable* interface is an empty interface containing no operation headings. So to make the *Weight* class comply to the *ObjectOutputStream* class's requirements we need only start it with the lines

```
import java.io.*;
public class Weight implements Serializable
```

no other changes are required.

The program in LISTING-11.11 sets up two *Weight* objects and writes them to a file.

LISTING-11.11

Writing Objects to a File

```
import Weight;
import java.io.*;

public class WritingWeights
{
  public static void main(String args[])
  {
      Weight w1 = new Weight(2,7);
      Weight w2 = new Weight(5,11);
      try
      {
          ObjectOutputStream objfile = new ObjectOutputStream
          ➥(new FileOutputStream("myobj.dat"));
          objfile.writeObject(w1);
          objfile.writeObject(w2);
          objfile.close();
      }
      catch(IOException ioe)
      {
          System.out.println(ioe.getMessage());
          System.exit(1);
      }
  }
}
```

Activity 11.15

Modify your *Distance* class definition as required and output two *Distance* objects to a stream using the method shown above.

Writing Aggregate Objects

When a class's attributes are themselves objects of other classes (as with the *Horse* class) the values held in these referenced objects are also written to the stream. For example, if a *Horse* object is streamed, the values held in the attributes *name, handicap* and *length* would all be written to the file.

Reading an Object from a Stream

To read back the objects written to a stream we need to use an *ObjectInputStream* object. This class is defined with complementary operations to the *ObjectOutputStream* class.

ObjectInputStream(InputStream is) — Creates an *ObjectInputStream* object linked to *is*.

Object readObject() — Returns the next object from the stream. It is necessary to cast the returned value to the appropriate class. This operation can throw a *ClassNotFoundException* which must be handled. This is not a subclass of *IOException.*

boolean readBoolean()
byte readByte()

short readShort()
char readChar()
int readInt(int)
long readLong()
float readFloat()
double readDouble() Each of the above return a primitive data value from the stream.

String readUTF() Returns a String from the stream.

close() Closes the stream.

The program in LISTING-11.12 reads and displays the *Weight* values written by the previous program.

LISTING-11.12

Reading Objects from a File

```
import Weight;
import java.io.*;

public class ReadingWeights
{
  public static void main(String args[])
  {
       Weight w1;
       Weight w2;
       try
       {
            ObjectInputStream objfile = new ObjectInputStream
            ↳(new FileInputStream("myobj.dat"));
            w1 = (Weight)objfile.readObject();
            w2 = (Weight)objfile.readObject();
            objfile.close();
            System.out.println("w1 = "+w1);
            System.out.println("w2 = "+w2);
       }
       catch(Exception ioe)
       {
            System.out.println("************");
            ioe.getMessage();
            System.exit(1);
       }
  }
}
```

Activity 11.16

Write a program to retrieve two *Distance* objects from a file.

The File Class

Introduction

As well as manipulating the contents of a file we may want to perform housekeeping operations on directories and files. For example, we might want to list the files held in a directory, find out when a file was last modified, or display how many bytes are in a file.

To perform these sort of operations we need to use a *File* class object.

File objects can be used to reference either a directory or a file in a directory; Java does not distinguish between these two situations.

Class Definition

The class methods are described below:

Constructors

File(String f)	Creates a *File* object that references the existing file or directory *f*. If *f* represents a file, it is assumed to be in the current directory. If *f* is a directory it is assumed to be a subdirectory off the current directory. This does not create a file or directory.
File(String p, String f)	Creates a *File* object that references the existing file or directory *f*. The location of *f* is given by *p*.
File(File p, String f)	Creates a *File* object that references the existing file *f*. The location of *f* is given by *p*.

Other Methods

boolean exists()	Returns *true* if the referenced item actually exists.
boolean isDirectory()	Returns *true* if the current object references an existing directory
boolean isFile()	Returns *true* if the current object references an existing file.

If we assume the C: drive of a computer has a file identified by the line

```
C:\java2\booksol\chapter11\mydata.dat
```

and that *chapter11* has a sub-directory named *solutions*

and that C:\java2\booksol\chapter11 is the current directory, then the program

```
import java.io.*;

public class FileInfo
{
    public static void main(String args[])
    {
        File dr = new File(args[0]);
        if(dr.exists())
        {
            if(dr.isFile())
                System.out.println("This is an existing file");
            if(dr.isDirectory())
                System.out.println("This is an existing
                ↳directory");
        }
        else
            System.out.println("Invalid file or directory");
    }
}
}
```

would give the following responses

Command line	Response
java FileInfo xxx.xxx	Invalid file or directory
java FileInfo mydata.dat	This is an existing file
java FileInfo chapter11	Invalid file or directory
java FileInfo solutions	This is an existing directory

String getName() Returns the name of the file or directory.

String getPath() Returns the path information from the current directory to the file or directory.

String getParent() Returns the parent of the last directory mentioned in the path information.

If we make the same assumptions about the current directory and position of the *mydata.dat* file then the program

```
import java.io.*;

public class FileInfo
{
    public static void main(String args[])
    {
        File dr = new File(args[0]);
        if(dr.exists())
        {
            System.out.println("Name   : "+ dr.getName());
            System.out.println("Path   : "+ dr.getPath());
            System.out.println("Parent : "+ dr.getParent());
        }
        else
            System.out.println("Invalid file or directory");
    }
}
```

responds to the line

```
FileInfo mydata.dat
```

with the output

```
Name   : mydata.dat
Path   : mydata.dat
Parent : null
```

This assumes FileInfo.class is held in the booksol directory.

However if the current directory is `C:\java2\booksol`, then the command

```
FileInfo chapter11\mydata.dat
```

displays

```
Name   : mydata.dat
Path   : chapter11\mydata.dat
Parent : chapter11
```

From the same current directory the line

```
FileInfo chapter11\solutions
```

displays

```
Name   : solutions
Path   : chapter11\solutions
Parent : chapter11
```

Some of the following operations assume the *File* object references a file; while others assume a directory is referenced.

boolean canRead()	Returns *true* if the file can be read.
boolean canWrite()	Returns *true* if the program has write access
boolean isHidden()	Returns *true* if the file is marked as hidden.
boolean setReadOnly()	Marks a file as read-only and returns *true* if the operation was successful.
boolean createNewFile()	Creates a new file. Returns *true* if successful.
boolean mkdir()	Makes a directory. Returns *true* if successful.
boolean delete()	Deletes the file or directory. Returns *true* if successful.
long length()	Returns the number of bytes in a file.
String[] list()	Returns an array of *String* objects giving names of the files in the directory.

Activity 11.17

Write a program that displays the number of bytes in the file you created in Activity 11.16. The file contains the two *Distance* objects.

Solutions

Activity 11.1

No solution required.

Activity 11.2

No solution required.

Activity 11.3

No solution required.

Activity 11.4

No solution required.

Activity 11.5

```
import Input;
import java.io.*;

public class Act11_5
{
    public static void main(String args[])
    {
        int idcode;
        String name;
        char sex;
        byte scores[] = new byte[3];

        System.out.print("Enter idcode : ");
        idcode = Input.readInt();
        System.out.print("Enter name : ");
        name = Input.readString();
        System.out.print("Enter sex : ");
        sex = Input.readChar();
        for(int c = 0; c < 3 ; c++)
        {
            System.out.print("Enter score "+(c+1)
            ↳+" : ");
            scores[c] = (byte)Input.readInt();
        }
        FileOutputStream myfile;
        try
        {
            myfile = new FileOutputStream
                    ↳("STUDENTS.DAT");
            myfile.write(idcode);
            myfile.write(name.getBytes());
            myfile.write(sex);
            myfile.write(scores);
            myfile.close();
        }
        catch(IOException e)
        {
            System.out.println(e.getMessage());
            System.exit(0);
        }
    }
}
```

Activity 11.6

No solution required.

Activity 11.7

No solution required.

Activity 11.8

Only the declaration of *myfile* needs to be changed.

```
import Input;
import java.io.*;

public class Act11_8
{
    public static void main(String args[])
    {
        int idcode;
        String name;
        char sex;

        System.out.print("Enter idcode : ");
        idcode = Input.readInt();
        System.out.print("Enter name : ");
        name = Input.readString();
        System.out.print("Enter sex : ");
        sex = Input.readChar();

        BufferedOutputStream myfile;
        try
        {
            myfile = new BufferedOutputStream
            ↳(new FileOutputStream("mydata.dat"));
            myfile.write(idcode);
            myfile.write(name.getBytes());
            myfile.write(sex);
            myfile.close();
        }
        catch(IOException e)
        {
            System.out.println(e.getMessage());
            System.exit(0);
        }
    }
}
```

Activity 11.9

Using the *writeChars()* statement the name is written as a sequence of Unicode (2-byte) characters.

The *writeUTF()* method writes ASCII (1-byte) characters. The characters are preceded by a 2-byte count of the number of characters written.

Activity 11.10

```
import java.io.*;

public class Act11_10
{
    public static void main(String args[])
    {
        int idcode;
        String name;
        char sex;

        DataInputStream myfile;
        try
        {

            myfile = new DataInputStream
            ↳(new FileInputStream("mydata.dat"));
            idcode = myfile.readInt();
            name = myfile.readUTF();
            sex = myfile.readChar();
            myfile.close();
            System.out.println("Idcode : "
            ↳+idcode+" Name : "+name+" Sex : "
            ↳+sex);
        }
        catch(IOException e)
        {
            System.out.println(e.getMessage());
            System.exit(0);
        }
    }
}
```

Activity 11.11

To add end-of-line characters after each data item simply use `println` rather than print in the output statements which change to

```
myfile.println(idcode);
myfile.println(name);
myfile.println(sex);
```

Activity 11.12

```
import java.io.*;
import Input;

public class Act11_12
{
    public static void main(String args[])
    {
        double num;
        RandomAccessFile myfile;
        try
        {
            myfile = new RandomAccessFile
            ↳("mynumbers.dat","rw");
            myfile.seek(0);
            for(int j = 0; j < 10 ; j++)
            {
                num = (Math.random()*100);
                myfile.writeDouble(num);
            }
            System.out.println("The file contains "
            ↳+myfile.length()+" bytes");
            myfile.seek(0);
            for(int j = 1; j <= 10 ; j++)
            {
                num = myfile.readDouble();
                System.out.println(j+" = "+num);
            }
            System.out.print("Which number(1 - 10)
            ↳:");
            int p = Input.readInt();
            while(p >= 1 && p <= 10)
            {
                myfile.seek((p-1)*8);
                num = myfile.readDouble();
                System.out.println(num);
                System.out.print("Which number(1
                ↳- 10):");
                p = Input.readInt();
            }
            myfile.close();
        }
        catch(IOException e)
        {
            System.out.println(e.getMessage());
            System.exit(0);
        }
    }
}
```

Activity 11.13

```
import java.io.*;
import Input;

public class Act11_13
{
    public static void main(String args[])
    {
        int idcode;
        String name;
        char sex;
        byte scores[] = new byte[3];
        try
        {
            RandomAccessFile myfile = new
RandomAccessFile("mydata.dat","rw");
            myfile.seek(0);
            System.out.print("Enter idcode : ");
            idcode = Input.readInt();
            while(idcode != -99)
            {
                System.out.print("Enter name : ");
                name = Input.readString();
                System.out.print("Enter sex : ");
                sex = Input.readChar();
                for(int c = 0; c < 3 ; c++)
                {
                    System.out.print("Enter score "
                    ↳+(c+1)+" : ");
                    scores[c]=(byte)Input.readInt();
                }
                myfile.writeInt(idcode);
                myfile.writeUTF(name);
                for(int c=1 ;c<=30-name.length();
                ↳ c++)
                    myfile.writeByte(32);
                myfile.writeChar(sex);
                myfile.write(scores);
                System.out.print("Enter idcode: ");
                idcode = Input.readInt();
            }
            myfile.close();
        }
        catch(IOException e)
        {
            System.out.println(e.getMessage());
            System.exit(0);
        }
    }
}
```

Activity 11.14

```
import java.io.*;
import Input;

public class Act11_14
{
    public static void main(String args[])
    {
        int idcode;
        String name;
        char namechars[] = new char[30];
        char sex;
        byte scores[] = new byte[3];
        byte temp;
        RandomAccessFile myfile;
        try
        {
            myfile = new RandomAccessFile
            ↳("mydata.dat","r");
            myfile.seek(0);
            for(int j = 0; j < 3 ; j++)
            {
                idcode = myfile.readInt();
                name = myfile.readUTF();
                myfile.skipBytes(30-name.length());
                sex = myfile.readChar();
                for(int c = 0; c < 3; c++)
                    scores[c]=myfile.readByte();
                System.out.print("id:"+idcode
                ↳+" name:"+name+" sex:"+sex);
                for(int c = 0; c < 3 ; c++)
                    System.out.print(" Score "
                    ↳+(c+1)+" : "+scores[c]);
                System.out.println();
            }
            System.out.println("File contains "
            ↳+myfile.length()/38 + " records");
            System.out.print("Which number(1-3):");
            int p = Input.readInt();
            while(p >= 1 && p <= 3)
            {
                myfile.seek((p-1)*41);
                idcode = myfile.readInt();
                name = myfile.readUTF();
                myfile.skipBytes(30-name.length());
                sex = myfile.readChar();
                for(int c = 0; c < 3; c++)
                    scores[c]=myfile.readByte();
                System.out.print("id:"+idcode+
                ↳" name:"+name+" sex:"+sex);
                for(int c = 0; c < 3 ; c++)
                    System.out.print(" Score "
                    ↳+(c+1)+" : "+scores[c]);
                System.out.println();
                System.out.print("Which number
                ↳(1-3):");
                p = Input.readInt();
            }
            myfile.close();
        }
        catch(IOException e)
        {
            System.out.println(e.getMessage());
            System.exit(0);
        }
    }
}
```

Activity 11.15

```
import Weight;
import java.io.*;

public class Act11_15
{
    public static void main(String args[])
    {
        Distance d1 = new Distance(1,2,3);
        Distance d2 = new Distance(5,0,11);
        try
        {
            ObjectOutputStream objfile = new
            ↳ObjectOutputStream(new FileOutputStream("myobj.dat"));
            objfile.writeObject(d1);
            objfile.writeObject(d2);
            objfile.close();
        }
        catch(IOException ioe)
        {
            System.out.println(ioe.getMessage());
            System.exit(1);
        }
    }
}
```

Activity 11.16

```
import Weight;
import java.io.*;

public class Act11_16
{
    public static void main(String args[])
    {
        Distance d1;
        Distance d2;
        try
        {
            ObjectInputStream objfile = new
            ↳ObjectInputStream(new FileInputStream("myobj.dat"));
            d1 = (Distance)objfile.readObject();
            d2 = (Distance)objfile.readObject();
            objfile.close();
            System.out.println("d1 = "+d1);
            System.out.println("d2 = "+d2);
        }
        catch(Exception ioe)
        {
            ioe.getMessage();
            System.exit(1);
        }
    }
}
```

Activity 11.17

```
import java.io.*;

public class Act11_17
{
    public static void main(String args[])
    {
        File filedetails = new File("myobj.dat");
        System.out.println("This file contains "
        ↳+filedetails.length()+" bytes");
    }
}
```

Chapter 12

Threads

This chapter covers the following topics:

Basic Concepts

Extending the Thread Class

Runnable Interface

Synchronisation

Thread Class

Thread Stages

Threads

Introduction

This chapter is designed to serve as an introduction to the idea of threads; a topic that even most professional programmers will have very little practical experience in creating.

When we execute a Java program that we've written, we expect that program to begin execution at the first line in *main()* and continue running until it reaches the last line in *main()*. At that point the program terminates.

But what happens when your computer is executing two or more programs at the same time. For example, most operating systems will allow you to run, say, a word processor at the same time as a spreadsheet. More obviously, if you execute two programs both of which display animation, both will continue to execute (although possibly at a reduced speed).

The machine manages to run two (or more) programs at the same time by allocating each a small amount of processor time. As one program's time is used up, it makes way for the next program to be given control of the processor. The programs continue to swap control of the processor until the programs are terminated. By giving each program a small enough slice (just a few milliseconds) of processor time we get the impression that both programs are executing at exactly the same time. In fact, this would only be truly possible if the computer had a separate processor for each program being executed.

This concept of giving the impression of executing more than one set of instructions at the same time can be extended to operate within a single program. So, for example, a program might calculate pi to a thousand places while at the same time drawing complex graphics on the screen. One everyday use of this technique is a printing request. All word processing applications have a Print option. When this option is chosen by the user, printing starts, but the user may continue to type and edit existing text.

These sections of a program which can be executed simultaneously are know as **threads**.

Java, unlike most programming languages, allows you to define threads within your program.

The idea behind how threads work in practice can be quite complicated if you're not familiar with the ideas and problems of parallel processing so we'll introduces the ideas and situations that can arise with a real-life situation.

Imagine two people arriving at the outpatients department in a hospital. They have to register at reception and are then ready to be seen. There is only one doctor working so only one can be seen at a time.

How is the doctor to choose which one to see first? If neither are seriously ill he may work on a first-come, first-served basis. However, if patient A has a more serious complaint he will be taken first.

Once the doctor begins dealing with the patient he may continue until treatment is complete. Alternatively, the doctor may require some examining equipment that is not available so he may ask the patient to wait until the equipment arrives and in the meantime deal with the second patient. The first patient may even be so caring of his fellow human beings that after a few minutes he insists that the doctor have a look at the second patient.

Eventually the patients will leave. In fact, they may leave at any stage in the process.

This apparently pointless tale parallels the processes involved in using threads within a program.

Now imagine a program containing two objects designed to be executed as separate threads within a program. Object A displays the letters of the alphabet while Object B displays the numbers 0 to 9. The threads now move through various stages or states:

Newborn

Initially, the threads are in are created and are in the *newborn* state. In the newborn state a thread has been allocated memory and its local variables initialised.

Runnable

By executing the thread's *start()* method it moves to a *Runnable* state. The thread is now waiting in a queue ready to be executed. threads with a higher priority are moved to the front of the queue. If the arriving thread has the same or lower priority than threads already waiting it is placed at the end of the queue.

Running

Once the processor becomes free the thread at the front of the queue begins running. The thread may keep control of the processor until it has completed its operation in which case it moves on to the dead state. However, the thread may have to give up control of the processor because it needs access to a temporarily unavailable resource (perhaps a printer or a file). It may even simply need to wait for a period of time to pass (remember the *Clock* object waited one second between each execution of the *tick()* method). In these situations the thread moves to the *Blocked* stage.

A thread may even give up its control of the processor in order to allow some other thread to be processed. In this case, the thread giving up control returns to the end of the *Runnable* queue and waits its turn once more.

Blocked

The thread has given up control of the processor and is awaiting access to a resource or for a set time to pass. When the reason for entering the blocked state is dealt with, the thread returns to the *Runnable* state.

Dead

When the thread is complete or has been abandoned at some other stage, it is considered to be in the *Dead* state.

The most important state is *Runnable* where the code within a thread is actually executed by the computer. Like a patient, a thread can be assigned a priority with higher priority threads moving to the front of the queue. As a general rule threads of a higher priority will be placed in the *Running* state before a lower priority thread. Even if a high priority thread has to return to the *Runnable* state it will be placed in the queue ahead of lower priority threads still waiting to be served.

A thread's priority is set as an integer value between 1 and 9, 5 being the default value. A priority of 1 means a thread has a very low priority and is unlikely to be assigned processor time until all other threads have been completed or are *Blocked.*

The Thread Class

There are two ways to create objects that will be threads. One is to create classes that are derived from Java's *Thread* class.

The *Thread* class contains methods to allow a thread to move from one state to another and determine the current state of a thread. The main methods of the class are:

void start() — This moves a thread from the *Newborn* to *Runnable* state.

void stop() — Terminates the thread. That is, the thread moves to the *Dead* state.

void yield() — Causes the thread to move from the *Running* state and return to *Runnable.* It is then placed at the end of the *Runnable* queue unless the thread's priority warrants a higher position in the queue.

void sleep(int millisecs) throws InterruptedException — Causes the thread to move to the *Blocked* state where it remains for millisec milliseconds before moving to the *Runnable* state.
Notice that this method may throw an exception which must be dealt with.

boolean isAlive() — Returns *true* if the thread *Runnable, Running* or *Blocked*; otherwise *false* is returned.

void setPriority(int p) — Sets the priority to *p.* 1 p must lie in the range 1(low priority) to 9 (high priority).

int getPriority() — Returns the current priority of the current thread.

void run() — This method needs to be overridden in your derived class with the logic you want the thread to execute when it is in the *Running* state.

Thread currentThread() — Returns a reference to the thread currently in the *Running* state.

No call to *run()* will ever appear in your programs. Instead the Java environment automatically executes the *run()* method of a thread as soon as it is placed in the *Running* state. When the *run()* method is completed, the thread terminates.

The diagram in FIG-12.1 shows the various states of a thread and how a thread may move between one state and another.

FIG-12.1

Thread States

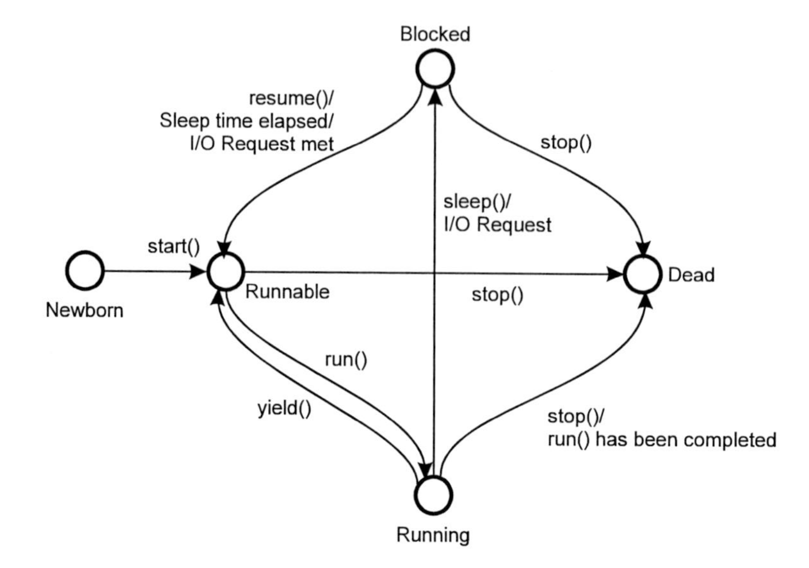

Implementing Threads

To show threads in operation we'll define two separate classes. The first of these, *Letters*, displays the letters of the alphabet. The code is:

```
public class Letters extends Thread
{
    public void run()
    {
        for(char c = 'A'; c <= 'Z' ; c++)
            System.out.print(c);
    }
}
```

In order to make a thread, the class has to extend the *Thread* class and override the inherited *run()* method.

The second class, *Numbers*, displays the values 0 to 9. Its code is:

```
public class Numbers extends Thread
{
    public void run()
    {
        for(int c = 0; c <= 9; c++)
            System.out.print(c);
    }
}
```

Finally, we need write a program that creates an object of each of the above classes and begins execution of each thread:

```
public class RunningThreads
{
    public static void main(String args[])
    {
        Numbers no = new Numbers();
        Letters let = new Letters();
        let.start();
        no.start();
    }
}
```

Once each thread moves to the *Runnable* state by calling their *start()* methods, the Java environment causes the *run()* method of each to be executed when they are allocated processor time.

What happens next depends on the operating system you are using. In Microsoft Windows each thread is allocated a limited amount of time before being returned to the *Runnable* state. This is known as **timeslicing**. Simpler operating system will allow each thread to run to completion before the next thread is allocated processor time.

Below is the result of executing *RunningThreads* program several times.

```
C:\jdk1.1.4\Threads>java RunningThreads
AB0123456789CDEFGHIJKLMNOPQRSTUVWXYZ

C:\jdk1.1.4\Threads>java RunningThreads
ABCDEFGHIJKLMNOPQRSTUVWXYZ0123456789

C:\jdk1.1.4\Threads>java RunningThreads
A012B3456789CDEFGHIJKLMNOPQRSTUVWXYZ

C:\jdk1.1.4\Threads>java RunningThreads
0ABCDEFGHIJKLMNOPQRSTUVWXYZ123456789

C:\jdk1.1.4\Threads>java RunningThreads
A012B34567C89DEFGHIJKLMNOPQRSTUVWXYZ

C:\jdk1.1.4\Threads>java RunningThreads
ABCDEFGHIJKLMNOPQRSTUVWXYZ0123456789
```

Notice that there is no way to predict which thread starts first, or how much output will be produced before one thread is replaced by another.

Activity 12.1

Type in and compile the *Letters* and *Numbers* class.

Type in the *RunningThreads* program and execute it.

Setting a Thread's Priority

By setting the *Letters* object's priority to a higher level we can affect the result.

If we change the priority of the thread displaying the letters as shown below

```
public class RunningThreads

{
    public static void main(String args[])
    {
        Numbers no = new Numbers();
        Letters let = new Letters();
        no.start();
        let.start();
        let.setPriority(7);        //Set to a high priority
    }
}
```

then the output changes to

```
    ABCDEFGHIJKLMNOPQRSTUVWXYZ0123456789
```

with the letters being display before any numbers.

Changing to a lower priority by modifying the *setPriority()* line to

```
let.setPriority(1);
```

gives the output

```
0123456A789BCDEFGHIJKLMNOPQRSTUVWXYZ
```

Notice that the *Letters* thread did not get exclusive use of the processor in this last display.

There is no guarantee of the exactly what sequence the threads will be processed in and your programs should make no assumptions in this area.

You may think that there are two threads running in the example above, but in fact, there are three:

The thread allocated to the *Letters* object
The thread allocated to the *Numbers* object
The *RunningThread* program

Even though the main application isn't a descendant of the *Thread* class it obviously needs to be allocated processor time and executed.

> **Activity 12.2**
>
> Modify your *RunningThreads*.java file's *main()* method as follows
>
> ```
> public static void main(String args[])
> {
>     Numbers no = new Numbers();
>     Letters let = new Letters();
>     let.start();
>     no.start();
>     for(int c = 0; c < 50; c++)
>         System.out.print('!');
> }
> ```
>
> Rerun the program.

Typical output of three runs is shown below.

```
C:\jdk1.1.4\Threads>java RunningThreads
!ABC0123456789!!!!!!!!!!!!!!!!!!!!!!!!!!!!!!!!DEFGHIJKLMNOPQRSTUVWXY
Z!!!!!!!!!!!!!!!!!

C:\jdk1.1.4\Threads>java RunningThreads
!ABCDEFGHIJKLMNOPQRSTUVWXYZ0123!!!!!!!!!!!!!!!!!!!!!4!56789!!!!!!!!!
!!!!!!!!!!!!!!!!!!

C:\jdk1.1.4\Threads>java RunningThreads
!ABCDEFGHIJKLMNOPQRSTUVWXYZ01!23456789!!!!!!!!!!!!!!!!!!!!!!!!!!!!!!
!!!!!!!!!!!!!!!!!!
```

Using yield()

By using the *yield()* method we can get more control of when a thread gives up control of the processor. For example, if we change the code for *Letter* and *Numbers* to

```
public class Letters extends Thread
{
    public void run()
    {
        for(char c = 'A'; c <= 'Z' ; c++)
        {
            System.out.print(c);
            yield();
        }
    }
}


public class Numbers extends Thread
{
    public void run()
    {
        for(int c = 0; c <= 9; c++)
        {
            System.out.print(c);
            yield();
        }
    }
}
```

Now when the we run the application typical outputs are

```
C:\jdk1.1.4\Threads>java RunningThreads
A01B2C3D4E5F6G7H8I9JKLMNOPQRSTUVWXYZ

C:\jdk1.1.4\Threads>java RunningThreads
A012BC3D45E6FG7H89IJKLMNOPQRSTUVWXYZ

C:\jdk1.1.4\Threads>java RunningThreads
A01B2CD3E4F56G7HI8J9KLMNOPQRSTUVWXYZ
```

Because of other possible delays, the output does not jump predictably from one thread to the other, but sharing between both is more even than before.

sleep()

Alternatively, we can put a thread into *Blocked* mode using the *sleep()* method. Because this throws an exception we need to use `try` and `catch` blocks.

The version of *Numbers* below demonstrates its use

```
public class Numbers extends Thread
{
    public void run()
    {
        for(int c = 0; c <= 9; c++)
        {
            System.out.print(c);
            try
            {
                sleep(2);
            }
            catch(InterruptedException ie)
            {
                return;
            }
        }
    }
}
```

Activity 12.3

Modify *Numbers* as shown above.

Rerun *RunningThreads* and examine the output.

Change the sleep time to 10 milliseconds and re-run the program.

How does this change affect the output?

The Runnable Interface

What if we wanted to make the *CountdownClock* class objects work in a separate thread? We can't declare *CountdownClock* class as a derivative of the *Thread* class since it is already a subclass of *Clock.*

To get round this we can declare a class as implementing the *Runnable* interface. This interface declares only one method, *run()*. Code for a version of *CountdownClock* is given below

```
import Clock;

public class CountdownClock extends Clock implements Runnable
{
    public CountdownClock()
    {
        super();
    }

    public CountdownClock(int h, int m, int s)
    {
        super(h,m,s);
    }
    public void tick()
    {
        int totalsec = hours*3600+minutes*60+seconds - 1;
        if(totalsec < 0)
            totalsec = 3600*24 - 1;
        hours = (totalsec / 3600)%24;
        minutes = (totalsec % 3600/60);
        seconds = totalsec%60;
    }
    public void run()
    {
        while(true)
        {
            System.out.print(toString()+"     \r");
            tick();
            try
            {
                Thread.sleep(1000);
            }
            catch(InterruptedException ie)
            {
                return;
            }
        }
    }
}
```

The *run()* function calls tick and then sleeps for 1 second before repeating an unending while loop.

To use a *CountdownClock* in a separate thread we need to create a *CountdownClock* object

```
CountdownClock cdc = new CountdownClock(0,0,30);
```

create a *Thread* class reference variable

```
Thread clockthread;
```

and use the *CountdownClock* object as the argument to the *Thread* class's constructor

```
clockthread = new Thread(cdc);
```

Now we can start the thread running:

```
clockthread.start();
```

and because the *run()* method contains an infinite loop and hence will not move to the *Dead* state automatically, we need to terminate the thread explicitly. One way to do this is to use the *stop()* method:

```
clockthread.stop();
```

```
import CountdownClock;
import Input;

public class UsingCdC
{
    public static void main(String args[])
    {
        CountdownClock cdc = new CountdownClock(0,0,30);
        Thread clockthread = new Thread(cdc);
        System.out.println("Press enter to stop");
        clockthread.start();
        char finish = Input.readChar();
        clockthread.stop();
    }
}
```

However, the *stop()* method is now deprecated because it has problems releasing all the resources of the thread when it dies. Instead the loop structure in the *run()* method should always be made finite, perhaps stopping when some Boolean attribute is set to *false*.

Activity 12.4

Type in and compile the version of *CountdownClock* given on the previous page.

Test the new class using the application coded above.

Add a private Boolean attribute named *terminate* to the *CountdownClock* class. This should be initialised to *false*.

Create a public method *setTerminate()* in *CountdownClock* which sets terminate to *true*.

Modify the *run()* method of *CountdownClock* to finish when *terminate* is *true*.

Modify *UsingCdC* so that *setTerminate()* is called when a key is pressed.

Test your program to check that the countdown stops when a key is pressed.

Synchronisation

Sometimes two or more threads can share common data. Consider the following *TextSorter* class:

```
import java.util.Arrays;

public class TextSorter
{
    private char text[];

    public TextSorter(String s)
    {
    text = s.toCharArray();
    }

    public  void sortText()
    {
        Arrays.sort(text);
    }

    public  void listText()
    {
        for(int c = 0; c < text.length; c++)
            System.out.print(text[c]);
    }
}
```

which fills a `char` array with the characters from a string. These characters can either be sorted using the *sortText()* method or listed using *listText()*. If a *Thread* derived class, *Sorting,* makes use of an object of the *TextSorter* class to sort the text:

```
public class Sorting extends Thread
{
    TextSorter a;

    public Sorting(TextSorter ts)
    {
        a = ts;
    }

    public void run()
    {
        a.sortText();
    }
}
```

and a second class, *Listing,* makes use of a *TextSorter* object to list the text:

```
public class Listing extends Thread
{
    TextSorter a;

    public Listing(TextSorter ts)
    {
        a=ts;
    }

    public void run()
    {
        a.listText();
    }
}
```

then an application could set up a thread from each of these two classes using the same *TextSorter* object:

```
TextSorter testdata = new TextSorter
    ↳("maryhadalittlelambitsfleecewaswhiteassnow");
Sorting t1 = new Sorting(testdata);
Listing t2 = new Listing(testdata);
```

Once running, thread *t1* could be displaced after only partially sorting the text; *t2* then takes over and begins to display the partially sorted text. But before this is complete control returns to *t1* and sorting continues. This time when *t2* takes over once more the characters have moved about within the char array and may even end up being displayed more than once as they change positions. LISTING-12.1 demonstrates the problem.

LISTING-12.1

Synchronisation Problrems

```
public class UsingUnSync
{
  public static void main(String args[])
  {
      TextSorter testdata = new TextSorter
          ↳("maryhadalittlelambitsfleecewaswhiteassnow");
      Sorting t1 = new Sorting(testdata);
      Listing t2 = new Listing(testdata);
      t1.start();
      t2.start();
  }
}
```

Typical output for this program are shown below:

```
aaaaaabcdeeeeefhhiiillllmmnorsssstttttwwwy     (sorted)
mmaehadaliihlelaabiaefleecswtswtttyrssnow     (partially sorted)
```

We can solve this problem by making sure that the *listText()* method of an object cannot begin execution until *sortList()* of the same object is completed and vice versa. Java lets us do this by adding the term `synchronized` to the method headings. When a `synchronized` method begins execution, it locks access to that object by any other `synchronized` methods until that routine is complete at which point it unlocks the object. The revised version of *TextSorter* being

```
import java.util.Arrays;
public class TextSorter
{
    char text[];

    public TextSorter(String s)
    {
        text = s.toCharArray();
    }

    public synchronized void sortText()
    {
        //Object locked here
        Arrays.sort(text);
        //Object unlocked here
    }

    public synchronized void listText()
    {
        // Object locked here
        for(int c = 0; c < text.length; c++)
            System.out.print(text[c]);
        //Object unlocked here
    }
}
```

Now, which ever of the two methods starts first will lock out the other until it is complete.

Solutions

Activity 12.1

No solution required.

Activiy 12.2

No solution required.

Activity 12.3

No solution required.

Activity 12.4

The final version of *CountdownClock* is shown below:

```
//import Clock;

public class CountdownClock extends Clock
implements Runnable
{
    private boolean terminate = false;

    public CountdownClock()
    {
        super();
    }

    public CountdownClock(int h, int m, int s)
    {
        super(h,m,s);
    }

    public void tick()
    {
        int totalsec = hours*3600+minutes*60
        ↳+seconds - 1;
        if(totalsec < 0)
            totalsec = 3600*24 - 1;
        hours = (totalsec / 3600)%24;
        minutes = (totalsec % 3600/60);
        seconds = totalsec%60;
    }

    public void setTerminate()
    {
        terminate = true;
    }

    public void run()
    {
        while(!terminate)
        {
            System.out.print(toString()+"  \r");
            tick();
            try
            {
                Thread.sleep(1000);
            }
            catch(InterruptedException ie)
            {
                return;
            }
        }
    }
}
```

The new version of *UsingCdC* is:

```
public class UsingCdC
{
    public static void main(String args[])
    {
        CountdownClock cdc =
        ↳new CountdownClock(0,0,30);
        Thread clockthread = new Thread(cdc);
        System.out.println("Press enter to stop");
        clockthread.start();
        char finish = Input.readChar();
        cdc.setTerminate();
    }
}
```

Chapter 13

GUI Applications Using AWT

This chapter covers the following topics:

- Adapters
- Button Class
- Checkbox Class
- CheckboxGroup Class
- Choice Class
- Color Class
- Creating an Application Window
- Creating Radio Buttons
- Event Classes
- Frame Class
- How to Write Event-Handlers
- List Class
- Label Class
- Layout Managers
- Listeners
- Scrollbar Class
- TextArea Class
- TextComponent Class
- TextField Class

GUI Applications Using AWT

Introduction

So far all our applications have been of a command prompt variety. There has been no sign of moveable windows with buttons, menus and edit boxes.

However, if we are to create a modern software package with a significant amount of user interaction then a **Graphical User Interface** (GUI) is almost a necessity.

Java allows use to achieve this by supplying a set of related classes for creating the basic components of such a system. Hence, we can use existing *Button*, *Label* or *TextField* classes to create the objects that populate our new software.

These GUI components need to be positioned within our application's window. With platform-specific software such components are usually placed at specific positions within the window and are of specified dimensions. However, when using Java, we have to keep in mind that our application may be run on many different platforms with varying screen resolutions, so absolute positioning and sizing of components can cause serious problems. Instead, Java employs a **layout manager** to decide on the position and size of the GUI components appearing in the application window.

Once positioned, components must be made to react to user input. For example, we will want something to happen when the user clicks on a button. A component is made to react to user input by adding a **listener** which states exactly which events a particular component should *listen* for. For each event we want a component to react to, we need to write a Java function. The function will be executed when the event occurs. For example, if an application contained a button and a label, we might make the button *listen* for being pressed and then write a routine, linked to the button pressed event, which changes the label's text to "*Button pressed*".

This chapter introduces the various features mentioned above; subsequent chapters then expand on the options available.

Creating an Application Window

The GUI components that we need are defined by Java in the **Abstract Windowing Toolkit** or **AWT** package. To use objects from the classes defined there we need to include the statement

```
import java.awt.*;
```

in our programs.

Any GUI application will appear within a window. Java's *Frame* class allows us to create such a basic window. One way to do this is to add a *Frame* object to *main()*. The logic required by the program is:

```
Create a Frame object
Set its size
Make the window (frame) visible
```

The code overleaf (LISTING-13.1) shows how this is done.

LISTING-13.1

Creating a Window Using a *Frame* Object

```
import java.awt.*;

public class Window
{
  public static void main(String args[])
  {
      Frame fm = new Frame();
      fm.setSize(300,100);
      fm.show();
  }
}
```

Activity 13.1

Type in the above program, compile and run it.

You should be able to see the window. Try moving, resizing and closing the window.

Notice that the close options don't work. You'll have to click on the DOS window and press Ctrl-C to cancel the program.

An alternative approach is to make our own class a descendant of the *Frame* class. This, more usual approach, is demonstrated in LISTING-13.2 below.

LISTING-13.2

Creating a Window Using a *Frame* Subclass.

```
import java.awt.*;

public class Window2 extends Frame
{
  public static void main(String args[])
  {
      Window2 fm = new Window2();
      fm.setSize(300,100);
      fm.show();
  }
}
```

Activity 13.2

Type in and test this second version of the program.

As you can see, there is very little difference in the two approaches when it comes to coding *main()*. This second version creates a *Window2* object rather than the *Frame* object of the earlier version. In both cases the screen should appear as shown in FIG-13.1.

FIG-13.1

A Basic Application Window

In general, we'll stick to this second approach, but highlight the differences between the two styles on occasion.

We can discover what else can be achieved in our window by examining the *Frame* class.

The Frame Class

As we have seen, the *Frame* class is used as the basis of a window-type application. We can use its methods to position and size the application window; set its title; set up a menu bar; decide which cursor shape is shown; and control the user ability to resized the window.

Constructors

Frame()	Creates an untitled window.
Frame(String s)	Creates a window with the value *s* in the title bar.

To add a title to our window we need to create a constructor for the *Window2* class and make it call the second of the above superclass constructors. The code is shown in LISTING-13.3.

LISTING-13.3

Creating a Window Title

```
import java.awt.*;
public class Window2 extends Frame
{
   public Window2(String s)
   {
       super(s);
   }

   public static void main(String args[])
   {
       Window2 fm = new Window2("Starting GUI");
       fm.setSize(300,100);
       fm.show();
   }
}
```

Activity 13.3

Modify your previous program as shown above so that the text "Starting GUI" appears in the title bar.

The code necessary to achieve the same effect when using a *Frame* object is shown in LISTING-13.4.

LISTING-13.4

Titling a *Frame* Object

```
import java.awt.*;

public class Window
{
   public static void main(String args[])
   {
       Frame fm = new Frame("Starting GUI");
       fm.setSize(300,100);
       fm.show();
   }
}
```

Displaying the Window

The size, position and visibility of the application window can be set using the following methods:

void setSize(int w, int h) — Sets the application window to *w* pixels wide by *h* pixels high.

void setBounds(int x, int y, int w, int h) — Sets the application window to *w* pixels wide by *h* pixels high. The top left corner of the window is at screen coordinates (*x*,*y*).

void show() — Causes the window to be made visible.

void hide() — Causes the window to become invisible.

The window is initially hidden, so a call to *show()* is necessary to display it.

An alternative to *show()* and *hide()* is *setVisible()* which can perform both the same tasks.

void setVisible(boolean b) — If *b* is *true*, the window is shown. If *b* is *false*, the window is hidden.

boolean isVisible() — Returns *true* if the window is visible; otherwise *false* is returned.

> **Activity 13.4**
>
> Modify your *Window2* program to use the *setBounds()* and *setVisible()* operations. These should replace the calls to *setSize()* and *show()*.
>
> Position the application window so that it occupies the centre of the screen.

Accessing the Window Title

The window title can be retrieved or changed later.

String getTitle() — Returns the string displayed in the window's title.

void setTitle(String s) — Sets the title to *s*.

Window Resizing

We can enable or disable resizing of the window by the user and also determine which of these two states the window is currently in.

void setResizable(boolean b) — The window can be resized if *b* is *true*, otherwise the window cannot be resized by the user.

boolean isResizable() — Returns *true* if the window can be resized; otherwise *false* is returned.

Activity 13.5

Add the line

```
fm.setResizable(false);
```

to your program.

Execute the program and try to resize the window by dragging the edges of the window.

Try to maximise and minimise the window.

Changing the Background Colour

The background colour of your window can be changed using the *setBackground()* method:

void setBackground(Color c)	Changes the applications background colour to *c*.
Color getBackground()	Returns the current colour of the background.

Notice that the parameter to this method is an object from the *Color* class. This class is defined within Java

The Color Class

Constants

Color white
Color lightGray
Color gray
Color darkGray
Color black
Color red
Color pink
Color orange
Color yellow
Color green
Color magenta
Color cyan
Color blue

These named colours can be used when a method requires a *Color* object as an argument.

Constructors

Color(int red, int green, int blue)	Creates a *Color* object whose colour is constructed from the specified amount of red, green and blue. These values should lie in the range 0 to 255.

Other Methods

int getRed()	Returns the value of the colour's red component.
int getGreen()	Returns the value of the colour's green component.
int getBlue()	Returns the value of the colour's blue component.
Color brighter()	Returns a colour one shade lighter than the current colour.
Color darker()	Returns a colour one shade darker than the current colour.

In our previous example we could make the window's background colour red by adding the line

```
fm.setBackground(Color.red);
```

Alternatively, we could create our own colour using the *Color* class constructor to supply an argument to *setBackground()*:

```
fm.setBackground(new Color(214,20,76));
```

Adding GUI Components

Introduction

Any self-respecting GUI application is going to contain components such as labels, buttons, edit boxes, checkboxes, etc.

Each of these items is defined as a class within the AWT package. To have such items appear in our application we need to create objects of the appropriate class (*Label*, *Button*, etc.) and add them to the window.

Probably the simplest of these components is the *Label*. This offers various constructors as we will see in a moment. However, the most obvious takes as an argument the string which is to form the text of the label.

LISTING-13.5 shows a first attempt at displaying a label to our application by adding a *Label* object as an attribute of the class.

LISTING-13.5

Adding a Label

```
import java.awt.*;

public class Window2 extends Frame
{
   private Label labA = new Label("This is a label!!!");

   public Window2(String s)
   {
        super(s);
   }

   public static void main(String args[])
   {
        Window2 fm = new Window2("");
        fm.setSize(300,100);
        fm.show();
   }
}
```

Activity 13.6

Type in and test the program.

As you can see there is no sign of the label.

The problem is that, although we have created the label as part of our class, it still needs to be added to the window in much the same way as we need to add values to a list.

This is done using the *add()* method.

The *add()* method is inherited by the *Frame* from one of its many ancestral classes. We will look at those classes later, but for the moment it is sufficient to know that *add()* takes as an argument the component to be added to the frame. In this case we need the line

```
add(labA);
```

which should be placed in the constructor as shown below:

```
public Window2(String s)
{
    super(s);
    add(labA);
}
```

> **Activity 13.7**
>
> Modify your code as shown above and run your program.

Your program should produce the display shown in FIG-13.2.

FIG-13.2

Adding a *Label* Object

If our program had used a *Frame* object (rather than create a descendant class) we could have achieved the same results by adding the line

```
fm.add(labA);
```

to *main()*, having previously added *labA* as an attribute of our class.

The Label Class

As a general rule, labels are used to show fixed text such as headings, instructions or identification for edit boxes, etc. but as a class in its own right, it has many methods.

Constants

int LEFT *int CENTER* *int RIGHT*	These constants are used when defining the horizontal alignment of the label's text.

Constructors

Label()	Creates a blank label.
Label(String s)	Creates a label displaying string *s*.
Label(String s, int align)	Creates a label whose text is horizontally aligned as specified by *align*. *align* will be one of the first three class constants listed above.

Getting and Setting Alignment

void setAlignment(int align)	Sets the alignment of the labels text to *align*. A *Label* class constant should be used for this parameter.
int getAlignment()	Returns the alignment of the label's text.

Getting and Setting Text

void setText(String s)	Sets the label's text to *s*.
String getText()	Returns the label's text.

The Button Class

To place a button in our window we need to create a *Button* class object. This class has the following methods:

Constructors

Button()	Creates a button without a caption.
Button(String s)	Creates a button with caption *s*.

Getting and Setting the Button's Caption

setLabel(String s)	Sets the caption of button to *s*
String getLabel()	Returns the button's caption.

Activity 13.8

By inserting the lines

```
private Button butA = new Button("Press Me");
add(butA);
```

at the appropriate points in your code, add a button to your application.

The program produces a suprising result as shown in FIG-13.3.

FIG-13.3

Adding a *Button* Object

The button seems to have taken over the whole screen.

An Introduction to Layout Managers

This brings us to the topic of layout managers. If you've ever used development programs such as Microsoft's Visual Basic or Borland's Delphi you'll be used to specifying exactly the position and size of all the components that you place in your application window. However, in Java, as we've seen, we simply add components without stating their size or position.

The reason for this is that Java employs something called a **Layout Manager** to determine where components are to be placed. There are several varieties of layout manager; each employing a different strategy for placing and sizing components.

Frame-based applications default to a *BorderLayout* manager. This manager recognises only five possible positions in which a component can be placed:

NORTH
SOUTH
EAST
WEST
or CENTER

as shown in FIG-13.4.

FIG-13.4

BorderLayout Positions

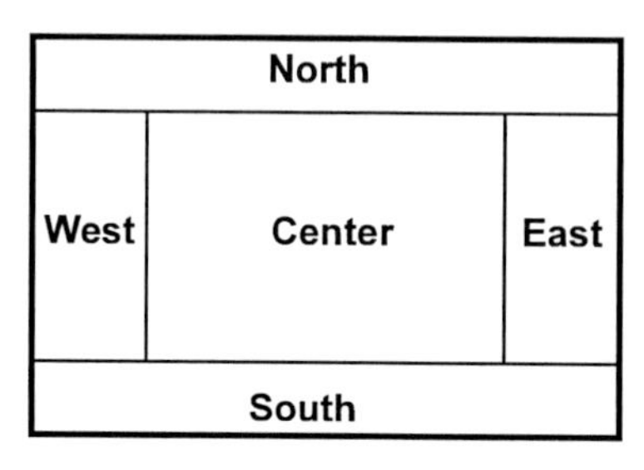

If no position is specified in the *add()* method, CENTER is assumed.

When we add a component, we should really state in which of these positions it is to be placed. This is done using a second variation of the *add()* method. As well as the parameter name, we need to add as a second argument one of the following:

```
BorderLayout.NORTH
BorderLayout.SOUTH
BorderLayout.EAST
BorderLayout.WEST
BorderLayout.CENTER
```

Activity 13.9

Change the *add()* statements of your program to read

```
add(labA, BorderLayout.NORTH);
add(butA, BorderLayout.SOUTH);
```

Run your program once more.

This time you should see the result shown in FIG-13.5.

FIG-13.5

Label and Button in a BorderLayout

An alternative version of *add()* allows the position to be given as a string containing one of the following values: *North,South,East,West,* or *Center*

This method has the format

```
add(String position, Component c)
```

but is overloaded so that we can reverse the order of the arguments:

```
add(Component c, String position)
```

Activity 13.10

Change your *add()* statements to

```
add("North",labA);
add("South",butA);
```

and re-run your program.

We'll look at the various layout managers in some detail later, but for the moment, we'll change to a different layout manager which allows many more components to be added.

The **FlowLayout Manager** places the component in rows. Much like words in a word processing document, components are placed starting at the top left. Subsequent components are placed on the same row until there is no more space and then the next row is used.

To change layout managers we use the method *setLayout()* in the *Frame* class and create a specific layout manager object as the argument.

```
setLayout(new FlowLayout());
```

With this layout we can revert to simple *add()* methods.

The new version of constructor is now coded as

```
public Window2(String s)
{
    super(s);
    setLayout(new FlowLayout());
    add(labA);
    add(butA);
}
```

which creates the window shown in FIG-13.6

FIG-13.6

Label and Button in a FlowLayout

Activity 13.11

Enter this new version of the constructor and check that your display is as shown.

What happens when you click on the "Press Me" button?

Listening

How are we going to get the button to react to being pressed?

Perhaps you have had some experience of other programming languages like Delphi or Visual Basic. In those languages every component has a list of events, such as clicking on a button, moving a mouse over an image or dragging an object across the screen, which it will recognise. The programmer can then write a piece of code and link it to a specific event. This piece of code is known as an **event handler**. When the event for which you have written the code occurs, the event handler is executed.

In Java, three steps are required to get a component to react to an event:

```
Tell the component to listen for a specific event
    or a set of events
Tell the component which object contains the event handler
Write the code of the event handler within the appropriate class
```

To demonstrate this we'll get the button, when pressed, to change the label's caption to "Button pressed". That is, we will get the button to listen for being pressed.

The button can be made to listen for various events. For example, we might get it to react to the mouse pointer moving over or moving off the button. We have to choose which event we want to listen for and then add the appropriate listener to the button.

The various events and the corresponding event handler names are defined in a set of *Event* interface classes.

One such interface is *ActionListener* which declares a method called *actionPerformed()*. It is this interface that we need to implement to get the button to react to being pressed.

Notice that we have no freedom of choice for the event handler name: it must be called *actionPerformed()*.

We also have to tell the button which object contains the event handler code to be executed when the button is clicked. We achieve all of this with a single statement of the form

```
component_name.addActionListener(obj_implementing_actionPerformed)
```

The most obvious approach for placing *actionPerformed()* is to include it in our own class. So we get *butA* to listen for being pressed with the statement

You will recall that *this* is a reference to the current object.

```
butA.addActionListener(this);
```

When the *addActionListener()* call is placed in a method of our *Frame* class descendant, then *this* refers to the window created in *main()*. That is, to the object *fm*.

and the *actionPerformed()* routine is coded as

```
public void actionPerformed(ActionEvent e)
{
    labA.setText("Button pressed");
}
```

As you can see, this routine takes a parameter of type *ActionEvent*. We'll look at this class later.

Only two more statements need to be added near the beginning of the program. First we need to import the appropriate classes from the package *java.awt.event* using the statement

```
import java.awt.event.*;
```

and lastly we need to state that our class implements the *ActionListener* interface:

```
public class Window2 extends Frame implements ActionListener
```

The complete program is shown in LISTING-13.6.

LISTING-13.6

Adding a Listener

```
import java.awt.*;
import java.awt.event.*;

public class Window2 extends Frame implements ActionListener
{
  private Label labA = new Label("This is a label!!!");
  private Button butA = new Button("Press Me");
  public Window2(String s)
  {
      super(s);
      setLayout(new FlowLayout());
      butA.addActionListener(this);  // Listen for butA
                                     // pressed
      add(labA);
      add(butA);
  }

  // *** Execute this if button pressed ***
  public void actionPerformed(ActionEvent e)
  {
      labA.setText("Button pressed");
  }

  public static void main(String args[])
  {
      Window2 fm = new Window2("Starting GUI");
      fm.setSize(300,100);
      fm.show();
  }
}
```

Activity 13.12

Type in and test the program above.

Activity 13.13

Add a second button (*butB*), showing the text "*Push Here*", to your program.

Add a listener to the button using the line

```
butB.addActionListener(this);
```

Run the program and check that both buttons will change the label's text.

The ActionEvent Class

The *ActionEvent* class is one of a family of class designed for use in event handling. For the moment we need only examine two of its methods:

Object getSource()	Returns a reference to the component that called the routine for which the *ActionEvent* object is the parameter (in this case, the routine is *actionPerformed()*).
String getActionCommand()	Returns a special string held in the component calling the event-handler.

The examples following demonstrate these two methods.

The *actionPerformed()* routine in LISTING-13.7 uses *getSource()* to check if *butA* has been pressed. The logic for the routine is

```
IF butA pressed THEN
    Set label's text to "butA pressed"
ELSE
    Set label's text to "butB pressed"
ENDIF
```

LISTING-13.7

Adding A Single Listener for Two Components

```
import java.awt.*;
import java.awt.event.*;

public class Window2 extends Frame implements ActionListener
{
  private Label labA = new Label("This is a label!!!");
  private Button butA = new Button("Press Me");
  private Button butB = new Button("Push Here");

  public Window2(String s)
  {
      super(s);
      setLayout(new FlowLayout());
      butA.addActionListener(this);
      butB.addActionListener(this);
      add(labA);
      add(butA);
      add(butB);
  }

  public void actionPerformed(ActionEvent e)
  {
      if(e.getSource() == butA)
          labA.setText("butA pressed");
      else
          labA.setText("butB pressed");
  }

  public static void main(String args[])
  {
      Window2 fm = new Window2("Starting GUI");
      fm.setSize(300,100);
      fm.show();
  }
}
```

The line

```
if(e.getSource() == butA)
```

checks to see if the reference address returned by *getSource()* is the same as that contained in *butA* (remember, *butA* is a reference to the *Button* object, not the *Button* object itself).

Activity 13.14

Type in and test your program.

In the next program we make use of the *getActionCommand()* method to return a string which has been previously assigned to the button.

Every component which implements the *addActionListener()* also contains a method called *setActionCommand()* which specifies the string to be returned when a *getActionCommand()* is executed for that component.

The program in LISTING-13.8 assigns the strings "butA pressed" and "butB pressed" to *butA* and *butB* respectively. That message is then retrieved in the *actionPerformed()* routine and assigned to the label's caption.

LISTING-13.8

Using ActionEvent's getActionCommand()

```
import java.awt.*;
import java.awt.event.*;

public class Window2 extends Frame implements ActionListener
{
  private Label labA = new Label("This is a label!!!");
  private Button butA = new Button("Press Me");
  private Button butB = new Button("Push Here");
  public Window2(String s)
  {
      super(s);
      setLayout(new FlowLayout());
      butA.setActionCommand("butA pressed");
      butB.setActionCommand("butB pressed");
      butA.addActionListener(this);
      butB.addActionListener(this);
      add(labA);
      add(butA);
      add(butB);
  }

  public void actionPerformed(ActionEvent e)
  {
      labA.setText(e.getActionCommand());
  }

  public static void main(String args[])
  {
      Window2 fm = new Window2("Starting GUI");
      fm.setSize(300,100);
      fm.show();
  }
}
```

Note the *setActionCommand()* calls in the constructor.

The line

```
labA.setText(e.getActionCommand());
```

gets the *ActionCommand* string associated with the object that caused *actionPerformed()* to be executed and assigns it to the label.

Since e, the parameter to *actionPerformed()* has a method *getSource()* which returns a reference to the object causing *actionPerformed()* to be executed, we should be able to use that reference to access the methods of that object.

For example, since *e.getSource()* will return a reference to a *Button* object in our examples, the expression

```
e.getSource().getLabel()
```

should return the caption of the button pressed.

Unfortunately, this won't work because *getSource()* assumes it is returning a reference to an instance of an *Object* and that class does not contain a method called *getLabel()*. To get this to work we need to cast the address returned to the actual class type involved. In this case, that means a *Button*. so the correct expression is

```
((Button)e.getSource()).getLabel();
```

Activity 13.15
Type in and test the program above.

Review

We've covered some complicated ideas in this section, so it worth having a look back at what we've done so far:

- **GUI applications** use classes held in the AWT package.
- **To create a GUI application** we define a class which is descended from the Frame class.
- **GUI components** such as buttons and labels are defined as attributes of the new class.
- **Each component has to be added** to the new class using the *add()* method.
- **The position of a component** is determined by the layout manager used.
- **Components that have to react** to user input need to be made to listen for the required event.
- **An event handler** has to be written for each event
- **The class containing the event handlers** must implement the appropriate interface
- **An object of the class in which the event handlers** are coded must be specified as a parameter when adding the listener.

FIG-13.7 illustrates where these various features appear in our previous program.

FIG-13.7

Steps for Creating a Basic GUI Application

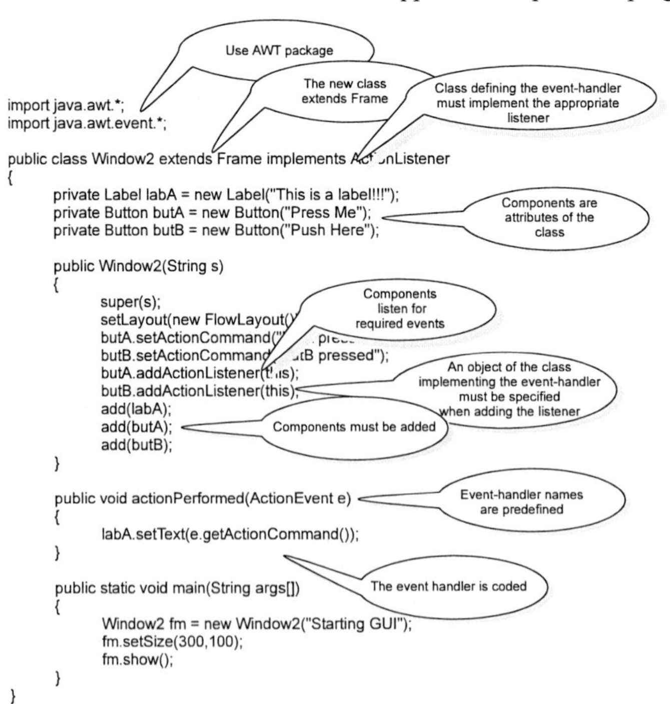

Activity 13.16

Write a program containing two buttons and two labels as shown below

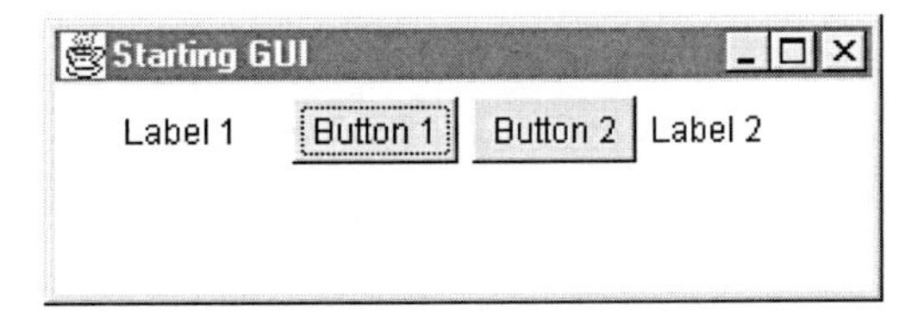

Write an event handler so that pressing the first button changes the first label to read *"Pressed"*, while pressing the second button changes the second label to read *"Pushed"*.

More About Event-Handlers

Implementing Event Handlers in Separate Classes

What happens if each button in our application requires an entirely separate handler? We would not be able to include both handlers within the existing *Window2* class since both routines need exactly the same heading:

```
public void actionPerformed(ActionEvent e)
```

Instead we need to create new classes in which we can place the required routines. For example:

```
class ActClass1 implements ActionListener
{
    public void actionPerformed(ActionEvent e)
    {
        Button temp = (Button)e.getSource();
        labA.setText(temp.getLabel());
    }
}

class ActClass2 implements ActionListener
{
    public void actionPerformed(ActionEvent e)
    {
        Button temp = (Button)e.getSource();
        labB.setText(temp.getLabel());
    }
}
```

If we use this approach, the *addActionListener()* calls used on the buttons must now reference objects from these classes:

```
butA.addActionListener(new ActClass1());
butB.addActionListener(new ActClass2());
```

The new classes can be defined as inner classes within the *Window2* giving them access to the attributes of the *Window2* class.

The complete code now becomes that shown in LISTING-13.9.

LISTING-13.9

Event Handlers Coded in a Separate Class

```
import java.awt.*;
import java.awt.event.*;

public class Window2 extends Frame
{
  Label labA = new Label("Label1");
  Label labB = new Label("Label2");
  Button butA = new Button("Press 1");
  Button butB = new Button("Press 2");

  public Window2(String s)
  {
      super(s);
      setLayout(new FlowLayout());
      butA.addActionListener(new ActClass1());
      butB.addActionListener(new ActClass2());
      add(labA);
      add(butA);
      add(butB);
      add(labB);
  }

  class ActClass1 implements ActionListener
  {
      public void actionPerformed(ActionEvent e)
      {
          Button temp = (Button)e.getSource();
          labA.setText(temp.getLabel());
      }
  }

  class ActClass2 implements ActionListener
  {
      public void actionPerformed(ActionEvent e)
      {
          Button temp = (Button)e.getSource();
          labB.setText(temp.getLabel());
      }
  }

  public static void main(String args[])
  {
      Window3 fm = new Window3("Starting GUI");
      fm.setSize(300,100);
      fm.show();
  }
}
```

Activity 13.17

Type in and test the program above.

Listening for the Mouse

A button can be made to listen for events other than being pressed. For example, it can listen and react to the mouse pointer moving over and away from its position on the screen.

As we've seen, we get a component to react to an event by listening for the event and writing an event handler. Event handlers are named in interface classes such as *ActionListener*.

Unlike *ActionListener*, which declares only one event handler name, the *MouseListener* interface contains several:

void mouseClicked(MouseEvent me)	Executed if a mouse button is pressed and released.
void mousePressed(MouseEvent me)	Executed if the mouse button is pressed.
void mouseReleased(MouseEvent me)	Executed if the mouse button is released.
void mouseEntered(MouseEvent me)	Executed if the mouse pointer moves over the component.
void mouseExited(MouseEvent me)	Executed if the mouse pointer moves away from the component.

To listen for these events we have to perform the same steps as before:

```
Add a listener to the component
Specify the object containing the event handlers
Write code for each event handler
```

The program in LISTING-13.10 demonstrates this by having a label listen for the various mouse events.

LISTING-13.10

The MouseListener Interface

```
import java.awt.*;
import java.awt.event.*;
public class ListenM extends Frame implements MouseListener
{
  private Label labA = new Label("Label-----------1");

  public ListenM(String s)
  {
      super(s);
      setLayout(new FlowLayout());
      labA.addMouseListener(this);
      add(labA);
  }
  public void mouseClicked(MouseEvent me)
  {
      labA.setText("Mouse Clicked");
  }
  public void mousePressed(MouseEvent me)
  {
      labA.setText("Mouse Pressed");
  }
  public void mouseReleased(MouseEvent me)
  {
      labA.setText("Mouse Released");
  }
  public void mouseEntered(MouseEvent me)
  {
      labA.setText("Mouse Entered");
  }
  public void mouseExited(MouseEvent me)
  {
      labA.setText("Mouse Exited");
  }

  public static void main(String args[])
  {
      ListenM fm = new ListenM("Starting GUI");
      fm.setSize(300,100);
      fm.show();
  }
}
```

NOTE: It is necessary to implement each of the operations defined in the *MouseListener* interface.

> **Activity 13.18**
>
> Type in the above program and test it.
>
> What messages appear when the mouse button is pressed and released over the label?
>
> Do all the buttons on the mouse activate the event handlers?

As you see, pressing a button while over the label causes several events

Button Pressed	This happens as the button is pushed down.
Button Released	This happens when the button is released.
Button Clicked	This happens after both press and release are processed.

Because release and pressed happen almost simultaneously, we are not aware of the label's caption changing to *Mouse released.*

> **Activity 13.19**
>
> Comment out the line of code with *mouseClicked()* and re-run the program.
>
> Check for the *Mouse released* message.

The MouseEvent Class

The *MouseEvent* object which is passed to each of the event handlers contains the same *getSource()* method we saw in the *ActionEvent* class earlier, but in addition, it contains several other methods specifically for retrieving mouse information:

int getX()	Returns the X ordinate of the mouse pointer.
int getY()	Returns the Y ordinate of the mouse pointer.

For example, the *mouseClicked()* event-handler could display the mouse position with the line

```
System.out.println("Mouse at("+me.getX()+","+me.getY()+")");
```

The *Point* class has two public attributes, *x* and *y*.

We could find the mouse coordinates with the line

```
Point mat =
me.getPoint();
```

and access the details using the expressions `mat.x` and `mat.y`

See page 446 for more details on the *Point* class.

Point getPoint()	Returns the co-ordinates of the mouse pointer as a *Point* object.
int getClickCount()	Returns the number of times the mouse button has been clicked.

> **Activity 13.20**
>
> Change the *mousePressed()* event handler to display the co-ordinates of the mouse position as the label's caption.

Notice that the co-ordinates given assume that (0,0) is the top left corner of the space allocated by the layout manager to the label - not the top-left of the screen or window.

Activity 13.21

Change the *mousePressed()* handler to display the number of times the mouse is clicked.Test your program. Try varying the delay between clicks and observe what effect this has on the count.

Listening for Key Presses

Pressing keys on the keyboard creates key events. When a key is pressed we naturally assume that the character represented by the key has its value transmitted to the program. However, things are a bit more complicated than that. It is often necessary to detect that some combination of keys is being pressed (e.g. Alt-Y). To do this Java can detect either the simple Unicode value of a key (as would be required when simple text is being entered) or the more complex codes required to detect key combinations. These second code types are known as **virtual key codes**.

The *KeyListener* interface declares operations for detecting both normal Unicode characters and virtual key codes. The operations defined are:

void keyTyped(KeyEvent ke)	Executed when a key has been pressed and released. Use this event if you need to get the Unicode value of the key pressed.
void keyPressed(KeyEvent ke)	Executes when a key is pressed down. Use this event if you want to get virtual key code of the key when it is pressed.
void keyReleased(KeyEvent ke)	Executes when a key is released.

The program in LISTING-13.11 highlights the differences between detecting a virtual key code and normal characters. The program sets up two labels, *labA* and *labB*. *labA* reacts to each *keyTyped* event by adding an asterisk to its caption; *labB* displays an extra asterisk on each *keyPressed* event.

LISTING-13.11

The KeyListener Interface

```
import java.awt.*;
import java.awt.event.*;

public class ListenK extends Frame implements KeyListener
{
  private Label labA = new Label("Label-----------1");
  private Label labB = new Label("Label-----------2");

  public ListenK(String s)
  {
       super(s);
       setLayout(new FlowLayout());
       labA.addKeyListener(this);
       add(labA);
       add(labB);
  }

  public void keyTyped(KeyEvent ke)
  {
       labA.setText(labA.getText()+"*");
  }

  public void keyPressed(KeyEvent ke)
  {
       labB.setText(labB.getText()+"*");
  }
```

continued on next page

LISTING-13.11
(continued)

The KeyListener Interface

```
    public void keyReleased(KeyEvent ke){}
    public static void main(String args[])
    {
        ListenK fm = new ListenK("Starting GUI");
        fm.setSize(300,100);
        fm.show();
        fm.labA.setText("");
        fm.labB.setText("");
    }
}
```

Activity 13.22

Type in and test the program above.

Press the *A* key.
Both labels should add an asterisk.

Press the *Shift* key.
Only labB *adds an asterisk.*

Experiment with other key presses.

What happens if you hold a key down for a few seconds?

The labels will stop displaying extra characters when they occupy all the space allocated by the layout manager. Re-run the program to continue your tests.

After you have entered several characters, additional key presses are not displayed on the screen. This is because the label's caption has grown to such an extent that it requires more space than was allocated by the layout manager for the label component. The layout manager allocates space for the label based on the number of characters in the label at start-up time: the longer the initial caption, the more horizontal space allocated.

It is because of this that the label's initial caption is a set of hyphens: this allocates enough space to allow several characters from the keyboard to be displayed before we run out of room.

Note also that the label is emptied in *main()*. By this point in the program the layout manager has already allocated space for the label, so removing its caption has no effect on the space allocated. It does, however, give us a blank label to which the characters typed can be added.

A second point to note from the program is that all the operations declared in the *MouseListener* interface must be defined - even if there is no code in the body of the method. If any operation is omitted, your class is treated as an abstract one.

The KeyEvent Class

The *KeyEvent* class, an object of which is a parameter to all *KeyListener* operations, offers several methods for manipulating and accessing the key pressed.

Methods of the class include

int getKeyCode() Returns the virtual key code of the key pressed as an integer. Use this routine with the *keyPressed* and *keyReleased* event handlers.

char getKeyChar() Returns the character associated with the key pressed. Use this method with the *keyTyped* event.

The program in LISTING-13.12 demonstrates the use of *getKeyChar()* to display the characters typed in one label and uses *getKeyCode()* to display the virtual key codes in a second label.

LISTING-13.12

Using getKeyChar() and getKeyCode()

```
import java.awt.*;
import java.awt.event.*;

public class ListenK extends Frame implements KeyListener
{
   private Label labA = new Label("Label-----------1");
   private Label labB = new Label("Label-----------2");

   public ListenK(String s)
   {
        super(s);
        setLayout(new FlowLayout());
        labA.addKeyListener(this);
        add(labA);
        add(labB);
   }

   public void keyTyped(KeyEvent ke)
   {
        labA.setText(labA.getText()+ke.getKeyChar());
   }

   public void keyPressed(KeyEvent ke)
   {
        labB.setText(labB.getText()+ke.getKeyCode());
   }

   public void keyReleased(KeyEvent ke){}

   public static void main(String args[])
   {
        ListenK fm = new ListenK("Starting GUI");
        fm.setSize(300,100);
        fm.show();
        fm.labA.setText("");
        fm.labB.setText("");
   }
}
```

Activity 13.23

Type in and test the program above.

Other Features of the KeyEvent Class

The *KeyEvent* class also defines a set of named constants for each possible virtual key code. The names of these constants begin with VK_ and end with the key name. Hence, the A key's virtual key code is named VK_A; the zero key is VK_0; the caps lock key is VK_CAPS_LOCK; the cursor up key is VK_UP; etc.

Since the key codes are only returned when a key is first pressed down (or eventually released) it might be difficult to detect when a key is continually held down. For example, a user might hold down the Shift key in order to enter several capital letters.

Activity 13.24

If the user pressed the following keys

```
Shift(held down)    A B C
```

and finally released the *Shift* key,

list the order of key events and the key values involved.

To make life a little easier at detecting the state of certain keys, the *KeyEvent* class includes the following methods:

boolean isShiftDown()	Returns *true* if the Shift key is currently held down; otherwise *false* is returned.
boolean isControlDown()	Returns *true* if the Control key is currently held down; otherwise *false* is returned.
boolean isAltDown()	Returns *true* if the Alt key is currently held down; otherwise *false* is returned.

A useful place to listen for key events is in an edit box where we can use it to control the keys accepted from the user. We'll look at this later.

The WindowListener Interface

Ever since we started producing GUI applications we've had a problem in terminating the application. In fact, we've had to resort to Ctrl-C. However, the *WindowListener*, designed as its name suggests, to handle window events, can be used to create a proper shut-down.

The *WindowListener* interface contains the following method declarations:

windowOpened(WindowEvent e)	Executed when the window is opened.
windowClosing(WindowEvent e)	Executes just before a window closes
windowClosed(WindowEvent e)	Executes just after a window has closed.
windowIconified(WindowEvent e)	Executes when a window is minimised to an icon.
windowDeiconified(WindowEvent e)	Executed when a window returns from an icon to its normal size.
windowActivated(WindowEvent e)	Executes when a window becomes the active window.
windowDeactivated(WindowEvent e)	Executes when a window stops being the active window.

To use these we must make our window listen for these events.

The program in LISTING-13.13 shows when each of these event are caught by displaying a message in the console window as each event occurs.

LISTING-13.13

The WindowListener

```
import java.awt.*;
import java.awt.event.*;

public class ListenW extends Frame implements WindowListener
{
  private Label labA = new Label("Controlling Windows");
  public ListenW(String s)
  {
      super(s);
      setLayout(new FlowLayout());
      addWindowListener(this);
      add(labA);
  }

  public void windowOpened(WindowEvent we)
  {
      System.out.println("Window opened");
  }

  public void windowClosing(WindowEvent we)
  {
      System.out.println("Window closing");
  }

  public void windowClosed(WindowEvent we)
  {
      System.out.println("Window closed");
  }

  public void windowIconified(WindowEvent we)
  {
      System.out.println("Window ToIcon");
  }

  public void windowDeiconified(WindowEvent we)
  {
      System.out.println("Window FromIcon");
  }

  public void windowActivated(WindowEvent we)
  {
      System.out.println("Window Activated");
  }

  public void windowDeactivated(WindowEvent we)
  {
      System.out.println("Window Deactivated");
  }

  public static void main(String args[])
  {
      ListenW fm = new ListenW("Starting GUI");
      fm.setSize(300,100);
      fm.show();
      fm.labA.setText("");
  }
}
```

Activity 13.25

Type in and test the program above.

Are there any events which never happen?

The *windowClosed()* event handler will only be executed when the window in question is not the main window of the application. We'll see an example of this later.

The WindowEvent Class

The *WindowListener* operations have a *WindowEvent* object as a parameter. This class contains the following operations:

Window getWindow()	Returns a reference to the window causing the event to happen.

As you can see, this is similar to the *getSource()* method available in other classes except that a *Window* object reference is returned.

Closing the Application Window

We've seen from earlier code that the application window is made visible using the *show()* method. It should therefore come as no surprise that there is a *hide()* method for making the window disappear. However, an invisible window is not the same as a terminated application. To achieve that we can use `System.exit(0).` as in previous, console based, applications.

Activity 13.26

Change the *windowClosing()* method so that it contains the following lines:

```
we.getWindow().setVisible(false);
System.exit(0);
```

Compile and run your program.

Does the program terminate when the Exit option is chosen from the menu and when using the Exit button at the top right of the window?

There are a few more listeners that we have yet to encounter. However, many of these are designed with specific GUI components in mind and we will come across them as we describe more of the components we can use within our GUI application.

Adapters

Introduction

If you've typed in the programs above, you'll appreciate that it's time-consuming not to say boring, having to create empty event handlers. And yet, if we implement an interface we have no choice in the matter.

To alleviate this problem, Java offers a set of classes which implement many of the *Listener* interfaces with empty routines. Collectively these are known as adapter classes or simply adapters.

WindowAdapter

For example, the class *WindowAdapter* contains coded, but empty, methods for all of the operations declared in the *WindowListener* interface.

By getting a class to extend the *WindowAdapter* class rather than implement the *WindowListener* interface, we need only override those event handlers that we need in our program instead of having to define every single method.

This alternative approach to handling window shutdown is shown in LISTING-13.14.

LISTING-13.14

Using an Adapter

```
import java.awt.*;
import java.awt.event.*;

public class ListenW2 extends Frame
{
  public ListenW2(String s)
  {
       super(s);
       addWindowListener(new WindowHandler());
  }

  class WindowHandler extends WindowAdapter
  {
       public void windowClosing(WindowEvent we)
       {
            we.getWindow().setVisible(false);
            System.exit(0);
       }
  }

  public static void main(String args[])
  {
       ListenW2 fm = new ListenW2("Starting GUI");
       fm.setSize(300,100);
       fm.show();
  }
}
```

> **Activity 13.27**
>
> Type in and test the program above.
>
> *Notice that the* addWindowListener() *creates an object of the inner class* WindowHandler.

Creating Anonymous Classes Using Adapters

Rather than create a named class that extends *WindowAdapter*, a very common approach to using any adapter is to create an anonymous descendant class. The code for the new class is placed in the parameter section of the *addWindowListener()* call and can be a bit confusing until you get used to this technique. LISTING-13.15 adapts the previous program to demonstrate this approach.

LISTING-13.15

Anonymous Adapter Classes

```
import java.awt.*;
import java.awt.event.*;

public class ListenW3 extends Frame
{
  public ListenW3(String s)
  {
       super(s);
       addWindowListener
```

continued on next page

LISTING-13.15
(continued)

Anonymous Adapter Classes

```
        (
            new WindowAdapter()
            {
                public void windowClosing(WindowEvent we)
                {
                    we.getWindow().setVisible(false);
                    System.exit(0);
                }
            }
        );
        add(labA);
    }


    public static void main(String args[])
    {
        ListenW3 fm = new ListenW3("Starting GUI");
        fm.setSize(300,100);
        fm.show();
        fm.labA.setText("");
    }
}
```

Other Adapters

Other adapters exist for every Listener that has more than one operation. So we have

MouseAdapter	which implements	*MouseListener*
KeyAdapter	which implements	*KeyListener*

Activity 13.28

Modify the program in LISTING-13.12 to use *KeyAdapter* instead of *KeyListener.*

Write two versions of the program: one using the inner class approach; the other an anonymous class.

Other GUI Components

The TextField Class

Any windows user will have come across edit boxes; in Java these are known as **text fields** and can be created within an application by creating a *TextField* object.

The class has the following methods:

Constructors

TextField()	Creates edit box of a minimum width.
TextField(int v)	Creates an edit box with space for *v* characters.
TextField(String s)	Creates an edit box containing *s* at start-up. Useful when a default entry is required.
TextField(String s int v)	Creates an edit box initially containing *s* with space for *v* characters.

Other Methods

void setEchoChar(char c)	Sets character placed in edit box on each key stroke to *c*.
char getEchoChar()	Returns the character used as echo.
boolean echoCharIsSet()	Returns *true* if an echo character has been set, otherwise *false* is returned.
void setColumns(int v)	Sets the width of the edit box for *v* characters.
int getColumns()	Returns the current column width of edit box.
String getText()	Returns the value displayed in the *TextField* object.

By adding an edit box attribute to our class with the lines such as

```
private TextField editA = new TextField();
add(editA);
```

we create a textfield component as shown in FIG-13.8.

FIG-13.8

Default TextField

As you can see the edit box is rather small. A second version of the constructor allows us to specify the number of columns in the edit box:

```
TextField t1 = new TextField(25);
```

which gives the result shown in FIG-13.9.

FIG-13.9

Specified Size TextField

> **Activity 13.29**
>
> Create an application containing a *TextField* and *Label.*
>
> Run your program and click in the edit box to give it focus. Enter the text "this is a test" in the box before pressing Enter.

Adding ActionListener to the TextField Component

It's also possible to get the edit box to react to an event in much the same way we did for the button component. For example, the *TextField* component can use the same *ActionListener* interface as a *Button* object. However, this time, the event is linked to pressing the Enter key rather than clicking on a button.

> **Activity 13.30**
>
> Modify the program you created in the last Activity so that the text placed in the edit box is copied to the label when the Enter key is pressed.

> **Activity 13.31**
>
> Modify your program so that when a numeric value is typed into the edit box, the label displays double that value (i.e. 12 in edit box shows 24 in label)
>
> Hint: You will need to convert the text in the edit box to a number; double it and then convert back to a string for storing in the label.
>
> What happens if you press a non-numeric key?

Using the KeyListener

Instead of waiting for the *Enter* key to be pressed we could update the label on each key press. To do this we'll need to attach the *KeyListener* to the *TextField* component:

We could, alternatively, use KeyAdapter.

We'll start the program with the statement

```
public class TestTextField extends Frame implements KeyListener
```

and then add the listener to the edit box:

```
txtA.addKeyListener(this);
```

Now we have to write the code for each of the three event handlers specified in the *KeyListener* interface. These are:

```
keyTyped(KeyEvent ke)
keyPressed(KeyEvent ke)
keyReleased(KeyEvent ke)
```

For this example, we'll only write meaningful code for the *keyReleased()* method. But we must code the others, even if, as is the case here, we create empty bodies for each method:

```
public void keyPressed(KeyEvent e)
{
}

public void keyReleased(KeyEvent e)
{
}

public void keyTyped(KeyEvent e)
{
    labA.setText(txtA.getText());
}
```

The complete program is shown in LISTING-13.16 below.

LISTING-13.16

Using the KeyListener with a TextField

```
import java.awt.*;
import java.awt.event.*;

public class UsingTextFields extends Frame implements
                                          ↳KeyListener
{
  private Label labA = new Label("Controlling Windows");
  private TextField txtA = new TextField(20);

  public UsingTextFields(String s)
  {
      super(s);
      setLayout(new FlowLayout());
      addWindowListener(new WindowHandler());
      txtA.addKeyListener(this);
      add(labA);
      add(txtA);
  }

  class WindowHandler extends WindowAdapter
  {
      public void windowClosing(WindowEvent we)
      {
          we.getWindow().setVisible(false);
          System.exit(0);
      }
  }

  public void keyPressed(KeyEvent e)
  {
  }

  public void keyReleased(KeyEvent e)
  {
  }

  public void keyTyped(KeyEvent e)
  {
      labA.setText(txtA.getText());
  }

  public static void main(String args[])
  {
      UsingTextFields fm = new UsingTextFields("Starting GUI");
      fm.setSize(300,100);
      fm.show();
      fm.labA.setText("");
  }
}
```

Activity 13.32

Modify the program you created in the last Activity so that the doubled value shown in the label updates on each key release.

Consuming Events

We still don't have any real control over which keys the user is going to press. Obviously in the program that doubles the value entered we don't want non-numeric characters to be placed in the edit box. We can achieve this by using **consuming the event**. Consuming an event prevents it from being passed on to a component. For example, we can detect and consume any non-numeric keys thereby preventing them from being placed within the edit box. This is done using the *MouseEvent* class's *consume()* method. LISTING-13.17 demonstrates this approach.

LISTING-13.17

Consuming Events

```
import java.awt.*;
import java.awt.event.*;

public class ConsumingEvents extends Frame implements
                                            ↳KeyListener
{
  private TextField txtA = new TextField(20);
  public ConsumingEvents(String s)
  {
      super(s);
      setLayout(new FlowLayout());
      addWindowListener(new WindowHandler());
      txtA.addKeyListener(this);
      add(txtA);
  }

  class WindowHandler extends WindowAdapter
  {
      public void windowClosing(WindowEvent we)
      {
          we.getWindow().setVisible(false);
          System.exit(0);
      }
  }

  public void keyPressed(KeyEvent e){}

  public void keyReleased(KeyEvent e){}

  public void keyTyped(KeyEvent ke)
  {
      char ch = ke.getKeyChar();
      //*** IF it's not a numeric key THEN consume it ***
      if(ch < '0' || ch > '9')
          ke.consume();
  }

  public static void main(String args[])
  {
      ConsumingEvents fm = new ConsumingEvents("Starting GUI");
      fm.setSize(300,100);
      fm.show();
  }
}
```

Activity 13.33

Type in and test the program above.

Linking More Than One Listener to a Component

We've made the *TextField* component react to the ENTER key being pressed by adding *KeyListener*, but we can add several listeners to the same component. So, for example, we can get that same edit box to listen for the mouse being moved over it. To do this we need to start by implementing the *MouseListener* to our application class:

```
public class UsingTextFields extends Frame implements
                                ↳KeyListener, MouseListener
```

Next the *TextField* component must be told to listen for these additional events:

```
txtA.addMouseListener(this);
```

Finally, we need to code the methods of the *MouseListener* interface.

The program in LISTING-13.18 displays the contents of the text field within the label as each key is pressed but also changes the label to read "over" when the mouse moves over the *TextField* component. This message is removed when the mouse moves off the *TextField* component.

LISTING-13.18

Multiple Listeners

```
import java.awt.*;
import java.awt.event.*;

public class UsingTextFields extends Frame implements
                        ↳KeyListener, MouseListener
{
  private Label labA = new Label("Controlling Windows");
  private TextField txtA = new TextField(20);

  public UsingTextFields(String s)
  {
      super(s);
      setLayout(new FlowLayout());
      addWindowListener(new WindowHandler());
      txtA.addKeyListener(this);
      txtA.addMouseListener(this);
      add(labA);
      add(txtA);
  }

  class WindowHandler extends WindowAdapter
  {
      public void windowClosing(WindowEvent we)
      {
          we.getWindow().setVisible(false);
          System.exit(0);
      }
  }

  public void keyReleased(KeyEvent e)
  {
      labA.setText(txtA.getText());
  }

  public void keyTyped(KeyEvent e){}
  public void mouseClicked(MouseEvent e){}
  public void mousePressed(MouseEvent e){}
  public void mouseReleased(MouseEvent e){}
```

Continued on next page

LISTING-13.18
(continued)

Multiple Listeners

```
    public void mouseEntered(MouseEvent e)
    {
        labA.setText("Over");
    }
    public void mouseExited(MouseEvent e)
    {
        labA.setText("");
    }

    public static void main(String args[])
    {
        UsingTextFields fm = new UsingTextFields("Starting GUI");
        fm.setSize(300,100);
        fm.show();
        fm.labA.setText("");
    }
}
```

> **Activity 13.34**
>
> Modify the program above replacing the Listener interfaces with the equivalent Adapters.
>
> (HINT: You'll need to use inner classes and assign the *TextField* component to new instances of these inner classes.)

The *TextField* class also inherits a set of methods from its parent class, *TextComponent*. That class is covered later in this chapter.

The Scrollbar Class

Scrollbars are implemented in Java AWT by the *Scrollbar* class. This class has the following features:

Constants

HORIZONTAL
VERTICAL

These are used within the constructor to determine the orientation of the scrollbar and are used in constructor calls.

Constructors

Scrollbar() Creates a default vertical scrollbar.

Scrollbar(int orientation) Creates a scroll bar with a given orientation Use Scrollbar.HORIZONTAL or Scrollbar.VERTICAL as the argument.

Scrollbar(int orientation, int initvalue, int thumbsize, int min, int max)
Creates a scrollbar that can be used to select a value from a sliding scale.
The arguments define the orientation; minimum and maximum values obtainable; the initial value of the scroll thumb position; and the stepsize when clicking in the arrows at either end of the scrollbar.

The program in LISTING-13.19 creates a default scrollbar as shown in FIG-13.19.

LISTING-13.19

Using Scrollbars

```
import java.awt.*;
import java.awt.event.*;

public class UsingScrollbars extends Frame
{
  private Scrollbar sb = new Scrollbar();

  public UsingScrollbars (String s)
  {
      super(s);
      setLayout(new FlowLayout());
      addWindowListener(new WindowHandler());
      add(sb);
  }

  class WindowHandler extends WindowAdapter
  {
      public void windowClosing(WindowEvent we)
      {
          we.getWindow().setVisible(false);
          System.exit(0);
      }
  }

  public static void main(String args[])
  {
      UsingScrollbars fm = new UsingScrollbars("Starting GUI");
      fm.setSize(300,100);
      fm.show();
  }
}
```

FIG-13.10

Default Vertical Scrollbar

We can get more control over the scrollbar by using a second version of the constructor:

```
Scrollbar(int orientation)
```

We use this version along with one of the constants, HORIZONTAL or VERTICAL, to determine the orientation of the scrollbar.

So, if we change the declaration of the scrollbar to

```
Scrollbar sb1 = new Scrollbar(Scrollbar.HORIZONTAL);
```

this creates the display shown in FIG-13.11.

FIG-13.11

A Horizontal Scrollbar

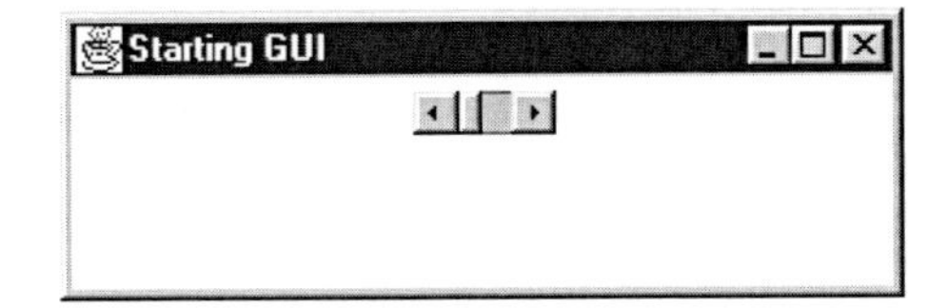

A final version of the constructor allows us to specify the range of values that the scrollbar represents, the initial value, the type of bar (vertical or horizontal) and the size of the scroll thumb. It has the format:

```
Scrollbar(int orientation, int initvalue, int thumbsize,
        ↳int min, int max)
```

> **Activity 13.35**
>
> Type in the application shown above, changing the scrollbar constructor line to
>
> ```
> Scrollbar sb = new Scrollbar(Scrollbar.HORIZONTAL,0,10,0,255);
> ```
>
> Run the application and try moving the scrollbar thumb.

The AdjustmentListener Interface

To get the scrollbar to do something useful we'll need to add a listener. For scrollbars we'd normally want to implement the *AdjustmentListener* interface which listens for adjustments to the position of the thumb in the scrollbar. This interface declares only one operation:

adjustmentValueChanged(AdjustmentEvent ae)	Executed when the scrollbar's thumb is moved.

The AdjustmentEvent Class

Constants

ADJUSTMENT_FIRST
ADJUSTMENT_LAST
ADJUSTMENT_VALUE_CHANGED
UNIT_INCREMENT
UNIT_DECREMENT
BLOCK_DECREMENT
BLOCK_INCREMENT
TRACK

These constants can be used when testing the type of adjustment made to the scrollbar. See LISTING-13.20..

Methods

int getValue()	Returns the value of the thumb.
int getAdjustmentType()	Returns the type of adjustment made.

The program in LISTING-13.20 updates a label's text according to the value of a scrollbar and the type of adjustment made.

LISTING-13.20

Using AdjustmentEvent

```
import java.awt.*;
import java.awt.event.*;

public class UsingScrollbars extends Frame
                    ↳implements AdjustmentListener
{
  private Scrollbar sb = new Scrollbar(Scrollbar.HORIZONTAL);
  private Label labA = new Label("Using Scrollbars");

  public UsingScrollbars (String s)
  {
      super(s);
      setLayout(new FlowLayout());
      addWindowListener(new WindowHandler());
      sb.addAdjustmentListener(this);
      add(sb);
      add(labA);
  }

  class WindowHandler extends WindowAdapter
  {
      public void windowClosing(WindowEvent we)
      {
          we.getWindow().setVisible(false);
          System.exit(0);
      }
  }

  public void adjustmentValueChanged(AdjustmentEvent ae)
  {
      int type = ae.getAdjustmentType();
      StringBuffer s = new StringBuffer();
      if (type == AdjustmentEvent.UNIT_INCREMENT)
          s.append("Unit Incr ");
      else if (type == AdjustmentEvent.BLOCK_INCREMENT)
          s.append("Block Incr ");
      else if (type == AdjustmentEvent.UNIT_DECREMENT)
          s.append("Unit Decr ");
      else if (type == AdjustmentEvent.BLOCK_DECREMENT)
          s.append("Block Decr ");
      else if (type == AdjustmentEvent.TRACK)
          s.append("Track ");

      labA.setText(ae.getValue()+" - "+s);
  }

  public static void main(String args[])
  {
      UsingScrollbars fm = new UsingScrollbars("Starting GUI");
      fm.setSize(300,100);
      fm.show();
  }
}
```

Activity 13.36

Type in the program above and attempt to get each adjustment type displayed in the label.

What is the maximum value possible?

You should have noticed that the possible range of values is zero to 90 - exactly 10 less than the range defined. This is because of the thumb's width (10). To overcome this we need to make the maximum value larger by the width of the thumb.

> **Activity 13.37**
>
> Modify the scrollbar so that a range of 0 - 100 is selectable.

The Checkbox Class

The *Checkbox* class is used to create checkboxes. However, it is also used to create radio buttons. We'll look at the two uses separately.

Constructors

Checkbox()	Creates a check box with no accompanying text.
Checkbox(String st)	Creates a check box with accompanying text. *st*
Checkbox(String st,boolean b)	Creates a check box with accompanying text. *st*. If *b* is *true*, the check box is ticked otherwise it is not.

The lines

```
private Checkbox cb1 = new Checkbox();
private Checkbox cb2 = new Checkbox("Check box 2");
private Checkbox cb3 = new Checkbox("Ticked", true);
private Checkbox cb4 = new Checkbox("Unticked",false);
```

result in the display shown in FIG-13.12.

FIG-13.12

Checkboxes

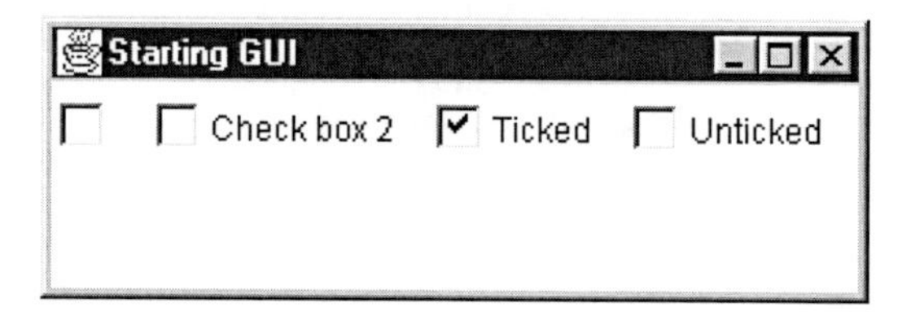

Methods

boolean getState()	Returns *true* if the current object is ticked; otherwise *false* is returned.
void setState(boolean b)	If *b* is *true* the current object is ticked; otherwise it is made blank.
String getLabel()	Returns the label associated with the checkbox.
void setLabel(String st)	Sets the checkbox label to *st*.

The ItemListener Interface

With checkboxes your program may not need to react to the checking of the box. Rather, it is more likely that the state of the boxes will be examined only when the user has completed his interactions. However, should you want to react to any change in a checkbox's status it should add an *ItemListener* and implement its single operation:

itemStateChanged(ItemEvent ie)	Executed when a checkbox's state changes.

The ItemEvent Class

Constants

ITEM_FIRST
ITEM_LAST
ITEM_STATE_CHANGED
SELECTED
DESELECTED

These are integer constants and can be used when checking the type of value returned by *getStateChanged()* below.

Methods

int getStateChanged()	Returns an integer representing the state of the checkbox.

The program in LISTING-13.21 demonstrates the use checkboxes and the *ItemListener* interface. The program represents a page from a multiple-choice test paper. The question appears with four possible answers, more than one of which may be correct. Each time the user clicks on an answer some random words of encouragement appear. When the "Stop" button is pressed, the score is displayed. One point is scored for a correct answer, 0.6 is deducted for a wrong one.

LISTING-13.21

Using ItemEvent

```
import java.awt.*;
import java.awt.event.*;

public class Quiz extends Frame implements
              ↳ItemListener, ActionListener
{
  private Checkbox choices[] = {new Checkbox("Edinburgh"),
      ↳new Checkbox("Glasgow"),new Checkbox("London"),
      ↳new Checkbox("Manchester")};
  private Label question = new Label("Which of the following
      ↳have populations of over 1 million?");
  private Label result = new Label("all correct");
  private Label comment = new Label("wwwwwwwwwwwwwwwwwww");
  private Button fin = new Button("Stop");

  public Quiz (String s)
  {
      super(s);
      setLayout(new FlowLayout());
      addWindowListener(new WindowHandler());
      add(question);
      for(int c = 0; c < choices.length; c++)
      {
          add(choices[c]);
          choices[c].addItemListener(this);
      }
      add(comment);
      add(result);
      add(fin);
      fin.addActionListener(this);
  }
```

continued on next page

LISTING-13.21
(continued)

Using ItemEvent

```
class WindowHandler extends WindowAdapter
{
    public void windowClosing(WindowEvent we)
    {
        we.getWindow().setVisible(false);
        System.exit(0);
    }
}

public void itemStateChanged(ItemEvent ie)
{
    String list[] = {"Are you sure?", "Is that a good choice?"
                ↳, "Any more?","Are you finished?"};
    int pick = (int)(Math.random()*4);
    comment.setText(list[pick]);
}

public void actionPerformed(ActionEvent ae)
{
    boolean correct[] = {false,false,true,true};
    double score = 0;
    for (int c = 0; c < choices.length; c++)
        if (choices[c].getState() == correct[c])
        {
            if (correct[c])
                score+=1;
        }
        else
            if(!correct[c])
                score -=0.6;
    result.setText("Score:"+score);
}


public static void main(String args[])
{
    Quiz fm = new Quiz("Starting GUI");
    fm.setSize(400,200);
    fm.show();
    fm.result.setText("");
    fm.comment.setText("");
}
}
```

Activity 13.38

Type in and test the program above.

Modify the program so that a "Next Question" button is added and when pressed results in a second question being posed.

The question should be

Which of the following planets have no moons?
Mars, Mercury, Saturn, Venus (correct answer: Mercury and Venus)

The *"Stop"* button should give the score gained over both questions.

Creating Radio Buttons

Whereas several checkboxes may be selected at the same time, radiobuttons are grouped together and only one can be selected at any time. When a new radiobutton is selected, the previously selected button is unselected.

We can create radiobuttons by grouping a set of *Checkbox* objects. To do this we need to call a new version of the *Checkbox* constructor:

Checkbox(String st,boolean b, CheckboxGroup cg)
Checkbox(String st,CheckboxGroup cg,boolean b)
Both of these constructors create a checkbox with text *st* belonging to group *cg*. If *b* is *true* the box is ticked. Only one box in a group can be ticked.

The CheckboxGroup Class

This class is designed for the sole purpose of grouping one or more *Checkbox* objects.

Constructor

CheckboxGroup() — Creates a *CheckboxGroup* object.

Methods

Checkbox getSelectedCheckbox() — Returns a reference to the currently selected radiobutton in the group.

Checkbox getCurrent() — Returns a reference to the radiobutton that has focus.

void setSelectedCheckbox(Checkbox rb) — Sets radiobutton *rb* to selected.

void setCurrent(Checkbox rb) — Sets radiobutton *rb* as the current button.

Example

The program in LISTING-13.22 allows the user to select between red, green and blue backgrounds for the application window. The program needs to set up a *CheckboxGroup* object

```
private CheckboxGroup options = new CheckboxGroup();
```

and then add the required radiobuttons to this group

```
private Checkbox ans1 = new Checkbox("Red",options,false);
private Checkbox ans2 = new Checkbox("Green",options,false);
private Checkbox ans3 = new Checkbox("Blue",options,false);
```

The first parameter gives the text of the radiobutton; the second specifies the *CheckboxGroup* the item is added to; and the third parameter indicates if the radiobutton is initially selected. The *Checkbox* components are then added to the application in the usual way:

```
add(ans1);
add(ans2);
add(ans3);
```

Each has to add an *ItemListener:*

```
ans1.addItemListener(this);
ans2.addItemListener(this);
ans3.addItemListener(this);
```

and finally the event handler needs code to check which radiobutton has been pressed and change the colour accordingly.

LISTING-13.22

Radiobuttons

```
import java.awt.*;
import java.awt.event.*;
public class Radio extends Frame implements ItemListener
{
  private  CheckboxGroup options = new CheckboxGroup();
  private  Checkbox ans1 = new Checkbox("Red",options,false);
  private  Checkbox ans2 = new Checkbox("Green",options,false);
  private  Checkbox ans3 = new Checkbox("Blue",options, false);

  public Radio (String s)
  {
      super(s);
      setLayout(new FlowLayout());
      addWindowListener(new WindowHandler());
      add(ans1);
      add(ans2);
      add(ans3);
      ans1.addItemListener(this);
      ans2.addItemListener(this);
      ans3.addItemListener(this);
  }

  class WindowHandler extends WindowAdapter
  {
      public void windowClosing(WindowEvent we)
      {
          we.getWindow().setVisible(false);
          System.exit(0);
      }
  }

  public void itemStateChanged(ItemEvent ie)
  {
      Checkbox temp;
      temp = (Checkbox)ie.getSource();
      if(temp==ans1)
          setBackground(Color.red);
      if(temp==ans2)
          setBackground(Color.green);
      if(temp==ans3)
          setBackground(Color.blue);
  }

  public static void main(String args[])
  {
      Radio fm = new Radio("Radio Buttons");
      fm.setSize(400,200);
      fm.show();
  }
}
```

Activity 13.39

Add two more radiobuttons to the above program which allow a darker or lighter shade to be picked.
HINTS: You'll need to add the new buttons to a different *CheckboxGroup*.
The current background colour can be obtained using *getBackground()*.
The colour shade can be changed using the *Color* class's *brighter()* and *darker()* methods.

The Choice Class

The *Choice* class implements a combobox-like component where the user can select from a list. Initially, the first item is selected by default.

Constructor

Choice()	Creates a combo box with no choices.

Methods

void add(String s)	Adds string *s* to the end of the list of options.
void insert(String s, int post)	Inserts *s* at position *post* in the list.
void remove(int post)	Removes the item at position *post.*
void remove(String s)	Remove the choice whose string is equal to *s*.
void removeAll()	Removes all entries from the choice.
void select(int post)	Selects the item at position *post.*
void select(String s)	Selects the item whose string is equal to *s*.
String getSelectedItem()	Returns a reference to the selected item.
int getSelectedIndex()	Returns the index of the selected item.
String getItem(int post)	Returns a reference to the choice at position *post.*
int getItemCount()	Returns the number of items in the list.

Example

A typical choice box is shown in FIG-13.13.

FIG-13.13

Choice

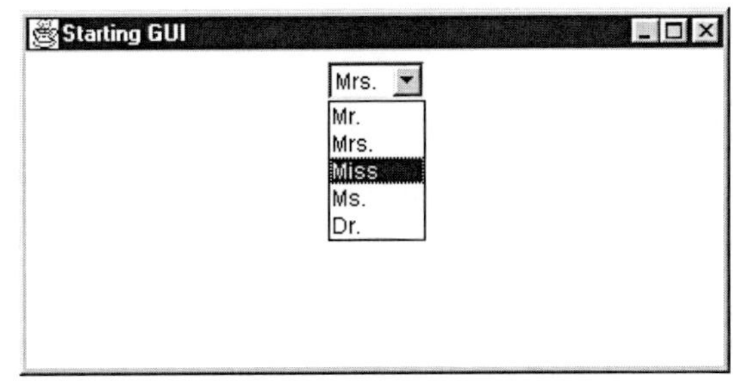

To set up a *Choice* object our class would contain the attribute

```
private Choice ch1 = new Choice();
```

To this the various options we wish to include should be added in the class constructor:

```
ch1.add("Mr.");
ch1.add("Mrs.");
ch1.add("Miss");
ch1.add("Ms.");
ch1.add("Dr.");
```

If your program needs to react to the user making a selection then, like the *Checkbox* component, a *Choice* component can be linked to the *ItemListener*.

The following program (LISTING-13.23) contains an edit box, choice box and a label. The edit box is to hold a surname while the choice box contains a title (Mr. Mrs., etc.) When both data-entry components contain information the label displays a greeting using the title and surname.

LISTING-13.23

Using Choice

```
import java.awt.*;
import java.awt.event.*;

public class UsingChoice extends Frame implements
      ⇳ItemListener, ActionListener
{
   private Choice ch1 = new Choice();
   private TextField txt = new TextField(25);
   private Label greeting = new Label("WWWWWWWWWWWWWWWWWWWWW");

   public UsingChoice(String s)
   {
      super(s);
      setLayout(new FlowLayout());
      addWindowListener(new WindowHandler());
      ch1.add("Mr.");
      ch1.add("Mrs.");
      ch1.add("Miss");
      ch1.add("Ms.");
      ch1.add("Dr.");
      ch1.addItemListener(this);
      txt.addActionListener(this);
      add(ch1);
      add(txt);
      add(greeting);
   }

   class WindowHandler extends WindowAdapter
   {
      public void windowClosing(WindowEvent we)
      {
         we.getWindow().hide();
         System.exit(0);
      }
   }

   public void itemStateChanged(ItemEvent ie)
   {
      if (!txt.getText().equals(""))
         greeting.setText("Good evening "+ch1.getSelectedItem()
            ⇳+" "+txt.getText());
   }

   public void actionPerformed(ActionEvent ae)
   {
      greeting.setText("Good evening "+ch1.getSelectedItem()
         ⇳+" "+txt.getText());
   }
```

continued on next page

LISTING-13.23
(continued)

Using Choice

```
    public static void main(String args[])
    {
        UsingChoice fm = new UsingChoice("Starting GUI");
        fm.setSize(400,200);
        fm.show();
        fm.greeting.setText("");
    }
}
```

Activity 13.40

Modify the program above by adding three checkboxes labelled "Rev", "Cpt." and "Hon." These options should be added or removed from the *Choice* component's list depending on the state of the checkboxes (checked = add to choice).

The List Class

The *List* class is similar in purpose to the *Choice* class, but it does not contain an area in which the selected item is placed. Instead, the selected item simply remains visible and highlighted with the list of options.

Constructors

List()	Creates a *List* object with default height. That is, there is space for four options. Where there's more a scrollbar is visible.
List(int h)	Creates a *List* with height *h*. That is, *h* options are visible.
List(int h, boolean b)	Creates a *List* object of height *h*, in which more than one item can be selected at any time if *b* is *true*.

Methods

void add(String s)	Adds *s* to the end of the options list.
void add(String s int post)	Adds *s* at position *post* in the options list.
void replaceItem(String s, int post)	Replace the option at position *post* with *s*.
void remove(int post)	Removes the item at position *post.*
void remove(String s)	Removes the option whose string matches *s*.
void removeAll()	Removes all options from the list.
int getItemCount()	Returns the number of options in the list.

String getItem(int post)	Returns the option at position *post.*
String[] getItems()	Returns an array of all items in the list.
int getSelectedIndex()	Returns the position of the selected item.
int[] getSelectedIndexes()	Returns an array of the positions of the selected items
String getSelectedItem()	Returns the text of the selected item
String[] getSelectedItems()	Returns an array of the text of the selected items
void select(int post)	Causes the option at position *post* to be selected.
void deselect(int post)	Deselects the option at position *post.*
boolean isIndexSelected(int post)	Returns *true* if the option at position *post* is currently selected.
boolean isMultipleMode()	Returns *true* if multiple selection is allowed.
void setMultipleMode(boolean b)	If *b* is *true*, multiple selection is allowed; otherwise multiple selection is disallowed.

Example

The program in LISTING-13.24 allows values from a left-hand list to be transferred to a right-hand list by selecting the required items and and clicking on the transfer button. A typical screen shot is shown in FIG-13.14.

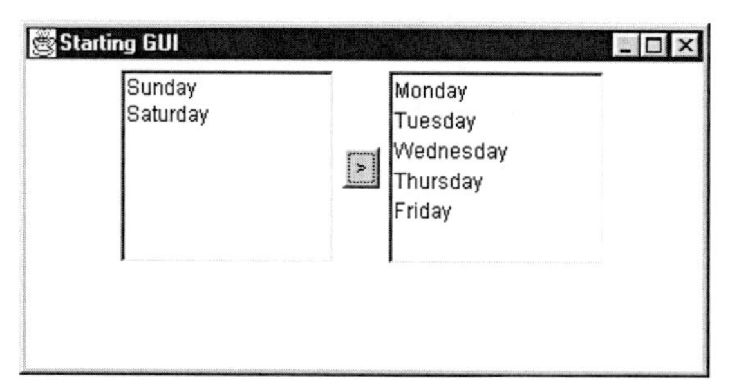

LISTING-13.24

Using the List Class

```
import java.awt.*;
import java.awt.event.*;

public class UsingList extends Frame implements ActionListener
{
   private List ch1 = new List(7, true);
   private List ch2 = new List(7,true);
   private Button selectedtoworking = new Button(">");
```

continued on next page

LISTING-13.24
(continued)

Using the List Class

```
    public UsingList(String s)
    {
        super(s);
        setLayout(new FlowLayout());
        addWindowListener(new WindowHandler());
        String days[] = {"Sunday","Monday","Tuesday","Wednesday",
            ↳"Thursday","Friday","Saturday"};
        for(int c = 0; c < days.length; c++)
            ch1.add(days[c]);
        add(ch1);
        selectedtoworking.addActionListener(this);
        add(selectedtoworking);
        add(ch2);
    }

    class WindowHandler extends WindowAdapter
    {
        public void windowClosing(WindowEvent we)
        {
            we.getWindow().setVisible(false);
            System.exit(0);
        }
    }

    public void actionPerformed(ActionEvent ae)
    {
        String selected[] = ch1.getSelectedItems();
        for(int c = 0; c< selected.length; c++)
        {
            ch2.add(selected[c]);
            ch1.remove(selected[c]);
        }
    }

    public static void main(String args[])
    {
        UsingList fm = new UsingList("Starting GUI");
        fm.setSize(400,200);
        fm.show();
    }
}
```

Activity 13.41

Type in and test the program above.

The TextArea Class

Whereas the *TextField* component allows only a single line of text, a *TextArea* object creates a user defined numbers of rows. This type of component might be useful for such things as an address or notes field in a form.

Constants

SCROLLBARS_BOTH
SCROLLBARS_VERTICAL_ONLY
SCROLLBARS_HORIZONTAL_ONLY
SCROLLBARS_NONE

These integer constants are used when specifying the scrollbar requirements of the *TextArea* object to be created.

Constructors

TextArea()	Creates an empty text area.
TextArea(String s)	Creates a text area initially containing *s*.
TextArea(int r, int c)	Creates a text area with *c* columns and *r* rows.
TextArea(String s, int r, int c)	Creates a text area with *c* columns and *r* rows containing *s*.
TextArea(String s, int r, int c, int scbr)	Creates a text area with *c* columns and *r* rows containing *s*. Visible scrollbars are determined by the value of *scbr*. Its value should be a named constant.

The lines

```
private TextArea ta1 = new TextArea();
private TextArea ta2 = new TextArea("String only");
private TextArea ta3 = new TextArea(5,30);
private TextArea ta4 = new TextArea("String,rows and cols",7,20);
private TextArea ta5 = new TextArea("String, cols, rows and
↳vertical scrollbars ",7,20,TextArea.SCROLLBARS_VERTICAL_ONLY);
```

give the display shown in FIG-13.15.

FIG-13.15

TextArea Objects

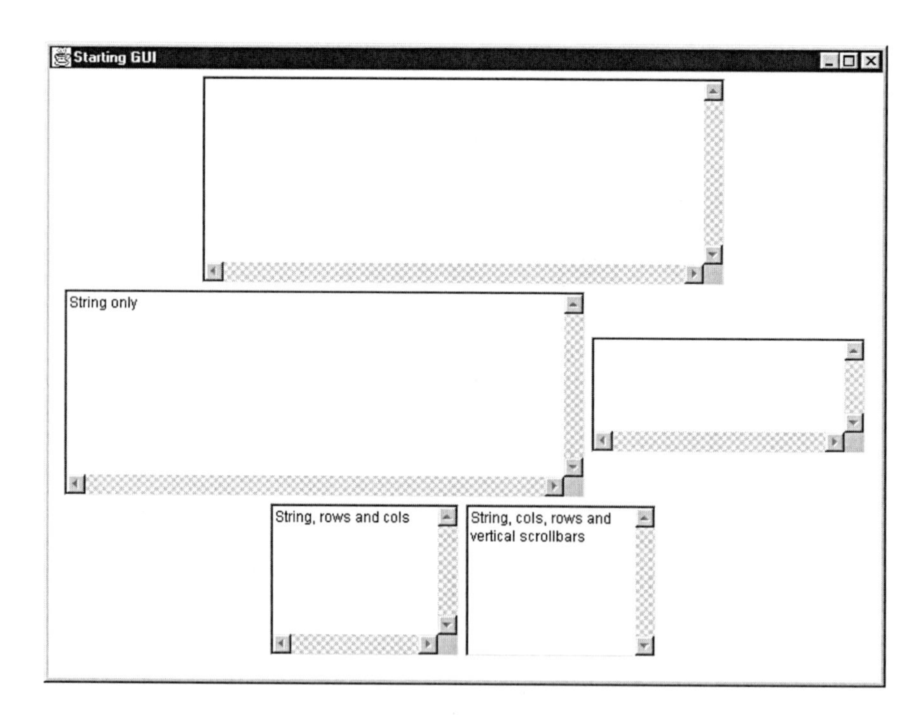

Notice that using only a vertical scrollbar restricts the width of the textarea and any text entered is automatically wrapped.

Methods

void append(String s)	Adds *s* to the end of the text.

void insert(String s, int post)	Adds *s* after the character at position *post*.
void replaceRange(String s, int st, int fin)	Replaces the text between positions *st* and *fin-1* with *s*.
int getRows()	Returns the number of rows.
void setRows(int r)	Sets the number of rows to *r*.
int getColumns()	Returns the number of columns.
void setColumns(int c)	Sets the number of columns to *c*.

Example

The program in LISTING-13.25 sets up a text area and 5 buttons each of which demonstrate different methods of the *TextArea* class.

LISTING-13.25

Using the TextArea Class

```
import java.awt.*;
import java.awt.event.*;

public class UsingTextArea extends Frame implements
ActionListener
{
  private TextArea tal = new TextArea("0123456789",5,30);
  private Button ops[] = {new Button("This at end"),new
Button("At post 5"), new Button("Replaced 2,3"),new Button(" 3
Extra rows"),new Button("10 extra columns")};

  public UsingTextArea(String s)
  {
      super(s);
      setLayout(new FlowLayout());
      addWindowListener(new WindowHandler());
      add(tal);
      for(int c = 0; c < ops.length; c++)
      {
          ops[c].addActionListener(this);
          add(ops[c]);
      }

  }

  class WindowHandler extends WindowAdapter
  {
      public void windowClosing(WindowEvent we)
      {
          we.getWindow().setVisible(false);
          System.exit(0);
      }
  }

  public void actionPerformed(ActionEvent ae)
  {
      Button temp = (Button)ae.getSource();
      int c = 0;
      while(ops[c] != temp)
          c++;
      switch(c)
      {
          case 0:
              tal.append("This at end");
              break;
```

continued on next page

LISTING-13.25
(continued)

Using the TextArea

```
            case 1:
                ta1.insert("XXXXX",5);
                break;
            case 2:
                ta1.replaceRange("AAAAAAAAA",2,3);
                break;
            case 3:
                ta1.setRows(ta1.getRows()+3);
                break;
            case 4:
                ta1.setColumns(ta1.getColumns()+10);
                break;
        }
    }

    public static void main(String args[])
    {
        UsingTextArea fm = new UsingTextArea("Starting GUI");
        fm.setSize(800,600);
        fm.show();
    }
}
```

Activity 13.42

Type in and test the program above.

Notice that you have to resize the application window before the change in size becomes apparent.

The TextComponent Class

There are two components we can use to allow user text input. These are the *TextField* component and the *TextArea* component. Both of these are derived from the *TextComponent* class. Although objects of this class cannot be created by the programmer, it contains several methods which are inherited by the *TextField* and *TextArea* classes. These operations fall into three main areas: get and setting the text held; getting and setting the selected area of the text; determining if the user may modify the text. These methods are:

String getText()	Returns the text held.
void setText(String s)	Sets the text held to *s*.
String getSelectedText()	Returns the selected area of text.
void select(int st, int fin)	Sets the selected area from character *st* to character *fin*-1.
int getSelectionStart()	Returns the position of the first selected character.
void setSelectionStart(int st)	Sets the start of the selected area to *st*.
int getSelectionEnd()	Returns the position of the last character in the selected area.

void setSelectionEnd(int fin)	Sets the end of the selected area to *fin*-1.
void selectAll()	Selects the complete text.
int getCaretPosition()	Returns the position of the text cursor.
void setCaretPosition(int post)	Moves the text cursor to position *post.*
boolean isEditable()	Returns *true* if the user can enter text.
void setEditable(boolean b)	If *b* is *true*, then the text component will accept data from the user; if *b* is *false*, no text will be accepted.

The TextListener Interface

A Listener interface available to subclasses of *TextComponent* is *TextListener*. This contains a single method:

void textChangedValue(TextEvent te)	This is executed when the contents of the text component are changed.

The TextEvent Class

This class contains no useful methods but, as with other Event classes it does contain the *getSource()* method.

Summary

This chapter has covered many aspects of GUI programming. These include the concepts of events, event-handlers, layout managers and the visual components. The next three chapter revisit these areas giving both an overview of the various options and more detail on particular aspects.

Solutions

Activity 13.1

No solution required.

Activity 13.2

No solution required.

Activity 13.3

No solution required.

Activity 13.4

```
import java.awt.*;

public class Window2 extends Frame
{
    public Window2(String s)
    {
        super(s);
    }

    public static void main(String args[])
    {
        Window2 fm = new Window2("Starting GUI");
        fm.setBounds(650,500,300,100);
        fm.setVisible(true);
    }
}
```

Activity 13.5

No solution required.

Activity 13.6

No solution required.

Activity 13.7

No solution required.

Activity 13.8

```
import java.awt.*;

public class Window2 extends Frame
{
    private Label labA = new Label("This is a
label!!!");
    Button butA = new Button("Press Me");

    public Window2(String s)
    {
        super(s);
        add(labA);
        add(butA);
    }

    public static void main(String args[])
    {
        Window2 fm = new Window2("Starting GUI");
        fm.setSize(300,100);
        fm.setBackground(Color.red);
        fm.show();
    }
}
```

Activity 13.9

No solution required.

Activity 13.10

No solution required.

Activity 13.11

Although the button gives the appears of being pressed, no other action results from clicking on the button.

Activity 13.12

No solution required.

Activity 13.13

```
import java.awt.*;
import java.awt.event.*;

public class Window2 extends Frame implements
ActionListener
{
    private Label labA = new Label("This is a
label!!!");
    private Button butA = new Button("Press Me");
    private Button butB = new Button("Push Here");

    public Window2(String s)
    {
        super(s);
        setLayout(new FlowLayout());
        // Listen for butA and butB
        butA.addActionListener(this);
        butB.addActionListener(this);
        add(labA);
        add(butA);
        add(butB);
    }

    // *** Execute this if button pressed ***
    public void actionPerformed(ActionEvent e)
    {
        labA.setText("Button pressed");
    }

    public static void main(String args[])
    {
        Window2 fm = new Window2("Starting GUI");
        fm.setSize(300,100);
        fm.show();
    }
}
```

Activity 13.14

No solution required.

Activity 13.15

No solution required.

Activity 13.16

```
import java.awt.*;
import java.awt.event.*;

public class Window2 extends Frame implements
ActionListener
```

```
{
    private Label labA = new Label("Label1");
    private Label labB = new Label("Label2");
    private Button butA = new Button("Press Me");
    private Button butB = new Button("Push Here");

    public Window2(String s)
    {
        super(s);
        setLayout(new FlowLayout());
        butA.addActionListener(this);
        butB.addActionListener(this);
        add(labA);
        add(butA);

        add(butB);
        add(labB);
    }

    // *** Execute this if button pressed ***
    public void actionPerformed(ActionEvent e)
    {
        if(e.getSource() == butA)
            labA.setText("Pressed");
        else
            labB.setText("Pushed");
    }

    public static void main(String args[])
    {
        Window2 fm = new Window2("Starting GUI");
        fm.setSize(300,100);
        fm.show();
    }
}
```

Activity 13.17

No solution required.

Activity 13.18

As the mouse pointer passes over the label, its text changes to *Mouse Entered*; when the pointer moves away, the label changes to *Mouse Exited.*

If the mouse button is pressed when over the label, its text changes to *Mouse Pressed.* If the mouse button is released while still over the label, it changes to *Mouse Clicked.*

This works for both left and right buttons.

Activity 13.19

The *Mouse Released* message no w appears when the mouse button is released.

Even without removing the *Mouse Clicked* message, it is possible to display the *Mouse Released* message by employing the following steps|:

move over the label
push down the mouse button
move away from the label
move back over the label
release the mouse button

Activity 13.20

```
import java.awt.*;
import java.awt.event.*;

public class ListenM extends Frame implements
MouseListener
{
    private Label labA = new
Label("Label-----------1");

    public ListenM(String s)
    {
        super(s);
        setLayout(new FlowLayout());
        labA.addMouseListener(this);
        add(labA);
    }

    public void mouseClicked(MouseEvent me)
    {
        labA.setText("Mouse Clicked");
    }

    public void mousePressed(MouseEvent me)
    {
        labA.setText("X:"+me.getX()+" Y:"+
        ↳me.getY());
    }

    public void mouseReleased(MouseEvent me)
    {
        labA.setText("Mouse Released");
    }

    public void mouseEntered(MouseEvent me)
    {
        labA.setText("Mouse Entered");
    }

    public void mouseExited(MouseEvent me)
    {
        labA.setText("Mouse Exited");
    }

    public static void main(String args[])
    {
        ListenM fm = new ListenM("Starting GUI");
        fm.setSize(300,100);
        fm.show();
    }
}
```

Activity 13.21

The *mousePressed()* routine should be changed to

```
public void mousePressed(MouseEvent me)
{
    labA.setText("Click count:"+
    ↳me.getClickCount());
}
```

It will be easier to see the results if you comment out the code in the other mouse event handlers.

Activity 13.22

Holding a key down causes the character to be entered repeatedly.

Activity 13.23

No solution required.

Activity 13.24

By adding a System.out.println() instruction to each handler we see that the event happen in the following sequence:

```
Key pressed ?
Key pressed A
Key typed A
Key released A
Key pressed B
Key typed B
Key released B
Key pressed C
Key typed C
Key released C
Key released ?
```

where ? marks the *Shift* key.

If any key is held for some time the KeyPressed event will repeat.

Activity 13.25

No solution required.

Activity 13.26

Both options cause the window to close.

Activity 13.27

No solution required.

Activity 13.28

Version 1 (Inner class)

```
import java.awt.*;
import java.awt.event.*;

public class Act13_28 extends Frame
{
    private Label labA = new
    ↳Label("Label-----------1");
    private Label labB = new
    ↳Label("Label-----------2");

    public Act13_28(String s)
    {
        super(s);
        setLayout(new FlowLayout());
        labA.addKeyListener(new KeyHandler());
        add(labA);
        add(labB);
    }

    class KeyHandler extends KeyAdapter
    {
        public void keyTyped(KeyEvent ke)
        {
            labA.setText(labA.getText()+"*");
        }

        public void keyPressed(KeyEvent ke)
        {
            labB.setText(labB.getText()+"*");
        }
    }

    public static void main(String args[])
    {
        Act13_28 fm = new Act13_28("Starting GUI");
        fm.setSize(300,100);
        fm.show();
        fm.labA.setText("");
        fm.labB.setText("");
    }
}
```

Version 2 (Anonymous class)

```
import java.awt.*;
import java.awt.event.*;
public class Act13_28 extends Frame
{
    private Label labA = new
    ↳Label("Label-----------1");
    private Label labB = new
    ↳Label("Label-----------2");

    public Act13_28(String s)
    {
        super(s);
        setLayout(new FlowLayout());
        labA.addKeyListener
        (
            new KeyHandler()
            {
                public void keyTyped(KeyEvent ke)
                {
                    labA.setText(labA.getText()+"*");
                }

                public void keyPressed(KeyEvent ke)
                {
                    labB.setText(labB.getText()+"*");
                }
            }
        );
        add(labA);
        add(labB);
    }

    public static void main(String args[])
    {
        Act13_28 fm = new Act13_28("Starting GUI");
        fm.setSize(300,100);
        fm.show();
        fm.labA.setText("");
        fm.labB.setText("");
    }
}
```

Activity 13.29

```
import java.awt.*;
import java.awt.event.*;

public class Act13_29 extends Frame
{
    private TextField txtA = new TextField(30);
    private Label labA =
    ↳new Label("xxxxxxxxxxxxxxxxxxxx");

    public Act13_29(String s)
    {
        super(s);
        setLayout(new FlowLayout());
        add(labA);
        add(txtA);
    }

    public static void main(String args[])
    {
        Act13_29 fm = new Act13_29("Starting GUI");
        fm.setSize(300,100);
        fm.show();
    }
}
```

Activity 13.30

```
import java.awt.*;
import java.awt.event.*;

public class Act13_30 extends Frame implements
ActionListener
{
    private TextField txtA = new TextField(30);
    private Label labA =
    ↳new Label("xxxxxxxxxxxxxxxxxxxx");

    public Act13_30(String s)
    {
        super(s);
        setLayout(new FlowLayout());
        txtA.addActionListener(this);
        add(labA);
        add(txtA);
    }

    public void actionPerformed(ActionEvent ae)
    {
        labA.setText(txtA.getText());
    }

    public static void main(String args[])
    {
        Act13_30 fm = new Act13_30("Starting GUI");
        fm.setSize(300,100);
        fm.show();
    }
}
```

Activity 13.31

```
import java.awt.*;
import java.awt.event.*;

public class Act13_31 extends Frame implements
ActionListener
{
    private TextField txtA = new TextField(30);
    private Label labA =
    ↳new Label("xxxxxxxxxxxxxxxxxxxx");

    public Act13_31(String s)
    {
```

```
        super(s);
        setLayout(new FlowLayout());
        txtA.addActionListener(this);
        add(labA);
        add(txtA);
    }

    public void actionPerformed(ActionEvent ae)
    {
        double value =
        ↳Double.parseDouble(txtA.getText())*2;
        labA.setText(""+value);
    }

    public static void main(String args[])
    {
        Act13_31 fm = new Act13_31("Starting GUI");
        fm.setSize(300,100);
        fm.show();
    }
}
```

An exception is thrown if a non-numeric value is entered.

Activity 13.32

```
import java.awt.*;
import java.awt.event.*;

public class Act13_32 extends Frame
{
    private TextField txtA = new TextField(30);
    private Label labA =
    ↳new Label("xxxxxxxxxxxxxxxxxxxx");

    public Act13_32(String s)
    {
        super(s);
        setLayout(new FlowLayout());
        txtA.addKeyListener
        (
            new KeyAdapter()
            {
                public void keyReleased
                ↳(KeyEvent ke)
                {
                    double value =
                    ↳Double.parseDouble(txtA.
                    ↳getText())*2;
                    labA.setText(""+value);
                }
            }
        );
        add(labA);
        add(txtA);
    }

    public static void main(String args[])
    {
        Act13_32 fm = new Act13_32("Starting GUI");
        fm.setSize(300,100);
        fm.show();
    }
}
```

Activity 13.33

No solution required.

Activity 13.34

```
import java.awt.*;
import java.awt.event.*;

public class Act13_34 extends Frame
{
    private Label labA = new Label("Controlling
    ↳Windows");
    private TextField txtA = new TextField(20);

    public Act13_34(String s)
    {
        super(s);
        setLayout(new FlowLayout());
        addWindowListener(new WindowHandler());
        txtA.addKeyListener(new KeyHandler());
        txtA.addMouseListener(new MouseHandler());
        add(labA);
        add(txtA);
    }

    class WindowHandler extends WindowAdapter
    {
        public void windowClosing(WindowEvent we)
        {
            we.getWindow().hide();
            System.exit(0);
        }
    }

    class KeyHandler extends KeyAdapter
    {
        public void keyReleased(KeyEvent e)
        {
            labA.setText(txtA.getText());
        }
    }
    class MouseHandler extends MouseAdapter
    {
        public void mouseEntered(MouseEvent e)
        {
            labA.setText("Over");
        }
        public void mouseExited(MouseEvent e)
        {
            labA.setText("");
        }
    }
    public static void main(String args[])
    {
        Act13_34 fm = new Act13_34("Starting GUI");
        fm.setSize(300,100);
        fm.show();
        fm.labA.setText("");
    }
}
```

Activity 13.35

```
No solution required.
```

Activity 13.36

The maximum value possible is 90.

Activity 13.37

To allow the full range of zero to 100 we need to set 110 as the upper limit. With a thumb 10 pixels wide, this gives the full 0 - 100 range.

```
Scrollbar sb =
new Scrollbar(Scrollbar.HORIZONTAL,0,10,0,110)
```

Activity 13.38

This is a more complex question than it first appears. Some of the local variables in the *actionPerformed()* method of the original need to become class attributes so they can be accessed by other operations.

Also the *Next Question* button needs to calculate the score for the current question before updating the label and checkboxes.

To achieve this the Next Question button is linked to two different handlers; one calculates the result of the current question and the other changes the text on the screen to show the next question.

```
import java.awt.*;
import java.awt.event.*;

public class Act13_38 extends Frame implements
ItemListener, ActionListener
{
    private Checkbox choices[] =
    ↳{new Checkbox("Edinburgh"),
```

```
↳new Checkbox("Glasgow"),
↳new Checkbox("London"),
↳new Checkbox("Manchester")};
private Label question =
↳new Label("Which of the following have
↳populations of over 1 million?");
private Label result = new Label
↳("all correct");
private Label comment =
↳new Label("wwwwwwwwwwwwwwwwww");
private Button fin = new Button("Stop");
private Button next = new Button
↳("Next Question");
private boolean correct[] =
↳{false,false,true,true};
private int score = 0;

public Act13_38 (String s)
{
    super(s);
    setLayout(new FlowLayout());
    addWindowListener(new WindowHandler());

    add(question);
    for(int c = 0; c < choices.length; c++)
    {
        add(choices[c]);
        choices[c].addItemListener(this);
    }
    add(comment);
    add(result);
    add(fin);
    add(next);
    fin.addActionListener(this);
    next.addActionListener(this);
    next.addActionListener
    ↳(new NextQuestionHandler());
}

class NextQuestionHandler
↳implements ActionListener
{
    public void actionPerformed(ActionEvent ae)
    {
        String options[]=
        ↳{"Mars","Mercury","Saturn","Venus"};
        boolean answers[] =
        ↳{false,true,false,true};
        for(int c = 0; c < choices.length; c++)
        {
            choices[c].setLabel(options[c]);
            choices[c].setState(false);
        }
        question.setText("Which of the
        ↳following planets have no moons?");
        for(int c = 0; c < answers.length; c++)
            correct[c] = answers[c];
    }
}

class WindowHandler extends WindowAdapter
{
    public void windowClosing(WindowEvent we)
    {
        we.getWindow().setVisible(false);
        System.exit(0);
    }
}

public void itemStateChanged(ItemEvent ie)
{
    String list[] = {"Are you sure?",
    ↳"Is that a good choice?", "Any more?",
    ↳"Are you finished?"};
    int pick = (int)(Math.random()*4);
    comment.setText(list[pick]);
}

public void actionPerformed(ActionEvent ae)
{
    for (int c = 0; c < choices.length; c++)
        if (choices[c].getState() == correct[c])
        {
            if (correct[c])
                score++;
        }
        else
            if(!correct[c])
                score -=0.6;
    result.setText("Score:"+score);
}

public static void main(String args[])
{
    Act13_38 fm = new Act13_38("Starting GUI");
    fm.setSize(400,200);
    fm.show();
    fm.result.setText("");
        fm.comment.setText("");
    }
}
```

Activity 13.39

```
import java.awt.*;
import java.awt.event.*;

public class Act13_39 extends Frame implements
↳ItemListener
{
    private CheckboxGroup options =
    ↳new CheckboxGroup();
    private Checkbox ans1 = new
Checkbox("Red",options,false);
    private Checkbox ans2 =
    ↳new Checkbox("Green",options,false);
    private Checkbox ans3 =
    ↳new Checkbox("Blue",options, false);
    private CheckboxGroup shades =
    ↳new CheckboxGroup();
    private Checkbox shade1 =
    ↳new Checkbox("Lighter",shades,false);
    private Checkbox shade2 =
    ↳new Checkbox("Darkerer",shades,false);

    public Act13_39 (String s)
    {
        super(s);
        setLayout(new FlowLayout());
        addWindowListener(new WindowHandler());
        add(ans1);
        add(ans2);
        add(ans3);
        add(shade1);
        add(shade2);
        ans1.addItemListener(this);
        ans2.addItemListener(this);
        ans3.addItemListener(this);
        shade1.addItemListener(this);
        shade2.addItemListener(this);
    }

    class WindowHandler extends WindowAdapter
    {
        public void windowClosing(WindowEvent we)
        {
            we.getWindow().setVisible(false);
            System.exit(0);
        }
    }

    public void itemStateChanged(ItemEvent ie)
    {
        Checkbox temp;
        temp = (Checkbox)ie.getSource();
        if(temp==ans1)
            setBackground(Color.red);
        if(temp==ans2)
            setBackground(Color.green);
        if(temp==ans3)
            setBackground(Color.blue);
        if(temp == shade1)
            setBackground
            ↳(getBackground().brighter());
        if(temp == shade2)
            setBackground
            ↳(getBackground().darker());
    }

    public static void main(String args[])
    {
        Act13_39 fm = new Act13_39
        ↳("Radio Buttons");
        fm.setSize(400,200);
        fm.show();
    }
}
```

Activity 13.40

```
import java.awt.*;
import java.awt.event.*;

public class Act13_40 extends Frame
↳implements ItemListener, ActionListener
{
    private Choice ch1 = new Choice();
    private TextField txt = new TextField(25);
    private Label greeting =
    ↳new Label("WWWWWWWWWWWWWWWWWWWW");
```

```
        private Checkbox extras[] =
        ➥{new Checkbox("Rev"),new Checkbox("Cpt"),
        ➥new Checkbox("Hon")};

        public Act13_40(String s)
        {
            super(s);
            setLayout(new FlowLayout());
            addWindowListener(new WindowHandler());
            ch1.add("Mr.");
            ch1.add("Mrs.");
            ch1.add("Miss");
            ch1.add("Ms.");
            ch1.add("Dr.");
            ch1.addItemListener(this);
            txt.addActionListener(this);

            add(ch1);
            add(txt);
            add(greeting);
            for(int c = 0; c < extras.length; c++)
            {
                extras[c].addItemListener
                ➥(new CheckboxHandler());
                add(extras[c]);
            }
        }

        class WindowHandler extends WindowAdapter
        {
            public void windowClosing(WindowEvent we)
            {
                we.getWindow().setVisible(false);
                System.exit(0);
            }
        }

        class CheckboxHandler implements ItemListener
        {
            public void itemStateChanged(ItemEvent ie)
            {
                Checkbox temp =
                ➥(Checkbox)ie.getSource();
                if (temp.getState())
                    ch1.add(temp.getLabel());
                else
                    ch1.remove(temp.getLabel());
            }
        }

        public void itemStateChanged(ItemEvent ie)
        {
            if (!txt.getText().equals(""))
                greeting.setText("Good evening "
                ➥+ch1.getSelectedItem()+" "
                ➥+txt.getText());
        }

        public void actionPerformed(ActionEvent ae)
        {
            greeting.setText("Good evening "
            ➥+ch1.getSelectedItem()+" "+
            ➥txt.getText());
        }

        public static void main(String args[])
        {
            Act13_40 fm = new Act13_40("Starting GUI");
            fm.setSize(450,200);
            fm.show();
            fm.greeting.setText("");
        }
    }
```

Activity 13.41

No solution required.

Activity 13.42

No solution required.

CHAPTER 14

The AWT Family Tree

This chapter covers the following topics:

Canvas Class

Component Class

Container Class

Dialog Class

Dimension Class

FileDialog Class

Font Class

FontMetrics Class

Graphics Class

Image Class

MediaTracker Class

Panel Class

Point Class

Rectangle Class

ScrollPane Class

Toolkit Class

Window Class

The AWT Family Tree

Introduction

The visual component classes that we examined in the last chapter are descended from the *Component* class while the *Frame* class is a descendant of the *Container* and *Window* classes. Since a class inherits its ancestor's features it is important to examine these other classes in order to realise the full potential of the classes we have already used.

The diagram in FIG-14.1 shows the main classes in the AWT family tree.

FIG-14.1

The AWT Family Tree

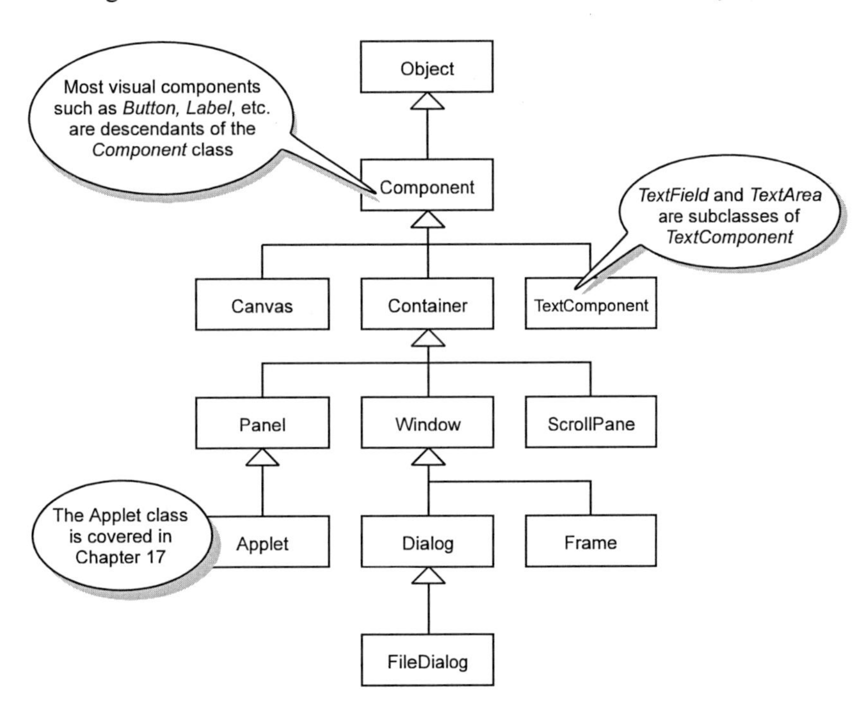

Before we look at the *Component* class in detail, there are several other minor classes whose objects are used by operations within the *Component* class that should be explained.

The Dimension Class

Objects of the *Dimension* class are used to define the width and height of components. The class has the following public attributes:

int width	Width of item.
int height	Height of item

Constructors

Dimension()	Creates a *Dimension* object with *width* and *height* set to zero.
Dimension(int w, int h)	Creates a *Dimension* object with *width* and *height* to *w* and *h* respectively.

Dimension(Dimension d)	Creates a *Dimension* object with identical values to *d*.

Other Methods

double getWidth()	Returns the value of *width* in `double` format.
double getHeight()	Returns the value of *height* in `double` format.
void setSize(double w, double h)	Sets the value of *width* and *height* to *w* and *h* respectively. Truncation will occur if *w* and *v* have a fractional part to their values.
void setSize(int w, int h)	Sets the value of *width* and *height* to *w* and *h* respectively.
void setSize(Dimension d)	Sets the value of *width* and *height* to *d.width* and *d.height* respectively.

The Point Class

This class gives the coordinates of a position in two-dimensional space. *Point* objects are often used to specify the position of the top left corner of a component.

Public Attributes

int x *int y*	These give the coordinates of a point.

Constructors

Point()	Creates a *Point* object with *x* and *y* set to zero.
Point(int xp, int yp)	Creates a *Point* object with *x* and *y* to *xp* and *yp* respectively.
Point(Point p)	Creates a *Point* object with identical values to *p*.

Other Methods

double getX()	Returns the value of *x* in `double` format.
double getY()	Returns the value of *y* in `double` format.
void setLocation(double xp, double yp)	Sets the value of *x* and *y* to *xp* and *yp* respectively. Truncation will occur if *xp* and *yp* have a fractional part to their values.

void setLocation(int xp, int yp)	Sets the value of *x* and *y* to *xp* and *yp* respectively.
void setLocation(Point d)	Sets the value of *x* and *y* to *d.x* and *d.y* respectively.
void move(int newx, int newy)	Sets the value of *x* and *y* to *newx* and *newy* respectively.
void translate(int addx, int addy)	Adds *addx* and *addy* to *x* and *y* respectively.

The Rectangle Class

This class is used to specify the position and size of a rectangular area.

Public Attributes

int x *int y*	These attributes are used to specify the coordinates of the top-left corner of the rectangle.
int width *int height*	The width and height of the rectangle.

Constructors

Rectangle()	Creates a *Rectangle* object with all attributes set to zero.
Rectangle(Rectangle r)	Creates a *Rectangle* object with all attributes set to the corresponding attributes of *r*.
Rectangle(int xp,int yp,int w,int h)	Creates a *Rectangle* object with *x = xp, y = yp, width = w* and *height = h.*
Rectangle(Point p, Dimension d)	Creates a *Rectangle* object with the top-left coordinates (*x* and *y*) set to *p.x* and *p.y*. The rectangle has the dimensions *d.width* and *d.height*.

Other Methods

double getX()	Returns the value of *x* as a `double`.
double getY()	Returns the value of *y* as a `double`.
double getWidth()	Returns the value of *width* as a `double`.
double getHeight()	Returns the value of *height* as a `double`.

Rectangle getBounds()	Returns the top-left coordinates and size of the current rectangle.
void setBounds(Rectangle r)	Sets all attributes of the current object to the corresponding attributes of *r*.
void setBounds(int xp, int xp, int w, int h)	Sets the current object attributes as follows: *x = xp, y = yp, width = w* and *height = h.*
Point getLocation()	Returns the values of *x* and *y* in a *Point* object.
void setLocation(int xp, int yp)	Sets the value of *x* and *y* to *xp* and *yp* respectively.
void setLocation(Point d)	Sets the value of *x* and *y* to *d.x* and *d.y* respectively.
void move(int newx, int newy)	Sets the value of *x* and *y* to *newx* and *newy* respectively.
void translate(int addx, int addy)	Adds *addx* and *addy* to *x* and *y* respectively.
boolean contains(Point p)	Returns *true* if the point *p* is inside the current rectangle, otherwise *false* is returned.
boolean contains(int x, int y)	Returns *true* if the position (x,y) is inside the current rectangle, otherwise *false* is returned.
boolean contains(Rectangle r)	Returns *true* if the rectangle *r* is entirely within the current rectangle, otherwise *false* is returned.
boolean contains(int xp, int yp, int h, int w)	Returns *true* if the rectangle whose top-left corner is at position (*xp,yp*) with width *w* and height *h* is entirely within the current rectangle, otherwise *false* is returned.

The Cursor Class

An object of this class is used to set the cursor shape displayed when the mouse pointer moves over a visual component such as a button.

Named Constants

int DEFAULT_CURSOR
int CROSSHAIR_CURSOR
int TEXT_CURSOR
int WAIT_CURSOR
int SW_RESIZE_CURSOR
int SE_RESIZE_CURSOR

int NW_RESIZE_CURSOR
int NE_RESIZE_CURSOR
int N_RESIZE_CURSOR
int S_RESIZE_CURSOR
int W_RESIZE_CURSOR
int E_RESIZE_CURSOR
int HAND_CURSOR
int MOVE_CURSOR

One of these values should be used as an argument to the class constructor. This determines the shape of the cursor on the screen.

Constructor

Cursor(int shape)

Creates a *Cursor* object. The shape of the cursor is determined by shape which should be one of the named constants given above.

Class Methods

Cursor getDefaultCursor()

Returns the default cursor used by the current operating system.

Other Methods

int getType()

Returns the *Cursor* object's cursor shape. The value returned should be tested against the named constants given above.

The Font Class

Objects of this class are used when the font of a text item, such as that which appears on a label or button, is to be specified.

Named Constants

int PLAIN
int BOLD
int ITALIC

These represent font styles. They can be used as arguments for operations of the class.

Although the *Font* class contains many operations, typically we will simply use the constructor to create the required font for the component.

Font(String name, int style, int size)

Creates a *Font* object using the font style specified by *name*. The named constants given above are possible values for *style* and determine the look of the text. *style* can be a combination of the named constants. For example, use the expression `Font.BOLD+Font.ITALIC` to create a bold italic style.

The characters will be *size* points high.A point is 1/72 of an inch.

You can use a named font such as Arial for the font style, but there is no guarantee that that specific font will be available on the machine running your program. Instead, one of the following generic terms will always work:

Serif
SansSerif
Monospaced
Dialog
DialogInput

The current settings for a component's font can be determined by the following operations:

int getStyle()	Returns the style used by the font. The integer returned will be equivalent to *Font.BOLD, Font.ITALIC, Font.PLAIN* or a combination of those.
int getSize()	Returns the font size in points.
String getName()	Returns the font name.
boolean isPlain()	Returns *true* if the font style is plain.
boolean isBold()	Returns *true* if the font style is bold.
boolean isItalic()	Returns *true* if the font style is italic.

The FontMetrics Class

Precise details of a font such as the height, ascent and descent values are known as **font metrics**. An explanation of these terms is shown in FIG-14.2.

FIG-14.2

Font Terms

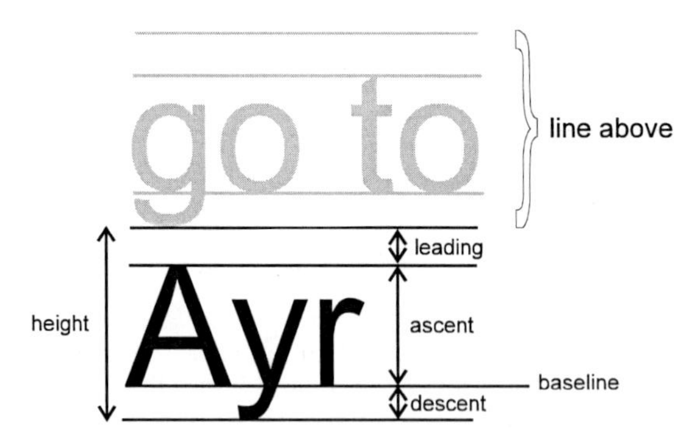

These details can also be retrieved using the following operation:

int getLeading()	Returns the leading value.
int getAscent()	Returns the ascent value.
int getDescent()	Returns the descent value.
int getHeight()	Returns the height value.

int charWidth(char ch) — Returns the width of *ch* if displayed on the screen using the current font settings.

int stringWidth(String s) — Returns the width of *s* if displayed on the screen using the current font settings.

The Component Class

The *Component* class is an abstract class which declares and defines various operations inherited by the visual components.

Some of the more important operations of the *Component* class are given below.

String getName() — Returns the name of a component. Each component is allocated a name by the Java environment. This is not its variable name as defined within the program.

void setName(String s) — Sets the name of a component.to *s*.

The program in LISTING-14.1 places a button on a GUI application and displays its name in the console window.

LISTING-14.1

Getting a Component's Name

```
import java.awt.*;

public class TestComp extends Frame
{
  private Button but1 = new Button("Press here");

  public TestComp(String s)
  {
      super(s);
      add(but1);
  }

  public static void main(String args[])
  {
      TestComp fm = new TestComp("Testing");
      fm.setLayout(new FlowLayout());
      fm.setSize(100,200);
      fm.show();
      System.out.println(fm.but1.getName());
  }
}
```

Activity 14.1

Enter the program above and execute it.

What name is given to the button?

We can create our own name for the component using *setName()*. For example, if we rewrite the constructor of the above program to read

```
public TestComp(String s)
{
```

```
        super(s);
        add(but1);
        but1.setName("new name");
    }
```

the program would then give the button name as *new name*.

Activity 14.2

Since the *Frame* class is also a descendant of *Component*, it has inherited the methods given here.

Set the name of the *TestComp* component created in your previous program to *my window* and display its name using *getName()*.

Component getParent() — Returns a reference to the parent of the current component. The parent of a component is the container to which it has been added.

Activity 14.3

If you added the line

```
System.out.println(fm.but1.getParent().getName());
```

to *main()* in your previous program, what name would be displayed on the screen?

setEnabled(boolean b) — Disables a component if *b* is set to *false*; enables a component if *b* is *true*.
By default, all components added to your program are enabled; their text is visible and they responded to events. A disabled component is normally greyed-out and will not respond to events.

Where button or menu options are not appropriate, they are often greyed-out. For example, the *Cut* and *Copy* options in a word processor's *Edit* menu will be greyed-out until some text or image has been selected. An example of a greyed-out button is shown in FIG-14.3.

FIG-14.3

A Disabled Component

boolean isEnabled() — Returns *true* if a component is enabled, otherwise *false* is returned.

The following lines in *main()* disable the *Button* object and display the message *false* in the console window.

```
fm.but1.setEnabled(false);
System.out.println(fm.but1.isEnabled());
```

We met this operation in the previous chapter in the description of the *Frame* class. As you can see now, the *Frame* class inherited the operation (and many others) from the *Component* class.

void setVisible(boolean b) — If *b* is *false*, the component is invisible and does not react to events. If *b* is *true* the component is visible and does react to events.

boolean isVisible() — Returns *true* if a component is visible, otherwise *false* is returned.

void setBackground(Color c) — Sets the background colour to *c*. This operation may not work with every component since the native operating system is responsible for creating AWT components.

Color getBackground() — Returns the background colour of the component.

The program in LISTING-14.2 displays a label with a yellow background.

LISTING-14.2

Changing Background Colour

```
import java.awt.*;

public class TestComp extends Frame
{
    private Label labl = new Label("This is a label");

    public TestComp(String s)
    {
        super(s);
        add(labl);
    }

    public static void main(String args[])
    {
        TestComp fm = new TestComp("Testing");
        fm.setLayout(new FlowLayout());
        fm.setSize(200,100);
        fm.show();
        fm.labl.setBackground(Color.yellow);
    }
}
```

void setForeground(Color c) — Sets the foreground colour to *c*. This operation may not work with every component since the native operating system is responsible for creating AWT components.

Color getForeground() — Returns the foreground colour of the component.

Activity 14.4

Type in the program in LISTING-14.2 making the foreground colour of the label red.

Run the program to check your results.

Change the colour of the window itself to grey.

void setSize(Dimension d) — Sets the width and height of a component to the values given in *d*. Sizes are given in pixels.

void setSize(int w, int h) — Sets the width and height of a component to *w* and *h* respectively. Sizes are given in pixels.

Dimension getSize() — Returns the width and height of the component as a *Dimension* object.

The program in LISTING-14.3 creates a button and then resizes it. Its new size is then displayed in the console window. Notice that we've already used *setSize()* as inherited by the *Frame* class.

LISTING-14.3

Setting a Component's Size

```
import java.awt.*;

public class TestComp extends Frame
{
   private Button but1 = new Button("Press here");

   public TestComp(String s)
   {
        super(s);
        add(but1);
   }

   public static void main(String args[])
   {
        TestComp fm = new TestComp("Testing");
        fm.setLayout(new FlowLayout());
        fm.setSize(200,150);
        fm.show();
        fm.but1.setSize(new Dimension(50,80));
        System.out.println(fm.but1.getSize());
   }
}
```

Activity 14.5

Type in and run the above program.

What happens to the button when the window is resized?

Resizing the window causes the layout manger to recalculate the position of the items in the frame.

void setLocation(Point p) — Changes the position of the top-left corner of a component to *p.x*, *p.y*. Coordinates are measured from the top-left corner of the current window.

void setLocation(int x, int y) — Changes the position of the top-left corner of a component to *x*, *y*. Coordinates are measured from the top-left corner of the current window.

Point getLocation() — Returns the position of the top-left corner of the component. Coordinates are measured from the top-left corner of the current window.

Point getLocationOnScreen() — Returns the position of the top-left corner of the component. Coordinates are measured from the top-left corner of the screen.

> **Activity 14.6**
>
> Write an application containing a button. When the button is pressed move the application window 50 pixels down and 80 pixels to the right and display the new coordinates of the window.

setBounds(Rectangle r) — Sets the position and size of the current component to those given by *r*.

setBounds(int xp, int yp, int w, int h) — Sets the position and size of the current component as follows:
x = *xp*, *y* = *yp*, *width* = *w* and *height* = *h*.

Rectangle getBounds() — Returns the position and size of the current component.

void setCursor(Cursor c) — Sets the cursor used when the mouse pointer is over the component to *c*. This method and the *Cursor* class were described in the previous chapter.

Cursor getCursor() — Returns the cursor used by the component.

Some components contain text. The next three operations can be used to change and determine the font used by a component. The operations make use of other font-related classes which are also described here.

void setFont(Font f) — Sets the font used by the component to *f*.

The program in LISTING-14.4 changes the font used on a button's caption.

LISTING-14.4

Changing Font Attributes

```
import java.awt.*;

public class TestComp extends Frame
{
  private Button but1 = new Button("Press here");

  public TestComp(String s)
  {
       super(s);
       add(but1);
  }
  public static void main(String args[])
  {
       TestComp fm = new TestComp("Testing");
       fm.setLayout(new FlowLayout());
       fm.setSize(200,150);
       fm.show();
       fm.but1.setFont(new Font("Monospaced",Font.BOLD,20));
  }
}
```

Activity 14.7

Type in and test the program above.

What problem occurs? Try resizing the window. Does this solve the problem?

If the program had set the text details in the constructor and before adding the button to the frame, the button would have displayed correctly. However, by changing the font after the button had been added and the frame displayed, the layout manager had already determined the size of the component. We'll see later how to solve this problem.

The *Component* class also contains a method for retrieving the current font setting:

Font getFont()	Returns the current font details.
FontMetrics getFontMetrics()	Returns a *FontMetric* object giving the details of the current font.

The next three routines from the *Component* class are called by some of the layout managers to determine the size of a visual component. We'll discuss these further later in this chapter.

Dimension getPreferredSize()	Returns the preferred size for a component. The FlowLayout manager calls this method to determine what space should be allocated to a component that is to be displayed.
Dimension getMinimumSize()	Returns the minimum size acceptable to a component. Even where a layout manager does attempt to size a component according to the preferred size, this may not be possible if the window is too small.
Dimension getMaximumSize()	Returns the largest size acceptable when the component is displayed.
void invalidate()	Causes the component to be marked as invalid. When a component is marked as invalid it indicates that the space allocated to it by the layout manager needs to be recalculated.
void validate()	This operation should be used on the container to which components have been added. It causes the components in that container to be checked. If any are marked as invalid, the layout manger reorganises the positioning of the components.

In the program in LISTING-14.4 the FlowLayout manager makes a call to the button's *getPreferredSize()* method to determine the size of the button. After the font size is changed, we need to persuade the layout manager to recalculate the size requirements. This can be done by invalidating the button and calling the frame's *validate()* operation.

On this occasion, the *invalidate()* line could be omitted, since changing the font sets the button as invalid.

Activity 14.8

At the end of *main()* in your previous program, add the lines

```
fm.butl.invalidate();
fm.validate();
```

Re-run the program.

Many (but not all) of the *addlistener* operations are also defined within the *Component* class. These are given below.

void addComponentListener(ComponentListener cl)
void addFocusListener(FocusListener fl)
void addKeyListener(KeyListener kl)
void addMouseListener(MouseListener ml)
void addMouseMotionListener(MouseMotionListener mml)
void addInputMethodListener(InputMethodListener iml)

These operations make the component listen for a given set of events. Each has its own set of events. The argument for each operation must be an object which implements the specified listener interface.

Not all of these listeners were discussed in the previous chapter. See Chapter 16 for a further discussion on listeners.

We can stop a component listening for a set of events by removing the appropriate listener. For each of the add Listeners above there is a corresponding remove Listener operation. For example, *void removeMouseListener(MouseListener ml)* removes the mouse listener

The visual components that we create have to be shown on the screen. For the most part AWT components are displayed by calls to the underlying operating system functions which create such objects. However, it is possible to define your own components and the details of exactly how these are to be drawn on the screen must be given. There are three main routines involved in this. They are listed here since they are first stated in the *Component* class, but later in this chapter we will demonstrate their use by constructing our own components.

void paint(Graphics g)	Draws the component on the screen.
void update(Graphics g)	Redraws the background to a component and then calls *paint()*.
void repaint()	Schedules a call to *update()*. *update()* will then be executed at the earliest time convenient to the system.

The Canvas Class

This is a simple class and is used for two main purposes. The first is to create gaps in the layout of components. A *Canvas* object can be added to a window in the same way we have previously added buttons and labels. Since a *Canvas* object is normally invisible we can create an apparent gap in the component layout. For example, if an application contains the lines

```
Button b1 = new Button("First");
Button b2 = new Button("Second");
        .
add(b1);
add(b2);
```

the resultant layout when using a *FlowLayout* is shown in FIG-14.4. However, if we add a *Canvas* object between these with the code:

```
Button b1 = new Button("First");
Button b2 = new Button("Second");
Canvas c1 = new Canvas(); //Zero argument constructor
        .
add(b1);
c1.setSize(50,50); //Canvas width and height default to zero
add(c1);
add(b2);
```

the layout now changes to that shown in FIG-14.5.

FIG-14.4

Initial Layout

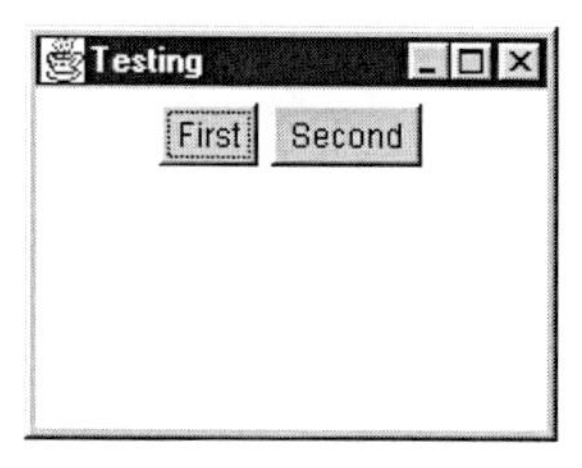

FIG-14.5

Layout With Canvas Added

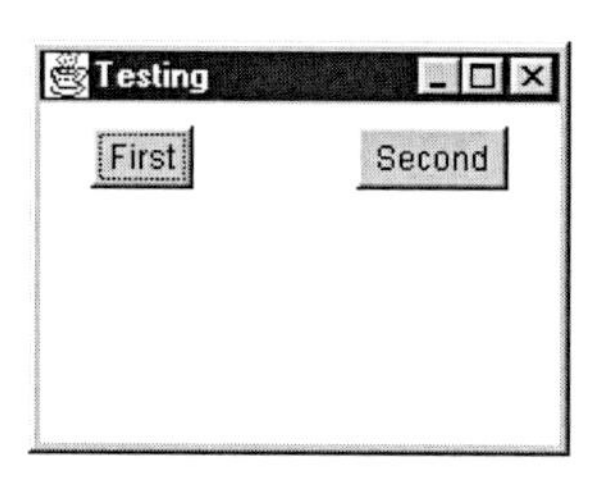

The second use of the *Canvas* class is as the superclass of a new class which overrides the *paint()* method to draw on the screen.

The paint method takes a *Graphics* object as an argument. It is this object that contains all the methods necessary to draw and display images. Details of the *Graphics* class are given below.

The Graphics Class

The *Graphics* class descends directly from the *Object* class, so it has few inherited methods. However, many of the operations it does define are equivalent to those we have met elsewhere.

You are unlikely ever to create an object of this class, rather you will make use of the *Graphics* object passed to *paint()* methods. A typical operation of the class is described below.

drawLine(int x1, int y1, int x2, int y2)	Draws a line between the points *(x1,y1)* and *(x2,y2)*.

Before looking at the other methods of the class, we'll create a short example of how the *Canvas* class can be subclassed and its *paint()* method overridden to create graphical output.

The program in LISTING-14.5 draws a diagonal line in *Canvas*-derived object.

LISTING-14.5

Drawing in a Canvas

```
import java.awt.*;

public class TestComp extends Frame
{
  Button b1 = new Button("First");
  Button b2 = new Button("Second");
  NewCanvas c1 = new NewCanvas();

  private class NewCanvas extends Canvas
  {
      public NewCanvas(){};
      public void paint(Graphics g)
      {
          g.drawLine(0,0,50,50);
      }
  }

  public TestComp(String s)
  {
      super(s);
      setLayout(new FlowLayout());
      add(b1);
      c1.setSize(50,50);
      add(c1);
      add(b2);
  }

  public static void main(String args[])
  {
      TestComp fm = new TestComp("Testing");
      fm.setSize(200,150);
      fm.show();
  }
}
```

Activity 14.9

Type in and test the program given above.

The layout manager automatically calls the paint() *method of every component added so there is no need for our own code to make this call.*

Other drawing operations of the *Graphics* class include:

void drawRect (int x, int y, int w, int h) Draws a rectangle whose top-left corner is at (x,y) and that is w pixels wide and h pixels high.

void drawOval(int x, int y, int w, int h) Draws the largest possible ellipse that can be enclosed in a rectangle whose top-left corner is at (x,y) and that is w pixels wide and h pixels high.

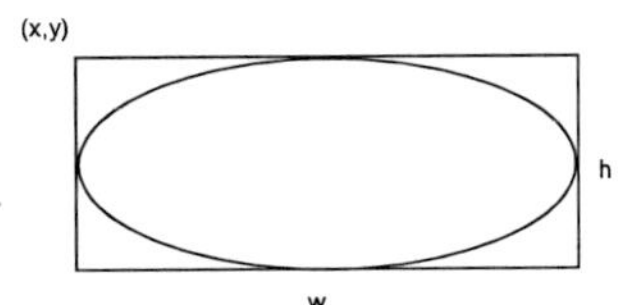

void drawRoundRect (int x, int y, int w, int h, int aw, int ah)

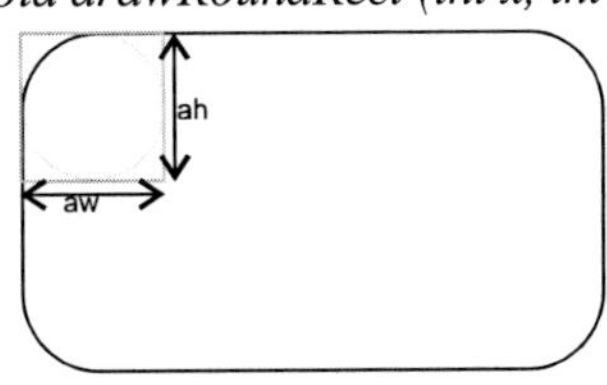

Draws a rectangle whose top-left corner is at (x,y) and that is w pixels wide and h pixels high. The corners of the rectangle are rounded. The degree of roundness is determined by the parameters *aw*, giving the arc's width and *ah*, giving the arc's height.

void drawArc (int x, int y, int w, int h, int stdeg, int arcdeg)

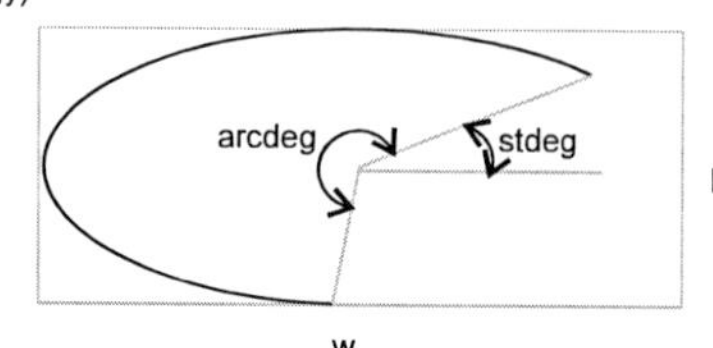

Draws a section of an elliptical arc. The ellipse is within the rectangle defined by *x,y, w* and *h*.
The part of the ellipse drawn starts at an angle of *stdeg* from the horizontal and covers *arcdeg* degrees.

void drawPolygon(int x[], int y[], int pnts)

Draws a polygon. The coordinates of each point on the polygon are stored in the arrays *x* and *y*. All x-ordinates are stored in *x*; the y-ordinates in *y*. The number of points on the polygon is given by *pnts*. A line connecting the first and last points given is also drawn.

void drawPolyline(int x[], int y[], int pnts)

Draws a an open-ended polygon through the points given by x and y. No line is drawn between the first and last points.

void draw3DRect (int x, int y, int w, int h, boolean raised)

Draws a rectangle whose top-left corner is at (*x,y*) and that is *w* pixels wide and *h* pixels high. A shadow 3D effect is added to the right and bottom lines if *raised* is *true*; otherwise the shadow is added to the top and left lines.

void drawString (String s, int x, int y)

Draws the string *s* using the current font and colour settings. The bottom left of the first character is positioned at (*x,y*).

void drawBytes (byte b[], int st, int cnt, int x, int y)

Draws as characters the contents of *b[st]* to *b[st+cnt-1]*. Drawing starts at position (*x,y*).

void drawChars (char c[], int st, int cnt, int x, int y)

Draws the characters *c[st]* to *c[st+cnt-1]*. Drawing starts at position (*x,y*).

void clearRect (int x, int y, int width, int height)

Draws a rectangle whose top-left corner is at (*x,y*) and that is *w* pixels wide and *h* pixels high. The rectangle is outlined and filled using the current background colour of the component.

void setColor (Color c)	Sets the colour to be used when drawing to *c*.
Color getColor()	Returns the current colour used for drawing.
public void setFont (Font f)	Sets the font to be used when drawing text to *f*.
Font getFont()	Returns the current font used for displaying text.
FontMetrics getFontMetrics()	Returns the font metrics for the currently specified font.
FontMetrics getFontMetrics (Font f)	Returns the font metrics for font *f*.
void fillRect (int x, int y, int w, int h)	Creates a filled rectangle whose top-left corner is at (*x,y*) and that is *w* pixels wide and *h* pixels high. The current drawing colour is used for all fills.

void fill3DRect (int x, int y, int w, int h, boolean raised)

Creates a filled 3D rectangle. The top-left corner is at (*x,y*) and that is *w* pixels wide and *h* pixels high.

void fillArc (int x, int y, int w, int h, int stdeg, int arcdeg)

Creates a filled "pie-slice". The ellipse is within the rectangle defined by *x, y, w* and *h*.
The part of the ellipse drawn starts at an angle of *stdeg* from the horizontal and covers *arcdeg* degrees.

void fillOval (int x, int y, int w, int h)	Draws the largest possible filled ellipse that can be enclosed in a rectangle whose top-left corner is at (*x,y*) and that is *w* pixels wide and *h* pixels high.

void fillPolygon (int x[], int y[], int pnts)

Draws a filled polygon. The coordinates of each point on the polygon are stored in the arrays *x* and *y*. All x-ordinates are stored in *x*; the y-ordinates in *y*. The number of points on the polygon is given by *pnts*. A line connecting the first and last points given is also drawn.

void fillRoundRect (int x, int y, int w, int h, int aw, int ah)

Draws a filled rectangle whose top-left corner is at (*x,y*) and that is *w* pixels wide and *h* pixels high. The corners of the rectangle are rounded. The degree of roundness is determined by the parameters *aw*, giving the arc's width and *ah*, giving the arc's height.

The program in LISTING-14.6 demonstrates many of these operations.

LISTING-14.6

Using paint() Methods

```
import java.awt.*;
public class TestComp extends Frame
{
   NewCanvas c1 = new NewCanvas();

   private class NewCanvas extends Canvas
   {
        NewCanvas(){};
        public void paint(Graphics g)
        {
             g.drawOval(0,0,30,50);
             g.drawRoundRect(70,0,50,80,10,20);
             g.drawArc(140,0,60,30,90,180);
             g.drawPolygon(new int[]{30,0,60},new int[]
                  ↳{100,150,150},3);
             g.drawPolyline(new int[]{110,80,140},new int[]
                  ↳{100,150,150},3);
             g.drawString("Hello",10,200);
             g.drawChars(new char[]{'A','B','C','D','E','F'},2,3,
                  ↳100,200);
             g.setColor(Color.red);
             g.fillRect(200,200,80,50);
             g.clearRect(210,210,60,30);
        }
   }

   public TestComp(String s)
   {
        super(s);
        c1.setSize(300,300);
        add(c1);
   }

   public static void main(String args[])
   {
        TestComp fm = new TestComp("Testing");
        fm.setSize(300,300);
        fm.show();
   }
}
```

The output produced by the above program is shown in FIG-14.6.

FIG-14.6

Output to a Canvas

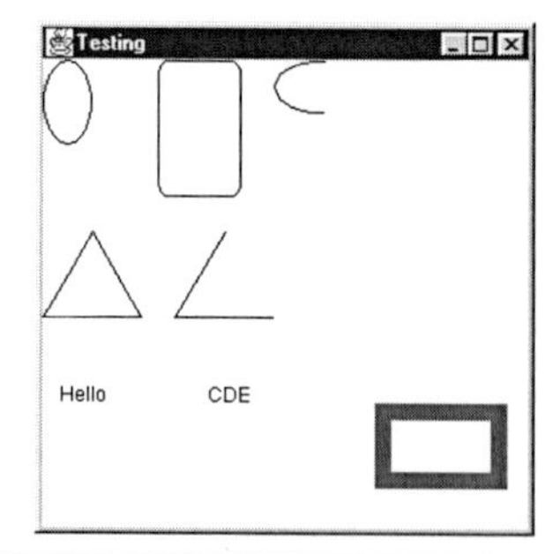

Activity 14.10

Using the same approach as the program in LISTING-14.6, produce a program that creates the image shown below.

The rectangle is red with white spots.

The *Graphics* class also contains methods for handling image file in GIF and JPEG format. We'll see how to use these in a few pages time.

The Container Class

The *Container* class is designed to hold components. Since the other classes we will examine later such as *Frame* and *Window* are derived from this class they inherit all its features.

Component add(Component c)	Adds component c to the container. It returns a reference to the added component.
Component add(String p, Component c)	Adds component *c* at position *p*. Used with *BorderLayout*. Typical values for *p* are "North", "South" etc.
Component add(Component c, int p)	Adds component *c* at position *p*. Used with layout managers that allow a position to be specified.
Component add(Component c, Object cons)	Adds component *c* applying constraints *cons*. Typical use would be with *GridBagLayout*.
void remove(Component c)	Removes component c from the container.
void remove(int p)	Removes the component at position *p* in the container.
int getComponentCount()	Returns the number of components in the container.
Component getComponent(int p)	Returns a reference to the component at position *p*.
Component[] getComponents()	Returns an array of references to the components in the container.
void setLayout(LayoutManager lm)	Sets up the layout manager for the container.
LayoutManager getLayout()	Returns a reference to the current layout manager.

The Panel Class

Panel objects can be used within an application to add to the flexibility of component layout. Use of this class is demonstrated in the next chapter. It has no new features; only those inherited from its ancestors. There are two constructors:

Panel()	Creates a new *Panel* object. The default layout manager is *FlowLayout.*

Panel(LayoutManager lm)	Creates a new *Panel* object with layout manager *lm*.

The Window Class

Although we might be tempted to associate this class with a full-blown window as appears in a GUI application, in fact, this is a very simple window that has no menus, or border and cannot be resized. It's probably most useful for creating a splash screen appearing when an application first loads. It is necessary to set the size of a Window object and make it visible. Default settings are zero width and height and invisible.

Constructors

Window(Frame f)	Creates a new *Window* object within *f*.
Window(Window w)	Creates a new *Window* object within *w*.

The program in LISTING-14.7 creates a small green window containing a button within the application's main window.

LISTING-14.7

Creating a Window Object

```
import java.awt.*;
public class TestComp extends Frame
{
  private Button but1 = new Button("Press here");
  private Window w;

  public TestComp(String s)
  {
      super(s);
      w = new Window(this);
      w.setLayout(new FlowLayout());
      w.setBounds(30,30,100,50);
      w.setBackground(Color.green);
      w.add(but1);
      w.setVisible(true);
  }
  public static void main(String args[])
  {
      TestComp fm = new TestComp("Testing");
      fm.setLayout(new FlowLayout());
      fm.setSize(200,150);
      fm.show();
  }
}
```

Activity 14.11

Type in and test the program given in LISTING-14.7.

Add a second, red *Window* object with the top left corner at (50,50) using the same width and height as before.

What happens as you click in each window?

Other methods of the *Window* class include:

void pack()	Sets the size of the window to the minimum size needed to show all the components that it contains.
void show()	Shows the window. Equivalent to *setVisible(true)*.
void hide()	Hides the window. Equivalent to *setVisible(false)*.
void dispose()	Releases resources allocated to the window. Normally, the garbage collector takes care of deallocating resources. However, in the case of windows, this should be done manually.
void toFront()	Brings the window to the front of all other windows.
void toBack()	Places the window behind all other windows.
Window getOwner()	Returns a reference to the container used as an argument to the window's constructor call.
void addWindowListener(WindowListener wl)	Adds the *WindowListener wl* to the window.
void removeWindowListener(WindowListener wl)	Removes the *WindowListener wl* from the window.
Toolkit getToolkit()	Returns a reference to a *Toolkit* object. This contains platform-dependent information. The *Toolkit* class is described below.

The Toolkit Class

Dimension getScreenSize()	Returns the current display mode size in pixels.
int getScreenResolution()	Returns the pixels per inch used on the screen.

The program in LISTING-14.8 displays the screen details in the console window.

LISTING-14.8

Retrieving Screen Information

```
import java.awt.*;

public class TestComp extends Frame
{
  public TestComp(String s)
  {
      super(s);
  }

  public static void main(String args[])
  {
      TestComp fm = new TestComp("Testing");
      fm.setSize(200,150);
      fm.show();
      System.out.println(fm.getToolkit().getScreenSize());
      System.out.println(fm.getToolkit().getScreenResolution());
  }
}
```

Toolkit getDefaultToolkit() — This class method returns a reference to the system toolkit.

The *Toolkit* class also contains operations for loading images. We'll look at loading images next and cover these routines at that point.

Adding Images

Java can display images held in **.gif** and **.jpg** format. The processes involved are complex but the actual lines of code required for most applications are simple.

The image itself is referenced by an *Image* class pointer:

```
Image ex;
```

An *Image*-derived object is created by the *getImage()* method defined in the *Toolkit* class. This method is given the name of the file to be loaded and initiates transfer of data from the file to the *Image* object in a separate thread:

```
ex = Toolkit.getDefaultToolkit().getImage("photo.jpg");
```

To display an image we need to use the *drawImage()* method defined in the *Graphics* class.

```
g.drawImage(ex,0,0,this);
```

The parameters for *drawImage()* give the *Image* object, *ex*; the position within the object for the top left corner of the image, (0,0), and a reference to the object on which the image is drawn, *this*.

The program in LISTING-14.9 demonstrates how these statements are used in a practical way. The program uses the following approach:

```
Create a Canvas derived class
Override its inherited paint() method to load and
↳display an image
```

The *paint()* method's logic is

```
Create an Image reference variable
Get the default toolkit for the system and call its
↳getImage() method
```

```
    (this loads the stated image and returns a reference to it)
Using the Graphic class's drawImage() to display the
↳image on screen
```

LISTING-14.9

Displaying an Image

```
import java.awt.*;

public class UsingImages extends Frame
{
   ImageCanvas ic = new ImageCanvas();

   private class ImageCanvas extends Canvas
   {
        Image ex;

        public ImageCanvas()
        {
             ex = Toolkit.getDefaultToolkit().getImage("photo.jpg");
        }

        public void paint(Graphics g)
        {
             g.drawImage(ex,0,0,this);
        }
   }

   public UsingImages(String s)
   {
        super(s);
        add(ic);
   }

   public static void main(String args[])
   {
        UsingImages fm = new UsingImages("Images");
        fm.setSize(300,300);
        fm.show();
   }
}
```

Activity 14.12

Load any small jpeg image into your current directory.

Rename the file "*photo.jpg*".

Type in and run the program above.

Activity 14.13

Modify your previous program so the name of the file can be given as part of the command line.

Test your program then return to the previous version of your program.

However, there's more going on in displaying an image than might at first be suspected.

Since image files are compressed they need to be reconstructed into a form suitable for display. The job of transferring data from the file and the conversion is done, in the new thread, by routines in the *ImageProducer* interface.

An object that implements the *ImageObserver* interface communicates with the *ImageProducer* object to determine the current progress in loading the image.

The *ImageObserver* interface, which declares a single operation, *imageUpdate()*, is implemented by the *Component* class and hence occurs in every AWT component.

As we said before, image loading takes place in a separate thread from the display. Java creates the new thread as soon as a request to load an image is executed. A separate thread is used because loading may take a considerable amount of time, especially if the image is being downloaded from the Internet. By handling this in a separate thread, the main program may continue with useful work while the downloading is taking place. This *imageUpdate()* method makes calls to the *paint()* method responsible for displaying the image as more and more of the image is loaded.

Next we'll start looking at each class and interface involved in LISTING-14.9

The Image Class

This is an abstract class from which derived classes are used to reference the image. Operations are included to find the dimensions of an image and rescale it.

Class Constants

int SCALE_DEFAULT
int SCALE_FAST
int SCALE_SMOOTH

int SCALE_REPLICATE *int SCALE_AREA_AVERAGING*	Theses are used as arguments when an image is to be scaled.
int getWidth(ImageObserver io)	Returns the width of an image in pixels. The argument would normally be the component into which the image is drawn. Returns -1 if the image details have not yet been loaded.
int getHeight(ImageObserver io)	Returns the height of an image in pixels. The argument would normally be the component into which the image is drawn. Returns -1 if the image details have not yet been loaded.

Activity 14.14

Add the line

```
System.out.println(ex.getWidth(this)+"  "+ex.getHeight(this));
```

as the last line of your *paint()* method.

Run your program.

You should see the values -1 -1 displayed initially and then the correct dimensions of your image. These will appear several times until the image eventually appears.

Image getScaledInstance(int w, int h, int method)

Returns a reference to a scaled version of the current image. The new image is *w* pixels wide and *h* pixels high. *method* defines the scaling method used. This should be one of the constant values given earlier.

Activity 14.15

Add the line

```
ex = ex.getScaledInstance(40,20,Image.SCALE_DEFAULT);
```

as the final line in the *ImageCanvas* class constructor.

Run the program.

You should see a smaller version of your image.

Image Handling Methods in the Toolkit Class and Graphics Class

To add images to our application we need to use operations from both the *Toolkit* class and the *Graphics* class. From the *Toolkit* class we use *getImage()*:

Image getImage(String file) — Returns a reference to an *Image*-derived object which contains the image held in *file*.

This is called after the *getDefaultToolkit()* returns the correct reference.

The *Graphics* class has two useful routines:

boolean drawImage(Image im, int x, int y, ImageObserver io)

Displays the image referenced by *im*. The image's top-left corner is at position (*x*,*y*). *io* reports on the loading progress. *io* normally has the value `this`, since all awt components implement the *ImageObserver* interface. The routines returns *true* if the image is drawn successfully.

boolean drawImage(Image im, int x, int y, int w, int h, ImageObserver io)

Displays the image referenced by *im*. The image's top-left corner is at position (*x*,*y*). *io* reports on the loading progress. The image is drawn with a width of *w* pixels and height *h* pixels. This gives a scaled version of the image.

The MediaTracker Class

There will be times when your program really needs to wait for an image to be completely loaded before continuing with other operations. To do this we can make use of a *MediaTracker* object, which, when linked to an image will report on its loading status.

For example, we saw before that the *getWidth()* routine returns -1 if we attempt to call it before the image's dimensions have been determined. By linking a *MediaTracker* object to the image we could make sure we don't attempt to call *getWidth()* before the image is loaded.

The basic operations we need from this class are:

Constructor

MediaTracker(Component c)	Creates a *MediaTracker* object linked to component *c*. The parameter *c* will be the object displaying the image, normally, `this`.

Methods

void addImage(Image im, int ID)	Links the *MediaTracker* object to the image *im*. An *ID* is assigned by the programmer to the image. It is this *ID* value that is used later. More than one image can be given the same *ID* value if they are to be considered a single group. For example, the images that make up an animation.
void waitForID(int ID)	Waits for the image associated with *ID* to load. When completed, *true* is returned. A possible *InterruptedException* may be thrown by this routine so this must be handled.

This class is used in the example shown in LISTING-14.10.

The ScrollPane Class

A *ScrollPane* object, as the name suggests, is a container incorporating scrollbars.

Unlike the others, this container can only contain one component. If you try to add a second component, the first is automatically removed.

Class Constants

int SCROLLBARS_AS_NEEDED *int SCROLLBARS_ALWAYS* *int SCROLLBARS_NEVER*	Possible values used in the

constructor. The value used determines when scrollbars appear.

Constructors

ScrollPane()	Creates a *ScrollPane* object. Scrollbars appear as needed.
ScrollPane(int bars)	Creates a *ScrollPane* object. Scrollbars appear as needed specified by *bars*. Possible values for *bars* are the class constants given above.

Methods

void setScrollPosition(int vp, int hp)	Sets the position of the vertical and horizontal scrollbars to *vp* and *hp* respectively.

A common reason for using a *ScrollPane* is to display a large image.

The program in LISTING-14.10 uses a *ScrollPane* and a *MediaTracker* object to display such an image.

The program employs the following logic

```
An inner ImageCanvas class is defined. This is extended from the
Canvas class and contains an Image component and ImageTracker
component.

The constructor for this inner class links the Image object to
an image file and the ImageTracker to the Image object.
The image is completely loaded and its size is used to set the
canvas size.

The paint() method draws the image.

The main class contains a ScrollPane object to which the image
is added.

The application window is smaller than the image which can be
examined by scrolling.
```

LISTING-14.10

Using the ScrollPane Class

```
import java.awt.*;

public class UsingScrollPane extends Frame
{
  ScrollPane sp = new ScrollPane(ScrollPane.SCROLLBARS_ALWAYS);

  private class ImageCanvas extends Canvas
  {
      Image ex;
      MediaTracker md;

      public ImageCanvas()
      {
          md = new MediaTracker(this);
          ex = Toolkit.getDefaultToolkit().
                ↳createImage("photo2.jpg");
          md.addImage(ex,0);
```

Continued on next page

LISTING-14.10
(continued)

Using the ScrollPane

```
            try
            {
                md.waitForID(0);
            }
            catch(InterruptedException ie)
            {}
            setSize(ex.getWidth(this),ex.getHeight(this));
        }

        public void paint(Graphics g)
        {
            g.drawImage(ex,0,0,this);
        }
    }

    public UsingScrollPane(String s)
    {
        super(s);
        ImageCanvas ic = new ImageCanvas();
        sp.add(ic);
        add(sp);
    }

    public static void main(String args[])
    {
        UsingScrollPane fm = new UsingScrollPane("Images");
        fm.setBounds(200,200,500,500);
        fm.show();
    }
}
```

Activity 14.16

Type in and run the program above using an appropriate image.

Zooming An Image

The next program is a more complete application with a scrollpane containing an image and a button which can be clicked to magnify the image size.

This introduces some new problems: the canvas containing the image must be resized on each zoom; and the layout manager for the scrollbar must recalculate the space required by the larger canvas

The code is given in LISTING-14.11.

LISTING-14.11

Image Zooming

```
import java.awt.*;
import java.awt.event.*;

public class UsingScrollPane extends Frame
↳implements ActionListener
{
    ScrollPane sp = new ScrollPane(ScrollPane.SCROLLBARS_ALWAYS);
    ImageCanvas ic;
    Panel options = new Panel();
    Button zoom = new Button("Zoom In");
    int newWidth, newHeight;

    private class ImageCanvas extends Canvas
    {
        Image ex;
        MediaTracker md;
```

Continued on next page

LISTING-14.11
(continued)

Image Zooming

```
        public ImageCanvas()
        {
            md = new MediaTracker(this);
            ex = Toolkit.getDefaultToolkit().
            ↳createImage("photo2.jpg");
            md.addImage(ex,0);
            try{md.waitForID(0);}
            catch(InterruptedException ie){}
            newWidth = ex.getWidth(this);
            newHeight = ex.getHeight(this);
            setSize(newWidth, newHeight);
        }

        public void paint(Graphics g)
        {
            g.drawImage(ex,0,0,newWidth, newHeight,this);
        }
    }

    private class WindowHandler extends WindowAdapter
    {
        public void windowClosing(WindowEvent we)
        {
            we.getWindow().hide();
            System.exit(0);
        }
    }


    public UsingScrollPane(String s)
    {
        super(s);
        addWindowListener(new WindowHandler());
        ic = new ImageCanvas();
        sp.add(ic);
        zoom.addActionListener(this);
        options.add(zoom);
        add("West",options);
        add("Center",sp);
    }


    public void actionPerformed(ActionEvent ae)
    {
        newWidth *=2;
        newHeight *=2;
        ic.setSize(newWidth, newHeight);
        repaint();
        validate();
    }


    public static void main(String args[])
    {
        UsingScrollPane fm = new UsingScrollPane("Images");
        fm.setBounds(200,200,500,500);
        fm.show();
    }
}
```

Activity 14.17

Type in and test the program above.

Add a second button which halves the width and height when clicked.

The Dialog Class

An object of the *Dialog* class creates the typical dialog box seen when messages, warnings or options are displayed by an application.

Dialog boxes fall into two main types: modal and non-modal. A modal dialog box stops the user from accessing any other windows of the current application until it has been closed. Less obviously, it blocks the thread that displayed the dialog box.

Non-modal dialog boxes cause none of these restrictions.

Constructors

Dialog(Frame f)	Creates a non-modal *Dialog* object. The object is linked to *f*.
Dialog(Frame f, boolean b)	Creates a *Dialog* object. If *b* is *true*, the dialog box is a modal one.
Dialog(Frame f, String s, boolean b)	Creates a *Dialog* object. If *b* is *true*, the dialog box is a modal one. The dialog box contains the title *s*.

Methods

boolean isModal()	Returns *true* if the dialog box is modal.
String getTitle()	Returns the dialog box title.
void setTitle(String s)	Sets the dialog box title to *s*.
void setResizable(boolean b)	If *b* is *false*, the dialog box cannot be resized.
boolean isResizable()	Returns *true* if the dialog box can be resized.
void show()	Shows the dialog box.
void hide()	Hides the dialog box.
void dispose()	Frees the resources allocated to the dialog box.

A *Dialog* object doesn't have any great capabilities so you need to create a derived class for any application in which it is to be used. The following class code creates a dialog box to be used when closing an application:

```
private class CloseDialog extends Dialog
    ↳implements ActionListener
{
    Button yes = new Button("Yes");
    Button no = new Button("No");
    Label lab1 = new Label("Terminate program?");
```

```
    public CloseDialog(Frame c)
    {
        super(c,"Closing Application",true);
        setLayout(new FlowLayout());
        addWindowListener(new WindowHandler());
        add(lab1);
        yes.addActionListener(this);
        no.addActionListener(this);
        add(yes);
        add(no);
        setSize(150,90);
    }

    public void actionPerformed(ActionEvent ae)
    {
        hide();
        dispose();
        if (ae.getSource()==yes)
            System.exit(0);
    }
}
```

In this case it is a private class for use within our previous program so that when an attempt is made to close the application the dialog box appears to give the user a last chance to change his mind and continue using the application.

The dialog box produced is shown in FIG-14.7.

FIG-14.7

A Closing Dialog

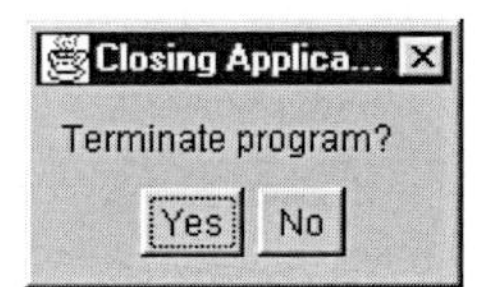

The complete program is shown in LISTING-14.12.

LISTING-14.12

Using a Closing Dialog

```
import java.awt.*;
import java.awt.event.*;

public class UsingScrollPane extends Frame implements
ActionListener
{
  ScrollPane sp = new ScrollPane(ScrollPane.SCROLLBARS_ALWAYS);
  ImageCanvas ic;
  Panel options = new Panel();
  Button zoom = new Button("Zoom In");
  int newWidth, newHeight;
  CloseDialog cl;

  private class ImageCanvas extends Canvas
  {
      Image ex;
      MediaTracker md;

      public ImageCanvas()
      {
          md = new MediaTracker(this);
          ex = Toolkit.getDefaultToolkit().createImage
          ↳("photo2.jpg");
          md.addImage(ex,0);
          try{md.waitForID(0);}
          catch(InterruptedException ie){}
```

Continued on next page

LISTING-14.12
(continued)

Using a Closing Dialog

```
            newWidth = ex.getWidth(this);
            newHeight = ex.getHeight(this);
            setSize(newWidth, newHeight);
        }

        public void paint(Graphics g)
        {
            g.drawImage(ex,0,0,newWidth, newHeight,this);
        }
    }

    private class CloseDialog extends Dialog
    ↳implements ActionListener
    {
        Button yes = new Button("Yes");
        Button no = new Button("No");
        Label lab1 = new Label("Terminate program?");

        CloseDialog(Frame c)
        {
            super(c,"Closing Application",true);
            setLayout(new FlowLayout());
            addWindowListener(new WindowHandler());
            add(lab1);
            yes.addActionListener(this);
            no.addActionListener(this);
            add(yes);
            add(no);
            setSize(150,90);
        }

        public void actionPerformed(ActionEvent ae)
        {
            hide();
            dispose();
            if (ae.getSource()==yes)
            {
                dispose();
                System.exit(0);
            }
        }
    }

    private class WindowHandler extends WindowAdapter
    {
        public void windowClosing(WindowEvent we)
        {
            cl = new CloseDialog((Frame)we.getSource());
            Point p = getLocationOnScreen();
            cl.setLocation(p.x+50, p.y+50);
            cl.show();
        }
    }

    public UsingScrollPane(String s)
    {
        super(s);
        addWindowListener(new WindowHandler());
        ic = new ImageCanvas();
        sp.add(ic);
        zoom.addActionListener(this);
        options.add(zoom);
        add("West",options);
        add("Center",sp);
    }
```

Continued on next page

LISTING-14.12
(continued)

Using a Closing Dialog

```
    public void actionPerformed(ActionEvent ae)
    {
        newWidth *=2;
        newHeight *=2;
        ic.setSize(newWidth, newHeight);
        repaint();
        validate();
    }

    public static void main(String args[])
    {
        UsingScrollPane fm = new UsingScrollPane("Images");
        fm.setBounds(200,200,500,500);
        fm.show();
    }
}
```

Activity 14.18

Modify your previous program to display a dialog box when closing the application.

Test the program.

The FileDialog Class

Our image viewing program is rather limited since the name of the file is written into the code. Any serious program should allow the user to select the file to be displayed. This can be done using a *FileDialog* object which displays filenames within a specified directory. AWT implements dialog boxes by calling that feature by simply displaying the file dialog box produced by the operating system under which it is running. Open or Save file dialog boxes can be displayed, but there is no practical difference between these other than possibly the title's text. There is no built in ability to actually load or save a file, the file dialog only returns the current directory and selected file name as String objects.

Constants

int LOAD *int SAVE*	These are used in other methods to determine which type of file dialog box is to be opened.

Constructors

FileDialog(Frame f)	Creates a *FileDialog* object. The object is linked to *f*. An open file dialog box is produced.
FileDialog(Frame f, String s)	Creates a *FileDialog* object. The box contains the title *s*. An open file dialog box is produced.
FileDialog(Frame f, String s, int m)	Creates a *FileDialog* object. The box contains the title *s*. *m* should be assigned one of the class constants and determines

which type of file dialog is displayed (LOAD or SAVE).

Methods

int getMode()	Returns the file dialog mode (LOAD or SAVE).
void setMode(int m)	Sets the file dialog mode.
String getDirectory()	Returns the currently selected directory.
void setDirectory(String d)	Sets the current directory to *d*.
String getFile()	Returns the name of the currently selected file.
void setFile(String f)	Sets the currently selected file to *f*.

The program in LISTING-14.13 is again an extension of the image displaying program which allows the image to be displayed to be selected using a file dialog. It contains an improved version of the *ImageCanvas* class that allows a named file to be drawn on the canvas.

LISTING-14.13

Using a File Dialog

```
import java.awt.*;
import java.awt.event.*;

public class UsingScrollPane extends Frame implements
ActionListener
{
   ScrollPane sp = new ScrollPane(ScrollPane.SCROLLBARS_ALWAYS);
   ImageCanvas ic;
   Panel options = new Panel();
   Button zoom = new Button("Zoom In");
   int newWidth, newHeight;
   FileDialog fd;
   CloseDialog cl;

   private class ImageCanvas extends Canvas
   {
       Image ex;

       public ImageCanvas()
       {
           loadImage("photo2.jpg");
       }

       public void loadImage(String s)
       {
           MediaTracker md;
           md = new MediaTracker(this);
           ex = Toolkit.getDefaultToolkit().createImage(s);
           md.addImage(ex,0);
           try{md.waitForID(0);}
           catch(InterruptedException ie){}
           newWidth = ex.getWidth(this);
           newHeight = ex.getHeight(this);
           setSize(newWidth, newHeight);
           repaint();
       }
```

Continued on next page

LISTING-14.13
(continued)

Using a File Dialog

```
    public void paint(Graphics g)
    {
        g.drawImage(ex,0,0,newWidth, newHeight,this);
    }
}

private class CloseDialog extends Dialog
↳implements ActionListener
{
    Button yes = new Button("Yes");
    Button no = new Button("No");
    Label lab1 = new Label("Terminate program?");

    CloseDialog(Frame c)
    {
        super(c,"Closing Application",true);
        setLayout(new FlowLayout());
        addWindowListener(new WindowHandler());
        add(lab1);
        yes.addActionListener(this);
        no.addActionListener(this);
        add(yes);
        add(no);
        setSize(150,90);
    }

    public void actionPerformed(ActionEvent ae)
    {
        hide();
        dispose();
        if (((Button)ae.getSource())==yes)
        {
            dispose();
            System.exit(0);
        }
    }
}

private class WindowHandler extends WindowAdapter
{
    public void windowClosing(WindowEvent we)
    {
        cl =new CloseDialog((Frame)we.getSource());
        Point p = getLocationOnScreen();
        cl.setLocation(p.x+50, p.y+50);
        cl.show();
    }
}

public UsingScrollPane(String s)
{
    super(s);
    addWindowListener(new WindowHandler());
    ic = new ImageCanvas();
    sp.add(ic);
    zoom.addActionListener(this);
    options.add(zoom);
    add("West",options);
    add("Center",sp);
    fd = new FileDialog(this,"Load File");
}

public void actionPerformed(ActionEvent ae)
{
    newWidth *=2;
    newHeight *=2;
    ic.setSize(newWidth, newHeight);
    repaint();
```

Continued on next page

LISTING-14.13
(continued)

Using a File Dialog

```
        validate();
    }

    public static void main(String args[])
    {
        UsingScrollPane fm = new UsingScrollPane("Images");
        fm.setBounds(200,200,500,500);
        fm.show();
        fm.fd.show();
        String filename;
        if ((filename = fm.fd.getFile()) != null)
            fm.ic.loadImage(fm.fd.getDirectory()+filename);
    }
}
```

Activity 14.19

Modify your previous program to include a file dialog for choosing the image to be loaded.

Adding a Menu Bar

Most GUI applications make use of a menu bar at the top of the window. We can achieve this in Java by adding a *MenuBar* object to our window. The *Frame* class contains methods that allow such a bar to be added or removed.

void setMenuBar(MenuBar b)	Adds menu bar *b* to the frame.
MenuBar getMenuBar()	Returns a reference to the menu bar object used by the frame. If no menu bar exists, `null` is returned.

A typical menu is shown in FIG-14.8.

FIG-14.8

A Typical Menu

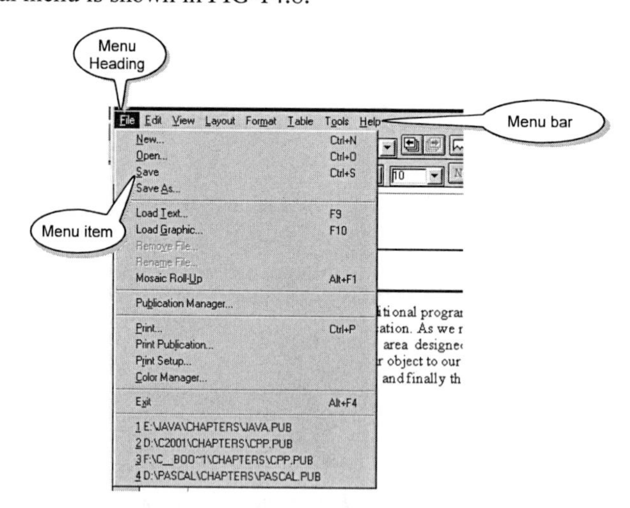

The menu bar consists of three distinct elements :

The menu bar itself
(a *MenuBar* object)
The main headings of the menu bar
(a set of *Menu* objects)

The menu items in each drop-down option
(a set of *MenuItem* objects)

We need to look at these three related classes before we can create a menu-driven application. The diagram in FIG-14.9 shows the relationship between the menu classes.

FIG-14.9

The Menu Classes

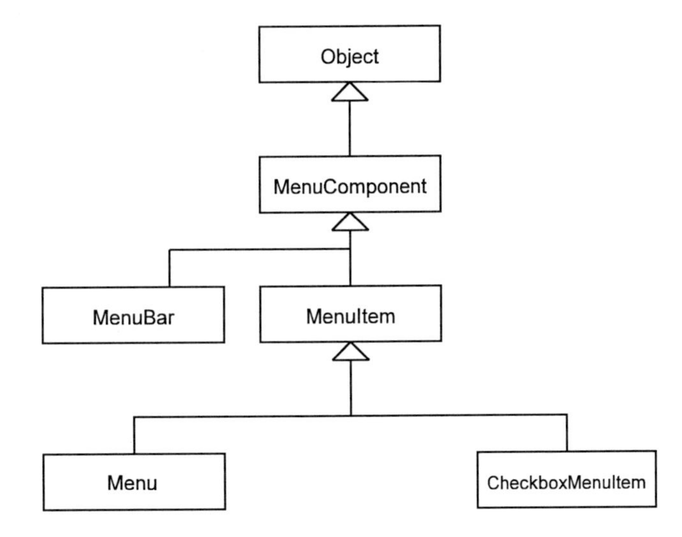

As you can see from the diagram above, menus are not derived from the *Component* class and so do not inherit the features of that class

The MenuComponent Class

This is an abstract class which defines some of the basic operations that the *Component* class adds to the other visual components. These operations include:

String getName()	Returns the name of a menu component. Each component is allocated a name by the Java environment. This is not its variable name as defined within the program.
void setName(String s)	Sets the name of a menu component.
Component getParent()	Returns a reference parent of the current component. The parent of a menu component is the container to which it has been added.
void setFont(Font f)	Sets the font used by the menu text to *f*.
Font getFont()	Returns the current font setting.

The MenuBar Class

As we have seen, using an object of this class allows us to add a menu bar to our window application. Objects of this class can hold a set of *Menu* objects. These objects give the main options of the menu bar.

Constructor

MenuBar()	Creates a new, but empty, menu bar.

Methods

void add(Menu m)	Adds *Menu* object *m* to the menu bar.
void remove(int p)	Removes the menu object at position *p*. The first menu object is at position zero.
void remove(MenuComponent mc)	Removes *mc* from the menu. *mc* may be a menu heading or menu item.
int getMenuCount()	Returns the number of items in the current menu bar.
Menu getMenu(int p)	Returns a reference to the *Menu* item at position *p* in the heading.

The MenuItem Class

Constructors

MenuItem()	Creates an empty *MenuItem* object. Its text can be set later.
MenuItem(String s)	Creates a *MenuItem* object showing the text *s*.
MenuItem(String s, MenuShortcut ms)	Creates a *MenuItem* object showing the text *s*. The menu shortcut is set to *ms*.

Methods

void setLabel(String s)	Sets the menu item's text to *s*.
String getLabel()	Returns the text of a menu item.
void setEnabled(boolean b)	If *b* is *true*, the menu item is enabled, otherwise it is disabled.
boolean isEnabled()	Returns *true* if the menu item is enabled, otherwise *false* is returned.
void setShortcut(MenuShortcut ms)	Sets the menu shortcut for the current item to *ms*.
MenuShortcut getShortcut()	Returns the shortcut for the menu item.
void deleteShortcut()	Removes the shortcut from the current item.

MenuItem getShortcutMenuItem(MenuShortcut ms)
Returns a reference to the item whose shortcut is *ms*.

void setActionCommand(String s) — Sets the *ActionCommand* string to *s*.

String getActionCommand() — Returns the *ActionCommand* string.

void addActionListener(ActionListener al) — Adds *ActionListener al* to the menu item. Use this to add an event-handler which will be executed when the menu item is selected.

void removeActionListener(ActionListener al)
Removes the *ActionListener al* from the menu item.

The Menu Class

Constructors

Menu() — Creates an empty *Menu* object. Its text can be set later.

Menu(String s) — Creates a *Menu* object showing the text *s*.

Menu(String s, boolean b) — Creates a *Menu* object showing the text *s*. If *b* is *true*, the menu heading is enabled.

Methods

int getItemCount() — Returns the number of menu items added to the current menu heading.

MenuItem getItem(int p) — Returns the menu item at position p. The first item is at position zero.

MenuItem add(MenuItem mi) — Adds *mi* as a menu item under the current heading. The item is added to the end of the list.

add(String s) — Creates a menu item with test *s* and adds it under the current heading. The item is added to the end of the list.

void insert(MenuItem mi, int p) — Adds *mi* as a menu item under the current heading. The new item is placed at position *p*.

void insert(String s, int p) — Creates a menu item with test *s* and adds it under the current heading. The new item is placed at position *p*.

void addSeparator()
Adds a horizontal line separator to the menu. It is added at the end of the list.

void insertSeparator(int p)
Adds a horizontal line separator to the menu. It is added at position *p* in the list.

void remove(int p)
Removes the item at position *p* in the list.

void remove(MenuComponent mc)
Removes the item *mc* from the current menu heading.

void removeAll()
Removes all items from the current menu heading.

The next few programs demonstrate how menus are used and implemented. The first of these, in LISTING-14.14 adds a menu bar, two menu headings and 3 options to each drop-down menu.

LISTING-14.14

Adding a Menu

```
import java.awt.*;
import java.awt.event.*;


public class UsingMenus extends Frame implements ActionListener
{
   private Label labA = new Label("Menu Option");
   private MenuBar mb = new MenuBar();
   private Menu menus[] = {new Menu("File"), new Menu("View")};
   private MenuItem menuitems[][] ={{new MenuItem("Open"),
   ↳new MenuItem("Save"), new MenuItem("Exit")},
   ↳{new MenuItem("Zoom"),new MenuItem("Negative"),
   ↳new MenuItem("Black & White")}};

   public UsingMenus(String s)
   {
        super(s);
        setLayout(new FlowLayout());
        addWindowListener(new WindowHandler());
        add(labA);
        setMenuBar(mb);
        for(int c = 0; c < menus.length; c++)
             mb.add(menus[c]);
        for(int c = 0; c < menus.length; c++)
             for(int j = 0; j < menuitems[c].length; j++)
                  menus[c].add(menuitems[c][j]);
   }

   class WindowHandler extends WindowAdapter
   {
        public void windowClosing(WindowEvent we)
        {
             dispose();
             System.exit(0);
        }
   }

   //*** We'll link to this later ***
   public void actionPerformed(ActionEvent e)
   {
        labA.setText(((MenuItem)e.getSource()).getLabel());
   }
```

Continued on next page

LISTING-14.14
(continued)

Adding a Menu

```
    public static void main(String args[])
    {
        UsingMenus fm = new UsingMenus("Starting GUI");
        fm.setSize(300,100);
        fm.show();
    }
}
```

Activity 14.20

Type in and run the program.

The first change we'll make is to add a separator before the *Exit* option

Activity 14.21

Add the line

```
menus[0].insertSeparator(2);
```

to the end of the *UsingMenus* class constructor.

Check that a separator has been correctly added.

Now we need the menu options to react when clicked. You may have noticed that only *addActionListener()* is available so we need to implement *ActionListener* and link it to each menu item. For the moment, we'll just make each menu item display its name in the label. To do this we'll change the constructor lines

```
for(int c = 0; c < menus.length; c++)
    for(int j = 0; j < menuitems[c].length; j++)
        menus[c].add(menuitems[c][j]);
```

to

Existing lines are in italics.

```
for(int c = 0; c < menus.length; c++)
    for(int j = 0; j < menuitems[c].length; j++)
    {
        menus[c].add(menuitems[c][j]);
        menuitems[c][j].addActionListener(this);
    }
```

Activity 14.22

Make the changes given above and test your program.

Shortcuts

People who use a package will often prefer to choose options using key strokes rather than by mouse clicking. All major GUI operating system allow for this option by holding down the Control key (or some other) and hitting a special character. For example, rather than clicking on *Menu* then *Open*, we might simply press Ctrl-O.

Java allows a shortcut to be added to each menu item. Although the shortcut can be added later, the easiest way is to include it as part of the *MenuItem*'s constructor.

In our own application we could add this shortcut by changing the object placed in the *menuitems* array:

The second line contains the changed item.

```
private MenuItem menuitems[][] ={{
    ↳new MenuItem("Open",new MenuShortcut('O')),
    ↳new MenuItem("Save"), new MenuItem("Exit")},
    ↳{new MenuItem("Zoom"),new MenuItem("Negative"),
    ↳new MenuItem("Black & White")}};
```

Activity 14.23

Add shortcuts to every menu item in your program as follows

Open	Ctrl-O
Save	Ctrl-S
Exit	Ctrl-Q
Zoom	Ctrl-Z
Negative	Ctrl-N
Black&White	Ctrl-B

Test each option ensuring the label's text changes correctly for each.

Cascading Menus

Some menus will naturally lead to other submenus. For example, in the *Zoom* option we might want to see a list of pre-defined options.

Since the *Menu* class is a subclass of *MenuItem*, it is possible to add a *Menu* object to an existing *Menu* object and hence create a submenu.

The following changes are required:

1. *Zoom* is no longer a *MenuItem* object and must be removed from the *menuitems* array:

Shortcuts are omitted for simplicity.

```
private MenuItem menuitems[][] ={{new MenuItem("Open"),
↳new MenuItem("Save"), new MenuItem("Exit")},
↳{new MenuItem("Negative"), new MenuItem("Black & White")}};
```

2. *Zoom* must be set up as a menu with menu items in its own right. This has been done in a separate method which returns a reference to the menu created:

```
private Menu createZoomSubmenu()
{
    MenuItem zoomitems[]={new MenuItem("50%"),
    ↳new MenuItem("100%"), new MenuItem("200%"),
    ↳new MenuItem("300%")};
    Menu zm = new Menu("zoom");
    for(int c = 0; c < zoomitems.length; c++)
        zm.add(zoomitems[c]);
    return zm;
}
```

3. The *Zoom* option must be added back at its original position. This code can be inserted at the end of the constructor:

```
menus[1].insert(createZoomSubmenu(),0);
```

Checkbox Menu Items

Some menus are used to select options which stay in place until deselected. For example, a menu headed *Font* might have option *Italic, Bold and Underline*. By adding these as *CheckboxMenuItem* objects, each can display a tick mark when selected as shown in FIG-14.10.

FIG-14.10

Checked Menu Items

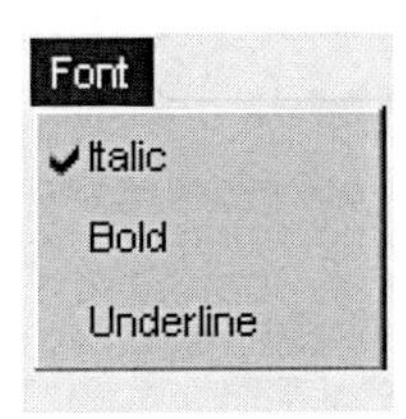

The *CheckboxMenuItem* class is defined as follows:

Constructors

CheckboxMenuItem()	Creates an empty *CheckboxMenuItem* object. Its text can be set later.
CheckboxMenuItem(String s)	Creates a *CheckboxMenuItem* object showing the text *s*.
Menu(String s, boolean b)	Creates a *CheckboxMenuItem* object showing the text *s*. If *b* is *true*, the menu item is checked.

Methods

boolean getState()	Returns *true* if the item is checked.
void setState(boolean b)	If *b* is *true* the item is checked, otherwise it is unchecked.
void addItemListener(ItemListener il)	Adds an *ItemListener* to the menu item.
void removeItemListener(ItemListener il)	Removes an *ItemListener* from the menu item.

Creating an ActionListener for Each Menu Item

So far we've linked each menu item to the same event handler. However, in a real application we'll need a separate handler for each item. For example, we could have the *Open* option of the previous programs display a *FileDialog* object and cause the *Exit* option to terminate the application.

To do this a *FileDialog* object, *fd*, is set up as an attribute of the class and the following lines added at the end of the constructor:

```
menuitems[0][0].addActionListener //Handler for open
(
    new ActionListener()
    {
        public void actionPerformed(ActionEvent ae)
        {
            fd.show();
        }
```

```
        }
);

menuitems[0][2].addActionListener // Handler for Exit
(
    new ActionListener()
    {
        public void actionPerformed(ActionEvent ae)
        {
            dispose();
            System.exit(0);
        }
    }
);
```

Activity 14.24

Return to your program which displays an image.

Add a menu with the following headings and options:

Heading	**Options**	**Submenu options**
File	*Open, Exit*	
View	*Zoom*	*50%, 100%, 200%*

Write handler for each menu option so that the task suggested by the option's text is implemented.

The *FileDialog* box should no longer open automatically, but only when Open is selected from the menu.

Creating Your Own Components

Introduction

As well as using the classes that come with the Java Development Kit, there is nothing to stop us creating our own visual component classes. As a general rule such classes are extended from the *Component* class.

In this section we'll see what's involved in doing that.

The Triangle Class

The *Triangle* class draws a simple triangular shape. It has methods to allow the colour and orientation of the triangle to be changed.

An informal definition of the class is given below:

Attributes

private int direction	The direction in which the triangle points. 0 = up; 1 = down
private Color fill	The colour used to fill the triangle.

Constructor

public Triangle create()	Creates a *Triangle* object. The orientation is up and the colour is red.

Methods

public void setDirection(int v)	Sets the direction of the triangle to *v*. If v = 0 the triangle points up, all other values of *v* make the triangle point down.
public void setColour(Color c)	Sets the triangle's colour to *c*.
public int getDirection()	Returns the current orientation of the triangle (0 = up; 1 = down).
public Color getColour()	Returns the current fill colour.
public void paint(Graphics g)	Draws the triangle.
public Dimension getPreferredSize()	Returns the width and height of the triangle.

This last routine returns the dimensions of the triangle and is called by some of the layout managers (e.g. *FlowLayout*). The method inherited from the *Component* class returns a width of 1 pixel and a height of 1 pixel.

The code for the Triangle class is given in LISTING-14.15.

LISTING-14.15

The Triangle Class

```
import java.awt.*;
import java.awt.event.*;

public class Triangle extends Component
{
      private int direction;//Direction of triangle 0=up 1=down
      private Color fill;   //Triangle's colour


   /** Creates triangle - defaults: up and red */
   public Triangle()
   {
      direction = 0;
      fill = Color.red;
   }


   /** Sets direction of triangle and redraw */
   public void setDirection(int v)
   {
      if (v==0)
         direction = 0;
      else
         direction = 1;
      repaint();
   }


   /** Sets colour of triangle and redraw */
   public void setColour(Color c)
   {
      fill=c;
      repaint();
   }


   /** Returns the direction of the triangle */
   public int getDirection()
   {
      return direction;
   }


   /** Returns the current fill colour */
   public Color getColour()
   {
      return fill;
   }


   /** Returns the dimensions of triangle */
   public Dimension getPreferredSize()
   {
      return new Dimension(20,20);
   }


   /** Draw triangle in specified colour and direction */
   public void paint(Graphics g)
   {
      g.setColor(fill);
      if(direction==0)
         g.fillPolygon(new int[]{0,20,10,0},
         ⇨new int[]{0,0,18,0},4);
      else
         g.fillPolygon(new int[]{0,20,10,0},
         ⇨new int[] {18,18,0,18},4);
   }
}
```

Activity 14.25

Type in and compile the *Triangle* class.

Create an application with a button, triangle and three radio buttons.

The button, when pressed should change the orientation of the triangle.

The radio buttons should be labelled red, green and blue. These should be used to select the triangle's colour.

Activity 14.26

Create a *Dice* class component. The definition of the class is

Attributes:

int value	(value showing on die 1 - 6)
Color facecolour	(Die body colour)
Color spotcolour	(Die spot colour)
int size	(Width and height of die in pixels)

Operations:

Dice create()	Creates a *Dice* object. The object is red with white spots and shows a random value (1 - 6). The die should be 100 pixels square.
void roll()	Randomly changes *value* (1 to 6)
void setFaceColour(Color c)	Sets *facecolour* to colour *c*.
void setSpotColour(Color c)	Sets *spotcolour* to colour *c*.
void setDieSize(int v)	Sets dimensions of die to *v* (must be 20 to 200)
int getValue()	Returns *value*
int getDieSize()	Returns *size*
Color getFaceColour()	Returns *facecolour*
Color getSpotColour()	Returns *spotcolour*

Overridden Methods:

void paint(Graphics g)	Draws die according to its attributes.
Dimension getPreferredSize()	Returns the *size* attribute for both width and height.
String toString()	Returns *value* as a string.

Create an application which tests the various features of the *Dice* class.

Solutions

Activity 14.1

The button is assigned the name *button0*.

Activity 14.2

The code for *main()* should be changed to

```
public static void main(String args[])
{
    Act14_02 fm = new Act14_02("Testing");
    fm.setName("my window");
    fm.setLayout(new FlowLayout());
    fm.setSize(100,200);
    fm.show();
    System.out.println(fm.getName());
}
```

Activity 14.3

Since the button is added to the frame, it is the parent of the button. Hence, the term

my window

would be displayed.

Activity 14.4

```
import java.awt.*;

public class Act14_04 extends Frame
{
    private Label lab1 =
    ↳new Label("This is a label");
    public Act14_04(String s)
    {
        super(s);
        add(lab1);
    }
    public static void main(String args[])
    {
        Act14_04 fm = new Act14_04("Testing");
        fm.setLayout(new FlowLayout());
        fm.setSize(200,100);
        fm.setBackground(Color.gray);
        fm.show();
        fm.lab1.setForeground(Color.red);
        fm.lab1.setBackground(Color.yellow);
    }
}
```

Activity 14.5

Although the program seems to ignore the instruction to resize the button, this does come into effect when the window is resized.

Activity 14.6

```
import java.awt.*;
import java.awt.event.*;

public class Act14_06 extends Frame
↳implements ActionListener
{
    private Button but1 =
    ↳new Button("Press here");

    public Act14_06(String s)
    {
        super(s);
        but1.addActionListener(this);
        add(but1);
    }
    public void actionPerformed(ActionEvent ae)
    {
        Point p = getLocation();
        p.translate(50,80);
        setLocation(p);
        System.out.println(getLocation());
    }

    public static void main(String args[])
    {
        Act14_06 fm = new Act14_06("Testing");
        fm.setLayout(new FlowLayout());
        fm.setSize(200,150);
        fm.show();
    }
}
```

Activity 14.7

The text is too large for the button.

Resizing solves the problem as the button takes on an more appropriate size.

Activity 14.8

The button resizes to accommodate the text at the start of the program without the need for resizing.

Activity 14.9

No solution required.

Activity 14.10

```
import java.awt.*;

public class Act14_10 extends Frame
{
    NewCanvas c1 = new NewCanvas();

    private class NewCanvas extends Canvas
    {
        NewCanvas(){};
        public void paint(Graphics g)
        {
            g.setColor(Color.red);
            g.fillRect(0,0,90,90);
            g.setColor(Color.white);
            g.fillOval(0,0,30,30);
            g.fillOval(60,0,30,30);
            g.fillOval(30,30,30,30);
            g.fillOval(0,60,30,30);
            g.fillOval(60,60,30,30);
        }
    }
    public Act14_10(String s)
    {
        super(s);
        c1.setSize(300,300);
        add(c1);
    }

    public static void main(String args[])
    {
        Act14_10 fm = new Act14_10("Testing");
        fm.setSize(300,300);
        fm.show();
    }
}
```

Activity 14.11

```
import java.awt.*;

public class Act14_11 extends Frame
{
    private Button but1 = new Button("Press here");
    private Window w;
```

```
        private Window w2;

        public Act14_11(String s)
        {
            w = new Window(this);
            w.setLayout(new FlowLayout());
            w.setBounds(30,30,100,50);
            w.setBackground(Color.green);
            w.add(but1);
            w.setVisible(true);
            w2 = new Window(this);
            w2.setBounds(50,50,100,50);
            w2.setBackground(Color.red);
            w2.setVisible(true);
        }

        public static void main(String args[])
        {
            Act14_11 fm = new Act14_11("Testing");
            fm.setLayout(new FlowLayout());
            fm.setSize(200,150);
            fm.show();
        }
    }
```

Activity 14.12

No solution required.

Activity 14.13

```
import java.awt.*;
public class Act14_13 extends Frame
{
    ImageCanvas ic;

    private class ImageCanvas extends Canvas
    {
        Image ex;
        public ImageCanvas(String s)
        {
            ex = Toolkit.getDefaultToolkit().
            ↳getImage(s);
        }

        public void paint(Graphics g)
        {
            g.drawImage(ex,0,0,this);
        }
    }

    public Act14_13(String s1, String s2)
    {
        super(s1);
        ic = new ImageCanvas(s2);
        add(ic);
    }

    public static void main(String args[])
    {
        if(args.length == 0)
        {
            System.out.println
            ↳("Need image file name");
            System.exit(0);
        }
        Act14_13 fm =
        ↳new Act14_13("Images", args[0]);
        fm.setBounds(200,200,500,500);
        fm.show();
    }
}
```

Activity 14.14

No solution required.

Activity 14.15

No solution required.

Activity 14.16

No solution required.

Activity 14.17

```
import java.awt.*;
import java.awt.event.*;

public class Act14_17 extends Frame
↳implements ActionListener
{
    ScrollPane sp =
    ↳new ScrollPane(ScrollPane.SCROLLBARS_ALWAYS);
    ImageCanvas ic;
    Panel options = new Panel();
    Button zoom = new Button("Zoom In");
    Button zoomout = new Button("Zoom Out");
    int newWidth, newHeight;

    private class ImageCanvas extends Canvas
    {
        Image ex;
        MediaTracker md;

        public ImageCanvas()
        {

            md = new MediaTracker(this);
            ex = Toolkit.getDefaultToolkit().
            ↳createImage("photo2.jpg");
            md.addImage(ex,0);
            try{md.waitForID(0);}
            catch(InterruptedException ie){}
            newWidth = ex.getWidth(this);
            newHeight = ex.getHeight(this);
            setSize(newWidth, newHeight);
        }

        public void paint(Graphics g)
        {
            g.drawImage(ex,0,0,newWidth,
            ↳newHeight,this);
        }
    }


    private class WindowHandler
    ↳extends WindowAdapter
    {
        public void windowClosing(WindowEvent we)
        {
            we.getWindow().hide();
            System.exit(0);
        }
    }

    public Act14_17(String s)
    {
        super(s);
        addWindowListener(new WindowHandler());
        ic = new ImageCanvas();
        sp.add(ic);
        zoom.addActionListener(this);
        zoomout.addActionListener(this);
        options.add(zoom);
        options.add(zoomout);
        add("West",options);
        add("Center",sp);
    }

    public void actionPerformed(ActionEvent ae)
    {
        if(ae.getSource()==zoom)
        {
            newWidth *=2;
            newHeight *=2;
        }
        else
        {
            newWidth /=2;
            newHeight /= 2;
        }
        ic.setSize(newWidth, newHeight);
        repaint();
        validate();
    }

    public static void main(String args[])
    {
        Act14_17 fm = new Act14_17("Images");
        fm.setBounds(200,200,500,500);
        fm.setMenuBar(new MenuBar());
        fm.show();
    }
}
```

Activity 14.18

```
import java.awt.*;
import java.awt.event.*;

public class Act14_18 extends Frame
↳implements ActionListener
{
    ScrollPane sp =
    ↳new ScrollPane(ScrollPane.SCROLLBARS_ALWAYS);
    ImageCanvas ic;
    Panel options = new Panel();
    Button zoom = new Button("Zoom In");
    Button zoomout = new Button("Zoom Out");
    int newWidth, newHeight;
    CloseDialog cl;

    private class ImageCanvas extends Canvas
    {
        Image ex;
        MediaTracker md;

        public ImageCanvas()
        {

            md = new MediaTracker(this);
            ex = Toolkit.getDefaultToolkit().
            ↳createImage("wall6.jpg");
            md.addImage(ex,0);
            try{md.waitForID(0);}
            catch(InterruptedException ie){}
            newWidth = ex.getWidth(this);
            newHeight = ex.getHeight(this);
            setSize(newWidth, newHeight);
        }

        public void paint(Graphics g)
        {
            g.drawImage(ex,0,0,newWidth,
            ↳newHeight,this);
        }
    }

    private class CloseDialog
    ↳extends Dialog implements ActionListener
    {
        Button yes = new Button("Yes");
        Button no = new Button("No");
        Label lab1 = new Label
        ↳("Terminate program?");

        CloseDialog(Frame c)
        {
            super(c,"Closing Application",true);
            setLayout(new FlowLayout());
            addWindowListener(new WindowHandler());
            add(lab1);
            yes.addActionListener(this);
            no.addActionListener(this);
            add(yes);
            add(no);
            setSize(150,90);
        }

        public void actionPerformed(ActionEvent ae)
        {
            hide();
            dispose();
            if(((Button)ae.getSource())==yes)
            {
                dispose();
                System.exit(0);
            }
        }
    }


    private class WindowHandler
    ↳extends WindowAdapter
    {
        public void windowClosing(WindowEvent we)
        {
            cl = new CloseDialog(
            ↳(Frame)we.getSource());
            Point p = getLocationOnScreen();
            cl.setLocation(p.x+50, p.y+50);
            cl.show();
        }
    }

    public Act14_18(String s)
    {
        super(s);
        addWindowListener(new WindowHandler());
        ic = new ImageCanvas();
        sp.add(ic);
        zoom.addActionListener(this);
        zoomout.addActionListener(this);
        options.add(zoom);
        options.add(zoomout);
        add("West",options);
        add("Center",sp);
    }

    public void actionPerformed(ActionEvent ae)
    {
        if(ae.getSource()==zoom)
        {
            newWidth *=2;
            newHeight *=2;
        }
        else
        {
            newWidth /=2;
            newHeight /= 2;
        }
        ic.setSize(newWidth, newHeight);
        repaint();
        validate();
    }

    public static void main(String args[])
    {
        Act14_18 fm = new Act14_18("Images");
        fm.setBounds(200,200,500,500);
        fm.setMenuBar(new MenuBar());
        fm.show();
    }
}
```

Activity 14.19

```
import java.awt.*;
import java.awt.event.*;

public class Act14_19 extends Frame
↳implements ActionListener
{
    ScrollPane sp =
    ↳new ScrollPane(ScrollPane.SCROLLBARS_ALWAYS);
    ImageCanvas ic;
    Panel options = new Panel();
    Button zoom = new Button("Zoom In");
    Button zoomout = new Button("Zoom Out");
    int newWidth, newHeight;
    FileDialog fd;
    CloseDialog cl;

    private class ImageCanvas extends Canvas
    {
        Image ex;

        public ImageCanvas()
        {
            loadImage("wall6.jpg");
        }

        public void loadImage(String s)
        {
            MediaTracker md;
            md = new MediaTracker(this);
            ex = Toolkit.getDefaultToolkit().
            ↳createImage(s);
            md.addImage(ex,0);
            try{md.waitForID(0);}
            catch(InterruptedException ie){}
            newWidth = ex.getWidth(this);
            newHeight = ex.getHeight(this);
            setSize(newWidth, newHeight);
            repaint();
        }

        public void paint(Graphics g)
        {
            g.drawImage
            ↳(ex,0,0,newWidth, newHeight,this);
        }
    }

    private class CloseDialog
    ↳extends Dialog implements ActionListener
    {
        Button yes = new Button("Yes");
        Button no = new Button("No");
        Label lab1 = new Label
        ↳("Terminate program?");
        CloseDialog(Frame c)
        {
            super(c,"Closing Application",true);
            setLayout(new FlowLayout());
            addWindowListener(new WindowHandler());
```

```
            add(lab1);
            yes.addActionListener(this);
            no.addActionListener(this);
            add(yes);
            add(no);
            setSize(150,90);
        }

        public void actionPerformed
        ↳(ActionEvent ae)
        {
            hide();
            dispose();
            if (((Button)ae.getSource())==yes)
            {
                dispose();
                System.exit(0);
            }
        }
    }

    private class WindowHandler
    ↳extends WindowAdapter
    {
        public void windowClosing(WindowEvent we)
        {
            cl = new CloseDialog((Frame)we.
            ↳getSource());
            Point p = getLocationOnScreen();
            cl.setLocation(p.x+50, p.y+50);
            cl.show();
        }
    }

    public Act14_19(String s)
    {
        super(s);
        addWindowListener(new WindowHandler());
        ic = new ImageCanvas();
        sp.add(ic);
        zoom.addActionListener(this);
        zoomout.addActionListener(this);
        options.add(zoom);
        options.add(zoomout);
        add("West",options);
        add("Center",sp);
        fd = new FileDialog(this,"Load File");
    }

    public void actionPerformed(ActionEvent ae)
    {
        if(ae.getSource()==zoom)
        {
            newWidth *= 2;
            newHeight *= 2;
        }
        else
        {
            newWidth /= 2;
            newHeight /= 2;
        }
        ic.setSize(newWidth, newHeight);
        repaint();
        validate();
    }

    public static void main(String args[])
    {
        Act14_19 fm = new Act14_19("Images");
        fm.setBounds(200,200,500,500);
        fm.setMenuBar(new MenuBar());
        fm.show();
        fm.fd.show();
        String filename;
        if ((filename = fm.fd.getFile()) != null)
            fm.ic.loadImage
            ↳(fm.fd.getDirectory()+filename);
        System.out.println
        ↳(fm.fd.getDirectory()+filename);
    }
}
```

Activity 14.20

No solution required.

Activity 14.21

No solution required.

Activity 14.22

No solution required.

Activity 14.23

```
import java.awt.*;
import java.awt.event.*;

public class Act14_23 extends Frame
↳implements ActionListener
{
    private Label labA = new Label("Menu Option");
    private MenuBar mb = new MenuBar();
    private Menu menus[] = {new Menu("File"),
    ↳new Menu("View")};
    private MenuItem menuitems[][] =
    ↳{{new MenuItem("Open",new MenuShortcut('O'))
    ↳,new MenuItem("Save",new MenuShortcut('S'))
    ↳, new MenuItem("Exit",new MenuShortcut('Q'))},
    ↳{new MenuItem("Zoom",new MenuShortcut('Z'))
    ↳,new MenuItem("Negative",new MenuShortcut('N')),
    ↳new MenuItem("Black & White",
    ↳new MenuShortcut('B'))
    ↳}};
    FileDialog fd =
    ↳new FileDialog(this,"Load File");

    public Act14_23(String s)
    {
        super(s);
        setLayout(new FlowLayout());
        addWindowListener(new WindowHandler());
        add(labA);
        setMenuBar(mb);
        for(int c = 0; c < menus.length; c++)
            mb.add(menus[c]);
        for(int c = 0; c < menus.length; c++)
            for(int j = 0; j < menuitems[c].length;
            ↳ j++)
            {
                menus[c].add(menuitems[c][j]);
                menuitems[c][j].
                ↳addActionListener(this);
            }
        menus[0].insertSeparator(2);
    }

    class WindowHandler extends WindowAdapter
    {
        public void windowClosing(WindowEvent we)
        {
            dispose();
            System.exit(0);
        }
    }

    public void actionPerformed(ActionEvent e)
    {
        labA.setText(((MenuItem)e.getSource()).
        ↳getLabel());
    }

    public static void main(String args[])
    {
        Act14_23 fm = new Act14_23("Starting GUI");
        fm.setSize(300,100);
        fm.show();
    }
}
```

Activity 14.24

```
import java.awt.*;
import java.awt.event.*;

public class Act14_24 extends Frame
↳implements ActionListener
{
    ScrollPane sp =
    ↳new ScrollPane(ScrollPane.SCROLLBARS_ALWAYS);
    ImageCanvas ic;
    int originalWidth, originalHeight;
    int newWidth, newHeight;
    FileDialog fd;
    CloseDialog cl;
    private MenuBar mb = new MenuBar();
    private Menu menus[] = {new Menu("File"),
    ↳new Menu("View")};
```

```
private MenuItem menuitems[] =
↳{new MenuItem("Open"),new MenuItem("Exit")};
private MenuItem zoomitems[]=
↳{new MenuItem("50%"),new MenuItem("100%"),
↳new MenuItem("200%")};

private Menu createZoomSubmenu()
{
    Menu zm = new Menu("zoom");
    for(int c = 0; c < zoomitems.length; c++)
    {
        zoomitems[c].addActionListener(this);
        zm.add(zoomitems[c]);
    }
    return zm;
}

public void actionPerformed(ActionEvent ae)
{
    if(ae.getSource()==zoomitems[0])
    {
        newWidth = originalWidth / 2;
        newHeight = originalHeight / 2;
    }
    else if(ae.getSource() == zoomitems[1])
    {
        newWidth  = originalWidth;
        newHeight = originalHeight;
    }
    else
    {
        newWidth  = originalWidth*2;
        newHeight = originalHeight*2;
    }
    ic.setSize(newWidth, newHeight);
    repaint();
    validate();
}

public Act14_24(String s)
{
    super(s);
    addWindowListener(new WindowHandler());
    setMenuBar(mb);
    for(int c = 0; c < menus.length; c++)
        mb.add(menus[c]);
    for(int c = 0; c < menuitems.length; c++)
            menus[0].add(menuitems[c]);
    ic = new ImageCanvas();
    sp.add(ic);
    add("Center",sp);
    fd = new FileDialog(this,"Load File");
    menus[1].insert(createZoomSubmenu(),0);
    menuitems[0].addActionListener
    (
        new ActionListener()
        {
            public void actionPerformed
            ↳(ActionEvent ae)
            {
                String filename;
                fd.show();
                if ((filename = fd.getFile())
                ↳!= null)
                    ic.loadImage(fd.
                    ↳getDirectory()+filename);
                ic.setSize(newWidth,newHeight);
                ic.validate();
            }
        }
    );
    menuitems[1].addActionListener
    (
        new ActionListener()
        {
            public void actionPerformed
            ↳(ActionEvent ae)
            {
                dispose();
                System.exit(0);
            }
        }
    );
}

public static void main(String args[])
{
    Act14_24 fm = new Act14_24("Images");
    fm.setBounds(200,200,500,500);
    fm.show();
}

private class ImageCanvas extends Canvas
{
    Image ex;

    public void loadImage(String s)
    {
        MediaTracker md;
        md = new MediaTracker(this);
        ex = Toolkit.getDefaultToolkit().
        ↳createImage(s);
        md.addImage(ex,0);
        try{md.waitForID(0);}
        catch(InterruptedException ie){}
        newWidth = originalWidth =
        ↳ex.getWidth(this);
        newHeight = originalHeight =
        ↳ex.getHeight(this);
        setSize(newWidth, newHeight);
    }

    public void paint(Graphics g)
    {
        g.drawImage(ex,0,0,newWidth,
        ↳newHeight,this);
    }
}

private class CloseDialog extends Dialog
↳implements ActionListener
{
    Button yes = new Button("Yes");
    Button no = new Button("No");
    Label lab1 = new Label
    ↳("Terminate program?");

    public CloseDialog(Frame c)
    {
        super(c,"Closing Application",true);
        setLayout(new FlowLayout());
        addWindowListener(new WindowHandler());
        add(lab1);
        yes.addActionListener(this);
        no.addActionListener(this);
        add(yes);
        add(no);
        setSize(150,90);
    }

    public void actionPerformed(ActionEvent ae)
    {
        hide();
        dispose();
        if(((Button)ae.getSource()) == yes)
        {
            dispose();
            System.exit(0);
        }
    }
}

private class WindowHandler
↳extends WindowAdapter
{
    public void windowClosing(WindowEvent we)
    {
        cl =new CloseDialog
        ↳((Frame)we.getSource());
        Point p = getLocationOnScreen();
        cl.setLocation(p.x+50, p.y+50);
        cl.show();
    }
}
}
```

Activity 14.25

```
import java.awt.*;
public class Act14_25 extends Frame
↳implements ActionListener,ItemListener
{
    Button b1 = new Button("Flip triangle");
    Triangle t1 = new Triangle();
    CheckboxGroup gr = new CheckboxGroup();
    Checkbox cb1 = new Checkbox("red",gr,true);
    Checkbox cb2 = new Checkbox("green",gr,false);
    Checkbox cb3 = new Checkbox("blue",gr,false);

    public Act14_25(String s)
    {
        super(s);
        setLayout(new FlowLayout());
        b1.addActionListener(this);
        cb1.addItemListener(this);
        cb2.addItemListener(this);
        cb3.addItemListener(this);
        add(b1);
        add(t1);
        add(cb1);
        add(cb2);
        add(cb3);
    }
```

```
    public void actionPerformed(ActionEvent e)
    {
        t1.setDirection(1-t1.getDirection());
    }

    public void itemStateChanged(ItemEvent e)
    {
        if(e.getSource()==cb1)
            t1.setColour(Color.red);
        else if(e.getSource()==cb2)
            t1.setColour(Color.green);
        else
            t1.setColour(Color.blue);
    }

    public static void main(String args[])
    {
        Act14_25 fm = new Act14_25("Triangle");
        fm.setBounds(200,200,500,500);
        fm.show();
    }
}
```

Activity 14.26

Code for *Dice* class:

```
import java.awt.*;

public class Dice extends Component
{
    private int value;
    private Color facecolour;
    private Color spotcolour;
    private int size;

    public Dice()
    {
        size = 100;
        value = (int)(Math.random()*6) + 1;
        facecolour = Color.red;
        spotcolour = Color.white;
    }

    public void roll()
    {
        value = (int)(Math.random()*6) + 1;
        repaint();
    }

    public void setFaceColour(Color c)
    {
        facecolour = c;
        repaint();
    }

    public void setSpotColour(Color c)
    {
        spotcolour = c;
        repaint();
    }

    public void setDieSize(int v)
    {
        if(v < 20 || v > 200)
            return;
        size = v;
        repaint();
    }

    public int getDieSize()
    {
        return size;
    }

    public int getValue()
    {
        return value;
    }

    public Color getFaceColour()
    {
        return facecolour;
    }

    public Color getSpotColour()
    {
        return spotcolour;
    }

    public String toString()
    {
        return (""+value);
    }

    public Dimension getPreferredSize()
    {
        return new Dimension(size,size);
    }

    public void paint(Graphics g)
    {
        g.setColor(facecolour);
        g.fillRect(0,0,size,size);
        g.setColor(spotcolour);
        int a = (int)(size/3);
        switch (value)
        {
            case 1: g.fillOval(a,a,a,a);
                    break;
            case 2: g.fillOval(0,0,a,a);
                    g.fillOval(2*a,2*a,a,a);
                    break;
            case 3: g.fillOval(0,0,a,a);
                    g.fillOval(2*a,2*a,a,a);
                    g.fillOval(a,a,a,a);
                    break;
            case 4: g.fillOval(0,0,a,a);
                    g.fillOval(2*a,2*a,a,a);
                    g.fillOval(2*a,0,a,a);
                    g.fillOval(0,2*a,a,a);
                    break;
            case 5: g.fillOval(0,0,a,a);
                    g.fillOval(2*a,2*a,a,a);
                    g.fillOval(2*a,0,a,a);
                    g.fillOval(0,2*a,a,a);
                    g.fillOval(a,a,a,a);
                    break;
            case 6: g.fillOval(0,0,a,a);
                    g.fillOval(2*a,2*a,a,a);
                    g.fillOval(2*a,0,a,a);
                    g.fillOval(0,2*a,a,a);
                    g.fillOval(0,a,a,a);
                    g.fillOval(2*a,a,a,a);
                    break;
        }
    }
}
```

The test application:

```
import java.awt.*;
import java.awt.event.*;
import Dice;

public class Act14_26 extends Frame implements
AdjustmentListener
{
    private Dice die = new Dice();
    private Button roll = new Button("Roll");
    private Label thrown = new Label(" XX");
    private Scrollbar size =
    ↳new Scrollbar(Scrollbar.HORIZONTAL,0,10,20,
    ↳210);
    private CheckboxGroup facecolours =
    ↳new CheckboxGroup();
    private CheckboxGroup spotcolours =
    ↳new CheckboxGroup();
    private Checkbox facecol[] =
    ↳{new Checkbox("Red",facecolours,true),
    ↳new Checkbox("Blue",facecolours,false),
    ↳new Checkbox("Green",facecolours,false)};
    private Checkbox spotcol[] =
    ↳{new Checkbox("White",spotcolours,true),
    ↳new Checkbox("Yellow",spotcolours,false),
    ↳new Checkbox("Black",spotcolours,false)};
    public Act14_26(String s)
    {
        super(s);
        setLayout(new FlowLayout());
        addWindowListener(new WindowHandler());
        add(die);
        add(roll);
        add(thrown);
        for(int c = 0; c< facecol.length ; c++)
        {
            add(facecol[c]);
            facecol[c].addItemListener
            ↳(new FaceHandler());
        }
        for(int c = 0; c< spotcol.length ; c++)
        {
            add(spotcol[c]);
            spotcol[c].addItemListener
            ↳(new SpotHandler());
        }
        add(size);
        size.addAdjustmentListener(this);
        roll.addActionListener
```

```
            (
                new ActionListener()

                {
                    public void actionPerformed
                    ↳(ActionEvent ae)
                    {
                        die.roll();
                        thrown.setText(die.toString());
                    }
                }
            );
        }

        public void adjustmentValueChanged
        ↳(AdjustmentEvent ae)
        {
            die.setDieSize(ae.getValue());
            if(die.getDieSize()>90)
            {
                die.invalidate();
                die.getParent().validate();
            }
        }

        public static void main(String args[])
        {
            Act14_26 fm = new Act14_26("Dice");
            fm.setSize(220,220);
            fm.show();
        }

        class WindowHandler extends WindowAdapter
        {
            public void windowClosing(WindowEvent we)
            {
                we.getWindow().hide();
                System.exit(0);
            }
        }

        class SpotHandler implements ItemListener
        {
            public void itemStateChanged(ItemEvent ie)
            {
                Checkbox temp = (Checkbox)ie.getSource();
                if(temp == spotcol[0])
                    die.setSpotColour(Color.white);
                else if(temp == spotcol[1])
                    die.setSpotColour(Color.yellow);
                else
                    die.setSpotColour(Color.black);
            }
        }

        class FaceHandler implements ItemListener
        {
            public void itemStateChanged(ItemEvent ie)
            {
                Checkbox temp = (Checkbox)ie.getSource();
                if(temp == facecol[0])
                    die.setFaceColour(Color.red);
                else if(temp == facecol[1])
                    die.setFaceColour(Color.blue);
                else
                    die.setFaceColour(Color.green);
            }
        }
    }
```

CHAPTER 15

Layout Managers

This chapter covers the following topics:

CardLayout

GridLayout

GridBagLayout

Review of BorderLayout

Review of FlowLayout

Working Without a Layout Manager

Layout Managers

Introduction

You will recall from Chapter 13 that a layout manager is responsible for positioning visual components on the screen.

Every class descended from the *Container* class is automatically associated with a layout manager. The default layout manager for a container can be overridden to allow us to make use of a different layout manager or even to eliminate their use entirely.

In Chapter 13 we made use of the *FlowLayout* and *BorderLayout* managers. In this chapter we'll review those layouts, look at two new layouts: *GridLayout* and *GridBagLayout*, and finally, see how to place components without a layout manager.

Review of BorderLayout

The program snippet below

```
public class Layouts extends Frame
{
    String position[] = {"North","South","East","West","Center"};
    Button but[] = {new Button("But1"),new Button("But2"),
    ↳new Button("But3"),new Button("But4"),new Button("But5")};

    public Layouts(String s)
    {
        super(s);
        addWindowListener(new WindowHandler());
        for(int c = 0; c < but.length; c++)
            add(position[c],but[c]);
    }
```

creates the layout shown in FIG-15.1

FIG-15.1

The Default BorderLayout

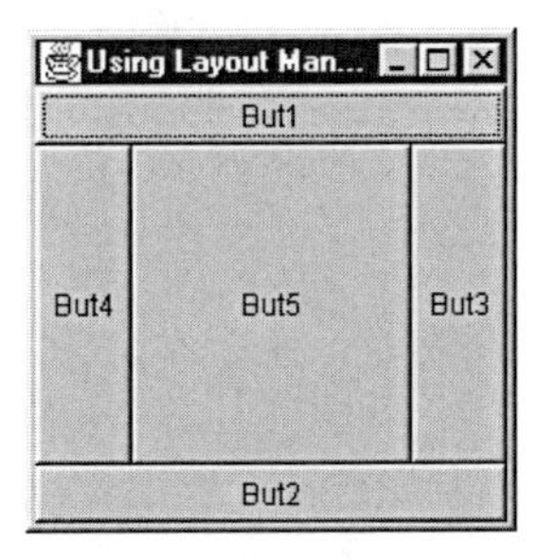

Descendants of the *Frame* class default to using the *BorderLayout* format. This offers only five positions for components. These positions are identified as *North, South, East, West* and *Center.*

Where possible the layout manager uses the preferred width value when placing the West and East components; their height is determined by the height of the frame. Preferred height values are used in placing North and South components but their width is set to fill the frame. The *Center* component's height and width is determined by the amount of space remaining when the other components have been placed. Where only a *Center* position is used, the component will fill the whole frame.

The *BorderLayout* class defines the following features

Constants

String NORTH
String SOUTH
String EAST
String WEST
String CENTER

These values can be used with the container's *add()* method.

Constructors

BorderLayout()	Creates a *BorderLayout* object.
BorderLayout(int vgap,int hgap)	Creates a *BorderLayout* object. When components are laid out a vertical gap of *vgap* pixels and a horizontal gap of *hgap* pixels is maintained between components.

By adding the line

```
setLayout(new BorderLayout(20,5));
```

to the previous example the layout shown in FIG-15.2 is obtained.

FIG-15.2

Adding Gaps to the BorderLayout

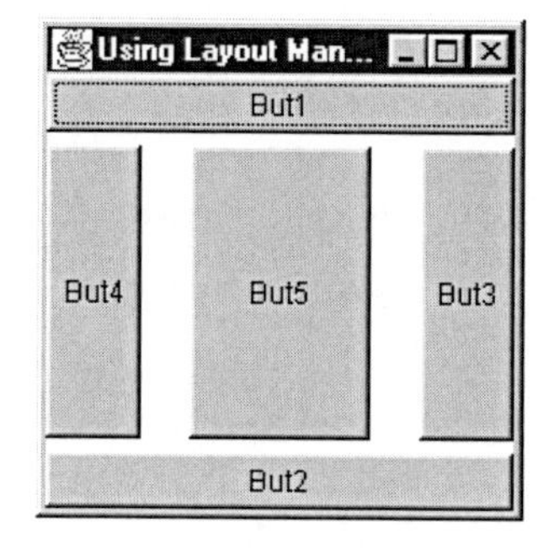

Other Methods

int getHgap()	Returns the horizontal gap setting.
void setHgap(int hgap)	Sets the horizontal gap to *hgap* pixels.
int getVgap()	Returns the vertical gap setting.
void setVgap(int vgap)	Sets the vertical gap to *vgap* pixels.

Review of FlowLayout

The *Flowlayout* manager places items one after another in rows, starting at the top of the container. When no space remains on the first row components are placed on the next row. The size of the components is taken from their preferred size.

The section of code below

```
public class Layouts extends Frame
{
    Button but[] = {new Button("But1"),new Button("But2"),
    ↳new Button("But3"), new Button("But4"), new Button("But5")};

    public Layouts(String s)
    {
        super(s);
        setLayout(new FlowLayout());
        addWindowListener(new WindowHandler());
        for(int c = 0; c < but.length; c++)
            add(but[c]);
    }
```

produces the layout shown in FIG-15.3

FIG-15.3

Default FlowLayout

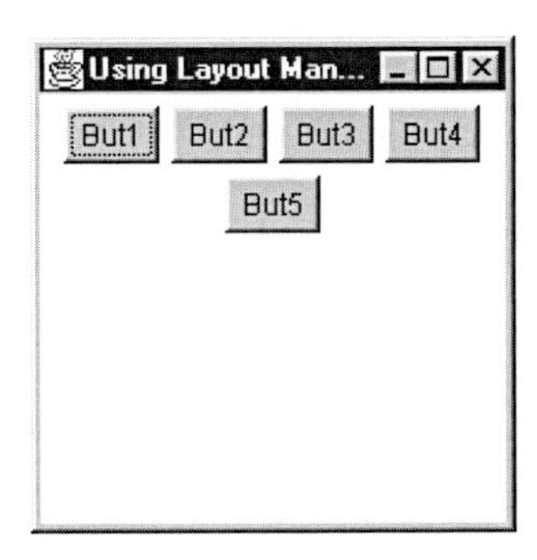

Notice from the figure that the last button is placed in the centre of the new row. This is caused by the alignment setting of the layout manager.

The main features of the *FlowLayout* class are given below:

Constants

int LEFT
int CENTER
int RIGHT

These values are used to set the alignment of the components.

Constructors

FlowLayout()	Creates a *FlowLayout* object.
FlowLayout(int align)	Creates a *FlowLayout* object. The alignment setting is defined by *align. align* should be one of the class constants shown above. The default alignment is CENTER.
FlowLayout(int align,int vgap,int hgap)	Creates a FlowLayout object with specified alignment, vertical gap and horizontal gap.

Using the line

```
setLayout(new FlowLayout(FlowLayout.LEFT));
```

to set up the layout manager gives the result shown in FIG-15.4

FIG-15.4

FlowLayout with Left Alignment

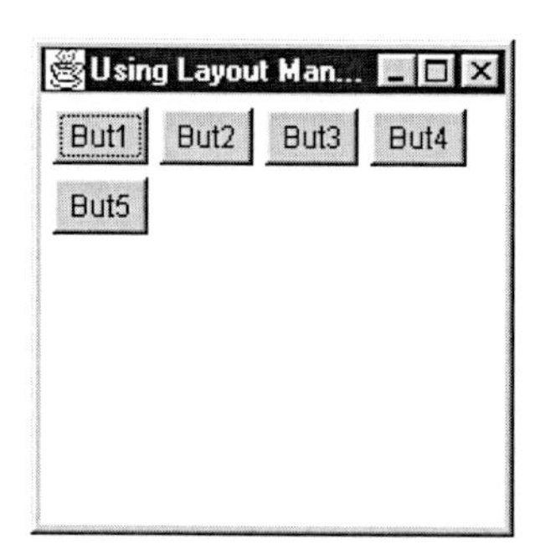

Other Methods

int getAlignment()	Returns the current alignment setting.
void setAlignment(int align)	Sets the alignment to align.
int getHgap()	Returns the horizontal gap setting.
void setHgap(int hgap)	Sets the horizontal gap to *hgap* pixels.
int getVgap()	Returns the vertical gap setting.
void setVgap(int vgap)	Sets the vertical gap to *vgap* pixels.

Using More than One Layout Manager

Since each *Container*-derived class automatically has its own layout manager and may contain components of its own, a common practice when trying to achieve specific layouts is to add a *Panel* container to the main *Frame* object and then add components to the panel. The *Panel* component defaults to using a *FlowLayout* manager.

In the following example the main *Frame* uses *BorderLayout*. A *Panel* is placed in the South location and three *Button* objects added to the panel.

```
Button but[] = {new Button("But1"),new Button("But2"),
new Button("But3")};
Panel p1 = new Panel();
public Layouts(String s)
{
    super(s);
    addWindowListener(new WindowHandler());
    add("South",p1);
    for(int c = 0; c < but.length; c++)
        p1.add(but[c]);
}
```

This gives the layout shown in FIG-15.5.

FIG-15.5

Using a Panel to Modify Layout

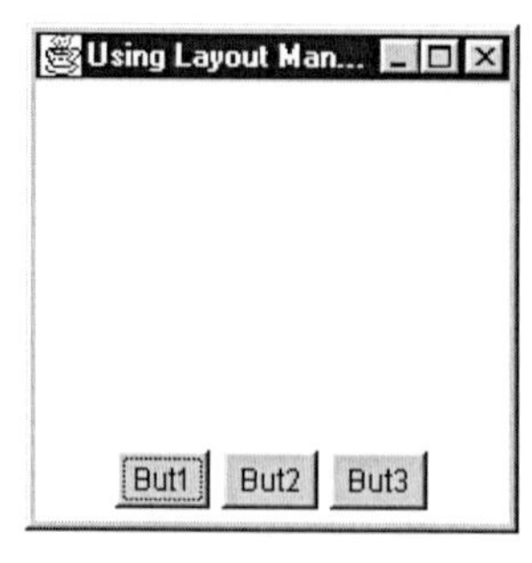

GridLayout

The *GridLayout* allows us to divide the container's area into a number of rows and columns. Each cell in this structure can then hold a component. The *add()* command adds components to each cell in turn starting at the top left cell. If you need something to be placed in the fifth cell, then it must be the fifth component added.

Cells are of equal size and components are stretched to fill the cell space.

The following code sets up five buttons in a 2 rows by 3 column grid.

```
Button but[] = {new Button("But1"),new Button("But2"),
↳new Button("But3"),new Button("But4"), new Button("But5")};

public Layouts(String s)
{
    super(s);
    setLayout(new GridLayout(2,3));
    addWindowListener(new WindowHandler());
    for(int c = 0; c < but.length; c++)
        add(but[c]);
}
```

The resulting layout is shown in FIG-15.6.

FIG-15.6

Default GridLayout Settings

One way to give the appearance of creating gaps is to add a *Canvas* object. These have no visible presence.

The following code adds a *Canvas* object before the last button:

```
Button but[] = {new Button("But1"),new Button("But2"),
↳new Button("But3"),new Button("But4"), new Button("But5")};

public Layouts(String s)
{
    super(s);
    setLayout(new GridLayout(2,3));
    addWindowListener(new WindowHandler());
    for(int c = 0; c < but.length; c++)
    {
        if(c == 4)
            add(new Canvas());
        add(but[c]);
    }
}
```

This produces the layout shown in FIG-15.7.

FIG-15.7

Adding a Canvas Object to Modify Placement

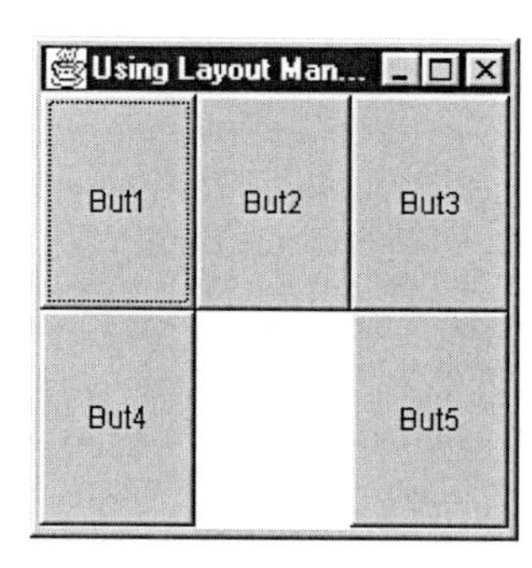

The *GridLayout* class has the following main features:

Constructors

GridLayout()	Creates a *GridLayout* object with 1 row and 1 column.
GridLayout(int rows, int cols)	Creates a *GridLayout* object with *rows* rows and *cols* columns.
GridLayout(int rows, int cols, int vgap , int hgap)	Creates a *GridLayout* object with *rows* rows and *cols* columns. There is a gap of *vgap* pixels between columns and *hgap* pixels between rows.

Other Methods

int getRows()	Returns the number of rows defined for the layout.
void setRows(int r)	Sets the number of rows to *r*.
int getColumns()	Returns the number of columns defined for the layout.
void setColumns(int c)	Sets the number of columns to *c*.
int getHgap()	Returns the horizontal gap setting.
void setHgap(int hgap)	Sets the horizontal gap to *hgap* pixels.
int getVgap()	Returns the vertical gap setting.
void setVgap(int vgap)	Sets the vertical gap to *vgap* pixels.

GridBagLayout

As the name suggests, this layout manager has some similarities to the previous one. However, this is the most complicated of the layout managers and requires some preliminary design of the layout before it can be used effectively.

It allows us to use a basic grid as before but a component may spread over several adjacent cells.

Let's assume we need to create the layout shown in FIG-15.8.

FIG-15.8

A GridBagLayout Arrangement

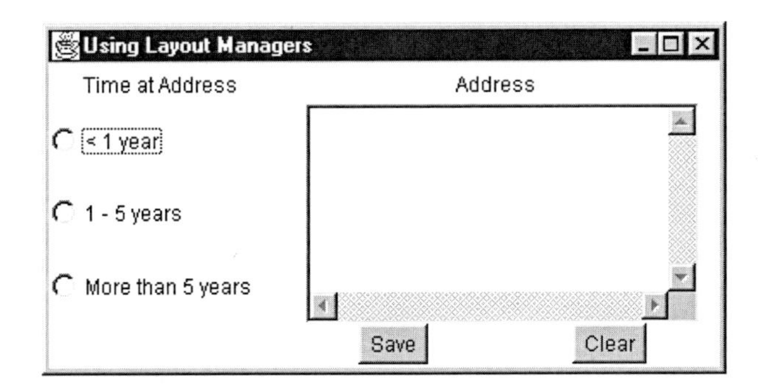

We begin by dividing the screen layout into rows and columns with a maximum of one component per cell, though one component may cover several cells. The result is shown in FIG-15.9.

FIG-15.9

Designing with a Grid

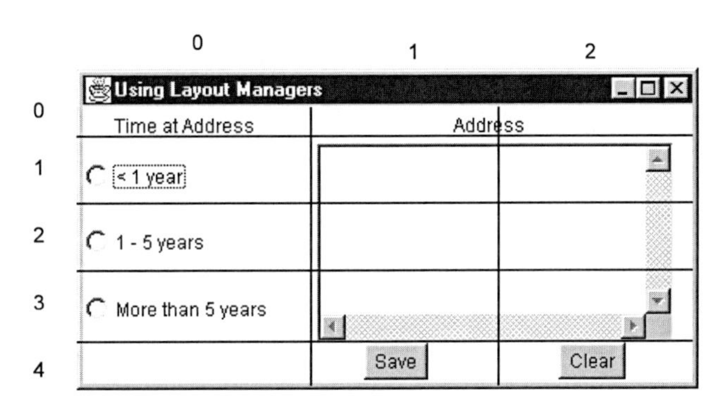

Notice that the rows and columns are numbered starting at 0. So the label "Time at Address" is in cell (0,0), while the "Clear" button is in cell (2,4). The "address" label covers two cells in the first row. The *TextArea* component is the largest covering two columns and three rows.

To demonstrate the steps required to construct this layout we'll begin using only *Button* components and replace these with the *Label, CheckButton* and *TextArea* components later, after we have mastered the use of this new layout manager.

We can start by declaring all the buttons we require:

```
Button but[] = {new Button("But1"),new Button("But2"),
new Button("But3"),new Button("But4"),new Button("But5"),
new Button("But6"),new Button("But7"),new Button("But8")};
```

In the constructor we need to state that we intend to use a *GridBagLayout*. However, rather than use the instruction

```
setLayout(new GridBagLayout());
```

we'll create a named *GridBagLayout* object

```
GridBagLayout layoutused = new GridBagLayout();
```

and then use that as the argument to *setLayout()*:

```
setLayout(layoutused);
```

Notice that the number of rows and columns is not given in the constructor. Instead, this is calculated automatically as we add components.

The GridBagConstraints Class

Next we need to create a *GridBagConstraints* object. This object is used to deliver information to the layout manager about the placement and size of a component.

It has several public attributes which we need to set. These are:

int gridx	Gives the column in which the component is to be placed.
int gridy	Gives the row in which the component is to be placed.
int gridwidth	Gives the number of columns the component is to be stretched over.
int gridheight	Gives the number of rows the component is to be stretched over.
double weightx	Determines the column width.
double *weighty*	Determines the row height.
int fill	Determines how the component expands to fill the cell.
int anchor	Determines the position of the component within a cell.

We need to create the object

```
GridBagConstraints gbc = new GridBagConstraints();
```

set its values as required. For the first button these will be:

```
gbc.gridx = 0;          //*** Placed in cell (0,0)
gbc.gridy = 0;
gbc.gridwidth = 1;      //*** Covers 1 column, 1 row
gbc.gridheight = 1;
gbc.weightx = 100;      //*** Cell column and row dimensions
gbc.weighty = 100;
```

Now the first component and its constraints are made known to the layout manager with the statement

```
layoutused.setConstraints(but[0],gbc);
```

and finally, the component can be added to the *Frame* container:

```
add(but[0]);
```

All of this has to be repeated for each component in turn. Rather than produce highly duplicated code we'll set up the constraints for each component in an array:

```
int compdetails[][]={{0,0,1,1},{1,0,2,1},{0,1,1,1},{0,2,1,1},
↳{0,3,1,1},{1,1,2,3},{1,4,1,1},{2,4,1,1}};
```

Next we'll create a helper routine to fill the *GridBagConstraints* object with details from the array:

```
private void setComponentConstraints(GridBagConstraints gbc,
↳int d[])
{
    gbc.gridx = d[0];
    gbc.gridy = d[1];
    gbc.gridwidth = d[2];
    gbc.gridheight = d[3];
    gbc.weightx = 100;
    gbc.weighty = 100;
}
```

Finally, the whole of the placement code is written:

```
int compdetails[][]={{0,0,1,1},{1,0,2,1},{0,1,1,1},{0,2,1,1},
↳{0,3,1,1},{1,1,2,3},{1,4,1,1},{2,4,1,1}};
Button but[] = {new Button("But1"),new Button("But2"),
↳new Button("But3"),new Button("But4"),new Button("But5"),
↳new Button("But6"),new Button("But7"),new Button("But8")};

private void setComponentConstraints(GridBagConstraints gbc,
↳int d[])
{
    gbc.gridx = d[0];
    gbc.gridy = d[1];
    gbc.gridwidth = d[2];
    gbc.gridheight = d[3];
    gbc.weightx = 100;
    gbc.weighty = 100;
}

public ButOnly(String s)
{
    super(s);
    GridBagLayout layoutused = new GridBagLayout();
    setLayout(layoutused);
    GridBagConstraints gbc = new GridBagConstraints();
    for(int c = 0; c <= 7; c++)
    {
        setComponentConstraints(gbc, compdetails[c]);
        layoutused.setConstraints(but[c],gbc);
        add(but[c]);
    }
    addWindowListener(new WindowHandler());
}
```

This produces the layout shown in FIG-15.10.

FIG-15.10

Creating the GridBagLayout

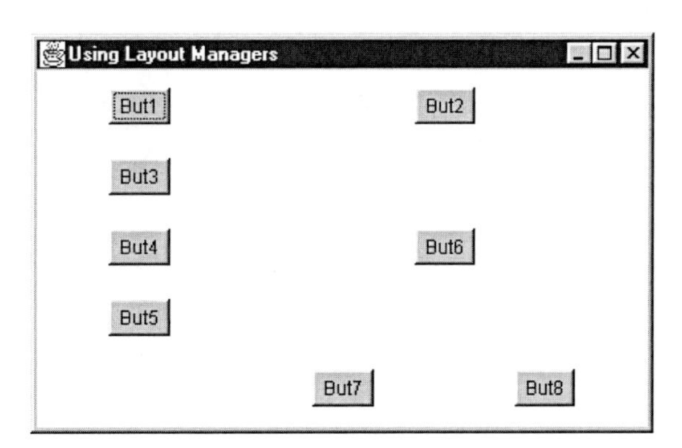

The buttons in the display are sized according to their preferred size.

fill

The fill attribute of the *GridBagConstraints* class has four possible values. These are

NONE	The components take on their preferred size. This is the default value.
BOTH	The component expands to fill the whole cell.
HORIZONTAL	The component's width expands to fill the cell, but height remains at the preferred size.
VERTICAL	The component's height expands to fill the cell, but its width remains at the preferred size.

Adding the line

```
gbc.fill = gbc.BOTH;
```

results in a new look to the application shown in FIG-15.11.

FIG-15.11

The *fill* Attribute set to BOTH

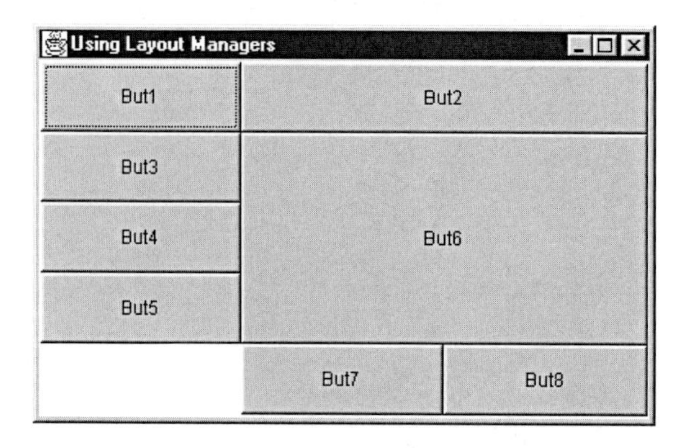

anchor

If a component does not fill its cell, then its position within that cell is determined by the value of the the *GridBagConstraints* 's *anchor* attribute.

This has nine possible values defined as named constants within the class. These are shown in FIG-15.12.

FIG-15.12

Cell Position Names

Cell

NORTHWEST	NORTH	NORTHEAST
WEST	CENTER	EAST
SOUTHWEST	SOUTH	SOUTHEAST

So if we change *But8* back to its original size and place it in the NORTHEAST position with the statements

```
gbc.fill = gbc.NONE;
gbc.anchor = gbc.NORTHEAST;
```

the layout produced is shown in FIG-15.13.

FIG-15.13

Positioning Within a Cell

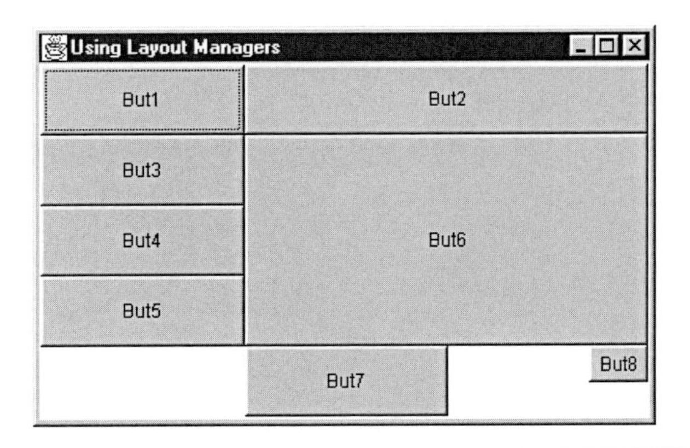

> **Activity 15.1**
>
> Create the layout of components shown in FIG-15.8.

Cell Dimensions

The *weightx* and *weighty* attributes of the *GridBagConstraints* object determines the width and height of rows and columns.

The complete width and height of the application is determined by the *setSize()* inherited from the *Frame* class. The *GridBagLayout* manager then has to divide this into rows and columns. The number of rows and columns can be calculated from the position stated for each component and the number of cells it spans (details given in the *gridx, gridy, gridwidth* and *gridheight* attributes). The width of a column is determined by the following formula:

```
largest weightx value in that column / sum of largest weightx
values in each column * width of the frame
```

In our example every cell had a weightx value of 100, and there were three columns in a frame 400 pixels wide. Applying these figures to the formula we can calculate that column one should have a width of

```
100/300*400
= 133 pixels
```

> **Activity 15.2**
>
> What effect would changing the *weightx* value for *But1, But3* and *But4* to zero make to the width of the first column?

> **Activity 15.3**
>
> How could we make column one have a width of approximately 25% of the frame width?

If every component in a column has its *weightx* value set to zero, the column won't disappear. Rather its width will be determined by the value returned by the *getMinimumSize()* of the largest component in that column.

CardLayout

You may be familiar with tabbed frames in various Microsoft Windows application. An example is shown in FIG-15.14 below.

FIG-15.14

Tabbed Pages

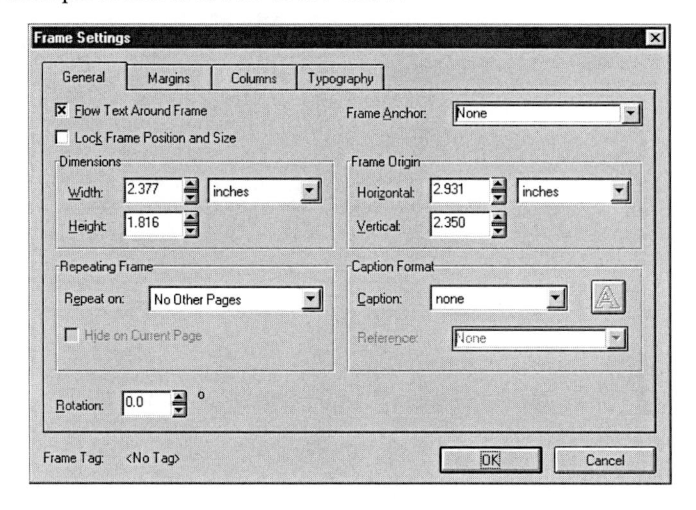

Each tab, *General, Margins, Columns* and *Typography*, when pressed makes visible the set of components linked with that tab. We can think of the set up as four tabbed cards. By selecting a particular tab, we place that card in front of the three others. It's from this comparison that the *CardLayout* class gets its name.

The Java implementation of this setup may not look quite as appealing as the Microsoft Windows version but it serves the same purpose.

We don't use the *CardLayout* on the whole window. Instead we stick with the *Frame*'s default *BorderLayout* (although another layout still could be used).

We now place a panel in the NORTH area of the *Frame* and another in the CENTER position. The NORTH panel is assigned a set of buttons; one for each tabbed area we wish to create.

Only one component can be placed on each *card*, so if we want a complex structure associated with each tab we need to define that structure in some other class and then add an object of that type to the required *card.* In the example that follows we create a private inner class defining this the required card layout:

```
class Card extends Panel
{
    private Label lab[] = new Label[3];
    private TextField txt[] = new TextField[3];

    public Card(String s[])
    {
        setBackground(Color.yellow);
        setLayout(new GridLayout(3,2));
        for(int c = 0; c < lab.length; c++)
            lab[c] = new Label(s[c]);
        for(int c = 0; c < 3; c++)
        {
            add(lab[c]);
            txt[c] = new TextField(30);
            add(txt[c]);
        }
    }
}
```

Three *Card* objects are then added, one on each layer. The full program is given in LISTING-15.1.

LISTING-15.1

Using CardLayout

```
import java.awt.*;
import java.awt.event.*;

public class UsingCardLayout extends Frame
↳implements ActionListener
{
   Button but[] =
   ↳{new Button("Personal"),new Button("Course"),
   ↳new Button("Results")};
   Card cards[] =
   ↳{new Card(new String[]{"Name","Age","Phone"}),
   ↳new Card(new String[]{"Course", "Class", "Year"}),
   ↳new Card(new String[]{"Passed","Failed","Average Score"})};
   Panel pcenter;
   CardLayout layoutused;

   public UsingCardLayout(String s)
   {
        super(s);
        addWindowListener(new WindowHandler());
        Panel pnorth = new Panel();
        for(int c = 0; c < 3; c++)
        {
             pnorth.add(but[c]);
             but[c].addActionListener(this);
        }
        add("North",pnorth);
        pcenter = new Panel();
        layoutused = new CardLayout();
        pcenter.setLayout(layoutused);
        add("Center", pcenter);
        pcenter.add(cards[0],"Personal");
        pcenter.add(cards[1],"Course");
        pcenter.add(cards[2],"Results");
   }

   class Card extends Panel
   {
        private Label lab[] = new Label[3];
        private TextField txt[] = new TextField[3];

        public Card(String s[])
        {
             setBackground(Color.yellow);
             setLayout(new GridLayout(3,2));
             for(int c = 0; c < lab.length; c++)
                  lab[c] = new Label(s[c]);
             for(int c = 0; c < 3; c++)
             {
                  add(lab[c]);
                  txt[c] = new TextField(30);
                  add(txt[c]);
             }
        }
   }

   class WindowHandler extends WindowAdapter
   {
        public void windowClosing(WindowEvent we)
        {
             we.getWindow().hide();
             System.exit(0);
        }
   }
```

continued on next page

LISTING-15.1

Using CardLayout

```
    public void actionPerformed(ActionEvent ae)
    {
        Button es = (Button)ae.getSource();
        layoutused.show(pcenter,es.getLabel());
    }

    public static void main(String args[])
    {
        UsingCardLayout fm =
        ↳new UsingCardLayout("Using Layout Managers");
        fm.setSize(400,120);
        fm.show();
    }
}
```

Activity 15.4

Type in and test the program given in LISTING-15.1.

Working Without a Layout Manager

We can eliminate layout managers from a container with the line

```
setLayout(null);
```

It now becomes the responsibility of the programmer to size and position the components. The program in LISTING-15.2 demonstrates the techniques required by adding three buttons to a frame.

LISTING-15.2

Working Without a Layout Manager

```
import java.awt.*;

public class NoLayout extends Frame
{
   private Button but[] = {new Button("Button 1"),
   ↳new Button("Button 2"),new Button("Button 3")};

   public NoLayout(String s)
   {
        super(s);
        setLayout(null);
        but[0].setBounds(20,20,70,40);
        but[1].setBounds(120,20,70,40);
        but[2].setBounds(220,20,70,40);
        add(but[0]);
        add(but[1]);
        add(but[2]);
   }

   public static void main(String args[])
   {
        NoLayout fm = new NoLayout("No Layout Manager");
        fm.setSize(400,200);
        fm.show();
   }
}
```

Activity 15.5

Type in and test the program above.

If you haven't yet become familiar with layout managers you may find the idea of eliminating them appealing. However, without a layout manager many of things that happen automatically now have to be programmed in. For example, is we add the lines

```
fm.but[0].setLabel("WWWWWWWWWWWWWWWWWWWWWWW");
fm.but[0].invalidate();
fm.validate();
```

to the end of *main()* in the previous program, the button, with its new label, is not automatically resized. The programmer would have to determine the width of the text and change the size of the button accordingly (possible also having to move the other buttons).

This Activity demonstrates the shortcomings of eliminating the layout manager.

Activity 15.6

Run the previous program again.

Maximise the window.

Reduce the window so all three buttons are not visible.

Activity 15.7

Restore the use of a layout manager by changing the program to read

```
import java.awt.*;

public class NoLayout extends Frame
{
  private Button but[] = {new Button("Button 1"),
  ↳new Button("Button 2"), new Button("Button 3")};

  public NoLayout(String s)
  {
      super(s);
      setLayout(new FlowLayout());
      add(but[0]);
      add(but[1]);
      add(but[2]);
  }

  public static void main(String args[])
  {
      NoLayout fm = new NoLayout("No Layout Manager");
      fm.setSize(400,200);
      fm.show();
  }
}
```

Run the program and reduce and maximise window size.

Repositioning no becomes automatic.

Add the three lines at the top of the page to main().

Redrawing is performed automatically.

Solutions

Activity 15.1

```
import java.awt.*;
import java.awt.event.*;

public class ButOnly extends Frame
{
    int
    compdetails[][]={{0,0,1,1},{1,0,2,1},{0,1,1,1},
    ↳{0,2,1,1},{0,3,1,1},{1,1,3,3},{1,4,1,1},
    ↳{2,4,1,1}};
    Button but[] = {new Button("But1"),
    ↳new Button("But2"),new Button("But3"),
    ↳new Button("But4"),new Button("But5"),
    ↳new Button("But6"),new Button("But7"),
    ↳new Button("But8")};

    private void setComponentConstraints
    ↳(GridBagConstraints gbc, int d[])
    {
        gbc.gridx = d[0];
        gbc.gridy = d[1];
        gbc.gridwidth = d[2];
        gbc.gridheight = d[3];
        gbc.weightx = 100;
        gbc.weighty = 100;
        gbc.fill = gbc.BOTH;
        gbc.ipadx = 10;
        gbc.ipady = 5;
    }

    public ButOnly(String s)
    {
        super(s);
        GridBagLayout layoutused =
        ↳new GridBagLayout();
        setLayout(layoutused);
        GridBagConstraints gbc =
        ↳new GridBagConstraints();
        for(int c = 0; c <= 7; c++)
        {
            setComponentConstraints
            ↳(gbc, compdetails[c]);
            layoutused.setConstraints(but[c],gbc);
            add(but[c]);
        }
        addWindowListener(new WindowHandler());
    }

    class WindowHandler extends WindowAdapter
    {
        public void windowClosing(WindowEvent we)
        {
            we.getWindow().hide();
            System.exit(0);
        }
    }

    public static void main(String args[])
    {
        ButOnly fm = new ButOnly
        ↳("Using Layout Managers");
        fm.setSize(400,250);
        fm.show();
    }
}
```

Activity 15.2

No effect since *But5*, which is in the same column, would still have the same weighting it is the largest weighting in the column that determines its width..

Activity 15.3

If no component in column 1 has a weighting of greater than 25 and the highest weightings in columns 2 and 3 total 75 then column 1 will be 25% of the total width.

Activity 15.4

No solution required.

Activity 15.5

No solution required.

Activity 15.6

No solution required.

Activity 15.7

No solution required

Chapter 16

Listeners and Event Handlers

This chapter covers the following topics:

Adapters

Component-Derived Classes and their Listeners

Event Classes

Listener Interface Relationships

Listeners and Event Handlers

Review

This chapter summarises the listeners and related classes we dealt with in Chapter 13. In addition, new listeners are introduced and explained.

TABLE-16.1 lists the main AWT components and the listeners to which they can be linked.

TABLE-16.1

Components and their Listeners

	ActionListener	AdjustmentListener	ComponentListener	ContainerListener	FocusListener	ItemListener	KeyListener	MouseListener	MouseMotionListener	TextListener	WindowListener
Button	✔		✔		✔		✔	✔	✔		
Checkbox			✔		✔	✔	✔	✔	✔		
CheckMenuItem			✔		✔	✔	✔	✔	✔		
Choice			✔		✔	✔	✔	✔	✔		
Container			✔	✔	✔		✔	✔	✔		
Label			✔		✔		✔	✔	✔		
List	✔		✔		✔	✔	✔	✔	✔		
MenuItem	✔		✔		✔		✔	✔	✔		
Scrollbar		✔	✔		✔		✔	✔	✔		
TextComponent	✔		✔		✔		✔	✔	✔	✔	
TextArea	✔		✔		✔		✔	✔	✔	✔	
TextField	✔		✔		✔		✔	✔	✔	✔	
Window			✔		✔		✔	✔	✔		✔

All listeners are defined as a set of related Interfaces (see FIG-16.1).

FIG-16.1

Interface Relationships

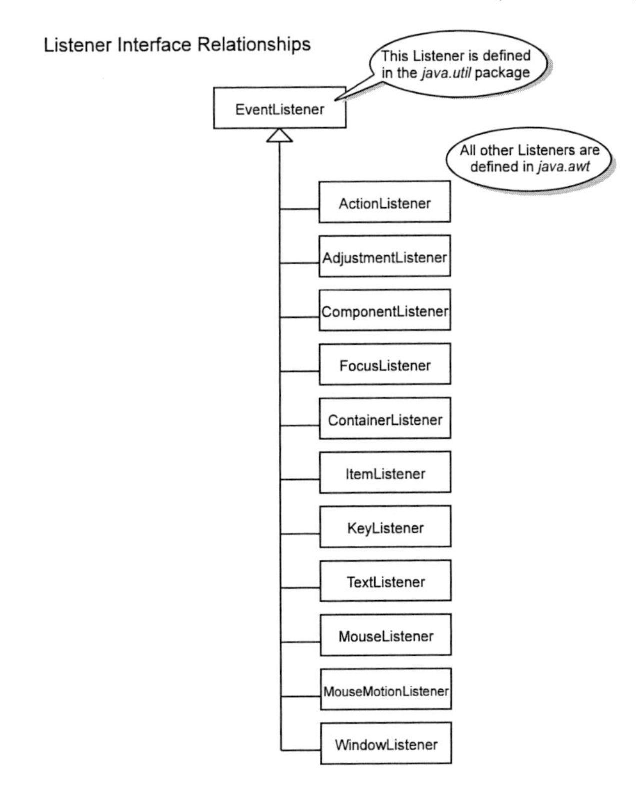

Listeners

EventListener is an empty interface. Other listener interfaces are given below.

Interface	*Methods*
`ActionListener`	`void actionPerformed(ActionEvent)`
`AdjustmentListener`	`void adjustmentValueChanged(AdjustmentEvent)`

`ComponentListener`	`void componentResized(ComponentEvent)`
	`void componentMoved(ComponentEvent)`
	`void componentShown(ComponentEvent)`
	`void componentHidden(ComponentEvent)`

`ContainerListener`	`void componentAdded(ContainerEvent)` `void componentRemoved(ContainerEvent)`
`FocusListener`	`void focusGained(FocusEvent)` `void focusLost(FocusEvent)`
`ItemListener`	`void itemStateChanged(ItemEvent)`

`KeyListener`	`void keyTyped(KeyEvent)`
	`void keyPressed(KeyEvent)`
	`void keyReleased(KeyEvent)`

`MouseListener`	`void mouseClicked(MouseEvent)`
	`void mousePressed(MouseEvent)`
	`void mouseReleased(MouseEvent)`
	`void mouseEntered(MouseEvent)`
	`void mouseExited(MouseEvent)`

`MouseMotionListener`	`void mouseDragged(MouseEvent)` `void mouseMoved(MouseEvent)`
`TextListener`	`void textValueChanged(TextEvent)`

`WindowListener`	`void windowActivated(WindowEvent)`
	`void windowDeactivated(WindowEvent)`
	`void windowClosing(WindowEvent)`
	`void windowClosed(WindowEvent)`
	`void windowOpened(WindowEvent)`
	`void windowIconified(WindowEvent)`
	`void windowDeiconified(WindowEvent)`

Adapters

Some of the more complex listeners have corresponding adapter classes which can be used in their place. The advantage of using an adapter is that only those listener methods required by the program need to be implemented; empty versions of all other methods are inherited.

Adapter Class	*Equivalent to*
`ComponentAdapter`	`ComponentListener`
`ContainerAdapter`	`ContainerListener`
`FocusAdapter`	`FocusListener`
`KeyAdapter`	`KeyListener`
`MouseAdapter`	`MouseListener`
`MouseMotionAdapter`	`MouseMotionListener`
`WindowAdapter`	`WindowListener`

Event Classes

The event classes used as parameters for the listener methods are also related (see FIG-16.2).

FIG-16.2

Event Classes

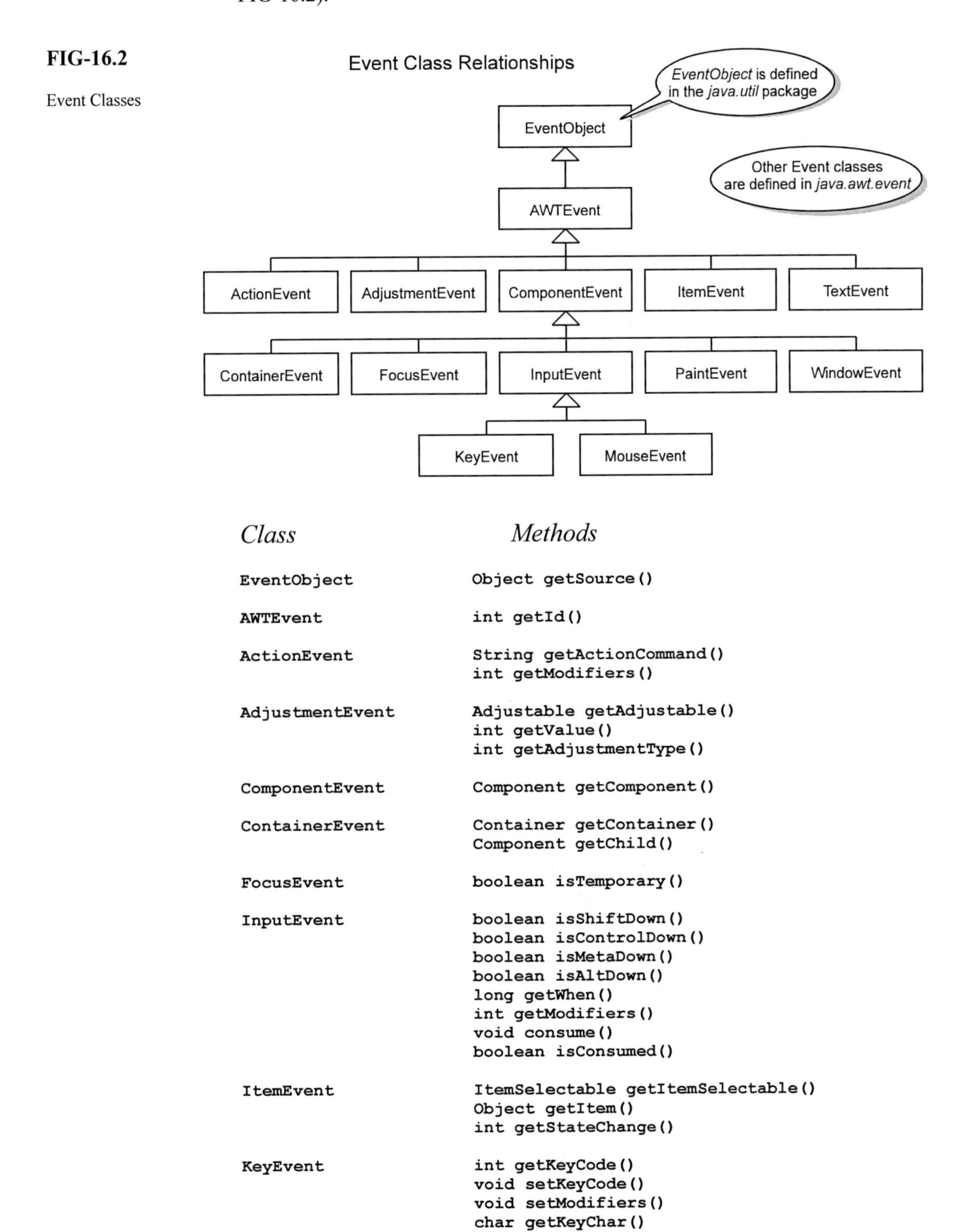

Class	*Methods*
`EventObject`	`Object getSource()`
`AWTEvent`	`int getId()`
`ActionEvent`	`String getActionCommand()` `int getModifiers()`

`AdjustmentEvent`	`Adjustable getAdjustable()`
	`int getValue()`
	`int getAdjustmentType()`

`ComponentEvent`	`Component getComponent()`
`ContainerEvent`	`Container getContainer()` `Component getChild()`
`FocusEvent`	`boolean isTemporary()`

`InputEvent`	`boolean isShiftDown()`
	`boolean isControlDown()`
	`boolean isMetaDown()`
	`boolean isAltDown()`
	`long getWhen()`
	`int getModifiers()`
	`void consume()`
	`boolean isConsumed()`

`ItemEvent`	`ItemSelectable getItemSelectable()`
	`Object getItem()`
	`int getStateChange()`

`KeyEvent`	`int getKeyCode()`
	`void setKeyCode()`
	`void setModifiers()`
	`char getKeyChar()`
	`void setKeyChar()`
	`boolean isActionKey()`

MouseEvent	int getClickCount() int getX() int getY() Point getPoint() void translatePoint(int x, int y) boolean isPopupTrigger()
PaintEvent	Rectangle getUpdateRect() void setUpdateRect(Rectangle r)
TextEvent	No additional methods
WindowEvent	Window getWindow()

FocusListener

As the user clicks on a visual component such as a button or editbox, that component becomes active. It is said to gain **focus**, the previously active component loses focus. By adding a *FocusListener* to a component we can determine when it gains or loses focus.

The *FocusListener* methods are:

void focusGained(FocusEvent fe)	This method executes when the listening component gains focus.
void focusLost(FocusEvent fe)	This method executes when the listening component loses focus.

The *FocusEvent* class contains only one method:

boolean isTemporary()	Returns *true* if the component has gained focus only temporarily.

The program in LISTING-16.1 contains a button and three radio buttons. As each gains focus a message giving that component's name is sent to the console window.

LISTING-16.1

FocusListener Events

```
import java.awt.*;
import java.awt.event.*;

public class List16_1 extends Frame implements FocusListener
{
   private Button create = new Button("Push to Create");
   private CheckboxGroup type =  new CheckboxGroup();
   private Checkbox radio[] =
   ↳{new Checkbox("Label",type,true),
   ↳new Checkbox("Button",type,false),
   ↳new Checkbox("TextField",type,false)};

   public List16_1(String s)
   {
        super(s);
        setLayout(new FlowLayout());
        create.addFocusListener(this);
        add(create);
        for(int c = 0; c < 3; c++)
        {
             radio[c].addFocusListener(this);
             add(radio[c]);
        }
   }
```

continued on next page

LISTING-16.1
(continued)

FocusListener Events

```
    public void focusGained(FocusEvent fe)
    {
        System.out.println(((Component)fe.getSource()).getName());
    }

    public void focusLost(FocusEvent fe)
    {
    }

    public static void main(String args[])
    {
        List16_1 fm = new List16_1("Listeners");
        fm.setSize(400,400);
        fm.show();
    }
}
```

Activity 16.1

Type in the program above and observe the effects of shifting focus between the four components.

Add a handler for *focusLost()* which displays the name of the component losing focus.

The ComponentEvent Class

A *Component* reference gives us access to more methods without having to cast the reference variable to some other class.

You may have noticed from FIG-16.2 that the *FocusEvent* class descends from the *ComponentEvent* class which defines a *getComponent()* method. This method is similar to *getSource()* inherited from the *EventObject* class. However, *getComponent()* returns a *Component* reference rather than the *Object* reference returned by *getSource()*. This gives us the opportunity to replace the expression

```
((Component)fe.getSource()).getName())
```

used in the previous program with the simpler

```
ge.getComponent().getname()
```

Activity 16.2

Make the suggested change to the focus handlers in your previous program.

ContainerListener

The *ContainerListener* can be used on a container component such as a *Frame* or *Panel.* Each time a component is added or removed the listening container will fire one of the following events:

void componentAdded(ContainerEvent ce) This method executes when a component is added to the listening container.

void componentRemoved(ContainerEvent ce) This method executes when a component is removed from the listening container.

The *ContainerEvent* class defines the following methods:

Container getContainer()	Returns a reference to the container to which the component has been added or removed.
Component getChild()	Returns a reference to the component being added or removed.

Normally, components are added to a container within the constructor. However, it is possible to add them later. The program in LISTING-16.2 allows the user to add labels, buttons or edit boxes by selecting the required component type and clicking on the *create* button. This program is an extension of LISTING-16.1.

LISTING-16.2

Adding Components Dynamically

```
import java.awt.*;
import java.awt.event.*;

public class List16_2 extends Frame implements ActionListener
{
  private Button create = new Button("Push to Create");
  private CheckboxGroup type =  new CheckboxGroup();
  private Checkbox radio[] =
  ↳{new Checkbox("Label",type,true),
  ↳new Checkbox("Button",type,false),
  ↳new Checkbox("TextField",type,false)};

  public List16_2(String s)
  {
       super(s);
       setLayout(new FlowLayout());
       create.addActionListener(this);
       add(create);
       for(int c = 0; c < 3; c++)
       {
            add(radio[c]);
       }
  }

  public void actionPerformed(ActionEvent ae)
  {
       Checkbox temp = type.getSelectedCheckbox();
       if(temp == radio[0])
       {
            Label l1 = new Label("XXX");
            add(l1);
       }
       else if (temp == radio[1])
       {
            Button l1 = new Button("AAA");
            add(l1);
       }
       else
       {
            TextField l1 = new TextField(20);
            add(l1);
       }
       validate();
  }

  public static void main(String args[])
  {
       List16_2 fm = new List16_2("Listeners");
       fm.setSize(400,400);
       fm.show();
  }
}
```

Activity 16.3

Type in and test the program above.

Now we'll add a listener to detect the components as they are added, displaying their generated name and the name of the container to which they are added. To this end, we'll need to implement *ContainerListener.* The lines of code required are:

```
public class List16_3 extends Frame implements ActionListener,
↳ContainerListener

addContainerListener(this);

public void componentAdded(ContainerEvent ce)
{
    System.out.print(ce.getChild().getName()+" added to ");
    System.out.println(ce.getContainer().getName());
}
```

Activity 16.4

Modify your last program to include the lines above and test the final code.

ComponentListener

The *ComponentListener* reacts to the resizing, moving and change in visibilty of a component. It contains the following methods:

void componentResized(ComponentEvent ce)
This method executes when a component is resized.

void componentMoved(ComponentEvent ce)
This method executes when a component is moved.

void componentShown(ComponentEvent ce)
This method executes when a component becomes visible.

void componentHidden(ComponentEvent ce)
This method executes when a component is hidden.

As we saw earlier, the *ComponentEvent* class has a single method, *getComponent()* which returns a reference to the component that initiated the event.

The program in LISTING-16.3 displays a *Dice* component with buttons to roll, resize, show and hide the *Dice* object.

Console messages are created for each *ComponentEvent* initiated by the die.

LISTING-16.3

Using ComponentListener

```
import java.awt.*;
import java.awt.event.*;


public class List16_3 extends Frame implements ActionListener,
↳ComponentListener
{
  private Dice die = new Dice();
  private Button controls[]  =
  ↳{new Button("Throw"),new Button("Resize"),
  ↳new Button("Hide"),new Button("Show")};


  public List16_3(String s)
  {
      super(s);
      setLayout(new FlowLayout());
      die.addComponentListener(this);
      add(die);
      for(int c = 0; c < 4; c++)
      {
           controls[c].addActionListener(this);
           add(controls[c]);
      }
  }

  public void componentResized(ComponentEvent ce)
  {
      System.out.println("Die resized");
  }

  public void componentMoved(ComponentEvent ce)
  {
      System.out.println("Die moved");
  }

  public void componentShown(ComponentEvent ce)
  {
      System.out.println("Die shown");
  }

  public void componentHidden(ComponentEvent ce)
  {
      System.out.println("Die hidden");
  }

  public void actionPerformed(ActionEvent ae)
  {
      Object temp = ae.getSource();
      if(temp == controls[0])
      {
           die.roll();
      }
      else if (temp == controls[1])
      {
           die.setDieSize((int)(die.getDieSize()*1.1));
           die.invalidate();
      }
      else if (temp == controls[2])
      {
           die.setVisible(false);
      }
      else
      {
           die.setVisible(true);
      }
      validate();
  }
```

continued on next page

LISTING-16.3
(continued)

Using ComponentListener

```
  public static void main(String args[])
  {
      List16_3 fm = new List16_3("Listeners");
      fm.setSize(400,400);
      fm.show();
  }
}
```

Activity 16.5

Type in and test the program given above.

What actions by the user causes a *componentMoved* event to occur?

MouseMotionListener

The *MouseMotionListener* handles two events. These are:

void mouseDragged(MouseEvent me)	This method executes when the mouse is dragged within the listening component.
void mouseMoved(MouseEvent me)	This method executes when the mouse is moved within the listening component.

Like the *MouseListener* (described in a previous chapter), these methods take as parameters *MouseEvent* objects.

The program in LISTING-16.4 places a *Canvas* component within the application frame and issues console messages when the mouse is moved or dragged within the canvas area.

LISTING-16.4

Using MouseMotionListener

```
import java.awt.*;
import java.awt.event.*;

public class List16_4 extends Frame implements
MouseMotionListener
{
  private Canvas cv = new Canvas();

  public List16_4(String s)
  {
      super(s);
      cv.addMouseMotionListener(this);
      add(cv);
  }

  public void mouseDragged(MouseEvent me)
  {
      System.out.println("Mouse dragged");
  }

  public void mouseMoved(MouseEvent me)
  {
      System.out.println("Mouse moved");
  }
```

continued on next page

LISTING-16.4
(continued)

Using MouseMotionListener

```
  public static void main(String args[])
  {
      List16_4 fm = new List16_4("Listeners");
      fm.setSize(400,400);
      fm.show();
  }
}
```

Activity 16.6

Type in and execute the program above.

You will have observed from Activity 16.6 that, unlike other events, dragging and moving the mouse creates events that triggers continuously, several times per second.

The program in LISTING-16.5 makes use of these events, and others from *MouseListener,* to create a simple drawing program.

LISTING-16.5

MouseMotionListener and Graphics

```
import java.awt.*;
import java.awt.event.*;

public class List16_5 extends Frame
↳implements MouseMotionListener
{
  private Canvas cv = new Canvas();
  private Point start = new Point();

  public List16_5(String s)
  {
      super(s);
      cv.addMouseMotionListener(this);
      cv.addMouseListener(new MousePressedHandler());
      add(cv);
  }

  public void mouseDragged(MouseEvent me)
  {
      Graphics g = cv.getGraphics();
      g.drawLine(start.x,start.y,me.getX(),me.getY());
  }

  public void mouseMoved(MouseEvent me)
  {
  }

  public static void main(String args[])
  {
      List16_5 fm = new List16_5("Listeners");
      fm.setSize(400,400);
      fm.show();
  }


  class MousePressedHandler extends MouseAdapter
  {
      public void mousePressed(MouseEvent me)
      {
          start = me.getPoint();
      }
  }

}
```

Points to Note

The *mousePressed()* method, defined in an extension of the *MouseAdapter* class, records the mouse pointer position when the mouse button is pressed.

The *mouseDragged()* method draws a line between that point and the current position. Since the *mouseDragged* event occurs continuously the overall effect is to create a series of lines originating from the starting position where the mouse button was first pushed down.

To draw on a component we need to obtain a reference to the *Graphic* component involved. You should recall that every component is drawn by the application making an automatic call to its *paint()* method. This method takes a *Graphics* object parameter. A separate *Graphics* object is created for each component within an application. To draw within a component we need to obtain a reference to its *Graphics* object. In the case of the *Canvas* component added to our application, this is done with the line

```
Graphics g = cv.getGraphics();
```

in the *mouseDragged()* method.

> **Activity 16.7**
>
> Enter and test the program in LISTING-16.5.
>
> What happens when the window is resized?

Rubber Banding

A common use of this press and drag activity is rubber-banding. In this technique a single line is drawn between the starting point and the current mouse position. Any movement of the mouse is reflected by a movement of the line.

We only need to make a simple change to the previous program to achieve this effect.

> **Activity 16.8**
>
> Implement rubber banding by adding or modifying lines in your previous program.
>
> Your program should contain the following lines:
>
> ```
> private Point finish = new Point();
>
> g.setColor(Color.white);
> g.drawLine(start.x,start.y,finish.x,finish.y);
> finish.x = me.getX();
> finish.y = me.getY();
> g.setColor(Color.black);
> g.drawLine(start.x,start.y,finish.x,finish.y);
> ```

TextListener

From TABLE-16.1 we can see that the *TextListener* is linked to the *TextComponent* class. Since *TextComponent* is the superclass for both *TextField* and *TextArea* it follows that both those classes inherit the ability to listen for this event.

TextListener defines a single method:

void textValueChanged(TextEvent)	This method executes when the contents of a text field changes.

The program in LISTING-16.6 demonstrates the use of this listener by creating a console message each time the text of an edit box changes.

LISTING-16.6

Using TextListener

```
import java.awt.*;
import java.awt.event.*;

public class List16_6 extends Frame implements TextListener
{
  private TextField txt = new TextField(20);

  public List16_6(String s)
  {
       super(s);
       setLayout(new FlowLayout());
       txt.addTextListener(this);
       add(txt);
  }

  public void textValueChanged(TextEvent te)
  {
       System.out.println("Text changed");
  }

  public static void main(String args[])
  {
       List16_6 fm = new List16_6("Listeners");
       fm.setSize(400,400);
       fm.show();
  }
}
```

Solutions

Activity 16.1

```
import java.awt.*;
import java.awt.event.*;

public class Act16_1 extends Frame
↳implements FocusListener
{
    private Button create =
    ↳new Button("Push to Create");
    private CheckboxGroup type =
    ↳new CheckboxGroup();
    private Checkbox radio[] =
    ↳{new Checkbox("Label",type,true),
    ↳new Checkbox("Button",type,false),
    ↳new Checkbox("TextField",type,false)};

    private String lastcomp = "None";
    public Act16_1(String s)
    {
        super(s);
        setLayout(new FlowLayout());
        create.addFocusListener(this);
        add(create);
        for(int c = 0; c < 3; c++)
        {
            radio[c].addFocusListener(this);
            add(radio[c]);
        }
    }

    public void focusGained(FocusEvent fe)
    {
        System.out.println
        ↳(fe.getComponent().getName()
        ↳+" has gained focus");
    }

    public void focusLost(FocusEvent fe)
    {
        System.out.println
        ↳(fe.getComponent().getName()
        ↳+" has lost focus");
    }

    public static void main(String args[])
    {
        Act16_1 fm = new Act16_1("Listeners");
        fm.setSize(400,400);
        fm.show();
    }
}
```

Activity 16.2

No solution required.

Activity 16.3

No solution required.

Activity 16.4

No solution required.

Activity 16.5

Resizing the die or the window causes the *componentMoved* event to occur.

Activity 16.6

No solution required.

Activity 16.7

When the window is resized all lines previously drawn disappear.

Activity 16.8

```
import java.awt.*;
import java.awt.event.*;

public class Act16_8 extends Frame
↳implements MouseMotionListener
{
    private Canvas cv = new Canvas();
    private Point start = new Point();
    private Point finish = new Point();

    public Act16_8(String s)
    {
        super(s);
        cv.addMouseMotionListener(this);
        cv.addMouseListener(
        ↳new MousePressedHandler());
        add(cv);
    }

    public void mouseDragged(MouseEvent me)
    {
        Graphics g = cv.getGraphics();
        g.setColor(Color.white);
        g.drawLine
        ↳(start.x,start.y,finish.x,finish.y);
        finish.x = me.getX();
        finish.y = me.getY();
        g.setColor(Color.black);
        g.drawLine
        ↳(start.x,start.y,finish.x,finish.y);
    }

    public void mouseMoved(MouseEvent me)
    {
    }

    public static void main(String args[])
    {
        Act16_8 fm = new Act16_8("Listeners");
        fm.setSize(400,400);
        fm.show();
    }

    class MousePressedHandler
    ↳extends MouseAdapter
    {
        public void mousePressed(MouseEvent me)
        {
            start = me.getPoint();
        }
    }
}
```

CHAPTER 17

Applets

This chapter covers the following topics:

Adding Components to an Applet

Applet Classs

How to Create an Applet

How to Add an Applet to a Web Page

Images in an Applet

Sound in an Applet

URL Class

Using Parameters with an Applet

Applets

Introduction

Most people associate the Java programming language with the Internet and the small programs, kown as **applets** that are found on so many Web pages. These applets differ from applications in the following ways:

- They must be imbedded within an HTML document
- They cannot write to files on the machine on which they are being executed.
- All applets are defined as classes descended from the Java's *Applet* class.
- Applets do not require a *main()* function.

Introducing the Applet Class

Since all applets are descended from the *Applet* class, perhaps we'd better start by learning something about this Java class.

The *Applet* class is a subclass of *Panel* as shown in FIG-17.1.

FIG-17.1

The Applet Class

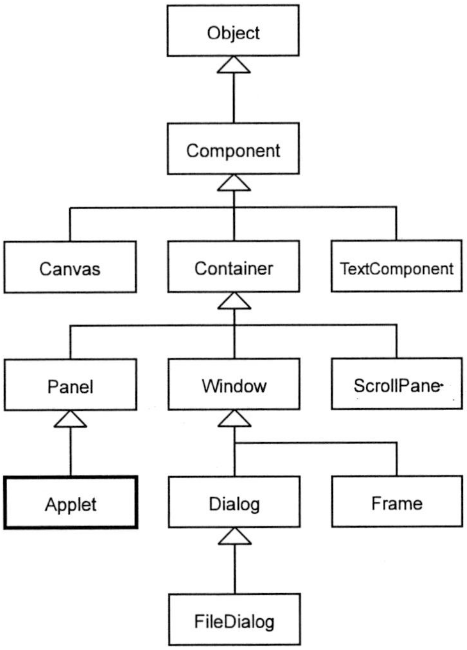

The *Applet* class is defined in the package

java.applet

Although it inherits many features from ancestral classes, there are four main methods which are declared within the *Applet* class. These are:

```
init()
start()
stop()
destroy()
```

All of these routines are called automatically by the Internet browser when an applet appears as part of a web page. All four are also empty in the *Applet* class and expected to be overridden in descendant classes as required.

init()

This routine is called by the browser as soon as the Java applet is loaded. Override this method if some type of one-off setting up operation is required.

start()

The *start()* operation is called each time the Web page containing the applet is visited. Override this routine if items need re-initialised on each visit to the page.

stop()

This is called when an applet is to be terminated. Termination may be caused by moving to another Web page.

destroy()

This method is called just before an applet is removed from memory.

Creating an Applet

To create an applet of our own we need to define a new class as a descendant of the *Applet* class and override all or some of the *Applet* class methods.

The following example (LISTING-17.1) simply outputs a message to the console window as each phase of the applet is executed.

LISTING-17.1

A First Applet

```
import java.applet.Applet;

public class FirstApplet extends Applet
{
  public void init()
  {
      System.out.println("init run");
  }

  public void start()
  {
      System.out.println("start run");
  }

  public void stop()
  {
      System.out.println("stop run");
  }

  public void destroy()
  {
      System.out.println("destroy run");
  }
}
```

Activity 17.1

Type in and save the program above (save as *FirstApplet.java*).

To execute an applet we must embed it within an HTML document.

It is assumed you already have a background knowledge of HTML and the tags used to create a web page.

Activity 17.2

Enter the following text

```
<html>
    <head>
        <title> Testing first applet</title>
    </head>
    <body>
        <h1> This appears when using a browser</h1>
        <applet code = "FirstApplet.class" width="200"
        ↳height="300"></applet>
    </body>
</html>
```

Save the file as *First.html.*

The only line that should be new to you is the one invoking the applet:

```
<applet code = "FirstApplet.class" width=200 height=300></applet>
```

which names the applet to be executed and specifies the dimensions (in pixels) to be allocated to it within the web page.

If the applet were in a different directory from the HTML document then path information would be required as part of the class name (e.g. “C:\FirstApplet.class”).

Running the Applet

There are two ways to execute the applet:

1. Load the HTML document into a browser that supports Java (making sure that Java is enabled).

2. Load the HTML document into **appletviewer** which comes as part of the Java software.

Activity 17.3

Test your new applet by executing the line

```
appletviewer First.html
```

Close the applet.

You should see all four messages in the console window.

Adding Components

Like an application, we can add any component to an applet. The *Applet* class defaults to using a *FlowLayout* manager but, as with other containers, this can be changed.

The next program (LISTING-17.2) implements a simple game of chance. It contains two dice, a button and two labels. The program implements the following logic:

```
On Start up:
       Set won count to zero
       Set lost count to zero
On button press:
    Roll both dice
    IF both show the same value or the total is 7 THEN
       Add 1 to the won count
    ELSE
       Add 1 to the lost count
    Update the labels to show the current number of wins and losses
```

LISTING-17.2

A Game Applet

```
import java.applet.Applet;
import java.awt.*;
import java.awt.event.*;
import Dice;

public class List17_2 extends Applet implements ActionListener
{
  private Dice die[] = {new Dice(), new Dice()};
  private Button play = new Button("Play");
  private Label result[] = {new Label("Won 0"),
  ↳new Label("Lost 0")};
  private int won=0, lost=0;

  public void init()
  {
      add(die[0]);
      add(die[1]);
      add(result[0]);
      add(result[1]);
      play.addActionListener(this);
      add(play);
  }

  public void actionPerformed(ActionEvent ae)
  {
      die[0].roll();
      die[1].roll();
      if(die[0].getValue() == die[1].getValue()
      ↳|| die[0].getValue()+die[1].getValue()==7)
          won++;
      else
          lost++;
      result[0].setText("Won :"+won);
      result[1].setText("Lost:"+lost);
  }
}
```

Images in an Applet

An applet can display JPEG and GIF images. The GIF image may be a static one or an animated GIF.

In an application we had to invoke methods of the *Toolkit* class to fetch an image. However, the *Applet* class includes methods of its own to perform this task.

Since applets will involve locating and loading images from remote sites, one of the parameters to these routines is a URL (a web-style address).

There are two versions of the operation. These are:

Image getImage(URL loc)	Returns a reference to the image at the address *loc*.
Image getImage(URL loc, String filename)	Returns a reference to the image identified by *filename* at address *loc*.

The URL Class

A *URL* object is used to contain a Web-style address. For example, *www.barrvillage.com*. The class is defined in the package *java.net* and hence, any program using a *URL* object must include the statement

```
import java.net.URL;
```

Constructors

In fact there are several constructors available for this class, but the simplest takes a single string

URL(String s)	Creates a URL object linked to the address location *s*. The constructor may throw a *MalformedURLException* which must be dealt with.

A typical call to this constructor might be

```
try
{
    URL imageat = new URL("http://www.crosswinds.net
    ↳/~alitardis/");
}
catch(MalformedURLException mue)
{
    System.out.println("Invalid URL");
}
```

It's also possible that the URL address refers to a file directory on a disk, in which case the constructor call might be

```
URL imageat = new URL("file:/C:/JavaAlistair/");
```

Once retrieved, the image can be displayed by overriding the inherited *paint()* method and making a call to the *Graphics* class's *drawImage()* method.

This will draw directly onto the applet's own canvas. Alternatively a *Canvas* class descendant can be defined and an object of that class added to the applet.

The applet in LISTING-17.3 displays *photo.jpg*.

LISTING-17.3

Displaying an Image

```
import java.applet.Applet;
import java.awt.*;
import java.net.*;

public class Images extends Applet
{
   Image im;

   public void init()
   {
        try
        {
             URL findat = new URL("file:/D:/JavaBook/Chapter17/");
             im = getImage(findat,"photo.jpg");
        }
        catch(MalformedURLException mue)
        {
             System.out.println("Invalid URL");
        }
   }

   public void paint(Graphics g)
   {
        g.drawImage(im,0,0,this);
   }
}
```

Activity 17.4

Type in and run the program above. You may have to change URL and file name details.

The *URL* class contains many other methods but none are relevant to image retrieval.

Rather than create a URL object directly as shown above, an easier way to derive the parameter required by *getImage()* is to make use of other methods defined in the *Applet* class which return *URL* objects:

URL getDocumentBase()	Returns the location of the HTML document containing the current applet.
URL getCodeBase()	Returns the location of the current applet.

Since these routines do not throw exceptions, the code required to display the image is more straight-forward. The revised version of the previous program is shown in LISTING-17.4.

LISTING-17.4

Using getCodeBase()

```
import java.applet.Applet;
import java.awt.*;
import java.net.*;

public class Images2 extends Applet
{
   Image im;
```

continued on next page

LISTING-17.4
(continued)

Using getCodeBase()

```
    public void init()
    {
        im = getImage(getCodeBase(),"photo.jpg");
    }

    public void paint(Graphics g)
    {
        g.drawImage(im,0,0,this);
    }
}
```

Sounds

An applet can play sounds in much the same way as it can display images.

Earlier versions of Java could only play 8KHz mono sound files in AU format. However, since Java 1.2 AIFF, WAV and three MIDI-based formats are supported.

There are two methods for playing a sound file directly:

void play(URL loc)	Plays the file specified by *loc*.
void play(URL loc, String filename)	Plays the file specified by *loc+filename*.

The program in LISTING-17.5 plays a sound file on start up.

LISTING-17.5

Playing a Sound File

```
import java.applet.Applet;

public class UsingApplets extends Applet
{
    public void start()
    {
        play(getCodeBase(),"wolf.wav");
    }
}
```

The *play()* method does not offer any control over the sound file. For example, we cannot terminate play early or automatically repeat playing. The *Applet* class offers two more methods which can be used to create an *AudioClip* object. This object is linked to the sound file and offers the extra control missing from the *play()* method.

AudioClip getAudioClip(URL loc)	Returns a reference to an object that implements the *AudioClip* interface. This object is linked to *loc*.
AudioClip getAudioClip(URL loc, String filename)	Returns a reference to an object that implements the *AudioClip* interface. This object is linked to *loc+filename*.

The AudioClip Interface

The *AudioClip* interface is in the *java.applet* package. It declares three methods:

play()	Plays the sound file.

loop()	Plays the sound file repeatedly
stop()	Stops playing of the sound file.

If you've created an applet that plays a sound file, make sure you override the applet's *stop()* method. The overridden method should terminate any sound files still playing.

The program in LISTING-17.6 links buttons to TV theme tunes. Pressing a button causes any sound currently playing to stop and the selected file is played. When the applet terminates, the currently playing file is halted.

LISTING-17.6

Using an AudioClip Object

```
import java.applet.*;
import java.awt.*;
import java.net.*;
import java.awt.event.*;


public class UsingApplets extends Applet
↳implements ActionListener
{
  private Button themes[] =
  ↳{new Button("Outer Limits"),new Button("Star Trek"),
  ↳new Button("The Twilight Zone")};
  private AudioClip sounds[] = new AudioClip[3];
  private int playing = 0;

  public void init()
  {
      for(int c = 0; c < themes.length; c++)
      {
          themes[c].addActionListener(this);
          add(themes[c]);
      }
      String filenames[]={"ol.wav","st.wav","tz.wav"};
      for(int c = 0; c < sounds.length; c++)
          sounds[c]=getAudioClip(getCodeBase(),filenames[c]);
  }

  public void actionPerformed(ActionEvent ae)
  {
      Object temp = ae.getSource();
      sounds[playing].stop();
      for(int c = 0; c < themes.length; c++)
          if(temp == themes[c])
          {
              playing = c;
              sounds[c].play();
              break;
          }
  }

  public void stop()
  {
      sounds[playing].stop();

  }
}
```

Activity 17.5

Substituting your own sound files, type in and run the program above.

Passing Parameters to an Applet

There are many sites on the Internet where you can download useful applets for inclusion in your own web site. For the most part only the bytecode *class* files are available; the author retaining the original source code.

Now, if the theme tune applet in the previous listing were available as a class file anyone intending to use it would run into a problem. The applet expects specific sound files to be available, but that may not be the case, or the web designer may want to use different files. Of course, with access to the source code, the file names could be changed, but how can this be done when only the class file is available?

Where some aspects of an applet may need to be modified when embedding it in a web page we need to add applet parameters to our code.

We'll see how this is done by writing a new version of the theme tune applet that makes use of parameters.

The applet designer has to identify which values in his program need to become parameters and to give names to these parameters. He then has to read the value assigned to these parameters using the *Applet* class's *getParameter()* method which is defined as:

String getParameter(String paraname)	Returns the value of the parameter named *paraname*. This value will be placed within the HTML document.

The steps required to change the applet code are:

1. Identify which values need to be assigned from parameters.

   For the theme tune we'll need to change the sound file names and the buttons' labels to parameters.

2. Assign names to each parameter.

   The button labels can be BUTTONTEXT1, BUTTONTEXT2, BUTTONTEXT3. The sound files can be FILE1, FILE2, FILE3.

3. Modify the code to read the values of the parameters.

   A typical line for setting a button label would be
   ```
   themes[0].setLabel(getParameter("BUTTONTEXT1"));
   ```
   and for file name assignment
   ```
   filenames[0] = getParameter("FILE1");
   ```

The complete program is given in LISTING-17.7

LISTING-17.7

Using Parameters

```
import java.applet.*;
import java.awt.*;
import java.net.*;
import java.awt.event.*;
```

continued on next page

LISTING-17.7
(continued)

Using Parameters

```
public class Parameters extends Applet
↳implements ActionListener
{
   private Button themes[] = {new Button(),new Button(),
   ↳new Button()};
   private AudioClip sounds[] = new AudioClip[3];
   private int playing = 0;

   public void init()
   {
        for(int c = 0; c < themes.length; c++)
        {
             themes[c].addActionListener(this);
             add(themes[c]);
        }
        themes[0].setLabel(getParameter("BUTTONTEXT1"));
        themes[1].setLabel(getParameter("BUTTONTEXT2"));
        themes[2].setLabel(getParameter("BUTTONTEXT3"));
        String filenames[] = new String[3];
        filenames[0] = getParameter("FILE1");
        filenames[1] = getParameter("FILE2");
        filenames[2] = getParameter("FILE3");
        for(int c = 0; c < sounds.length; c++)
             sounds[c]=getAudioClip(getCodeBase(),filenames[c]);
   }

   public void actionPerformed(ActionEvent ae)
   {
        Object temp = ae.getSource();
        sounds[playing].stop();
        for(int c = 0; c < themes.length; c++)
             if(temp == themes[c])
             {
                  playing = c;
                  sounds[c].play();
                  break;
             }
   }

   public void stop()
   {
        sounds[playing].stop();

   }
}
```

The applet now requires several additional tags to assign values to the parameters. A new version of *First.html* is shown below (see LISTING-17.8).

LISTING-17.8

Specifying Parameters in an HTML File

```
<html>
   <head>
        <title> Testing first applet</title>
   </head>
   <body>
        <h1> This appears when using a browser</h1>
        <applet code = "Parameters.class" width="250" height="300">
             <param name="BUTTONTEXT1" value="Rawhide">
             <param name="BUTTONTEXT2" value="I Dream of Jeannie">
             <param name="BUTTONTEXT3" value="Laurel & Hardy">
             <param name="FILE1" value="raw.wav">
             <param name="FILE2" value="idoj.wav">
             <param name="FILE3" value="lah.wav">
        </applet>
   </body>
</html>
```

Activity 17.6

Enter and compile the program given in LISTING-17.7.

Create your own version of the HTML file shown in LISTING-17.8 with parameters specifying your own sound files.

Where several related values need to be passed as parameters as with the sound file names, a single string can be used with a separating character between each value. Using this technique the HTML file could give the file names using the line

```
<param name="FILES" value="raw.wav|idoj.wav|lah.wav">
```

The Java program needs code to separate out the parts of this parameter. For clarity this is done in a separate routine which contains the following logic:

```
Assign the parameter from the HTML code to a string
Add a '|'  to the end of the string
Extract each substring terminated by the '|' character
↳storing these as the file names
```

The code for the routine is:

```
public void getFileNames(String filenames[])
{
    String temp = getParameter("FILES")+'|';
    int startat = 0;
    int foundat;
    foundat = temp.indexOf('|',startat);
    for(int c = 0; foundat != -1 && c < filenames.length; c++)
    {
        filenames[c] = temp.substring(startat,foundat);
        startat = foundat+1;
        foundat = temp.indexOf('|',startat);
    }
}
```

The *init()* method calls this routine with the line

```
getFileNames(filenames);
```

Activity 17.7

Change your previous program to allow both the file names and the button labels to be input using only two strings.

Make the required changes to the HTML file and test your code.

Other Parameter Types

Not all parameters required by an applet are going to be strings. For example, we might want to pass the applet's background colour or its dimensions as parameters in the HTML document.

In the HTML document such parameters need to be given as strings. For example:

```
<param name="BACKGROUND" value="FF0000">
```

Within the applet itself such parameters can be read and converted as necessary:

```
String temp = getParameter("BACKGROUND");
int colourvalue = Integer.parseInt(temp,16);
setBackground(new Color(colourvalue));
```

The Web Designer and Class Parameters

From the sound files example, we can see that the web page designer needs detailed knowledge of what `<param>` tags he may need when using a Java applet. Of course, such information should be included in the documentation produced by the applet designer. But since documentation and class files may end up separated, another method of tackling this is to override the *getParameterInfo()* which is included in the applet class. This is designed to return a two-dimensional array of strings detailing the parameters that may be used. Normally, this would be used to return the name, type and description of each possible parameter.

In the sounds applet the *getparameterInfo()* method might be coded as:

```
public String[][] getParameterInfo()
{
    return new String[][]
    {
        {"BUTTONS", "String array", "Label for three buttons.
        ↳Separate each label using | "},
        {"FILES","String array", "Name of sound files.
        ↳Separate each with |. Include file extension"}
    };
}
```

The details could then be displayed with an application such as

```
public class DisplayParaDetails
{
    public static void main(String args[])
    {
        Parameters p = new Parameters();
        String temp[][]=p.getParameterInfo();
        for(int row = 0; row < temp.length;  row++)
            for(int col = 0; col < temp[row].length; col++)
                System.out.println(temp[row][col]);
    }
}
```

Solutions

Activity 17.1

No solution required.

Activity 17.2

No solution required.

Activity 17.3

No solution required.

Activity 17.4

No solution required.

Activity 17.5

No solution required.

Activity 17.6

No solution required.

Activity 17.7

```
import java.applet.*;
import java.awt.*;
import java.net.*;
import java.awt.event.*;

public class Parameters extends Applet
implements ActionListener
{
    private Button themes[] = {new Button(),new
Button(),new Button()};
    private AudioClip sounds[] = new AudioClip[3];
    private int playing = 0;
    public void init()
    {
        for(int c = 0; c < themes.length; c++)
        {
            themes[c].addActionListener(this);
            add(themes[c]);
        }
        getButtonNames();
        String filenames[] = new String[3];
        getFileNames(filenames);
        for(int c = 0; c < sounds.length; c++)
            sounds[c]=getAudioClip(getCodeBase(),filenames[c
]);
    }


    public void actionPerformed(ActionEvent ae)
    {
        Object temp = ae.getSource();
        sounds[playing].stop();
        for(int c = 0; c < themes.length; c++)
            if(temp == themes[c])
            {
                playing = c;
                sounds[c].play();
                break;
            }
    }

    public void stop()
    {
        sounds[playing].stop();

    }

    public void getFileNames(String filenames[])
    {
        String temp = getParameter("FILES")+'|';
        int startat = 0;
        int foundat;
        foundat = temp.indexOf('|',startat);
        for(int c = 0; foundat != -1 &&
        ↳c < filenames.length; c++)
        {
            filenames[c] =
            ↳temp.substring(startat,foundat);
            startat = foundat+1;
            foundat = temp.indexOf('|',startat);
        }
    }

    public void getButtonNames()
    {
        String temp = getParameter("BUTTONS")+'|';
        int startat = 0;
        int foundat;
        foundat = temp.indexOf('|',startat);
        for(int c = 0; foundat != -1 &&
        ↳c < themes.length; c++)
        {
            themes[c].setLabel(temp.substring(
            ↳startat,foundat));
            System.out.println(themes[c].getLabel());
            startat = foundat+1;
            foundat = temp.indexOf('|',startat);
        }
    }
}
```

The HTML file neeeded would be

```
<html>
    <head>
        <title> Testing Sound Applets </title>
    </head>
    <body>
        <h1> TV Themes </h1>
        <applet code = "Parameters.class"
           ↳width="250" height="300">
        <param name = "BUTTONS" value =
     ↳"Rawhide|I Dream of Jeannie|Laurel & Hardy">
        <param name = "FILES" value =
     ↳"raw.wav|idoj.wav|lah.wav">
        </applet>
    </body>
</html>
```

CHAPTER 18

Swing

This chapter covers the following topics:

Adding a Menu

Basic Concepts

ButtonGroup Class

JApplet Class

JButton Class

JCheckBox Class

JFrame Class

JLabel Class

JRadioButton Class

Look and Feel

Using Swing Components

Introduction

The Swing components are designed as a replacement for the AWT components.

AWT components work by making calls to the underlying operating system in order to create buttons, edit boxes and radio buttons, etc. This has always caused problems with some aspects of portability. In addition, the features offered by the AWT class methods have been limited to what is possible within the operating systems.

A few Swing classes still need to use the operating system to create instances.

These are JFrame, JWindow, JDialog and JApplet.

The Swing components overcome these problems by being written entirely in Java and without reference to the underlying operating system's components.

As a general rule, Swing contains the same type of components as AWT. However, Swing class names start with J. Hence, while AWT defines a *Button* class, Swing defines a *JButton* class. Many of the methods in the Swing classes match those of the equivalent AWT component, but often additional features will have been added.

The main features added by Swing are:

- Increased methods available for each visual component.
- The ability to define specific "look and feel" for visual components. This allows components such as button and edit boxes to take on the look of a specific operating system or recognised design.
- Components are drawn on the screen using *paintComponent()* rather than the *paint()* method used by AWT.
- Automatic double buffering to handle such problems as screen flicker.

It is not the intention of this chapter to cover all of the components available in Swing. Many are similar in operation to their AWT equivalents and by this point you should be familiar with using the Java documentation to discover more details about a given class. However, a few components are covered here along with some of the more important differences between AWT and Swing.

Activity 18.1

Some of the exercises that follow require small GIF images (approx. 32 x 32 pixels).

1. Create or copy a coloured GIF image of this size.
2. Produce a black and white copy of the image and an embossed version of the image.
3. Repeat this process for two other GIF images so that you finish up with 9 separate GIF files.

Call the files: *image1col.gif, image1bw.gif, image1emb.gif, image2col.gif, image2bw.gif, image2emb.gif, image3col.gif, image3bw.gif, image3emb.gif* and save them in your Java directory.

Creating a First Swing-Based Application

Swing components are held within the package *javax.swing*, so we need to start with the import statement:

```
import javax.swing.*;
```

To create an application, the class containing *main()* should be derived from the *JFrame*:

```
public class StartingSwing extends JFrame
```

An object of this class will act as the main window of your application.

However, GUI objects such as buttons and edit boxes are not placed directly onto this frame. Instead, the frame employs a *JRootPane* object to hold these other components. Even that isn't the end of the story, for the root pane itself consists of four parts:

A menu bar area.	You must place a *JMenuBar* object if you intend to create a traditional menu driven application.
A content pane.	This is where the GUI components are placed. This is a *JPanel* object.
A layered pane.	Conceptually, this is rather like a set of acetates placed on top of each other. One layer (acetate) contains the menu bar area and contents pane while other layers can be used to place separate floating items such as pop-up menus. This is a *JLayeredPane* object.
A glass pane	If we continue the analogy, this acts as a piece of glass covering our collection of acetates.

You can get at these various parts of the root pane object using the following methods of the *JFrame* class:

Container getContentPane()	Returns the contents pane. Cast the returned item to a *JPanel* object for full access.
JMenuBar getJMenuBar()	Returns the menu bar.
JLayeredPane getJLayeredPane()	Returns the layered pane.
Component getGlassPane()	Returns the glass pane.

We'll look at each part in turn with a few examples to make things a little clearer.

In this first program using Swing, we'll recreate the button-pressing example of the earlier AWT application: when the button on the application is pressed, the contents of a label are changed to match that of the button.

As we saw before with AWT components, items such as buttons and labels are positioned using a layout manager. By default, the contents pane uses a *BorderLayout* manager.

The program uses the following logic

```
Define the button and label as attributes of the class
In the constructor
    Call the  super-class constructor to set the application's
    title bar
    Get a reference to the application's contents pane
    Add the button and label to the contents pane
In actionPerformed()
    Copy the button's text to the label
In main()
    Create an object of our new class
```

The code is given in LISTING-18.1 below

LISTING-18.1

Getting Started with Swing

```
import javax.swing.*;
import java.awt.event.*;

public class StartingSwing extends JFrame
↳implements ActionListener
{
   JButton b1 = new JButton("Hello");
   JLabel lab1 = new JLabel("This changes");

   public StartingSwing()
   {
        super("First Swing");
        JPanel pane = (JPanel)getContentPane(); // Get content pane
        b1.addActionListener(this);
        pane.add("North",b1);
        pane.add("South",lab1);
   }

   public void actionPerformed(ActionEvent e)
   {
        lab1.setText(b1.getText());
   }

    public static void main(String args[])
    {
       StartingSwing sw = new StartingSwing();
    }
}
```

Notice that the *JButton* class defines a *getText()* method rather than the *getLabel()* method of the *Button* class. The older method is also available but has been deprecated.

Activity 18.2

Type in and run the program given above.

You won't see very much! But the machine is doing something. You'll probably have to press Ctrl-C to get the DOS prompt back.

Making the Application Visible

We need to add the instruction

```
sw.setVisible(true);
```

as the last line in *main()*. This makes sure that the window running our application is visible. Alternatively, we can use the call

```
sw.show();
```

which has the same effect.

Activity 18.3

Insert one of the lines above for showing your application window and re-run your program.

This time you should see the minimal window shown below.

Drag on the sides of the window to resize it. Now you should see the label and button.

Click on the button. The label's text should change.

Try closing the application window.

Closing the Application

Although clicking the exit option closes the window, it does not terminate the program, so again you will need to use Ctrl-C to regain a prompt.

To solve this problem, we need a *WindowAdapter*-derived object in which the *windowClosing()* method is overridden. The code required is given below and should be added to *main()*.

```
sw.addWindowListener
    (
        new WindowAdapter()
        {
            public void windowClosing(WindowEvent e)
            {
                System.exit(0);
            }
        }
    );
```

A second method of closing the window, if you're using Java 2 release 1.3 or higher, is to call the *JFrame* class's *setDefaultCloseOperation()* method. This takes a *JFrame* class constant as an argument. That value is *JFrame.EXIT_ON_CLOSE*.

We do this with the line

```
sw.setDefaultCloseOperation(JFrame.EXIT_ON_CLOSE);
```

which should be added to *main()*.

If using Java 2 ver 1.3 use the second method of closing the application window. For earlier Java versions use the *WindowAdapter* approach.

Activity 18.4

Add the above code to the end of *main()*. Retest your program.

It should close correctly now.

Initial Window Size

We can set the initial size of the window in the same three ways available for AWT applications.

The first is to use the *pack()* method inherited from *JFrame* which sizes the window in such a way that all components within it will be visible. To do this just add the line

```
sw.pack()
```

before making the window visible.

An alternative approach is to use the *setSize()* method also inherited from *JFrame* in which the width and height of the Window can be given in pixels. For example:

```
sw.setSize(300,150);
```

> **Activity 18.5**
>
> Try each approach by adding the appropriate line to *main()*.

The second option above positions the window at the top left of the screen. A final way of specifying not only the initial size of the window, but also its position is to use

```
sw.setBounds(200,200,500,350);
```

This call requires the coordinates of the top-left and bottom-right corners of the window.

> **Activity 18.6**
>
> Try this last method of sizing and positioning the application window.

Visual Components: Look and Feel

Using AWT components, the buttons, labels and windows etc. took on the look of the operating system on which they were running. Since components were created by making calls to functions in the underlying operating system this is hardly surprising.

However, Swing components offer the programmer the ability to choose a certain style or **look** for an applications components and for that look to remain identical irrespective of the platform on which the application is run. Hence, we can choose a Microsoft Windows look, a Motif look or a native Java look for our application.

As well as setting the look of a component we can also determine how it reacts to events. So, for example, with AWT, while selecting multiple items from a list might require a Shift+click operation on one system, Ctrl+shift might be required on another. This is known as the component **feel**.

With Swing this feel aspect can also be selected.

This concept of being able to choose the look and feel of components without any need to rewrite code is known as **pluggable look and feel.**

The UIManager Class

UI stands for User Interface.

There are several classes involved in manipulating the look and feel of Swing components. The most important of these is the *UIManager* class. It contains the *setLookAndFeel()* method which is used to set the look and feel.

Normally, three styles will be available on a Windows machine: Windows, Motif and Java. The default is *Java look and feel.*

Detailed manipulation of the look and feel is outside the scope of this text. Examine the java help files for more details on the UIManager class.

The Swing Hierarchy

Our first application has already introduced many new classes from the Swing or Java Foundation Classes (JFC). The diagram in FIG-18.1 shows many of the classes mentioned in this text.

FIG-18.1

The Swing Family Tree

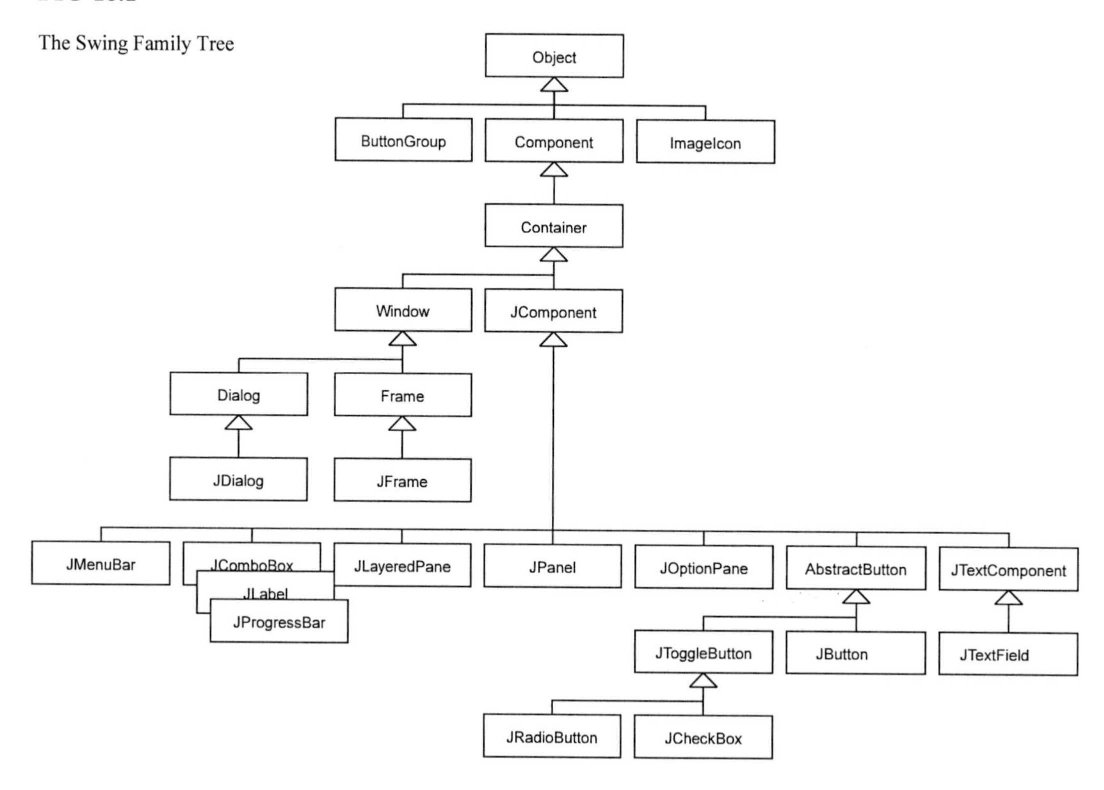

The JButton Class

This class is a descendant of the *AbstractButton* class from which it inherits many methods.

Constructors

There are four versions of the constructor:

JButton()	Creates an unlabelled button.
JButton(String s)	Sets the caption on the button to *s*.
JButton(Icon m)	Shows image *m* as an icon on the button.
JButton(String s,Icon m)	Shows image *m* and text *s* on the button.

Icon is an Interface defined within the Swing components.

To add an image to the button we need to create an object of any class that implements the *Icon* interface. One such class is *ImageIcon*.

We can create an object of this class using a statement such as

This requires a string identifying the image's file name. Normally, small gifs are used.

```
private ImageIcon pic = new ImageIcon("image1bw.gif");
```

and then use the object as the argument for the button's constructor:

```
private JButton b1 = new JButton(pic);
```

Alternatively, we can create an anonymous *ImageIcon* object as the constructor's argument

```
private JButton b1 = new JButton(new ImageIcon("image1bw.gif"));
```

The program in LISTING-18.2 illustrates the use of a button icon.

LISTING-18.2

Using a JButton

```
import javax.swing.*;
import java.awt.event.*;

public class Swing2 extends JFrame implements ActionListener
{
  private ImageIcon pic = new ImageIcon("image1bw.gif");
  private JButton b1 = new JButton(pic);
  private JLabel lab1 = new JLabel("This changes");

  public Swing2()
  {
      super("First Swing");
      JPanel pane = (JPanel)getContentPane();
      b1.addActionListener(this);
      pane.add("North",b1);
      pane.add("South",lab1);
   }

   public void actionPerformed(ActionEvent e)
   {
      lab1.setText("Pressed");
   }

   public static void main(String args[])
   {
      Swing2 sw = new Swing2();
      sw.setBounds(200,200,500,350);
      sw.show();
      sw.setDefaultCloseOperation(JFrame.EXIT_ON_CLOSE);
   }
}
```

Activity 18.7

Modify your program to add a small GIF file as an icon on the button.

The button's caption should read Hello.

Changing the Button's Icon

We can specify that the button should display a different icon when pressed using the *setPressedIcon(Icon m)* method.

Activity 18.8

Add the statement

```
b1.setPressedIcon(new ImageIcon("image1emb.gif"));
```

as the third line of your program's constructor.

Run your program and click the mouse in the button.

You should see the second (embossed) image appear while the button is held down.

We can use another image when the mouse simply moves over the button without clicking. We can specify the image to be shown using *setRolloverIcon(Icon)*, but in addition we need to enable the rollover effect using *setRolloverEnabled(boolean)*

Activity 18.9

Add the statements

```
b1.setRolloverIcon(new ImageIcon("image1col.gif"));
b1.setRolloverEnabled(true);
```

to the constructor in your program.

Test the effect by moving the mouse over the button.

If a button is disabled (using *setEnabled(false)*) the normal icon is greyed-out automatically but it is also possible to specify a different icon for this state using *setDisabledIcon(Icon)*.

Other Button Effects

We can add a hint, or tool-tip as Java refers to it, to a Button object using the method *setToolTipText(String)*. This method is inherited from *JComponent* and so can be used on any other descendant component.

The hint specified will appear when the mouse hovers over the component.

> **Activity 18.10**
>
> Add the line
>
> ```
> b1.setToolTipText("Press button to change label");
> ```
>
> to the constructor.
>
> Run the program and hover the mouse pointer over the button.

An accelerator key can be set for the button using *setMnemonic(char)*. With this set we can use the *Alt* key and the specified character to activate the button.

> **Activity 18.11**
>
> Set *H* as the accelerator key of your button.

You can also set the font of the buttons label using *setFont(Font)*. For example:

```
b1.setFont(new Font("Arial",Font.BOLD,20));
```

The position of the text and icon on a label can be modified using *setHorizontalTextPosition(int)* and *setVerticalTextPosition(int)*. For this purpose *JButton* defines the class constants

```
JButton.LEFT
JButton.CENTER
JButton.RIGHT
JButton.TOP
JButton.BOTTOM
```

Typical statements would be:

```
b1.setHorizontalTextPosition(JButton.LEFT);
b1.setVerticalTextPosition(JButton.BOTTOM);
```

The JLabel Class

This class, like AWT's *Label* class, is designed to display text. However, like *JButton*, an image can be linked to that text. The text can be accessed and changed as can the image. Objects of this type can listen for events and can display a hint when the mouse is moved over it.

Some of the methods are described below:

Constructors

JLabel(String s) — Sets the label to the specified string.

JLabel(String s, int position) — Sets the label to string *s* and justifies it horizontally in accordance with *position*. Named values for *position* are:

```
JLabel.LEFT
JLabel.CENTER
JLabel.RIGHT
```

JLabel(Icon c)	Sets the label to show image *c*.
JLabel(Icon c , int position)	Sets the label to show image *c* justified in accordance with *position*.
JLabel(String s, Icon c, int position)	Sets the label to string *s*, with image *c* justified in accordance with *position*.

Various examples are shown in FIG-18.2 below:

FIG-18.2

JLabel Constructors

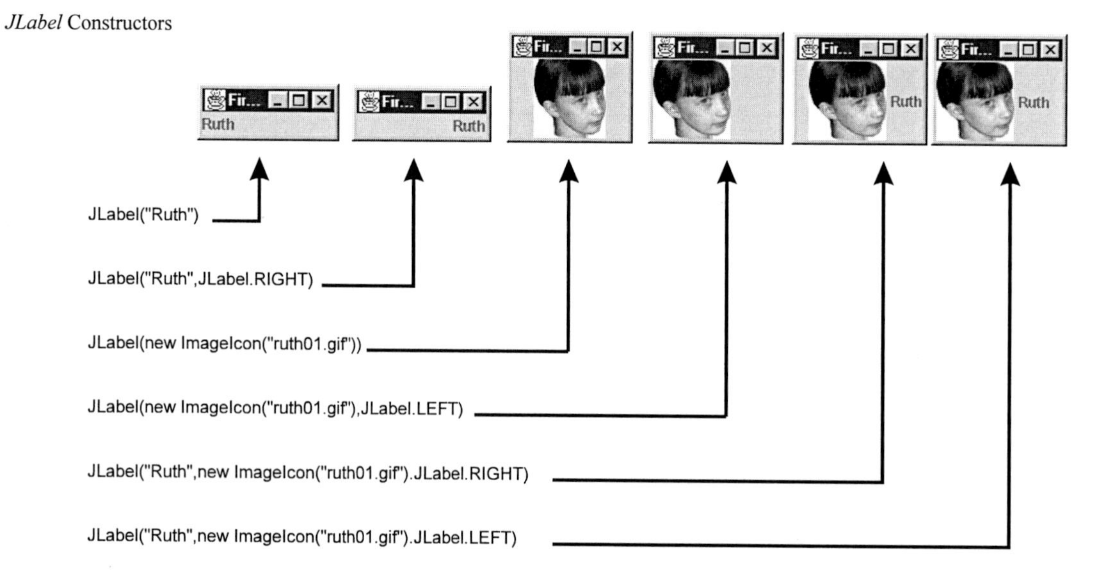

Text-Related Methods

Manipulation of the label's text can be achieved using the following methods.

String getText()	Returns the label's caption.
void setText(String s)	Sets the label's caption to *s*.
void setFont(Font f)	Sets the font of the label's text to *f*.
void setForeground(Color c)	Sets the text colour to *c*.

Icon-Related Methods

As well as displaying text, a label may also contain an icon. A second icon can be defined when the label is marked as disabled.

Icon getDisabledIcon()	Returns the separate image used when the label is disabled. There may be none, in which case `null` is returned.
Icon getIcon()	Returns the normal image associated with the label. If there is none, `null` is returned.
setDisabledIcon(Icon c)	Sets the image to be used when the label is disabled to *c*.

setIcon(Icon c)	Sets the image used when the label is enabled to *c*.

Some effects are shown in FIG-15.3 below.

FIG-18.3

JLabel Icon-Related Methods

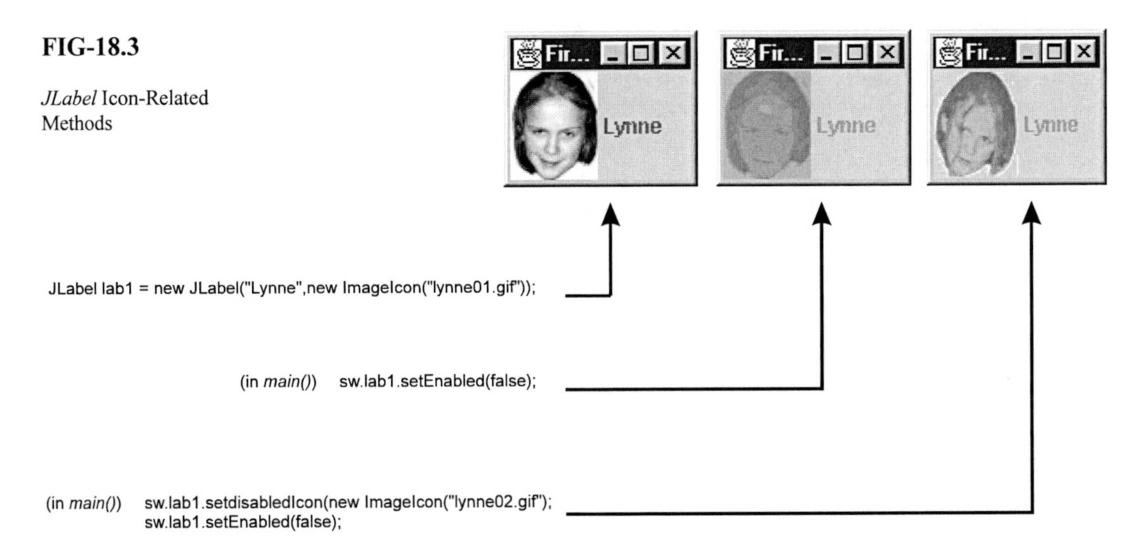

Alignment-Related Methods

These routines adjust the positions of the text and image attributes of the label relative to each other or within the rectangular area assigned by the layout manager to the label component.

int getHorizontalAlignment()	Returns how the text/image is aligned horizontally within the label's display area. Possible values are:
	`JLabel.LEFT`
	`JLabel.CENTER`
	`JLabel.RIGHT`

int getHorizontalTextPosition()	Returns the horizontal position of the text component relative to the image component. Possible values are the same as above.
int getIconTextGap()	Returns the gap (in pixels) between the image and text components.

int getVerticalAlignment()	Returns the vertical alignment of the text/image within the rectangular area assigned by the layout manager to the label component. Possible values are:
	`JLabel.TOP`
	`JLabel.CENTER`
	`JLabel.BOTTOM`

void setHorizontalAlignment(int p)	Sets the components alignment within the allocated space to *p*. *p* should be one of the named constants:
	`JLabel.LEFT`
	`JLabel.CENTER`
	`JLabel.RIGHT`

The results of each option are shown in FIG-18.4 below.

FIG-18.4

JLabel
Alignment-Related
Methods

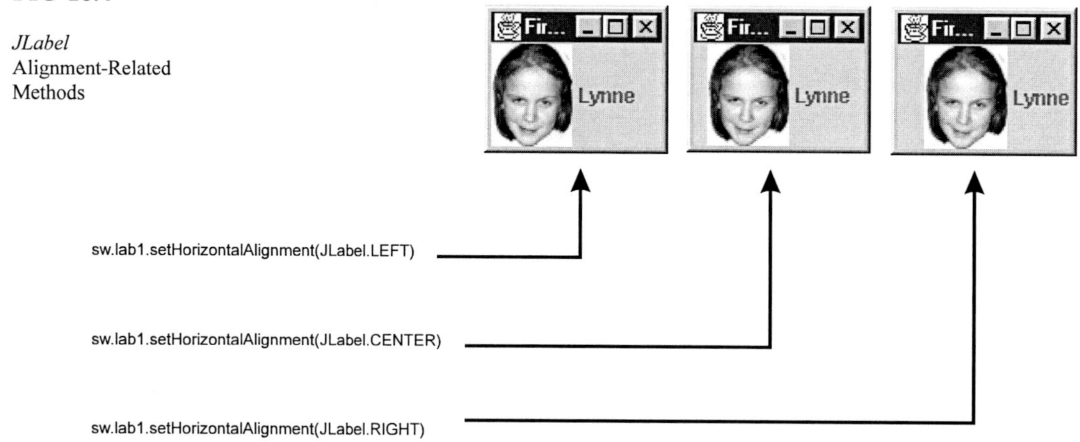

void setHorizontalTextPosition(int p) Sets the text's horizontal position relative to the image. Possible positions are
`JLabel.LEFT`
`JLabel.CENTER`
`JLabel.RIGHT`

The results of each option are shown in FIG-18.5 below.

FIG-18.5

JLabel
HorizontalTextPosition()

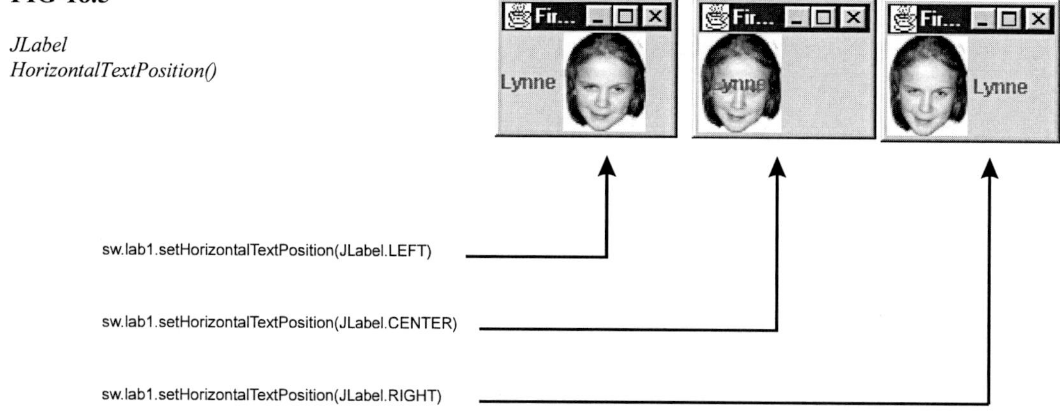

void setIconTextGap(int g) Sets the gap between the image and text components to *g* pixels.

Examples are shown in FIG-18.6 below.

FIG-18.6

JLabel
setIconTextGap()

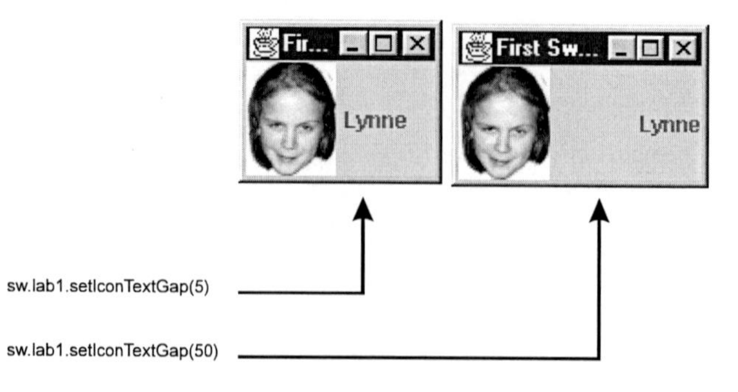

void setVerticalAlignment(int p)

Sets the components alignment within the allocated space to *p*. *p* should be one of the named constants:

```
JLabel.TOP
JLabel.CENTER
JLabel.BOTTOM
```

Examples are shown in FIG-18.7 below.

FIG-18.7

JLabel setVerticalAlignment()

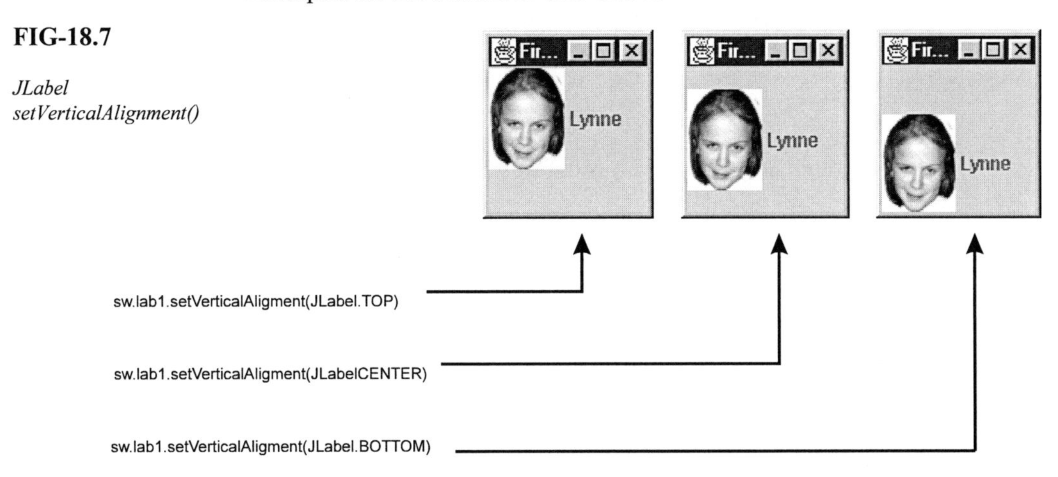

void setVerticalTextPosition(int p)

Sets the text's vertical position relative to the image. Possible positions are

```
JLabel.TOP
JLabel.CENTER
JLabel.BOTTOM
```

Examples are shown in FIG-18.8 below.

FIG-18.8

JLabel setVerticalTextPosition()

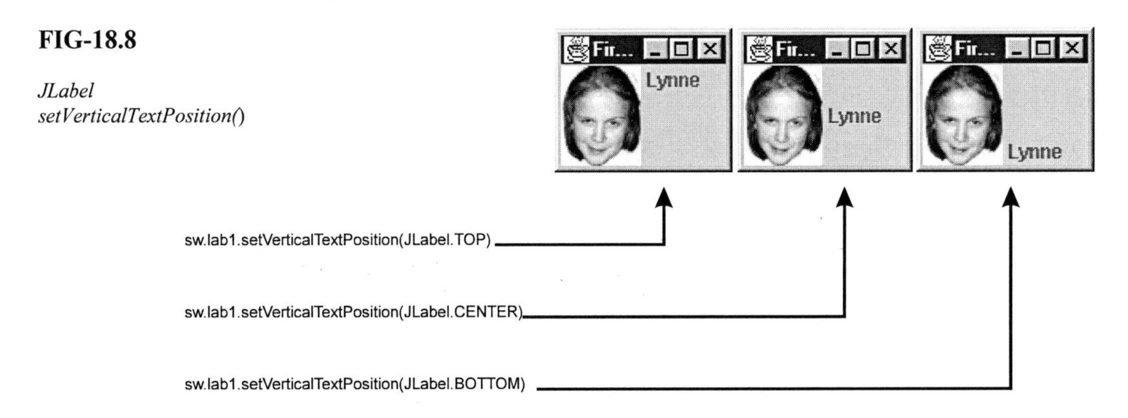

Other JLabel Features

Like *JButton*, *JLabel* is a descendant of *JComponent* and from there it inherits many methods including

```
setToolTipText(String s)
```

Use *setEnabled(false)* to disable the label.

This method is inherited from the *Component* class.

Activity 18.12

Create a program containing two buttons and a label. The first button, when pressed, should cause the label to be disabled, the second button should re-enable it.

JCheckBox

Swing's class for creating checkboxes has a rather extended set of ancestors and hence inherits many features. However, its basic purpose remains to allow the user to select an option clicking on the checkbox. The box shows its current state by displaying (or not) a check mark in a boxed area. The boxed area can be replaced by an image if an *Icon* parameter is used in the constructor. What follows is a description of many of the class's features:

Constructors

There are no less than seven constructors but these are variations on the text, icon and initial state of the object to be created.

JCheckBox()	No Text; no icon; unchecked.
JCheckBox(String s)	Displays text *s*; no icon; unchecked.
JCheckBox(String s, boolean b)	Displays *s*; no icon; checked if *b* is *true*.
JCheckBox(Icon c)	Displays image c; no text; unchecked.
JCheckBox(Icon c, boolean b)	Displays image *c*; no text; checked if *b* is *true*.
JCheckBox(String s Icon c)	Displays text *s*; image *c*; unchecked.
JCheckBox(String s, Icon c, boolean b)	Displays text *s*; image *c*; checked if *b* is true.

The program in LISTING-18.3 creates a checklist group with only text features.

LISTING-18.3

Using *JCheckBox*

```
import javax.swing.*;
import java.awt.event.*;
import java.awt.*;

public class SwingCheck extends JFrame
↳implements ActionListener
{
  JLabel lab1 = new JLabel("Classmates");
  JCheckBox ck1[] =      {    new JCheckBox("Lynne"),
                              new JCheckBox("Laura"),
                              new JCheckBox("Ruth")
                         };


  public SwingCheck()
  {
      super("First Swing");
      JPanel pane = (JPanel)getContentPane();
      pane.setLayout(new GridLayout(5,1));
      pane.add(lab1);
      pane.add(ck1[0]);
      pane.add(ck1[1]);
      pane.add(ck1[2]);
  }
```

continued on next page

LISTING-18.3
(continued)

Using *JCheckBox*

```
    public void actionPerformed(ActionEvent e)
    {
        lab1.setText(((JButton)e.getSource()).getText());
    }

   public static void main(String args[])
   {
        SwingCheck sw = new SwingCheck();
        sw.pack();
        sw.show();
        sw.setDefaultCloseOperation(JFrame.EXIT_ON_CLOSE);
   }
}
```

The display from the above program is shown in FIG-18.9. Part a) shows the initial display while b) shows the display after Lynne and Ruth are selected.

FIG-18.9

Using CheckBox

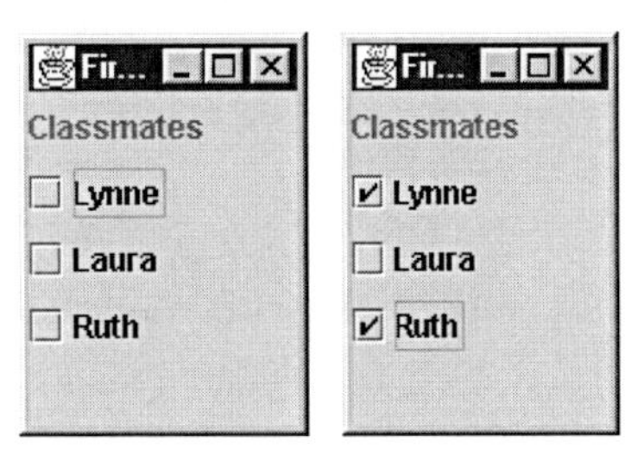

a) Initial State   b) Lynne and Ruth Selected

Using Images in a Checkbox

If, however, we use images in the checkbox, the image specified is used for an unchecked box. Since this image replaces the rectangle shown in text-only checkboxes, a second image needs to be specified for display when the checkbox is selected. This is done using the method:

`setSelectedIcon(Icon c)`   Image *c* is shown when the checkbox is selected.

The code snippet below defines an image-based checkbox array:

```
    JCheckBox ckbx[] =
    {
            new JCheckBox("Lynne",new ImageIcon("lynneem.gif")),
            new JCheckBox("Laura",new ImageIcon("lauraem.gif")),
            new JCheckBox("Ruth",new ImageIcon("ruthem.gif"))
    };
```

The alternative images are then set up with the lines:

```
    ckbx[0].setSelectedIcon(new ImageIcon("lynnec.gif"));
    ckbx[1].setSelectedIcon(new ImageIcon("laurac.gif"));
    ckbx[2].setSelectedIcon(new ImageIcon("ruthc.gif"));
```

A complete program is shown in LISTING-18.4 below.

LISTING-18.4

Images in a CheckBox

```
import javax.swing.*;
import java.awt.event.*;
import java.awt.*;
```

continued on next page

LISTING-18.4
(continued)

Images in a CheckBox

```
public class SwingCheck extends JFrame
↳implements ActionListener
{
  JLabel lab1 = new JLabel("Classmates");
  JCheckBox ckbx[] =
  {
       new JCheckBox("Lynne",new ImageIcon("lynneem.gif")),
       new JCheckBox("Laura",new ImageIcon("lauraem.gif")),
       new JCheckBox("Ruth",new ImageIcon("ruthem.gif"))
  };

  public SwingCheck()
  {
       super("First Swing");
       JPanel pane = (JPanel)getContentPane();
       pane.setLayout(new GridLayout(5,1));
       ckbx[0].setSelectedIcon(new ImageIcon("lynnec.gif"));
       ckbx[1].setSelectedIcon(new ImageIcon("laurac.gif"));
       ckbx[2].setSelectedIcon(new ImageIcon("ruthc.gif"));
       pane.add(lab1);
       pane.add(ckbx[0]);
       pane.add(ckbx[1]);
       pane.add(ckbx[2]);
  }


   public void actionPerformed(ActionEvent e)
   {
      lab1.setText(((JButton)e.getSource()).getText());
   }

  public static void main(String args[])
  {
       SwingCheck sw = new SwingCheck();
       sw.pack();
       sw.show();
       sw.setDefaultCloseOperation(JFrame.EXIT_ON_CLOSE);
  }
}
```

Activity 18.13

Type in and test the program above using your own images.

Typical displays from the program are shown in FIG-18.10.

FIG-18.10

Images in a CheckBox

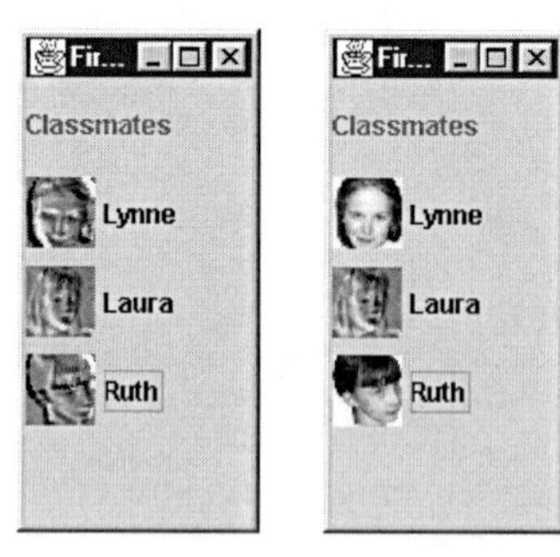

a) Initial State b) Lynne and Ruth selected

Other methods which manipulate the image shown are similar to those already covered in the *JButton* class:

setDisabledIcon(Icon c)	Image *c* is shown when the checkbox is disabled.

setRolloverIcon(Icon c)	Image *c* is displayed when the mouse moves over the checkbox. However, the checkbox must be rollover enabled.
setRolloverEnabled(boolean b)	If *b* is *true*, and a different image has been specified, moving the mouse over the checkbox will change its image component to that specified using *setRolloverIcon()*.

Text and Icon Positioning Methods

void setHorizontalTextPosition(int p)	Sets the text's horizontal position relative to the image. Possible positions are:
	`JCheckBox.LEFT`
	`JCheckBox.CENTER`
	`JCheckBox.RIGHT`

int getHorizotalTextPosition()	Returns the horizontal position of the text component relative to the image component. Possible values are the same as above.

void setVerticalTextPosition(int p)	Sets the text's vertical position relative to the image. Possible positions are:
	`JCheckBox.TOP`
	`JCheckBox.CENTER`
	`JCheckBox.BOTTOM`

int getVerticalTextPosition()	Returns the vertical position of the text component relative to the image component. Possible values are the same as above.

void setHorizontalAlignment(int p)	Sets the components alignment within the allocated space to *p*. *p* should be one of the named constants:
	`JCheckBox.LEFT`
	`JCheckBox.CENTER`
	`JCheckBox.RIGHT`

int getHorizontalAlignment()	Returns how the text/image is aligned horizontally within the label's display area. Possible values are as above.

void setVerticalAlignment(int p)	Sets the components alignment within the allocated space to *p*. *p* should be one of the named constants:
	`JCheckBox.TOP`
	`JCheckBox.CENTER`
	`JCheckBox.BOTTOM`

int getVerticalAlignment()	Returns the vertical alignment of the text/image within the rectangular area assigned by the layout manager to the label component. Possible values are as above.

Display-related Methods

void setForeground(Color c)	Changes the text colour to *c*.
void setBackground(Color c)	Changes the component's background colour to *c*.
void setFont(Font f)	Sets the font used by the checkbox's text to *f*.

Other Useful Methods

void setMnemonic(char c)	Sets *c* as the accelerator key. The first occurrence of character *c* in the checkbox's text is underlined.
void setToolTipText(String s)	Sets the hint shown when the mouse hovers over the checkbox component.
void setSelected(boolean b)	Sets the checkbox to selected if *b* is *true*, else it is set to unselected.
boolean isSelected()	Returns *true* if the checkbox is selected, otherwise *false* is returned.
String getText()	Returns the text (if any) shown with the checkbox.

Events

The usual event to listen for with a checkbox is the *ItemListener*. This interface contains the method

```
itemStateChanged(ItemEvent e)
```

which is executed whenever the associated checkbox is clicked.

The program in LISTING-18.5 demonstrates the use of this by displaying the name of the last checkbox to be selected.

LISTING-18.5

Using Checkboxes

```
import javax.swing.*;
import java.awt.event.*;
import java.awt.*;

public class CheckDemo extends JFrame implements
ActionListener,ItemListener
{
   JLabel lab1 = new JLabel("Classmates");
   JLabel lab2 = new JLabel();
   JCheckBox ckbx[] =
   {
        new JCheckBox("Lynne",new ImageIcon("lynneem.gif")),
        new JCheckBox("Laura",new ImageIcon("lauraem.gif")),
        new JCheckBox("Ruth",new ImageIcon("ruthem.gif"))
   };
```

LISTING-18.5
(continued)

Using Checkboxes

```
    public CheckDemo()
    {
         super("First Swing");
         JPanel pane = (JPanel)getContentPane(); // Get content pane
         pane.setLayout(new GridLayout(5,1));
         ckbx[0].setSelectedIcon(new ImageIcon("lynnec.gif"));
         ckbx[1].setSelectedIcon(new ImageIcon("laurac.gif"));
         ckbx[2].setSelectedIcon(new ImageIcon("ruthc.gif"));
         ckbx[0].addItemListener(this);
         ckbx[1].addItemListener(this);
         ckbx[2].addItemListener(this);
         pane.add(lab1);
         pane.add(ckbx[0]);
         pane.add(ckbx[1]);
         pane.add(ckbx[2]);
         pane.add(lab2);
    }

    public void actionPerformed(ActionEvent e)
    {
         lab1.setText(((JButton)e.getSource()).getText());
    }

    public void itemStateChanged(ItemEvent e)
    {
         JCheckBox ptr = (JCheckBox)e.getSource();
         if (ptr.isSelected())
              lab2.setText(ptr.getText());
    }


    public static void main(String args[])
    {
         CheckDemo sw = new CheckDemo();
         sw.pack();
         sw.show();
         sw.setDefaultCloseOperation(JFrame.EXIT_ON_CLOSE);
    }
}
```

Activity 18.14

Modify the program above (using your own images and text) so that the bottom label shows the names of all the items selected. The list should be updated each time a checkbox is changed.

JRadioButton

Unlike AWT, Swing has a separate class for radio buttons. However, it contains many of the same operations as the *JCheckBox* class and can be used with an image in place of the normal circular selection mark.

Constructors

Again, there are seven constructors but these are variations on the text, icon and initial state of the object to be created.

JRadioButton()	No Text; no icon; unchecked.
JRadioButton(String s)	Displays text *s*; no icon; unchecked.
JRadioButtonString s, boolean b)	Displays *s*; no icon; checked if *b* is *true*.

JRadioButton(Icon c)	Displays image c; no text; unchecked.
JRadioButton(Icon c, boolean b)	Displays image *c*; no text; checked if *b* is *true*.
JRadioButton(String s Icon c)	Displays text *s*; image *c*; unchecked.
JRadioButton(String s, Icon c, boolean b)	Displays text *s*; image *c*; checked if *b* is *true*.

Other Methods

setDisabledIcon(Icon c)	Image *c* is shown when the checkbox is disabled.
setRolloverIcon(Icon c)	Image *c* is displayed when the mouse moves over the checkbox. However, the checkbox must be rollover enabled.
setRolloverEnabled(boolean b)	If *b* is *true*, and a different image has been specified, moving the mouse over the checkbox will change its image component to that specified using *setRolloverIcon()*.

void setHorizontalTextPosition(int p)	Sets the text's horizontal position relative to the image. Possible positions are:
	`JRadioButton.LEFT`
	`JRadioButton.CENTER`
	`JRadioButton.RIGHT`

int getHorizotalTextPosition()	Returns the horizontal position of the text component relative to the image component. Possible values are the same as above.

void setVerticalTextPosition(int p)	Sets the text's vertical position relative to the image. Possible positions are:
	`JRadioButton.TOP`
	`JRadioButton.CENTER`
	`JRadioButton.BOTTOM`

int getVerticalTextPosition()	Returns the vertical position of the text component relative to the image component. Possible values are the same as above.

void setHorizontalAlignment(int p)	Sets the components alignment within the allocated space to *p*. *p* should be one of the named constants:
	`JRadioButton.LEFT`
	`JRadioButton.CENTER`
	`JRadioButton.RIGHT`

int getHorizontalAlignment()	Returns how the text/image is aligned horizontally within the label's display area. Possible values are as above.

void setVerticalAlignment(int p)	Sets the components alignment within the allocated space to *p*. *p* should be one of the named constants: `JRadioButton.TOP` `JRadioButton.CENTER` `JRadioButton.BOTTOM`
int getVerticalAlignment()	Returns the vertical alignment of the text/image within the rectangular area assigned by the layout manager to the label component. Possible values are as above.
void setForeground(Color c)	Changes the text colour to *c*.
void setBackground(Color c)	Changes the component's background colour to *c*.
void setFont(Font f)	Sets the font used by the checkbox's text to *f*.
void setMnemonic(char c)	Sets *c* as the accelerator key. The first occurrence of character *c* in the checkbox's text is underlined.
void setToolTipText(String s)	Sets the hint shown when the mouse hovers over the checkbox component.
void setSelected(boolean b)	Sets the checkbox to selected if *b* is *true*, else it is set to unselected.
boolean isSelected()	Returns *true* if the checkbox is selected, otherwise *false* is returned.
String getText()	Returns the text (if any) shown with the checkbox.

The following code creates one text-only radio button and an image based one:

```
JRadioButton b1 = new JRadioButton("Text only");
JRadioButton b2 = new JRadioButton("Lynne",
                     ↳new ImageIcon("lynneem.gif"));
```

The image specified for the second radio button is the one used when the button is not selected, so we need a call to *setSelectedIcon()* to specify the image to be shown when the button is selected:

```
b2.setSelectedIcon(new ImageIcon("lynnec.gif"));
```

Screen dumps of the selected and unselected states are shown in FIG-18.11.

FIG-18.11

Radiobuttons with Images

a) Unselected

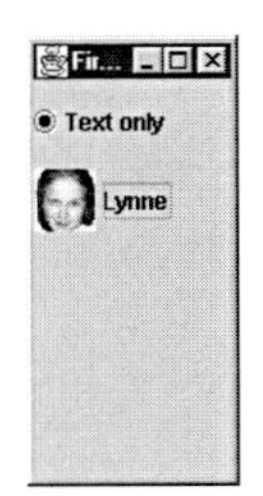

b) Selected

Radio buttons are usually grouped so as to represent a set of mutually exclusive user options. To do this we need to link the radio buttons to a *ButtonGroup* object.

ButtonGroup

The *ButtonGroup* class has an empty constructor:

`ButtonGroup()`	Creates a *ButtonGroup* object used to hold mutually exclusive options. These options are often *JRadioButton* objects but may be of other classes.

We can then add or remove items from the group:

`add(AbstractButton b)`	Adds item *b* to the group.
`remove(AbstractButton b)`	Removes item *b* from the group.

Menus

Introduction

Most traditional programs use a menu bar to host the drop-down menu options for the application. As we mentioned earlier, the Swing layout of a *JFrame* object has a specific area designed for this purpose. To make use of it we need to add a *JMenuBar* object to our application. This in turn is populated with the main options of the bar. These are *JMenu* objects which are added to the *JMenuBar* object. Finally the items to be shown in the drop-down section are added. These are *JMenuItem* objets which are added to the appropriate *JMenu* object.

A typical menu is shown in FIG-18.12 below.

FIG-18.12

A Typical Menu

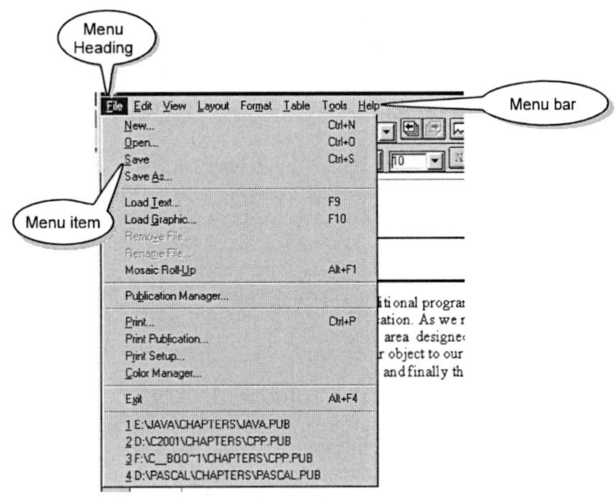

Adding a JMenuBar

We can start creating a menu by defining, as attributes of our class, the various components we will need. In this example, we are going to start with a menu bar containing one menu: *File*. This menu contains four items: *New; Open; Save* and *Save As*. The declarations required for this are

```
private JMenuBar menubar = new JMenuBar();

private JMenu filemenu = new JMenu("File");

private JMenuItem newitem = new JMenuItem("New");
private JMenuItem openitem = new JMenuItem("Open");
private JMenuItem saveitem = new JMenuItem("Save");
private JMenuItem saveasitem = new JMenuItem("Save As");
```

Next we need to add these to our application. This is a little different from adding the buttons and labels from previous examples.

If you recall, a Swing application is constructed from a *JFrame* object which contains a *JRootFrame* object which in turn contains a menu bar area, a contents pane, a layered pane and a glass pane.

We start by telling the root pane that a menu bar is to be used. To do this we need a reference to the root pane using JFrame's *getRootPane()* and then call the root pane's *setJMenuBar()* method. The code required (which is placed in the constructor) is

```
JRootPane pane = getRootPane();
pane.setJMenuBar(menubar);
```

Next we add the menu heading to the menubar

```
menubar.add(filemenu);
```

And finally the menu items to the menu heading:

```
filemenu.add(newitem);
filemenu.add(openitem);
filemenu.add(saveitem);
filemenu.add(saveasitem);
```

The complete code for the program is shown in LISTING-18.6 below

LISTING-18.6

Creating a Menu

```
import javax.swing.*;
import java.awt.event.*;
import java.awt.*;

public class MenuTest extends JFrame
{
  private JMenuBar menubar = new JMenuBar();
  private JMenu filemenu = new JMenu("File");
  private JMenuItem newitem = new JMenuItem("New");
  private JMenuItem openitem = new JMenuItem("Open");
  private JMenuItem saveitem = new JMenuItem("Save");
  private JMenuItem saveasitem = new JMenuItem("Save As");

  public MenuTest()
  {
      super("First Swing");
      JRootPane pane = getRootPane();
      pane.setJMenuBar(menubar);
      menubar.add(filemenu);
      filemenu.add(newitem);
      filemenu.add(openitem);
      filemenu.add(saveitem);
      filemenu.add(saveasitem);
   }

   public static void main(String args[])
   {
      MenuTest sw = new MenuTest();
      sw.setBounds(200,150,200,200);
      sw.setVisible(true);
      sw.addWindowListener
      (
          new WindowAdapter()
          {
              public void windowClosing(WindowEvent e)
              {
                  System.exit(0);
              }
          }
      );
   }
}
```

The display produced is shown in FIG-18.13.

FIG-18.13

The Menu Created

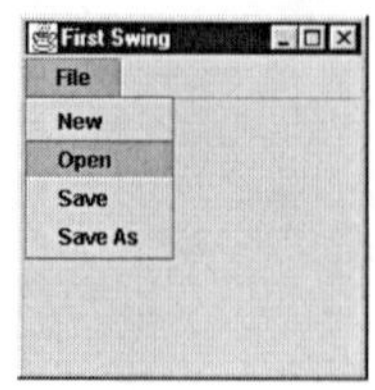

Creating Applets Using JApplet

Introduction

Swing replaces the *Applet* class with the *JApplet* class. It's from this new class that you should create a descendant class when creating your own applet.

However, only Netscape support the latest Swing *JApplet* class in their browser, for other browsers a plug-in will be required. For this reason, Swing applets are not heavily used on the Internet and are possibly more useful in an Intranet environment.

JApplet is a descendant of *Applet* and so retains the *init() start() stop()* and *destroy()* methods.

Like *JFrame, JApplet* contains a contents pane to which visual components such as buttons and edit boxes should be added.

The default layout manager is *BorderLayout (Applet* uses *FlowLayout)*.

Double buffering is automatic and should stop flicker in animated applications.

JApplet Example

The following applet (LISTING-18.7) allows the user to enter a temperature in Fahrenheit and convert it to Celcius.

LISTING-18.7

Creating a JApplet

```
import javax.swing.*;
import java.awt.event.*;
import java.awt.*;

public class SwingApplet extends JApplet implements
ActionListener
{
  JTextField txt = new JTextField(10);
  JButton convert = new JButton("Press to Convert");
  JLabel lab1 = new JLabel("..........");

  public void init()
  {
      JPanel panel = (JPanel)getContentPane();
      panel.setLayout(new GridLayout(3,2));
      panel.add(txt);
      panel.add(new JLabel("Fahrenheit"));
      panel.add(new Canvas());
      panel.add(lab1);
      panel.add(new JLabel("Celcius"));
      panel.add(convert);
      }

  public void actionPerformed(ActionEvent ae)
  {
      int celsius = (int)((Integer.parseInt(txt.getText())+40)
      ↳*5/9-40+0.5);
      lab1.setText(""+celsius);
  }
}
```

Solutions

Activity 18.1

No solution required.

Activity 18.2

No solution required.

Activity 18.3

No solution required.

Activity 18.4

No solution required.

Activity 18.5

No solution required.

Activity 18.6

No solution required.

Activity 18.7

No solution required.

Activity 18.8

No solution required.

Activity 18.9

No solution required.

Activity 18.10

No solution required.

Activity 18.11

No solution required.

Activity 18.12

```
import javax.swing.*;
import java.awt.event.*;
import java.awt.*;

public class DisableLabel extends JFrame
↳implements ActionListener
{
    JLabel lab1 = new JLabel
    ↳("Label can be disabled");
    JButton enable = new JButton
    ↳("Press to Enable");
    JButton disable = new JButton
    ↳("Press to disable");

    public DisableLabel()
    {
        super("Disabling Components");
        JPanel pane = (JPanel)getContentPane();
        pane.setLayout(new FlowLayout());
        pane.add(lab1);
        enable.addActionListener(this);
        disable.addActionListener(this);
        pane.add(enable);
        pane.add(disable);
    }

    public void actionPerformed(ActionEvent ae)
    {
        if(ae.getSource()==enable)
            lab1.setEnabled(true);
        else
            lab1.setEnabled(false);
    }

    public static void main(String args[])
    {
        DisableLabel sw = new DisableLabel();
        sw.pack();
        sw.show();
        sw.setDefaultCloseOperation
        ↳(JFrame.EXIT_ON_CLOSE);
    }
}
```

Activity 18.13

No solution required.

Activity 18.14

```
import javax.swing.*;
import java.awt.event.*;
import java.awt.*;

public class Act18_14 extends JFrame
↳implements ItemListener
{
    JLabel lab1 = new JLabel("Classmates");
    JLabel lab2 = new JLabel();
    JCheckBox ckbx[] =
    {
        new JCheckBox("Lynne",
        ↳new ImageIcon("lynneem.gif")),
        new JCheckBox("Laura",
        ↳new ImageIcon("lauraem.gif")),
        new JCheckBox("Ruth",
        ↳new ImageIcon("ruthem.gif"))
    };


    public Act18_14()
    {
        super("First Swing");
        JPanel pane = (JPanel)getContentPane();
        pane.setLayout(new GridLayout(5,1));
        ckbx[0].setSelectedIcon
        ↳(new ImageIcon("lynnec.gif"));
        ckbx[1].setSelectedIcon
        ↳(new ImageIcon("laurac.gif"));
        ckbx[2].setSelectedIcon
        ↳(new ImageIcon("ruthc.gif"));
        ckbx[0].addItemListener(this);
        ckbx[1].addItemListener(this);
        ckbx[2].addItemListener(this);
        pane.add(lab1);
        pane.add(ckbx[0]);
        pane.add(ckbx[1]);
        pane.add(ckbx[2]);
        pane.add(lab2);
    }

    public void itemStateChanged(ItemEvent e)
    {
        JCheckBox ptr = (JCheckBox)e.getSource();
        if (ptr.isSelected())
            lab2.setText((lab2.getText()+"  "
            ↳+ptr.getText()).trim());
        else
        {
            String nametogo = ptr.getText();
            StringBuffer selectednames =
```

```
            ↳new StringBuffer(lab2.getText());
            int start = lab2.getText().indexOf(nametogo);
            int fin = nametogo.length()+start;
            selectednames.delete(start,fin);
            lab2.setText(new String(selectednames).trim());
        }
    }

    public static void main(String args[])
    {
        Act18_14 sw = new Act18_14();
        sw.pack();
        sw.show();
        sw.setDefaultCloseOperation(JFrame.EXIT_ON_CLOSE);
    }
}
```

Index

M

N

O

P

R